Rhetorics of Display

Studies in Rhetoric/Communication
Thomas W. Benson, Series Editor

87

Rhetorics of *Display*

Edited by Lawrence J. Prelli

The University of South Carolina Press

Published by the University of South Carolina Press
Columbia, South Carolina 29208

www.sc.edu/uscpress

Manufactured in the United States of America

27 26 25 24 23 22 21 20 19 18
10 9 8 7 6 5 4 3 2

Library of Congress Cataloging-in-Publication Data

Rhetorics of display / edited by Lawrence J. Prelli.
    p. cm.— (Studies in rhetoric/communication)
Includes bibliographical references and indexes.
ISBN–13: 978-1-57003-618-7 (cloth : alk. paper)
ISBN–10: 1-57003-618-7 (cloth : alk. paper)
ISBN–13: 978-1-57003-619-4 (pbk. : alk. paper)
ISBN–10: 1-57003-619-5 (pbk. : alk. paper)
  1. Visual communication—Philosophy. 2. Appearance (Philosophy) 3. Image (Philosophy)
4. Exhibitions—Philosophy. 5. Rhetoric—Philosophy. I. Prelli, Lawrence J., 1955– II. Series.

P93.5.R49 2006
302.2301—dc22   2005035454

"Envisioning Postcommunism: Budapest's Stalin Monument," by Beverly James, appeared
in slightly different form in *Imagining Postcommunism,* by Beverly James (Texas A&M
University Press).

Contents

Illustrations

Series Editor's Preface

In *Rhetorics of Display,* Lawrence J. Prelli and his colleagues explore the mutual illuminations of the concepts of rhetoric and display as the showing forth of appearances with persuasive designs or consequences. The contributors disclose rhetoric through the lens of display, and display through the lens of rhetoric. To show forth a claim, an appearance, a truth, a state of affairs, a policy, a speaker, or an audience—through words spoken or written, or through images, structures, or any other human creation—is to engage in rhetoric. The authors gathered here show how display works as a figure, motive, and effect in rhetoric, and how a variety of modes of display in monuments, landscapes, commemorations, public demonstrations, visual images, and the human body are motivated by and may be illuminated from a rhetorical perspective.

The book begins with a theoretical and historical overview of what it means to conceive of display in rhetorical terms, illustrating how theorists and critics, ancient and modern, have addressed the issues. The following chapters demonstrate the impulse of the book's title. These critical analyses of a series of cases are not forced into the straightjacket of "*the* theory of rhetoric and display," but cohere around the exploration of *rhetorics* of display, exhibiting a high degree of theoretical rigor that is responsive to the situated diversity of the cases.

Editor Prelli has grouped the essays in a series of dialectical pairs—the verbal depiction of the visual and the visual depiction of the verbal; the disposition of place and the placing of disposition; demonstrations as rhetorical display and rhetorical displays as demonstrative; epideictic identifications and divisions. Prelli and his collaborators engage in a lively rethinking of a long rhetorical history and an energetic re-viewing of a variety of displays, from the *Titanic* to Tiananmen, from the Irish famine to a warehouse fire in Massachusetts, from Saratoga to Budapest, from a South African prison to Colin Powell. The essays open new perspectives and create new connections for students and working scholars interested in rhetoric, public memory, visual rhetoric, cultural studies, interpersonal communication, media, and related subjects.

THOMAS W. BENSON

Acknowledgments

One of the most pleasant aspects of completing a book project is that it affords the opportunity to tell colleagues and friends that you appreciate them for their contributions and support. That opportunity does not present itself as often as one might wish in the workaday world of academia, so I hope here to realize it as fully as possible. I am very grateful to colleagues in the Department of Communication at the University of New Hampshire who saw the potential of this project from its very inception. Lawrence Rosenfield sparked the generative insight that, although our work was distributed among rhetorical, media, interpersonal, and cultural studies, we still shared significant interests that clustered around the study of communicative forms of display. Without his inspiration, this book never would have been conceived, let alone brought to completion. James Farrell, Beverly James, Joshua Meyrowitz, and John Shotter offered support at various stages of this project. Sometimes their support was direct, at other times subtle, but always exceptional and of considerable personal importance to me. Colleagues and visitors who participated in department colloquia together offered, through their commentaries and projects, an illuminating range of variations on the central theme that communicative "displays," whatever they might be, are rhetorically constituted, as well as politically and culturally consequential. For that collective effort, I thank John Adams, Phebe Chao, Patrick Daley, John Erni, James Farrell, Jan Golinski, S. Michael Halloran, Sally Jacoby, Beverly James, Joshua Meyrowitz, Lawrence Rosenfield, David Smith, John Shotter, and Mari Boor Tonn.

The authors of this book's chapters were, without exception, diligent, scholarly, and amiable. I owe them all a debt of gratitude for making my editorial work as intellectually stimulating as it was personally pleasurable. Any distinction I might venture to boast for myself as editor is contingent upon the scholarly acumen of the writers I was fortunate to corral for this project. I also am grateful for the group of reviewers who were as generous with their time as they were skilled in their craft; they would make an enviable editorial board for a top-flight scholarly journal: John Adams (Hamilton College), Floyd D. Anderson (State University of New York College at Brockport), Stephen Browne (Pennsylvania State University), David Birdsell (Baruch College at the City University of New York), Phebe Chao (independent scholar), Sonja Foss (University of Colorado at Denver), James Farrell (University of New Hampshire), Gerard Hauser (University of Colorado at Boulder), Robert Ivie (Indiana University), Beverly James (University of New Hampshire), Henry

Krips (University of Pittsburgh), Carolyn Miller (North Carolina State University), Richard Morris (Arizona State University), Lester Olson (University of Pittsburgh), Christine Oravec (University of Utah), Lawrence Rosenfield (University of New Hampshire), Craig Smith (California State University at Long Beach), and David Watters (University of New Hampshire). So distinguished a group of authors and reviewers makes it plain for all to see that any blemishes remaining in the chapters collected in this book surely must be mine.

I also am quite fortunate to work at a university that offers an array of programs and resources to foster scholarship. I want to thank Dean Marilyn Hoskin and Associate Dean Thomas Trout of the College of Liberal Arts for making resources available to overcome obstacles associated with this project. Among those resources are the Palmer Fund, the Alumni Gifts Fund, and the James Fund. I also want to thank the Office of the Vice President for Academic Affairs and its University Faculty Scholars Program, which made it possible for me to take a much needed semester leave from teaching to work nearly full-time on this book.

Many others contributed to this project in different ways since its inception. Students in my two undergraduate seminars on rhetorics of display provided a thoughtful audience for rehearsal of themes that eventually constituted the conceptual spine of this book. Dayna Angelone, Daniel Corrigan, Jamie Elliott, Lauren Hopke, Aaron Williams, Zachary Breault, Alexandra Buchalski, Aaron Robarge, and Melissa Stevenson remain in my thoughts as exemplars of teaching's pleasures and privileges. Conversations with James Grew, Esq., a graduate from our undergraduate program, were relevant, engaging, and pleasurable. John Rouman, professor emeritus of classics at the University of New Hampshire, provided valuable technical assistance, and John A. Campbell of the University of Memphis provided helpful bibliographical advice. I also benefitted from conversations with department colleagues Jennifer Borda, R. Michael Jackson, and Mardi Kidwell, particularly pertaining to bibliographical matters. I appreciate communication graduate Jamie Elliott's help compiling the first draft of the book's selected bibliography, English department graduate students Andrea Minnis's and Spencer Henderson's work on its subsequent revision, and undergraduate student Kim Hartford's assistance with final citation checks. Reference librarians Louise Buckley, Peter Crosby, Valerie Harper, Deborah Watson, Deanna Wood, and David Severn always made visits to UNH's Dimond Library as pleasurable as they were productive. Always pleasurable and productive, too, were my frequent trips to Karen Baker's Country Bookseller Bookstore in Wolfeboro, New Hampshire. I also thank Doug Prince, manager of the university's Photographic Services Department, for his advice and skill preparing the book's graphics for submission to the University of South Carolina Press.

I am obliged to the editors and staff at the University of South Carolina Press for their service and advice. Series editor Tom Benson was a source of uncommon perspective both at the project's inception and near its completion. Barry Blose, acquisitions editor, saw the merit of this project from the start and offered firm, patient, and thoughtful guidance throughout the entire process leading to its completion.

Any large project, upon completion, invites reflection on life's experiences along the way and on the friends who shared them. My friend John Adams was always generous with his time at the right times; he has been a source of good cheer and wise advice almost as long as I have known him. So, too, was my friend and former teacher Ted Smith III. Ted and his wife, Rosemary, opened my eyes to displays that I had never before seen and that were wonderful to behold. Ted's death and the death of another former teacher, Richard B. Gregg, make publication of this book without their imagined contributions bittersweet. Conversations and outings with Phebe Chao and Roger Sorkin were always rich in pleasurable enthusiasms that elevated the spirit and filled the mind. Patricia Woodbury, an especially dear friend of my wife's, was an important presence in our lives together until her recent and untimely death. She, too, is missed very much. All of these friends in their different ways command "acknowledgment," which, to my mind, attests to the significance of this book's subject. Whatever else rhetorics of display might be, surely they include our efforts to somehow fix in memory our gratitude for significant encounters with important others whose presences and absences, together, upon reflection, disclose life's most poignant meanings. Above all others, I am grateful for my wife, Terri Winters, who reminds me every day that, although more remains concealed than is revealed as our experience of life unfolds, what matters is the quality of the disclosures encountered along the way. I dedicate my work in this book to her.

Rhetorics of Display

Lawrence J. Prelli

1

*R*hetorics of Display *An Introduction*

This is a book about rhetorics of display. "Display" evokes commonplace associations about (1) "how things look or appear," (2) exhibition or demonstration, and (3) showiness or ostentation.[1] "Rhetoric" summons similar commonplace associations: rhetoric often is said to deal with appearances rather than reality; to manifest demonstrations and exhibitions of feelings and commitments rather than of reason and sound judgment; and to involve exaggerated style or ostentatious self-display rather than sober presentation of substantial matters for impartial consideration. But these commonplace correspondences obscure the full range of "displays" that could be said to operate rhetorically—that is, persuasively—when they engage with those who become audience to them. Nor do they enable consideration of how rhetorical or persuasive acts manifest or display how things appear to those addressed. This book opens consideration of the many ways that displays operate rhetorically and that rhetorics enact display. When we suspend the pejorative connotations popularly associated with the words "rhetoric" and "display," we find that much of what appears or looks to us as reality is constituted rhetorically through the multiple displays that surround us, compete for our attention, and make claims upon us.

The chapters in this book together explore a representative and diverse assortment of displays and how they rhetorically manifest the ways that phenomena, persons, places, events, identities, communities, or cultures appear before those who become audience to them. Displays are manifested rhetorically through the verbally generated "image" in speeches and literature. Displays appear rhetorically in sketches, paintings, maps, statistical graphs, photographs, and television and film images. Displays are manifested rhetorically in the homes we inhabit and in the many places we visit—museums and exhibitions, memorials and statuary, parks and cemeteries, casinos and theme parks, neighborhood street corners and stores. Displays are manifested rhetorically in the "demonstration" of a scientific finding, of a political grievance, of a preferred identity. In whatever manifestation, displays also anticipate a responding audience whose expectations might be satisfied or frustrated, their values and interests affirmed, neglected, or challenged.

Rhetorics of Display is the first book-length work that offers a conceptually focused perspective on rhetorical studies of display. That focus does not mean that the authors share the same theoretical, critical, or methodological approaches in their studies; clearly they do not, but that diversity in approach helps to disclose the richly textured and multifaceted rhetorical workings of displays. But all the studies in this book—as rhetorical studies—presume that the meanings manifested rhetorically through display are functions of particular, situated resolutions of the dynamic between revealing and concealing. Put directly, whatever is revealed through display simultaneously conceals alternative possibilities; therein is display's rhetorical dimension. Rhetorical analyses of displays proceed from that presumption, probing its situated manifestations, assessing the implications of that which is manifested for those who become audience to it. Whether constituted through vocal enunciation, textual inscription, visual portrayal, material structure, enacted performance, or some combination, rhetorical study of displays proceeds from the central idea that whatever they make manifest or appear is the culmination of selective processes that constrain the range of possible meanings available to those who encounter them.

One of the claims of this book is that rhetorics of display are nearly ubiquitous in contemporary communication and culture and, thus, have become the dominant rhetoric of our time. Attempts to relate rhetoric and display certainly did not originate with this book. The history of the communication arts can be read as a series of transformations in how rhetoric is associated with and dissociated from display in thought and practice. I make no pretense of giving an exhaustive account of that history in this introduction, but in the first of three sections, I want to offer a series of historical exhibits or vignettes—displays, if you will—that exemplify some of the distinctive attempts to draw and redraw that relationship in rhetorical theorizing and practice. From that exhibition, the chapters included in this book and related current scholarship in rhetorical studies appear within a wider perspective that underscores some of the distinctive—as well as not so distinctive—features of how rhetoric and display are related and studied in our times. The second section of the introduction articulates the central themes that together offer a comprehensive perspective on contemporary rhetorical studies of display. Ongoing scholarly projects and lines of inquiry in contemporary rhetorical studies coalesce around these articulated themes and, thus, imply strongly that rhetorics of display could very well be the dominant rhetoric of our day. The introduction ends with a third section that previews this book's chapters in relation to the themes elucidated in the second section.

Rhetoric and Display: Some Historical Vignettes

The rhetoric of display is an idea of ancient lineage, traceable to the Greek word *deiktikos,* which meant "exhibit," "show forth," "make known"; it is the opposite of the verb "conceal." According to Aristotle, the rhetoric of display was one of two ways of exhibiting or making known. Richard McKeon, philosopher and historian of rhetoric, explained that Aristotle modified the verb *deiktikos* to form the words *apodeiktikos* and *epideiktikos* and, thus, to distinguish logical and rhetorical forms of "showing forth."[2] "Apodeictic" meant show forth "from" or "by," as in the demonstration of a well-ordered scientific proof. "Epideictic" meant show forth "on" or "for," as in the disclosure of a person's virtue through an eloquent ceremonial speech.[3] The manifestations of rhetorical display were thus separated from demonstrative processes of "making known" through scientific proving.

Many students of classical rhetoric associated Aristotle's discussion of display oratory in his *Rhetoric* with amusement or diversion; epideictic "showing forth" became rhetorical "showing off" through stylistic ostentation and verbal self-display. From that vantage, the rhetoric of display paled in public significance when compared with the oratory of politics and of law. Lawrence W. Rosenfield, critic of rhetoric and aesthetics, deepened appreciation of the rhetoric of display when he explained that the term *epideixis* ("to shine or show forth") does not mean "mere display," as though orators simply were exhibiting their skills; rather, it means making manifest or highlighting the fleeting "appearance" of excellence in human experience that otherwise would remain "unnoticed or invisible."[4] At its best, epideictic calls for collective acknowledgment of virtue's presence; it "acts to unshroud . . . notable deeds in order to let us gaze at the aura glowing from within."[5] The orator's task is not to demonstrate or prove virtue but, through verbal ornament and stylistic embellishment, to "set an example" of excellence for listeners to behold and "take heed of its meaning."[6] Those who "behold" excellence Aristotle aptly called "witnesses" (*theoroi*).[7] They are called to gaze upon the reality of excellence disclosed through the exemplary instances manifested before them and, through intensified awareness and contemplation, undergo an epiphany or otherwise draw inspiration from the epideictic encounter.[8] According to Rosenfield's reading, Aristotle's epideictic is oratory of paramount civic importance since it commands members of a community to join together in thoughtful acknowledgment, celebration, and commemoration of that which is best in human experience.[9]

Aristotle's sharp distinction between rhetorical display and logical proof collapsed in the writings of Roman rhetoricians who called epideictic "demonstrative oratory" and thus signaled the intermingling of qualities of proving—making known "from" or "by"—with rhetorical display—showing forth "on" or "for." According to McKeon, Cicero's demonstrative oratory of praising virtue (*laudatio*) and censuring vice (*vitupera*) merged "the certainties and necessities of proof" with "the estimations and necessities of action."[10] Quintilian later puzzled over this shift from epideictic to demonstrative, wondering how Roman writers derived "demonstration" from the Greek "epideictic," which meant "display rather than demonstration," and then applied it to the narrower category of *laudatio,* which the Greeks called "encomium." He speculated that the terminological change was not, in fact, derived from the Greek but was a Roman innovation: "But it may be that Romans are not borrowing from the Greek when they apply the title *demonstrative,* but are merely led to do so because praise and blame demonstrate the nature of the object with which they are concerned."[11] Thus, we might surmise that Roman *laudatio* demonstrates a person's praiseworthiness "by" or "from" conventional understandings of life's values and virtues. As Gerard Hauser argues, display oratory became for the Romans "a special mode of proof," though they did not go so far as to consider the demonstrations of scientific proving as rhetorical displays.[12]

Jeffrey Walker details an alternative sophistic view of epideictic in Greco-Roman antiquity that extended the range of rhetorical display beyond the oratory of public ceremony to encompass all discourses that shape the beliefs and desires constituting a culture.[13] His perspective is based partly on the sophistic theory of Hermogenes of Tarsus, who broadened panegyric to include not only epideictic speeches but also the "literary discourses" of philosophy, history, and poetry.[14] That broadening meshes nicely with Aristotle's distinction between two kinds of audience function. The discourse of *pragmatikon*—the oratory of politics and of law—is addressed to an audience of *kritai,* or decision makers, who are empowered through direct public action—such as a vote—to decide whether to enact a policy or a law, whether to convict those accused of crimes, or whether a particular penalty is just. The discourse of *epideiktikon* is addressed to an audience of *theoroi,* or observers, who are not called upon to cast votes but, according to Walker, "to form opinions about and in response to the discourse presented."[15] Epideictic thus functions as a "suasive 'demonstration,' display, or showing forth (*epideixis*) of things, leading an audience of *theoroi* to contemplation (*theoria*), possible insight, and to formation of opinions and desires on matters of philosophical, social, ethical, and cultural concern."[16] As Walker explains it:

> "Epideictic" appears as that which shapes and cultivates the basic codes of value and belief by which a society or culture lives; it shapes the ideologies and imageries with which, and by which, the individual members of a community identify themselves; and, perhaps more significantly, it shapes the fundamental grounds, the "deep" commitments and presuppositions, that will underlie and ultimately determine decision and debate in particular pragmatic forums. As such, epideictic suasion is not limited to the reinforcement of existing beliefs and ideologies or to merely ornamental displays of clever speech (though clearly it can serve such purposes as well). Epideictic can also work to challenge or transform conventional beliefs—plainly the purposes of Plato's dialogues, Isocrates' panegyrics, what remains of Gorgias's epideictics (particularly *Helen* and the surviving paraphrases of *On the Nonexistent*), and the sophistic or Protagorean practice of antilogy that is parodied in the "speech of Lysias" in Plato's *Phaedrus*. All such discourses, again, are "epideictic" according to the late-sophistic theory of Hermogenes of Tarsus, and according to the definition I am emphasizing here. When conceived in positive terms and not simply in terms of lack, epideictic discourse reveals itself . . . as the central and indeed fundamental mode of rhetoric in human culture.[17]

For Walker, then, epideictic cannot be relegated to secondary importance or dismissed as "mere display" relative to the "rhetoric of practical civic business" because the discourses of *epideiktikon* constitute the very grounds of culture upon which the much narrower discourses of *pragamatikon* depend.[18]

The fifteenth- and sixteenth-century Renaissance humanists offer a view of epideictic as aesthetic, moralizing display. Epideictic poets and orators advanced conventional moral standards of civic humanism by adducing "images," "patterns," or "examples" of virtue ornamented to please audiences aesthetically, move their sentiments, and, perhaps, induce them to emulate exemplified deeds in their own civic conduct.[19] According to Rosenfield, this kind of epideictic readily is seen as display oratory in the sense wrongly attributed to Aristotle's original formulation. The poet or orator could presuppose dogmatic assumptions about right moral conduct as they exhibited their artistic talents in richly detailed examples that comported with received standards of decorum. Aesthetic execution of conventional moralizing exemplars thus became the central focus of rhetorical display—rather than disclosing quite unconventional, extraordinary manifestations of excellence—with the corollary expectation that audiences would register their pleasure by bestowing praise (or blame) upon the artists in accord with the perceived "virtuosity" of their performances.[20]

This transformation in epideictic is part of a larger shift in thought signaled by Leon Battista Alberti's *De pictura* (1435) and its first systematic presentation of fixed-point perspective. Alberti showed how excellent artistic execution brought a profusion of details into proportionate, ordered, visual perspective. The science of perspective that Alberti explained not only permeated the Renaissance arts but also presaged the stance of detached observer so central to the emergence of modernist sciences. Alberti's elaboration of fixed-point per-spective and other components of the painter's art invites a view of the artist as a detached but self-conscious and shrewd observer of how things that are seen "appear." Based upon that learning, the artist can re-create similar appearances through artful merger of mat-ter and form manifested in the shadings, textures, and colors that constitute the painting's visual display. Much as the artist must be sufficiently detached to observe material and for-mal means available for enacting aesthetic creation, members of the audience also become detached and even passive viewers of the art, as though spectators at a performance.[21]

Renaissance humanists theorized and practiced a visual aesthetic that integrated the arts through rhetorical—and especially epideictic—categories.[22] Alberti saw the art of painting as rhetorical display in that the elements of visual composition operated accord-ing to the precepts of rhetoric, and the art itself aimed at giving spectators "a heightened sense of *virtù*" comparable to the task Cicero assigned to his ideal orator in *De oratore*.[23] The traditional arts of rhetorical display—poetry and oratory—exhibited a decidedly visual consciousness parallel to that of the visual arts. Emphasis on the visual rather than cog-nitive in oratorical display is illustrated by epideictic preachers who beseeched their audi-ences "to 'look,' to 'view,' to 'gaze upon'" exhibited actions and deeds rather than "to think," "to meditate," "to consider."[24] An audience, of course, might also reflect upon actions and deeds displayed, but it must first hear them described in a "word-picture."[25] Orators and poets thus crafted their examples of virtue or vice by investing their narratives with quali-ties conducive to imaginative seeing through *ekphrasis,* or detailed description.[26] The com-monplace humanist expressions "Painting is mute poetry and poetry a speaking picture" and "*ut pictura poesis*" ("as is painting, so is poetry") are fitting epigrams for the Renais-sance integration of the verbal and visual arts as modes of rhetorical display.[27] Both the speaking picture (the poet's *pictura,* or verbal exemplary narrative) and the silent poetry (the painter's *istoria,* or visual narrative) are conceived in terms of making visible idealized images or patterns or examples of people and events limned with moral meanings so that audiences could "gaze upon" and, perhaps, strive to mirror or otherwise emulate them in their own conduct.[28] The visual aesthetic and moralizing implications of Renaissance epi-deictic extended to architecture and urban design (the piazza).[29] Landscape gardening and park design, too, exhibited a similar "epideictic semiotic" that glorified republican civic ideals while affording visitors opportunities for "re-creation" so that they could resume full participation in civic life.[30]

Renaissance humanists presumed that all aesthetic displays are rhetorical performances before audiences capable of appraising the virtuosity of their execution. The attending pub-lic, educated in rhetorical precepts, could enjoy the pleasures of aesthetic discernment and judgment, bestowing praise or its opposite, with the artist's fame—more than the subject's —hanging in the balance.[31] Art criticism itself became something of an epideictic art of display, exhibiting critics' discernment and judgment as they assigned praise or blame.[32] Castiglione's *Book of the Courtier* serves as a paradigm for enacted rhetorical displays before appraising audiences.[33] The courtier's performance is manifested through self-display. The act of characterizing oneself as an aesthetic creation is comparable to the efforts of the painters, poets, and playwrights of the day to develop characterizations worthy of praise.[34] The courtier attempts to appear before others in socially advantageous ways, striking a graceful pose while exhibiting *sprezzatura,* or a kind of "negligent diligence," that conceals the artistry behind the performance.[35] But Castiglione also anticipated that audiences were positioned to respond as critics of the rhetorically enacted performance. He not only sketched "the conduct of the gracious courtier" but also depicted the "responses with which the courtier's audience should properly reward his performance."[36]

The "showings" of the arts were rhetorical displays, but rhetorical displays were not thought to constitute knowledge in the physical and theological sciences. The discourses of the sciences included overt rhetorical displays as well as dialectical arguments about the probable, but the processes of establishing certain knowledge were recognized as the domain of apodeictic "demonstration."[37] During the scientific revolutions of the seventeenth and eighteenth centuries, "making known" was the "showing forth" of certainty increasingly aided by disciplined methods of logical and mathematical reasoning or by instruments and technologies for attending more closely to objects under observation. The writings of Descartes mark a convenient starting point for tracking the trajectory of these developments: he formulated procedures for making relevant facts visible through algebraic representation and diagraming in a step-by-step process for solving problems in his *Rules for the Direction of the Intellect* (or *Regulae*); he described a disciplined method of thought for arriving at clear and distinct ideas in his *Discourse on Method;* and he brought algebraic equations into visual, geometric representation through what we now call Cartesian coordinates.[38] Galileo would make another convenient starting point. His use of the telescope arguably is among the first in a long line of subsequent instrumental and technological innovations that scientists would use "to disclose, probe, isolate, measure, represent, or otherwise bring to attention the objects of investigation."[39] "Making known" from the Renaissance up until and through the Enlightenment became associated with visualizing forms of demonstration that enabled the seeing of objects—whether ideas in the mind or things in the world—with ever greater clarity, accuracy, and precision.

Eighteenth-century rhetoric and poetics grounded principles for verbally enacted rhetorical displays on the primary presumption of Enlightenment thought that human attainments are founded upon the psychological predisposition to believe what we experience through the visual sense. Isaac Newton's development of nonrhetorical processes of "making known" through the observational method, as well as the emergence of philosophical empiricism, influenced that development.[40] Since oratory and poetry could not make audiences actually see objects directly through the senses, theories of rhetoric and poetics incorporated a network of interconnected psychological and aesthetic concepts for understanding how words could engage powers of imaginative seeing. For instance, in his *Philosophy of Rhetoric,* George Campbell predicated his theory of "moral reasoning" upon that primary presumption. Influenced by David Hume's empirical philosophy, Campbell explained how poets and orators needed to verbalize experiences so vividly that the image evoked would possess such "vivacity" as to seem the product of sense experience rather than of imagination.[41] Dramatic and visual arts are immediately present before spectators and, thus, might be expected to deeply "impress" them, but Henry Home (Lord Kames) explained that the verbal arts could, through accurate description, so vividly evoke imagery that audiences would undergo the fantasy of "ideal presence," as if transported to the scene and actually perceiving the event or object rather than hearing or reading a verbal account.[42] Given the primary presumption that "seeing is believing," Adam Smith, Hugh Blair, James Beattie, Archibald Alison, and others stressed the need for orators and poets to make use of descriptive "verbal portraiture" to create "concrete, specific, clear, factual, picturesque imitations" of the phenomenal world.[43] And those verbal portraits engaged with the audience's moral as well as aesthetic senses, prompting their discernment of beauty in accord with received standards of taste and stimulating sentiments conducive to the experience of sympathy, benevolence, and other moral virtues.[44]

Twentieth-century rhetoricians Richard McKeon, Chaim Perelman, and Kenneth Burke offer ideas that broaden the range of displays that are considered rhetorical and the kinds of rhetorical phenomena that are manifested through display.[45] They also are among the scholars who presaged what I will contend is a major development in rhetorical studies today. McKeon offered an expansive view of "demonstrative rhetoric" as a "productive art" of showing or manifesting facts or values in all fields of discourse and action.[46] Alluding to the political demonstrations during the late 1960s and early 1970s, McKeon claimed that critical reactions against and declining faith in the apodeictic certainties of nineteenth-century idealist and materialist metaphysics brought about a transformation of demonstration from "proof to manifestation" that he thought was among the significant, distinguishing phenomena of the rhetoric of his times. "Demonstration" applied as much to actions that "show forth" feelings and commitments as it did to "making known" through inferential patterns and rules of proof. But, from McKeon's perspective, both are products of a demonstrative rhetoric conceived as a universal, productive, inventive art of discourse and action that constitutes and makes known all facts and values through rhetorical exhibiting, presenting, and manifesting.[47]

Chaim Perelman's concept of "presence" broadens the range of rhetorical display to encompass nearly all verbal emphasis in discourses addressed to situated audiences.[48] According to Perelman, "Choosing to single out certain things for presentation in a speech draws the attention of the audience to them and thereby gives them a *presence* that prevents them from being neglected."[49] Presence is identified with rhetorical display through "presentation": "the *displaying* of certain elements on which the speaker wishes to center attention in order that they may occupy the foreground of the hearer's consciousness [emphasis added]."[50] Presence is, as Carroll Arnold put it, a matter of emphasis or highlighting, of "actively bringing thoughts . . . before the minds of the audience addressed."[51] Perelman acknowledges that displays making an object visually present have rhetorical influence, but he is concerned primarily with verbal emphases that make "realities . . . distant in time and space" present to an audience's consciousness even as they allow alternative possible realities to fade from conscious attention.[52] Hence, all arguments for Perelman exhibit a partiality in perspective since they consist of a "preliminary selection of facts and values," of a "specific description in a given language," and of "an emphasis which varies with the importance given them."[53] Rhetorical display creates presence for these selected elements through presentational forms that shape how the substance of discourse appears in the minds of audiences addressed.[54]

Kenneth Burke's theory of dramatism, which depicts all of human relations as "symbolic drama," offers a perspective of direct relevance to rhetorical studies of display. Burke's dramatism maintains that since humans literally possess a "special aptitude for 'symbolic action,'" drama affords a literal vocabulary for the study of human relations in terms of action.[55] Burke's dramatism is predicated on a view of language as "symbolic action." His concept of "terministic screens" depicts all language use as rhetorical insofar as our choice of words enacts a partial perspective toward a situation by simultaneously directing attention toward some meanings while deflecting consideration of others.[56] The very use of verbal symbols, then, is meaningful symbolic action laced with rhetorical motivations and inclinations. Accordingly, Burke offers his "pentad" as a critical vocabulary for mapping linguistic depictions in terms of action—acts, scenes or settings, agents or actors, agencies or instruments, purposes or goals—with the aim of disclosing the motives behind enacted symbolic dramas.[57] He also stresses that symbolic drama indelibly permeates social hierarchies or orders. Inevitably, as we encounter symbols of authority, status conflicts, and prestige issues, we find ourselves violating rules (what Burke calls the "thou shalt nots") that constitute social hierarchies and, thus, manifest much of the drama of our lives. Violation of hierarchical rules generates guilt and the corresponding desire for atonement and redemption. From Burke's vantage, much of the drama of our lives consists in agonistic struggles to expiate guilt through purifying symbolic acts—acts of mortification or of scapegoating—that foster a sense of movement toward redemption and restoration of place within the hierarchy.

Burke's dramatism is even more far-reaching in its implications for rhetorical studies of display than Perelman's "presence" and McKeon's view of demonstrative rhetoric as a universal, productive art. Display is manifested in the screening or attention-directing function of language; language highlights, points out, or shows forth even as it diminishes, ignores, or conceals. Display is involved in terminological enactments of symbolic dramas that exhibit, consciously or unconsciously, attitudes and motivations. Display is rhetorically manifested in the symbolism of hierarchical rules, in our experiences of adhering to them or violating them, and in our undergoing guilt should we violate the "thou shalt nots," with corresponding desires for redemption. Burke's depiction of human life literally as symbolic drama carries the all-encompassing implication that life itself, insofar as it is experienced by symbolizing animals, consists largely, if not entirely, of rhetorically enacted performances or displays.[58]

These vignettes show that questions about how rhetoric and display are related did not originate in our time but are of long-standing significance in the history of the communication arts. McKeon, Perelman, and especially Burke imply that rhetorical displays manifest and permeate communication and culture far beyond what the earlier vignettes exhibited, but those earlier characterizations still yield distinctive perspectives that have resonance even today. "Showing forth" through rhetorical disclosure still often is distinguished from nonrhetorical processes of "making known" through logic, mathematics, and science; but it also is the case that we could work out the implications of Burke's, McKeon's, and even Perelman's ideas to challenge that distinction and mount the argument that all acts of "showing forth" and of "making known" are rhetorically manifested displays. However one might stand on that issue, we still experience rhetorical displays in the classical sense of ceremonial speeches that seek to inspire audiences with images and exemplars of the excellent and wonderful in human experience. We also encounter rhetorical display in discourses and actions that constitute and show forth the opinions, facts, or values that manifest the grounds of argument and proof—if not of what Walker called the "codes of value and belief" that constitute an entire society or culture. Surely we still encounter multiple aesthetic creations that attract attention and work to please us, even as they exhibit moral—or moralizing—implications. The means of emphasis, amplification, or ornament conceived in the past ranged across the inducements of verbal figures, visual images, material structures, and enacted performances. These remain among the resources of rhetorical display even today in our televisual, mass-mediated culture. And the anticipated orientation of those who become audience to rhetorical displays still varies along a continuum running from the engaged, contemplative witness to the passive, pleasure-seeking spectator.

Nearly all of the chapters in *Rhetorics of Display* analyze or theorize relationships between rhetoric and display as manifested in the communicative practices and cultural contexts of our times. Some of those studies transform ideas encapsulated in the historical vignettes for fresh application in disclosing the situated rhetoric of particular contemporary forms of display. Not only do the ideas of McKeon, Perelman, and Burke still generate theoretical insight and lend critical utility, but, depending upon the display examined and its situated context, so, too, do the ideas of Aristotle, Quintilian, Castiglione, and others. Even when not explicitly treated, specific relationships between rhetoric and display that were articulated in the past periodically echo throughout these chapters. However, the studies collected here move beyond those ideas by examining cases that afford opportunities for theorizing new understandings about displays as rhetorical and about rhetoric as display. Without at all rejecting resources from the past whenever they have utility, the essays in this book offer exemplars for fresh thinking about a range of rhetorical displays that, together, mark out the leading themes of an emerging field of rhetorical inquiry that is especially suited to our times.

A characteristic feature of rhetoric in our times is the absence of widely authoritative standards for gaining compliance and commitment from audiences. In the absence of taken-for-granted standards, we find ourselves amidst multiple, ever-changing, and always-contestable manifestations of interest and worth. The amplifications of multiple visual, textually inscribed, or televisual images exhibit before us a plurality of conceptions of fact and of value, of attitudes and judgments. The places we visit or inhabit embody in their physical structures and material ornaments symbolic inducements that work to dispose our attitudes, emotions, or sentiments. Our encounters with others enact displays of self and of others that imply who we desire or otherwise take ourselves to be. We always are potentially an audience to these multiple displays, sometimes as thoughtful witnesses but oftentimes as passive spectators of the passing show who hope, at best, to be amused. But the general conclusion to be drawn is that whatever is "displayed" or "made manifest"— whatever commands and sustains attention relative to a vast field of competitors— addresses a claim about value and attitude to those who somehow become audience to it. In view of the nearly ubiquitous nature of display in contemporary communication and culture, it is tempting to conclude that the rhetoric of "manifestation" and "showing"—the rhetoric of display—is the dominant rhetoric of our times.

It is not surprising, then, that rhetorical studies are today coalescing around themes related to display. In the next section I identify some of those themes and suggest that they together mark out a comprehensive perspective on a newly emerging—though far from new—field of rhetorical inquiry I call rhetorical studies of display.

Rhetorical Studies of Display

Peter Wollen characterized studies presented during the 1993 Dia Center for the Arts conference on visual display and subsequently published in the book *Visual Display: Culture*

Beyond Appearances as concerned with unlocking various manifestations of rhetoric that, in turn, worked to occlude or otherwise conceal truths behind visual displays.[59] Displays such as shrines and curiosity cabinets, wax and other museums, statistical graphics in classical economics, medical displays and displays about medicine, performances of ethnicity, sports and art exhibitions, images in science fiction films, and others manifest rhetorics that conceal "truths" behind whatever they visually reveal. But since rhetoric always offers opportunities for "decipherment and unmasking," Wollen tells us, we always can learn to approach the world of spectacle "with skepticism, to locate it within history, to decipher its signs, to deflect its imaginary power."[60] These studies of visual display are depicted as cutting through illusory rhetorical manifestations of visual displays to gain revelations of "culture beyond appearances."

Visual Display is an important and provocative collection of essays that resonates with the generative idea for this book on rhetorics of display: whatever is rhetorically manifested through displays also necessarily conceals. Wollen's distinction between rhetorics of display and the truths about culture behind or beyond them also raises an important related issue. To be sure, we can argue about a visual display in its situated context, point out what it may conceal, and explore the political, cultural, and artistic implications of whatever our criticisms reveal. At the same time, our efforts to disclose truths are complicated by the introduction of our own critical perspectives. Even skeptical acts of "decipherment and unmasking" depend upon perspectives that necessarily foreclose alternative possible meanings even as they disclose purported truths and, thus, conceal as well as reveal. There is, to put it directly, no way to see that which is displayed as it really is, unencumbered by our own partial points of view.

Three recent essay collections indicate current scholarly interest in themes directly related to rhetorical studies of display. The first two of the three collections I shall discuss are decidedly rhetorical studies written primarily by rhetoricians. One is *Defining Visual Rhetorics,* edited by Charles A. Hill and Marguerite Helmers.[61] This book explores the rhetorical operations of visual displays. The studies reveal the "visual rhetoric" manifested in photographs, in painting, in embroidery, in film, in advertising, in graphical displays, in the upscale shopping market, and in the home. The chapters together indicate that an important dimension for rhetorical studies of display is how visual displays influence our attitudes and feelings, shape and reinforce our beliefs and values, and constrain what we write, say, or otherwise think about them. The second is *Rhetorical Bodies,* edited by Jack Selzer and Sharon Crowley.[62] This book examines rhetorical relationships between the symbolic and the material. The studies explore those rhetorical relationships as manifested in public memorials, medical dissections, literal acts and political images of cannibalism, body images in poetry, photographs of the body, and the verbal "figuring" or "inscribing" of types of embodied persons. As a collection, this book indicates that both verbal inducement of body images in relation to material practices and the symbolic dimensions of the material as manifested in built structures and in corporeal forms are important aspects of display. The third is *The Politics of Display: Museums, Science, Culture,* edited by Sharon Macdonald. Macdonald characterizes the volume as exploring "the processes involved in, and the political consequences of" display in science museums and exhibitions since, "of all types of public display, it is these that have most frequently presented themselves as, and been thought to be, outside—or above—politics."[63] Most of the studies in this book are not conceived as rhetorical analyses, but as they work to expose the play of politics behind science museums and exhibitions, they also imply that what is displayed before the public as unequivocal and celebrated achievements are manifested through the "selections, styles, and silences" of rhetoric.[64] This book thus suggests that museums, exhibitions, and other presentations are displays of rhetorical interest and significance.

Other ongoing projects in rhetorical studies intersect with these themes and, thus, further indicate the significance of display in contemporary rhetorical studies. For example, consider rhetorical studies of public memory.[65] Rhetorical studies of public memory grapple with tensions between revealing and concealing characterized in terms of remembrance and forgetfulness, recollection and amnesia. Rhetorics that constitute public memory are displays that manifest contingent resolutions of those tensions, whether through speeches, photographs or films, memorials or monuments, or exhibitions and other public performances. Rhetorical studies of public memory expose those situated rhetorics and their special allures and inducements; they thus reawaken contingently resolved tensions associated with remembering and forgetting and thereby show that public memory always is potentially contestable. And they do so by questioning what is and is not remembered, whose interests become present in public memory and whose remain absent, who has authority to define public memory and who challenges and counters that authority, and what constitutes past transgressions and who is accountable for them. And, perhaps above all, these studies examine rhetorics of public memory that often are overtly epideictic and, thus, imply an additional parallel, if not direct, association with studies of rhetorical display. Full understanding of the rhetorics that constitute public memory requires attention to how they manifest assumptions about what is worth remembering about the past and about whether the remembered is worthy of praise or condemnation, acknowledgment or disparagement, celebration or lamentation.

As the books surveyed here and the entries to the selected bibliography indicate, contemporary rhetorical studies often coalesce around or intersect with themes related to rhetorical display. Rhetorical studies of display are distinguishable from other studies in that they presuppose in their theoretical and critical practices the classical idea that to display is to "show forth" or "make known," which, in turn, implies its opposite—to conceal. That dynamic between revealing and concealing—deepened and extended by contemporary rhetorical theorists and critics—is the core presumption behind rhetorical studies of display. Hence, the studies collected in *Rhetorics of Display* presume that displays are rhetorical because the meanings they manifest before situated audiences result from selective processes and, thus, constitute partial perspectives with political, social, or cultural implications. Rhetorical studies typically disclose the partiality of displays by reawakening tensions contingently resolved through those selective processes. Thus, the rhetorics of display often are deconstructed by exploring how those situated resolutions conceal even as they reveal, what meanings they leave absent even as they make others present, whose interests they mute as well as whose they emphasize, what they condemn as well as celebrate, and so on. This is so regardless of whether those rhetorics are enunciated through speech, inscribed in linguistic texts, depicted visually, circulated and viewed electronically, embodied in material structures or materialized in bodily form, or enacted through exhibitions, demonstrations, or other performances.

The perspective on rhetorical studies of display offered here, then, incorporates the presumption that displays are constituted rhetorically through situated resolutions of the core dynamic between revealing and concealing. Put otherwise, rhetorics of display are manifested through processes of what I shall call "rhetorical selectivity."[66] There are at least four overlapping but distinguishable selective processes that manifest the rhetoric of displays. These four selective processes designate the organizing themes of a perspective on rhetorical studies of display in contemporary scholarship. Rhetorical studies of display examine rhetorical selectivity manifested in (1) the verbal depiction of the visual and the visual depiction of the verbal; (2) the disposition of place and the placing of disposition; (3) demonstrations as rhetorical display and rhetorical displays as demonstrative; and (4) epideictic identifications and divisions. I shall discuss these themes in turn.

I earlier mentioned Kenneth Burke's trenchant observation that all meaning, insofar as it is mediated through language, is inherently persuasive because language use is a selective process that conceals even as it reveals. Using Burke's language, words direct attention toward some possible meanings and simultaneously deflect from consideration meanings that would be implied with different words.[67] And this notion of verbally directed "seeing" is literally intended since observations made about experiences are "implicit in the terminology you have chosen, whether your choice of terms was deliberate or spontaneous."[68] Even so "natural" and sensual an experience as walking along a forested trail in northern New England is mediated through language. For example, some might see only an undifferentiated grouping of sparrows flutter across the path before them, while those terminologically equipped to see distinctive markings would be impressed by the variety of birds: chipping sparrows, white-throated sparrows, white-crowned sparrows, slate-colored juncos. The point is that without verbally directed attention, much of what we do see would remain unseen. This acquired verbal capacity for directed seeing is exhibited in any field guide for classification of the birds and is put to full use in books that promise to instruct readers on how to read the surrounding habitat or environment. One such book teaches a vocabulary needed to "read the forested landscape" by directing attention to signs indicative of events in the forest's past. Thus, the reader learns to see signs of previous pasturage, of logging, of fire, of blow-downs, and of blights that, quite literally, would otherwise have remained unseen.[69] These examples illustrate that much of the rhetoric of display is manifested through selective processes of terminological depiction of the visual.

But selectivity also is at work in visual as well as in verbal dimensions of display. Paintings, sketches, photographs, and other visual images are rhetorical in that they, too, emphasize some meanings even as they diminish or conceal others. Peter Burke observed that visual images operate according to conventions and styles, including the style of realism that has (as would any style) "its own rhetoric."[70] W. J. T. Mitchell characterized his essays in iconology as a "rhetoric of images" in the dual sense that they are studies both of "what to say about images" and of "'what images say'—that is, the ways in which they seem to speak for themselves by persuading, telling stories, or describing."[71] Art historian Michael Ann Holly contended that the "rhetoric of the image" manifested in Renaissance paintings prescribed and prefigured "rhetorical strategies" that art historians such as Jacob Burckhardt incorporated in their own interpretive accounts.[72] Thus, the visual as well as the linguistic "cajoles" and "persuades":

> By using it [rhetoric] to refer to pictorial constructs (especially those of the Renaissance, the age that was itself obsessed with the power of rhetoric) rather than linguistic principles, I intend to underscore its classical power to cajole: "the art of

expressive speech or discourse . . . persuasive or moving power" in dictionary terms; in Quintilian's, "The task of the artist is to persuade, while the power of persuasion resides in the art. Consequently, while it is the duty of the orator to invent and arrange, *invention* and *arrangement* may be regarded as belonging to rhetoric." Just as obviously, any viewer (or listener) for that matter has a mind of her or his own, a situatedness in history, a context for understanding that ultimately shapes what she or he chooses to see. Cajolery is not tantamount to indoctrination. Yet to ignore totally the shaping impulses of the work as it throws itself into—or even forms its trajectory through—time is to deny the power of images, and ultimately to fool our-selves into thinking that there is some truth for the asking in the abstract, away from context, away from rhetoric, away from imagining, away from history.[73]

"As often as language teaches us to see," Holly wrote, "art instructs us in telling. The exchange works actively in both directions."[74] That point is generalizable. Visual depictions rhetorically constrain our verbal responses, much as verbal depictions rhetorically con-strain what we are prompted to see. Rhetorical studies of display examine the nexus of visual and verbal depictions that selectively manifest the rhetoric of displays.[75] Words shape what we imagine or actually see. Names, labels, and narratives direct attention to whatever purportedly is significant or desirable about visually displayed objects. Thus, Halloran and Clark indicate that an ordinary lump of metal becomes a valued object—a musket ball used during the American Revolution; Jorgensen-Earp points out how ordinary objects salvaged from the *Titanic*'s debris field on the ocean floor become valued as sacred relics from a hallowed grave site or as rare artifacts that must be conserved for study and under-standing.[76] But visual images also constrain what we plausibly can say, or write, or even think about them. Consider, for example, the widely circulated photographic image of Pfc. Lynndie England, posing with "thumbs up" before helpless, naked captives at the Abu Ghraib prison in Iraq. Susan Sontag wrote that we see not only on this and other similar images "expressions of satisfaction at the acts of torture being inflicted" but also the "deep satisfaction of being photographed" presumably for lighthearted circulation among friends: "The events are in part designed to be photographed. The grin is for the camera. There would be something missing if, after stacking the naked men, you couldn't take a picture of them."[77] This account of the soldiers photographed as "having fun" while performing degrading and humiliating acts is difficult to contest based on the visual evidence.[78]

Displays also are manifested rhetorically through the structures of built places. The material structure of a place's tangible features resonates with symbolic implications gen-erated through selective namings, conventions, styles, narratives, and rituals. Places are thus disposed rhetorically in their physical design so that their arrangement works to dispose the attitudes, feelings, and conduct of those who visit, dwell within, or otherwise encounter them.[79] As Halloran and Clark succinctly put it, places exert influence,[80] and rhetorical studies of display often examine the manifestation of that influence in relationships be-tween the dispositions of places and the placings of dispositions.[81] Gambling casinos are structured to stimulate pursuit of desires. Cathedrals are designed to inspire awe and rev-erence. Memorials are constructed to encourage contemplation and remembrance. All three are places that do the rhetorical work of redisposing the inclinations of those who enter them from the familiar, everyday world. Of course, the rhetoric of places also is manifested in the workplace, the home, and other ordinary places since they, too, are arranged and adorned in ways that redispose and regulate the inclinations of those who dwell within them. All constructed and designed places can be considered as material embodiments of preferred attitudes, feelings, and valuings. Thus, an important dimension of the rhetoric manifested in display is the symbolic resonance of material places that inclines those who occupy them to experience social meaning from particular, selectively structured vantage points or perspectives.

One example of how built structures exhibit rhetorical qualities is Richmond, Virginia's, famous tree-lined boulevard, Monument Avenue. Before 1996, a drive along Monument Avenue brought successively into view a series of impressive monuments to Confederate president Jefferson Davis and generals J. E. B. Stuart, Stonewall Jackson, and Robert E. Lee. (Also included is a monument to naval commander Matthew Fontaine Maury.) Erected between 1890 and 1929, the monuments together manifested in material form an internally consistent narrative, with each offering an exemplar of the Confederate leadership's valor and statesmanship.[82] That consistency was visibly disrupted with the unveiling, on July 10, 1996, of statuary commemorating African American tennis player and Richmond native son Arthur Ashe Jr. for his achievements as an athlete, literacy spokesman, and AIDS activist. A drive along Monument Avenue today either begins or ends with the Ashe statue, tennis racket in one hand and books in the other, surrounded by children with upturned faces and outstretched arms. The Ashe monument commemorates civic virtues exhibited by ordinary citizens for the benefit of their community (which includes the presence of children) rather than those of great leaders in service to a political or military cause. And, of course, the presence of Ashe as the exemplar of those virtues itself functions as a material synecdoche of African American emergence into metropolitan, regional, and national civic life—a synecdoche jarringly incongruous with the embodied Confederate story celebrating leaders who defended a cause that barred that political possibility. The incongruity experienced when moving from one to the other material emplacement of clashing attitudes and values illustrates the general point that selective composition, design, and placement of built structures manifest some meanings even as they conceal others and, thus, operate rhetorically.

Displays also are rhetorically manifested through enacted demonstrations. "Demonstration" denotes a much wider range of meanings than anticipated by Aristotle's sharp distinction between "proving" and "rhetorical display."[83] It still is not unusual for people to think in terms of irrefutable proof when discussing the demonstrations of science, logic, or mathematics, but they would as readily associate demonstrations with the showings of individual and group feelings and convictions through protest rallies, candlelight vigils, picket lines, and parades.[84] As demonstrations, both are rhetorical displays through portrayal, exhibition, and presentation. To demonstrate, then, is to enact a rhetorical performance that anticipates the presence of others; it is the staging of a spectacle to be seen. Standing for the national anthem before the start of a professional baseball game is a staged performance that demonstrates identification of spectators, players, and the game itself with patriotism; other public gatherings, such as theater productions or musical concerts, do not require spectators to demonstrate that particular allegiance, though theatergoers and concertgoers might well be expected, through their personal comportment, to demonstrate some other sort of allegiance. The performative aspect of demonstrations is revealed whenever the virtuosity of their execution is questioned, as would be the case, for instance, of accusing someone of acting badly by refusing to stand for the anthem before the game. But that refusal, of course, might itself manifest a demonstration of convictions and feelings that run against those enacted by the ritual—an entirely different staged performance.

Many rhetorical displays exhibit demonstrative qualities of proof, manifestation, and performance. The rhetorical displays of scientists and other technical communicators often involve adducing proof for claims through staged performances that "make known" noteworthy features of some occurrence or event or object by simulation, exhibition, or presentation.[85] Museums of science and art create the rhetorical displays of exhibits and exhibitions that, often at one stroke, prove (through making purported facts known), make manifest (by showing valued artifacts for immediate inspection), and enact (through staging the context for viewing purported facts and valued objects). The "image events" that display much of what constitutes the new rhetoric of emerging social movements also exhibit these demonstrative qualities.[86] Rhetorical displays in much of politics, advertising, and entertainment are performances that manifest or show forth, through televisual and other images, the values, sentiments, and desires presumably taken for granted as proof of the worthiness (or the reverse) of particular events, personalities, and products. Rhetorical displays that exhibit demonstrative qualities might very well permeate daily life. People do demonstrate or act out preferred identities and conceptions of self through words and deeds that enact, with varying degrees of virtuosity, self-portrayals exhibiting the "right" attitudes and feelings or proving the "right" commitments and allegiances.[87]

Displays manifest through verbal and visual depiction, through the disposition of place, through demonstration—or all three—specific, situated, rhetorical resolutions of the dynamic between concealing and revealing.[88] And such rhetorical resolutions exhibit partial perspectives—an orientation, a point of view, a way of seeing—that both open and restrict possibilities for meaning for those who become audience to them. What rhetorician Richard Weaver wrote about linguistic forms of rhetoric applies to all forms of rhetorical display: displays emphasize and diminish, amplify and mute, select and omit, disclose and conceal, and, thus, exhibit perspectives that "embody an order of desire."[89] The perspectives they enact are laced with assumptions about what is or is not desirable or to be valued, about what is and is not praiseworthy, about what ought and ought not to be.[90] In that respect, displays exhibit epideictic qualities. To claim that displays exhibit epideictic qualities does not imply the privileging of any particular order of goods or values. The displays we encounter in our daily lives make manifest a wide variety of possible conceptions of the good, or values, that compete for our potential interest and desire. But they all do manifest rhetorically some particular order of desire that necessarily places some conceptions of the good before others and, thereby, works to influence those who become audience to them.[91]

The assertion that displays have an epideictic dimension does not entail the view that audiences necessarily respond as contemplative *theoroi;* nor does it rule out that possible response. Depending on the situated context, audiences could function along one or more of the lines of response exhibited earlier in the vignettes. Audiences still are engaged as thoughtful witnesses or stimulated as passive spectators; they can participate in authentic experiences that inspire or in aesthetic experiences that please; they can take part in manifesting the grounds of knowledge or of political thought or action; they can pursue entertainments that excite, provoke, or, perhaps, merely relieve boredom. These are among the possible inclinations of situated audiences as they respond to exhibited values with some degree of enthusiasm or detachment, praise or blame, acknowledgment or disparagement, celebration or disdain, affirmation or disavowal.

Displays are manifested in anticipation of appearing before some situated audience, but those who actually become audience to them bring to the encounter their own orientations or points of view; they themselves "embody an order of desire" whose more or less settled patterns of valuing and attitudinizing may or may not resonate with the meanings disclosed before them. Monument Avenue originally addressed southern white audiences, perhaps calling up nostalgic and romantic images of the Old South, but the statuary of Confederate leaders today evoke different sentiments and valuings from many, if not most, whites who become audience to them; they surely would resonate in the same way with very few— if any—African Americans. We can see from this example that the valuings and attitudes made to appear through display are potentially contestable and subject to being rearranged in accord with some distinctive, alternative "order of desire." In that respect, a display confronts audiences with what Burke called "possibilities of classification in its partisan" and, we should add, "unifying" facets.[92] If we accept Burke's view, rhetorics of display, like all rhetoric, incorporate resources of identification and of its inescapable counterpart, division. It does not matter whether the display is intended for us as the addressed audience.[93] Opportunities for identification and division arise regardless of who becomes audience to the display. It is not surprising, then, that we encounter displays nearly on a daily basis that somehow engage with our sense of belonging and identity, with our sense of social relationships, and with our sense of history.[94] We might find that a display affirms our identity, magnifies our interests, and celebrates our values, but it also might generate feelings of being ignored, belittled, debased, or diminished. And, as often is the case, it might leave us ambivalent, disengaged, or indifferent. Insofar as displays manifest some particular, situated ordering of desires, their rhetorical dimension invites us to do some attitudinizing of our own, whether through expressions of identification, alienation, or some intermediate inclination.

The next section presents this book's chapters according to the four pivotal themes that together define the perspective toward contemporary rhetorical studies of display that I have offered here.

Structure of the Book

Rhetorics of Display contains studies that exhibit different theoretical and critical approaches, but each study, as a rhetorical study, presumes that whatever becomes manifest or appears through display is the culmination of selective processes that constrain the range of possible and permissible meanings available to those who become audience to them. The rhetorics examined in these chapters are always situated and, thus, contingent resolutions of the dynamic between revealing and concealing that enable partial and always potentially contestable perspectives. The authors thus examine how displays open and foreclose possibilities for meaning and with what consequences for those who become audience to them. The chapters furnish exemplars that disclose rhetorical manifestations of displays through (1) the verbal depiction of the visual and the visual depiction of the verbal; (2) the disposition of place and the placing of disposition; (3) demonstrations as rhetorical display and rhetorical displays as demonstrative; and (4) epideictic identifications and divisions.

The Verbal Depiction of the Visual and the Visual Depiction of the Verbal

The chapters in this section direct attention to verbal depictions of the visual and visual depictions of the verbal as manifesting the rhetorics of displays under examination. In chapter 2, Cheryl R. Jorgensen-Earp discloses how verbal narratives framed objects seen at the *Titanic* exhibition in Chicago through a rhetoric of display that reawakened the sense of *Titanic*'s place in public memory while legitimating the controversial project of disturbing the *Titanic*'s resting site for commercial exploitation. The controversy involved two conflicting metaphorical systems. Critics of salvage evoked a "sacralizing" system of metaphor that depicted the sunken ship as a tomb, the seabed as hallowed ground, and the salvagers as no better than grave robbers for disturbing them. Defenders of salvage turned to a "secularizing" metaphorical system in which the ship and seabed became an archeological dig and the salvagers heroic, entrepreneurial adventurer-scientists. The exhibition drew positive associations from both systems in two narratives that brought visitors to a simulated site of the *Titanic*'s sinking. One displayed objects within the familiar tragic narrative about the night when the great ship sank. The other enacted a memorializing story in which a piece of the ship's hull became a simulated grave marker situated in sand at an ersatz gravesite. Both narratives induced visitors to see *Titanic* objects as valuable both as scientific artifacts and as sacred relics, thus reconciling otherwise conflicting implications of the opposed metaphorical systems. The exhibition, then, was a celebration of science's secular powers of retrieval and restoration that, by displaying objects otherwise consigned to oblivion at the bottom of the sea, afforded visitors opportunities to contemplate and memorialize the meaning of the *Titanic* tragedy.

In chapter 3, James Michael Farrell examines nineteenth-century British newspaper accounts of the Irish famine that enacted what he calls an "economy of display," combining the visual image of an artist's sketch and an accompanying verbal description to induce emotional and moral responses from readers. This analysis shows that, although the sketches are affecting in both respects, verbal depictions heighten their emotional and moral power. Both verbal and pictorial images functioned figuratively by synecdoche, representing part of the "horrible spectacle" that they attempted to depict. Farrell shows that these synecdoches were accomplished through the verbal trope of describing the indescribable and the visual trope of representing the unrepresentable, which, respectively, alluded to the full magnitude of suffering beyond the expressive powers of words and images. But Farrell also illustrates, with examples of exclusively verbal accounts of the famine, that verbal description—what rhetoricians traditionally called *ekphrasis*—surpasses visual portrayal in so firing the imagination that the scene of suffering is made, as Kames would have it, "ideally present" to the consciousness of readers. Whether through verbal or visual depiction, or a combination of the two, the famine was evoked in ways that stimulated readers' powers of imaginative witnessing so that they, in turn, could display in their sympathetic responses a "right appreciation of suffering" in accordance with standards of taste and sensibility expected of Britain's social elite.

In chapter 4, I investigate how maps and other graphics used during a World Court case about placement of an international maritime boundary between the United States and Canada in the Gulf of Maine manifested a rhetoric of visual *taxis* that both structured how the gulf's major features were seen and disposed the attitudes of those who saw them. This study attends to how visual patterns and images participate in rhetorical displays that engage the nearly ubiquitous dynamic between literalizing metaphorical associations as factual attributes and refiguring purportedly factual attributes as metaphorical or otherwise fanciful. The United States advanced as a purported fact the claim that the Northeast Channel—a deepwater trench—is a "natural boundary" in the gulf area and, as such, a suitable location for the legal boundary, which, among other functions, would divide jurisdiction over separate, intact commercial fish stocks. Images and patterns exhibited on U.S. graphics invited viewers to see natural boundary associations as factual attributes of the Northeast Channel *as it is* rather than as resemblances for thinking about the channel *as if* it were a natural boundary. Canada sought to refigure those attributes as mythic, fanciful, or merely metaphorical, even as they, too, urged a presumably factual perspective on natural boundaries of their own. Both parties enacted a visual rhetoric of display that invited viewers to see the gulf's features through "structures" that would incline them toward preferred partisan perspectives on the most desirable legal resolution of the conflict.

In chapter 5, Robert Hariman and John Louis Lucaites show that the famous "man confronting tanks" photograph exemplifies what they define as a photographic icon. Through their close inspection of visually manifested assumptions that constitute this widely celebrated image, Hariman and Lucaites disclose how it ideologically constrains or "screens" the range of plausible interpretations that viewers could bring to the event that it depicts. The image manifests an abstract modernist aesthetic that decontextualizes the event, placing the viewer in an objective perspective for seeing the man and the tanks as figures against an almost grid-like background. Concealed from view is the lush context of local cultural expression, its rich variety of colors, textures, and details. The image enacts a stark realist drama between absolute state power and the opposition of the solitary individual. The drama's immediate outcome is not in doubt, but it also is harbinger of the inevitable triumph of liberal individualism as the unquestioned ideology of globalization. Concealed from view are political possibilities including that of Chinese democratic self-determination that might offer an alternative vision for a global society beyond that of endless assimilation into Western liberal-democratic culture. The photographic icon of the man confronting tanks, then, becomes an exemplar for global order that enables Westerners to see this complex political event in their own image, "celebrating" liberal-democratic culture and diminishing alternative cultural visions, circumscribing and restricting political possibility.

The Disposition of Place and the Placing of Disposition

Chapters in this section highlight relationships between the "dispositions" or structures of material places and the dispositions or "structures" of attitudes exhibited by those who encounter them. In chapter 6, S. Michael Halloran and Gregory Clark discuss national park landscapes as rhetorical displays of places sacred to an American civic religion. The sublimity of the nature parks and the symbolism of redemptive sacrifice at the historical parks function as an epideictic that prompts visitors to overcome differences and join together as a congregation of citizens sharing a common American identity. Halloran and Clark exploit parallels with religious encounters with the sacred in their analysis of Saratoga Battlefield National Historical Park as a special place in American civic religion. Visitors participate in secular "rituals of observation" that parallel the Catholic ritual of the stations of the cross as they drive along the park's tour road, visit stations marked by important symbols, imagine specific events that transpired there, and, perhaps, contemplate their meaning for American identity. Halloran and Clark consider whether the symbolically resonant displays encountered during that journey afford visitors opportunities for undergoing the kind of individually transcendent and thoughtful experience that Rosenfield assigned to the *theoroi* of Aristotle's epideictic: an experience of inspiration or epiphany analogous to what Mircea Eliade characterized as the religious experience of "hierophany," or the temporary irruption of the sacred into our present, time-bound, profane world.

In chapter 7, Beverly James shows how a Stalin statue once located at Procession Square in the center of Budapest and subsequent depictions of its destruction during the 1956 Hungarian revolution are rhetorical displays that inclined audiences toward distinctive kinds of "beholding." She details the rhetorical qualities of the gargantuan statue's monumental visual presence—designed in accord with principles of socialist realist iconography—and how it compelled observers to behold the all-powerful state and its restrained vision of political possibility. In contrast, depictions of the statue's destruction enabled audiences to undergo what James called, following Rosenfield, thoughtful "epideictic beholding" of an event disposed toward open political possibility. That event persisted in public memory since the Hungarian revolution as an inspiring exemplar of resistance to tyranny. James speculates that epideictic beholding possesses a largely overlooked subversive potential for pursuit of human autonomy. Beholding depictions of the Stalin statue's destruction is not a matter of celebrating meaningless iconoclasm nor of rehearsal of taken-for-granted values and attitudes but an opportunity to contemplate an inspiring vision of emancipation.

In chapter 8, Victoria J. Gallagher develops and applies a heuristic framework for comparative study of commemorative memorials and monuments based on Richard Merelman's work on "cultural projection," contemporary studies of rhetorical genres, and studies of public memory. Her comparative study of the Martin Luther King Jr. Memorial and Center for Nonviolent Social Change and the Stone Mountain Park Confederate Memorial discloses the similarities and differences in their respective commemorative contexts, their particular manifestations of generic patterns of commemoration, their cultural projections of relationships between dominant and subordinate groups, and their enacted social visions. The King memorial and center combine dominant and subordinate cultural projections so that visitors are inclined to acknowledge their racial identities and contemplate prospects for collaborative biracial social action. The Confederate memorial, in its celebration of Confederate sacrifice and valor, projects white hegemony that, at the time of its completion in 1970, seemed the Old South's response to the civil rights movement of the 1950s and 1960s. But that projection has dimmed amidst the glare of the de-raced southern theme park and former Olympic venue that is Stone Mountain Park. While the King memorial and center project for its predominantly African American visitors a culturally blended vision of biracial social action and change, Stone Mountain Park projects a de-raced place of fun, entertainment, and consumption that both white and black visitors enjoy, albeit, as Gallagher notes, often "separately but equally."

In chapter 9, Lawrence W. Rosenfield discusses Las Vegas casino hotels as sites of rhetorical displays that amplify the theme that "desires aroused set one free." He examines the visual topoi and sensual imagery that manifest that theme and, thereby, circumvent common sense, stimulate desire, and encourage excessive consumption. Visitors encounter rhetorical allures that arouse desires through topoi that exhibit abundance, promise effort-lessness of movement, and enact fantasies in which visitors can escape the burdens of daily life and participate in a celebration of excess through unrestrained, immediate satisfaction of desires and appetites. Rosenfield thus shows how the themed casino resort hotels along the Vegas strip exploit stock Hollywood images or stereotypical images about tourist hot spots through enacted, sensual displays that entrance visitors with fantasies of uninhibited, easy, immediate, safe indulgence.

In chapter 10, Richard Morris studies gravescapes—"memorials and the landscape containing them"—as material displays that rhetorically manifest a distinctive ethos or worldview about the recalcitrant reality of death. He explains the cultural and rhetorical significance of three gravescape traditions that are enacted through displays of the icons, inscriptions, mottos, and shapes of the memorials and by their location, arrangement, and appearance within the landscape that contains them. The stark memento mori gravescape reminds visitors of the ephemeral nature of physical existence and of the inevitability of divine judgment, with everlasting life or damnation hanging in the balance. The lush romantic garden gravescape inclines visitors to find individual inspiration and pathos in the harmony of life and death in nature. The expansive heroic lawn cemetery disposes vis-itors to see immortality in the deeds of the honored dead who surmounted life's obstacles through exercise of reason, ambition, and strength. Morris details these material displays and their cultural and rhetorical significance, showing how those adhering to an ethos or worldview were equipped to answer the most fundamental questions of human existence.

Demonstrations as Rhetorical Display and Rhetorical Displays as Demonstrative

The chapters in this section direct attention to relationships between demonstrations as rhetorical display and rhetorical displays as demonstrative. "Demonstration" brings into view associations about rhetorical displays as proofs, manifestations, and performances. In chapter 11, Gerard A. Hauser discloses all three in his analysis of Indres Naidoo's narrative account of demonstrative displays of dissidence in the notorious Robben Island Prison during South African apartheid. Hauser offers a perspective on demonstrative displays that extends McKeon's notion of demonstrative discourse and action as a productive resource for rhetorical creation to the political prisoner's body as the locus for invention of resistance that both challenges oppressive power and discloses the power of the oppressed. The pris-oners' bodies constitute the "place" for resisting their warders' and guards' efforts to dehu-manize or criminalize them through physical degradation, humiliation, and torment and for enacting displays of their humanity and dignity as "prisoners of conscience." Hauser accounts for the power of Naidoo's narrative displays of those embodied, demonstrative acts in terms of evincing for readers, through verbal depictions and episodic form, what Quintilian called a fantasia, or imagined visualization, of the place of struggle. Turning to the work of Bakhtin, Hauser discusses how these demonstrative displays (whether directly witnessed or imaginatively seen) enacted a dialogue between official authority and moral conviction that manifested for readers of conscience self-evident proof of their commit-ment to political change.

Jerry Blitefield in chapter 12 examines political demonstrations as rhetorical displays in his study of the community organizing practices of Saul Alinsky's Industrial Areas Foun-dation (IAF). The IAF attempts to redistribute the imbalance of power between otherwise dispersed community groups and a city's power elite. Drawing from Kenneth Burke, Blite-field explains that the strategy for organizing involves strengthening newly emerging organizational identifications by creating sharp divisions from adversaries. That strategy is enacted through demonstrative tactics—which the IAF calls "actions"—that make the organization manifestly present to power brokers as a force for social change. A successful action is a visible, public demonstration that the organization has acquired power and that defenders of the status quo have, to some degree, lost power. These actions manifest this shifting power balance through what Blitefield calls "premonitory proof." The action is proof of the group's capacity to challenge and disrupt established power relationships, and it is premonitory in that its successful enactment implies the possibility of future reenactment—unless, of course, the group's demands are met. This and other aspects of IAF actions require a successful, staged performance before an anticipated responding audience. Among the qualities of successful performance is the reversal of conventional rhetorical relationships so that the powerful find themselves as spectators who can only witness and contemplate the implications of the group's rhetorically enacted spectacle of collective power, shared grievance, and demands for change.

In chapter 13, John Shotter offers a comprehensive perspective that shows how encounters with displays open possibilities for manifesting or showing otherwise invisible but real presences. The presences manifested through rhetorical display are analogous with perceptual experience of the invisible but real presence of a three-dimensional image asserting itself between the viewer and the planar surface of a stereogram. But the liminal world opens to disclose those presences only when we are rightly oriented to see them. The presence encountered is neither a subjective projection of categorical expectations onto the displayed nor is it an impartial description of the displayed but rather an agentic presence disclosed contingently through the orchestrated interplay of a mutually responsive, dialogically structured interaction. Shotter applies this perspective on the dynamic disclosure of agentic presences where we least would expect to encounter them: the sciences. Behind objective, mechanical descriptions of phenomena are scientists' efforts to so orchestrate their performative interactions that they attain "relationally responsive understandings" of agentic presences that otherwise could not be disclosed to them. Though Shotter does not elaborate the point, the vantage he offers shows how all rhetorical displays are potentially demonstrative in that whatever they "show forth" during encounters with them constitutes a kind of proof that resists our subjective impositions, but only if we remain open to its disclosure as participants in an orchestrated, relational, dialogical performance. Shotter's perspective resonates with the other two studies collected in this section, much as those studies inform his perspective.

Epideictic Identifications and Divisions

Rhetorical displays are manifested through emphases and de-emphases that exhibit "orders of desire." Those who become audience to them exhibit a wide range of possible responses depending upon whether the valuings and attitudes displayed resonate with their own preferences and inclinations. Whatever else they might be, encounters with displays always are to some degree epideictic in the sense that they animate moral (or moralizing) presumptions about what constitutes the worthwhile and worthless, the praiseworthy and blameworthy, the significant and insignificant. An important aspect of the rhetorics of display, then, is that they manifest possible relationships with audiences that open or restrict opportunities for community through identification, estrangement, or some intermediate inclination. These epideictic identifications and divisions become especially salient during encounters with displays that enact conceptions of ethos, identity, or image.

In chapter 14, John C. Adams returns rhetorical display to its classical origins in public eulogy in his study of the educational function of epideictic. Central to discharging that function is the display of paradigm cases that manifest concrete instances of widely admired public virtues for the audience's acknowledgment and commemorative observance. Adams stresses that audiences themselves must be predisposed to participate in these celebratory encounters. They must possess the right culturally prompted "linguistic predisposition" to remain open to speech as a vehicle of virtue's disclosure and to the corollary possibility that speakers can offer, without calculation of advantage, guileless testaments to a common sense of loss and to a shared appreciation for the very best qualities of human association. Audiences myopically inclined toward skepticism, if not cynicism, are blind to even the most brilliant illumination of virtue's presence in epideictic display. Audiences open to displays of civic virtues such as courage and sacrifice in behalf of others have potential to find actualized in the paradigm cases identification-inducing exemplars that transcend the otherwise multiple divisions that permeate so much of public life through display of qualities of human excellence. Using former president Bill Clinton's eulogy of six firefighters killed during a warehouse fire in Worcester, Massachusetts, as a case study, Adams shows how epideictic can evoke an ethos enabling citizens to find in civic virtue a model of concord amidst the discord of public political life, provided that they are rightly predisposed to acknowledge its display when actually exhibited before them.

In chapter 15, John Nguyet Erni pursues a spatial theory of identity through the exemplar of "queer" culture's manifestation in the particular locale of South Beach in Miami, Florida. The figure of the queer, from Erni's perspective, does not emerge from imposing categories that assign some essentializing, stabilizing, authentic meaning, nor by exploring contrasts between fixed depictions of dominant and marginal communities. Rather, queerness is exhibited in cultural narratives about tourism, economics, architecture, social gentrification, and exile politics at South Beach that coalesce around and are most understandable within "queer spatial terms." Moreover, this queer spatiality manifests a way of being queer that is dynamically and spontaneously exhibited in everyday performances of queer life that together constitute the visible sexual community of the South Beach "scene." Erni thus eschews metaphysical claims about finding deep meaning and identity in places and instead directs attention to the manifestation of queerness in shifting surface appearances of style rather than settled queer "truth," in sensual, embodied variety rather than sterile, abstract uniformity, in movement across rather than permanence within space. Erni himself enacts in his chapter an epideictic performance that celebrates a community of queerness by showing, hinting at, or making visible its dynamic spatial and temporal placings at South Beach.

In chapter 16, Phebe Shih Chao discusses tattoos and body piercings ranging from the threatening and confrontational to the trendy and fashionable as embodied displays of identity transformation. Following Kenneth Burke's theory of symbolic drama, Chao examines these practices as rituals that enable wearers to cast off unwanted aspects of their identities and exhibit "purified" versions of themselves. Thus, tattoo and piercing are symbolic acts of identity transformation that implicate wearers (and viewers) in dramas about social guilt. From that vantage, getting a tattoo or a piercing is an act of redemptive identification that purges impurities not by passing them onto a scapegoat but, rather, through self-vic-timage. Guilt is purged, then, through the catharsis of undergoing symbolic—and literal —mortification of the flesh. Chao discusses how displays of visible "emblems of transfor-mation" embodied in the form of a tattoo or piercing and the responses of those who see them manifest tensions between identification and division that are central to Burke's rhet-oric of motives. Having cleansed guilt associated with some undesired, "polluted" aspect of their former selves, the tattooed and pierced not only acquire a desired, more purified iden-tity but also realign their social identifications and divisions with implications for how oth-ers see them and their motives. Both those who display tattoos and piercings and those who behold them are thus inevitably implicated within ongoing symbolic dramas in which they struggle to overcome social guilt through redemptive acts of mortification, scapegoat-ing, or both, that reveal their social identifications and divisions.

In chapter 17, Mari Boor Tonn shows how Colin Powell's Jamaican immigrant ancestry is exhibited to enact what Shelby Steele called a bargain for American racial innocence. Tonn also draws on Burke's dramatism—including his "pentad"—as she details how Pow-ell's self-portrayal and others' portrayals of him sealed that bargain in narratives granting white racial innocence for which Powell secured prestige, popularity, and power in return. Powell is the hero in a Jamaican Horatio Alger story who, through hard work and perse-verance, transcended race and attained success in American society. This immigrant tale becomes a moralizing exemplar for distinguishing the qualities of a "good" black persona from a "bad" black persona. White Americans thus see Powell's good black persona as a redemptive symbol of racial reconciliation and racial healing that absolves them of guilt for racial tensions. The burden for those tensions is shifted onto the scapegoat of native Ameri-can "blackness" that purportedly exhibits a self-defeating preoccupation with race as an excuse for personal failures. Native black experience is thereby concealed while whites are pardoned for racial transgressions. Powell, the racial redeemer, can at once capitalize on his blackness while distancing himself from associations about blackness that make whites uncomfortable, thus exemplifying the bargainer for racial innocence.

In the final chapter, Joshua Meyrowitz examines what he calls the "collaborative con-struction of intimacy" in which politicians, journalists, and the public focus on the public display of private, embodied experiences rather than engage substantive public issues not easily associated with personal bodily experience. Politicians and their handlers readily enact self-characterizing disclosures of familial and other private intimacies to curry favor with voters, though they are quick to invoke a zone of privacy whenever journalists raise questions about private behaviors that contradict and, thus, reveal artifice, if not dissem-bling, behind the self-portrayals. Meyrowitz tracks how national politicians revealed per-sonal intimacies between themselves and their spouses and children, their parents, and their siblings during the 1996 Democratic and Republican National Conventions. Displays of intimacy have the effect of insulating the "personalized" politician from criticism about policy decisions. Meyrowitz then moves on to detail how private intimacy displays are enabled through the environmental medium of electronic communication—particularly television—in contrast with the medium of print. The consequence is that policy delibera-tion is superseded by a hollow spectacle of posing leaders and debunking "insider" views that leave the public cynical about all politics but also sufficiently entertained to watch, increase ratings and, thus, continue the spectacle. Meyrowitz thus offers a view of American politics as an orchestrated performance in which politicians become televisual, democratic versions of Castiglione's courtier as they seek to impress their benefactors—the voters—with the virtuosity of their enacted public displays of private intimacies, for which they anticipate, in return, the honors of public office.

The chapters are organized as exemplars for highlighting one of the four central themes that together constitute the structure of this book, but each chapter contains analyses that could be used to exhibit one or more of the other themes as well. Consider some alternative possible arrangements. Rosenfield's discussion of visual topoi, Hauser's examination of verbal enactments of imaginative fantasia, Shotter's reflections on invisible but real presences, and Tonn's elaboration of terministic screens that display Colin Powell also engage the theme that rhetorical displays are manifested through verbal depiction of the visual and visual depiction of the verbal. Similarly, Blitefield's analysis of the management of space to enact impressive spectacles and Erni's "placing" of sexuality in South Beach also readily inform the theme that rhetorical displays are exhibited through disposing places and placing dispositions. Jorgensen-Earp's discussion of the exhibition and performance of narratives about the *Titanic,* my account of the use of visual displays to prove or undermine purported facts during a World Court case, Chao's study of tattoos and body piercings as enacting symbolic dramas in corporeal forms, and Meyrowitz's account of manifesting televisually the private in public relate to the theme of demonstrations as rhetorical display and rhetorical displays as demonstrative. Finally, all of the chapters are relevant to the theme of epideictic identifications and divisions, though Halloran's and Clark's analysis of the epideictic dimensions of Saratoga Battlefield National Park, James's study of epideictic beholding, Morris's discussion of three "ethotic" gravescape traditions, and Gallagher's study of the rhetoric of dominant and subordinate cultural projections might appear more directly related than others. These examples do not exhaust possible relationships and connections between the chapters and the four themes that structure this book. In any case, the fact that the chapters could be used to amplify one or another of the four themes not only suggests the complexity of the displays that they examine and of the analyses that they contain but also indicates that the book's conceptual structure comes fairly close to capturing the distinctive but overlapping ways that displays are rhetorically manifested in all of their rich variety.

   It turns out, then, that book editors enact a rhetoric of display that involves selective emphasis and de-emphasis, highlighting and muting; the chapters I offered as exemplary of specific themes could have been exhibited differently, with different implications. But a similar point could be made about the authors themselves. The authors cannot illuminate all that they could possibly disclose about the rich and multilayered displays under their examination; they must select and omit, emphasize and mute. No less than with the displays whose rhetoric they study, the criticisms and analyses they offer exhibit the partiality of their own perspectives that, in turn, are limned with implications and presumptions about what is more or less significant or insignificant, worthwhile or worthless, praiseworthy or blameworthy, celebratory or lamentable. In an important respect, the authors anticipate an audience of *theoroi,* and their chapters call upon that audience to consider, contemplate, and, perhaps, even make use of the lines of thought and insight that are shown forth from the analyses contained within. The audience called upon, our readers, come to this book equipped with their own perspectives; you, too, embody an order of desire consisting of valuings and attitudinizings that may or may not resonate with whatever the chapters assembled here disclose for your consideration. *Rhetorics of Display* invites your participation in epideictic encounters through which we are enjoined in contemplation and subsequent conversation about the dominant rhetorics of our time.

Notes

1. Ludmilla Jordanova, "Medicine and Genres of Display," in *Visual Display: Culture beyond Appearances,* ed. Lynne Cooke and Peter Wollen, 216 (New York: Free Press, 1995).

2. Richard McKeon, "The Uses of Rhetoric in a Technological Age: Architectonic Productive Arts," in *The Prospect of Rhetoric,* ed. Lloyd F. Bitzer and Edwin Black, 58 (Englewood Cliffs, N.J.: Prentice Hall, 1971).

3. Ibid., 58.

4. Lawrence W. Rosenfield, "The Practical Celebration of Epideictic," in *Rhetoric in Transition: Studies in the Nature and Uses of Rhetoric,* ed. Eugene E. White, 135 (University Park: Pennsylvania State University Press, 1980); also see his account of mere display at 131–34.

5. Ibid., 135.

6. Ibid., 135–36.

7. Ibid., 140, 147.

8. Ibid., 146. For a different reading, see Gerard Hauser's depiction of Aristotle's epideictic orator as one who "teaches" by asking audiences to witness "virtuosity as it is revealed in the lives of exemplary citizens"—virtuosity that, according to Aristotle's ethical doctrine, exhibits balanced emotional and moral dispositions. The orator's narrative examples of "lived virtue" not only certify "virtue's worldly appearance" but also encourage mimesis of ideals nobler than mere advantage. Only when "observers" and "witnesses" are suitably instructed to recognize and attest to virtue can they later be called upon to temper unruly passions, look beyond partisan self-interest, and meet the higher demands of the public good when making and applying the laws. Rosenfield contends that Aristotle's epideictic has no teaching or didactic function. Gerard A. Hauser, "Aristotle on Epideictic: The Formation of Public Morality," *Rhetoric Society Quarterly* 29, no. 1 (Winter 1999): 5–23, especially 13–17. (Compare with Rosenfield at 140–41, 146.)

9. Rosenfield, "Practical Celebration," 146–47. For an overview of rhetoric and display in classical Greek rhetorical theory, see John Poulakos and Takis Poulakos, *Classical Greek Rhetorical Theory* (New York: Houghton Mifflin, 1999), 61–87. On Aristotle's epideictic, see, in addition to Rosenfield's and Hauser's essays, Christine Oravec, "'Observation' in Aristotle's Theory of Epideictic," *Philosophy and Rhetoric* 9 (1976): 162–74. For detailed studies of displays associated with ancient Greek ritual and ceremony, see E. L. Bowie, "Early Greek Elegy, Symposium and Public Festival," *Journal of Hellenic Studies* 106 (1986): 13–35; Michael F. Carter, "The Ritual Functions of Epideictic Rhetoric: The Case of Socrates' Funeral Oration," *Rhetorica* 9 (1991): 209–32; W. R. Conner, "Tribes, Festivals and Processions: Civic Ceremonial and Political Manipulation in Archaic Greece," *Journal of Hellenic Studies* 107 (1987): 40–50; William D. Furley, "Praise and Persuasion in Greek Hymns," *Journal of Hellenic Studies* 115 (1995): 29–46; Takis Poulakos, "The Historical Intervention of Gorgias's *Epitaphios:* The Genre of Funeral Oration and the Athenian Institution of Public Burials," *Pre/Text* 10 (1989): 90–99; and Donovan J. Ochs, *Consolatory Rhetoric: Grief, Symbol, and Ritual in the Greco-Roman Era* (Columbia: University of South Carolina Press, 1993), 37–83.

10. McKeon, "Uses of Rhetoric," 58–59.

11. Quintilian, *Institutio Oratoria,* trans. H. E. Butler (Cambridge, Mass.: Harvard University Press, 1920), 3.4.12–14.

12. See Hauser, chapter 11, this volume, 232.

13. Jeffrey Walker, *Rhetoric and Poetics in Antiquity* (Oxford: Oxford University Press, 2000).

14. Ibid., 114–15.

15. Ibid., 8–9.

16. Ibid., 9.

17. Ibid., 9–10.

18. Ibid., vii, 10.

19. O. B. Hardison Jr., *The Enduring Monument: A Study of the Idea of Praise in Renaissance Literary Theory and Practice* (1962; repr., Westport, Conn.: Greenwood Press, 1973), 52; John W. O'Malley, *Praise and Blame in Renaissance Rome: Rhetoric, Doctrine, and Reform in the Sacred Orators of the Papal Court, c. 1450–1521* (Durham, N.C.: Duke University Press, 1979), 71–73; and for discussion of the relationship of epideictic with civic humanism, see Lawrence W. Rosenfield, "Central Park and the Celebration of Civic Virtue," in *American Rhetoric: Context and Criticism,* ed. Thomas W. Benson, 228–30 (Carbondale: Southern Illinois University Press, 1989).

20. Rosenfield, "Central Park and the Celebration of Civic Virtue," 234–38.

21. See John R. Spencer's discussion of Alberti's concern with vision and visibility and the use of the mathematical system of perspective in the introduction to Leon Battista Alberti, *On Painting,* trans. John R. Spencer, 2nd ed. (New Haven: Yale University Press, 1966), 17–23.

22. For an overview, see chapter 5, "Renaissance Reintegration" (254–93) and chapter 7, "Rhetoric and the Sister Arts" (340–74) in Brian Vickers, *In Defense of Rhetoric* (Oxford: Clarendon Press, 1988).

23. John R. Spencer, "*Ut rhetorica pictura:* A Study in Quattrocento Theory of Painting," *Journal of the Warburg and Courtauld Institutes* 20 (1957): 26–44; esp. 39, 43–44.

24. O'Malley, *Praise and Blame in Renaissance Rome,* 63.

25. Ibid.

26. Ibid.; Brian Vickers, *In Defense of Rhetoric,* 291; Rosenfield, "Central Park and the Celebration of Civic Virtue," 237. Michael Baxandall, who turns to Hermogenes' account of *ekphrasis* as a style that "must contrive to bring about seeing through hearing," illustrates its use by Renaissance writers in their depictions of visual art. See his *Giotto and the Orators: Humanist Observers of Painting and the Discovery of Pictorial Composition, 1350–1450* (Oxford: Oxford University Press, 1971), 85–87, 90–96.

27. "Painting is mute poetry and poetry a speaking picture" appears in Plutarch but is attributed to Simonides. "*Ut pictura poesis*" is a throwaway line in Horace's *Ars Poetica.* Both became justifications for theorizing about sensory interrelationships between the visual and verbal arts. For a comprehensive discussion see John Graham, "*Ut pictura poesis,*" in *Dictionary of the History of Ideas,* ed. Philip P. Weiner (New York: Scribner's, 1973), 4:465–76. Also see O'Malley, *Praise and Blame in Renaissance Rome,* 63–65.

28. For discussion of *pictura* in relation to adducing verbal examples or patterns of virtue or vice, see Hardison Jr., *The Enduring Monument,* 52–57. Alberti's concept of *istoria* is explained in Spencer, introduction to *On Painting,* 23–28. Also see Baxandall's detailed discussion of the elements of a "cognitive style" that artists shared with viewers in *Painting and Experience in Fifteenth-Century Italy,* 2nd ed. (Oxford: Oxford University Press, 1988), 29–108.

29. See Rosenfield, "Central Park and the Celebration of Civic Virtue," 228–29; Vickers, *In Defense of Rhetoric,* 343n11, 353.

30. Rosenfield, "Central Park and the Celebration of Civic Virtue," 238–59.

31. Ibid., 234. Alberti depicted the painter's acquiring fame as a chief aim of painting. See Spencer, *On Painting,* 89.

32. Baxandall, *Giotto and the Orators,* 45. Baxandall portrays Alberti's *De pictura* as filling a "niche" by laying out a system of precepts enabling more informed viewing of paintings. See 124–25, 129.

33. Baldesar Castiglione, *The Book of the Courtier,* trans. George Bull (New York: Penguin, 1967).

34. Rosenfield, "Central Park and the Celebration of Civic Virtue," 227, 253, 254–55; Lawrence Manley, *Convention 1500–1750* (Cambridge: Harvard University Press, 1980), 112–16.

35. This point is based partly on Eduardo Saccone's translation of *sprezzatura* as "an art without art, a negligent diligence, an inattentive attention," quoted in Jennifer Richards, "Assumed Simplicity and the Critique of Nobility; or, How Castiglione Read Cicero," *Renaissance Quarterly* 54 (2001): 461n3. See Richards's interpretation of the influence of Cicero's portrayal of "assumed simplicity," or *dissimulatio,* in *De oratore* on Castiglione's depiction of *sprezzatura,* particularly in the first book of the *Courtier* (ibid., 460–86). She contends her reading shows "that the practice of *sprezzatura* challenges, rather than produces, the aristocratic disdain often regarded as Castiglione's legacy" (ibid., 461). Also see Eduardo Saccone, "*Grazia, sprezzatura, affettazione* in the *Courtier,*" in *Castiglione: The Ideal and the Real in Renaissance Culture,* ed. Robert W. Hanning and David Rosand, 57 (New Haven: Yale University Press, 1983).

36. Rosenfield, "Central Park and the Celebration of Civic Virtue," 227.

37. For discussion of relationships among rhetoric, dialectic, and demonstration in Renaissance science, see Jean Dietz Moss, *Novelties in the Heavens: Rhetoric and Science in the Copernican Controversy* (Chicago: University of Chicago Press, 1993), 1–23. For a commentary on epideictic dimensions of Galileo's *Dialogue,* see Brian Vickers, "Epideictic Rhetoric in Galileo's *Dialogo,*" *Annali dell'Istituto e Museo di Storia della Scienza di Firenze* 8 (1983): 69–102.

38. See Philip Fisher's illuminating discussion of Descartes' visualizing procedures in relation to the passion of "wonder" or "astonishment" in *Wonder, the Rainbow, and the Aesthetics of Rare Experience* (Cambridge, Mass.: Harvard University Press, 1998), 41–50, 57–67.

39. Jan Golinski, *Making Natural Knowledge: Constructivism and the History of Science* (Cambridge: Cambridge University Press, 1998), 133. Golinski provides a constructionist account of the "specially manufactured instruments" through which scientists attended to phenomena during his useful overview of relevant case studies ranging from the early modern period to the twentieth century (133–61).

40. Hauser discusses this point in chapter 11, 252n15.

41. George Campbell, *The Philosophy of Rhetoric,* ed. and rev. intro. by Lloyd F. Bitzer (Carbondale: Southern Illinois University Press, 1988), 81. Moral reasoning involved conscious thought about the evidence of experience (46–49). Campbell distinguished the probabilities of moral reasoning from the certitudes of "demonstrative" reasoning, which he saw as abstract and only narrowly applicable (43–46). For an account of Campbell's thought, including Hume's influences, see Bitzer's introduction, viii–li. For Bitzer's succinct discussion of Campbell's principle of vivacity, see xxxii–xxxiv.

42. Henry Home, Lord Kames, *Elements of Criticism* (1762; repr., New York: Johnson Reprint, 1970), 1:104–27. See James Farrell's discussion of "ideal presence" and related aesthetic and moral concepts as having rhetorical purchase within educated circles well into the nineteenth century in chapter 3.

43. Gerard A. Hauser, "Empiricism, Description, and the New Rhetoric," *Philosophy and Rhetoric* 5 (1972): 24–44; the quotation is on 27.

44. See the discussion in Garry Wills, *Inventing America: Jefferson's Declaration of Independence* (New York: Vintage, 1978), 193–206.

45. These and other rhetoricians were part of a much wider interest among scholars during the latter half of the twentieth century in understanding the pervasiveness of "display" in our political, psychological, social, and cultural lives. Consider but a few examples; others abound.

Erving Goffman contended that "life itself is a dramatically enacted thing" involving manifold displays and managed images during the "presentation of self" before others in everyday social life (Goffman, *Presentation of Self in Everyday Life* [Garden City, N.Y.: Doubleday-Anchor, 1959], 72). Daniel Boorstin discussed the "Graphic Revolution" and how its all-pervasive visual imagery has so saturated American society that illusion seems more persuasive and real than reality itself; we are so awash in "the image," thought Boorstin, that pseudoevents and other images are supplanting ideas as the coin of public life (Daniel Boorstin, *The Image: A Guide to Pseudo-Events in America* [1961; repr., New York: Harper and Row, 1964]). Guy Debord wrote that we live in a "society of the spectacle" that has transformed experience into endless and empty encounters with transitory, abstract, and commodified images (Debord, *The Society of the Spectacle* [1967; repr., Detroit: Black and Red, 1983]). Jacques Lacan's psychoanalytic theory of looking posits that, in the world of spectacle, we not only look but also are looked at or fall under "the gaze" (Lacan, *The Four Fundamental Concepts of Psycho-Analysis,* trans. Alan Sheridan, ed. Jacques-Alain Miller [New York: W. W. Norton, 1978]). Based on an analysis of prisons, Michel Foucault advanced the idea of "panopticism," or the notion that people are organized within institutions to maximize social control through the constant surveillance of the "disciplinary gaze" (Foucault, *Discipline and Punish: The Birth of the Prison,* trans. Alan Sheridan [New York: Pantheon, 1977]). Neil Postman, following the work of Marshall McLuhan, argued that the advent of the television medium of "discourse" was catalyst of an already-developing transition in consciousness from a print-based to an image-based culture with the consequence that education, politics, religion, or any other subject presented televisually is structured to entertain and stimulate pleasure rather than invite serious thought, authentic feeling, or vital conviction (Postman, *Amusing Ourselves to Death: Public Discourse in the Age of Show Business* [New York: Penguin, 1985]). Neal Gabler, following Boorstin and Postman, argued that life itself has become an assemblage of "public life movies" starring "celebrities" from the worlds of politics, business, education, the arts, sports, and other fields and "personal life movies" starring everyone else whose sense of themselves is besotted with the imagery of entertainment and celebrity to the extent that they, too, enact performances supported by the right costuming, props, and stage sets (Gabler, *Life the Movie: How Entertainment Conquered Reality* [New York: Knopf, 1998]). "Dramatic enactment" or "presentation," "the image," "the spectacle," "the gaze," "the panopticon," "the movie" are but a sampling of conceptual "lenses" that offer distinctive angles for thinking about life experiences as showing and seeing, exhibiting and beholding, manifesting and witnessing, performing and spectating, seeing and being seen; put directly, they look to disclose from different vantages how much of life is manifested through display.

46. McKeon, "Uses of Rhetoric," 59–60. Also see "Discourse, Demonstration, Verification, and Justification," in *Démonstration, Vérification, Justification,* ed. Philippe Devaux, 44–45 (Paris: Nauwelaerts, 1968).

47. McKeon thus transformed classical forms of "epideictic" and "demonstrative" oratory for contemporary application as a universal productive art of "invention."

48. Chaim Perelman, "Choice, Presence, and Presentation," in *The Realm of Rhetoric* (Notre Dame, Ind.: University of Notre Dame Press, 1982), 33–40. Also see C. Perelman and L. Olbrechts-Tyteca, *The New Rhetoric: A Treatise on Argumentation,* trans. John Wilkinson and Purcell Weaver (Notre Dame, Ind.: University of Notre Dame Press, 1969), 115–41. A useful commentary is Robert E. Tucker's "Figure, Ground and Presence: A Phenomenology of Meaning in Rhetoric," *Quarterly Journal of Speech* 87 (2001): 396–414. John Shotter offers a critical reading of Perelman's idea of presence (and Tucker's commentary) in chapter 13, 287–88n38.

49. Perelman, "Choice, Presence, and Presentation," 35.

50. Perelman and Olbrechts-Tyteca, *The New Rhetoric,* 142.

51. Carroll C. Arnold, introduction to Perelman, *The Realm of Rhetoric,* xiii.

52. Perelman, "Choice, Presence, and Presentation," 35.

53. Ibid., 34.

54. Ibid., 36–40. Also see Perelman and Olbrechts-Tyteca, *The New Rhetoric,* 142–83. Perelman and Olbrechts-Tyteca also develop a conception of the contemporary "epideictic genre" as serving the educational function of inculcating and reinforcing accepted values and attitudes. In contrast with McKeon, they take Aristotle's notion of epideictic as the point of theoretical departure rather than Roman demonstrative oratory. See *The New Rhetoric,* 47–54. John C. Adams extends the notion of contemporary epideictic as educational in chapter 14.

55. Kenneth Burke, "Dramatism," in *International Encyclopedia of the Social Sciences,* vol. 7, ed. David L. Sills, 448, 445–52 (New York: Macmillan, 1968). This article gives a good overview of dramatism for those unfamiliar with Burke's work. For a comprehensive account of dramatism, see William H. Rueckert, *Kenneth Burke and the Drama of Human Relations,* 2nd ed. (Berkeley: University of California Press, 1982).

56. Kenneth Burke, "Terministic Screens," in *Language as Symbolic Action: Essays on Life, Literature, and Method* (Berkeley: University of California Press, 1966), 45–62.

57. Burke elaborates the dramatistic pentad in *A Grammar of Motives* (1945; repr., Berkeley: University of California Press, 1969). For examples illustrating use of the pentad as a critical method, see Mari Boor Tonn, Valerie A. Endress, and John N. Diamond, "Hunting and Heritage on Trial: A Dramatistic Debate over Tragedy, Tradition, and Territory," *Quarterly Journal of Speech* 79 (1993): 165–81; David S. Birdsell, "Ronald Reagan on Lebanon and Grenada: Flexibility and Interpretation in the Application of Kenneth Burke's Pentad," *Quarterly Journal of Speech* 73 (1987): 267–79; and Floyd D. Anderson and Lawrence J. Prelli, "Pentadic Cartography: Mapping the Universe of Discourse," *Quarterly Journal of Speech* 87 (2001): 73–95.

58. Jerry Blitefield discusses Burke's concepts of identification and symbolic form in chapter 12, Phebe Shih Chao examines identification and division in relation to Burke's guilt-purification-redemption cycle in chapter 16, and Mari Boor Tonn makes use of Burke's concept of terministic screens and applies his dramatistic pentad in chapter 17.

59. Peter Wollen, introduction to *Visual Display: Culture beyond Appearances,* ed. Lynne Cooke and Peter Wollen, 9–13 (New York: The New Press, 1998).

60. Ibid., 13.

61. Charles A. Hill and Marguerite Helmers, eds., *Defining Visual Rhetorics* (Mahwah, N.J.: Lawrence Erlbaum, 2004).

62. Jack Selzer and Sharon Crowley, eds., *Rhetorical Bodies* (Madison: University of Wisconsin Press, 1999).

63. Sharon Macdonald, preface to *The Politics of Display: Museums, Science, Culture* (New York: Routledge, 1998), xi.

64. Sharon Macdonald, "Exhibitions of Power and Powers of Exhibition: An Introduction to the Politics of Display," in *Politics of Display,* 2. Two chapters of that book that are noteworthy as rhetorical studies are Steven W. Allison-Bunnell, "Making Nature 'Real' Again: Natural History Exhibits and Public Rhetorics of Science at the Smithsonian Institution in the Early 1960s," 77–97, and Thomas F. Gieryn, "Balancing Acts: Science, *Enola Gay* and History Wars at the Smithsonian," 197–228. Also see Macdonald's afterword, "From War to Debate?" 229–235, where she speculates about what we might call a "new rhetoric" for "displaying" science before the public that would feature public debate *about* science rather than seek public understanding *of* science through exhibition of its decided facts and its demonstrable public virtues.

65. See Kendall R. Phillips, ed., *Framing Public Memory* (Tuscaloosa: University of Alabama Press, 2004). This discussion is based partly on Phillips's introduction, 1–14. For useful overviews,

see Stephen H. Browne, "Reading, Rhetoric and the Texture of Public Memory," *Quarterly Journal of Speech* 81 (1995): 237–65, and Barbie Zelizer, "Reading against the Grain: The Shape of Memory Studies," *Critical Studies in Mass Communication* 12 (1995): 214–39. In addition to the essays in *Framing Public Memory,* see as examples the following case studies: Tamar Katriel, "Sites of Memory: Discourses of the Past in Israeli Pioneering Settlement Museums," *Quarterly Journal of Speech* 80 (1994): 1–20; Stephen H. Browne, "Remembering Crispus Attucks: Race, Rhetoric and the Politics of Commemoration," *Quarterly Journal of Speech* 85 (1999): 169–87; M. Lane Bruner, "Strategies of Remembrance in Pre-Unification West Germany," *Quarterly Journal of Speech* 86 (2000): 86–107; Marouf Hasian Jr., "Anne Frank, Bergen-Belsen, and the Polysemic Nature of Holocaust Memories," *Rhetoric and Public Affairs* 4 (2001): 349–74; Bryan Hubbard and Marouf Hasian Jr., "Atomic Memories of the *Enola Gay:* Strategies of Remembrance at the National Air and Space Museum," *Rhetoric and Public Affairs* 1 (1998): 363–85; and Ekaterina V. Haskins, "'Put Your Stamp on History': The USPS Commemorative Program *Celebrate the Century* and Postmodern Collective Memory," *Quarterly Journal of Speech* 89 (2003): 1–18. In *Rhetorics of Display,* the chapters by Cheryl R. Jorgensen-Earp (chapter 2), Robert Hariman and John L. Lucaites (chapter 5), Michael Halloran and Gregory Clark (chapter 6), Beverly James (chapter 7), and Victoria J. Gallagher (chapter 8) contribute to this project.

66. I use the expression "rhetorical selectivity" with the caveat that the processes it designates need not necessarily imply deliberate choice or planning, though displays often are rhetorically strategic in view of goals or functions. But selective processes also can—and often do—involve unreflected or unconscious habit, inclination, or impulse.

67. Burke, "Terministic Screens," in *Language as Symbolic Action,* 44–47, and *Rhetoric of Motives* (1950; repr., Berkeley: University of California Press, 1969), 43.

68. Burke, "Terministic Screens," 47.

69. Tom Wessels, *Reading the Forested Landscape: A Natural History of New England* (Woodstock, Vt.: Countryman Press, 1997).

70. Peter Burke, *Eyewitnessing: The Uses of Images as Historical Evidence* (Ithaca, N.Y.: Cornell University Press, 2001), 30. Peter Burke's discussion of visual evidence as both reflecting and distorting social reality parallels Kenneth Burke's focus on verbal reflecting and deflecting in his discussion of terministic screens. See 30–31.

71. W. J. T. Mitchell, *Iconology: Image, Text, Ideology* (Chicago: University of Chicago Press, 1986), 1–2.

72. Michael Ann Holly, *Past Looking: Historical Imagination and the Rhetoric of the Image* (Ithaca, N.Y.: Cornell University Press, 1996), 9, 24–25. Holly does not contend "that the work of art possesses unchanging ontological status" but does claim "that a viewer's . . . relation to a work of art is prescribed, assigned in advance by a system of representation which I call rhetorical" (ibid., 14). See the discussion of how Burckhardt's "perspectivism" as a historian was influenced by an analogue of perspectivism exhibited in Renaissance paintings and elaborated systematically by Alberti (ibid., 36–48, 53–54, 72–79).

73. Ibid., 26–27.

74. Ibid., 11.

75. There is a rich scholarly literature in rhetorical studies that can inform analyses of the verbal-visual nexus of display. That body of literature started to develop during the 1970s to the 1980s and includes Thomas W. Benson's and Martin J. Medhurst's work on the rhetoric of film images (Benson, "Joe: An Essay in the Rhetorical Criticism of Film," *Journal of Popular Culture* 8 [1974]: 610/24–618/32; "The Rhetorical Structure of Frederick Wiseman's *High School,*" *Communication Monographs* 47 [1980]: 233–61; and "The Rhetorical Structure of Frederick Wiseman's *Primate,*" *Quarterly Journal of Speech* 71 [1985]: 204–17; Medhurst and Benson, "*The City:* The

Rhetoric of Rhythm," *Communication Monographs* 48 [1981]: 446–67; Medhurst, "*Hiroshima, Mon Amour:* From Iconography to Rhetoric," *Quarterly Journal of Speech* 68 [1982]: 345–70); Sonja K. Foss's inquiries into the rhetoric of visual art and imagery (Foss, "Rhetoric and the Visual Image: A Resource Unit," *Communication Education* 31 [1982]: 55–66; "Judy Chicago's *The Dinner Party:* Empowering of Women's Voice in Visual Art," in *Women Communicating: Studies of Women's Talk,* ed. Barbara Bate and Anita Taylor, 9–26 [Norwood, N.J.: Ablex, 1988]; and "A Rhetorical Schema for the Evaluation of Visual Imagery," *Communication Studies* 45 [1994]: 213–24); Lester Olson's studies of rhetorical iconology (Olson, "Portraits in Praise of a People: A Rhetorical Analysis of Norman Rockwell's Icons in Franklin D. Roosevelt's 'Four Freedoms' Campaign," *Quarterly Journal of Speech* 69 [1983]: 15–84; "Benjamin Franklin's Pictorial Representations of the British Colonies in America: A Study in Rhetorical Iconology," *Quarterly Journal of Speech* 73 [1987]: 18–42; *Emblems of American Community in the Revolutionary Era* [Washington, D.C.: Smithsonian, 1991]; and *Benjamin Franklin's Vision of American Community: A Study in Rhetorical Iconology* [Columbia: University of South Carolina Press, 2004]); Kathleen Turner's articulation of a rhetorical perspective for examining comic strips (Turner, "Comic Strips: A Rhetorical Perspective," *Central States Speech Journal* 28 [1977]: 24–35); and Martin J. Medhurst's, Michael D. DeSousa's, and Denise M. Bostdorff's studies of the rhetoric of political cartoons (Medhurst and DeSousa, "Political Cartoons as Rhetorical Form: A Taxonomy of Graphic Discourse," *Communication Monographs* 43 [1981]: 197–236; Bostdorff, "Making Light of James Watt: A Burkean Approach to the Form and Attitude of Political Cartoons," *Quarterly Journal of Speech* 73 [1987]: 43–59). Michael Osborn contributed an important, grounded theoretical reflection on verbal and visual aspects of "rhetorical depiction" (Osborn, "Rhetorical Depiction," in *Form, Genre, and the Study of Political Discourse,* ed. Herbert W. Simons and Aram A. Aghazarian, 79–107 [Columbia: University of South Carolina Press, 1986]). Also of interest, though not directly inspecting the visual-verbal theme, is Robert L. Scott's essay on rhetoric and Diego Rivera's painting (Scott, "Diego Rivera at Rockefeller Center: Fresco Painting and Rhetoric," *Western Speech Communication* 41 [1977]: 71–82).

Rhetorical studies relevant to examination of the verbal-visual nexus have continued to accumulate through the turn of the twenty-first century, with essays in *Defining Visual Rhetorics* among the most recent. Both Olson and Foss continued their significant lines of inquiry as already indicated in the above citations. In addition, there are two essays that are usefully read together when considering this theme: Gregory Clark's, S. Michael Halloran's, and Allison Woodford's study of the visual rhetoric of nineteenth-century landscape painting and Halloran's essay on how nineteenth-century writers depicted the landscape in "picturesque" terms. Together, they enable focused consideration, respectively, of the visual dimension of the verbal and of the verbal dimension of the visual (Clark, Halloran, and Woodford, "Thomas Cole's Vision of 'Nature' and the Conquest Theme in American Culture," in *Green Culture: Environmental Rhetoric in Contemporary American Culture,* ed. Carl G. Herndl and Stuart C. Brown, 261–80 [Madison: University of Wisconsin Press, 1996]; Halloran, "The Rhetoric of Picturesque Scenery: A Nineteenth-Century Epideictic," in *Oratorical Culture in Nineteenth-Century America,* ed. Gregory Clark and S. Michael Halloran, 226–46 [Carbondale: Southern Illinois University Press, 1993]). Barbie Zelizer's book on photojournalism and accounts of atrocity and Cara A. Finnegan's work on the uses and circulation of documentary photographs examine rhetorical relationships between images and words and between visual and textual contexts (Zelizer, *Remembering to Forget: Holocaust Memory through the Camera's Eye* [Chicago: University of Chicago Press, 1998]; Finnegan, *Picturing Poverty: Print Culture and FSA Photographs* [Washington, D.C.: Smithsonian, 2003]). Of related interest is John Louis Lucaites's essay on documentary photojournalism (Lucaites, "Visualizing 'The People': Individualism vs. Collectivism in *Let Us Now Praise Famous Men,*" *Quarterly Journal of Speech* 83 [1997]: 269–88). Studies in "visual argument" engage issues about whether and, if so, how arguments are manifested visually as well as verbally. David S. Birdsell and Leo Groarke, David Fleming, J. Anthony Blair, Randall Lake and Barbara Pickering, Cara A. Finnegan, and Gretchen S. Barbatsis conducted studies along that theme (Birdsell and Groarke, "Toward a Theory of Visual Argument," *Argumentation and Advocacy* 33 [Summer 1996]: 1–10; Fleming, "Can Pictures Be Arguments?" *Argumentation and Advocacy* 33 [Summer 1996]: 11–22; Blair, "The Possibility and Actuality of Visual Arguments," *Argumentation and Advocacy* 33 [Summer 1996]: 23–39; Lake and Pickering, "Argumentation, the Visual, and the Possibility of Refutation: An Exploration," *Argumentation* 12 [1998]: 79–93; Finnegan, "The Naturalistic Enthymeme and Visual Argument: Photographic Representation in the 'Skull Controversy,'" *Argumentation and Advocacy* 37 [Winter 2001]: 133–49; Barbatsis, "'Look and I Will Show You Something You Will Want to See': Pictorial Engagement in Negative Political Campaign Commercials," *Argumentation and Advocacy* 33 [Fall 1996]: 69–80). Included among other informative work are rhetorical studies of embroidery by Maureen Daly Goggin (Goggin, "Visual Rhetoric in Pens of Steel and Inks of Silk: Challenging the Great Visual/Verbal Divide," in *Defining Visual Rhetorics,* 87–110); of political cartoons by Janis Edwards and Carol K. Winkler (Edwards and Winkler, "Representative Form and the Visual Ideograph: The Iwo Jima Image in Editorial Cartoons," *Quarterly Journal of Speech* 83 [1997]: 289–310; and Edwards, *Political Cartoons in the 1988 Presidential Campaign: Image, Metaphor, Narrative* [New York: Garland, 1997]); of presidential photographic opportunities by Keith V. Erickson (Erickson, "Presidential Rhetoric's Visual Turn: Performance Fragments and the Politics of Illusionism," *Communication Monographs* 67 [2000]: 138–57, and his "Presidential Spectacles: Travel and the Rhetoric of Political Illusionism," *Communication Monographs* 65 [1998]: 141–53); of iconic photographs by Robert Hariman and John L. Lucaites (Hariman and Lucaites, "Dissent and Emotional Management in a Liberal-Democratic Society: The Kent State Iconic Photograph," *Rhetoric Society Quarterly* 31 [2001]: 5–31); and of painting by Marguerite Helmers, Henry Krips, and Stephen Happel (Krips, "Rhetoric, Ideology, and the Gaze: *The Ambassadors'* Body," in *At the Intersection: Cultural Studies and Rhetorical Studies,* ed. Thomas Rosteck, 186–205 [New York: Guilford, 1999]; Helmers, "Framing the Fine Arts through Rhetoric," in *Defining Visual Rhetorics,* 63–86; Happel, "Picturing God: The Rhetoric of Religious Images and Caravaggio's *Conversion of St. Paul,*" in *Rhetorical Invention and Religious Inquiry: New Perspectives,* ed. Walter Jost and Wendy Olmsted, 323-55 [New Haven, Conn.: Yale University Press, 2000]). The "translation" of literary works into feature films marks an important potential site for investigating the verbal-visual theme. For work related to that topic, though without detailing the visual aspects of the "translations," see Wayne J. McMullen and Martha Solomon, Brenda Cooper and David Descutner, and G. Thomas Goodnight (McMullen and Solomon, "The Politics of Adaptation: Steven Spielberg's Appropriation of *The Color Purple,*" *Text and Performance Quarterly* 14 [1994]: 158–74; Cooper and Descutner, "'It Had No Voice to It': Sidney Pollack's Film Translation of Isak Dinesen's *Out of Africa,*" *Quarterly Journal of Speech* 82 [1996]: 228–50; Goodnight, "The Firm, the Park and the University: Fear and Trembling on the Postmodern Trail," *Quarterly Journal of Speech* 81 [1995]: 267–90).

76. Respectively, chapters 6 and 2.

77. Susan Sontag, "Regarding the Torture of Others: Notes on What Has Been Done—and Why—to Prisoners by Americans," *New York Times Magazine,* May 23, 2004, 28.

78. Ibid., 24–29, 42. Even those who sought to justify or excuse the soldiers' actions tended to see the soldiers photographed as "having fun" before the camera. Radio talk-show host Rush Limbaugh, for example, verbally reframed the images as analogous to college fraternity pranks and "initiation rituals" that were justifiable as "having a good time" necessary for emotional release from the pressures of a war zone. Sontag depicted those remarks as part of an America "in which the fantasies and the practice of violence are seen as good entertainment, fun" (ibid., 28–29).

79. Garry Wills's discussion of the nineteenth-century rural cemetery movement in relation to romanticism illustrates how displays are rhetorically manifested through arrangements of place that dispose the attitudes of those who visit them. The picturesque rural cemetery created a natural place designed to enable sensitive visitors to undergo "liminal" or "threshold" experiences from which they could intuit or grasp spiritual insight. The romantics imagined permanence immanent to transitory nature, which, in turn, could be contemplated within the cycles of the seasons, in the borderlands between living and dying, between time and eternity, the past and future. Wills's analysis discloses the "placing" of disposition in cemeteries such as Mount Auburn Cemetery. See Garry Wills, *Lincoln at Gettysburg: The Words That Remade America* (New York: Simon and Schuster, 1992), 63–89. Also see Richard Morris's detailed discussion of what we might call the "placings" of disposition that constitute this and two other gravescape traditions in chapter 10.

80. See chapter 6, 142.

81. An early study of rhetorical aspects of architecture in Nazi Germany by Charlotte L. Stuart was published in 1973, but essays informing this theme started accumulating from about the mid-1980s until the present (Stuart, "Architecture in Nazi Germany: A Rhetorical Perspective," *Western Speech* 37 [1973]: 253–63). Relatively early work includes studies of the Vietnam Veterans Memorial by Harry W. Haines, Sonja Foss, A. Cheree Carlson and John E. Hocking, Peter Ehrenhaus, and Richard Morris (Haines, "'What Kind of War?': An Analysis of the Vietnam Veterans Memorial," *Critical Studies in Mass Communication* 3 [1986]: 1–20; Foss, "Ambiguity as Persuasion: The Vietnam Veterans Memorial," *Communication Quarterly* 34 [1986]: 326–40; Carlson and Hocking, "Strategies of Redemption at the Vietnam Veterans' Memorial," *Western Journal of Communication* 52 [1988]: 203–15; Ehrenhaus, "The Vietnam Veterans Memorial: An Invitation to Argument," *Journal of the American Forensic Association* 25 [1988]: 54–64, and "Silence and Symbolic Expression," *Communication Monographs* 55 [1988]: 41–57; Richard Morris, "The Vietnam Veterans Memorial and the Myth of Superiority," in *Cultural Legacies of Vietnam: Uses of the Past in the Present,* ed. Richard Morris and Peter Ehrenhaus, 199–222 [Norwood, N.J.: Ablex, 1990]). In addition, any sampling from this literature should include two exemplary essays: Rosenfield's study of New York City's Central Park in relation to the epideictic tradition of civic humanism that presumed "character traits, such as pride, cooperation, dignity, and common sense, could be instilled and enhanced by visiting a garden landscape"; and Carole Blair's, Marsha S. Jeppeson's, and Enrico Pucci Jr.'s study of the Vietnam Veterans Memorial and how it inclines visitors to participate in open-ended expression of multiple, individual, and often competing possibilities for the Vietnam War's meaning—a disposition that we might call the "postmodern" attitude (Rosenfield, "Central Park and the Celebration of Civic Virtue," 221–66; Blair, Jeppeson, and Pucci, "Public Memorializing in Postmodernity: The Vietnam Veterans Memorial as Prototype," *Quarterly Journal of Speech* 77 [1991]: 263–88). Two exemplary book-length works are Richard Morris's investigation of American "gravescape" traditions and Gregory Clark's study of the rhetoric of American landscapes (Morris, *Sinners, Lovers, and Heroes: An Essay on Memorializing in Three American Cultures* [Albany: State University of New York Press, 1997]; Clark, *Rhetorical Landscapes in America: Variations on a Theme from Kenneth Burke* [Columbia: University of South Carolina Press, 2004]). Other essays that inform this theme include Roxanne Mountford's work on the pulpit as gendered "rhetorical space," Carole Blair's study of memorial sites as exemplars of rhetoric's materiality, Carole Blair's and Neil Michel's study of the Astronauts Memorial, Cheryl R. Jorgensen-Earp's and Lori A. Lanzilotti's study of shrines, Victoria J. Gallagher's work on the Birmingham Civil Rights Institute, and Greg Dickinson's studies of Starbucks and of Old Pasadena (Mountford, "On Gender and Rhetorical Space," *Rhetoric Society Quarterly* 30 [Winter 2001]: 41–71; Blair, "Contemporary U.S. Memorial Sites as Exemplars of Rhetoric's Materiality," in *Rhetorical Bodies,* 16–57; Blair and Michel, "Commemorating in the Theme Park Zone: Reading

the Astronauts Memorial," in *At the Intersection,* 29–83; Jorgenson-Earp and Lanzilotti, "Public Memory and Private Grief: The Construction of Shrines at the Sites of Public Tragedy," *Quarterly Journal of Speech* 84 [1998]: 150–70; Gallagher, "Memory and Reconciliation in the Birmingham Civil Rights Institute," *Rhetoric and Public Affairs* 2 [1999]: 303–20; Dickinson, "Joe's Rhetoric: Finding Authenticity at Starbucks," *Rhetoric Society Quarterly* 32 [Fall 2002]: 5–27, and "Memories for Sale: Nostalgia and the Construction of Identity in Old Pasadena," *Quarterly Journal of Speech* 83 [1997]: 1–27).

82. This analysis is based partly on Kirk Savage's commentary in "The Past in the Present: The Life of Memorials," *Harvard Design Magazine* (Fall 1999): 17–18; also see Sanford Levinson's discussion of the controversy about the Ashe statue in *Written in Stone: Public Monuments in Changing Societies* (Durham, N.C.: Duke University Press, 1998), 115–19.

83. As discussed earlier, McKeon formulated an expansive perspective on demonstrative rhetoric that encompassed all "showing" or "making known" through demonstrations, exhibitions, and presentations, regardless of whatever specific forms they might take in discourse and action.

84. Early scholarly literature on political demonstrations developed during the protests and nonverbal displays that characterized much of the political rhetoric of the late 1960s and early 1970s. As I explained earlier, McKeon pointed to those protests and nonverbal displays as evidence that warranted a broadened understanding of demonstrative rhetoric. See the studies by Thomas W. Benson and Bonnie Johnson ("The Rhetoric of Resistance: Confrontation with the War Makers, Washington, D.C.," *Today's Speech* 16 [September 1968]: 35–42), James R. Andrews ("Confrontation at Columbia: A Case Study in Coercive Rhetoric," *Quarterly Journal of Speech* 55 [1969]: 9–16), Robert L. Scott and Donald K. Smith ("The Rhetoric of Confrontation," *Quarterly Journal of Speech* 55 [1969]: 1–8), Richard B. Gregg ("The Ego-Function of the Rhetoric of Protest," *Philosophy and Rhetoric* 4 [1971]: 71–91), and John Waite Bowers and Donovan J. Ochs (*The Rhetoric of Agitation and Control* [Reading, Mass.: Addison-Wesley, 1971]). Also see David Berg, who stressed the importance of the mass media—particularly television—to successful demonstrative performance, and two essays by Franklyn Haiman (the second a retrospective piece updating the first) on the legal and moral implications of what Leland Griffin called the "body rhetoric" of nonverbal street protests (Berg, "Rhetoric, Reality, and Mass Media," *Quarterly Journal of Speech* 58 [1972]: 255–63; Haiman, "The Rhetoric of the Streets: Some Legal and Ethical Considerations," *Quarterly Journal of Speech* 53 [1967]: 99–114, and his "Nonverbal Communication and the First Amendment: The Rhetoric of the Streets Revisited," *Quarterly Journal of Speech* 68 [1982]: 371–83; Griffin, "The Rhetorical Structure of the 'New Left' Movement: Part 1," *Quarterly Journal of Speech* 50 [April 1964]: 127 [quoted in Haiman, "The Rhetoric of the Streets: Some Legal and Ethical Considerations," 102]).

85. Displays of graphical devices during technical communication are also demonstrative performances subject to criticism. For an example, consider Edward Tufte's study of the thirteen charts that Morton Thiokol engineers developed when assessing whether to oppose launching the ill-fated space shuttle Challenger. The engineers had debated at length the possibility that cold weather could lead to a catastrophic O-ring failure and were inclined against going ahead with the launch. Tufte critiqued their performance, showing how the engineers failed to convince NASA officials because they did not effectively *display* a pattern among the data that easily could have been recognized as the basis for their concern. Edward R. Tufte, *Visual Explanations: Images and Quantities, Evidence and Narrative* (Cheshire, Conn.: Graphics Press, 1997), 39–51.

86. Kevin Michael DeLuca's analysis of image events enacted by Earth First!, Act Up, and Queer Nation discloses qualities that resemble the three senses of demonstration discussed here. These body rhetorics have "argumentative force," they manifest feelings and commitments symbolically, and they are performances enacted in anticipation of an audience. See his "Unruly

Arguments: The Body Rhetoric of Earth First!, Act Up, and Queer Nation," *Argumentation and Advocacy* 36 (Summer 1999): 9–21. Of related interest is DeLuca and Jennifer Peeples, "From Public Sphere to Public Screen: Democracy, Activism, and the 'Violence' of Seattle," *Critical Studies in Media Communication* 19 (2002): 125–51. Also see DeLuca's detailed study of image events as rhetorical tactics in environmental activism, *Image Politics: The New Environmental Activism* (New York: Guilford, 1999).

87. The work of Kenneth Burke, discussed earlier, and of Erving Goffman offer perspectives that afford productive points of departure for thinking about the "demonstrative" qualities of self (and other) portrayal in daily life. Other scholarship that can inform and stimulate studies along the theme of examining rhetorical displays as demonstrative and demonstrations (exhibitions, presentations) as rhetorical display includes S. Michael Halloran's and David Procter's studies of enacted spectacles, Tamar Katriel's study of Israeli Youth Movement ceremonials, Bryan C. Taylor's investigation of a controversy over an exhibit portraying the use of atomic bombs near the end of the Second World War at the National Air and Space Museum, and Marouf Hasian Jr.'s account of the U.S. Holocaust National Memorial Museum. (Halloran, "Text and Experience in a Historical Pageant: Toward a Rhetoric of Spectacle," *Rhetoric Society Quarterly* 31 [Fall 2001]: 5–17; Procter, "The Dynamic Spectacle: Transforming Experience into Social Forms of Community," *Quarterly Journal of Speech* 76 [1990]: 117–33; Katriel, "Rhetoric in Flames: Fire Inscriptions in Israeli Youth Movement Ceremonials," *Quarterly Journal of Speech* 73 [1987]: 444–59; Taylor, "The Bodies of August: Photographic Realism and the Controversy at the National Air and Space Museum," *Rhetoric and Public Affairs* 1 [1998]: 331–61; and Hasian Jr., "Remembering and Forgetting the 'Final Solution': A Rhetorical Pilgrimage through the U.S. Holocaust Memorial Museum," *Critical Studies in Media Communication* 21 [2004]: 64–92). Also see Cameron Shelley's distinction between rhetorical and demonstrative modes of visual argument, as well as suggestive work on visual manifestations of demonstration in Thomas W. Benson's analysis of the televisual construction of "proof" in a *60 Minutes* episode (Shelley, "Rhetorical and Demonstrative Modes of Visual Argument: Looking at Images of Human Evolution," *Argumentation and Advocacy* 33 [Fall 1996]: 53–68; Benson, "Killer Media: Technology, Communication Theory, and the First Amendment," in *Rhetorical Dimensions in Media: A Critical Casebook,* ed. Martin J. Medhurst and Thomas W. Benson, 2nd ed., 378–97 [Dubuque, Iowa: Kendall/Hunt, 1991]). Studies of rhetorical displays enacted during demonstrations and protest actions include (in addition to sources cited in notes 84 and 86), Adrienne E. Christiansen and Jeremy J. Hanson on the protest actions of Act Up, Karen A. Foss and Kathy L. Domenici on the displays of the Mothers of the Plaza de Mayo, Sara Hayden on participants' statements before the Million Mom March, and John Arthos Jr.'s account of the pledge ceremony conducted by Louis Farrakhan at the Million Man March (Christiansen and Hanson, "Comedy as Cure for Tragedy: Act Up and the Rhetoric of AIDS," *Quarterly Journal of Speech* 82 [1996]: 157–70; Foss and Domenici, "Haunting Argentina: Synecdoche in the Protests of the Mothers of the Plaza de Mayo," *Quarterly Journal of Speech* 87 [2001]: 237–58; Hayden, "Family Metaphors and the Nation: Promoting a Politics of Care through the Million Mom March," *Quarterly Journal of Speech* 89 [2003]: 196–215; Arthos Jr., "The Shaman-Trickster's Art of Misdirection: The Rhetoric of Farrakhan and the Million Men," *Quarterly Journal of Speech* 87 [2001]: 41–60). Other studies direct attention to the performative dimensions of distinct kinds of rhetorical display, including Walter H. Beale's essay on epideictic discourse as performative, Katriel's investigations of Israeli pioneer settlement museums as "ideological and performative arenas," Carole Blair's and Neil Michel's study of the performative aspects of the Civil Rights Memorial in Montgomery, Alabama, Suzanne M. Daughton's inspection of "iconic enactment" in the text of an Angelina Grimke speech, Robert Hariman's and John L. Lucaites's analysis of an "iconic photograph" in relation to "performing civic identity," and Marguerite

Helmer's consideration of the performative dimensions involved in experiencing a painting hanging in a museum (Beale, "Rhetorical Performative Discourse: A New Theory of Epideictic," *Philosophy and Rhetoric* 11 [1978]: 221–46; Katriel, "'Our Future is Where Our Past Is:' Studying Heritage Museums as Ideological and Performative Arenas," *Communication Monographs* 60 [1993]: 69–75, and her "Sites of Memory: Discourses of the Past in Israeli Pioneering Settlement Museums," 1–20; Blair and Michel, "Reproducing Civil Rights Tactics: The Rhetorical Performances of the Civil Rights Memorial," *Rhetoric Society Quarterly* 30 [Spring 2000]: 31–55; Daughton, "The Fine Texture of Enactment: Iconicity as Empowerment in Angelina Grimke's Pennsylvania Hall Address," *Women's Studies in Communication* 18 [1995]: 20–43; Hariman and Lucaites, "Performing Civic Identity: The Iconic Photograph of the Flag Raising on Iwo Jima," *Quarterly Journal of Speech* 88 [2002]: 363–92; and Helmers, "Painting as Rhetorical Performance: Joseph Wright's *An Experiment on a Bird in an Air Pump*," *Journal of Advanced Composition* 21 [Winter 2001]: 71–95).

88. Theoretical and critical studies might emphasize one or another of these three themes, but displays integrate them in situated rhetorical practice. For a study that attends to all three, see Robert H. Byer's account of Daniel Webster's Bunker Hill Monument speech. He accounts for the experience of "beholding" monumental sublimity in terms of (1) the monument's immediate, imposing, physical presence, (2) Webster's skillful generation of presence through "word painting," and (3) Webster's own dynamic presence, embodied in his oratorical performance. His analysis of Nathaniel Hawthorne's depictions of ruins is offered as a "dialectical" alternative to conventional "monumental" practices. That alternative underscores the point that values and beliefs are transitory rather than permanent, as shown in the passing of the communities that once embodied them in material structures that remain only as ruins. Robert H. Byer, "Words, Monuments, Beholders: The Visual Arts in Hawthorne's *The Marble Faun*," in *American Iconology*, ed. David C. Miller, 163–85 (New Haven, Conn.: Yale University Press, 1993).

89. Richard Weaver, "Language Is Sermonic," in *Language Is Sermonic: Richard M. Weaver on the Nature of Rhetoric*, ed. Richard L. Johannesen, Rennard Strickland, and Ralph T. Eubanks, 211 (Baton Rouge: Louisiana State University Press, 1970).

90. Weaver's definition of rhetoric as "an art of emphasis embodying an order of desire" captures the dual assumptions of selectivity and valuation that I contend are central to understanding displays as rhetorical. This definition is related to a view of language as "sermonic" in the sense that whenever we use language, our selection of words discloses the values, attitudes, and purposes that we hold and, at least by implication, want others to share. Weaver focused on linguistic selectivity and valuing, but I contend that the emphases and de-emphases manifesting the valuational or "moralizing" implications of display are not restricted to verbal displays, but also constitute visual, material, and demonstrative displays (ibid., 201–25).

91. The perspective I present here invites examination of epideictic qualities exhibited in contemporary rhetorical displays in all of their rich verbal, visual, material, and demonstrative variety. Other relevant and potentially useful perspectives are also available to guide inquiries into contemporary manifestations of epideictic. As mentioned earlier, McKeon and Perelman and Olbrechts-Tyteca contributed distinctive and widely applicable understandings of contemporary epideictic. Some commentators on Aristotle's epideictic imply that his original conception, once properly understood, remains applicable to specific communicative forms and situations today (See Hauser, "Aristotle on Epideictic," 17–20; Rosenfield, "Practical Celebration of Epideictic," 131, 141–42, 146–48). Other scholars reconceive epideictic presumably to strengthen its contemporary applicability and relevance (see for example Beale, "Rhetorical Performative Discourse," 221–46; Celeste Michelle Condit, "The Functions of Epideictic: The Boston Massacre Orations as Exemplar," *Communication Quarterly* 33 [1985]: 284–98; Cynthia Miecznikowski Sheard, "The Public Value of Epideictic Rhetoric," *College English* 58 [1996]: 765–94). Critical studies disclose

epideictic qualities across a wide range of distinct kinds of rhetorical display. Much of this work has centered on contemporary eulogy and other public oratory (See Brooke Rollins, "The Ethics of Epideictic Rhetoric: Addressing the Problem of Presence through Derrida's Funeral Orations," *Rhetoric Society Quarterly* 35 [Winter 2005]: 5–23; John M. Murphy, "'Our Mission and Our Moment': George W. Bush and September 11th," *Rhetoric and Public Affairs* 6 [2003]: 607–32 and "Epideictic and Deliberative Strategies in Opposition to War: The Paradox of Honor and Expediency," *Communication Studies* 43 [1992]: 65–78; Bonnie J. Dow, "The Function of Epideictic and Deliberative Strategies in Presidential Crisis Rhetoric," *Western Journal of Speech Communication* 53 [1989]: 294–310; Amos Kiewe, "Framing Memory through Eulogy: Ronald Reagan's Long Good-Bye," in *Framing Public Memory,* 248–66; Denise M. Bostdorff, "George W. Bush's Post-September 11 Rhetoric of Covenant Renewal: Upholding the Faith of the Greatest Generation," *Quarterly Journal of Speech* 89 [2003]: 293–319; Michael P. Sipiora, "Heidegger and Epideictic Discourse: The Rhetorical Performance of Meditative Thinking," *Philosophy Today* 35 [1991]: 239–53). Other critical work discloses epideictic qualities in nonoratorical forms of display ranging from press releases aimed at addressing a crisis in the image of professional baseball (Gray Matthews, "Epideictic Rhetoric and Baseball: Nurturing Community through Controversy," *Southern Communication Journal* 60 [1995]: 275–91) and print advertisements designed to advance corporate interests (Richard E. Crable and Steven L. Vibbert, "Mobil's Epideictic Advocacy: 'Observations' of Prometheus-Bound," *Communication Monographs* 50 [1983]: 380–94), through documentary film (Thomas W. Benson, "The Rhetorical Structure of Frederick Wiseman's *Primate,*" *Quarterly Journal of Speech* 71 [1985]: 216–17) and television talk show interactions (Robert McKenzie, "Audience Involvement in the Epideictic Discourse of Television Talk Shows," *Communication Quarterly* 48 [2000]: 190–203), to the discourses of science (Dale L. Sullivan, "The Epideictic Rhetoric of Science," *Journal of Business and Technical Communication* 5 [1991]: 229–45) and the "displays" of critical scholarship (Michael Carter, "Scholarship as Rhetoric of Display: Or, Why is Everybody Saying All Those Terrible Things about Us?" *College English* 54 [1992]: 303–13; Dale L. Sullivan, "The Epideictic Character of Rhetorical Criticism," *Rhetoric Review* 11 [1993]: 339–49). Regardless of the perspective preferred or of the particular form of display examined, displays manifest rhetorics with qualities that invite examination as epideictic.

92. Kenneth Burke, *A Rhetoric of Motives,* 22.

93. For a good example of how rhetorical displays can generate "misidentifications" yielding unintended divisions, see Gary C. Woodward's account of the controversy surrounding sculptor John Ahearn's social-realist representations of ordinary South Bronx residents in statuary placed at the intersection of Jerome Avenue and 169th Street (*The Idea of Identification* [Albany: State University of New York Press, 2003], 105–12). Woodward describes the sculptures of three residents in the midst of unremarkable street activities:

> "Raymond," a lean young Hispanic man in sneakers, black pants, and a black hooded sweatshirt, is kneeling next to his pit bull. The dog is looking into the distance; his master has a downward gaze suggesting he is occupied with his own thoughts. "Daleesha" is a thin 14-year-old girl in mid-stride on rollerskates, the whiteness of her footgear contrasting sharply with a colorful Batman t-shirt. With her hair in a topknot and her legs slightly bent, she looks like any adolescent who has confidently mastered a new thrill. "Carey" is a heavy muscular black man without a shirt. A basketball is tucked under his right arm. And his left foot rests on an enormous boom box, which seems to clearly announce his presence on the street (107).

A controversy ensued immediately after the sculptures were installed on their pedestals that involved questioning Ahearn's motives for choosing these three subjects and not seeking prior approval from "the community." Accusations of racism were made. His defenders, including

Woodward, pointed out class motives behind the expectation that his subjects should have been more idealized images of middle-class or professional African Americans. Ahearn, citing respect for his critics, took the statues down one week after he had installed them. Displays engage with the expectations of those who become audience to them, often in unintended ways.

94. See Woodward's discussion of identification and the concept of identity in *Idea of Identification*, 21–43. For an exemplary critical study of identification and the constitution of identity, in the context of cinematic display, see Ekaterina V. Haskins, "Time, Space, and Political Identity: Envisioning Community in *Triumph of the Will*," in *The Terministic Screen: Rhetorical Perspectives on Film*, ed. David Blakesley, 92–106 (Carbondale: Southern Illinois University Press, 2003). Also see Gregory Clark's insightful exploration of this theme in relation to American tourist landscapes in *Rhetorical Landscapes in America*.

Part 1

The Verbal Depiction of the Visual and the Visual Depiction of the Verbal

2

$\mathcal{S}$atisfaction of Metaphorical Expectations through Visual Display *The* Titanic *Exhibition*

Late in the evening of April 14, 1912, the Royal Mail Ship *Titanic*, making her maiden voyage from Southampton to New York, struck an iceberg and sustained a series of gashes along her hull. Although the sea that night was smooth "like polished glass"[1] and there were some two hours and forty minutes between impact and sinking, only an estimated 705 passengers and crew survived. The purportedly unsinkable *Titanic* carried few lifeboats, an oversight leading to the deaths of some 1,522 men, women, and children.[2] International controversy quickly followed as Britain and America held separate inquiries. At both hearings, ample blame for the tragedy was distributed to those connected in any official capacity with the voyage.

Early in the morning of September 1, 1985, an American and French research crew aboard the U.S. Navy research vessel *Knorr* discovered the remains of the *Titanic* at the bottom of the North Atlantic.[3] It quickly became apparent that, after seventy-three years, the *Titanic* had lost none of her ability to generate international controversy. This time, the major players had shifted to the scientific communities of America and France and, by extension, to the community of oceanographic science of the world. The issue this time was not who was to blame for the sinking and loss of life but what should be done with *Titanic* now that she was found.

A hearing was brought before the House Committee on Merchant Marine and Fisheries on October 29, 1985, to debate the merits of HR 3272, the *RMS Titanic Maritime Memorial Act of 1985*. This bill, brought by Rep. Walter Jones of North Carolina, was overwhelmingly passed and signed into law by President Reagan in late 1986.[4] HR 3272 designated that the *Titanic* is an international maritime memorial and that "pending . . . international agreement or guidelines, no person should physically alter, disturb or salvage the R.M.S. *Titanic* in any research or exploratory activities which are conducted."[5]

HR 3272 turned out to be a toothless law. The United States did not have legal jurisdiction over the *Titanic* site, which was located 367 miles southeast of Newfoundland. Indeed, even Canada, which opposed salvage, would have difficulty sustaining any claim to jurisdiction since the *Titanic* site is located in what is widely regarded as the "high seas." Walter Lord, the author of two popular *Titanic* accounts—*A Night to Remember* and *The*

Night Lives On—expressed the generally accepted belief that "the sea belongs to no one, and there are few funds for guarding a patch of ocean."[6] Independent salvagers were unlikely to allow the law or the operation's difficulty to deter them. As perennial salvager Jack Grimm of Abilene said, "You can do anything you're big enough to do out there."[7] Cunard Lines (which purchased the White Star line) admitted to having no claim; survivors' or victims' relatives could only with difficulty prove ownership of personal items; and claims by an insurance company and Douglas Woolley, an Englishman, to hold title to *Titanic* remained unproven.[8] *Titanic*, it seems, belonged to no one and to everyone.

Ambiguities about the ownership of *Titanic*'s remains are matched by uncertainties over the public significance of the site. As Stephen Browne reminds us, "public memory, though claimed by many, is the sole property of none."[9] With the failure of legal remedy, the "rhetorical battleground"[10] of public memory would decide the fate of the rediscovered *Titanic*. This chapter examines rhetoric that emerged during the initial contest over *Titanic*'s remains and the way that this discourse sought to stabilize both public attitudes toward salvage and the place of the rediscovered *Titanic* in public memory. I first contend that, by treating the *Titanic* as a gravesite, opponents of salvage constructed a cluster of sacralizing metaphors that served to constrain and guide appropriate commemoration. Proponents of salvage countered with a cluster of secularizing metaphors that delegitimized the presumptive view of *Titanic* as a gravesite and substituted an alternative set of thoughts and actions. I then examine the display of salvaged artifacts in *Titanic:* The Exhibition. This exhibit relied on dramatic visuals and the familiar received narrative of the *Titanic* disaster to bring exhibit patrons to a simulated site of *Titanic*'s sinking. By co-opting the sacralizing metaphors, exhibitors resisted characterization as defilers of the sacred ground and sought post hoc legitimacy for the secular interests underlying the exhibit.

Public Memory and the Site of Tragedy

After a wealth of studies on such memorials and museums as the Vietnam Veterans Memorial, the United States Holocaust Memorial Museum, and the Civil Rights memorials and museums in Atlanta, Montgomery, and Memphis,[11] the negotiated and contested nature of the act of memorializing is well established. It has become a given in rhetorical studies of public memory that public memorials give voice to both a view of the present and recommendations for the future by constructing a view of the past.[12] Yet the majority of these studies concern memorials constructed at locations removed, in space as well as time, from the events being commemorated. Memorials and monuments built on land set aside for the purpose of commemoration are thoroughly, in Browne's terms, "produced" as opposed to "given" texts.[13] The location for the memorial, its size, prominence, and ability to establish a presence in the public mind are points for intense negotiation. A chosen location becomes a part of the meaning of the memorial, for it speaks to the importance of the commemorated person or event in our public lives.

Although all commemorative sites have potential as focal points for mourning and public memory, there is an essential difference between memorials constructed in selected locations and those constructed at the sites of public tragedies. What Blair, Jeppeson, and Pucci note concerning the ability of public monuments to "'sacralize' individuals, places, and ideas"[14] rings particularly true when the memorial is constructed at a location touched by violent death. Sites of public tragedy take on an atmosphere of the holy.[15] The actual locations of tragic events generate both an expectation of memorialization and a constraint upon the discourse and action deemed appropriate to the site. As Edward Linenthal maintains, there is "a primal attraction to scenes of destructive power, to the shattered landscape and shattered people that bear witness to such events."[16] With that attraction comes a particular "emotional empathy"[17] with those who died there. James McPherson speaks, for example, of the figurative "presence of ghosts" on the Gettysburg battlefield.[18] With tragic sites, it is as if "the ground itself . . . was transformed" by events that occurred there. The sense that the site itself is "holy ground," baptized by the blood spilled there, applies a distinct pressure on those who would memorialize at the site. Preservation and commemoration become part of the effort to guarantee "the sanctity of the site," to establish "the purity of the sacred environment."[19]

This is not to say that memorials constructed in chosen space necessarily lack a sense of the holy. For example, the Vietnam Veterans Memorial is considered "sacred ground," particularly by veterans, a place made holy not simply by its commemorative power but by its function as a site of reunions. Yet such sites are "a human construction."[20] There is a palpable difference between the new World War II memorial in its much-debated location on the National Mall in Washington, D.C., and the USS *Arizona* Memorial in Pearl Harbor. The latter is quite literally a tomb, and it still today serves as an active gravesite. Any *Arizona* survivor has the right to have his ashes placed at the bottom of the ship's open gun turrets. The sufferings of those who died in 1941 at that place—not less than the remains of some one thousand men still entombed there—give to the *Arizona* Memorial a "charged environment"[21] that cannot be duplicated in any other location.

With memorials at the sites of tragedies, viewers are particularly sensitive to false notes that destroy the illusion of oneness in time to the event and the faithful re-creation of the experience of the original participants. For that reason, the displacement of room 307, Dr. King's room in the Lorraine Motel section of the National Civil Rights Museum, is not simply an issue of historic accuracy but of viewer-affective response. The movement and duplication of the room potentially hinders the viewer's vicarious participation, the sense of time travel sought by pilgrims to a particular historic location.[22]

For some mourners, violent death turns the site of a public tragedy into the symbolic deathbed of the victims.[23] Visitors to the site of the sinking of *Titanic* stand over a liminal space, the threshold crossed by those who died. Thus, journeys to the site of the sinking take on the nature of a pilgrimage (albeit a secular one),[24] and during this pilgrimage the contact with the gateway of death allows a vicarious sense of oneness with the dead.[25] Visitors to the site of the sinking often comment on a tendency to mentally place themselves not with the survivors but with those standing at the rail watching the last lifeboat pull away. This projection is more than a mental exercise and constitutes a point of modern cultural identification. According to David Stennard, modern individuals facing their own deaths "often do so with a sense of its meaninglessness and of their own insignificance."[26] Such cannot be said about those who died on the *Titanic,* if contemporary accounts of its sinking are to be believed. Writers used the drama of the final moments to invest the victims' deaths with significance, whether as proof of modern technological hubris, of class struggles, or even of the pros and cons of women's suffrage.[27]

Seen in the context of a pilgrimage, the battle over the salvage of articles from the *Titanic* takes on a new significance. These mundane objects from 1912 daily life—dishes, chamber pots, satchels, hand mirrors—become relics from the holy site, imbued with a power from their previous contact with the deceased.[28] Some potentially salvageable objects clearly point up the connection between the fascination with *Titanic,* the liminality of the site, and the quasi-holy nature of *Titanic* artifacts. No object does this more clearly than the pair of men's boots found on the ocean floor, each boot lying next to the other in such a fashion that the viewer can clearly picture the body that once filled them. Although some bodies were recovered immediately after the sinking, most of the dead of the *Titanic* simply disappeared. During the modern exploration of the wreck, no remains were located, the bodies having been crushed by the depths, swept away by currents, or removed by ocean scavengers. These boots serve as a metaphor for our human condition: we all disappear, finally, leaving behind us the detritus of our lives as the fragile proof that we ever existed.

Alan Radley points out how objects become a "tangible record of human endeavour" even though they were not created for that purpose.[29] In part because they manage simply to survive into the present, artifacts become a hook on which to hang an interpretation of the past. Artifacts help us to remember; thus, they "play a central role in the memories of cultures and individuals."[30] Key to understanding the importance of the *Titanic* artifacts is acknowledgment of the way possessions of the deceased are valued in our individual lives. "Possessions," Radley claims, "are marked by their mnemonic quality, as a gateway to recapturing experiences and the satisfaction of relationships with loved ones who are now either dead or at some distance."[31] Individual families may choose to leave the deceased's bedroom or study untouched ("just the way he left it") or may refuse to sell even valuable items connected with the deceased. By doing so, families choose to hold key possessions "in suspension—untouched—making them sacred in their being marked as being beyond disposal or exchange."[32] The human need to designate certain objects as sacred helps to explain why the decision to prevent or allow salvage was ultimately an issue of public memory rather than legality.

Even in comparison to other public tragedies, memorializing the *Titanic* disaster poses a particular challenge. In contrast to the Murrah building site in Oklahoma City,[33] the site of the *Titanic* disaster is an unlikely location for either a temporary or a permanently constructed memorial. Further, the decision about *Titanic* salvage was a commemorative issue argued on the vernacular rather than official level. Official commemoration emphasizes a collective construction of public memory that speaks in a language of "timelessness and sacredness."[34] Vernacular commemoration reflects a culture representing "an array of specialized interests,"[35] and these community interests are reflected in language that "speaks of rights."[36] In the case of *Titanic,* only an organized (and very narrow) scientific community possessed the technology needed to access the site, and that community served as gatekeeper to the numerous salvagers and promoters seeking access. These salvagers and businessmen, together with the scientists and conservators who made recovery possible, served as one viewpoint in the debate over salvage.

Testimony and commentary that challenged salvage and favored a memorializing treatment of *Titanic* came from a variety of sources. Dr. Robert Ballard, the American leader of the discovery expedition, was vocal in this regard in a variety of scientific and popular settings. From the memorial service he held for the *Titanic* victims shortly after discovery to his initial attempts to safeguard public knowledge of *Titanic*'s precise location, his position that the wreck should remain untouched was consistent and clear. Ballard's view was shared by most of the Woods Hole Scientific Community, the *Titanic* Historical Society, survivors, and relatives of victims. Thus the debate over *Titanic* salvage and the subsequent display of the artifacts serves as a case study to illuminate Bodnar's claim that "public memory remains a product of elite manipulation, symbolic interaction, and contested discourse."[37] An examination of the metaphors that served as "powerful symbolic expressions" of this clash of competing interests gives insight into the multivocal nature of the debate over public commemoration.[38]

The Titanic *as Site of Metaphorical Contention*

The initial step for this study is to uncover the metaphors controlling the issue of appropriate commemoration.[39] A particular metaphor defines the object, designates our proper attitude toward the object, and negatively characterizes those who do not share this attitude. Finally, the metaphor completes its task by indicating the appropriate future actions to take in respect to the object.[40] In the case of the *Titanic,* metaphors clustered around two differing characterizations of the site of the tragedy: a sacralizing system of metaphors and an opposing secularizing system. These primary metaphors and their variations served to characterize the agents in the oceanographic/salvage communities, to condemn or laud specific behaviors by these agents, and to advocate appropriate actions in regard to *Titanic.* These same metaphors would later structure the display of *Titanic* artifacts, visually extending the argument about salvage to the general public.

Sacralizing the *Titanic* Site

For those who wished to treat the remains of *Titanic* as a permanent, intact memorial, the controlling metaphor was to describe it, first and foremost, as a *gravesite.* According to hearing testimony by Dr. John Brinnin, maritime history professor, the *Titanic* is a "*tomb* and a *reliquary,*"[41] as can be seen by the "many poignant personal *relics*" photographed by the expedition.[42] To disturb a *tomb* is to disturb "the bodies of those *entombed* within," particularly distressing to one survivor, for "a friend of hers remains within its hull."[43] Jon Hollis testified that to disturb *this tomb* may mean seeing "remains removed or moved to pick up a platter."[44] Edward Kamuda, general secretary of the *Titanic* Historical Society, maintained that the hull itself is "a *gravestone* for the 1,500 people who died."[45] Therefore, according to Robert Ballard, the entire area surrounding the *Titanic* is, or should be, "*hallowed ground.*"[46]

One element necessary to support a gravesite metaphor is a sense of whose grave it actually is. The rediscovered *Titanic* becomes the primary figure among the deceased. It is easy to personify the *Titanic* as a great lady, largely because of traditional references to a ship as "she." Dr. Robert Ballard could be counted on for an expression of anthropomorphic zeal:

> The *Titanic* is truly gone for good, home-ported at last. She'll never be raised and for that I'm sad, but content . . . Although she is still awesome in her dimensions, she is no longer the *graceful lady* that sank five days into her maiden voyage in April 1912. Her beauty has faded; she is broken in two and age has withered her . . . In future, when I think of the *Titanic,* I will see her bow sitting upright on the bottom, dignified despite the decay and, finally, at rest.[47]

Accordingly, *Newsweek* dramatically stated that "the *grave* of the *Titanic*"[48] had been found, and the *Seattle Post-Intelligencer* further maintained that her "*corpse*" had been "*prowled*" by scientists.[49] Despite the indignities, she is "in beautiful condition," even "gorgeous."[50]

Leslie Pink and Leonard Brown of the *Titanic* Preservation Trust likened exploring inside *Titanic* to "trespassing with intent to do damage in a *graveyard*."[51] But these characterizations are kind compared to the most common accusation that what salvagers were really doing was robbing that graveyard. According to the metaphors of *Titanic* as a tomb or a female corpse at rest, what are we to think of those with "a spirit less of reverence for the dead than gain for the living?"[52] According to *Titanic* historians John Eaton and Charles Haas, they are "*plunderers* and *armchair salvage experts*."[53] Jon Hollis maintained at the committee hearing that they are little more than "*thieves in the night*. They are *grave robbers, pirates* and *turncoats*"[54] who through their "*buccaneering*"[55] would willingly "destroy for profit what belongs to all the world."[56] Because they prey off of the dead, they are "*vultures*,"[57] "*scavengers*,"[58] "*grim reapers* of profit"[59] who would have the wreck "*cannibalized*"[60] for their own ends.

If these metaphors condemn particular behavior, they also point clearly to appropriate actions. The action implicit in the gravesite metaphor (the act of memorializing) was made explicit in a call for an international maritime memorial. Much like the USS *Arizona,* the *Titanic* would remain in place as a *maritime tomb,*[61] with visits permitted to the ocean surface over the wreck. The wreck itself could be photographed and studied. Dr. Robert Ballard was quoted as saying, "It is better to photograph a *graveyard* than to rob the objects lying there."[62] Ballard himself was upheld as a model of proper respect for the dead implied by the primary gravesite metaphor. When a cable from the *Titanic* was accidentally snagged and brought to the surface, Ballard had the cable dropped overboard immediately. He even had the crewmen wash their hands on the off chance that some *Titanic* rust remained.[63] His respect was cited approvingly by Walter Lord as a "sensitivity that verged on piety."[64] Such Ballard stories—and there were many—took on a mythic-instructive air.

Secularizing the *Titanic* Site

Those who favored allowing the salvage of *Titanic* on an unlimited, free-market basis also testified at the hearing before the maritime committee and presented their case in the popular press. One ready outlet for presenting the salvage case was the *National Review,* whose editor, William F. Buckley Jr., showed considerable interest in salvage. On September 25, 1987, he wrote an article in response to Sen. Lowell P. Weicker's bill to ban the import of *Titanic* artifacts into America for commercial gain.[65] He later outlined a series of arguments: first, that leaving the artifacts at the bottom of the North Atlantic would not "consecrate" them, and second, that Congress had no "business telling an adult American what he can and what he cannot purchase from a willing seller, if you're not talking drugs or machine guns."[66] Following this article, the French IFREMER (Institut Français de Recherche pour l'Exploitation de la Mer) oceanographic team invited Buckley along to dive with the expedition to view the *Titanic.*[67] This journey solidified Buckley's support for the salvage of artifacts. Also favoring salvage was the French IFREMER oceanographic team, which had long felt slighted in both publicity and compensation for the discovery of the *Titanic* remains. They were joined by independents who tried for years to discover and salvage *Titanic* and businesspeople—such as Westgate Productions and Ocean Research Exploration Ltd.—who stood to profit from salvage.

For those who favored unregulated salvage, the key metaphor for the site of disaster and the discovered remains of *Titanic* was to equate it with an *archeological site.* In support of this metaphor, touchstones of history needed to be found to prove that the application to *Titanic* was compatible. William F. Buckley claimed to feel no more a "voyeur" viewing *Titanic* than he did viewing the Nile tombs or the catacombs in Lima.[68] The Nile tombs analogy quickly became the focal point of anxiety for salvagers. Bruno Chomel de Varagnes, director of the IFREMER expedition, felt that the same arguments for memorializing *Titanic* could be made regarding the Egyptian pyramids. This, he felt, could mean the "end to all archeological research."[69] Buckley wondered whether, if the gravesite metaphor and the opposition to salvage held sway, we would "need to return to the Pyramids everything that has been taken from them."[70]

Just as those who preferred building a memorial to allowing salvage made a human connection to the ship, those who favored unrestricted salvage worked to distance the public from any feeling of warmth toward the ship herself. According to Captain W. F. Searle of the U.S. Navy, the *Titanic* is a "hulk."[71] It—notice, not "she"—is merely a "wreck, 882 feet long, 46,000 tons of twisted steel."[72] Outside of its "creaky *carapace*,"[73] Buckley stated, such "oddments as plates, wine bottles, jewelry, strongboxes" are spread in "chaotic arrangements."[74]

These language strategies were employed to gain the distance needed to see the wreck as an archeological site. The general problem according to salvagers was that, as one *National Review* reader put it, "Senator Weicker and all those people just don't understand *archeology*."[75] Nor did they understand archeologists. The next work of the metaphoric clusters would be to rehabilitate the image of salvagers. If the *Titanic* is no longer primarily a gravesite, then its explorers are no longer grave robbers. They are, Buckley claimed, "above all *adventurers, pioneer types*" who have "refreshed a legend . . . making possible scientific and historic discoveries."[76] To say that these "*adventurers-entrepreneurs*"[77] exploited *Titanic* is, Buckley further stated, like saying "Gauguin exploited Tahiti" or "Quaker Oats exploits Iowa."[78] There exist, according to Robert Chappaz of Taurus International, technical consultants for the salvage operation, "no *monkey business,* no *greedy vultures*,"[79] only *heroic explorers,* described by the *New York Times* as "kind of *like Lucas and Spielberg doing 'Indiana Jones.'*"[80] They are "scientists,"[81] who "by law must earn their research funds."[82] They are not exploiting; they are excavating. They are not plundering; they are preserving.

In a 1999 article on underwater salvage for *Preservation* magazine, Adam Goodheart referred to the deep oceans as "a *closed time capsule*."[83] The implications of this metaphor are telling, for time capsules are created with the expectation that they will be opened one day. Goodheart described the value of shipwrecks: "[E]ach freezes in time a particular moment in history, the moment of its sinking. Each is, in a sense, a *small-scale Pompeii*. And like the *ash of Vesuvius,* the ocean can, under certain conditions, be an extraordinary preservative environment."[84] Placed so close to the time-capsule metaphor, the sense is that the natural deep-water preservation is in some way purposeful, almost as if the artifacts have been waiting to be discovered and removed.

Finally, these metaphors point toward appropriate action, a different action than was implied by the gravesite and related metaphors. An archeological site is to be explored; the archeologists, according to Buckley, are to retrieve "from utter uselessness artifacts that, for some people, exercise an alluring historical appeal."[85] Further, Chappaz maintained, we should follow the wisdom of the archeological past in dealing with *Titanic*, for "we preserve it better by bringing these things up and putting them in museums for the public."[86] Thus, the competing central metaphor (archeological site) finally led to a call for action in direct opposition to the gravesite metaphor.

During the years between the debate over the *RMS Titanic Maritime Memorial Act* and the 2000 exhibition of artifacts examined in this chapter, the legal fate of *Titanic* and her artifacts followed a twisted path. Despite media and public pressure, IFREMER conducted a 1987 salvage expedition for Titanic Ventures, a limited partnership.[87] On October 28, 1987, Westgate Productions presented a "live" opening of the second-purser's safe, hosted by Telly Savalas. The Las Vegas host, the game-show format where four experts waited to examine the contents, the fact that the show was telecast at 2:00 A.M. Monte Carlo time (to cash in on U.S. prime time)[88] led the show to be roundly condemned as "a circus."[89] Titanic Ventures sold the eighteen hundred artifacts from this expedition and its salvage interests to RMS *Titanic* Inc.,[90] which contracted the French team for a 1993 salvage operation. In 1994, a U.S. federal court order gave RMS *Titanic* Inc. salvor-in-possession rights to the *Titanic* wreck.[91] The first exhibition of *Titanic* artifacts opened at the National Maritime Museum in Greenwich, England, that same year.[92]

Although the gravesite metaphor did not have sufficient power to prevent salvage, business interests became trapped in the constraints of their own secularizing metaphor. If the *Titanic* wreck is an archeological site, then its artifacts can no longer be equated with "stamps or coins" to be bought and sold by collectors.[93] They are archeological finds to be studied and preserved in a museum rather than allowed to decay at the ocean bottom. Thus, in order to make this argument for preservation and in its initial attempts to be awarded salvor-in-possession, RMS *Titanic* Inc. accepted the implications of its own preferred metaphoric system and agreed to a contingency not to sell artifacts "piecemeal" but to keep the collection intact for public display.[94]

RMS *Titanic* Inc., shareholders, as part of a for-profit organization, chafed under these restrictions. Before he was ousted by stockholders in 1999, the company's then-president, George Tulloch, vigorously explored a variety of entrepreneurial avenues that fell just short of selling the artifacts.[95] Technically, Tulloch walked a fine line when he sold eighty thousand lumps of coal brought up from the ocean floor. These fragments were pieces of the larger lumps of coal salvaged, and—in order to claim that the artifacts were not actually sold—each new owner did not "buy" the coal but paid a twenty-five-dollar "fee" in order to act as a "conservator."[96] These efforts did not satisfy company shareholders. In replacing Tulloch with Arnie Geller, RMS *Titanic* Inc. signaled a more aggressive profit orientation that did not escape international attention. During the 1999 expedition to the wreck site, the company put out a news release declaring its "absolute right" to sell recovered gold, currency, and coins.[97] Two days following the statement, U.S. District Judge J. Calvitt Clarke Jr., based in Norfolk federal court and the overseer of *Titanic* salvage since 1992, slapped an emergency order on the company forbidding such sales. RMS *Titanic* Inc.'s new stance alienated the French government, which no longer agreed to provide submersibles for salvage. In December 1999, IFREMER threatened a lawsuit if artifacts were sold.[98]

By the time of the 2000 exhibition, then, RMS *Titanic* Inc. found itself in an increasingly untenable position. Not only did RMS *Titanic* Inc. have to defend against those opposed to all salvage efforts, but it also was now alienated from some of the very scientific community that originally supported the salvage, conservation, and public display of artifacts. The exhibition designers faced two rhetorical tasks.[99] They needed to bolster the secularizing metaphors, reestablishing the salvagers' bona fides as archeologists and conservators. More important, the exhibitors needed to reach out to opponents, particularly the paying public, steeped in the romance of *Titanic* as a gravesite. The need to co-opt the powerful rhetoric of the opposition forced the reconciliation of conflicting metaphors in *Titanic:* The Exhibition.

Titanic: *The Exhibition and the Narrative Reconciliation of Metaphors*

The conflict between sacralizing and secularizing metaphorical systems created enduring tensions in the public memory of *Titanic,* tensions that the artifact exhibitors needed to mitigate or resolve.[100] The remainder of this chapter will analyze the version of *Titanic:* The Exhibition displayed at the Museum of Science and Industry in Chicago from February 18 through September 4, 2000.[101] The work of *memoria* accomplished by *Titanic:* The Exhibition actually takes the form of two distinct narratives whereby the metaphors of the salvage dispute are given visual fulfillment. As Stephen Browne has said, it is the "labor of narratives to return the past to the present and say 'behold.'" The tension between the exhibit's dual narratives underscores that the salvage debate is less a proprietary dispute and more an argument about the way public memory is properly constructed.[102]

In my view, *Titanic:* The Exhibition constructs two narratives for the viewer: "*Titanic's* Endless Voyage" and "Memorializing through Science." The viewer's first encounter with the exhibit, a "tease" located beside the ticket lines on the lower floor of the museum, initiates themes pertinent to these two narratives. The centerpiece of this sneak preview display is the two-ton connecting rod bearing originally housed in one of *Titanic's* engines. It is now encased in glass and covered by a water-and-sodium-carbonate solution through which an electric current runs, a combination causing rust encrustation to fall away. The viewer is dramatically informed by an inscription, "You are witnessing its conservation." The remainder of this preview display consists of a three-minute film where salvors/explorers are superimposed over images of Captain Smith and first-class victim John Jacob Astor and where the deck of the sunken ship is juxtaposed with Edwardian film of children romping and adults being served refreshments on a liner's deck. Then the film scans the *Titanic's* debris field past bottles, stacks of egg plates, and a bedstead. Artifacts are shown raised in baskets and handled gently during the work of conservation. And, on the other side of the display, the very egg plates seen in the film are there, cleaned and wedged in sand in a glass case. A colorful banner beckons with offers to

Board
> the Mighty Ship

Stroll
> the Decks

Admire
> the Treasures . . . silverware, dishes, finery

Gaze
> at the stars in the North Atlantic sky

Feel
> the chill of the night air

Understand
the tragedy and why it happened
Learn
how science is bringing *Titanic* to us today
Experience
the unforgettable story of the *Titanic*

The display previews and legitimizes the primary themes emphasized in the exhibit proper. The banner offers an impossibility: to return in time and inhabit the sensory universe of people long deceased. Science is the mediator through salvage and conservation, "bringing *Titanic* to us" to be boarded at will, a vicarious experience of tragedy cleansed of its actual terror and pain.

Of the exhibit's thirteen rooms, eleven are given over to the mythic retelling of the familiar story of *Titanic*'s sinking. Patterning itself after the received version of *Titanic* as Greek tragedy, it is a tale of humanity's hubris, our overreaching pride in our own technological accomplishments.[103] In an atmosphere laden with irony and heavy on portents, the familiar characters file across the stage to mouth lines frozen by history. All builds to the climactic point of the sinking, providing the cathartic comeuppance for the technological human's attempt to outdo God. Because this story remained unchanged all the years that the wreck lay undiscovered, this tale would apparently favor leaving *Titanic* untouched, its myth intact, its lessons eternal. Yet the exhibitors cleverly co-opt the myth as a narrative stage set, a backdrop for the salvaged artifacts. The two remaining rooms give the salvage rationale its own mythic rendition (for orientation to the exhibit floorplan see figure C1). These dual narratives seek to reconcile the competing metaphors of the earlier salvage dispute, claiming the power of both metaphor clusters to support the display of *Titanic* artifacts.

Narrative One: *Titanic*'s Endless Voyage

Before entering the exhibit, visitors are given "boarding passes" with the names of *Titanic* passengers at the top. This device—which is used successfully at the Holocaust museum—encourages an identification[104] between visitors and passengers that is maintained unevenly throughout the exhibition. During my first visit to the exhibit, my adolescent son plunged ahead through the crowd to check the wall of survivors in the final room and returned cheerfully to inform me that we were dead crew members. A subsequent visit cast me in the more hopeful role of Mrs. James Vivian Drew (Lulu Thorne Christian), a second-class passenger who survived the sinking.

Visitors are diverted immediately from these subjective musings after they pass single file through a dark-blue curtained hall into the first room of the exhibit. In the middle of this small circular room, the visitor sees the *Titanic*'s bell—one of the Chicago exhibition's prize artifacts—dramatically lit from above and suspended over a bed of sand (see figure C2). The bell also is the exhibition's most controversial artifact, because the *Titanic*'s crow's nest was reportedly destroyed in the process of its retrieval during the 1987 salvage operation.[105] As viewers circle the bell on their right, they can view photographs of artifacts as they appeared on the sea floor—a propeller, garden bench, hatch—along the dark blue enclosing walls to their left. Thus, the room's setting creates the sense of viewing the bell in the ocean depths from which it was recovered. The inscription on the wall reads:

On the night of April 14, 1912 Lookout Frederick Fleet rang this bell three times with the warning—Iceberg right ahead. This bell, along with the other objects recovered from the ocean floor, bring to life the true story of the RMS *Titanic*.[106]

Gone is the subjective role of a specific passenger boarding *Titanic* on April 10, 1912, blind to the tragedy to come, replaced by an omniscient view that sees the scope of the *Titanic* story over time. This circular room is the ouroboros, the iconic snake swallowing its tail, where the past meets the present, the beginning meets the end. The bell that signaled the rising action of *Titanic's* moral drama is seamlessly joined to the rationale for the present experience.

A short hallway containing only an office desk and chair and a stained-glass window artifact heralds the conception of *Titanic*. Beside large photos of White Star chairman J. Bruce Ismay and Harland and Wolff's William Pirrie, the accompanying text describes the moment in July 1907 when the two men agreed to build the sister ships *Titanic* and *Olympic*. Visitors take a short step from conception to birth when they turn to enter a large room with a detailed model of the ship at its center. As they circle the model, they become equipped with a conceptual map of what they will see in the remaining exhibit. Recovered artifacts in clear cases surrounding the model recall the 1912 workman (a pulley, a man's leather work boot, awls, a tape measure), and large photographs reveal the creators and their creation (the drafting room of Harland and Wolff, the engine, the boilers). This room establishes the scene in which the drama of the "endless voyage" will unfold. Simultaneously, this part of the exhibit clarifies that the *Titanic* sinking was not a play. By recalling those who designed and built her, this room argues that *Titanic* is history, an actual event that the exhibit promises to recreate for the viewer.

Whatever the conscious intent of the exhibitors, an unintended counter-reading to the exhibit also becomes possible: the juxtaposition of the ersatz and the real. In one corner of the room a video invites us to "[m]arvel at the construction of the *Titanic* at Harland and Wolff's Belfast works." Only by buying the video in the gift shop does one learn that the ship under construction is the *Olympic*. The fact that the ships were identical cannot gloss that the vision offered is a spurious experience. The need to give the artifacts context leads to a continuing interplay between the real and the false, between the artifactual and the artificial, between 1912 reality and imaginative reconstruction. Throughout, this counter-reading competes with the exhibitors' preferred interpretation of the exhibit as history, accurately recreated through preservation and display.

Past its scenic element, this room is also responsible for the thematic establishment of *Titanic* as Greek tragedy. Quickly, the familiar characters are brought on stage: the cowardly Ismay, who escaped the sinking in a lifeboat, and second officer Lightholler, who manned his post to the end and survived by sheer chance. As tragic hero, we are given designer and passenger Thomas Andrews, whose hopeful vision is presented as hubris: "The *Titanic* is now about complete and will, I think, do the old Firm credit tomorrow when we sail." And as Greek chorus we have anonymous voices on the optional audio program:

Man's voice—"Why, she *is* a lifeboat!"
Woman's voice—"To call a ship unsinkable is flying in the face of God."

And there is also the contemporaneous description of the *Belfast Observer*:

. . . a ship so monstrous and unthinkable that it dwarfed the very mountains by the water. Everything was on a nightmare scale.

As presented, the portents of disaster, of the nightmare coming true, are so heavy that it is a wonder the ship was allowed to sail. Even the ragtime music that plays in this room ("Glow Worm," "Oh, You Beautiful Doll") takes on a sinister cast in light of our privileged view. This narrative "backshadowing"[107] allows us to view the past from the vantage of the present with all paths leading to an unavoidable end; it also implies that the signs pointing to that inevitable end were as visible in 1912 as they are today. The pride of the builders, the first-class flaunting of wealth, and the third-class anticipation of a brighter future are framed by our superior knowledge of impending doom. Thus, visitors experience a pleasurable sense of irony as they pass through the subsequent stages of the exhibition in anticipation of the final ending.

The stage is now prepared yet bare, lacking only the ensemble cast to take their positions in first class, on the bridge, in third class. The third room, the Passenger Gallery, is mainly notable for the solidarity it attempts with the working class. Over a large photograph of male, third-class passengers is the inscription, "Among the 710 third-class passengers were many immigrating to America to pursue their dreams." The voice-over is that of second-class passenger Lawrence Beesley: "Looking down from the boat deck, I often noticed how the third-class passengers were enjoying every moment of the time." From our vantage point in the present, the third-class passengers are easily viewed as childlike, hopeful—the innocents embarking not for a new life but for near-certain death. The third-class passengers appear only in the crowd scenes of this morality play. In the *Titanic* myth, they function not as individuals but as collective types—symbolic, as the modern viewer chooses, of the hope of the new world or the evils of class discrimination.

Rooms four through eight may be viewed as a single unit, for they fulfill, to the extent possible, the exhibition's promised opportunity to "[b]oard the mighty ship." Exhibit-goers wend their way from top to bottom through *Titanic*, walking between mock-ups of a first-class bedroom and the Verandah Café, past the grand staircase, a third-class cabin, the cargo area, and, finally, past the giant boilers and through the watertight doors of the engine room. Artifacts recovered from *Titanic*'s debris field appear in display cases within ersatz versions of their purported rooms of origin. Thus, the Verandah Café displays dishes, silverware, and still-corked bottles of champagne now half-full of a greenish liquid. In the third-class passageway is a door lock, the metal number for room two, and a Kaiser dictionary. The few but appropriate items for the cargo hold include fragments of a suitcase, a shirt collar manufactured in the Strand, London, and a passenger suitcase tag. And beside the impressive stage-set doors of *Titanic*'s massive boilers, an iron wrench and recovered coal summon images of the "black gang" responsible for stoking the fires. Thus, the meaning of recovered items for visitors is a function of the dynamic interplay between displayed artifacts and their artificial settings, between material texts and their constructed, material contexts.

Perhaps the largest number of individual artifacts is found surrounding the first-class bedroom: a Doulton Co. sink with its taps reading "Hot," "Cold," and "Waste"; a case containing a chamber pot, spittoon, travel clocks; a case with jewelry, a bedpost, a pendulum lamp. A wall-sized display case contains row upon row of personal items: toothbrushes and a cherry toothpaste jar, soapboxes and soap dishes, lint brushes and hairbrushes, a straight razor and a Gillette box with razors still inside, and a bottle of Purganol Daguin. More than any of the other rooms, this area uses items of creature comforts and bodily needs to capture a lost time and the vanished people of *Titanic*. Yet, the reality of the artifacts must rely on the artifice of the stage setting as a context and reminder of their use. Like all artifacts, the *Titanic*'s objects are divorced from their time. They achieve their grip on us through an uneasy analogy: the hand that held that object is gone; my hand exists but is soon to be gone. Visitors thus experience a powerful if fleeting sense of identification with the dead.

The visitor's experience of identification is unstable because the room's setting conveys the aura of old-fashioned Main Street pharmacy displays where new, authentically inauthentic shelves and counters are stocked with actual bottles of leftover medicine. The effect is cold; the artifacts easily can become simple detritus devoid of larger meaning. To maintain any impact when viewing the artifacts, I had to repeat a mental mantra: This was on the *Titanic*. This was on the bottom of the ocean. The person who used this shaving brush / this razor / this purgative may have died a hideous death (or not) but was there at that place / at that moment. This is the effect feared by Ballard that, removed from the site of tragedy, the artifacts will die, will be drained of their meaning. For some viewers, the simulated setting cannot maintain the verisimilitude needed to situate the artifacts within a larger context of meaning.

The exhibitors apparently anticipated this response and utilized several techniques to reanimate the artifacts on exhibit. Life is literally injected by the occasional appearance of actors in period costume. The impressive duplication of the grand staircase appears to be one primary point where human interaction is deemed necessary by the exhibitors (see figure C3). During my first viewing, an elegant older man, impersonating first-class staff, stood by the staircase to answer questions. His presence seemed primarily designed to impart the fact that the staircase before us was built to the blueprint of the ship itself from skylight to floor. To anachronistic or inappropriate questions ("Did you survive?"), he invariably replied, "You'll have to ask the captain." On my second time through, the staff member was replaced by a young African American man who played the role of Joseph La Roche of second class, the only black male passenger on *Titanic*. Although the actor did not attempt to duplicate the accent of the Haitian-born LaRoche, he was an appropriate choice to portray the twenty-five-year-old who was destined to perish in the sinking. To justify his presence on the grand staircase, LaRoche explained that "we" are allowed to tour the ship this day—April 10, 1912—because we are still docked in Southampton. Both actors revealed with great relish that the staircase floor was the "latest" invention, linoleum, an anachronistic joke relying on a modern cultural perception of cheapness for the humorous incongruity.

A second framing technique for the artifacts only affected viewers who purchased the audio tour. At the foot of the grand staircase, the listener hears faint music, murmurs of conversation, and a tinkling of glass as a man's voice says:

> Imagine that you are joining the spectacle of dinner in first class on the night of April 14, 1912, with everyone turned out in their finest, with the gilded chandelier glowing above, and the orchestra playing. This is a fairy tale world. At the top of the grand staircase there is a clock. It reads 11:30, midway through the final hour of Sunday,

April 14, 1912. In first class, the gala dinner is over. Throughout the ship, passengers and crew make ready for another peaceful night at sea. But in ten minutes all that will change. [The distant sound of a ticking clock, then (very faintly) a bell ringing, and a voice, "Iceberg, right ahead, sir!"]

The knowledge of approaching death hidden amidst the champagne glasses and elegant attire—the skull beneath the skin—allows viewers less a feeling of superiority than one of consubstantiality.[108] Only the passage of nearly ninety years could allow identification with the Edwardian mega-wealthy. The same anticipatory move without identification occurs at the third-class bedroom. After describing the roar of the engines in third class, the audio concludes, "Those who can adapt to the noise sleep soundly. Some won't even be disturbed by the strange scraping sound that will soon reverberate through the massive steel hull."

It is noteworthy that we are not asked to imagine ourselves as third-class passengers. Projection into the *Titanic* myth generally requires that we be on the boat deck boarding, or choosing not to board, the lifeboats. The primary *Titanic* films, *A Night to Remember* and James Cameron's *Titanic*, find ways to bring third-class characters up to the boat deck for the finale.[109] It is also notable that there is no representation of second-class accommodations.[110] The *Titanic* drama is always told as a series of polar opposites: the rich / the poor; the brave / the cowardly, the doomed / the survivors, women and children (the weak) / men (the strong), the worthy survivor (Molly Brown) / the unworthy survivor (J. Bruce Ismay). It is a myth that seeks dichotomies for dramatic impact and resists efforts at a more nuanced reading.

The final two rooms of the exhibit's initial narrative are given over to the actual disaster rather than exposition and anticipation. The first, called The Strike and Sinking, is one of the most effective and affecting of the entire exhibit. The viewer entering the rectangular, dimly lit, and dark-blue curtained space is confronted initially by such technical artifacts as the navigational compass, the base of the telegraph, and a pair of binoculars (the "misplaced" ones of the crow's nest?). In the center are two pillars of television monitors repeatedly playing a silent, computer-generated representation of *Titanic*'s collision, breaking apart, and sinking. Then at the end of the room is the interactive centerpiece: an actual, frozen "iceberg." The iceberg stands before a curtain of deep blue with pinpoint lights of stars and randomly generated quotes that appear against the night sky. These are the words of the dead, a reminder of the key players and romantic stories of that early morning:

I will not be parted from my husband. As we have lived so will we die. Together.

Mrs. Isidor Straus 12:30

We're dressed up in our best and are prepared to go down like gentlemen.

Benjamin Guggenheim

For God's sake, go! It's your last chance. Go!

Jacques Futrelle (to his wife) 1:07[111]

The iceberg itself is invitingly carved with different-sized handprints, and the nearby sign reads:

Touch the Iceberg

On the night of April 14, 1912, the waters of the North Atlantic were a frigid 28 degrees. Because salt water freezes at a lower temperature than fresh water, the ocean that night was colder than this iceberg.

How Long Can You Keep Your Hand on the Ice?

Imagine what it must have been like trying to swim in that water. Most who lost their lives that night did not drown. They died from hypothermia—they froze to death.

This interactive element provides sensory identification with the lost passengers: the silence, the stars in the dark blue sky, the pleasingly familiar monologues, and the numbing cold of the iceberg. Even the squeals of children and comments of adults are whispered as they snatch their hands away from the cold. Viewers linger here individually and in small groups, silently reading quotes as they appear and fade away. Achieved here is the telescoping of time, the oneness with the past sought by all historic exhibits. Ironically, the effect is achieved independent of any artifact.

The Aftermath Gallery closes out the first ten rooms and the received tale of *Titanic*'s sinking. Although this area has some of the more interesting artifacts—spectacles and their case, a derby hat, a child's toy airplane kit—the room is dominated by the prop lifeboat from the Cameron film. There is a scrapbook kept by a passenger on the rescue ship *Carpathia,* and "Molly Brown," a lively actress squeezed into period costume, emerges to hold a conversation about events on the lifeboats. This room consigns *Titanic* to the past, to the memories of survivors and the representations of popular culture. Thus, the first narrative of the exhibit takes *Titanic* not just from birth to death but from conception to public memory.

Narrative Two: Memorializing through Science

Three rooms remain in the exhibit. Room twelve, the Memorial Gallery, will return to the aftermath of *Titanic* and its legacy for good or ill. Yet, straddling room twelve are the two rooms where the second narrative, explicitly justifying salvage, takes place. Certainly, the first ten rooms provide a tacit argument for recovery through whatever pleasure or understanding the viewer may glean from the artifacts. Rooms eleven and thirteen, however, are pure justificatory rhetoric where both sets of metaphoric clusters constructed during the salvage debate are employed in an apologia for disturbing *Titanic*'s remains. The co-opting of the gravesite metaphor occurs visually as soon as the viewer enters room eleven, Discovery and Recovery. Looming darkly to the viewer's left is the "Big Piece," the section of hull raised from the ocean floor in 1998. The unlit interior of the hull actually forms the left wall of a narrow passageway so that the viewer moves from inside the ship, around the end of the piece, to view its dramatically lit exterior (see figure C4).[112]

The placement of the Big Piece with its back to the previous exhibit functions in two ways. First, it situates the preceding ten rooms as located within the interior of the ship. We are now left standing ostensibly in the debris field surrounding the ship. Display cases scattered throughout the room contain uncleaned stacks of dishes, a hot water tank, and a ceramic pot—all wedged in sand as they would exist *in situ*. But in this room the Big Piece is displayed as much more than an artifact; instead, it is situated as a gravestone, a marker to the body of the ship stretching out behind it. Above all, it is presented as an authentic memorial in steel to the dead. The memorializing function of the Big Piece is reinforced in the audio tour when *Titanic* "conservator and preserver, Stephen Pennick" makes these dedicatory remarks: "We can never bring the whole ship to the surface even if we wanted to. It will simply disintegrate. But we can bring back the thing that will keep the memory of the people alive and will serve as a memorial to this great tragedy." From this view it is the authentic thing (the touchstone) that provides the memory; it is the object that allows the past to be recalled.[113] By embodying the act of memorializing, the Big Piece fulfills Kenneth Burke's requirement that the scene properly "contain" the act that occurs there.[114] When visitors move from the interior to the exterior side of the Big Piece, then, they not only change places but also shift perspectives. The memorial, in the simulated form of the *Titanic* resting on the sea floor, works to evoke a constellation of meanings associated with the sacralizing system of metaphor. The Big Piece is more than artifact since it comes from and represents hallowed ground. As displayed, it concentrates *Titanic*'s essence into the only appropriate—and only publicly accessible—memorial. The Big Piece thus becomes a simulated grave marker at a simulated gravesite. Surrounding objects are displayed not as "artifacts," cleaned up for conservation and study, but as "relics" whose meaning is retained when seen in their original condition as retrieved from their underwater graveyard.

The exhibitors, thus, come full circle: by means of an artifact (the hull) salvaged from the site of the wreckage, they simulate the original site that opponents to salvage claimed as sacred and inviolate. They, then, co-opt the anti-salvage gravesite imagery and its sacralizing system of associations. Combined, the simulation and gravesite imagery are used to fashion a justification for salvaging operations and subsequent exhibitions of *Titanic* artifacts. Science becomes savior, the only means of conserving *Titanic* against the onslaught of blind, remorseless nature. The audio portion for room eleven claims, "The ship is being slowly consumed by metal-eating bacteria which give it these colors. This is why we must recover what we can from the site, because in a few years, perhaps a decade or two, there will be virtually nothing left. It will simply be gone."[115] The exhibit thus glosses any hint of controversy. A physical juxtaposition between the memorial and science as savior tacitly underscores a purported absence of conflict or tension between the two.

The Memorial Gallery (room twelve) displays, on facing walls, newspaper front pages announcing the disaster and the memorial wall where visitors may find the names on their boarding passes among lists of the saved or the lost. More emotionally powerful in the Chicago exhibit was the section of room twelve given over to the local tragedy of the SS *Eastland*, "Chicago's *Titanic*." The *Eastland* hosted a pleasure cruise on July 24, 1915, taking twenty-five hundred passengers to the Western Electric picnic. The ship, made top-heavy by the lifeboats required of passenger ships since the *Titanic* disaster, suddenly rolled over at its berth in the Chicago River. Over eight hundred people died, including twenty-two entire families, making the *Eastland* one of the nation's worst disasters. This initially jarring intrusion into the *Titanic* story actually yields an intense level of identification with victims of both disasters. Unlike *Titanic*, photographers were present to record the *Eastland* disaster and the immediate rescue attempts. Particularly arresting is the enlarged photograph of a middle-aged man clutching the dripping body of a young child dressed in best, go-to-the-picnic clothes. He stares in shock straight at us, across the decades, drawing the viewer into the reality and horror of sudden death.[116] By further prompting identification with the dead, room twelve reinforces the memorializing motives of the exhibit. This room strengthens the bond between its own hallowing of the sacred and the celebration of secular science found in the adjoining rooms.

Finally, in the Conservation Gallery (room thirteen) science holds sway with videos of exploration and conservation and even a live "laboratory" demonstration of conservation techniques. Although the salvors have the exhibit stage to themselves, they cannot help shadowboxing an opponent who is not there. The audio in the Conservation Gallery again presents the voice of Stephen Pennick:

> All of us *who walk on this side* cherish these objects and the people they represent. But in the end it is really up to you to decide their true value. We believe the memory of *Titanic*'s 2,228 people is worth preserving, and we hope you will agree. [emphasis added]

This self-declaration of love and sensitivity implies the existence of an opposing viewpoint. Only those aware of the original controversy would know the views of those who walk on the other side of the salvage debate. Yet, at this point, exhibit visitors would receive opposition to salvage as implausible if not mean-spirited. Memory of the dead is now served, not subverted, by science. Through science, the past is given a physical presence by the retrieval of objects that have long been lost. Here, the choice is clear: memory only answers to the summons of science; the past can only be maintained by its physical rendering in the present.

Conclusion

William F. Buckley often reiterated his feeling that at some point the public metaphoric focus had to change. He anticipated the shift from a view of the wreck as the grave of the passengers to a focus on the fascinating aspects of the items they left behind them. At some point, he claimed, the public must

> put down the glasses that see only tales of distress and suffering and pick up the other set, which focuses on science and history, on surviving artifacts—the sort of things that bring us to museums for whatever reason.[117]

Our fascination with the *Titanic* and the objects that were connected to her in some way is part of our desire for an "authentic encounter"[118] with the past she represents. When viewed through the ocean depths, the objects lying at the site of the tragedy retain the power to evoke a sense of that liminal space between life and death. Removed from that site, they lose much of their evocative potential for those who view the actual location of the event as a necessary component of *Titanic*'s public memory. Walter Lord voiced the feeling of many opposed to salvage: "To me the mystique of the *Titanic* was one of the wonderful things about it—the mystique of not knowing what happened once it slipped beneath the waves. And they've certainly ended that. Pulling these things up out of the water, you take away the mystery."[119]

The "displacement" of artifacts from the ocean depths surrounding the real *Titanic* to the exhibition's stage set marks a shift in both physical location and time. Location becomes, as Victoria Gallagher tells us, "a context out of which the artifact emerges and becomes meaningful."[120] Shifting the artifacts' locale visually pulls them away from the site of *Titanic*'s death to a modern context for her rebirth. Cleaning and conserving the artifacts further erases their ninety years on the ocean bottom, returning them to the time of their original creation and use. For some viewers, then, the juxtaposition of the artificial and the artifactual is problematic, because it negates the possibility of an authentic encounter. Other exhibit patrons readily embrace an appearance of authenticity *as* authenticity. For these viewers the juxtaposition of the artificial stage set and the artifact provides necessary cues for understanding. The essentializing of history, the past boiled down to the recognizable components of a historic period, is more pleasurable for some than the overlapping of time crowded upon time found in actual historic sites. Erasing this messy temporality facilitates understanding but at the risk of triggering what Blair, Jeppeson, and Pucci call "a touristic, consumptive response."[121]

It is the idea of a contextual encounter with history that now animates Robert Ballard's opposition to salvage. He describes the *Titanic* as a "laid out . . . battlefield, like a disaster site. It's like going to the battlefield at Gettysburg the day after the battle." Because conditions in the deep ocean "preserve the event," maintaining the original context retains the liminal feel of the site of death.[122] Ballard's anticipation of "remote touring" through fiber optics allows him to confront the archeological site metaphor directly. Those who first explored the tombs in Egypt had the impulse "to box everything up and ship it to London because no one would ever come there to see it." Yet these archeologists could not foresee 747s and rental cars that could have taken people to the now-emptied Egyptian tombs where today they find "nothing but graffiti."[123] Ballard envisions a day when electronic visitors to the *Titanic* wreck site will ask:

> "Why has that crow's-nest been destroyed?" Well, some salvors went after the bell. They destroyed the crow's-nest to get it. "I don't want the bell, I want to see the crow's-nest! I want to see where the guys were standing when they saw the iceberg." Gone![124]

An equally romantic view is presented by scientists attached to the salvage operations. Charles Pellegrino, in his fascinating book *Ghosts of the Titanic,* claims that his contact with the toy airplane salvaged from a suitcase "got to me, like a punch in the stomach," triggering thoughts of a child waiting for his gift at home and the father who would never arrive to deliver it.[125] Pellegrino compares the collection of artifacts to a vehicle of scientific discovery for the common man rather than a profit-making venture for elites: "As meteorites are a poor man's space program, archeological artifacts are indeed a pauper's time machine." He situates the *Titanic* site firmly in the realm of archeology, claiming that what "addicts" him to all archeology "is the uncanny tendency for inanimate objects to pull you back through time." For Pellegrino the special nature of *Titanic's* artifacts is their connection to known people and a time not that long removed from our own, a "familiarity . . . [that] both chills and warms the bones." But it is the final metaphor in this series where the common ground between Pellegrino and Ballard becomes obvious. "Every shipwreck," Pellegrino states, "is a time portal, a seagoing town flash-frozen."[126] The debate comes down to the appropriate means of crossing that portal.

The sacralizing and secularizing metaphor systems in the *Titanic* controversy have an appearance of autonomy and consistency that is easily belied. Are gravesites always to be left untouched? Are archeological sites always to be explored? The tensions between "veneration and curiosity"[127] are apparent in the exhibit narratives, and the boundary between veneration and physical "defilement" is more porous than it first appears. There are sites of tragedy where a profit motive is more clearly an issue of defilement. Business interests have, for example, encroached upon the edges of the Alamo and the Gettysburg sites, leading columnist Russell Baker to describe such battlegrounds: "Fertilize it with the blood of heroes and it brings forth a frozen-custard stand."[128] In the case of *Titanic,* however, profit comes from the exhibition itself, a display possible only through salvage and conservation. Whether the salvage and conservation of artifacts from a wreck site constitute defilement is a complicated issue now faced by the National Park Service in its administration of the USS *Arizona.* If the NPS takes steps to preserve the wreck site or to remove and conserve primary artifacts, is this "defilement through intrusion" at a gravesite? If they allow time and the elements to slowly deteriorate the *Arizona,* is this "defilement through neglect"?[129]

Titanic: The Exhibition does not resolve this paradox. Ultimately, the exhibitors appropriate a romantic narrative of uncommon ironies and tragedy as justification as much as memorialization. By the end of the exhibit, it is IFREMER and film of the robot *Nautile*'s exploits that are emphasized. In a story of danger and scientific bravery, the explorers/adventurers of IFREMER travel, according to one display banner, to depths where the pressure is "enough to implode any diving vessel and crush its passengers to dust." A video in exhibit room eleven of the struggle to raise the Big Piece in a storm replaces the controversial *should* it be raised with the dramatic *how* of scientific triumph. The exhibitors share with the designers and builders of *Titanic* the same enthusiasm for technological advance, the same technological hubris, that they framed so ironically in the opening rooms of the exhibit.

Nonetheless, the exhibitors' affection for the *Titanic* myth and their skill in visually constructing her narrative are palpable. Exhibit-goers not steeped in the polemics over salvage would likely find fulfillment of their sense of the sacred. This satisfaction for some viewers of the sacralizing metaphorical system comes courtesy of its co-optation. The exhibitors' promise to "bring to life" the story of *Titanic* becomes a pledge to preside over her rebirth. By emphasizing the raising of the Big Piece from the ocean depths, the exhibitors symbolically take part in her resurrection, a visual metaphor for life overcoming death. In this view, archeology completes rather than compromises the sacredness of the gravesite. *Titanic:* The Exhibition provides a narrative reconciliation of competing metaphorical systems, although the practical needs of science and the sacred may ultimately remain irreconcilable.

There are aspects to the *Titanic* salvage case that make it unusual but not unique. How we treat such sites as Ground Zero in New York City may be controlled by our sense that a death site is a gateway into another world and must be hallowed in some way. The World Trade Center attack has intruded into the modern psyche in much the same way that the *Titanic* disaster compelled the feelings and imaginations of 1912. Artifacts of Ground Zero, particularly the tattered flag pulled from the rubble and raised over the site during the rescue efforts, are set apart as relics symbolic of national trauma. Yet, Ground Zero is some of the more expensive real estate in Manhattan, and images from the terrorist attack are already being used to promote a wide variety of products, companies, and services. Whether a sense of the sacred can co-exist over time with these secular pressures remains to be seen.

It is instructive that in the Cameron film of the *Titanic,* the now-elderly survivor, Rose, gives her necklace to the ocean depths, an artifact of the *Titanic* that survived the sinking yet symbolically belongs to the wreck. And in the film, this same character returns in her death (or is it a dream?) to a ship restored to original glory, where she is greeted expectantly and applauded by the "waiting dead."[130] It is as if all objects and people touched by this particular site of death remain as relics made sacred by the event. The salvage and display of *Titanic* artifacts remind us that controlling the fate of the sacred is limited in a secular world.

Notes

The author would like to thank Lawrence Prelli, Stephen Browne, and Richard Morris for their guidance in the development of this essay. She also would like to thank Brian Wedge and the exhibition staff at Clear Channel Exhibitions for their assistance and for their permission to reproduce the floor plan and photographs from the 2000 exhibition.

1. Wyn Craig Wade, *The Titanic: The End of a Dream* (New York: Penguin Books, 1980), 231.

2. The number of *Titanic* survivors has long been a topic for debate, as has the number of those lost in the sinking. The final report of the 1912 United States Senate inquiry listed 706 as saved and 1,517 as lost. The British inquiry of the same year gave the final numbers as 711 saved and 1,490 lost (Titanic Inquiry Project, http://www.titanicinquiry.org [last accessed July 30, 2005]). Modern estimates vary just as widely, and I have chosen to use the statistics presented at the *Titanic* exhibition that is the object of this study.

3. Jamie Murphy, "Down into the Deep," *Time,* August 11, 1986, 50.

4. John P. Eaton and Charles A. Haas, *Titanic: Destination Disaster; The Legends and the Reality* (New York: W. W. Norton, 1987), 137–38.

5. U.S. Congress, House, *RMS Titanic Maritime Memorial Act of 1985,* 99th Cong., 1st sess., November 21, 1985, Report 99–393, 2.

6. Walter Lord, *The Night Lives On* (New York: Jove Books, 1987), 211.

7. William D. Marbach, "The Sea Gives up a Secret," *Newsweek,* September 16, 1985, 46.

8. Erik Eckhom, "Legal Issues Are Raised by *Titanic,*" *New York Times,* September 7, 1985, 29.

9. Stephen H. Browne, "Reading, Rhetoric, and the Texture of Public Memory," *Quarterly Journal of Speech* 81 (1995): 245.

10. Sacvan Bercovitch, *The Rites of Assent: Transformations in the Symbolic Construction of America* (New York: Routledge, 1993), 355.

11. See, for example, A. Cheree Carlson and John E. Hocking, "Strategies of Redemption at the Vietnam Veterans' Memorial," *Western Journal of Speech Communication* 52 (1988): 203–15; Carole Blair, Marsha S. Jeppeson, and Enrico Pucci Jr., "Public Memorializing in Postmodernity: The Vietnam Veterans Memorial as Prototype," *Quarterly Journal of Speech* 77 (1991): 263–88; Richard Morris, "The Vietnam Veterans Memorial and the Myth of Superiority," in *Cultural Legacies of Vietnam: Uses of the Past in the Present,* ed. Richard Morris and Peter Ehrenhaus, 199–222 (Norwood, N.J.: Ablex, 1990); Sonja K. Foss, "Ambiguity as Persuasion: The Vietnam Veterans Memorial," *Quarterly Journal of Speech* 34 (1986): 326–40; E. T. Linenthal, *Preserving Memory: The Struggle to Create America's Holocaust Museum* (New York: Viking Penguin, 1995); Victoria J. Gallagher, "Remembering Together: Rhetorical Integration and the Case of the Martin Luther King, Jr. Memorial," *Southern Communication Journal* 60 (1995): 109–19; and B. J. Armada, "Memorial Agon: An Interpretive Tour of the National Civil Rights Museum," *Southern Communication Journal* 63 (1998): 235–43.

12. Blair, Jeppeson, and Pucci, "Public Memorializing in Postmodernity," 283n.

13. Browne, "Reading, Rhetoric, and the Texture of Public Memory," 245.

14. Blair, Jeppeson, and Pucci, "Public Memorializing in Postmodernity," 271.

15. Cheryl R. Jorgensen-Earp and Lori Lanzilotti, "Public Memory and Private Grief: The Construction of Shrines at the Sites of Public Tragedy," *Quarterly Journal of Speech* 84 (1998): 159.

16. Edward Linenthal, *Sacred Ground: Americans and Their Battlefields* (Urbana: University of Illinois Press, 1991), 92.

17. James M. McPherson, "Gettysburg," in *American Places: Encounters with History,* ed. William E. Leuchtenburg, 264 (Oxford: Oxford University Press, 2000).

18. Ibid., 264.

19. Linenthal, *Sacred Ground,* 65, 5.

20. Peter Ehrenhaus, "Silence and Symbolic Expression," *Communication Monographs* 55 (1988): 52, 48.

21. Linenthal, *Sacred Ground,* 189.

22. Mabel O. Wilson, "Between Rooms 307: Spaces of Memory at the National Civil Rights Museum," *Harvard Design Magazine,* Fall 1999, 28–31.

23. Jorgensen-Earp and Lanzilotti, "Public Memory and Private Grief," 159.

24. Leah R. Vande Berg, "Living Room Pilgrimages: Television's Cyclical Commemoration of the Assassination Anniversary of John F. Kennedy," *Communication Monographs* 62 (1995): 56.

25. Ibid., 57.

26. David E. Stennard, *Death in America* (Philadelphia: University of Pennsylvania Press, 1975), xi.

27. Stephen Biel, *Down with the Old Canoe: A Cultural History of the Titanic Disaster* (New York: W. W. Norton, 1996).

28. Vande Berg, "Living Room Pilgrimages," 50.

29. Alan Radley, "Artefacts, Memory and a Sense of the Past," in *Collective Remembering,* ed. David Middleton and Derek Edward, 48 (London: Sage, 1990).

30. Ibid., 57.

31. Ibid., 50.

32. Ibid., 54.

33. Edward T. Linenthal, *The Unfinished Bombing: Oklahoma City in American Memory* (New York: Oxford University Press, 2001).

34. John Bodnar, *Remaking America: Public Memory, Commemoration, and Patriotism in the Twentieth Century* (Princeton, N.J.: Princeton University Press, 1992), 13–14.

35. Ibid., 14.

36. Browne, "Reading, Rhetoric, and the Texture of Public Memory," 245.

37. Bodnar, *Remaking America,* 20.

38. Ibid., 16.

39. Many of these metaphors emerged during the testimony given about HR 3272, the *RMS Titanic Maritime Memorial Act,* in the hearing before the Committee on Merchant Marine and Fisheries on October 29, 1985 (U.S. Congress, House, 99th Cong., 1st sess., Report 99–393). I also examine articles in the popular press from 1985 to 1987 that presented the competing discourses over the appropriateness of salvage.

40. George Lakoff and Mark Johnson, *Metaphors We Live By* (Chicago: University of Chicago Press, 1980).

41. House Committee on Merchant Marine and Fisheries, testimony of Dr. John Malcolm Brinnin, professor emeritus in maritime history, Boston University, *RMS Titanic Maritime Memorial Act: Hearing on Bill 3272,* 32. I have italicized for emphasis the metaphors discussed in this study.

42. Robert D. Ballard, *The Discovery of the Titanic* (Wisconsin: Madison Publishing, 1987), 192.

43. House Committee, Marylin J. Powers, letter written for Caroline Horwath (survivor), *RMS Titanic Maritime Memorial Act,* 31.

44. House Committee, Jon Hollis, *RMS Titanic Maritime Memorial Act,* 23.

45. "Hulk of *Titanic* Reported Intact," *New York Times,* September 4, 1985, sec. A. The article is citing Edward Kamuda, general secretary of the Titanic Historical Society.

46. Robert D. Ballard, "Epilogue for *Titanic,*" *National Geographic,* October 1987, 461.

47. Ballard, "The Discovery," 213.

48. Marbach, "The Sea Gives up a Secret," 44.

49. "TV Probes Mysteries of the *Titanic,*" *Seattle Post-Intelligencer,* October 28, 1987.

50. Marbach, "The Sea Gives up a Secret," 44. Some of the metaphors extended the woman image to its extreme, treating the *Titanic* as a hostess who is still gracious and "after 74 years . . . has guests" (quoted in Eaton and Haas, *Titanic: Destination Disaster,* 144). Even her current peril is due to her feminine nature, for, as Charles Sachs testified before the House committee, it is up to her protectors to prevent the "commercial *rape* of *Titanic* [emphasis added]" (House Committee, testimony of Charles I. Sachs, *RMS Titanic Maritime Memorial Act,* 111).

51. Eaton and Haas, *Titanic: Destination Disaster,* 138.

52. Anne Steacy, "Treasure Quest in a Tomb," *Macleans,* August 3, 1987, 42.

53. Eaton and Haas, *Titanic: Destination Disaster,* 136.

54. Michael D. Lemonick, "Tempest over the *Titanic,*" *Time,* August 3, 1987, 56. Lemonick is quoting Jon Hollis.

55. "Respecting the *Titanic,*" *Washington Post,* September 15, 1985, sec. D.

56. House Committee, Charles Ira Sachs, letter, *RMS Titanic Maritime Memorial Act,* 111.

57. Quoted in William F. Buckley Jr., "Excavating the *Titanic,*" *National Review,* September 25, 1987, 65.

58. "Respecting the *Titanic,*" sec. D.

59. House Committee, Sachs, *RMS Titanic Maritime Memorial Act,* 111.

60. House Committee, Powers, *RMS Titanic Maritime Memorial Act,* 31.

61. House Committee, Jack Fields, *RMS Titanic Maritime Memorial Act,* 3.

62. Barbara Huston, "Finder Cites a *Titanic* Atrocity," *Seattle Post Intelligencer,* October 29, 1987.

63. Eaton and Haas, *Titanic: Destination Disaster,* 147.

64. Lord, *The Night Lives On,* 210.

65. Buckley, "Excavating," 65.

66. William F. Buckley Jr., "Down to the Great Ship," *New York Times Magazine,* October 18, 1987, 93.

67. Ibid., 93.

68. Ibid., 79.

69. Lemonick, "Tempest over the *Titanic,*" 56.

70. Buckley, "Excavating," 65.

71. House Committee, testimony of Capt. W. F. Searle, U.S. Navy, retired, *RMS Titanic Maritime Memorial Act,* 87.

72. House Committee, Jack Grimm, *RMS Titanic Maritime Memorial Act,* 73.

73. Buckley, "Excavating," 65.

74. Ibid., 65.

75. Buckley, "Down," 93.

76. Ibid., 93.

77. William F. Buckley, "*Titanic* Bound," *National Review,* October 9, 1987, 70.

78. Buckley, "Down," 93.

79. Ken Ringle, "French Plan to Open *Titanic*'s Safe on T.V.," *Washington Post,* August 14, 1987, sec. A.

80. "Television Special from *Titanic* is Planned," *New York Times,* February 10, 1987, sec. C.

81. Ringle, "French Plan," sec. A.

82. Ibid.

83. Adam Goodheart, "Into the Depths of History," *Preservation,* January/February 1999, 40.

84. Ibid., 40.

85. Buckley, "Excavating," 65.

86. Ringle, "French Plan," sec. A.

87. Paul Heyer cleverly writes that, at this point, Ballard's desire that *Titanic* rest in peace turned into an IFREMER desire to "wrest a piece" (Paul Heyer, *Titanic Legacy: Disaster as Media Event and Myth* [Westport, Conn.: Praeger, 1995], 147.)

88. "*Titanic* Atrocity," *Seattle Post-Intelligencer,* October 29, 1987.

89. Ringle, "French Plan," sec. A. It was claimed that the "safe-cracking spectacular in Monte Carlo" (ibid.), as Rep. Walter Jones called it, was largely staged, for the bag of coins "found" in the previously opened safe may actually have come from a nearby satchel ("*Titanic* Atrocity"). Even Telly Savalas, attired in foul-weather gear— apparently to withstand the North Atlantic cold— and sporting incongruous, large sunglasses, was actually filmed on the deck of the *Nadir* in the Caribbean several weeks after the expedition took place (Reed Karaim, "Raiding the *Titanic,*" *Civilization,* December 1997–January 1998, 46).

90. Ricardo J. Elia, "*Titanic* in the Courts," *Archaeology* 54, no. 1 (January/February 2001), http://www.archaeology.org/0101/etc/titanic2.html (last accessed July 28, 2005).

91. In 1998, RMS *Titanic* Inc. attempted to use its position as salvor-in-possession to prevent visits by others to the *Titanic* site and the photographing of the wreck. A court injunction initially upheld this right to restrict access; however, the ruling was overturned on appeal. The Supreme Court refused to hear the case, thus denying the company exclusive video and photography rights (ibid.).

92. All that remains in Greenwich is a small section on underwater exploration. Films of the *Titanic* wreck site, and a wonderfully eerie holographic film of the wreck's dangling chandelier, are accompanied by a written description that reads:

> Underwater archeologists explore wrecks for information about the past: objects of little apparent interest or financial value can yield a great deal. Modern archeological techniques aim to produce maximum information with minimum site disturbance preserving as much as possible for future study. Archeology costs money; it does not make it.

However, the film's accompanying female voice-over reveals a stance that is part justification and part mea culpa: "Should we intrude? Is our quest for knowledge or for profit? As with all such scenes, curiosity prevails. We are only human after all" (Explorers Exhibit, National Maritime Museum, Greenwich, England, July 1999).

93. Buckley, "*Titanic* Bound," 71.

94. Marc Davis, "Judges Fear Two Interests in *Titanic* Case May Conflict," *Virginian-Pilot,* September 25, 2001, http://www.pilotonline.com/news/nw0925tit.html (last accessed August 23, 2002).

95. Tulloch proves to be an interesting man and one torn between profit and respect for the emotional impact of *Titanic.* Tulloch sought as much media coverage as possible for his "return" of a gold watch to survivor Edith Brown Haisman after the artifact was confirmed to have belonged to her father. Originally, however, restorers working for Tulloch had offered the watch to the elderly pensioner for a recovery fee of twenty thousand dollars. When she could not afford the fee, Tulloch loaned her the watch for the remainder of her life (she was then ninety-six), reclaimed the watch upon Haisman's death at one hundred, and the watch is now included in the traveling exhibit of *Titanic* artifacts (Karaim, "Raiding the *Titanic,*" 49). On the other hand, Tulloch sought to return to family members a satchel found in the debris field apparently belonging to Richard Leonard Beckwith, a first-class survivor. The Beckwiths returned the satchel, because the jumble of jewelry and valuables inside "gave them the creeps." This artifact, among other clues, may indicate looting in the final hours of *Titanic.* By the 1996 expedition, Tulloch would raise only twenty new objects to guarantee that his conservators could handle them (Charles Pellegrino, *Ghosts of the Titanic* [New York: William Morrow, 2000] 52–56, 254–55.)

96. Karaim, "Raiding the *Titanic*," 49.

97. Mark Davis, "Judges Fear."

98. Mark Davis, "*Titanic* Salvage Company Fights Pact Restricting Dives," *Virginian-Pilot*, April 5, 2000, http://www.imacdigest.com/titanic.html, January 17, 2002 (last accessed August 23, 2002).

99. The exhibitors from Clear Channel Entertainment responsible for the Chicago *Titanic* exhibit consisted of John Norman, president and chief operating officer; Tom Zaller, vice president, production; Mark Lach, exhibit designer / vice president, design; Brian K. Wedge, senior creative director; Mark Tischler, vice president, marketing and sales; and Brad Nuccio, marketing director.

100. Exhibitions and museums are sites where the clash over public memory is often virulent and political. The difficulties inherent in the construction of the Holocaust Museum and the controversy over the *Enola Gay* exhibit at the National Air and Space Museum are prime examples (see Linenthal, *Preserving Memory;* Bryan Hubbard and Marouf A. Hasian Jr., "Atomic Memories of *Enola Gay:* Strategies of Remembrance at the National Air and Space Museum," *Rhetoric and Public Affairs* 1 (1998): 363–85; and Edward T. Linenthal and Tom Engelhardt, eds., *History Wars: The Enola Gay and Other Battles for the American Past* [New York: Henry Holt, 1996]).

101. The touring exhibition of salvaged *Titanic* artifacts actually consists of three exhibits appearing simultaneously in various cities. Quite obviously, since the primary artifacts recovered from the wreck are one-of-a-kind—the ship's bell, the ship's whistles, the grand staircase cherub, the "Big Piece" of the hull, the first-class passenger door—these particularly iconic items must be divided among the three exhibits. More common and duplicated relics of the passengers (suitcases, toiletries, letters) and the ship (bottles, plates, workmen's tools) are also divided among the exhibits. Of course, mock-ups of *Titanic*'s rooms and the general layout may be replicated at will to appear in each exhibit. Therefore, the visual display in Chicago's exhibition is in some ways unique, although representative of the viewer's experience in each exhibit.

102. The author would like to thank Stephen Browne for these ideas shared during his insightful oral response to an earlier version of this study.

103. Discussions of *Titanic* that follow the Greek tragedy line are numerous. One of the best may be found in chapter 7, "The Unsinkable Ship," in Richard Howell, *The Myth of the Titanic* (New York: St. Martin's Press, 1999). But my favorite quote along these lines comes from Charles Pellegrino: "The tale of the *Titanic* has all the wondrous horror of a Greek tragedy penned by God with Shakespeare as his muse" (Pellegrino, *Ghosts of the Titanic,* 286).

104. Kenneth Burke, *A Rhetoric of Motives* (Berkeley: University of California Press, 1969), 20–21.

105. Heyer, *Titanic Legacy,* 147.

106. The inscriptions in the exhibit were recorded amid jostling crowds and in darkened rooms. Punctuation and capitalization may not be completely accurate but will be presented as originally recorded.

107. Gary Saul Morson, *Narrative and Freedom: The Shadows of Time* (New Haven: Yale University Press, 1994), 234. According to Morson, "backshadowing" implies that the signs pointing to a particular end were as visible in the past as they are in retrospect.

108. Burke, *A Rhetoric of Motives,* 20–21.

109. In a fine study of James Cameron's *Titanic,* Janice Rushing and Thomas Frentz point out that third-class passenger Jack Dawson, the Leonardo DiCaprio character, inexplicably can move without constraint about the great ship (Janice Hocker Rushing and Thomas S. Frentz, "Singing Over the Bones: James Cameron's *Titanic,*" in *Critical Studies in Media Communication* 17 [2000]: 20).

110. According to Brian Wedge of Clear Channel Entertainment, the 2002 *Titanic* exhibition in Chicago included a second-class bedroom display.

111. I cannot explain the impossible precision in giving the time for some quotations and the complete absence of time notation for others.

112. A docent stands in front of the Big Piece inviting the viewer to travel its length to a touch-tank containing a very small piece of the riveted hull. Through a narrow opening, an adult may insert a few fingers or a small child an entire hand to touch the hull, a not-completely-satisfying outlet for the desire to touch the Big Piece itself.

113. I would again like to thank Stephen Browne for his insights in this area.

114. Kenneth Burke, *A Grammar of Motives* (Berkeley: University of California Press, 1969), 15.

115. Before owning the archeological site metaphor, the exhibitors must gently shuffle to the side the more famous, anti-salvage discoverer of *Titanic,* Robert Ballard. "In 1995," the audio continues, "a team led by Jean Louis Michelle and Dr. Robert Ballard discovered the wreck." Retiring Ballard to secondary position, it is one of the few times that anything remotely connected to him will be mentioned.

116. The reader can find this same photograph on page 121 in George W. Hilton, *Eastland: Legacy of the Titanic* (Stanford: Stanford University Press, 1995).

117. Buckley, "Down," 93.

118. Peter Ehrenhaus, "The Vietnam Veterans Memorial: An Invitation to Argument," *Journal of the American Forensic Association* 25 (1988): 60.

119. Karaim, "Raiding the *Titanic,*" 51.

120. Gallagher, "Remembering Together," 113.

121. Blair, Jeppeson, and Pucci, "Public Memorializing in Postmodernity," 278.

122. Goodheart, "Into the Depths of History," 43–44.

123. Ibid., 44.

124. Ibid., 44.

125. Pellegrino, *Ghosts of the Titanic,* 31.

126. Ibid., 55–56.

127. Linenthal, *Sacred Ground,* 189.

128. Ibid., 115.

129. Ibid., 199–200.

130. Carlson and Hocking, "Strategies of Redemption," 211.

James Michael Farrell

3

"*T*his Horrible Spectacle"

Visual and Verbal Sketches of the Famine in Skibbereen

In February 1847, artist James Mahoney of Cork was commissioned by the *Illustrated London News* "to visit a seat of extreme suffering, viz, Skibbereen and its vicinity." The editors of the paper were interested in "ascertaining the accuracy of the frightful statements received from the west, and of placing them in unexaggerated fidelity before our readers." Directed by his commission, Mahoney offered to the paper "the graphic results of his journey, accompanied by such descriptive notes as he was enabled to collect whilst sketching the fearful incidents and desolate localities."[1]

The Mahoney illustrations in the *Illustrated London News* are among the most well-known images of the Great Hunger. A dozen of his drawings appeared in the weekly newspaper in a two-part article in February 1847, and his work is credited with "bringing the plight of the Famine victims to the notice of the British public; his emotive sketches were instrumental in eliciting an extremely generous response to the appeal by the British Relief Association in the early part of 1847."[2] This chapter will examine James Mahoney's work as an object lesson in the rhetoric of display. In particular, the chapter will explore both the artistic and rhetorical features of the illustrations, as well as the descriptive and emotional elements of the accompanying narrative, as a way to achieve insight into how image and text collaborate for rhetorical effect. A close examination of several of the illustrations, along with a detailed study of Mahoney's "descriptive notes," reveals a visual and verbal rhetoric cooperating in an economy of display. Mahoney's rhetoric of display, designed chiefly to engage the imagination and sympathy of the reading audience, is explained in terms of eighteenth-century moral and aesthetic theory. That theoretical perspective illuminates the primacy of the verbal narrative in the moral drama Mahoney enacts and depicts, and furthermore lends insight into the class implications of Mahoney's visual and verbal treatment of the Irish famine victims.

Between 1845 and 1850, more than a million Irish men, women, and children died of starvation, typhus, dysentery, or other famine-related diseases. Perhaps as many as a million and a half more left Ireland to avoid death, emigrating to North America, England, or Australia. News of the Irish famine was quickly spread throughout Great Britain, Europe, and North America. However affecting, few of the news accounts offered visual images of the suffering in Ireland. One exception was the work of James Mahoney for the *Illustrated London News*.

Examining Mahoney's commission, we begin to understand the evidentiary status and persuasive value of the visual image within the performance of nineteenth-century discourse. Mahoney is directed "to visit a seat of extreme suffering" and to thereby become himself an eyewitness to the "unmitigated sufferings of the starving peasantry." Although the newspaper notes that Mahoney "must already have been somewhat familiar with such scenes of suffering in his own locality, Cork," nevertheless a substitution of his local experience would not suffice. He was instead sent to "desolate localities" where he would personally witness, and so represent with his work, the "fearful incidents" of the famine.

Mahoney's editors were especially concerned that his illustrations and descriptions be undertaken "with the object of ascertaining the accuracy of the frightful statements received from the west." The previously published reports of the famine seemed incredible, and the newspaper wished to have its own eyewitness confirmation to verify "the accounts from the Irish provincial papers." To some, the regular stories of widespread starvation and the horrific narratives of suffering and death must have seemed exaggerated. The *Illustrated London News,* however, assured readers that Mahoney, having already seen the suffering in Cork, "cannot be supposed to have taken an extreme view of the greater misery at Skibbereen" and that therefore the "graphic results of his journey" would represent the scenes he actually witnessed and would place them "in unexaggerated fidelity before our readers."[3]

In sending an illustrator to witness the suffering, the *Illustrated London News* no doubt understood that a sketch from an artist on the scene could lend credibility to the written descriptions that had frequently been published in London papers. There was something in the sketch, in the visual representation of the scene, that was more trustworthy as an immediate and authentic representation of the "truth" being reported. At the same time, it is significant that Mahoney's sketches were accompanied by his own descriptive notes that contextualized the scenes depicted and added detail and depth he was incapable of capturing in his illustration. We need to explore the relationship of the visual and verbal presentation of the famine and assess their rhetorical function both separately and in combination, aiming to understand how sketch and narrative each contribute to accomplishing the goals of this particular rhetoric of display.

Sketching the "Horrible Spectacle"

In his study of the rhetoric of the sketch in British romanticism, Richard Sha maintains that, as a visual form, the sketch is "convincingly spontaneous, original, and natural." The "hasty brushwork and shading, broken lines, roughness, and irregularity" encourage viewers to credit the sketch as a representation of "the artist's spontaneous and authentic feelings." Moreover, in contrast to finished portraits and detailed painted landscapes, the sketch can rely on the presumption that "less finish, less labor, and less fastidiousness to form is more aesthetic, more truthful." At the same time, writes Sha, "the sketch bases its claims to aesthetic status on shared negatives—incompletion, irresolution, lack of finish," and consequently response to the sketch "entails construing absences as meaningful rather than as mere absences."[4]

WOMAN BEGGING AT CLONAKILTY.

1. Sketch by James Mahoney. *Illustrated London News,* February 13, 1847. Used with the permission of the Illustrated London News Picture Library

In figure 1 we see the rhetoric of the sketch at work. Mahoney's *Woman Begging at Clonakilty* is among the most affecting of his illustrations.[5] A starving Irish mother, in the unmistakable pose of a Madonna, yet displaying the extreme effects of starvation, grasps her infant child close to her bosom in her right arm and extends in her left hand a small dish as a depository for the charity of those moved by her pitiable condition. While the illustration is presented to readers as witnessing to the "accuracy" of other famine narratives, Mahoney's illustration is unfinished. While the sketch purports to offer a scene in "unexaggerated fidelity," it nevertheless represents an incomplete picture that invites the viewer to "construe absences as meaningful." In Mahoney's sketch, only the upper body of the woman is depicted, and we see in detail only the woman's face and hands. Mahoney leaves what are undoubtedly the most extreme effects of her starvation hidden by the cloak and shawl that veil her emaciated frame and limbs. While we see evidence of her hunger in her thin fingers, her deep-set eyes, and her careworn face, the image alone does not make it obvious that she is starving. It is rather left to the viewer to complete the picture and to imagine the complete physical detail of the starving body.

The sketch also represents the woman and child out of context. There is no landscape or cabin interior in which she is situated. By implication, there is no narrative context to aid our understanding of the image. Where is the woman's husband, or her neighbors, or the relief officials in Clonakilty? We get no sense of the history or the politics or the personal tragedy that led to the moment when Mahoney captures her image in a "spontaneous and authentic" sketch. Represented as a dependent supplicant, the woman is convincingly sketched in the subject position and relates directly to the viewer through the immediacy of Mahoney's rendering. But the implicit narrative of the sketch is also incomplete and remains necessarily silent about those who may, or may not, have responded to her pathetic appeal for aid. Whatever story might accompany the sketch is not made obvious by the details of the picture itself. It is left for the viewer to imagine or for the reporter to write.

Only the babe in the woman's arms shares the scene of misery with her. The presence of the infant, literally wrapped in swaddling clothes, renders the sketch as a religious icon and so enhances the moral demand on the viewer. Still, the child depicted is itself indistinct. Only the head of the baby is visible, and the face is drawn in profile with very little detail. What remains in these "absences" are questions to be answered by the viewer. While presumably the child belongs to the woman, we nevertheless wonder, is the child male or female? Has the child eaten or nursed? Is the child awake or asleep? The unfinished quality of Mahoney's sketch, while attesting to the "truth," invites the viewer to construct a narrative that can adequately contextualize the picture and answer the questions raised by its "incompletion and irresolution." We find, then, that the sketch itself, however "spontaneous and accurate" it appears and however much "unexaggerated fidelity" it offers, nevertheless constructs its "truth" by demanding of the viewer considerable interpretive exercise.

As it is, however, neither James Mahoney nor the *Illustrated London News* will risk such interpretive chaos and imprecision. The full impact of the sketch is achieved only when Mahoney offers his own accompanying descriptive note. Like the visual sketch, the descriptive note testifies to the authenticity of previous famine stories. It is Mahoney's firsthand account of the starvation in Clonakilty and corroborates those stories that described horrible suffering throughout the west of Ireland. But, Mahoney's eyewitness account also provides the spatial and temporal context for *Woman Begging at Clonakilty* and frames his visual sketch within a narrative display of "the greater misery at Skibbereen."

To accompany the sketch, the *Illustrated London News* printed Mahoney's written account of his visit:

I started from Cork, by the mail (says our informant), for Skibbereen, and saw little until we came to Clonakilty, where the coach stopped for breakfast; and here, for the first time, the horrors of the poverty became visible, in the vast number of famished poor who flocked around the coach to beg alms. Amongst them was a woman carrying in her arms the corpse of a fine child, and making the most distressing appeal to the passengers for aid to enable her to purchase a coffin and bury her dead little baby. This horrible spectacle induced me to make some inquiry about her, when I learned from the people of the hotel that each day brings dozens of such applicants into the town.[6]

Relying on the conventions of detailed descriptive writing, Mahoney informs his readers of the moment when "for the first time the horrors of the poverty became visible." In his eye-witness report of what was "visible" to him, he relates the story of being approached by the woman begging at Clonakilty. Mahoney's testimony, then, lends to his sketch further credibility as a "spontaneous and authentic" representation, because the narrative makes clear that the sketch was executed at the very moment when "the horrors of the poverty became visible."

Mahoney's story, however, takes an unexpected turn. What was obviously a pathetic scene when depicted merely visually in his sketch becomes a "horrible spectacle" when he, and we, learn that the infant in its mother's arms is dead. What had appeared in the sketch to be a mother seeking aid for a starving child turns out in the narrative to be a mother distracted by grief begging alms to bury an infant corpse.[7] It is a turn of events that was hardly to be imagined by those who first saw the sketch and sought to "construe its absences as meaningful." Like the reader who views his sketch, Mahoney, in response to the "horrible spectacle," is induced to "make some inquiry about her." In this way Mahoney now becomes more than a witness; he is our deputy, the one with whom we identify and who acts on our behalf. He enacts the very response called for by his own narrative and illustration, reacting as we might to circumstances that challenge our morality and humanity. Yet, what he learns is that the woman begging at Clonakilty is merely one of "dozens of such applicants" who come to the town each day.

Mahoney's narrative, then, also fails to fully satisfy our desire for context and personal detail. His inquiries are never answered, and we learn nothing more about the particular woman begging at Clonakilty. Instead, it is given out that the woman is representative of many such distressed mothers, and in her anonymity she is therefore made to represent the famine to readers in both the descriptive narrative and in the sketch of the illustrator. Thus, while the sketch and narrative compete in being authentic illustrations of the famine, neither can function as a literal representation of the suffering. The story and sketch of the *Woman Begging at Clonakilty* serve to represent the famine by synecdoche, and it is left to the reader again to imagine the extent and horror of "the greater misery at Skibbereen."

The case of *Woman Begging at Clonakilty,* then, begins to reveal some of the fundamental aspects of the rhetoric of visual and verbal display. With this particular example, we understand that the totality of the impression on a reader and viewer is made by a collaboration of image and word within an economy of display. While the image of Mahoney's sketch is powerful on its own, the heartrending narrative that accompanies it compounds and sharpens its impact. The visual sketch confirmed the authenticity of famine suffering, functioning as an eyewitness representation of a moment in the midst of that calamity. The verbal narrative, on the other hand, provided more detail, allowed the full play of imagination by sympathetic readers, and displayed "scenes" of misery more affecting than anything that could be drawn by the artist's pencil. At the same time, both the image and the text function figuratively, representing by synecdoche only part of the greater suffering to which

they refer. Neither the sketch nor the story, alone or in combination, can reveal the full portion of this poor woman's suffering, nor precisely articulate the wider extent of the famine
disaster in Ireland. That rhetorical work is accomplished in the imagination of the reader,
who implicitly understands both the image and the narrative as representative and suggestive.

The need for firsthand verification of the reports of starvation meant that readers of
the *Illustrated London News* had first to believe that Mahoney's representations were true.
He confessed his own skepticism about some of the published reports, which he took to be
merely "highly-coloured pictures, doubtless, intended for a good and humane purpose."
Yet, as his narrative affirmed, "each step that we took westward brought fresh evidence of
the truth of the reports of the misery." As a credible witness, Mahoney implies a sense of
immediacy in recounting the impression first made on him by the scenes he observed.
Passing through Shepperton Lakes, "the distress became more striking." Finally arriving at
Skibbereen, "I witnessed such scenes of misery and privation as I trust it may never be
again my lot to look upon." Like other witnesses to the famine, however, Mahoney was
challenged by the inadequacy of words and pictures and confessed his inability to capture
and convey the complete wretchedness of those he encountered. "Neither pen nor pencil
ever could portray the misery and horror, at this moment, to be witnessed in Skibbereen."
In an ironic turn, then, it becomes the inadequacy of the witness's words and pictures that
fortifies his credibility as a reporter of the events he was sent to describe and draw.

Mahoney tells us of a multitude of "scenes of misery and privation" but selects only one
or a few to represent each "desolate locality" he visits. The readers and viewers are solicited
to acknowledge Mahoney's firsthand authority and trust his selection of the scene as most
indicative of the general conditions he observed. Yet this struggle to represent suffering
reveals a significant feature of the rhetoric of display in this case. As Mahoney acknowledges
his inability to truthfully depict "this scene of horror," he invites readers to engage their
imaginations, to participate in completing the scene by supplying images from their own
mental reserves that he cannot requisition from his "pen nor pencil."

Mahoney's confessed incapacity to represent the sufferings he witnessed through verbal or visual images itself operates to prefigure how readers are to imagine the famine. His
descriptions and his sketches are but partial displays of greater suffering—verbal and visual
synecdoches—which direct readers to imaginatively envision the full extent of the horrors
that pressed upon him. The avowed inability of a writer to verbally represent suffering is
what Sean Ryder called the "trope of indescribability."[8] In this instance, we see that
Mahoney attempts to describe the suffering he encountered in cottages where "the dying,
the living, and the dead" were "lying indiscriminately upon the same floor, without anything between them and the cold earth, save a few miserable rags upon them." But he also
confesses that he there "witnessed almost indescribable indoor horrors" and thus invites
readers to put themselves imaginatively in his place and gather impressions similar to those
he himself experienced during his "melancholy visit."

Just as there is a verbal trope of indescribability, we see in the work of James Mahoney
a corresponding visual trope of the unrepresentable in which the artist also acknowledges
the inadequacy of his pictorial craft to re-present the scenes of misery he witnessed. In
drawing sketches, Mahoney follows a rhetorical strategy similar to that observable in his
verbal narrative. He allows the display of suffering to remain incomplete, partly occluded

to encourage the viewer to enter the scene by imagination. Each sketch thus functions as a synecdoche, a scene that is but a partial display of a wider spectacle of starvation, disease, and misery. Through this verbal and visual suggestion and approximation, Mahoney induces readers to go beyond his words and pictures to imagine and calculate the far-reaching and overwhelming consequences of the Irish Famine.

We see the work of both these synecdochic tropes—that of the indescribable and the unrepresentable—in Mahoney's account of his visit to the site of *The Village of Mienies* (see figure 2). Mahoney shows a partly tumbled rural cabin. In the foreground two miserable figures—a man and a woman, dressed in ragged clothing, apparently weakened by starvation, with vacant and indistinct faces—bow their heads to the ground as if in humiliation. Other cottages in the background occupy what appears as little more than a stony wasteland, an abandoned landscape of desperation. Here is one of the "desolate localities" to which Mahoney was originally sent and that he selects to illustrate. *The Village of Mienies* is made to represent visually the "distressed district of Skibbereen, and its neighbourhood." Like *Woman Begging at Clonakilty,* this sketch, by synecdoche, represents a larger truth and in this instance gives evidence of Mahoney's report that "the worst feature presenting itself, at this moment, all through the West, is the entire abandonment of agricultural occupation." During his entire excursion "from Clonakilty round to Dunmanway, not more than ten or a dozen fields seemed to have been prepared for the spring."[9]

At the same time, his sketch of the village also shows the inadequacy of the image to carry off the rhetorical work alone. We must rely on the descriptive notes to give us further information about *The Village of Mienies.* In his report of February 13, Mahoney ends his

THE VILLAGE OF MIENIES.

2. Sketch by James Mahoney. *Illustrated London News,* February 20, 1847. Used with the permission of Illustrated London News Picture Library

account by telling readers, "Having returned to Skibbereen, my next object was to seek out the truth of the following extract from Dr. Donovan's Diary, as published in *The Cork Southern Reporter,* of Jan. 26." The extract reported:

> A man of the name of Leahey died in the parish of Dromdaleague about a fortnight ago; his wife and two children remained in the house until the putrescent exhalations from the body drove them from their companionship with the dead; in a day or two after, some persons in passing the man's cabin, had their attention attracted by a loud snarling, and on entering found the gnawed and mangled skeleton of Leahey contended for by hungry dogs.[10]

Note that in the first place Mahoney is drawn to the scene by the necessity to corroborate the account that had been published. He first informs his readers, "This, I need not tell you, I looked upon as designed for an effect; and so I started for Dromdaleague." But the account of what he found upon his inspection is postponed until the next week when, along with the continued narrative, his sketch *The Village of Mienies* is printed among the illustrations.

Mahoney continues his narrative, informing readers that "we soon reached Dromdaleague, where I called upon the Rev. J. Creedon, and inquired of him as to the fate of Leahey. 'Not only do I know the statement to be true' replied the reverend gentleman, 'but I also prepared the man for death, and am ready to accompany you to the spot.'" Mahoney's narrative, then, enlists the reader to accompany him and the Reverend Creedon to "the village of Mienies, where the house of Leahey is situated, and of which I send you a sketch."[11] The village in the sketch, we come to learn, is the very one where the snarling dogs had gnawed the corpse of the expired Mr. Leahey. Indeed, the ambiguity of Mahoney's report implies that his sketch perhaps depicts the very cabin in which that gruesome scene was first witnessed. The dilapidated cabin exterior, itself appearing "gnawed and mangled," seems to signify both the general disorder of the country, as well as the moral insult to Leahey's humanity that transpired within its walls. The combination of narrative detail and visual sketch leads us to wonder if the people in the scene may have known Leahey or whether they had perhaps witnessed the horrible mutilation of his emaciated corpse. We are unable to see inside the darkened cabin door, but our imagination enters to investigate whether evidence remains there to corroborate Mahoney's testimony that "not only was the account of Leahey's house in the Diary true, but the case was even more disgusting than there stated." Mahoney informs the readers that "horrifying as it was, the man's mother, who found the dogs about him, after having first lain him across the few remaining sparks of fire upon the floor, went out to beg as much as would purchase a coffin to bury him in."[12] Though we cannot see the faces of those in Mahoney's sketch, it is left to us to ask if the woman might be Leahey's wife or mother, if the man might be one of those who "found the gnawed and mangled skeleton of Leahey." We wonder what has happened to Leahey's children, and we inevitably draw the mental analogy between this case and the earlier one of another mother begging alms "to purchase a coffin" for her dead child.

The authenticity of the representation is assured by Creedon's testimony and also by Mahoney, who vouches for the spontaneity and immediacy of his sketch by assuring us he was taken "to the spot" to draw the scene. Together, the sketch and narrative conspire to draw us into the scene making us vicarious spectators of suffering, indirect witnesses of the truth that the misery in Ireland is not exaggerated. The narrative describes what cannot be represented by the sketch. The illustration suggests what is otherwise "indescribable" in words. Both the image and text approximate the wider suffering and enlist the imagination of the reader to augment the depiction. Image and text collaborate to affirm the truth and to elicit an emotional and moral response from the newspaper's readers.

Directing Public Sympathy

Had the editors of the *Illustrated London News* been concerned merely with ascertaining the truth of the incredible reports of suffering in Ireland, we might say that James Mahoney had accomplished his goal of verifying those terrible accounts by providing "on the spot" sketches and narratives of the terrible starvation he saw. Yet the editors had a further rhetorical goal in mind. In the preface to its second installment of Mahoney's work, the paper announced that its "main object in the publication of this Series of Illustrations is to direct public sympathy to the suffering poor of these localities, a result that must, inevitably, follow the right appreciation of their extent and severity."[13] Beyond affirming the truth, the objects sketched for our contemplation by James Mahoney were expected to summon an emotional and moral response. Mahoney himself is specific about his hopes for such a reaction. "Bearing in mind the horrifying scenes that I have just witnessed," he writes, "I entreat you to do the best you can for so much suffering humanity."[14] The next critical task, then, is to examine how the display of that Irish suffering, in sketch and narrative, was meant to arouse the sympathetic response expected from the subscribers of the newspaper.

The sympathetic response was one closely connected to a particular mode of rhetorical appeal, an appeal based on a specific understanding of the moral, social, and psychological relationship among author, reader, and subject. By the 1840s, the theoretical and philosophical vocabulary of "sympathy" had become commonplace in the academic treatments of rhetoric and literature, and that vocabulary allows us to investigate with some profit the idea of "display" as a central term in the generation of sympathy for victims of the famine.[15]

Sympathy, wrote Adam Smith, is accomplished by exercise of the imagination. "As we have no immediate experience of what other men feel, we can form no idea of the manner in which they are affected, but by conceiving what we ourselves should feel in the like situation," he explained in *Theory of Moral Sentiments*. "By imagination," he continued, "we place ourselves in his situation, we conceive ourselves enduring all the same torments, we enter as it were into his body, and become in some measure the same person with him."[16] Certainly, such a sympathetic response would be anticipated from—even obligatory for—those who were firsthand witnesses of a "horrible spectacle," such as the Irish Famine. But what of those who were not present to see the distress nor to "visit a seat of extreme suffering?" The readers of the *Illustrated London News,* along with others who encounter suffering from a distance, must rely on the depictions of the writer and artist. James Mahoney and other famine correspondents must use their narratives and illustrations to "make immediate what was heretofore a distant evil."[17]

The rhetoric of sympathy, in the first place, requires the representation of the scene of suffering as an eyewitness account. Mahoney, for instance, tells readers that, in one town, "I saw the dying, the living, and the dead." He is on the scene and is present at the moment of the suffering—a point he emphasizes, for instance, in the presentation of his sketch *Boy and Girl at Cahera* (see figure 3). "This first Sketch is taken on the road, at Cahera, of a

BOY AND GIRL AT CAHERA.

3. Sketch by James Mahoney. *Illustrated London News*, February 20, 1847. Used with the permission of the Illustrated London News Picture Library

famished boy and girl turning up the ground to seek for a potato to appease their hunger," he reports. Mahoney places himself at the scene—"on the road"—as the eyewitness, stressing what Sha called the "the spontaneous delineation" of the "artist's feelings on the spot."[18] With his accompanying report, Mahoney offers a survey of the larger surroundings that also emphasizes his presence in the scene he describes. "Not far from the spot where I made this sketch," he writes, "and less than fifty perches from the high road, is another of the many sepulchres above ground, where six dead bodies had lain for twelve days, without the least chance of interment, owing to their being so far from town."[19]

Taking both the sketch and narrative together, we again see that visual illustration provides an incomplete picture of suffering, one that is supplemented by the detail of the descriptive note. The sketch itself is a vivid portrait of abject hunger, with the emaciated figures of two barefooted, mangy-haired children, their clothing in rags, scratching at the earth in search of a morsel of food. The children stare out at us to acquire both our spectatorship and our sympathy. We are compelled by our humanity to respond to an illustration that invites us to place ourselves in the situation of those depicted. As Smith explains, to the witness the "horror arises from conceiving what they themselves would suffer, if they really were the wretches whom they are looking upon."[20] At the same time, the sketch shows us only one narrow parcel of a wider landscape. While the image focuses on the two children, the description guides our imagination to another spectacle, "not fifty perches [rods —about 275 yards] from the high road," occupied not by the desperate starving but by "dead bodies" that had "lain for twelve days." Like the scene of the dogs gnawing at the corpse of Leahey, this image from Cahera was perhaps too graphic to be depicted by the artist, too unambiguously offensive for Victorian sensibilities to witness directly. Here again, we see how Mahoney describes the visually unrepresentable in words that induce readers to imagine a wider vicinity of misery. We imagine the "dead bodies" and easily come to realize that the children, like Mahoney, also see the "many sepulchres above ground" that both foretell their doom and make their search for food more urgent. In this instance, too, the children are selected by Mahoney to betoken that wider scene and to therefore serve as the visual representatives of both the living and the dead.

Of necessity, however, this intimate identification with those who suffer requires verbal depictions that present the objects of sympathy—starving children, diseased peasants, grieving mothers, even dead bodies—in language that is direct, detailed, and, most of all, vivid. The discourse must allow the reader to enter the scene of suffering and to experience, vicariously, the same agonies as those on whom he fixes his gaze. "For as to be in pain or distress of any kind excites the most excessive sorrow," Smith reasons, "so to conceive or to imagine that we are in it, excites some degree of the same emotion, in proportion to the vivacity or dulness of the conception."[21] Not surprisingly, the descriptions of the Irish famine, more than not, focused on what Elizabeth Clark has called "the gruesome tribulations of the body." In her study of antislavery writing of the 1840s and 1850s, Clark noted the commonplace use of "graphic, vivid language of a kind then thought unsuitable for polite society" and explains that such rhetorical display was necessary to acquire sympathy. "Sympathy was a complex process," Clark writes, "in which the observer's willed attentiveness to another's suffering gave rise to an intuitive empathic identification with the other's experience."[22] It is a style of rhetoric Stephen Browne has called "sentimental," and it inevitably involves "graphic modes of depiction" and "extensive and explicit images of the inflicted body."[23]

Adam Smith understood the connection between vivid depiction and sympathy, but it was left to his fellow Scot, Henry Home, Lord Kames, to articulate the psychological process that was understood to be the foundation of sympathetic discourse. To accomplish a sympathetic response, a writer must strive to create an "ideal presence." "An important event," Kames writes, "by a lively and accurate description, rouses my attention and insensibly transforms me into a spectator: I perceive ideally every incident as passing in my presence." This "ideal presence," Kames explains, enables "the power of speech to raise emotions, and depends entirely on the artifice of raising such lively and distinct images as are here described." Significant for our study of Mahoney's sketches and descriptions, Kames notes that "this power belongs also to painting." Yet the preferred mode is discursive, "for our passions cannot be raised by painting to such a height as can be done by words." Without ideal presence, "our sympathy would be confined to objects that are really present, and language would lose entirely that signal power it possesseth, of making us sympathize with beings removed at the greatest distance of time as well as of place."[24]

The *Illustrated London News* relied on the ability of James Mahoney to create an "ideal presence" that would allow its readers to "sympathize with beings removed at the greatest distance." Mahoney's effort to combine visual and verbal images, then, reflects an economy of display. In this economy, the illustration and the narrative work together efficiently, with the sketch illustrating the chief image of the narrative and the descriptive notes adding facts and interpretation that cannot be depicted visually. The visual image compresses the appeal into a communicative gesture apprehended immediately by the reader. The verbal report manages the interpretation of the picture by adding context and detail. Together, the visual and verbal displays inspire, direct, and constrain the imagination of the reader.

As we have seen, the emphasis on the vivid display of suffering, especially on the "gruesome tribulations of the body," is evident in both James Mahoney's sketches and his descriptive notes. Yet, they are present too in the lengthy passages quoted by Mahoney from the diary of Dr. Donovan. Mahoney refers to the diary as the doctor's "graphic account," and indeed, Donovan provides a detailed description of a visit to a cabin located in the midst of a burying ground. However, in the instance of Donovan's report, the economy of display is disrupted. The doctor's description was written before Mahoney's arrival and was composed without benefit of an accompanying sketch. In this instance, writer and artist are separate individuals attending to their tasks at different times. The greater burden on the writer is evident in the increased detail of his account:

> This shed is exactly seven feet long, by about six in breadth. By the side of the western wall is a long newly-made grave; by either gable are two of shorter dimensions, which have been recently tenated; and near the hole that serves as a doorway is the last resting-place of two or three children; in fact, the hut is surrounded by a rampart of human bones, which have accumulated to such a height that the threshold, which was originally on a level with the ground, is now two feet beneath it. In this horrible den, in the midst of human putrefaction, six individuals, males and females, labouring under most malignant fever, were huddled together, as closely as were the dead in the graves around. . . . I thrust my head through the hole of entrance, and had immediately to draw back, so intolerable was the effluvium; and though rendered callous by a companionship for many years with disease and death, yet I was completely unnerved at the humble seen [sic] of suffering and misery that was presented to my view; six fellow creatures were almost buried alive in this filthy sepulchre.[25]

Here, Donovan expends considerably more verbal effort to craft detail than Mahoney had done in his description of the woman at Clonakilty or the children at Cahera. Donovan's experience is communicated as a vivid, sensuous encounter with the horror in the cabin. His report refers to sights, sounds, and smells and offers details about dimensions of the cabin and a surrounding graveyard overwhelmed by the accumulation of dead bodies. In his recounting, Donovan features "the gruesome tribulations of the body" as he reveals "six individuals, males and females, labouring under most malignant fever . . . almost buried alive in this filthy sepulchre."

Donovan also stresses his literal entrance into the cabin and then his drawing back from the "effluvium." The conflict between this impulse to witness and the instinct to survive is echoed by Mahoney, who informs readers that Donovan "begged me not to go into the house, and to avoid coming into contact with the people surrounding the doorway." Both Donovan's diary entry and Mahoney's descriptive note position the authors in the midst of disease and death, compelled by scientific curiosity and the necessity of corroboration to overcome fear of contagion and "go into the house." The verbal image, however, also functions as a metaphor for the sympathetic response of the reader, who must also "enter into" the experience of those suffering, though such spectators might, like Donovan, be driven back by the "humble scene of suffering and misery" described in "graphic, vivid language of a kind then thought unsuitable for polite society."[26] Sympathy, as Clark wrote,

THE HUT OR WATCH-HOUSE IN THE OLD CHAPEL YARD.

4. Sketch by James Mahoney. *Illustrated London News,* February 13, 1847. Used with the permission of the Illustrated London News Picture Library

demands a "willed attentiveness to another's suffering," and with our imaginations we overcome initial reluctance and are compelled to follow Donovan into the cabin and experience vicariously the "horrible den" that "unnerved" this veteran physician.

Mahoney supplements Donovan's description with a sketch of the exterior of the cabin (see figure 4). The illustration attests to the existence of "this shed" and to the surrounding graveyard and "rampart of human bones," thereby confirming the facts to which Donovan testified. But the sketch by Mahoney is of the exterior of the cabin only and so, as with *The Village of Mienies,* offers an incomplete, unexpectedly veiled representation. The disease and death contained within are exposed only by Donovan's verbal narrative and by the imagination of the viewer. It is left to the power of "ideal presence," of a "lively and accurate description," to accomplish the emotional and moral connection with the reader and enable us to "sympathize with beings removed at the greatest distance." As Kames had suggested, the descriptive narrative of suffering, more than the visual illustration, is the primary vehicle by which an author achieves a sympathetic resonance with his audience. Within an economy of display, the artistic work of Mahoney's illustration could substitute for some of the descriptive work in Donovan's narrative and so could have made the representation more efficient. However, the moral and emotional labor would still be accomplished chiefly by words.

That Mahoney's illustrations had mainly a supplementary function within his economy of display is further demonstrated by several other affecting reports sent from Skibbereen during the same period. We see in these other examples of eyewitness accounts an exclusive reliance on a verbal rhetoric of display as the means of representing Irish misery and arousing the sympathy of readers. On Christmas Eve in 1846, for example, the *London Times* published a letter from Nicholas Cummins, a county magistrate from Cork. The letter, written only six weeks before Mahoney's visit, reported on the distressing progress of disease and starvation in the district of Skibbereen. Cummins wrote of what "[I have] seen myself within the last three days," having been inspired to "personally investigate the truth of several lamentable accounts which had reached me, of the appalling state of misery to which that part of the country was reduced." The writer promised to "state simply what I there saw."[27] As it was with Mahoney's reports, Cummins's letter was motivated in part by the persistent public disbelief about the magnitude of Irish suffering and by the necessity of verifying the accounts reaching readers in London. Such skepticism made published eyewitness reports like those of Cummins valuable as documentary evidence. The testimony of an eyewitness, who had himself set out to "investigate the truth," confirmed the news from Ireland, dispelled incredulity, and aroused a public response to the famine.[28] Although unaccompanied by any illustration, the testimony of Nicholas Cummins is compelling. Upon arriving at Skibbereen, he was

> surprised to find the wretched hamlet apparently deserted. I entered some of the hovels to ascertain the cause, and the scenes that presented themselves were such as no tongue or pen can convey the slightest idea of. In the first, six famished and ghastly skeletons, to all appearance dead, were huddled in a corner on some filthy straw, their sole covering what seemed a ragged horse cloth, their wretched legs hanging about naked above the knees. I approached with horror, and found by a low moaning they were alive—they were in fever, four children, a woman, and what had once been a man. It is impossible to go through the detail. Suffice it to say, that in a few minutes I was surrounded by at least 200 such phantoms, such frightful spectres as no words can describe. By far the greater number were delirious, either from famine or from fever. The demonic yells are still wringing in my ears, and their horrible images are fixed upon my brain. My heart sickens at the recital, but I must go on. . . . In another case, decency would forbid what follows, but it must be told. My clothes were nearly torn off in my endeavor to escape from the throng of pestilence around, when my neckcloth was seized from behind by a grip which compelled me to turn. I found myself grasped by a woman with an infant in her arms, and the remains of a filthy sack across her loins—the sole covering of herself and babe. The same morning, the police opened a house on the adjoining lands, which was observed shut for many days, and two frozen corpses were found, lying upon the mud floor, half devoured by the rats. A mother, herself in a fever, was seen the same day to drag out the corpse of her child, a girl about 12, perfectly naked, and leave it half covered with stones. In another house, within 500 yards of the cavalry station at Skibbereen, the dispensary doctor found seven wretches lying, unable to move, under the same cloak. One had been dead many hours, but the others were unable to move either themselves or the corpse.[29]

In his letter, Cummins employs a rhetoric of vivid description, a style that aims to compose a scene for readers to witness and that portrays the sensuous details of suffering. As readers we are meant to see what he saw, to hear what he heard, to feel what he felt. Cummins is physically surrounded, even assaulted by the scene the way a reader might be by the adjectives in his appalling description. Like Mahoney had done, Cummins identifies in particular the presence of women and children and employs synecdoche, stressing that the few individuals within the one cabin he visited quickly become "at least 200 such phantoms." At the same time, Cummins repeatedly employs a trope of indescribability. He confesses his incompetence, and sometimes his reluctance, to accurately depict the misery to which he was a witness. He explicitly pushes himself beyond the bounds of propriety in order to capture the scene and authenticate the death and wretchedness, even to the point of relating an image of rat-eaten corpses, a scene as gruesome as that which took place in the village of Mienies.

In a similar report, Elihu Burritt, an American philanthropist, also described Skibbereen during the famine and offered extracts from his journal for newspaper publication. On February 20, 1847, Burritt recorded his "first walk through this Potter's Field of destitution and death," where he saw "in every tenement we entered, enough to sicken the stoutest heart." As he toured Skibbereen with a Reverend Fitzpatrick, he "entered the graveyard, in the midst of which was a small watch-house." Whether the hut was the very same as that described and sketched by James Mahoney is not certain, but the dimensions are an exact match, and the description is familiar:

> This miserable shed had served as a grave where the dying could bury themselves. It was seven feet in length and six in width, and was already walled around on the outside with an embankment of graves, half way to the eaves. The aperture of this horrible den of death would scarcely admit of the entrance of a common-sized person. And into this noisome sepulchre living men, women, and children went down to die—to pillow upon the rotten straw—the grave clothes vacated by preceding victims surrounding them. Here they lay as closely to each other as if crowded, side by side, on the bottom of one grave. Six persons had been found in this fetid sepulchre at one time, and with only one able to crawl to the door to ask for water. Removing a board from the entrance of this black hole of pestilence, we found it crammed with wan victims of famine, ready and anxious to perish. A quiet, listless despair broods over the population, and death reaps a full harvest.[30]

The next day, Burritt, with the same Dr. Donovan who accompanied Mahoney, visited another location in Skibbereen, where he witnessed "the wretchedness of this little mud-city of the dead and dying." As others had done, Burritt strained to communicate the scene he witnessed. "I can find no language nor illustration sufficiently impressive to portray the spectacle," he wrote. After "a most horrifying spectacle" had met his eyes, he confessed, "I have lain awake for hours struggling mentally for some graphic and truthful similes, or new elements of description, by which I might convey to the distant reader's mind some tangible image of this object." The "object" was a famine-stricken child, "[a] boy about twelve years of age," held up by his mother. "The cold, watery-faced child was almost naked, and his body was swollen to nearly three times its usual size." In the same cabin, another child, "a thin-faced boy of two years," exhibited similar symptoms, "its cold, naked arms were not much larger than pipe-stems, while its body was swollen nearly to the size of a full grown person." Emphasizing that such scenes were representative, Burritt asked that readers "group these apparitions of death and disease into the spectacle of ten feet square, and then multiply it into three-fourths of the hovels in this region of Ireland, and he will arrive at a fair estimate of the extent and degree of its misery."[31]

All of the features of the vivid rhetoric of sympathy are in evidence in Burritt's description. He places himself as an eyewitness in the midst of suffering, within the domestic interior of cabins struck by disease and starvation. His account is a true rendering of the wretched conditions he observed, shared with "distant readers." As Burritt's editor notes, his journal entries were "written by him on the spot at the close of each day's observations." His narrative emphasizes the "gruesome tribulations of the body" and offers factual and sensuous detail aimed at creating an "ideal presence" that encourages a "willed attentiveness to another's suffering." The imagination of the reader is engaged by the conspicuous employment of the trope of indescribability. At the same time, his account is self-consciously synecdochic, inviting readers to "multiply" the suffering and imagine the full "extent and degree" of Irish misery.

The Right Appreciation of Suffering

The editors of the *Illustrated London News* had sought to "direct public sympathy" by printing Mahoney's work and instructed readers that such sympathy would "follow the right appreciation" of the suffering at Skibbereen. But as the editorial comments indicate, sympathy for the "suffering poor of these localities" was not entirely an inevitable or natural reaction to either the sketches of James Mahoney or the detailed verbal reports he or other writers provided. Rather, the anticipated response required a "right appreciation" for the suffering.[32] The sketches and narratives were meant to engage the imagination of the viewer, who, with a developed moral sense, would, by act of will, enter into that suffering. By imagining oneself in the situation of the sufferers—the distressed, the starving, the diseased, the mourning—readers and viewers engaged in an emotional and moral action that demonstrated their humanity, moral sense, and indeed "taste."

The editors of the *Illustrated London News,* like Adam Smith, Lord Kames, and their contemporary Hugh Blair, understood that sympathy was a learned response. The moral sense, like taste, was both improvable with time and experience and a token of class identification. According to Blair, one's taste extended to "the moral beauties" and was "a most improvable faculty." Principles of taste in matters of morals required sympathy and could "acquire authority," he maintained, from "consulting our own imagination and heart, and from attending to the feelings of others." Moreover, there was an "immense superiority which education and improvement give to civilized, above barbarous nations, in refinement of taste." Therefore, "correctness of taste" (what the editors called "right appreciation") represented to Blair "the sentiments of mankind in polished and flourishing nations."[33]

Adam Smith agreed. "As taste and good judgment, when they are considered as qualities which deserve praise and admiration, are supposed to imply a delicacy of sentiment and an acuteness of understanding not commonly to be met with," he wrote, "so the virtues of sensibility and self-command are not apprehended to consist in the ordinary, but in the uncommon degrees of those qualitites."[34] Cultivation of this virtue, Kames explained, was accomplished primarily through the "ideal presence" made possible in literature: "Examples drawn from real events, are not so frequent as to contribute much to a habit of virtue . . . [nature] therefore shows great wisdom, to form us in such a manner, as to be susceptible of the same improvement from fable that we receive from genuine history. By this admirable contrivance, examples to improve us in virtue may be multiplied without end."[35] But of course, the Irish famine *was* "genuine history." It was an authentic case for the application of the "improved" virtue of refined individuals, who, once assured that the accounts of suffering were presented with "unexaggerated fidelity," would exercise their "right appreciation" of the "genuine history" and dutifully respond in the manner expected of their class. In an age when other tokens of class were increasingly uncertain, frequently challenged, or threatened with erosion—language, learning, property, politics, the arts—here was a social domain in which the "civilized" portion of society could exercise its cultivated faculties and demonstrate its good breeding.[36]

In his descriptive notes, Mahoney implicitly acknowledges the class implications at work in his narrative. He refers to the fact that the Irish themselves (whom Blair would have considered "the rude and untaught vulgar," from a "rude and uncivilized nation") lacked the proper sympathy for their own countrymen.[37] "All sympathy between the living and dead seems completely out of the question," Mahoney wrote. "I saw from 150 to 180 funerals of victims to the want of food, the whole number attended by not more than 50 persons; and so hardened are the men regularly employed in the removal of the dead from the workhouse, that I saw one of them, with four coffins in a car, driving to the churchyard, sitting upon one of the said coffins, and smoking with much apparent enjoyment."[38] At the same time, Mahoney is at pains to demonstrate his own refined moral sensibility, informing readers of how "the horrors of the poverty became visible" to him and how such scenes were "truly heart-rending."

The importance of such class identifications is evident in another of Mahoney's powerful illustrations. As the editors indicate, the sketch depicts the visit of the local vicar to the "hut of a poor man named Mullins." Mahoney tells us that, in contrast to the callous, unsympathetic, and "hardened" nature of the native Irish peasant class, the vicar, Dr. Traill, was a man "whose humanity at the present moment is beyond all praise." Mahoney had witnessed "the efforts of the Vicar's family to relieve the afflictions around them." He had also seen firsthand "his daughters returning from their work of charity in the poorest portion of the town."[39]

In figure 5, *Mullins's Hut at Scull,* Dr. Traill is portrayed prominently in the foreground of the cabin interior. He is shown in profile and is drawn with significantly more facial detail than any of the other figures in the illustration. His outfit displays the marks of his class—distinct from those he visits—as Mahoney draws him dressed in shoes, pressed trousers, overcoat, scarf, and top hat. He is seated on a chair—the only visible piece of furniture in the cabin—with his legs crossed and his arm resting on his lap. By contrast, the illustration shows a rough cabin interior; ragged curtains or blankets hang from a loft above the seated vicar, who is clearly out of his element. A small pile of turf fuel is to one side; the dirt floor is strewn with straw. Six other people are visible. Three indistinct figures kneel behind and partially obscured by the vicar, another with barely visible features lays upon the straw in the corner, and two, apparently children, are seen faintly, drawn indistinctly as mere outlines at the cabin door. As with Mahoney's other drawings, this sketch invites our imagination to add features and narrative context. From the sketch alone, we receive little personal detail either about the visitor or the afflicted family. We recognize primarily the class distinction between the seated, well-dressed vicar and the remaining occupants of the

MULLINS'S HUT, AT SCULL.

5. Sketch by James Mahoney. *Illustrated London News,* February 20, 1847. Used with the permission of the Illustrated London News Picture Library

cabin. The principal message of the visual display, then, is the chief action sought by the entire series of Mahoney's illustrations: he means to have readers cross the threshold of class and enter into the wretched hovels and intense suffering of the Irish. The portrait of the vicar is the example; he is the representative of a class to whom the experience of the Irish is alien and remote. Just as the figures in the other sketches came to represent the wider experience of misery, the Reverend Traill here is the exemplary "illustration" for those who must respond and are responding to the famine.

The economy of display and the strategy of synecdoche are made evident here when the editors of the *Illustrated London News* provide narrative details to accompany *Mullins's Hut at Scull.* The Mullins hut, they suggest, is "a specimen of the in-door horrors of Scull." The account explains that the sketch depicts Mullins,

who lay dying in a corner upon a heap of straw, supplied by the Relief Committee, whilst his three wretched children crouched over a few embers of turf, as if to raise the last remaining spark of life. This poor man, it appears, had buried his wife some five days previously, and was, in all probability, on the eve of joining her, when he was found out by the untiring efforts of the Vicar, who, for a few short days, saved him from that which no kindness could ultimately avert. Our artist assures us that the dimensions of the hut do not exceed ten feet square, adding that, to make the sketch, he was compelled to stand up to his ankles in the dirt and filth upon the floor.[40]

Both the narrative and the sketch, then, emphasize the necessity of the privileged class—whether by physical visit or imagination—to cross the threshold and enter into the cabins of the suffering. The sketch by James Mahoney provides an example for our action. *Mullins's Hut at Scull* shows us the interior of the hovel and stresses the presence of the vicar in the midst of this "specimen of in-door horrors" giving evidence of his "humanity." The narrative tells us that the artist, too, is literally in the scene. It is Mahoney who both provides precise dimensions and describes himself as "up to his ankles" in the interior environment of a cabin visited by starvation and disease. But, while the artist is the invisible representative of the reader, the vicar is clearly portrayed as the visible embodiment of sympathy and the representative of his class. He is shown in the midst of the suffering, having not only entered into, but also having "found out," that distress to which he applied his sympathy and charity. To the extent that London readers identified with the vicar (an identification made easier by the detail with which his portrait is sketched), they saw themselves within the Mullins hut, confronting the "gruesome tribulations of the body" and having to determine for themselves how far their sympathy could extend.

The narrative informs us that the prone figure in the sketch is the father of the Mullins family. The remainder of the unidentified people in the scene are apparently children who, if the prophecy of the narrative is fulfilled, will soon become orphans. Yet neither the children nor their dying father is given a voice in the narrative or even drawn with any precise detail. They remain essentially anonymous sufferers, like those depicted in the other sketches. The moral authority to represent their suffering is here transferred to the vicar, to the artist, and to the *Illustrated London News,* who together serve as agents of "vicarious spectatorship,"[41] a role for which a "vicar"—one appointed to act for another—is especially well suited.

Significantly, however, the vicar, as the most visible agent of that spectatorship, is doing nothing. His is a posture of inaction; he neither attends to the sick nor feeds the hungry children. He is merely present on the scene, and in this way he accomplishes what is minimally required of the moral and sympathetic spectator.[42] He serves as a witness to suffering and enters into the experience of the wretched, but he refrains from, and so discourages, any action that might suggest the social, political, or economic responsibility of his class for the conditions depicted.[43] In this sense, the vicar can be seen as successfully engaged in "a game of social performance" that in particular demonstrates not only his refined sympathies, but at the same time his ability to engage "the distancing mechanisms required to perform in the intricate theatre of bourgeois culture." As Stephen Hartnett explains in his recent essay on sentimental rhetoric, "too much sympathy was a weakness, a liability."[44]

The image of the vicar, then, implicitly reinforces prevailing views of the causes of the famine, as well as the fundamental class assumptions that constrain the reading public.[45] That such views should be reflected by the work of the illustrator and writer, even as he stood "up to his ankles in the dirt and filth upon the floor," is not surprising, for while Mahoney sought to elicit sympathy, he was himself constrained by nineteenth-century social decorum, his own economic dependence on his employer, and the political reality of Irish colonial status.[46]

This rhetoric of display, then, both exploits and confirms well-defined class relationships that obligate "civilized" readers to respond appropriately and to exhibit a sympathy coincidental with their station as social superiors with refined tastes and morals. The "right appreciation" of such narratives becomes a gesture of class identification and offers one antidote to the erosion of class status associated with other social activity and cultural performance. The representation of the suffering body marks the Irish as alien, diseased, even abandoned by God. Ultimately, then, insofar as famine narratives participate in this reaffirmation of class hegemony, they affirm both the privileged status of the narrator (who speaks for the victims of famine) and the reader (who is meant to respond sympathetically in accord with his refined morals). The alien Irish victim remains silent and subject to the gaze of the vicarious spectator. Such was the cost of sympathy.[47]

Conclusions

This chapter has undertaken a study of the particular representational strategy employed by James Mahoney in his Irish famine illustrations. Sent to the scenes of utter desolation in famine-stricken Ireland, Mahoney became a reluctant witness to suffering as terrible as any observed or described in the nineteenth century. As the witness "on the spot," he stands in as our representative who must then employ his artistic and literary skills to "represent" the terrible misery it was his mission to chronicle.

Mahoney's rhetoric of sympathy relies throughout on an economy of display in which both image and word collaborate to induce an emotional and moral response from the readers of the *Illustrated London News*. The analysis here has shown that the artistic attributes of the sketch, as a genre of visual representation, are particularly suited for conveying a message of authenticity about the subject matter depicted. As such, they answer the immediate need for verification about the extent of Irish suffering. At the same time, as a necessarily "incomplete" rendering, the sketch relies on the interpretive work of the audience to fill in "absences" as "meaningful." In this way, the sketch is especially useful in the accomplishment of a moral rhetoric that seeks to engage the imagination and acquire the sympathy of an audience.

Mahoney's sketches invited the readers to "enter into" the scenes they observed and then to complete the picture of misery by employing their own imaginative resources. Mahoney's images, then, worked mainly by approximation and suggestion, representing selected aspects of suffering that readers augmented by imagination. Overcome by the nightmare of disease and starvation, and constrained by his inability to illustrate the complete picture of horror, Mahoney relied on the trope of the visually unrepresentable, a goad to imagination that indirectly expressed the overwhelming circumstances he witnessed.

Insofar as the images of James Mahoney represented merely part of a wider misery, they functioned as synecdoche, visual figures that required verbal interpretation in the descriptive notes that accompanied them. In these narrative notes, Mahoney employed a sentimental style of vivid description that often focused on the "gruesome tribulations of the body." This vivid sympathetic rhetoric afforded an "ideal presence" to the suffering victims of famine and placed moral demands on an audience induced, again, to employ their imaginations by placing themselves in the circumstances of those who suffered from disease or starvation. As the chapter has suggested, although the famine illustrations enabled the efficiency of Mahoney's economy of display, the most penetrating impression, and the most compelling of the moral demands, came primarily from these verbal narratives. Like the descriptions of other famine writers, Mahoney's rhetoric repeatedly and consistently turned to a verbal "trope of indescribability." The fact that words, like his artistic skills, failed to fully capture the complete picture of suffering shifted the burden of full description to the imaginations of his readers. As those enlisted to have a "right appreciation" for the suffering of the Irish, readers of Mahoney's accounts would offer a gesture of their own class standing by responding imaginatively and sympathetically to his images and stories. Just as Mahoney himself had done, they too would enter into the scenes of privation and death and, by a "willed attentiveness" to Irish misery, discharge the moral burden upon them.

The critical study of James Mahoney's famine illustrations suggests that a comprehensive understanding of the rhetoric of display will necessarily involve interpretation of individual images as synecdoche, as visual tropes that represent a wider landscape of social reality. While a given image might capture a particular moment, or even convey the essence of the circumstances from which it is snatched, it will ever implicitly acknowledge its own inadequacy and incompleteness. However useful the sketch, the painting, or the photograph might be as an icon of "reality," it concedes as well the necessity of interpretation, the desire for imagination, and the expectation of narrative contextualization. It is only the very rare image that transcends the need for a narrative and makes a substantial moral demand for sympathy and action on its own.[48] Even then, such an image or photograph stands in synecdochic relation to the residue of reality that is not conveyed. By its nature as a static display, it remains merely a rhetorical token of the "indescribable" and the "unrepresentable" in our sometimes terrible human experience. The singular image can only approximate that which "no tongue or pen can convey the slightest idea of."

Notes

1. "Sketches in the West of Ireland.—By Mr. James Mahoney," *Illustrated London News,* February 13, 1847. For a discussion of the coverage of the famine by the *Illustrated London News,* see Leslie Williams, "Irish Identity and the *Illustrated London News,* 1846–1851: Famine to Depopulation," in *Representing Ireland: Gender, Class, Nationality,* ed. Susan Shaw Sailer, 59–93 (Gainesville: University Press of Florida, 1997).

2. Noel Kissane, "James Mahoney's Famine Illustrations," in *The Irish Famine: A Documentary History* (Dublin: National Library of Ireland, 1995), 114.

3. *Illustrated London News,* February 13, 1847. Although for months the London papers had been reporting on the worsening conditions in Ireland, the descriptions of horrible suffering, of widespread disease and starvation, taxed the imagination and were met with disbelief. The editors of the *Times,* for example, questioned the reports of severe conditions in Ireland. "The moderation and the confidence of the age will scarcely allow us to speak of 'a famine,'" the *Times* editorialized. While acknowledging that "the food of the masses" was "seriously deficient" and that "it is very possible for millions to be reduced very low," the paper assured readers that "the mention of that gloomy word is not necessarily associated with the dreadful images of ancient or of barbarous scarcity. Famine adapts itself to the civilized state" (*London Times,* September 22, 1846).

Even newspapers that became convinced by the reports of Irish misery reveal an awareness of the skepticism of London readers. "We grieve to be obliged to say," wrote the *London Morning Chronicle,* "that our knowledge of our correspondent's sources of information compels us to regard the statements of his letter as coming nearer to the real truth, and the whole truth, of a matter which perhaps no man living is capable of yet comprehending in all its horrible integrity, than anything which we have yet presented to our readers" ("State of the Country–Spread of Destitution," *London Morning Chronicle,* reprinted in *Boston Daily Atlas,* November 9, 1846).

In private correspondence, skepticism about the extent of famine suffering was met with repeated guarantees of veracity. Aware of the reluctance of correspondents to credit firsthand reports as genuine, eyewitnesses writing private appeals emphasized that "these plain facts are stated without exaggeration, in terms as cold as if we had not hearts to feel the misery around us." They affirmed that their narratives conveyed "ungarnished and unexaggerated statements of facts, which are alas too true and which we are prepared, if necessary, to verify by affidavits." See Liam Swords, *In Their Own Words: The Famine in North Connacht, 1845–1849* (Dublin: The Columba Press, 1999), 105, 86.

4. Richard C. Sha, *The Visual and Verbal Sketch in British Romanticism* (Philadelphia: University of Pennsylvania Press, 1998), 1–4.

5. *Illustrated London News,* February 13, 1847. All of the place names indicate villages and townships within the poor law union of Skibbereen, to the southwest of Cork city. Skibbereen was among the most dreadfully affected areas during the famine.

6. All quotations in this section are from James Mahoney's narrative in the *Illustrated London News,* February 13, 1847.

7. Once beginning with the impression that the illustration recalls the classic religious icon of the Madonna, the revelation that the child in the mother's arms is dead may now also suggest that the illustration doubles as a "pietà" and thereby elicits further our "pity."

8. See Sean Ryder, "Reading Lessons: Famine and the *Nation,* 1845–1849," in *Fearful Realities: New Perspectives on the Famine,* ed. Chris Morash and Richard Hayes, 161 (Dublin: Irish Academic Press, 1996).

9. *Illustrated London News,* February 20, 1847.

10. Ibid., February 13, 1847.

11. Ibid., February 20, 1847.

12. Ibid.

13. Ibid.

14. Ibid.

15. While most of the theoretical texts I draw on are from the eighteenth century, many were still in wide use in 1847. More to the point is the fact that the ideas were common intellectual currency.

16. Adam Smith, *Theory of Moral Sentiments* (1759; repr., Indianapolis, Ind.: Liberty Classics, 1982), 9.

17. Stephen H. Browne, "'Like Gory Spectres': Representing Evil in Theodore Weld's *American Slavery as It Is,*" *Quarterly Journal of Speech* 80 (1994): 280. Browne's essay provides several interesting and helpful parallels from the American abolitionist movement of the same era.

18. *Illustrated London News,* February 20, 1847; Sha, *Visual and Verbal Sketch,* 3.

19. *Illustrated London News,* February 20, 1847.

20. Smith, *Theory of Moral Sentiments,* 10.

21. Ibid., 9.

22. Elizabeth Clark, "'The Sacred Rights of the Weak': Pain, Sympathy, and the Culture of Individual Rights in Antebellum America," *Journal of American History* 82 (1995): 465, 476, 481.

23. Browne, "Like Gory Spectres," 287, 289.

24. Henry Home, Lord Kames, *Elements of Criticism* (1762; repr., New York: Johnson Reprint Company, 1967), 1:107, 110, 113, 117, 122.

25. *Illustrated London News,* February 13, 1847.

26. Clark, "Sacred Rights of the Weak," 481.

27. Cecil Woodham-Smith, *The Great Hunger* (New York: Harper and Row, 1962), 162.

28. Indeed, publication of the Cummins letter in the *Boston Evening Transcript* on January 29, 1847, seems to have led directly to the organization of an important famine-relief meeting at Faneuil Hall.

29. Woodham-Smith, *The Great Hunger,* 162–63.

30. Elihu Burritt, *A Memorial Volume Containing a Sketch of His Life and Labors, with Selections from His Writings and Lectures, and Extracts from His Private Journals in Europe and America,* ed. Charles Northend (New York: D. Appleton and Company, 1879), 43–44. See also "Continued Distress in Ireland—Famine and Pestilence, Horrible Scenes" in *The National Era* 1 (April 1847), which offers extracts of Burritt's journal to American readers with the assurance that the account will "awaken feelings of horror and pity." For another example of such descriptive writing, see "Capt O'Brien to Col Jones," March 2, 1847, in Swords, *In Their Own Words,* 146–47.

31. Burritt, *A Memorial Volume,* 46–47.

32. *Illustrated London News,* February 20, 1847.

33. Hugh Blair, *Lectures on Rhetoric and Belles Lettres* (1784; reprint, ed. Harold F. Harding [Carbondale: Southern Illinois University Press, 1965]), 1:19, 23, 24, 31–32.

34. Smith, *Theory of Moral Sentiments,* 25.

35. Kames, *Elements of Criticism,* 126–27.

36. On the instability of various cultural tokens of nineteenth-century class identity, see Ken Cmiel, *Democratic Eloquence: The Fight over Popular Speech in Nineteenth-Century America* (Berkeley: University of California Press, 1990), esp. 55–93; see also S. Michael Halloran, "The Rhetoric of Picturesque Scenery: A Nineteenth-Century Epideictic," in *Oratorical Culture in Nineteenth-Century America: Transformations in the Theory and Practice of Rhetoric,* ed. Gregory Clark and S. Michael Halloran, 226–46 (Carbondale: Southern Illinois University Press, 1993).

37. Blair, *Lectures on Rhetoric and Belles Lettres,* 1:19, 32.

38. *Illustrated London News,* February 20, 1847.

39. Ibid.

40. Ibid.

41. Browne, "Like Gory Spectres," 287.

42. In his analysis of Theodore Weld's *American Slavery as It Is,* Stephen Browne makes the argument that the text provided "the satisfactions of moral exhaustion" in which "Northern readers could indulge a kind of vicarious horror while never really abridging the distance between Northern class identity and the realities of Southern slavery." As Browne explains, "The overwhelming emphasis on the slave's body and its brutal violation" allowed for "a form of response which took emotional intensity to be at once the means and end of moral commitment" and encouraged a "confusion of spectatorship with moral action" (Browne, "Like Gory Spectres," 279, 286, 289, 291).

43. Others, such as Dr. Donovan, did not so refrain. As the coroner investigating the death of Denis Kennedy, Donovan issued a verdict that the deceased "died of starvation caused by the gross neglect of the Board of Works." See Woodham-Smith, *The Great Hunger,* 141. Significantly, that episode from Donovan's experience is not reported by Mahoney or the *Illustrated London News.*

44. Stephen Hartnett, "Fanny Fern's 1855 *Ruth Hall,* the Cheerful Brutality of Capitalism and the Irony of Sentimental Rhetoric," *Quarterly Journal of Speech* 88 (February 2002): 6.

45. The two main narratives that "explained" the famine, and that were repeatedly articulated in the mainstream press, either identified the famine as a "natural" disaster and therefore a "visitation" of a vengeful God or blamed the famine on the Irish themselves, who are usually depicted as savage, immoral, superstitious, lazy, violent, and "uncivilized." In both cases, the Irish are

branded as both alien and deserving of their fate. See, for example, Thomas Gallagher, *Paddy's Lament: Ireland 1846–1847, Prelude to Hatred* (New York: Harcourt Brace Jovanovich, 1982), 83–90 and Christopher Morash, *Writing the Irish Famine* (Oxford: Clarendon, 1995), esp. 11–29, 99–127. See also "The Famine and the Sword," *Boston Evening Transcript*, March 3, 1847.

46. As Leslie Williams has argued, the *Illustrated London News* coverage reflected an editorial assumption about the "otherness of the Irish" and sought repeatedly to discourage armed rebellion and to minimize thoughts of English "political or social responsibility" ("Irish Identity," 90).

47. Following Hartnett's argument, however, we might propose that Mahoney and other famine witnesses had little choice in the representational strategy they chose. Moreover, ironically, their strategy may have undermined the class hegemony implied by their images and narratives. Mahoney's focused attention on the personal distress of an individual encourages a sentimental response and an essentially emotional relationship between the subject and the reader. While it is a response that implicitly discourages consideration of the famine in political and economic terms, it may have encouraged some readers "to consider dramatic political and economic changes that, prior to the emotional cathexis prompted by sentimental texts, seemed absurd or imprudent." Hartnett suggests that the "emotionally over-determined language" of mid-nineteenth-century sentimentalism was often symptomatic of "deeper difficulties in comprehending historical transformations that are not yet explainable or translatable in terms other than the personal." To Hartnett, a turn to sentimentalism is characteristic of the need to explain "dramatic political and economic changes" in the language of "the intricate yet always fragmentary experiential fabric of everyday life." The need to "express the inexpressible" he argues, led nineteenth-century sentimentalists to "explain the inexplicable by reducing it to immediate sensations."

Ironically, then, according to Hartnett's account, the employment of a sentimental rhetoric in the case of the famine witnesses might be understood as a "representational strategy" by Mahoney and others "that provides familiar emotional terms to help readers bridge the increasing gap between immediate experiences . . . and the incomprehensible historical forces" dominating Irish politics and economics. The famine images, then, serve as the familiar term, the metaphor for the colonial political and economic exploitation of Ireland by Great Britain, a metaphor whose full implications were not yet fully worked out nor perhaps even acknowledged by the nineteenth-century readers whose response remains, for the time, chiefly sentimental. But, as Hartnett recognizes, such a thesis is "difficult to prove" and in the case of famine representation exceedingly so; for famine discourse seems to have done little to undermine the view of Ireland in the colonial imagination of Great Britain. Moreover, many famine-era Irish writers (John Mitchel, William Smith O'Brien, and Archbishop John MacHale, for instance) explicitly situated the famine within a context of necessary political and economic change, to little effect. See Harnett, "Fanny Fern's 1855 *Ruth Hall*," 1–18.

48. A case in point is the compelling Pulitzer Prize–winning photograph of a starving Ethiopian mother and child by the *Boston Globe*'s Stan Grossfeld, taken during the Ethiopian famine of 1984. The image bears a striking structural and thematic resemblance to Mahoney's *Woman Begging at Clonakilty*.

Lawrence J. Prelli

4

*V*isualizing a Bounded Sea

A Case Study in Rhetorical Taxis

In 1984, a chamber of the International Court of Justice (ICJ) drew a boundary that divided United States and Canadian jurisdiction over resources in the Gulf of Maine.[1] At stake was Georges Bank, then site of one of the world's most productive fisheries. The dispute began when both countries declared exclusive fisheries zones that extended two hundred nautical miles from their coastlines, effectively excluding foreign fishing vessels and opening a potential economic bonanza for their own fishermen. In the Gulf of Maine, however, jurisdictional claims overlapped, leaving 17,650 square nautical miles in dispute, including 5,450 at Georges Bank.[2] The two governments agreed to use the first ad hoc chamber of the World Court to adjudicate the dispute and impose a single maritime boundary deciding jurisdiction over both the fisheries and seabed resources.[3]

The United States had to adjust its case to evolving legal and political constraints.[4] The United States had argued during earlier negotiations that Georges Bank was part of its continental shelf,[5] but an international tribunal subsequently rendered a decision that implied geological arguments were irrelevant to shelf delimitation cases unless the disputed area was located between two discrete continental shelves.[6] U.S. geologists told legal strategists that they could not "keep a straight face" if asked to make that claim about the disputed area in the gulf, so the argument was lost to U.S. strategists.[7] Moreover, the conflict's political motive had shifted from shelf resources (oil and gas prospects) to the commercial fisheries.[8] Fishing industry lobbies and their political supporters—led by the New England congressional delegation—claimed that Georges Bank belonged under exclusive U.S. jurisdiction because it was an "American" bank. The United States was left with the difficult burden of finding an alternative strategy capable of persuading an international tribunal that awarding the entire disputed area to the United States would be "equitable."[9]

An important feature of the new U.S. strategy was a bold and unprecedented argument that turned resource management and conservation into a legal principle for maritime boundary delimitation.[10] According to that "equitable" principle, maritime boundary decisions should facilitate resource conservation and management whenever and wherever possible. The United States applied that principle to purportedly factual and legally relevant circumstances in the gulf area. One of those circumstances was the Northeast Channel—a deep water trench in the Gulf of Maine—that the United States claimed was a "natural boundary" dividing both seabed and water column resources between Georges Bank and the Scotian Shelf.[11] The United States argued that the natural boundary at the Northeast Channel is a "significant break" in the seabed that divides the continental shelf and "stands between" commercial fish stocks living in separate "ecological regimes" over Georges Bank and the Scotian Shelf.[12] Accordingly, running the legal boundary along the "natural boundary" at the Northeast Channel "makes it both possible and appropriate to manage the stocks over Georges Bank separately from the stocks over the Scotian Shelf."[13] That proposal—which leaves Georges Bank under exclusive U.S. jurisdiction—*was* "equitable" based on the conservation principle, since it enabled single-state jurisdiction over intact ecological regimes and, thereby, presumably fostered better resource management and conservation than is possible under bilateral arrangements.[14] In contrast, the United States argued that Canada's proposed boundary ignored the gulf's "natural boundary," split the Georges Bank regime between the parties, and undermined efforts to conserve already overburdened resources by exposing them to conflicting management approaches.[15]

The efficacy of the conservation argument required that the tribunal accept as a relevant fact the claim that the Northeast Channel is a "natural boundary" dividing Georges Bank and Scotian Shelf "ecological regimes" in the gulf area. The rhetorical advantage of that prospect is clear. Natural boundaries, unlike legal boundaries, are not artificial things that can be contrived for purposes of economic self-interest,[16] political horse trading, or extensions of national power; instead, they are empirical realities that can only be discovered and described using the best available science. Thus, if the United States could convince the tribunal of the "fact" that the Northeast Channel is a natural boundary, then the court might be inclined to endorse the conservation principle as a new "impartial" standard for "equitable" maritime boundary division that could resonate with growing international demand for better conservation of the world's resources.

Canada, for its part, had to convince the tribunal that the natural boundary claim is "myth" without "basis in law or fact."[17] Canada argued that the Northeast Channel is not a "significant break" in the continental shelf, which is a "single, continuous, uninterrupted feature" in the gulf area.[18] Nor does the Northeast Channel divide the water column into separate "ecological regimes."[19] According to Canada, there are no bounded ecological regimes to separate at the Northeast Channel, since the flora and fauna within the gulf's waters are part of a "single," "complex" ocean system forming a "continuum" that "extends throughout the Gulf of Maine area from northeast to southwest."[20] According to Canada, the natural boundary claim is not objective fact established with science but political fiction invented out of distortion, exaggeration, and selectivity.[21] Any purportedly "natural" boundary only masks "political factors," since it, like any other, simply marks where a state wants to extend its legal jurisdiction.[22] Thus, from Canada's vantage, a decision awarding Georges Bank to the United States would be "utterly devoid of equity."[23]

This chapter explores rhetorical displays that exhibited the Gulf of Maine's central features through visual and verbal depiction. The two parties used more than two hundred maps and other graphics to augment written and oral pleadings, moving one participant to portray the case as "a war of images."[24] I shall examine how selected graphics incorporated visual structures that both shaped how the gulf's features were seen and disposed the attitudes of those who saw them. This is a study, then, in the rhetoric of visual *taxis*. In traditional rhetorical theory of oratory, the Greek word *taxis,* the Latin word *dispositio,* and the English word "arrangement" all pointed to the same phenomenon: the materials of a speech had to be structured strategically within coherent patterns of thought for maximum persuasive effect with particular, targeted audiences.[25] Today, rhetorical considerations of *taxis* go beyond oratory to include the structural dimensions of symbols, both visual and verbal. I suggest that visual structures can participate in the dynamic between literalizing metaphorically generated associations as factual attributes and refiguring purportedly factual claims as metaphorical. Of particular interest here is how the United States' visual structures augmented verbal depictions to establish "natural boundary" associations as literal and factual and Canada's efforts to refigure them as metaphorical or otherwise fanciful. Since metaphor is integral to this analysis, I begin by discussing metaphor in relation to visual *taxis.*

Visual Taxis and the Literalization of Metaphor

Both U.S. and Canadian lawyers struggled to delineate the Gulf of Maine's definitive geographical features. Part of that struggle involved what Robert Ivie described as the temptation to literalize metaphors.[26] A metaphor becomes literal whenever we no longer discriminate between "tenor" and "vehicle" but imagine the tenor to *be* the vehicle and, thus, *identical* with "the very thing which it only resembles."[27] As awareness of interaction between tenor and vehicle fades, a literal structure emerges that, in turn, becomes a potential rhetorical resource in the form of an accepted premise, "ground," or factual support for warranting otherwise disputable claims. Though Ivie did not pursue the point, the process of literalizing the metaphorical is reversible.[28] Challenges to purportedly literal structures often involve efforts to refigure them as mere resemblances rather than assertions of identity, reanimating faded tensions between tenor and vehicle that mark those structures as metaphorical.

Ivie directed attention to war rhetoric in his studies,[29] but the dynamic between literalizing the metaphorical and refiguring the literal is nearly ubiquitous to all thought and discourse. Following Kenneth Burke, Ivie acknowledged "the necessity of extending the figurative to the literal world" and its potential for literalizing once-figurative relationships.[30] Ernesto Grassi, following Giambattista Vico, contended that even the most rational philosophies involve the unfolding of a terminological logic traceable to and structured by original—but concealed or forgotten—metaphorical insight.[31] Hayden White, following Burke and Vico, identified metaphor as the primary of four master tropes that "prefigure" all historical and literary modes of thought, including the most rational or logical.[32] Max Black, following I. A. Richards, located metaphorical processes at the core of scientific creativity, where initially "heuristic" models of phenomena (x is *like* y) eventually can acquire ontological status within particular empirical domains (x *is* y).[33] All of these commentators presupposed the presence of literalized metaphors that they, in turn, refigured in their critical work.

Exploring the dynamic between literalizing the metaphorical and refiguring the literal requires that we reconceive the relationship between the literal and the figurative as a matter more of degree than of kind. As White put it, distinctions between "the literal and figurative, fictional and factual, referential and intensional dimensions of language" are examined productively as "the poles of a linguistic continuum between which speech must move in the articulation of any discourse whatsoever, serious or frivolous."[34] What "counts" as fact or fiction, literal or figurative, referential or intensional along that continuum is a function of how symbols are used within specific, situated contexts.[35]

How is the metaphorical transformed into the literal (or the reverse) in particular, situated discourses? An answer presupposes some perspective on metaphor's structure and function. Black contended that metaphors are structured through interaction of two domains of thought: the principal subject, or what the metaphor is about, and the subsidiary subject, or the metaphor that inclines us to think about the principal subject in its terms.[36] Meanings are shaped through interaction of these two domains: "A memorable metaphor has the power to bring two separate domains into cognitive and emotional relation by using language directly appropriate to the one as a lens for seeing the other; the implications, suggestions, and supporting values entwined with the literal use of the metaphorical expression enable us to see a new subject matter in a new way."[37] For Black, metaphor functions as a "screen," and commonplaces associated with the subsidiary subject, or metaphorical system, constitute the "network of lines upon the screen." So organized, the principal subject is "'seen through' the metaphorical expression."[38]

Black's use of visual terms to depict metaphor's primary function offers a clue to an important resource for engaging the dynamic between literalizing the metaphorical and refiguring the literal. His reference to varying screens that shape how we "see" a principal subject joins a tradition dating back to Aristotle, who himself thought that the proper function of metaphor is "to point out or show, to 'make visible'" relationships that otherwise would remain concealed.[39] Contemporary commentators acknowledge that the richest metaphors enable us to "see" or to "visualize" one thing in terms of another.[40] This visual imagery about metaphorical "seeing"—though itself metaphorical—points to an important literalizing resource. No resource has greater rhetorical power for ushering the shift from the metaphorical to the literal than the experience of seeing associations not as points of resemblance but as identifiable attributes inhering in actual, visible structures. The imagined seeing of resemblances then recedes from awareness, leaving a residue of thought no longer qualified as the result of "as if" thinking; instead, resemblances become attributes, characteristics, and qualities of the principal subject "as it is"[41] that, together, constitute a structure of identity.

How can we examine the functioning of visual structures to literalize the metaphorical? With minor amendment, Black's theory of metaphor can capture the creative, interactive process involved when visual symbols contribute to that dynamic.[42] Black's perspective is limited to *linguistic* metaphor and does not account for visual symbols that could induce, strengthen, or extend commonplaces associated with a particular structure of metaphorical or literalized "seeing." Susanne Langer's distinction between "presentational" and "discursive" symbols brings visual symbols within analytical reach.

According to Langer, presentational or nondiscursive symbols involve "a direct *presentation* of an individual object";[43] they appear in immediate sense experience, so "the mind reads" them "in a flash, and preserves" them in a "disposition or an attitude."[44] Presentational symbols are grasped immediately as holistic structures or patterns;[45] the elements that constitute them appear simultaneously. In contrast, discursive symbols are articulated during ongoing linear processes of speaking or writing when the elements that comprise them are brought successively into play. Discursive symbols are amenable to analysis into the discrete units of meaning—the words—that comprise them, but presentational symbols are much less susceptible to such analysis. Presentational symbols consist of elements that, when taken separately, are not discrete units of meaning but mere splotches of color or squiggles of line. Though presentational symbols display visual patterns that are recognizable across different contexts, the specific visual elements that comprise this or that individual instance of a pattern lack the independent significance and fixed meaning of words that, together, form discursive symbols—including metaphors—according to syntactical rules.[46]

Presentational symbols contribute to metaphorical systems by evoking commonplace associations that constrain how one thing is seen in terms of another. Take, for instance, a television commercial for an insurance company that contains a visual narrative showing a father comforting a frightened child while the verbal narrative emphasizes the security that life insurance affords those who purchase that particular company's policies. The subsidiary subject is the relationship between fathers and their children that, in turn, evokes associations that filter or screen how we see the principal subject—the relationship between the insurance company and its prospective adult male clients. Affective and cognitive associations about fathers providing secure childhoods form the network of lines on the screen through which adult male viewers are invited to see the insurance company's relationship to them. The vehicle of this metaphor—its subsidiary subject—remains unstated since it is carried through presentational rather than discursive symbolism.[47]

Our holistic and immediate experience of presentational symbolism underscores its power as a persuasive resource for literalizing metaphorically generated associations as factual. In the insurance commercial, affective associations from giving and receiving protection become literalized insofar as adult viewers actually can feel warmth, tenderness, and attachment and become inclined to affirm those associations. Of course, associations can be refigured by pointing out less appealing implications that otherwise might remain unnoticed—for example, the attitude that men are like children in their need for protection from a beneficent, all-powerful corporate father. Nevertheless, presentational symbols can influence attitudes in ways that literalize metaphorical associations as though actually experienced.

Presentational symbols can be examined as discrete structures, but they often are incorporated within visual patterns that interrelate them and constrain the range of plausible audience "readings." In their study of "the *taxis* of the visual," Kress and van Leeuwen inventory structural patterns that order and interrelate presentational symbols in visual displays.[48] Their inventory has rhetorical perspective, since it presumes that meanings are shaped visually through selections of symbols and structures that, necessarily and simultaneously, conceal some meanings even as they reveal others.[49] The visual patterns inventoried are a survey of culturally available structures imposed on visual symbols that constrain how audiences perceive and think about them. Kress and van Leeuwen, at least in principle, extend to visual symbols a premise about "arrangement" found in traditional rhetorical theory of oratory. In Roman rhetoric manuals we find surveys of options for arranging discovered materials for maximum impact with specific targeted audiences.[50] Though not avowedly sharing those strategic aims, Kress and van Leeuwen's compendium of patterns guides critical examination of visual arrangement practices and, in principle at least, applies also to strategic production of visual designs.[51] Whether critical or productive in application, their inventory extends the premise of classical rhetorical theory that disposition has significant rhetorical consequences from oratorical and other verbal patterns to visual design structures.[52]

Kress and van Leeuwen inventory variations on two kinds of visual design structures: narrative and conceptual. Both contain symbols called "participants" that "are perceived as distinct entities which are salient . . . to different degrees because of their different sizes, shapes, colour, and so on."[53] But the two general kinds of pattern interrelate participants differently. Narrative patterns relate participants with "vectors"—symbols for functions, actions, or processes. In narrative structures, at least one participant functions actively as the vector's origin while at least one other participant functions as the vector's passive recipient.[54] These patterns impose temporal relationships on visual symbols; they "present unfolding actions and events, processes of change, transitory spatial arrangements."[55] Conceptual patterns, in contrast, impose logical or spatial relationships on participants. Participants are symbolized "in terms of their generalized and more or less stable and timeless essence."[56] These symbols for fixed, unchanging categories are then interrelated visually as parts and whole, as genus and species, or as some other categorical relationship.

In the next section, I examine the United States' and Canada's base maps to show how they visually structured the gulf's geographical features in ways that simultaneously worked to incline viewers toward support of their respective legal claims.

Visual Disposition and the Disposition of Attitudes

Maps are products of cartographic persuasion and, thus, offer partial perspectives that constrain the range of meaningful readings available to those who use them.[57] Maps selectively symbolize bounded entities, imposing relationships among them. How ambiguities about placement of "edges" or "boundaries"[58] are resolved when delineating mapped features is central to this rhetorical process. A boundary or edge divides and separates; whatever is on one side is set apart from whatever is on the other. Both sides become discrete features—wholes unto themselves—but remove the boundary and all discreteness vanishes, leaving one single, homogeneous feature. Much of a map's persuasiveness depends on how visual elements (placement, shape, hue, size) are combined to induce a partial perspective in which some features and interrelationships come into view while others are minimized, if not concealed. The United States' and Canada's base maps show how visual structures selectively symbolize and interrelate features seen and, thereby, work to shape the attitudes of those who see them.

Locating Central Features

For illustration of the U.S. base map consider figure C5 (the base map actually would include all features shown here *except* the proposed boundary line). The Northeast Channel is the central locus of discontinuity in the entire mapped area.[59] The channel's shape appears using a one-hundred-fathom contour line, connecting the gulf's interior with the continental shelf edge. All three features appear in light blue, standing out from darker adjacent banks and shelf area. The channel seemingly divides the Gulf of Maine area into two "sides." To its southwest is the area labeled "Georges Bank," symbolized in a darker shade of blue and appearing with a fifty-fathom contour line. The bank is part of an undifferentiated seabed along southern New England and coasts farther to the southwest, contiguous with the American mainland. To the channel's northeast is a large area labeled

"Scotian Shelf," consisting of a differentiated seabed of unlabeled lighter blue basins and labeled darker blue banks of variable sizes and shapes (Browns Bank, German Bank, Roseway Bank, LaHave Bank, Emerald Bank, Sable Island Bank, Middle Bank, Censo Bank). The banks are revealed in size and number against the pale shelf backdrop on the Scotian side of the Gulf of Maine—right off Nova Scotia. Thus, the map presents a view of the gulf area as two sides divided at the central locus, the Northeast Channel.

In contrast, consider figure C6 as an example of Canada's base map (again, the base map actually would include all features shown *except* the proposed boundary line).[60] Georges Bank is the central feature within the Gulf of Maine area. Using a sixty-meter contour line, the bank appears smaller than on figure C5, but its darker blue shape stands out against paler surrounding area. The Great South Channel appears on the bank's southwestern side, effectively decentering the Northeast Channel. Beyond the Great South Channel is another distinctive feature: the Nantucket Shoals. The shoals—not Georges Bank— blend within an undifferentiated seabed that is contiguous with the U.S. mainland. To the bank's north and northwest is the interior Gulf of Maine, a differentiated seabed of labeled basins —Georges Basin, Wilkinson Basin, Jordan Basin—that clearly are separate from the Northeast Channel. To the bank's immediate northeast is shelf area and, of course, the Northeast Channel. Beyond the Northeast Channel is a visually inconspicuous and, thus, seemingly insignificant area consisting of unlabeled basins and mostly unlabeled banks. (That area, the Scotian Shelf, also is unlabeled.) Browns Bank is the only labeled seabed feature there, but it appears in the same small font and style of insignificant features such as the gulf's interior basins. Other banks, all unlabeled, recede from view, their outlined forms appearing in the same color as surrounding shelf area. Only Sable Island Bank and part of Browns Bank have a darker color that stands out against shelf area, but Sable Island Bank's large size is obscured by the map's edge, and Browns Bank is minimized by Georges Bank's larger presence. Georges Bank, then, is the central and most significant seabed feature within this view of the Gulf of Maine area, but without special "natural" or "spatial" relationship to surrounding features.

Placement of different features at the gulf's center indicates disagreement about their relative importance. According to Kress and van Leeuwen, "For something to be presented as Centre means that it is presented as the nucleus of the information on which all the other elements are in some sense subservient. The Margins are these ancillary, dependent elements."[61] On figure C5, the Northeast Channel is the central locus of division, with all other features, including Georges Bank, acquiring significance in relation to it. Visually, the significance of Georges Bank is its location on the "U.S. side" of the channel. On figure C6, Georges Bank is central in significance, with other features, including the Northeast Channel, acquiring importance relative to it. Visually, with the absence of distinct "sides," the southwestern tip of Nova Scotia appears to possess as much significance in relation to the bank as the Massachusetts coastline near Cape Cod.[62] These different central placements, then, invite the tribunal to adopt orientations toward the Gulf of Maine that, simultaneously, frame how the two parties want them to see the legal issues before them.

Figuring Georges Bank

Georges Bank is the central locus of the legal dispute, so how it is configured on maps will at one stroke relate the bank spatially to other gulf features and rhetorically to the parties' legal claims. Accordingly, the United States and Canada developed different presentational symbols for the bank whose display could help literalize metaphorical associations that were preferable from their respective legal positions. The United States argued that "Georges Bank is an extension of the Atlantic Coastal Plain into and under the sea"[63] and explained that the coastal plain extended "to the shoreline, where it plunges beneath the sea to form the continental shelf extending to the northeastern edge of Georges Bank."[64] Canada depicted Georges Bank as "a large, detached, oval-shaped bank defined by the Great South Channel and the Northeast Channel . . ."[65] These prosaic depictions actually were generated from metaphors: "Georges Bank is an American peninsula" and "Georges Bank is an island." Canada's chief science advisor made the strategy explicit:

> We acknowledged that Georges Bank had some very important ecosystem characteristics to it, but implied that it was an island . . . in-between Cape Cod and Southwest Nova Scotia, but separate from them both. . . . And, this island concept, it created a thing. Instead of an extension it was an island. An island can be divided up between two parties.[66]

The difference is consequential: should the chamber associate the bank with sovereign U.S. territory—as though it was a submarine "American" peninsula—it would be more inclined against putting that area in "foreign" hands; however, should it see the bank as a submerged island in between sovereign territories, it would be more disposed to find "equity" in division.

Consider again how Georges Bank appears on figure C5. The bank appears continuous with U.S. coastal waters, contiguous with the U.S. mainland, and separate from Canadian waters (due to the Northeast Channel's central presence). The bank visually evokes associations of attachment, appendage, and affiliation with the U.S. mainland so that we are disposed to see it as an *American* bank. In contrast, consider again the bank's appearance on figure C6. The centrally placed bank is separate from U.S. coastal waters and contiguous only with the Great South Channel to its west and with "deeper" shelf area and the Northeast Channel to its east. The two channels seemingly frame the bank in between southeastern New England and southwestern Nova Scotia. Thus, the bank evokes associations of detachment, separation, or independence from terrestrial features—both U.S. and Canadian—so that we come to see it as an *international* bank. Both parties, then, designed presentational symbols to literalize preferred but metaphorically generated associations about the site of contention.

It is not surprising, then, that each side sought to refigure the other's visually implied "literal" associations by *naming* the visual vehicle evoking them. The United States wrote: Canada "contends that Georges Bank is a detached bank, separated both from the Scotian Shelf and from the East Coast Continental Shelf of the United States. Canada in effect seeks to characterize Georges Bank as a *topographic island* [emphasis added]."[67] Canada not only named the "peninsula" vehicle but also designed maps to ridicule its implications.[68] One map, "The United States Boundary Proposal Treats Georges Bank as Part of the Emerged Land Domain of the United States," displayed the bank as a peninsula extending from southern New England at Cape Cod to the Northeast Channel. The imaginary peninsula consisted of "Nantucketland" and "Georgesland," cast in the same color as the real peninsula at Nova Scotia. (The Great South Channel is reduced to insignificance as a tiny, thin, light blue strip between those two "lands.") The other map, "The United States Boundary Proposal Denies the Existence of Nova Scotia," switched vehicles, and Nova Scotia became "Scotia Bank," appearing in the same dark blue as Georges Bank. These hidden metaphors, Canada complained, illustrated U.S. attempts "to justify the unjustifiable . . . [which] would make it necessary to refashion geography, reorder nature, revise history, and rewrite the law of maritime boundaries."[69] For contrast, Canada pointed to figure C6 and its proposed boundary line as "firmly rooted in equity, in law and in reality."[70]

Imposing Disposition

How "bounded" features like Georges Bank and the Northeast Channel are interrelated within visual design structures is my next consideration. According to Kress and van Leeuwen's inventory of visual structures, the two base maps are analytical and topographical variations on the general, conceptual pattern. Comparison of differences between the two maps' analytical and topographical structures will show further how visual *dispositio* or *taxis* works rhetorically to structure the attitudes of those who see the maps. I shall discuss those two structures in turn.

An analytical pattern relates a whole called the "carrier" with specific parts called "possessive attributes."[71] Attributes are "singled out as criterial in the given context . . . while others are ignored, treated as non-essential and irrelevant."[72] Accordingly, analytical structures relate carriers and constituent attributes as wholes and parts. Carriers can contain attributes that, in turn, function as carriers containing another layer of attributes, and so on. As we shall see, the two base maps exhibit different attributes as "criterial" and, thus, invite different attitudes.

Both maps display the same carrier—the Gulf of Maine area—that possesses both administrative and natural attributes. The seabed areas on figures C5 and C6 are depicted primarily as natural features, though the contour lines on both maps (sometimes accompanied with numbers signifying depth) and the grids on figure C6 show that their constituent features are known and charted. I have shown that the Northeast Channel and Georges Bank appear respectively as the central seabed features on figures C5 and C6, with Georges Bank seen as a peninsula on one and as an island on the other. But no federal jurisdictions or other zones of administrative influence are marked out in ways that encompass these and other seabed features, though line symbols were added to the base maps to support specific points of argument about one or the other nation's purported influence—or the lack thereof—over the contested area. How terrestrial features relate to natural seabed features is an important difference in how the two base maps structure attitudes toward legal claims advanced in the case.

Figure C5 emphasizes "natural" and de-emphasizes administrative attributes of terrestrial features. State and provincial boundary lines are absent and, thus, divert attention from those administrative entities. Nova Scotia is seen as a peninsula connected to the mainland by the Chignecto Isthmus rather than a province connected to Canada by a provincial boundary line. Labeled islands, all but the smallest cast in gray (the shading for land on U.S. maps), appear along the U.S. coast (Nantucket Island, Martha's Vineyard, Block Island, Long Island), within the gulf's interior (Grand Manan Island), southwest and southeast of Nova Scotia (Seal Island and Sable Island), and in the distant northeast (Cape Breton Island and Prince Edward Island). Capes are displayed along New England (Cape

Cod, Cape Ann, Cape Elizabeth) and Nova Scotia (Cape Sable and Cape Canso) coasts, with Cape Breton farther to the northeast. All capes and islands are readily seen as natural features. Only the two federal governments are circumscribed as bounded administrative entities by bold lines and large font labels. All other jurisdictional units appear as point symbols for eleven U.S. and three Canadian coastal cities (one at southwestern Nova Scotia), with all points and labels in uniform font size and style.

Figure C6 exhibits a more diverse and layered array of administrative attributes, with less emphasis on natural features. Federal jurisdiction again appears as two areas bounded by the boldest lines and labeled in the largest font, but embedded within them is a second bounded administrative layer of states and provinces—all delineated with lines and labels. On this map, Nova Scotia is a province marked by a boundary rather than a peninsula indicated by an isthmus. Embedded within the bounded states and provinces are labels and point symbols for cities, but they too are distinguished with two distinct font sizes and styles. In contrast, terrestrial entities that are seen as natural rather than administrative are limited, at best, to labeled islands and capes, including the addition of several labeled islands in the gulf area and of several capes along Nova Scotia.

Kress and van Leeuwen distinguished spatially structured analytical patterns into those that are read as *exhaustive* of a carrier's attributes and those that are read as *inclusive* in the sense that they show only some of the carrier's attributes.[73] That distinction identifies important differences in the analytical structures on the two maps. Both exhaust federal administrative attributes in the gulf's terrestrial area, but only figure C6 exhibits an exhaustive layer of provincial and state attributes embedded within them. Figure C6 also embeds an inclusive structure of cities within the state and provincial layer that highlights differences with font size and boldness of labels. Thus, Boston, New York, Halifax, St. John, Montreal, and Quebec stand out as more significant or powerful sites (economic, political, or cultural) relative to other cities and towns, such as the half-dozen fishing villages scattered along the southwestern Nova Scotia coast. In comparison, figure C5 renders state and provincial jurisdiction invisible, descending from the federal level to an inclusive attribute layer of selected cities and towns, uniformly depicted without regard to differences.

We now can see how the base maps' visual structures incline viewers to adopt particular attitudes toward any of the features added to them, including the proposed boundary lines. Figure C5 invites map readers to see the conflict as between nations over control of a bank that has stronger natural and spatial affinities with U.S. territory than with territories on the "other side"—the implied Canadian side—of the Northeast Channel. Against that backdrop, the United States' proposed boundary line appears superimposed on the natural seabed environment. The line's beginning and ending points lack connection to any administrative entity in the area, U.S. or Canadian, on land or at sea. The line's sharp, angular features contrast with the curvaceous contours of "natural" seabed features such as Browns Bank and German Bank, suggesting that legal divisions are artificial things imposed on the organic, natural world.[74] The line goes in a northwest to southeast direction, with starting and ending points implying that the United States could claim portions of both German Bank and Browns Bank. Instead, the United States "adjusts" the line's direction to avoid severing those banks and, thus, apparently puts concern for the natural environment's integrity before economic and political self-interest. An additional implication, of course, is that Canada's proposed boundary puts politics and economic self-interest before concern for the natural environment, since it would split Georges Bank, severing that natural feature. The solution? The Northeast Channel stands out as though nature itself has shown where to run the boundary. Put the boundary along that "natural" place, and both nations will have exclusive control over resources on their own respective "sides," which, in turn, will benefit resource conservation. Equity thus can be served by awarding the United States all of Georges Bank based on a new resource conservation and management precedent.

Figure C6 invites readers to see the conflict as between two nations over resources at an "international" bank in between southwestern Nova Scotia and southeastern New England that involves parties of unequal power. Against that backdrop, Canada's line runs in a southerly direction from the international land boundary terminus through centrally located, narrowly circumscribed Georges Bank at points equidistant to southwestern Nova Scotia and southeastern New England. Thus, the line is consistent with current international boundary relationships and is anything but arbitrary or artificial. Moreover, unlike the U.S. proposal, the line considers unequal power relationships between the two parties. The small fishing villages located along Nova Scotia's coasts and participating in that province's relatively modest, largely rural economy will gain a share of Georges Bank's much-needed bounty along with U.S. coastal cities participating in southern New England's more powerful and diverse economy. How could Canada propose a more "equitable" solution than splitting the centrally located bank with its more powerful neighbor? Again, there is an additional implication. The U.S. line fails to acknowledge political relationships and responsibilities, using concern for conservation as cover for pursuing the interests of the more powerful at the expense of the weaker. Canada's smoothed boundary line implies a fit with the natural world, but the geography it "respects" clearly is the gulf's *political* geography.

Displaying Objectivity

Both base maps sanctioned these quite-partisan implications with the visual stance of impartiality. Viewers are invited to adopt an attitude of dispassionate openness toward mapped features. After all, the maps purportedly furnish accurate and precise information based on sophisticated projection and scaling systems. The maps' topographical structures maintain and reinforce that attitude of impartiality, since each can be "read as accurately representing the physical spatial relations and the relative location of the possessive attributes."[75] The legends underscore that mapped features and spatial relationships are not arbitrary but are founded on careful measurement and computation. Thus, each map includes ratio scales for horizontal distance and bathymetric scales for seabed depth. But differences between the two topographical structures expose partisan inclinations concealed behind objectivity's display.

The United States and Canada measured bathymetric contours differently and, thus, gave different views of the gulf's seabed. For example, consider the display of the Great South Channel. Canada created a five-map graphic, "Effects Produced by Selective Representation of Bathymetric Contours," to show "that any feature of the shelf can be emphasized or made to disappear, depending on the contour intervals depicted."[76] The United States, Canada charged, used "selective labeling and selective bathymetry" to conceal the Great South Channel, display Georges Bank as "a kind of physical 'natural prolongation' of Massachusetts,"[77] and depict the Northeast Channel as cutting "across the entire breadth of the continental shelf."[78] Canada, in contrast, chose contours according to principles of accuracy and comprehensiveness to offer an "objective view" of the Gulf of Maine area.[79] The United States countered that Canada's five-map graphic exposed Canada's manipulation of bathymetry for strategic purposes. The map sequence lacked "logical order"[80] since it was arranged "to ensure that the sixty-meter-depth contour is highlighted," which, in turn, brought the Great South Channel into view.[81] The United States created a new six-map series that displayed the same contours "logically," by adding them "one at a time, in order from deep to shallow, to illustrate the relative significance of the bathymetric features."[82] The result? The Great South Channel lacks significance since it appeared last in the sequence.[83]

At stake in debates about appropriate scaling measures is the legitimacy of the maps' topographic structures. Map readers become aware of selective processes when features appearing on one map are different or are absent on another map. The need to account for those differences complicates the attitude that one is acquiring an accurate, precise, and impartial spatial analysis. Features might appear on maps as the product of partisan, persuasive strategy rather than of science. Such doubts would incline map readers—in this case, the chamber—to turn away from complicated issues of scale to find less contested and more stable factors upon which to make decisions.

In the next section, I examine how the United States combined visual with verbal depictions of the gulf's features to literalize a network of associations generated from what I will call a "bounded sea" system of metaphor.

Literalizing the Metaphorical: A Bounded Sea

During oral testimony, Dr. Robert Edwards, U.S. chief science advisor, explained that "boundaries and/or discontinuities are formed where two dissimilar areas meet"[84] and proceeded to show that geomorphological, climatic, and biotic boundaries coincided at the Northeast Channel. As a geomorphological boundary, Edwards said, the Northeast Channel is as much a "fixed" discontinuity as "mountains, valleys and shorelines, that separate or bisect plains and plateaux."[85] Edwards used a three-dimensional computer image to show that the Northeast Channel was the "critical" geomorphological feature on the gulf's seabed, dividing "Georges Bank, on the west, from Browns Bank in the southwestern part of the Nova Scotian Shelf on the east."[86] This reinforced written pleadings where the United States had argued that the Northeast Channel is a "significant" natural boundary because it was the only major "break" in the continental shelf's surface within the Gulf of Maine area.[87]

The Northeast Channel's geomorphological significance as a fixed locus of discontinuity was buttressed during written pleadings partly by an unstated riparian analogy. According to the U.S. geological narrative, the channel had ancient riparian origins as one of "two major drainage systems" in the area, with the other located "over what is now the western part of Georges Bank" (that is, the Great South Channel). During a later glacial period, "a tongue of the ice sheet covering the Gulf of Maine advanced though what is now the Northeast Channel, reaching the open sea. The scouring action by the ice sheet widened and deepened the Channel, and gave it its present U-shaped profile."[88] When the last glacier receded, the Northeast Channel's site was protected from glacial outwash deposits, but the western drainage system was "inundated" and "choked," leaving as its remnant the Great South Channel: "an ill-defined, shallow depression on the southwestern part of Georges

Bank." Today, as a result, the Great South Channel fails to reach "the seaward edge of the continental shelf," while the Northeast Channel is "four to five times deeper and does extend to the seaward edge of the continental slope."[89] The Northeast Channel, unlike its much shallower counterpart, is the Gulf of Maine basin's only "direct and deep access to the Atlantic Ocean" and is, thus, the "gateway through which deep (greater than two hundred meters) oceanic water enters the Gulf of Maine Basin."[90] Why does that difference make the Northeast Channel "significant"? The answer is due partly to an implied riparian association. The Northeast Channel divides or separates the continental shelf area from its origin in the deep basin until it meets the shelf edge, much as a river divides or bisects terrestrial areas from its source of origin until it meets the sea.

The Northeast Channel not only separates Georges Bank from the Scotian Shelf, but also functions to determine the movements and characteristics of bounded water masses above the gulf's geomorphological features.[91] Edwards used figure C7, "Water Circulation in the Gulf of Maine Area," to show how "water circulates through the area following a serpentine path that divides the area into three major regimes": the northwest-to-southeast "pass-through" pattern over the Scotian Shelf, the large clockwise gyre over Georges Bank, and the large counterclockwise gyre over the Gulf of Maine basin.[92] The Northeast Channel directs deep Atlantic water from the continental slope into the basin, "gradually mixing up through the water to the top, mixing with the surface waters from the Scotian Shelf, and changing the character of what follows from that point on."[93]

The circulation map embeds a "narrative pattern" against the analytical and topographical backdrop of the U.S. base map.[94] Arrow lines symbolize water currents as "vectors,"[95] indicating active, directional movement. Their curvaceous shapes and different sizes symbolize the dynamism and variable power of natural forces,[96] creating a sense of movement among the passive, stationary, and inert features of a static, unchanging, geomorphological scene. But the scene's passive features constrain those movements. The Northeast Channel is seen as the gateway through which large water currents both enter and exit the gulf's basin. The deep ocean current (symbolized with a large red arrow) moves southwestward until it splits at the mouth of the channel near the continental slope, with one branch passing through the channel until it enters the interior basin, where it splits again. The current retains its massive volume (the "branches" equal the size of the original "trunk"), filling the basin continuously, interacting and blending with surface currents. Surface currents (symbolized with medium blue arrows) move southwestward along the Scotian Shelf until drawn into the gulf's interior where they are resisted, diverted, and assimilated into a single large current. That large surface current (the large blue arrow) then winds around the western and southern "edges" of the basin, along the north side of Georges Bank, and exits through the Northeast Channel, where it resumes its southwestern journey along the continental shelf edge. Meanwhile, smaller surface currents (symbolized with small blue arrows) spin off and form a small gyre on Browns Bank (the small, clockwise arrow), a large, counterclockwise gyre over the basin, and a large clockwise gyre over Georges Bank.

The map's visual structure tells a story of active movement and passive resistance in which dynamic serpentine water currents move among the stationary features of a static, topographic scene to form distinct, bounded water columns. The central locus of that scene is the Northeast Channel, where the main "characters"—the massive ocean currents—enter and exit the Gulf of Maine basin and, thus, complement the implied "river in the sea" associations. Thus, the channel is again seen as the gulf's central locus of natural division and separation. In addition, the channel directs massive currents to make the "supporting cast" of bounded, distinctive water "regimes" appear at Georges Bank and the Scotian Shelf, as well as in the interior basin.

The United States argued that Scotian Shelf waters from the Labrador Current and continental slope waters entering through the Northeast Channel created three climatic regimes distinguishable by salinity concentrations and temperature distributions.[97] As a result, "marked fronts" emerge between the bounded regimes whenever they come into contact.[98] The United States explained that fronts separating different water bodies "are similar to the familiar weather fronts that separate cold air masses from warm air masses"[99] in that both give rise to climatic boundaries. Of special significance is the well-defined front that exists over the Northeast Channel "between the waters of Georges Bank and those of the Scotian Shelf"[100] that can "limit movement and exchange between regimes of many species of marine organisms."[101]

The United States produced remotely sensed satellite images of sea surface temperature to help literalize the idea of "fronts" between different bounded water regimes.[102] One image superimposed temperature gradients to mark out "where fronts form between the contrasting regimes of Georges Bank and of the Gulf of Maine Basin and between those of the Scotian Shelf and of the Gulf of Maine Basin."[103] Edwards used that image during oral pleadings to show gradients "on the eastern tip of Georges Bank" and "on the western side of Browns Bank" that are "bordering the Northeast Channel."[104]

The Northeast Channel is therefore the site of a climatic as well as a geomorphological boundary. According to Edwards, "The significance to the oceanography of the Gulf of Maine area, of the higher salinity and more consistently temperatured slope water, is that it is injected into the Gulf of Maine Basin through the Northeast Channel, radically altering the character of the water of the Basin and subsequently that of Georges Bank."[105] That "injection" creates a "*dichotomy* . . . between the waters of the Scotian Shelf and the waters of the Gulf of Maine Basin and Georges Bank [emphasis added]."[106]

When different climatic regimes make contact, the fronts that arise between them resist assimilation of one regime into the other and thereby limit interchange of marine organisms between them. Boundaries evidently work from restraints *within* as well as resistance from *without* different regimes to "define and integrate the biological communities."[107] The food chain is one biotic restraint on the movements of marine organisms in the Georges Bank and Scotian Shelf regimes. Simply put, marine organisms will follow their food sources: "The distribution and abundance of phytoplankton and zooplankton, the initial links in the marine food chain, determine to a large extent the location of other species, including commercial fish and shellfish that feed upon them."[108] Since phytoplankton lack locomotive powers, they are retained by the water patterns and characteristics that define the Georges Bank and Scotian Shelf regimes. Zooplankton feed on phytoplankton, larger organisms feed on zooplankton, and so on, up through the entire chain of predator-prey linkages to the commercial fish stocks. All are tethered together as links in a chain that keeps them within one or the other regime. One easily extends that chain to include American and Canadian predators that, evidently, should prey on commercial fish stocks contained within their own respective ecological regimes.

The United States used remotely sensed images of chlorophyll data to literalize associations about bounded "ecological regimes" containing aquatic food chains, one of which appears as figure C8.[109] The description that accompanies the image relates variable phytoplankton concentrations to the gulf's central, bounded features: "In the Gulf of Maine area, phytoplankton are most plentiful in the well-mixed waters along the coast, in the mouth of the Bay of Fundy, and over Georges Bank. Phytoplankton are also plentiful over the shallower banks of the Scotian Shelf. They are not plentiful in the Northeast Channel or in the center of the Gulf of Maine Basin."[110] Thus, the different phytoplankton concentrations show that the Northeast Channel again serves as a natural boundary dividing the Georges Bank and Scotian Shelf "ecological regimes."

We can see (or learn to see) on figure C8 the discrete bounded shapes of Georges Bank and the Scotian Shelf as easily as the familiar shapes of Long Island, Cape Cod, and Nova Scotia. The Northeast Channel, appearing in green, follows its course from the interior Gulf of Maine basin toward the black, deeper ocean waters farther seaward, separating the two banks. Indeed, Georges Bank and Nova Scotia are readily seen as symmetrical features of the gulf's environment; the peninsula under the sea seems the mirror image of the peninsula above the sea. When these configurations are seen, natural boundary associations seem literal and factual. But what are we actually "seeing"? The discrete shapes of Georges Bank, the Northeast Channel, and the Scotian Shelf are presentational symbols standing for those natural features; they are not representational copies of those features, per se, but highly processed images of large aggregates of data. Discrete shapes emerge from mathematical correlations between a chlorophyll concentration gradient and a color gradient, and the color gradient is of central importance to how the image is seen.[111]

Any notion of gradient is prefigured by what classical rhetoricians called *incrementum*. *Incrementum* is the figure of speech that constructs a series according to some increasing quality.[112] Here we have an instance of visual *incrementum* that displays chlorophyll concentration increases on each side of the Northeast Channel. Start from the green channel and look toward either the southeastern New England or the southwestern Nova Scotia coasts, and chlorophyll concentrations increase as they progress from yellow to orange-red and to a darker, brown-red. The channel, then, is seen as the locus of division between the two contrary, ascending color series.

The United States also claimed that water currents and climatic fronts retained the fish eggs and larvae of commercially important fish species and, thus, worked to separate them into discrete stocks on Georges Bank and the Scotian Shelf. For instance, the United States wrote that many stocks are divided because "the gyre formed by the waters overlying Georges Bank and the gyre overlying Browns Bank keep free-floating eggs and larvae of the fish and shellfish that inhabit these separate areas within their respective ecological regimes, where they mature, grow, and ultimately may be harvested. The water circulation patterns also help to prevent free-floating eggs and larvae of one regime from entering the other. Similarly, mature fish and shellfish of many species normally do not cross the Northeast Channel between Georges Bank and the Scotian Shelf."[113] Regardless of whether stocks were retained by food chains or by current patterns, stock separations and divisions were visually amplified with a graphic that implied the presence of an obstacle to interchange from one regime to the other at the Northeast Channel.

In its memorial, the United States literalized associations about the Northeast Channel as the central "natural" locus of division between commercial fish stocks using the graphic presented here as figure C9.[114] Figure C9 shows "sharp stock divisions at the Northeast Channel in 12 of the 16 species depicted."[115] Using yellowtail flounder as an example, the

United States said the horizontal bars showed a "sharp division marked by a separation between the stocks . . . at the Northeast Channel, and a less well-defined division between the stocks . . . west of Georges Bank."[116] That example illustrated that the "natural boundary" at the Northeast Channel "divides the Georges Bank regime from that of the Scotian Shelf," divides "many species of fish and shellfish into separate stocks," and, thus, "makes it both possible and appropriate to manage the stocks over Georges Bank separately from the stocks over the Scotian Shelf."[117] But the chart visually implied an additional association about the boundary's "dividing" and "separating" functions.

The chart is structured with a topological pattern. Kress and van Leeuwen explain that this pattern is "read as accurately representing the logical relations between participants, the way in which participants are connected to each other (whether they have common boundaries, or are partially or wholly included in each other, in which sequence they are connected, and so forth) but not the actual physical size of the participants or their distance from each other. . . . "[118] Here, sixteen important commercial species are related to a common boundary at the Northeast Channel to show whether they divide into discrete Georges Bank (in blue) and Browns Bank (in green) stocks or remain single, continuous stocks. The two banks mark potential stock locations within the gulf area, with Block Island and LaHave Bank symbolizing outlying locations to the southwest and to the northeast. Solid horizontal bars designate "range limits" for the fish stocks. The chart's structure resembles that of subway maps insofar as each bar tracks possible destinations along a linear, spatial sequence. We are invited by the chart's descriptive title to follow the horizontal blue bars from left to right across Georges Bank, and as we do, our readings are disrupted at the vertical line symbolizing the Northeast Channel, even if the blue bar continues—as it does in four cases—through that line. The sense of disruption is amplified when horizontal blue bars stop before the vertical line and then reappear in dark green on the other side, thus distinguishing separate stocks. These visual disruptions are easily associated with the presence of an obstacle that, somehow, impedes interchange between stocks on the two banks.

We can demonstrate how this visual arrangement generates the "obstacle" illusion by violating anticipated reading patterns. Read right to left *away* from the Northeast Channel across Georges Bank, and you see that haddock and cusk ranges end and longfin begin *within* Georges Bank, while redfish end near the bank's edge and scallops just beyond that edge. Are there unseen barriers or obstacles to passage of stocks at those locations? All others go beyond Georges Bank and reach, in variable strengths (lesser amounts are indicated with light green lines), as far southwest as Block Island. Read left to right *away* from the Northeast Channel across Browns Bank, and yellowtail stock end slightly beyond that bank's edge, lobster end within Browns Bank, and scallops both begin and end within Browns Bank. What impedes movement of those stocks? All other stocks continue to LaHave Bank, evidently, in strength. These alternative readings do not readily suggest the presence of barriers to passage; only readings disrupted by the vertical line invite that implication.

The United States did not frequently depict the Northeast Channel as a "barrier" during written pleadings, but during oral pleadings that word was used interchangeably with natural "boundary." This shift in terminological emphasis might have been due partly to a felt need to address before the tribunal Canada's accusation that the United States failed to cite any scientific work that "describes three separate and identifiable regimes in the Gulf of Maine area or that describes the Northeast Channel as a 'natural boundary.'"[119] That criticism implies that "ecological regimes" and "natural boundary" are ad hoc constructs rather than legitimate scientific terminology. During his testimony, Edwards used the published work of Canadian scientists who called the Northeast Channel a "barrier" to the movements of cod and haddock and, at the prompting of the U.S. lawyer, made the nationality of the source abundantly clear.[120] He acknowledged that there was no scientific work that "explicitly labels the three areas we have discussed as 'regimes,'" but stressed that scientists "as a matter of course" recognize them as "distinct areas for a variety of scientific and management purposes."[121] Indeed, the United States and Canada had "recognized for decades" the "existence of separate stocks in one or more of these three regimes" in "all attempts to conserve and manage the marine resources of the area."[122] "If a general fact is well known and accepted," Edwards said, "individuals do not feel the need to state it in writing, although acceptance of that fact, and what it implies, may underlie other work that they do."[123] At the conclusion of his testimony, then, Edwards affirmed as facts that "the Northeast Channel does form a natural boundary or barrier, and that there are separate stocks on Georges Bank."[124]

U.S. written and oral pleadings were replete with verbal and visual depictions that evoked a network of what I have called "bounded sea" associations, inviting a view of the Gulf of Maine as consisting of a "natural boundary" at the Northeast Channel separating and dividing discrete bounded "ecological regimes" on each of its sides. The Northeast Channel is a natural boundary with qualities of a river in the sea, of a weather front, of the limits of food chains, of a barrier. Whether verbalized explicitly or visually implied, those associations are literalized as factual attributes of the Northeast Channel *as it is* and not as metaphorical resemblances portraying the Northeast Channel *as if* it were a "natural boundary." Hence, the Northeast Channel *is* a natural locus of separation and division, of dichotomies and discontinuities splitting the gulf area, of obstacles to passage or interchange of fishing stocks. It does stand between two discrete bounded entities: the Georges Bank and Scotian Shelf regimes. For its part, Canada sought to refigure these purported facts and their implied and verbalized attributes as fanciful, thereby disrupting the view of the gulf's marine environment that the United States wanted the tribunal to take.

Refiguring the Literal: An Unbounded Sea

Canada contended that the gulf area does not consist of bounded ecological regimes divided by a natural boundary at the Northeast Channel, arguing instead that it is best seen as part of a climatic and biotic "continuum" or "integrated ocean system."[125] Though rejecting the possibility of natural boundaries in the sea and disavowing any interest in mounting its own "natural boundary theory," Canada's legal strategists could not escape the need to delineate "discontinuities" that bounded their proposed continuum or ocean system.[126] Any notion of spatial continuity implies discontinuity; a continuum must begin and end somewhere. Hence, Canada argued for discontinuities or limits—in other words, natural boundaries!—that set their proposed continuum apart from its surrounding environment. The proposed continuum extended from the northeastern boreal waters of the Canadian offshore environment through the Gulf of Maine to a "transition zone" in the vicinity of the Great South Channel, the Nantucket Shoals, and Cape Cod.[127] Georges Bank, its flora and fauna, are thereby tied more closely "to the Canadian offshore environment than to that of the United States."[128] Not at all incidentally, by shifting attention to species rather than stocks, Canada claimed that commercially important fish reached their range limits at the transition zone near the Great South Channel.[129] "Georges Bank stocks" no longer could be seen as "somehow synonymous with 'United States stocks'"; instead, seen from a species orientation, "many of the fish stocks on Georges Bank are far more closely associated with waters off Nova Scotia than with waters southwest of Georges Bank."[130]

Even as Canada delineated purportedly more significant natural discontinuities in the area,[131] they drew upon incongruous common-sense associations about the sea to portray the United States' "natural boundary" as the necessary result of exaggeration and distortion. Those criticisms associated "boundaries" with terrestrial barriers so that U.S. boundary depictions seemingly exhibited qualities contrary to the open, dynamic, and featureless sea:

> The sea, it need hardly be said, is a fluid environment: a dynamic, not static, medium. Its fundamental characteristics are its openness and relative uniformity. Unlike the land, the sea is not marked by geographically fixed discontinuities or boundaries. Changes in water properties that do exist are gradual and highly variable in location. . . . Only inordinate distortions of scale and serious oversimplifications can sustain any hypothesis of "natural boundaries" in the water column.[132]

Similarly, Canada argued that the U.S. proposal to consider "natural features" in determining maritime boundaries was based on a "false analogy" with land features. Land features —such as mountains or deserts—are conspicuous, but the sea is "generally featureless"; it "has no natural barriers."[133] In any case, Canada contended, even associating land features with natural boundaries is a misnomer since legal boundaries always are artificial and political; to think it more "natural" to locate a line in one place rather than another is illusory.[134]

In its countermemorial, Canada identified the purported natural boundary at the Northeast Channel with a "so-called stock barrier,"[135] using the words "boundary" and "barrier" interchangeably during criticism of U.S. portrayals of the stock divisions on figure C9. Adding twelve species to the sixteen the United States displayed on that figure, Canada argued that fourteen of the twenty-eight traversed the Northeast Channel in commercially important numbers.[136] "Ten (mackerel, pollock, shortfin squid, bluefin tuna, swordfish, saury, American shad, spiny dogfish, alewife, Atlantic salmon)" migrated "throughout all the areas the United States Memorial describes as 'separate and identifiable ecological regimes,' completely ignoring the 'boundaries' of all of them. The Northeast Channel does not separate stocks of these species." The remaining four—lobster, cusk, angler, argentine —actually concentrated in the channel, which, therefore, is "far from being a barrier." Of the other fourteen, twelve are not impeded by either the barrier or the ecological boundaries.[137] Longfin do not range far enough to the northeast to even reach the channel, so it cannot "represent a stock barrier for this species." Butterfish reach the limit of their migratory range at Georges Bank, so their absence on Browns Bank is not due to a boundary. Stocks of redfish, American plaice, witch flounder, and white hake do not abut the channel, which, therefore, "cannot be represented as a stock barrier for these species." Silver hake and red hake have stocks at Georges Bank that cross into the basin, thus "'violating' the limits" of two regimes. Atlantic herring stocks intermingle during their life histories "by crossing the 'boundaries' of all three alleged 'regimes.'" Haddock, cod, and scallops form "equally important stock discontinuities *within* so-called 'ecological regimes' as they do *between* 're-gimes.'" Thus, in all but two cases (yellowtail flounder and witch flounder), stocks did not "in fact" divide due to a barrier or boundary at the Northeast Channel.[138]

During oral pleadings, the two parties contested the legitimacy of calling the Northeast Channel a stock "boundary" or "barrier." The United States defended its display of stock divisions on figure C9 by arguing that Canada accepted all but one of them when negotiating the failed East Coast Fisheries Agreement. Why, then, should Canada reject them now?[139] Part of Edwards's testimony elaborated on six of the original twelve stock divisions, including the use of Canadian research mentioned earlier that claimed, among other things, that the Northeast Channel mounts a "barrier" to haddock and cod.[140] During cross-examination of Edwards, Canada returned to figure C9 to criticize the purported boundary divisions for four of the six stocks he did not mention in his testimony.[141] The Canadian lawyer amplified the point that longfin could not be divided into separate stocks by the Northeast Channel since there was no longfin stock on the Scotian side to separate from the stock on the Georges Bank side.[142] Canada also advanced the criticism that claims about the Northeast Channel separating stocks between the two sides were "inexact" for cusk, based on insufficient information for white hake, and wrong for redfish.[143]

At the end of his cross-examination, Canada worked to confound Edwards's earlier attempts to distinguish and qualify different kinds of boundaries. In his testimony, Edwards tried to distinguish geomorphological from climatic boundaries by claiming that the former are as "geographically fixed" as those found on the land, while the latter are more variable across space and time.[144] Neither are "impenetrable walls" that mount "absolute obstacles to the passage of organisms," Edwards explained, but both still "discourage passage."[145] Similarly, he had qualified understanding of fish stocks in relation to ecological "boundaries": "The three regimes in the Gulf of Maine area are not surrounded by walls."[146] Thus, the existence of discrete stocks on Georges Bank does not mean that individual members remain there during their entire life histories. Canada ignored such subtleties and conflated geomorphological boundaries in the seabed with climatic and, by implication, biotic boundaries in the water column: all became "fixed boundaries in the sea."[147] The penultimate moment came when Edwards was asked near the end of cross-examination whether he always believed in the idea of fixed boundaries in the sea. After ignoring Edwards's attempt to again distinguish geomorphological from climatic boundaries, the Canadian lawyer directed attention to one of Edwards's articles where he wrote, "Terrestrial ecosystems are relatively stable in their geographic boundaries and in their persistence. . . . In the ocean, boundaries and distribution of ecosystems change constantly."[148]

On the final day, the United States suddenly minimized the importance of calling the Northeast Channel a "natural boundary" in favor of depicting it merely as a locus of division and separation between stocks. A U.S. lawyer argued, "In [figure C9] the United States illustrated that the Northeast Channel divides—and here I will use the word, or limits—separate stocks of 12 and [*sic*] 16 commercially important species in the Gulf of Maine area. You may call this a natural boundary if you wish, or you may simply refer to it as a stock division. Whatever it is called, the Northeast Channel limits the range of these 12 species."[149] He then contended that since Canada criticized only four of the stocks during cross-examination, "we can assume that Canada does not seriously dispute the other information shown" on figure C9.[150] The United States turned again to technical papers used in

Canada's memorial to show that they referred to "'discrete'—that is the word that Canada uses—stocks of haddock, cod, yellowtail flounder, and Atlantic herring found on Georges Bank" and contained other depictions that comported with U.S. portrayals of all but one of the remaining species on the figure.[151] Indeed, before moving on to argue that fisheries institutions have used the Northeast Channel as a "stock division," he compared Canada's "new-found skepticism" at the trial—which "flies in the face of what long has been accepted in the scientific community"—with suggesting "that the Earth is at the centre of the solar system."[152]

Canada invited the tribunal to see the claim that the Northeast Channel is a natural boundary dividing two ecological regimes as an invention, ad hoc theory, or "myth" used by the United States in the attempt to secure all of Georges Bank for its own nationals. Canada's criticisms generated incongruous associations about the sea and boundaries that, if accepted, would render the United States' purportedly factual natural boundary claim "merely" metaphorical. Hence, the natural boundary's alleged qualities as a locus of separation and division, of dichotomies and discontinuities, of obstacles to passage or interchange are transformed from factual attributes of the Northeast Channel *as it is* into metaphorical associations for screening thought about the Northeast Channel *as if* it were a natural boundary. To accept the idea that the Northeast Channel is literally, in fact, a natural boundary required overlooking what Canada presumed throughout its criticisms were incongruous, common sense "factual" attributes about the sea *as it is:* its fluidity, its openness, its dynamism, its uniformity. And legal issues are settled by applying the law to facts, not to invented fictions.

Canada apparently succeeded in refiguring the United States' purported facts about natural boundaries as metaphorical and, thus, as irrelevant to legal adjudication. The chamber set aside technical distinctions between geomorphological and water column boundaries and turned instead to commonplace associations about natural boundaries and about the ocean that rendered them mutually incompatible:

> The Chamber is not . . . convinced of the possibility of discerning any genuine, sure and stable "natural boundaries" in so fluctuating an environment as the waters of the ocean, their flora and fauna. It has thus reached the conviction that it would be vain to seek, in data derived from the biogeography of the waters covering certain areas of sea-bed, any element sufficient to confer the property of a stable natural boundary— and what is more, one serving a double purpose—on a geomorphological accident which influences superadjacent waters but which is clearly inadequate to be seen as a natural boundary in respect of the sea-bed itself.
>
> The Chamber accordingly considers that the conclusion to be drawn in respect of the great mass of water belonging to the delimitation area is that it too essentially possesses the same character of unity and uniformity already apparent from an examination of the sea-bed, so that, in respect of the waters too, one must take note of the impossibility of discerning any natural boundary capable of serving as a basis for carrying out a delimitation of the kind requested of the Chamber.[153]

Genuine natural boundaries are "stable," the sea "fluctuates"; boundaries "differentiate," the sea is "uniform." The two cannot be joined. To do so is more myth than science, more metaphor than fact. Therefore, the chamber did not even need to address the question upon which the U.S. conservation argument hinged: whether the "legal-political operation" of boundary delimitation should follow, whenever possible, discernable natural boundaries. In this case, the chamber concluded "there are no geological, geomorphological, ecological or other factors sufficiently important, evident and conclusive to represent a single, incontrovertible natural boundary."[154]

Conclusions

Displays involve showing, making manifest, exhibiting. Visual *taxis* functions rhetorically both in shaping how features of the displayed are shown or made manifest and in disposing the attitudes of those who become audience to them. I have focused on the relationship of visual *taxis* to the verbal dynamic between literalizing metaphorically generated associations as factual and refiguring purportedly factual attributes as metaphorical. This chapter has shown that presentational symbols can function as literalized metaphors and that culturally available patterns of visual narration or logic can interrelate presentational symbols in ways that integrate metaphorical associations within coherent, literalized perspectives. Examination of both levels of visual *taxis* enables us to orient ourselves within a visual display's perspective and discern how it functions rhetorically to structure attitudes and associations. Several implications follow from the analyses conducted in this chapter.

This chapter offers a rhetorical perspective on the design and use of sophisticated graphics in practical communication that directs attention to how visual structures selectively symbolize and interrelate features seen and, thereby, dispose the attitudes of those who see those features through that "structured" perspective. For example, the base maps invited the tribunal to adopt partial orientations toward the gulf's marine environment through placement of different features at the center and the margins, through display of distinct visual metaphors and presentational symbols, and through imposition of analytical patterns. Commentators on the technical use of graphics in forensics acknowledge and sometimes tellingly illustrate their persuasive functions, but they generally stress securing understanding through display of accurate, clear, and relevant information.[155] In contrast, attention to the rhetoric of visual *taxis* would emphasize how graphical displays are selectively constituted and, thus, enact partial points of view. The mere presence of selectivity is not insidious, since it is indelibly involved in constituting visual displays, but the fact that visual displays necessarily must conceal even as they reveal is itself an important rhetorical resource for those who create or evaluate visual evidence.

The display of scientific objectivity is an important dimension of many visual graphics. We saw how visual structures incorporated in the base maps implied neutrality and impartiality even as they inclined viewers to adopt subtly partisan perspectives. Maps and satellite images, in particular, enact a "top-down," "god-like" perspective that is "the angle of maximum power," which, in turn, is evocative of "objective knowledge."[156] But any appearance of pure objectivity is illusory, since visual depictions always are limned with selections that, if revealed, expose the play of partiality behind the displays. Thus, we saw how the two parties attempted to snap that illusion by questioning motives behind the selection of specific scales or simply by exhibiting different configurations of the features seen on the maps. The chamber was probably susceptible to those appeals, since they were concerned about "having the wool pulled over their eyes" by technical manipulation, as one participant put it.[157] Of course, not all audiences would be troubled by simple exposure of selectivity. For example, an audience expert in marine ecology would not necessarily reject U.S. graphics based on Canada's criticisms, even should it dismiss natural boundary claims. Such an audience is likely to see the displays as more or less accurate approximations or resemblances of natural patterns rather than as depicting findings that are exclusively either right or wrong, true or false.

This chapter examined how visual *taxis* relates to the dynamic between literalizing the metaphorical and refiguring the literal. That dynamic itself points to an important dimension of the rhetoric of display. Metaphor, strictly understood, is rhetorical display through verbally pointing out or showing otherwise unseen relationships. Metaphors become literalized when awareness of vehicle-tenor interactions fades; *as if* resemblances thus become attributes of identity or qualities of the thing *as it is.* I contended that this shift from the metaphorical to the literal is accomplished through visual as well as verbal depiction. Presentational symbols and visual patterns for interrelating them function to structure perspectives so that metaphorically generated associations are seen as identifiable attributes of the tenor or principal subject as it is rather than imagined as points of resemblance between vehicle and tenor, subsidiary and principal subject. In the gulf case, maps and other graphics were rhetorical displays that exhibited, made manifest, or "showed forth" literalized metaphors and corollary associations as indisputable facts, grounds, and premises that could then, in turn, be used in support of more contestable claims. But those displays were subject to challenge, since literalizing tendencies are reversible. Whether through visual or verbal depiction, vehicle-tenor interactions can be reanimated; factual attributes can be refigured as "mere" resemblances. The United States and Canada thus enacted visual and verbal displays that participated in both countervailing tendencies of this rhetorical dynamic. For instance, each party exhibited Georges Bank as a literalized metaphor and sought to refigure the other's visual portrayal. And, of course, at the center of the dispute was the United States' exhibition of the fact that the Northeast Channel is a natural boundary and Canada's refiguring of that purported fact and its corollary associations as metaphorical or otherwise fictional.

The Canadians prevailed rhetorically with the court in refiguring natural boundary claims as metaphorical. We can infer the chamber's standard for finding facts about technical matters from its decision. In its quest for impartial grounds, the chamber wanted results from the debate between the two parties that were sufficient "to clear away all doubt, at least as regards certain of the technical aspects debated."[158] The United States was decidedly disadvantaged in meeting so exacting a standard for establishing the "fact" that the Northeast Channel is a natural boundary and, thus, a suitable location for the legal boundary. The more the United States had to defend or qualify claims about the existence of a natural boundary between two bounded "ecological regimes" in the gulf's water column, the less likely the tribunal would come to accept it as an unambiguous fact. As it turns out, all Canada needed to do was render "natural boundary" or "barrier" designations sufficiently ambiguous or theoretical so that they seemed bereft of the objective (that is, undebatable, uncontested) facts that the chamber wanted as its basis for forming an impartial decision.[159] It is not surprising, then, that the chamber relied on proverbial knowledge about the sea (its fluidity, featurelessness, uniformity, continuity, instability, unpredictability) and about natural boundaries (solid, fixed, conspicuous) when assessing what became a relatively complex "theory" of natural boundaries.[160]

The ICJ chamber's straightforward dismissal of U.S. natural boundary claims should not be taken to mean that alternative resolutions of this particular manifestation of the literalizing-refiguring dynamic are not possible. The United States was not wrong, nor was Canada right, in any absolute sense. Details about stock "boundaries" and "barriers" are arguable, but it was not implausible for the United States to emphasize that discrete stocks of several commercially important fish species would largely remain intact for managerial purposes if a jurisdictional line were drawn along the Northeast Channel. As the United States stressed during oral pleadings, Canadians evidently agreed with that portrayal in other, nonforensic contexts. Indeed, some Canadian scientists literally referred to the Northeast Channel as a stock "barrier," evidently unaware of its metaphorical or fictive qualities. For practical purposes, then, one could call the Northeast Channel a "natural" boundary dividing stocks and do so as though describing it as it is; it limits, separates, or divides intact stocks found on Georges Bank from those found on the Scotian Shelf. Similarly, Canada's emphasis on the sea's commonplace attributes to refigure "natural boundary" associations could itself be challenged as insufficiently factual with its own arguments about the natural marine environment. Canada marked out a continuum with a "transition zone" or locus of discontinuity that divided the distribution of cold and warm water fish species. From that vantage, discontinuities, divisions, limits, boundaries, and barriers seem literally to describe the sea as it is. Moreover, since those apparently factual attributes are not humanly created, why not call them natural? Indeed, if we accept those factual attributes we must also reconsider the alleged uniformity, featurelessness, and unboundedness of the sea. Are those features merely metaphorical, mythical, or fictive when applied to the purported transition zone? Evidently, Canada, too, was engaged in literalizing boundary or barrier associations even as it sought to refigure similar associations as counterintuitive and counterfactual given commonplace—but not necessarily scientific—understandings of the sea.

Examination of how particular manifestations of the literalizing-refiguring dynamic are played out rhetorically involves attending to the influences of the situated context and audience. One consideration that relates to a general problem of technical communication is whether untrained audiences are prepared to distinguish metaphorical from literal depictions of complex subject matters. When technical information is communicated to an untrained audience, forms of visual demonstration are often deployed along with metaphors and other verbal means of simplifying and clarifying complex material to enhance comprehension. But the use of metaphors encounters special communicative obstacles with untrained audiences since they usually cannot think about the technical subject *on its own terms*. Put slightly otherwise, when offered a metaphor to enhance understanding, they cannot always distinguish the tenor from the vehicle. C. S. Lewis would call such metaphors "pupillary" to distinguish them from the "master" metaphors wielded by the more technically proficient who *can* express the tenor on its own terms, or at least in terms other than that of the single, simplifying vehicle.[161] As a result, the technically uninitiated audience, unaware of alternative possibilities for thought and expression, might take that which only resembles the tenor to be the tenor itself; they thus treat metaphors as though they have been literalized. Literalizing tendencies are further reinforced when exhibited in some visual form, as in the case of images of the ozone hole or the Gulf Stream.

The dynamic between literalizing the metaphorical and refiguring the factual is nearly ubiquitous to situated language use, but we can anticipate distinctive kinds of situations where visual *taxis* will participate in that dynamic. The study in this chapter shows that the adversarial ethic of Anglo-American legal procedures makes it difficult to literalize metaphors, through verbal or visual means, since they always are potentially open to rebuttals and, thus, refiguration; yet, forensic pleading is replete with cases in which visual exhibitions prevail rhetorically. What is needed are studies of the rhetoric of visual *taxis* that is operative in such cases. Visual displays other than graphical depictions of purportedly impartial scientific information can also be studied in terms of how visual *taxis* relates to the literalizing-refiguring dynamic. "Demonstrative showings" exhibited in the bodily actions of guerrilla theater or in the spectacles of rallies, street demonstrations, and marches could be considered as visual manifestations of this dynamic. As Hauser and Blitefield show in this volume, demonstrative actions constitute a kind of bodily "proving" or structuring of perspective in which "claims" are advanced as indisputable, as certain, or as a "matter of fact." And, of course, demonstrations, too, can be refigured as manifesting fiction rather than fact, the "merely" metaphorical rather than the literal. Celebratory situations involving praise of people, ideas, or practices are promising for studies of how verbal depictions engage the literalizing-refiguring dynamic, since they typically invite efforts to literalize metaphors without expectation of efforts to critically refigure them. Visual *taxis* often is involved in less obvious "celebrations" that we encounter on a nearly daily basis. For example, celebrations of scientific and technological prowess through televisual and other displays of sophisticated images of phenomena ranging from the molecular to the astronomical, from the extraordinary discovery displayed on the nightly news to the familiar weather patterns seen on the nightly weather report. These and other often subtle celebratory displays also invite consideration of how visual *taxis* operates rhetorically to literalize the metaphorical as fact and to refigure the factual as metaphorical.

Notes

1. *Case Concerning Delimitation of the Maritime Boundary in the Gulf of Maine Area (Canada v. United States of America),* 1984 ICJ 246 (October 12, 1984) (hereinafter *Gulf of Maine*).

2. Davis R. Robinson, David A. Colson, and Bruce C. Rashkow, "Some Perspectives on Adjudicating before the World Court: The Gulf of Maine Case," *American Journal of International Law* 79 (1985): 579n5. For the legal context behind the unilateral declarations, see Mark B. Feldman and David Colson, "The Maritime Boundaries of the United States," *American Journal of International Law* 75 (1981): 754–56.

3. Jan Schneider, "The Gulf of Maine Case: The Nature of an Equitable Result," *American Journal of International Law* 79 (1985): 541–42; and Paul D. McHugh, "International Law—Delimitation of Maritime Boundaries," *Natural Resources Journal* 25 (1985): 1025–26.

4. See the account of political and legal contexts in Lawrence J. Prelli and Mimi Larsen Becker, "Learning from the Limits of an Adjudicatory Strategy for Resolving United States-Canada Fisheries Conflicts: Lessons from the Gulf of Maine," *Natural Resources Journal* 41 (2001): 450–55.

5. Feldman and Colson, "Maritime Boundaries," 758–59; Robinson and others, "The Gulf of Maine Case," 591.

6. Robinson and others, "The Gulf of Maine Case," 591n38.

7. Interview with deputy agent and counsel for the United States in the Gulf of Maine case, Washington, D.C., July 29, 1997.

8. Ibid.

9. For discussion of that U.S. strategy, see Prelli and Becker, "Learning from the Limits of an Adjudicatory Strategy for Resolving United States-Canada Fisheries Conflicts,"456–58.

10. Memorial of the United States of America, *I.C.J. Pleadings* (Delimitation of the Maritime Boundary in the Gulf of Maine Area) 2, submitted September 27, 1982, 247–51; also see 183–97 (hereinafter U.S. Mem.). Legal documents filed with the ICJ are called memorials, counter-memorials, and replies. A memorial presents the initial case, framing and responding to the points at issue. A countermemorial responds to the adversary's memorial and strengthens the case initially conveyed in one's own memorial. A reply responds to the adversary's challenges mounted in its countermemorial and further sharpens arguments central to one's own case. All citations to these documents are by paragraph number.

11. U.S. Mem., 296.

12. U.S. Mem., 31, 58.

13. U.S. Mem., 58.

14. U.S. Mem., 249–50, 316–17. For discussion of the "failure" of bilateral and multilateral agreements to foster conservation, see 189–92.

15. Counter-Memorial of the United States of America, *I.C.J. Pleadings* (Delimitation of the Maritime Boundary in the Gulf of Maine Area) 4, submitted June 28, 1983, 313, 349–57 (hereinafter U.S. CM); also see U.S. Mem., 318, 329.

16. Reply of the United States of America, *I.C.J. Pleadings* (Delimitation of the Maritime Boundary in the Gulf of Maine Area) 5, submitted December 12, 1983, 168 (hereinafter U.S. Rep.). The United States here contrasts the permanence of natural features with more transitory socioeconomic concerns.

17. Reply of Canada, *I.C.J. Pleadings* (Delimitation of the Maritime Boundary in the Gulf of Maine Area) 5, submitted December 12, 1983, 162 (hereinafter Can. Rep.).

18. Counter-Memorial of Canada, *I.C.J. Pleadings* (Delimitation of the Maritime Boundary in the Gulf of Maine Area) 3, submitted June 28, 1983, 168 (hereinafter Can. CM).

19. Ibid., 169.

20. Ibid., 182.

21. Can. Rep., chapter 3, 162–200 passim.

22. Can. CM, 529.

23. Can. Rep., 84.

24. Interview with economic advisor for Canada in the Gulf of Maine case, Halifax, Nova Scotia, Canada, July 31, 1997.

25. Within that tradition the first visual depiction of verbal speech structure is the *arbor picta*, which, according to Otto A. Dieter, dates to the early fourteenth century and is, thus, the earliest extant visual aid. The *arbor picta* visually compares the structure of a type of medieval sermon with the structure of a tree. See Floyd Douglas Anderson, "*Dispositio* in the Preaching of Hugh Latimer," *Speech Monographs* 35 (1968): 452–54; Harry Caplan, "A Late Mediaeval Tractate on Preaching," in *Of Eloquence: Studies in Ancient and Mediaeval Rhetoric*, ed. Anne King and Helen North, 57–60, 76, 77–78 (Ithaca, N.Y.: Cornell University Press, 1970); and Otto A. Dieter, "*Arbor Picta*: The Medieval Tree of Preaching," *Quarterly Journal of Speech* 51 (1965): 123–44.

26. Robert L. Ivie, "The Metaphor of Force in Prowar Discourse: The Case of 1812," *Quarterly Journal of Speech* 68 (1982): 240.

27. I. A. Richards, *Philosophy of Rhetoric* (1936; repr., London: Oxford University Press, 1976), 101.

28. Kenneth Burke's idea that the imaginative can become "bureaucratized" resembles Ivie's literalizing process and implies its reversibility. The implications of bureaucratic terms are never fully perfected or completed since opportunities always are available for spinning off unforeseen and incongruous meanings that re-imagine the bureaucratic. See Kenneth Burke, *Attitudes toward History*, 3rd ed. (Berkeley: University of California Press, 1984), 225–29, 308–14; also see

his *Permanence and Change: An Anatomy of Purpose,* 3rd ed. (Berkeley: University of California Press, 1984), 69–163.

29. Ivie, "The Metaphor of Force in Prowar Discourse," 240–53; also see his "Literalizing the Metaphor of Soviet Savagery: President Truman's Plain Style," *Southern Speech Communication Journal* 51 (Winter 1986): 91–105, and "Metaphor and the Rhetorical Invention of Cold War 'Idealists,'" *Communication Monographs* 54 (1987): 165–82.

30. Ivie, "Metaphor of Force in Prowar Discourse," 240.

31. Ernesto Grassi, *Rhetoric as Philosophy: The Humanist Tradition* (University Park: Pennsylvania State University Press, 1980), 4–8, 35–41, 43–46.

32. Hayden White, *Tropics of Discourse: Essays in Cultural Criticism* (Baltimore, Md.: Johns Hopkins Press, 1978), 1–25.

33. Max Black, *Models and Metaphors: Studies in Language and Philosophy* (Ithaca, N.Y.: Cornell University Press, 1962), 38–44, 226–29, 236–37. Thomas S. Kuhn included this distinction among the elements of a field's "disciplinary matrix" in *The Structure of Scientific Revolutions,* 3rd ed. (Chicago: University of Chicago Press, 1996), 184; also see his "Second Thoughts on Paradigms," in *The Essential Tension: Selected Studies in Scientific Tradition and Change* (Chicago: University of Chicago Press, 1977), 297–98.

34. Hayden White, *Figural Realism: Studies in the Mimesis Effect* (Baltimore, Md.: Johns Hopkins University Press, 1999), 17.

35. In response to the idea that the literal-figurative distinction is unworkable, since all language is metaphorical, Kenneth Burke contended that critical use of his far-reaching theory of dramatism would prove impossible without it. His defense is telling, since few scholars have extended further than Burke the ideas that language is in important respects metaphorical and that thought and expression are prefigured. Clearly, analysis of metaphor cannot proceed apace without that distinction. See Burke's remarks in Bernard L. Brock, Burke, Parke G. Burgess, and Herbert Simons, "Dramatism as Ontology or Epistemology: A Symposium," *Communication Quarterly* 33 (1985): 22–24, 25, 31–32, esp. 27–28. A good statement of his view on language is in "Terministic Screens," *Language as Symbolic Action: Essays on Life, Literature, and Method* (Berkeley: University of California Press, 1966), 44–62; on the prefiguration of thought and expression, see "Four Master Tropes," appendix D in *A Grammar of Motives* (1945; repr., Berkeley: University of California Press, 1969), 503–17.

36. Black, *Models and Metaphors,* 39–40.

37. Ibid., 236–37.

38. Ibid., 41.

39. Paul Ricoeur, "Between Rhetoric and Poetics," in *Essays on Aristotle's "Rhetoric,"* ed. Amelie Oksenberg Rorty, 346 (Los Angeles: University of California Press, 1996).

40. Commentators find visual imagery irresistible when discussing metaphor. Burke saw metaphor as the organizing source of "perspective," while Grassi pointed to metaphor's generative, prerational power of original "insight" into relationships previously unseen. Richards is the exception who proves the rule. He claimed commentators allude to a metaphorical kind of seeing that, in turn, blinds them to metaphors that do not function to make us "see" or "visualize" at all. See Richards, *Philosophy of Rhetoric,* 98, 128–32; Burke, *Permanence and Change,* 89–96; *Grammar of Motives,* 503–4; Grassi, *Rhetoric as Philosophy,* 7, 33.

41. The distinction is Black's, in *Models and Metaphors,* 228–29.

42. For a study examining how the interaction view of metaphor can be applied to the visual arts, see Carl R. Hausman, *Metaphor and Art: Interaction and Reference in the Verbal and Nonverbal Arts* (Cambridge: Cambridge University Press, 1989).

43. Susanne K. Langer, *Philosophy in a New Key: A Study in the Symbolism of Reason, Rite, and Art,* 2nd ed. (New York: New American Library, Mentor, 1951), 89.

44. Ibid., 91.

45. Ibid., 89.

46. Ibid., 86–88. The general patterns of visual symbols, such as the pietà or the swastika, are recognizable, but specific, detailed, visual elements—subtle shadings, turns of line, precise configurations of shape—that together comprise this or that particular instance of those patterns are not so readily recognizable beyond initial viewing contexts. Thus, general visual patterns can and particular line squiggles and color splotches cannot be cataloged in symbol dictionaries.

47. For a discussion of visual rhetoric, including visual metaphor, in commercial advertising, see Linda M. Scott, "Images in Advertising: The Need for a Theory of Visual Rhetoric," *Journal of Consumer Research* 21 (1994): 252–73.

48. Gunther Kress and Theo van Leeuwen, *Reading Images: The Grammar of Visual Design* (1996; repr., London: Routledge, 2001), 1, 232.

49. Ibid., 6, 11–12, 43–45.

50. For Roman examples of strategic thinking about arrangement decisions, see Harry Caplan, trans., *Rhetorica ad Herennium* (Cambridge, Mass.: Harvard University Press, 1954), 3.10.18 (also see the more general discussion at 3.9.17–3.10.17), and Quintilian's *Institutio Oratoria,* vol. 2, trans. H. E. Butler (Cambridge, Mass.: Harvard University Press, 1966), 5.12.14.

51. Kress and van Leeuwen, *Reading Images,* 12–14.

52. For discussion of strategic dispositional thinking, see Gerard A. Hauser, *Introduction to Rhetorical Theory* (New York: Harper and Row, 1986), 165.

53. Kress and van Leeuwen, *Reading Images,* 47.

54. Ibid., 48, 74. They call these participants "actors" and "goals."

55. Ibid., 56.

56. Ibid.

57. For discussion of maps as persuasive devices, see Denis Wood, *The Power of Maps* (New York: Guilford Press, 1992); Mark Monmonier, *How to Lie with Maps,* 2nd ed. (Chicago: University of Chicago Press, 1996); and Judith A. Tyner, "Persuasive Cartography," *Journal of Geography* 81 (July–August 1982): 140–44.

58. Richard B. Gregg contended that "edging" or "bounding" or "bordering" is one of several major cognitive principles at the core of all human perceptual, conceptual, and symbolic experience. See his *Symbolic Inducement and Knowing: A Study in the Foundations of Rhetoric* (Columbia: University of South Carolina Press, 1984), 38–51, 132–33; also see Hauser's useful summary of Gregg's work in *Introduction to Rhetorical Theory,* 162–64.

59. Figure C5 originally appeared as figure 30 in U.S. Mem., "Boundary in the Gulf of Maine Area Proposed by the United States."

60. Figure C6 is Canada's second base map, which was used after the memorial stage. According to a Canadian legal strategist, the U.S. graphics exhibited superior technical and visual qualities and, thus, required Canada to improve upon the comparatively modest graphics in its memorial. The particular use of that base map shown here originally appeared as figure 57 in Can. CM, "The Canadian Line Respects the Geography of the Gulf of the Maine Area." Interview with deputy agent for Canada in the Gulf of Maine case, Ottawa, Ontario, Canada, August 18, 1997.

61. Kress and van Leeuwen, *Reading Images,* 206.

62. Cape Cod and the islands of Martha's Vineyard and Nantucket somewhat complicate this view. Canada argued that both the "aberrant protrusion" of Cape Cod and the islands marred the relative symmetry between Massachusetts and western Nova Scotian coastlines. More important, from Canada's vantage, those features had "disproportionate" influence on their preferred geometrical method of boundary division—"equidistance"—leading to "inequitable" results. The

solution? Exclude those features from the analysis. See Memorial of Canada, *I.C.J. Pleadings* (Delimitation of the Maritime Boundary in the Gulf of Maine Area) 1, submitted September 27, 1982, 33, 305, 346–51, 428 (b) and (f) (hereinafter Can. Mem.).

63. U.S. Mem., 32.

64. Ibid., 32n1.

65. Can. Mem., 23.

66. Interview with science expert for Canada in the Gulf of Maine case, Bedford, Nova Scotia, Canada, August 1, 1997.

67. U.S. CM, 36; see the U.S. rebuttal of this depiction at 41–44.

68. Can. CM, 727, figure 55 and figure 56.

69. Can. CM, 727.

70. Ibid., 728.

71. Kress and van Leeuwen, *Reading Images,* 89.

72. Ibid., 90.

73. Ibid., 97.

74. Ibid., 53.

75. Ibid., 101.

76. Can. Rep., 171. The graphic appears as figure 3 in Can. CM, "Effects Produced by Selective Representation of Bathymetric Contours."

77. Can. CM, 38.

78. Can. Rep., 171.

79. Ibid., 171.

80. U.S. Rep., 213.

81. Ibid., 213n3.

82. Ibid., 213. The graphic appears in U.S. Rep. as figure 11, "Successive Representation of Bathymetric (Depth) Contours Depicted in Figure 3 of the Canadian Counter-Memorial."

83. U.S. Rep., 214.

84. Evidence of Dr. Edwards, witness and expert called by the government of the United States of America, *I. C. J. Pleadings* (Delimitation of the Maritime Boundary in the Gulf of Maine Area) 6 (Oral Proceedings), April 18, 1984, 397 (hereinafter Evidence; all references by page number).

85. Evidence, 397.

86. Ibid., 400.

87. U.S. Mem., 30–31; U.S. CM, 37–40.

88. U.S. Mem., 31.

89. Ibid., 33; also see U.S. CM, 38.

90. Annex 1 to the Counter-Memorial of the United States of America, "The Marine Environment of the Gulf of Maine Area," *I.C.J. Pleadings* (Delimitation of the Maritime Boundary in the Gulf of Maine Area) 4, submitted June 28, 1983, 6, 8 (hereinafter U.S. CM Annex 1).

91. U.S. Mem., 39–46; U.S. CM, 52–54.

92. Evidence, 402–3; also see U.S. Mem., 41; U.S. CM Annex 1, 14–17. Figure C7 originally appeared as figure 5 in U.S. Mem.

93. Evidence, 403.

94. As indicated earlier, narrative patterns depict processes of change and transition (Kress and van Leeuwen, *Reading Images,* 56).

95. Ibid., 57.

96. Kress and van Leeuwen observe that larger-sized arrows visually "amplify" vectorial relationships (ibid., 70).

97. Evidence, 404–7; also see U.S. CM Annex 1, 18–28.

98. U.S. Mem., 46.

99. Ibid.

100. Ibid.

101. Ibid., 40.

102. The data were collected on the National Oceanic and Atmospheric Administration's (NOAA) 5 satellite on June 14, 1979. Images of those data were included in U.S. CM Annex 1 as figure 11, "Surface Temperature and Temperature Gradients."

103. U.S. CM Annex 1, 19.

104. Evidence, 405.

105. Ibid., 406–7.

106. Ibid., 407.

107. U.S. Mem., 40.

108. Ibid., 47.

109. The data were collected with the Coastal Zone Color Scanner (CZCS) aboard the NOAA Nimbus 7 satellite on June 14, 1979. The image appeared in U.S. Mem. as figure 6, "Phytoplankton concentrations along the east coast of North America from south of New York City to Nova Scotia."

110. U.S. Mem., 49.

111. What this image actually displayed was the focus of a technical dispute. Canada contended that the wavelengths used failed to distinguish suspended sediments from chlorophyll and, thus, that the red shading gives an exaggerated portrayal of chlorophyll concentrations. Moreover, Canada referred to the image as a "snapshot" of a "given instant" that conveyed the misleading impression that these concentrations are far more stable over time than they actually are. The United States retorted that the image shows a pattern that recurs annually and is not an isolated snapshot and offered additional images, including a four-year sequence that showed similar patterns recurring at the same time each year. See Can. CM, 194; U.S. Rep., 217.

112. Jeanne Fahnestock examines this and other figures in the discourse and graphics of science in *Rhetorical Figures in Science* (New York: Oxford University Press, 1999). For *incrementum,* see ix, 91–93, 95–96, 98–99, 101, and figure 3.1 at 100.

113. U.S. Mem., 54.

114. The graphic originally appeared in U.S. Mem. as figure 7, "Ranges of stocks of sixteen commercially important species, in a zone extending from Block Island (Rhode Island), across Georges Bank, the Northeast Channel, and Browns Bank to LaHave Bank."

115. U.S. Mem., 57.

116. Ibid., 57.

117. Ibid., 58.

118. Kress and van Leeuwen, *Reading Images,* 101. This pattern is distinguished from topographical structures since it does not interrelate participants through accurate, scalable, spatial relationships.

119. The U.S. lawyer raised that criticism for Edwards's reply in Evidence, 421. Also see Can. Rep., 195.

120. Evidence, 412–13.

121. Ibid., 421.

122. Ibid., 422.

123. Ibid.

124. Ibid.

125. Can. CM, 168–70, 182, 199.

126. Ibid., 170; Can. Rep., 165, 180.

127. Can. Rep., 180–82; also see 169, 176 and Can. CM, 182.

128. Can. CM, 199; also Can. Rep., 188.

129. Can. CM, 203–7.

130. Can. CM, 202.

131. In addition to the transition zone near the Great South Channel, Canada also directed attention to the "Shelf-Slope Front," as the more "commonly recognized front" in the area that runs "along the continental shelf ridge, separating shelf water from slope water farther offshore" (Can. CM, 188).

132. Can. Rep., 179.

133. Can. CM, 531.

134. Ibid., 529.

135. Ibid., 212.

136. Ibid., 212 (a).

137. Ibid., 212 (b)–(f).

138. Ibid., 212 (g).

139. Argument of Mr. Bruce C. Rashkow, counsel for the government of the United States, *I. C. J. Pleadings* (Delimitation of the Maritime Boundary in the Gulf of Maine Area) 6 (Oral Proceedings), April 16, 1984, 361–63 (all references by page number).

140. Evidence, 412–16.

141. Ibid., 428–33. Canada also criticized U.S. depictions of herring stock, which Edwards did discuss in his testimony, at 433–34.

142. Ibid., 428.

143. Ibid., 431–33.

144. Ibid., 398–99.

145. Ibid., 399.

146. Ibid., 416.

147. Ibid., 434.

148. Ibid., 434–35.

149. Argument of Mr. David A. Colson, deputy agent for the government of the United States of America, *I. C. J. Pleadings* (Delimitation of the Maritime Boundary in the Gulf of Maine Area) 6 (Oral Proceedings), April 19, 1984, 440–41.

150. Ibid., 441.

151. Ibid., 441, 441–42.

152. Ibid., 442. For discussion of how institutions had, for managerial purposes, used the Northeast Channel as a locus of stock divisions, see 442–44.

153. *Gulf of Maine*, 54–55 (all references by paragraph number).

154. *Gulf of Maine*, 56. Nevertheless, the chamber still concluded that a political boundary need not follow a natural boundary even if it were established incontrovertably (ibid., 56).

155. For examples, see Larry Gillen, ed., *Photographs and Maps Go to Court* (Falls Church, Va.: American Society for Photogrammetry and Remote Sensing, 1986), and Gregory P. Joseph, *Modern Visual Evidence* (New York: Law Journal Seminars-Press, 1992).

156. Kress and van Leeuwen, *Reading Images,* 149.

157. Interview with deputy agent and counsel for the United States. Also see Prelli and Becker, "Learning from an Adjudicatory Strategy for Resolving United States-Canada Fisheries Conflicts," 473.

158. *Gulf of Maine,* 53.

159. The court based its decision on purportedly "neutral" principles and facts that neither of the parties disputed during pleadings. When it came to "relevant circumstances" in the case, an

acceptable fact evidently was an uncontested fact. The chamber's approach was at least partly due to difficulties handling complex scientific arguments in the ICJ. On these matters, see Prelli and Becker, "Learning from the Limits of an Adjudicatory Strategy for Resolving United States-Canada Fisheries Conflicts," 467–69, 473–75.

160. Black distinguished the "proverbial knowledge" of metaphor from the systematic complexity of theory underlying scientific models in *Models and Metaphors,* 239.

161. Clive S. Lewis, "Bluspels and Flananferes: A Semantic Nightmare," in *Rehabilitations and Other Essays* (1939; repr., Freeport, N.Y.: Books for Libraries Press, 1972), 135–58, esp. 140–41.

5

$\mathscr{L}$iberal Representation and Global Order

The Iconic Photograph from Tiananmen Square

The photographic images that appear in daily newspapers, weekly newsmagazines, and a variety of other media are an important mode of representation not because of their news value, which often is limited, but because of their relationship to civic identity, thought, and action. We believe that photojournalism is one of the cultural practices underwriting modern, liberal-democratic polity. Indeed, in the modern era, which is defined in part by large, heterogeneous states linked through technologies of mass communication, citizenship may depend on visual modalities that can fill in the relationship of the abstract individual to the impersonal state. Think of the typical Fourth of July picture of the child eating her ice cream cone in front of an American flag: this thoroughly conventional image communicates the social embodiment, psychological reassurance, and political idealism that once were provided by civic performances in oratory, while it can be much more widely disseminated. The same holds during times of crisis: think of the image of three firefighters looking up at the flag they have raised at Ground Zero in New York City.

The extent to which photojournalism can reinforce democratic identification can be put to the test by examining its most notable work: the iconic photograph. We define iconic photos as those photographic images produced in print, electronic, or digital media that (1) are widely recognized, (2) are understood to be representations of historically significant events, (3) activate strong emotional identification or response, and (4) are reproduced across a range of media, genres, or topics.[1] Examples include the "Migrant Madonna" with her children staring past the camera into the Great Depression, the soldier and nurse caught in a powerful embrace on V-J Day in Times Square, the Vietnamese girl running in terror from a napalm attack, and the plumes of smoke displayed as the Challenger explodes in the blue sky over Florida.

The iconic photograph's significance as a mode of political representation can be explicated by analysis of the individual image according to a set of critical assumptions. Because they are valued as artistic achievements within public media, iconic photos must be structured by familiar patterns of artistic design. Because of their position and frequent reproduction in public media, iconic photographs function as a mode of civic performance.[2] In addition, performative engagement is inevitably emotional: it activates available structures of feeling within the audience to define, enhance, or restrain the emotional dimension of an event. Finally, within the performative space created by the iconic photo there occurs a series of transcriptions that provides multiple codings of the event.[3]

We believe that images become iconic because they coordinate a number of motifs from within the social life of the audience, each of which would suffice to direct audience response and which together provide a public audience with sufficient means for comprehending potentially unmanageable events. Because the camera records the décor of everyday life, the photographic image becomes capable of directing the attention across a field of gestures, interaction rituals, social types, political styles, artistic genres, cultural norms, and other signs as they intersect in any event. Needless to say, these strong patterns of identification are sure to include hierarchies of social dominance and related figures of ideological control. Thus, the icon does not so much record an event as it organizes a field of interpretations to manage a basic contradiction or recurrent crisis within the political community; consequently, the icon can continue to shape public understanding and action long after the event has passed or the crisis has been resolved pragmatically.

In short, the iconic photograph provides the public audience with "equipment for living" in the form of specific images that can be more or less useful to a democratic society.[4] They can provide important social, emotional, and mnemonic resources for democratic identity, thought, and action, but they also can constrain public memory regarding specific historical events and political attitudes regarding large-scale social change. When an historical event is represented iconically, the result may be a reconnection with those tacit, ground-level resources of democratic life or another alignment of the historical record and public opinion with larger structures of domination. As these options are both articulated visually, there never is a sure demarcation between them, even for a single audience.

This ambiguity between civic connection and ideological control is particularly significant in the visual coverage of world politics. American experience of foreign affairs depends almost completely on mass media coverage of distant places and opaque cultures; unlike in domestic politics, public representations in world politics are almost never tested against individual experience. Photojournalism becomes especially influential in this context. Photojournalism records features of the world that seem to be apprehensible at a glance, reinforcing the assumption that cultural differences are mere inflections of an otherwise common humanity. The problem is that this "common humanity" is defined within the aesthetic and cultural conventions familiar to American audiences. Iconic photographs, then, can exert considerable influence over public understanding of foreign affairs by framing events from a dominant point of view rather than providing a point of entry into other cultures.

The image of a man standing before a row of tanks at Tiananmen Square is a case study in iconic appeal—and in ideological representation. We argue that the photo subordinates Chinese democratic self-determination to a vision of global order. This vision is grounded in the aesthetic conventions of cultural modernism, which reinforces a liberal ideology of individualism and "apolitical" social organization. The photo is, at one stroke, both a progressive celebration of human rights and a restriction of the political imagination regarding alternative and perhaps better versions of a global society.

Spectacles of Dissent

The drama in Tiananmen Square began as a series of demonstrations memorializing the reformer Hu Yaobang in mid-April 1989.[5] By organizing around the Monument to the

People's Heroes in the square, the demonstrators defined themselves as the heirs of the demonstration of May 4, 1919, that had inaugurated the political movements defining modern China. After a series of clashes with the police, on April 21 students began a continuous occupation of the square. Over the following weeks the protest mushroomed into a prolonged confrontation between students and urban workers on the one side and the Chinese government on the other. Events soon exceeded the abilities of the leaders on either side: government officials refused to meet with student leaders, a *People's Daily* editorial condemned the students in language reminiscent of a previous persecution, demonstrators participated in hunger strikes, and by May 29 there were one million people marching and milling about in the square in violation of a government order to disperse.

During the next few days the crowds melted away, leaving a much smaller cohort still camped in the square, but the escalation toward violence continued: increased deployment of troops was being met by organized resistance throughout the city, often by workers and other citizens. An advance of several thousand soldiers into the square on the morning of June 3 followed the past month's pattern of confrontation, standoff, and military retreat. Then, the deluge: In the evening, new troops launched a sustained, violent assault to clear the streets and the square. Tanks crashed through barricades as automatic weapons were fired into the crowds and at the fleeing demonstrators. Hundreds were killed—some mashed by tanks or other heavy vehicles—while many others were wounded. Sporadic violence continued for several days, but the public protest was broken, and in the following weeks thousands of demonstrators or other dissidents were imprisoned, some to be executed.

The first icon of the demonstration was not the still photo of the man and the tank, but a thirty-seven-foot-tall statue crafted by art students and modeled on the Statue of Liberty (see figure 6, *Goddess of Democracy*). Labeled the *Goddess of Democracy* (a revealing shift in nomenclature) by the demonstrators and positioned facing the government's giant portrait of Mao, the statue was featured prominently (and for obvious reasons) in various photos and live coverage in the American media.[6] The statue would be a fitting icon for the event, and for reasons that may not be obvious: seemingly a direct insertion of Western ideals into Chinese public culture, it was in fact intentionally altered to reflect a process of appropriation. Although seemingly a universal symbol of liberty, it became festooned with flags, banners, flowers, and other signs that defined the monument within a cultural milieu largely illegible to the Western audience. Ironically, the statue also continued a civic republican tradition of figural representation that has become antique in the West. The goddess still is included in some montages commemorating the event, but its status as a marker of democratic ideals has largely been displaced.

The dominant image today is of a man standing before a row of tanks (figure 7, "Man Confronting Tanks").[7] He is an anonymous figure in black pants and a white shirt; they are standard battle tanks in the generic camouflage used by every modern army.[8] He clearly has positioned himself in front of the lead tank to stop its forward movement. The tank has stopped, but its commander remains within; it could lurch forward to crush the man, yet there is no indication of any movement on either side. To Western observers, it is the premier image of the dramatic events in Tiananmen Square. "There is only one streetscene in China worth remembering in Western eyes. . . . this streetscene was transformed into iconography. . . . The man and the tank would live on beyond the few tense moments of the encounter to become a permanent and universal symbol."[9]

6. *Goddess of Democracy.*
Used with the permission
of *Chinese News Digest*

Nor should that be surprising, for the image had the benefit of a media blitz. As David Perlmutter has documented, video and still images of the man before the tank dominated newscasts, newspaper and newsmagazine coverage, and public commentary (including a speech by President George Bush).[10] It became the framing device for both journalistic and political representation of the Tiananmen protest. In subsequent years, the image has dominated visual histories, particularly those produced in the public media, and has become a stock image at Web sites and on posters in English, Chinese, and French advocating dissent and democratization.[11] The image has become "one of the defining iconic images of the 20th century, like a monument in a vast public square created by television."[12] This ascension culminated in the unknown man's selection by *Time* as one of the twenty most influential "leaders and revolutionaries" of the twentieth century.[13] He was, of course, neither a leader nor a revolutionary, and Perlmutter's argument seems inescapable: the iconic status of the photo was a product of the Western media elite.

This photographic icon also has displaced the Monument to the People's Heroes that was the point of origin for the protest in Tiananmen Square. As Wu Hung has stated, the demonstrations and massacre combined to redeem the memorial site as "a living monument that wove people's recollections of their struggle and death into a whole. Surrounding

7. "Man Confronting Tanks." Photograph by Stuart Franklin. Used with the permission of Magnum Photos

it a new public emerged."[14] The difference between the two monuments, one stone and the other photographic, is a difference not only between Chinese and Western understanding of the events in Tiananmen Square, but also between the national articulation of Chinese public culture and a global public sphere constituted by the Western media. As the image of the man and the tank achieved iconic status, it has acquired the ability to structure collective memory, advance an ideology, and organize or disable specific forms of emotional display and other resources for political action. As we shall see, the photo of the man and the tank constitutes liberalism as the dominant mentality for an emerging global order.

Seeing Like a State

The photograph of the man confronting the row of tanks is a picture of contrasts: the lone civilian versus the army; the vulnerable human body versus mechanized armor; "human hope and courage challenging the remorseless machinery of state power."[15] These dramatic differences lead directly to the predominant appropriation of the photo as a critique of authoritarian regimes and a celebration of liberal-democratic values. We do not intend to make light of this performance of civic virtue; indeed, that is exactly what we believe is one of the primary functions of the iconic image. Nonetheless, the Cold War is over, and practices of both cultural and political representation today have to contend with complicated processes of superimposition and contextual reconfiguration. Thus, the image's reprise of a dramatic conflict between freedom and oppression is only one in a series of transcriptions.

Although situated at the center of the composition, it does not comprise the only order of perception activated by the composition as a whole.

The key to our revaluing of this image is to see that the dramatic standoff is positioned within a modernist perspective toward pictorial space. This larger aesthetic frame unfolds from the vantage of the photographer, who is above and at some distance from the scene. From this vantage, one looks down on the scene from a safe place that is not included within it; the tank commander has no knowledge of the camera.[16] The tanks are still impersonal, but so is the scene as a whole. The viewer is disconnected from the scene—positioned as a distant spectator who can neither be harmed by nor affect the action unfolding below. The viewer of the picture acquires the neutral, "objective" stance of the camera. As James Scott has demonstrated, whenever we view unfolding events with an objective detachment afforded by a purportedly neutral point of view, we are "seeing like a state." By contrast with the swirl of people and banners around the *Goddess of Democracy* in the square, this scene is highly "legible" to the Western viewer. "Legibility implies a viewer whose place is central and whose vision is synoptic. . . . This privileged vantage point is typical of all institutional settings where command and control of complex human activities is paramount."[17] The (authoritarian) state that is positioned within the picture is subordinated (for a liberal-democratic audience) to the individual standing freely before it, but both of these alternatives are subordinated to the modernist scheme of representation that dominated governmental and most other institutional practices in both capitalist and socialist regimes in the late-twentieth century.

Thus, it is not surprising that the photograph depicts an event unfolding in an open, almost-completely deserted public space. The field on which the man and tank are positioned is a model of the abstraction characterizing modernist design: It is a flat, uniform, concrete surface of a city street, designed for modern transportation technologies such as the bus visible at the upper border of some versions of the photograph. It is devoid of any place to sit, congregate, or talk, and its dimensions are not to human scale—that is, for personal transactions—but rather built to accommodate the flow of vehicular traffic. The traffic pattern is evident from the only symbols on the surface: straight, parallel lines in white or yellow and white directional vectors that are either straight or at right angles. There is no ornamentation, and there are no words. Take out the representational figures in the center, and you have a modernist painting in the tradition of Mondrian.

The use of these modernist conventions is not merely an artistic coincidence, for it activates the realist style of political representation, which has been the dominant means for rationalizing power in international relations. By withdrawing emotionally from the swirl of events to assume a topographical perspective, the prince—or political analyst—sees the historical event as a tableau determined by "an abstract world of forces (functionally equivalent, socially barren entities like military units or nation-states or transnational corporations)."[18] This perspective is defined as much or more by what it excludes as by what it features. The banners, costumes, and swirl of bodies creating a carnival atmosphere in the square, the songs, parades, and other forms of public emotionality, the pamphlets, speeches, and constant din of talk all are replaced by an empty, regimented space marked by force-flow vectors and dominated by the organized deployment of uniform, interchangeable military machines. The one visible human being in the scene also conforms perfectly to dictates of this style, for he is a model of self-control. "One survives in this world through strategic calculation of others' capacity to act and through rational control of oneself."[19] Standing erect, poised, overcoming the natural impulse to flee from danger, acutely gauging the will of the unseen tank commander opposing him, the man's bold act of heroism also is an incarnation of realism's rational actor. His immobile, balanced stance and the clean lines of his modern, black and white attire provide aesthetic confirmation of this attitude.[20] More to the point, this rational self-control by the individual, which in turn is part of a larger mentality of viewing political reality in respect solely to calculations of self-interest and power, constrains identification with the Chinese reform movement. Rather than being pulled inside the mass demonstrations for popular democracy, this realist reproduction of the event encourages the viewer to look for the preponderance of power and to assess options in terms of a calculation of benefits and risks.

Additional elements of the photo reinforce this realist mentality. Any photograph is silent, but this one is a portrait of political action without speech. (Actually, a crowd of on-lookers was shouting throughout the scene, but that was not recorded by the photograph.) Tanks are not exactly built for negotiation, while they perfectly embody the essential definition of the modern state—its monopoly on force. The man is silent, using his body rather than his voice in a gesture that converts vocal protest to nonviolent resistance, a recognizable form of political action capable of balancing material coercion—for a moment. The scene's composition provides an allegory for the profound imbalance within the realist view of the world between force and morality. Moral, social, or cultural constraint on force is always precarious, held in place by the goodwill that is a sure casualty in violent or prolonged conflict and weakened further as speakers are silenced. The man stops the tanks, and his symbolic power—for example, his capacity to represent national identity, citizenship, civic rights, or the value of the individual person—temporarily, precariously, is capable of balancing the coercive power that is moving toward him. These symbolic values are represented through an absence—the empty space at his back that at once corresponds to the real, material tanks on the other side and predicts the inevitability of his giving way to their advance. The composition itself is predictive, as the tanks already have advanced across most of the pictorial field along the lines and vectors on the street indicating the forward direction of the traffic. As those lines correspond to the right-to-left diagonal line across the picture frame, they connote movement from their starting point toward their destination behind the man (and behind and to the side of the viewer, who may not be targeted but is being outflanked). The message seems clear: in this confrontation, force will prevail.

This conclusion is the more plausible because the only figure shown is male. One man stands against a mechanized army unit, the epitome of masculine power. This ideological grammar provides an additional basis for realist projections, as ideas of pluralism, cooperation between different social groups, and dialogue become less plausible in a monotonic system while conventional norms of rationality, emotional control, and hierarchical command become more plausible. It also may underscore the extent to which the photograph portrays the Chinese government as a threat rather than an actual perpetrator of violence. Tanks such as those stopping here had been churning through the square to destroy whoever had not left fast enough, and other pictures of the aftermath of that violence depict government-induced disorder while eliciting identification with the pain and relative innocence of the victims. The iconic photo, however, remains a gestural dance of masculine display. Within this gendered space, as in realism itself, there is far more attention paid to threats than to actual violence (which often proves embarrassing, if only because it reveals hidden complexities in motive and response). And this focus on *potential* violence gives a particular shape to the event. On the one hand, it is the preferred modality of state power: more efficient, less accountable, less capable of unintended consequences such as martyrdom, more transferable across the entire state apparatus of procedures and officials. On the other hand, it increases and inflects the man's representative power. It becomes easier to see him as a figure of revolution rather than of gradual change, a precursor to dramatic reversal of the picture's vectors rather than an endogenous transformation of a complex system. In short, a world of masculine display is a world of force fields and threats, of pushing and backing down and sudden reversals rather than difference and negotiation and mutual change, and of imposition and resistance rather than cooperation. As the viewer looks down from above, there is nothing that can jar one out of these assumptions. A poster celebrating democratic revolution reproduces the act of seeing like a state, a perspective that supports hardliners on each side of the Chinese conflict while overlooking less legible, more encultured forms of democratic reform.

From this vantage, there is much less dissonance between liberalism and realism than often is presumed.[21] Force prevails in the photo, but only as long as it is present, and it can never be present all the time, particularly if a modern economy is to thrive. Thus, the show of force will not prevail over time, the time of modernization. The photo is a literal depiction of realism and a prophetic representation of liberalism. (These modes of representation are appropriate to each doctrine and can coexist without direct contradiction.) According to that prophecy, arbitrary authority cannot stand against the innate human desire for freedom and the rule of law. The tank's hesitation portends the eventual triumph of liberalism and individual self-determination. The man's vulnerability keeps the door open to the continued need for force, however, particularly when both liberalism and realism contrast themselves to mass movements, power vacuums, and other harbingers of anarchy. Individual freedom and a world of forces, self-determination and rational calculation, an authoritarian present and a liberal future—these potentially difficult conjunctions are smoothed over by their aesthetic coordination within the conventions of modernism.

Any representation is a partial record of its object, but modernist representation is based on especially severe reductions in information. Whether for the purpose of artistic autonomy or rational administration, the approach is the same: surface variation, local knowledge, provisional arrangements, mixed categories, and social complexity are all subordinated to processes of reduction and abstraction and, when geared toward production, to processes of standardization and regimentation.[22] With few exceptions, the orientation is toward the universal rather than the parochial, the geometric rather than the organic, the functional rather than what is customary, an "international style" in architectural design and bureaucratic practices rather than attention to cultural differences and vernacular politics. And, as Scott remarks, "The carriers of high modernism tended to see rational order in remarkably visual aesthetic terms. For them, an efficient, rationally organized city, village, or farm was a city that *looked* regimented and orderly in a geometrical sense."[23] This way of seeing allows the agent to identify economies in resource use that serve specific interests, especially the interest of administrative control.

The extent of representational reduction achieved by the tank photo is evident only in respect to its context as that is defined by other accounts and especially other photos and video clips of the events in the square.[24] Whatever its full effect, the reduction certainly is one of considerable degree. From a day when one million people were congregating in the square, this photograph shows only a single individual. Instead of a crowd milling about amorphously amidst statues, banners, tents, kites, food vendors, and cultural icons, an individual is standing still in a perfectly balanced posture in an empty public space. Instead of noise, sirens, cacophony (and, in respect to written reports, the smells of food, garbage, and urine), there is silence and a general anesthesia of sensory engagement. Instead of parades and a constant flow of motorbikes, ambulances, trucks, and other vehicles, there are tanks stopped in a broad but deserted street. Instead of displays of public emotionalism, there is an act of calculated immobility. And, as already noted, instead of violence there is merely the threat of violence.[25]

It is easy at this point to say that the photo sanitizes the event to support the imposition of state power in a manner reflecting continued collusion among states or between state power and the mass media. This interpretation is too limited, however. If nothing else, that was not the immediate effect of the photograph. The contrast with the events surrounding the scene depicted was, at the time, experienced as a continuous and mutually validating flow of events. The extensive reduction accomplished within the pictorial frame occurred amidst a welter of information that was already known and a sense of historical moment that was being experienced and celebrated. Thus, the reduction is not merely the elimination of information, but rather a process for dealing with an excess of information and feelings. The iconic reduction works to intensify a mediated experience and to organize it.

The intensification of experience occurs by concentrating the energies generated by an event into specific, concrete images. There is no focus to a crowd, but our attention naturally zeros in on a lone figure in a square. Likewise, the government, heretofore represented only through long shots of buildings, now becomes visible in the condensation symbol of the battle tank. In a corresponding obversion, the public becomes known largely by its absence—an empty street, emptied because people have been fleeing from danger. In their place is only the man, the *individuated aggregate* capable of both representing collective experience and eliciting identification from an audience habituated to individualism.[26] The necessity of focusing on the individual in liberal representation is underscored by the fact that Chinese citizens had been stopping army vehicles for many days, and there are many photos of these successful acts of resistance—but always of the citizens acting in groups. There is only one photo of an individual acting by himself, yet that is the one that became iconic.

This reduction of a month-long mass demonstration before government buildings to a single moment in which a lone individual stands up to a tank condenses the entire conflict into an image of exquisite drama; information is lost, but in its place is the potential for a celebration of political liberty. This potential should not be underestimated. A compensatory shift from the material reality of power to a celebration of the possibility of future freedoms may be one way in which the photo continues to underwrite democratic polity. Democracy may always require an unreasonable amount of hope of the sort found in idealistic performances of individual dissent, and liberal democracy may require a strong association of political expression with individual self-assertion. This figure of dissent does not exist in a neutral space, however.

The photo's reduction of the experience is not just a suppression of facts, but rather the construction of a political scenario. Through reduction of the Chinese demonstration to this iconic moment, the photograph transforms the event from an episode in Chinese national history into a parable about the future global order. This transformation flows out of what is left after the reduction: in place of the pluralism evident in the square (which was a mélange of Chinese constituencies, Japanese fashions, American consumer products, and the world press), there remains only an iconography of modernism. In place of calls for public accountability and democratic participation in governance, there is a symbol of personal liberty and individual rights. Instead of a massed public confronting an enclaved leadership, there is the categorical difference between the individual and the state. In this scenario, political action occurs within a modernist terrain where state power and calculations of risk still predominate. The fundamental historical question is whether Western liberalism will achieve global hegemony, and the key to this drama is to give individuals the leverage that comes from participation in open markets and coverage by the Western media. Change is achieved through the actions of ordinary people acting as individual entrepreneurs, and it goes without saying that change will occur gradually while still-muscular totalitarian regimes grind slowly to a halt and ponder how to redirect their large, awkward machinery.

To summarize thus far, the iconic photo of the man standing before the tank is a paradigmatic case of modernist simplification. Through a series of reductions and intensifications of the political conflict erupting in Tiananmen Square, the photo restructures that conflict on the terms most legible and reassuring within a Western narrative of the continued expansion of modern technologies, open markets, and liberal ideals throughout the world. The universal validity of those scientific, economic, and political principles is implied by their depiction within the modernist "international style" of representation and by their extension without modification across the globe. These processes are evident in a photo that carries only the most muted sign of Chinese identity—the star on the army tank—while being constituted throughout by characteristic signs and figures of modernism. In this narrative, the state contracts to its most elemental functions while economic activity and a corresponding individualism expand without limit except as they are channeled by modern technologies of production, transportation, and communication. The image could be taken, and has been taken, anywhere in the world.

The photo's simplification of the Chinese conflict can have such comprehensive implications because it reproduces one of the fundamental achievements of modernism. As Scott observes, the development of the modern state required a comprehensive standardization of names, measures, jurisdictions, currencies, languages, and other signifying practices previously under local control. In every case, standardization was accomplished through simplification and in conjunction with "that other revolutionary political simplification of the modern era: the concept of a uniform, homogeneous citizenship." Taking France as his leading example, Scott argues that "[i]n place of a welter of incommensurable small communities, familiar to their inhabitants but mystifying to outsiders, there would rise a single national society perfectly legible from the center. The proponents of this vision well understood that what was at stake was not merely administrative convenience but also the transformation of a people. . . . The abstract grid of equal citizenship would create a new reality: The French citizen."[27]

A similar transformation is created on the grid of the Beijing street. In place of the welter of signs, most of them unreadable to those outside of China, and a dense, mass gathering that cannot be taken in as a whole, there is a transparent, perfectly legible depiction of a modern individual standing in an empty, uniform public space before a generic symbol of routinized state power. The photo has in a stroke transformed Chinese political identity into the "uniform, homogeneous citizenship" of the modern era. This is a layered transformation: it converts one or more forms of Chinese citizenship into another; it seamlessly integrates Chinese citizenship into a universal order of human rights (such that this citizenship, like any state currency, is convertible with any other); it elevates all civic identity into this universal form that now applies primarily to the global order rather than to any specific nation.[28] What once was the basis for the transformation of France from a premodern collage of local prerogatives into uniform jurisdiction of a modern state now becomes the basis for transforming national identities into the uniform economy of rights in a global order. And just as the earlier change in Europe was accomplished through the standardization of names, languages, and measures, so does the global order work through a standardization of signs. This common emphasis on matters of representation does not extend to continued administrative centralization, however. The center of the global order is the lens of the camera.

The Liberal Future

This strong positioning of liberalism is evident in other media portrayals of the Tiananmen Square protest. The film *The Gate of Heavenly Peace* is a fitting example due to both its overall excellence and its use of the tank photo as a framing shot.[29] The narrative begins with action shots of the carnage and casualties along with interviewees reacting to the attack by the army, follows with video footage of the man's encounter with the tank, then with similar tape from a state "news" voice-over that emphasizes the tank commander's restraint, and then again a bit later with the original clip to frame the rest of the film.[30] As the story develops, three basic political alternatives emerge: the authoritarian state, the popular democracy movement, and a doctrine of individual self-realization. The state is represented by its army and by officials who divide into two mutually limiting camps of hardliners and reformers. The popular movement of students, workers, and intellectuals likewise splits into two contradictory camps of pragmatic pluralists and neoauthoritarian demagogues. The third alternative of liberalism cannot be paralyzed by division because it already is completely fragmented into an unknown number of individual lives. These individuals include most prominently an articulate pop singer who celebrates self-expression and the mother of a murdered boy who emphasizes the importance of taking small, individual actions to achieve happiness.

By the end of the film, the state has lost all legitimacy, and popular democracy has failed. The swirling montage of the opening shots of the demonstrators is fading into memory, while the thrice-performed iconic standoff between the individual and the state remains the elemental political scenario awaiting resolution. The film ends with pictures of the boy who was killed while observing the demonstration. Like the man before the tank, he was not a demonstrator, just someone caught and then caught up in the event. His mother says, "Should we simply wait for another chance to start a Democracy Movement like 1989? Would that save China? I don't think so. The only way to change our situation is for each one of us to make a personal effort. Every small action counts." The narrator concurs: "When people abandon hope for a perfect future and faith in great leaders, they are returned to the common dilemmas of humanity. And there—in personal responsibility, in civility, in making sacred the duties of ordinary life—a path may be found."[31] Popular democracy has been transcribed into the "utopian" political theory that was the standard categorization of communism by the West during the Cold War. Genuine, justifiable political emotion has been depicted as unrealistic desire, and public grief over the loss both of lives and of freedom has been reduced to the experience of a single person's private mourning.[32] Liberalism is the practical alternative—the only alternative for a real world. The last shot of the film is not of a demonstration, not of the million people protesting in the square, nor of their leaders speaking before them. It is the picture, as from the family photo album, of the boy's face.

The film and the iconic photo articulate a common narrative of the ascent of liberalism in a global context. Each sublimates an interrupted democratic movement into the projection of a liberal future. Our point is not that the complexity expected of a China expert is missing from public documentary media, but rather that another culture's articulation of democratic self-assertion has been reconstituted according to the aesthetic and political conventions of the Western audience. Both texts fulfill Anne Norton's observation that "[l]iberalism has become the common sense of the American people, a set of principles unconsciously adhered to, a set of conventions so deeply held that they appear (when they appear at all) to be no more than common sense."[33] Instead of a possible "second center" for the emergence of a global culture, we see another version of ourselves. Instead of a more hybrid modernity, we see the familiar patterns of modernization. Instead of a deep yearning for democracy, we see an open space for individual self-assertion.

The modernist image is itself a complex design that is open to varied uses, however. The modern simplifications of uniform measures and uniform rights were both liberatory and the infrastructure of a comprehensive extension of disciplinary power. Likewise, modernist representation can articulate individual rights while it subordinates those forms of cultural identity that do not fit into its scheme of legibility. The universal constitution of Chinese citizenship reassures the Western audience that the global society will develop on familiar terms, yet it certainly is a progressive development for those dissidents who are in exile, and there is no question that China needs more liberty, not less. Rather than decide between choices that are not mutually exclusive, it is more useful to consider how this iconic photo organizes all political ideas within the projection of an imagined future. As Norton has remarked, "Representation is not merely a form of governance, it is also the means we use to create ourselves in a new world order."[34]

This rationalizing of historical change always depended on the capacity to transport the design principles of modernism across cultural borders. An "international style" should be the same style and the infrastructure of a modern civilization should be based on the same technologies and engineering whether one is in New York or São Paulo or Tehran. People have a vexing habit of preferring their own way of life, however, and so the modernist project encounters continual frustrations. It is just at this point, the problem of extending modernism, that modern visual media play a decisive role. As Scott remarks, "One response to this frustration is a retreat to the realm of appearances and miniatures—to model cities and Potemkin villages, as it were. . . . The effect of this retreat is to create a small, relatively self-contained, utopian space where high-modernist aspirations might more nearly be realized."[35] Scott defines the definitive cases as the theme park and museum, and the expansion and likely effects of these media in first-world societies is well documented. But there is another, much cheaper, and more portable example of a "small, relatively self-contained, utopian space": the photograph. Here the aesthetic effect of miniaturization is perfectly realized and completely normative. When the photo's composition is itself a model of modernist design, its predictive potency becomes enormous: "Just as the architectural drawing, the model, and the map are ways of dealing with a larger reality that is not easily grasped or manageable in its entirety, the miniaturization of high-modernist development offers a visually complete example of what the future looks like."[36] When a democratic revolution becomes compressed to a man and a tank seen at a distance— miniature figures that could be toys—and that surface is a plane surface marked as a grid— as if it were a game board—then a complex, partially illegible historical process has been represented as a model of the modern world's characteristic social order. Once again, the future is a modern future, achieved by modern technologies projecting the continued extension in space and time of universal values, values that are known to be universal because they are legible, transportable, and rational.

We should not romanticize indigenous development—Chinese democracy could be not only less liberal but also less democratic than one would wish—but it does hold out the possibility of a richer global civil society. Stated otherwise, a decidedly democratic global society would produce a heteronomous modernity, while a global liberalism is more likely to produce the homogenous social order of late-modern design.[37] The iconic image from Tiananmen Square obscures the idea that there might be alternative forms of modernization and that a global society could develop according to a different logic than expansion of and assimilation into Western liberal-democratic culture.

Despite its visual nature, the photo reinforces the modernist norms of print culture, including an emphasis on universal legibility and rationality achieved by abstraction and opposed to the excess and lack of linear perspective characterizing the political spectacle. As such, it holds the line against the hybridization of postliterate societies and the alternative modernities they might generate. Perhaps that line needs to be held for awhile, particularly if the core values of individual liberty and human rights are to be maintained amidst overwhelming processes of commodification. As always, and contrary to the aesthetic values of this iconic photo, it depends on the context. The man stopping the tank can be a model of democratic dissent or a parable of liberal hegemony, symbol of a new world order and a masking of its true cost.

Notes

1. See also Robert Hariman and John Louis Lucaites, "Dissent and Emotional Management in a Liberal-Democratic Society: The Kent State Iconic Photograph," *Rhetoric Society Quarterly* 31 (2001): 5–32, and *Icons of Liberal Democracy: Public Culture in the Age of Photojournalism* (Chicago: University of Chicago Press, forthcoming).

2. Like other performances, iconic photographs are situated, reflexive, aesthetically marked examples of restored behavior presented to an audience. Our sense of performance is drawn primarily from work in anthropology. Richard Bauman summarizes this perspective in "Performance," in *International Encyclopedia of Communications* (New York: Oxford University Press, 1989), 3:262–66; see also *Verbal Art as Performance* (Prospect Heights, Ill.: Waveland Press, 1984). Dwight Conquergood argues for extending performance theory to public discourse in "Rethinking Ethnography: Towards a Critical Cultural Politics," *Communication Monographs* 58 (1991): 179–94.

3. The term "transcription" comes from Umberto Eco, whose example points to both the larger operation of shifting between visual and verbal semiotics and to the specific shifts in meaning that occur as the reader is cued by specific narratives or interpretive terms to different patterns in and extending beyond the composition. Umberto Eco, "Critique of the Image," in *Thinking Photography,* ed. Victor Burgin, 33 (London: Macmillan, 1992). Eco discusses what we call iconic photographs in *Travels in Hyper Reality* (New York: Harcourt Brace, 1986), 216–17.

4. Kenneth Burke, "Literature as Equipment for Living," in *The Philosophy of Literary Form: Studies in Symbolic Action,* 3rd ed. (Berkeley: University of California Press, 1973), 293–304.

5. Despite a high degree of consistency among the various accounts of the massacre, there is a surprising variation regarding some details: even different dates are used. Fortunately for our purposes, the disputed or otherwise questionable circumstances are not relevant to our analysis of how the iconic photo constructs a model of global order that deflects attention from Chinese democratic display. For example, it doesn't matter that most viewers of the photo assume erroneously that it is taken in Tiananmen Square, that the man is a student, and that the tanks are on the assault. For the record, we have relied on the following sources: Craig Calhoun, *Neither Gods nor Emperors: Students and the Struggle for Democracy in China* (Berkeley: University of California Press, 1994); Craig Dietrich, *People's China: A Brief History,* 2nd ed. (New York: Oxford University Press, 1994); George Black and Rogin Munro, *Black Hands of Beijing: Lives of Defiance in China's Democracy Movement* (New York: John Wiley, 1993); Chu-Yuan Cheng, *Behind the Tiananmen Massacre* (Boulder, Colo.: Westview Press, 1990); Human Rights in China, *Children of the Dragon: The Story of Tiananmen Square* (New York: Macmillan, 1990); Tony Saich, *The Chinese People's Movement: Perspectives on Spring 1989* (Armonk, N.Y.: M. E. Sharpe, 1990); Associated Press, *China: From the Long March to Tiananmen Square* (New York: Henry Holt, 1990); Scott Simmie and Bob Nixon, *Tiananmen Square* (Seattle: University of Washington Press, 1989); Donald Morrison, ed. *Massacre in Beijing: China's Struggle for Democracy* (New York: Warner, 1989). Chronologies are available in Saich, *The Chinese People's Movement* and *Massacre in Beijing.*

6. See, for example, Virtual Museum of China '89, May, 1989 (Part 2), China News Digest International, http://museums.cnd.org/China89/8905–2.html, and Tiananmen Square Multimedia Exhibit, History Wiz, http://www.historywiz.com/goddess.htm (last accessed January 3, 2003). A black-and-white print is in *Media Studies Journal* (Winter 1999): 121, which also contains commentary by Melinda Liu, "The Goddess of Democracy," 120. The statue's demolition is shown in *The Gate of Heavenly Peace,* directed by Carma Hinton and Richard Gordon (Long Bow Group, 1995). Wu Hung reports on the students' decision to not make a literal reproduction of the American model, as had been done in Shanghai, in "Tiananmen Square: A Political History of Monuments," *Representations* 35 (1991): 110. Tsao Tsing-yuan provides a more detailed account of the statue's synthesis of several artistic models in "The Birth of the Goddess of Democracy," in *Popular Protest and Political Culture in Modern China,* ed. Jeffrey N. Wasserstrom and Elizabeth J. Perry, 2nd ed., 140–47 (Boulder, Colo.: Westview Press, 1994). We also should note that the distinction between "liberalism" and "democracy" applies only within Western political discourse; in the context of Chinese language and political history, "liberal" has no association with private property, and "democracy" has no association with pluralism. (We are indebted to Jeffrey Wasserstrom for his help on this question of translation.) All of our arguments are about the representation of China in the West, and they apply to Chinese political debate only as Western representations are cycled back into that society.

7. Because the scene was recorded in several photographs and two video clips, reproductions include a number of variations on this iconic image reflecting, for example, small changes in the man's stance from one second to another. In addition, any photo can be cropped in various ways. The image we have selected is the one used in many of the reproductions and particularly those

that are most prominently placed. It also seems to be the central image in the range of variations. The photo is one from several rolls taken on June 5, 1989, by Stuart Franklin from the balcony of the Beijing Hotel on Changan Boulevard overlooking the square. For a full-page, color reproduction of this image, see Richard Lacayo and George Russell, *Eyewitness: 150 Years of Photojournalism,* 2nd ed. (New York: Time, 1995), 164. A slightly smaller cropping in black-and-white is widely available as a poster. An array of five shots from Franklin's roll that show the beginning, middle, and end of the confrontation is in Human Rights in China, *Children of the Dragon,* 189–93. The other frequently reproduced image, which can be distinguished by the top of a street light in the lower right foreground, was taken by AP photographer Jeff Widener. It can be seen on the last page (318) of Associated Press, *China: From the Long March to Tiananmen Square* and at Tanks in Tiananmen Square, HistoryWiz, http://www.historywiz.com/tiananmentanks.htm (last accessed June 25, 2002). A third image often seen was taken by Charles Cole of *Newsweek.* It can be seen at Photo District News: Twentieth Anniversary, http://www.pdn-pix.com/20years/photojournalism/04_charlie_cole.html (last accessed June 25, 2002). Our analysis applies to each of these photos and related variants.

8. The man is often identified as a student, but it is more likely that he was a worker. "My dissident friends and I did our very best to find the man in the photo, but to no avail. I really wanted to meet him; he was such a perfect symbol of our cause. He was probably a worker. If he'd been a student, our networks would have found him. . . . it's just as well he was photographed from the back. That protected him" (report of an interview with Wang Dan in Marie-Monique Robin, *The Photos of the Century: 100 Historic Moments* [Koln: Evergreen, 1999], no. 88). Because the man's actual cultural designation is not legible in the photo, his generic modern dress then keys the dominant frame of reference. On the role of black dress in the ascendancy of modernity, see John Harvey, *Men in Black* (Chicago: University of Chicago Press, 1995). We believe that a similar generalization might apply to the tanks: Their only specific marking is the dull red star not unlike the red insignia on Soviet tanks or the dull blue and white star on U.S. tanks, and the Chinese T-59 is a variant on the Soviet T-55, which has been used as well by a number of other countries, including Israel. Retrofit and gun conversion packages are available from the British companies of Oceonics Vehicle Technology and Royal Ordinance Nottingham. See Christopher Foss, *Jane's Main Battle Tanks,* 2nd ed. (United Kingdom: Jane's Publishing Company, 1986), 11–14, 88–94, 163, 185–86. As one curious example of iconic dissemination, the Tiananmen Square photo now is used in one technical display: Federation of American Scientists, Military Analysis Network, Type 80 Specifications, http://www.fas.org/man/dod-101/sys/land/row/type-80.htm (last accessed June 25, 2002).

9. Michael Dutton, *Streetlife China* (Cambridge: Cambridge University Press, 1998), 17. Dutton specifies the symbol as one "of resistance to terror" that captures all that the West abhorred about Chinese communism. We hope to demonstrate that, as some of our sources attest, a wider range of meanings is available. There is no doubt, however, that the image is valued because it "fits so nicely with the story we [Westerners] expect to see" (Richard Gordon, "One Act, Many Meanings," *Media Studies Journal* [Winter 1999]: 82).

10. David D. Perlmutter, *Photojournalism and Foreign Policy: Icons of Outrage in International Crises* (Westport, Conn.: Praeger, 1998), 66–71.

11. The photo is included in the following visual histories, among others: Lacayo and Russell, *Eyewitness: 150 Years of Photojournalism,* 164; Vicki Goldberg, *The Power of Photography: How Photographs Changed Our Lives* (New York: Abbeville Press, 1991), 251; *Great Images of the Twentieth Century: The Photographs That Define Our Times* (New York: Time Books, 1999), 16; Richard B. Stolley, ed., *Our Century in Pictures* (Boston: Little, Brown, 1999), 375, and *Our Century in Pictures for Young People* (Boston: Little, Brown, 2000), 203; Robin, *The Photos of the Century: 100 Historic*

Moments, no. 88; Peter Stepan, *Photos That Changed the World* (Munich: Prestel, 2000), 162–63; *Time, Great Events of the 20th Century* (New York: Time, 1997), 52. It is used on many Web sites as the only or key visual representation of the protest: for example, CNN.com, "The Lingering Legacy of Tiananmen Square," http://www.cnn.com/WORLD/asiapcf/9905/28/tiananmen.legacy/ (last accessed June 25, 2002); The Freedom Forum, "Nearly 10 Years On, Bloody Crackdown at Tiananmen Square Stirs Vigorous Debate," http://www.freedomforum.org/templates/document .asp?documentID=5817 (last accessed June 25, 2002).

12. Gordon, "One Act, Many Meanings," 82.

13. Perlmutter quotes the London *Guardian* of June 4, 1992 (*Photojournalism and Foreign Policy,* 66). The *Time* selection, including an essay by Pico Iyer that celebrates "The Unknown Rebel" as a hero in a new "republic of the image," is at Time, "The Unknown Rebel," http://www.time.com/ time/time100/leaders/profile/rebel.html (last accessed June 25, 2002).

14. Wu Hung, "Tiananmen Square," 104.

15. The quoted text is from the narration in *The Gate of Heavenly Peace.* The transcript is available at "The Film," http://tsquare.tv/film/transcript01.html (last accessed June 25, 2002). It also is used in Gordon, "One Act, Many Meanings," 83. The emphasis on the *individual* assertion of liberty is evident in many appropriations of the image: see, for example, the billboard by the Foundation for a Better Life, "Sometimes it's a lone voice," http://www.forbetterlife.org/billboards/ billboard_detail.php?bb=square (last accessed June 25, 2002).

16. Note Stuart Franklin's comment that "'It really isn't a great picture, because I was much too far away'" (Robin, *The Photos of the Century,* n.p.). The pertinent norm of photojournalism, especially in respect to war or revolution, is that the photographer should be in the middle of the action, a virtual participant, in contrast to the distant or posed compositions of most other professional photography. See Susan D. Moeller, *Shooting War: Photography and the American Combat Experience* (New York: Basic Books, 1989), 9. Perlmutter notes the unusual distance for the Tiananmen icon and spins his wheels trying to explain it away (*Photojournalism and Foreign Policy,* 79–80).

17. James C. Scott, *Seeing Like a State: How Certain Schemes to Improve the Human Condition Have Failed* (New Haven: Yale University Press, 1998), 79.

18. Robert Hariman, *Political Style: The Artistry of Power* (Chicago: University of Chicago Press, 1995), 36.

19. Ibid.

20. Note also that the video version of the incident shown in *The Gate of Heavenly Peace* reveals a more complicated political scenario: while the close-in shot leaves a larger visual field outside the frame, the tank attempts to maneuver around the man, who dodges back and forth to stay in front of it and then clambers on board to *talk* to the crew through a viewing slit. All this activity appears ad hoc, aesthetically ragged, perhaps impulsive. In this view, historical action is much more a matter of micropolitical interactions that develop through improvisation and talk among people whose perspectives are likely to reflect their standpoints within the event.

21. Scholars in international relations are accustomed to seeing realism and liberalism defined as opposing theories of world politics. From that perspective, the analysis in this paper then will appear confused or ignorant. To avoid this misunderstanding, it is important to specify the level of analysis: We are not making claims about theoretical arguments in the social sciences. We are examining one instance of how realism and liberalism function as political discourses within public media. When political ideas operate in the "real world" of political actors speaking among themselves and before others to persuade, manipulate, rationalize, and otherwise use speech and other symbolic forms as modes of action, they typically use varied and often seemingly contradictory appeals. They do so because they have to address multiple audiences, represent multiple

constituencies, provide flexible responses to contingent events, and so forth. Moreover, these potential contradictions often are managed through incorporation into encompassing norms of representation. So it is that liberalism and realism can be conjoined within a common modernism. See also Francis A. Beer and Robert Hariman, eds., *Post-Realism: The Rhetorical Turn in International Relations* (East Lansing: Michigan State University Press, 1996).

22. Criticisms of modernist aesthetics now are legion. In part due to our emphasis on the conventions of modernist visual art, we have been influenced most directly by Scott and by Charles Jencks, *What Is Postmodernism?*, 4th ed. (London: Academy Editions, 1996), and *Late-Modern Architecture and Other Essays* (New York: Rizzoli, 1980). See also Brian Wallis, ed., *Art after Modernism: Rethinking Representation* (New York: New Museum of Contemporary Art, 1984).

23. Scott, *Seeing Like a State*, 4.

24. The coverage in *Newsweek* is illustrative. The June 12 cover screams "Bloodbath," and the June 19 cover declares a "Reign of Terror." Both covers and the other photos accompanying the story document the carnage in vivid, emotionally powerful images. The tank photo—"'A single student standing in front of a tank': Among the indelible images of the upheaval in Tiananmen, a lone demonstrator blocks an armored column on Changan Avenue"—is the last visual record of the confrontation in the streets; it is followed by portraits of establishment leaders and military police. By contrast with prior images, it is dispassionate, measured, and orderly. This reduction also functions as a transition within the magazine's visual narrative from past to present, from popular protest to official power, from domestic upheaval to global actors.

25. These contrasts are evident in the documentary video coverage throughout *The Gate of Heavenly Peace,* as well as the experiential account provided by Geremie Barmé, "Beijing Days, Beijing Nights," in *The Pro-Democracy Protests in China: Reports from the Provinces,* ed. Jonathan Unger, 35–58 (Armonk, N.Y.: M. E. Sharpe, 1991), which also is at http://www.tsquare.tv/links/Beijing_Days.html (last accessed June 25, 2002). It is crucial to remember that these differences in representation are not merely matters of taste; they are endorsements of different modes of political agency. Jeffrey N. Wasserstrom's observation on student protests in Shanghai puts the point clearly: "[W]hat made these protests so powerful was their efficacy as *symbolic performances* that questioned, subverted, and ultimately undermined official rituals and spectacles. Lacking economic clout and generally shunning violence, students had to rely primarily upon their ability to move an audience. This they did through the use of oratory, song, gestures, and other forms of symbolic actions. In short, they made all the techniques actors use in aesthetic forms of drama serve the purposes of the *political theater* of the street" (*Student Protests in Twentieth-Century China: The View from Shanghai* [Stanford: Stanford University Press, 1991], 5). See also Esherick and Wasserstrom, "Acting out Democracy: Political Theatre in Modern China," in *Popular Protest and Political Culture in Modern China,* 32–69. The symbolic resources for political performance are some of the most basic forms of democratic knowledge, and their suppression in the realm of representation then underwrites other political modalities such as money or guns. This is one of the direct linkages between Cold War rhetoric and the emerging discourse of global order.

26. For discussion of this trope, see John Louis Lucaites, "Visualizing 'The People': Individualism and Collectivism in *Let Us Now Praise Famous Men*," *Quarterly Journal of Speech* 83 (1997): 269–89.

27. Scott, *Seeing Like a State,* 32.

28. What drops out of this transformation is the recognition of any translation problem between the Western idea of human rights and Chinese political culture. See Xia Yong, "Human Rights and Chinese Tradition," in Dutton, *Streetlife China,* 23–41.

29. *The Gate of Heavenly Peace.* The Web site maintained by the Long Bow Group on the film summarizes and provides some references regarding discussion of the film, as well as additional

information and links regarding the protest and government actions (http://tsquare.tv/ [last accessed June 25, 2002]).

30. The film's use of the photo is further evidence of its iconic status: it is used to orient the Western viewer to the historical event—"a moment that would come to symbolize the hope and the tragedy of those spring days"—and its appropriation in other media is highlighted (transcript of *The Gate of Heavenly Peace,* http://tsquare.tv/film/transcript01.html [last accessed June 25, 2002]).

31. Ibid.

32. Contrast this deflection of public mourning with Wu Hung's observation that a vital, grassroots, dissident public emerged in Beijing in 1976 through the experience of grieving together over the death of Zhou Enlai ("Tiananmen Square," 102–4). The public may have required rational-critical debate (occurring in private settings), but it emerged from public mourning mediated by visual arts (the monument in the square, the wreaths and banners placed there, and so forth). Such "sentimental" acts may be far more important to democratic life than is acknowledged; if so, their suppression within modernist schemes of representation is incipiently antidemocratic.

33. Anne Norton, *Republic of Signs: Liberal Theory and American Popular Culture* (Chicago: University of Chicago Press, 1993), 1.

34. Ibid., 3.

35. Scott, *Seeing Like a State,* 256.

36. Ibid., 258.

37. See also Calhoun, *Neither Gods nor Heroes,* 189–90.

Part 2

*T*he Disposition of Place
and the Placing of Disposition

6

_N_ational Park Landscapes and the Rhetorical Display of Civic Religion

Images are not just a particular kind of sign, but something like an actor on the historical stage, a presence or character endowed with legendary status, a history that parallels and participates in the stories we tell ourselves about our own evolution from creatures "made in the image of a creator," to creatures who make themselves and their world in their own image.

W. J. T Mitchell[1]

The rhetorical power inherent in the visual experience of a symbolic place is best understood using Aristotle's third category of the rhetorical work of generating and maintaining public identity—the "epideictic." Epideictic rhetoric does not _argue_ the ideas or ideals that bind people into community so much as it _displays_ them to a witnessing public. Lawrence W. Rosenfield observes that anciently the epideictic provided an audience with "the opportunity of beholding a common reality," of "joining with our community in giving thought to what we witness," and of thereby experiencing together the "luminosity" of the values and aspirations they share.[2] His insight resonates with Kenneth Burke's comment that, for symbol users, "nature gleams secretly with a most fantastic shimmer of words and social relationships."[3] Together, Rosenfield and Burke help us understand the rhetorical power of a publicly significant place. As diverse individuals encounter such a place—one that "gleams" with common meaning—they share a common rhetorical experience.

Our project in this chapter is to examine the rhetorical functioning of such publicly significant places. The case we focus on is, broadly, the national parks of the United States; more specifically, a farmhouse along the tour road in the Saratoga National Historical Park. This park—one of the smaller ones in the National Park System—commemorates what is generally regarded as the pivotal battle of the American Revolution, in which colonists turned back a 1777 British offensive from Canada into New York. Our examination has two parts. First, we will explore the rhetorical functioning of landscape in general, suggesting that the public landscapes constituted by the U.S. national park movement display symbols that enable citizens to participate in a civic religion. Second, we will probe more deeply the idea of a civic religion and describe in some detail the rhetorical display of symbols at the Saratoga National Historical Park to reflect on how the experience of touring the battlefield —and perhaps other U.S. national parks—might work as a civic religion.

Rhetorical Landscapes and Civic Religion in America

J. B. Jackson, a cultural geographer and American cultural historian, has noted that when we refer to a "sense of place," we mean not just *atmosphere* but also *influence*. As he put it, when we view or visit a symbolic place,

> [t]he experience varies in intensity; it can be private and solitary, or convivial and social. The place can be a natural setting or a crowded street or even a public occasion. What moves us is our change of mood, the brief but vivid event. And what automatically ensues, it seems to me, is a sense of fellowship with those who share the experience, and the instinctive desire to return, to establish a custom of repeated ritual.[4]

People tend to encounter and examine landscapes aesthetically, but that aesthetic experience has the rhetorical function of prompting them to imagine alternative identities for themselves. As Burke would put it, scene invites transformation of one's sense of self. And in his short history of the term "landscape," J. B. Jackson connects the aesthetic function of scenery directly with the rhetorical function of influencing individual identity in collective ways:

> In the eighteenth century, *landscape* indicated scenery in the theater and had the function of discreetly suggesting the location of the action or perhaps the time of day [and] there is no better indication of how our relation to the environment can change over the centuries than in the role of stage scenery. Three hundred years ago Corneille could write a five-act tragedy with a single indication of the setting: "The action takes place in the palace of the king." If we glance at the work of a modern playwright, we will probably find one detailed description of a scene after another, and the ultimate in this kind of landscape . . . is the contemporary movie. Here the set does much more than merely identify the time and place and establish the mood. By means of shifts in lighting and sound and perspective, the set actually creates the players, identifies them, and tells them what to do.[5]

Place works rhetorically, then, as "a composition of man-made or man-modified spaces to serve as infrastructure and background for our collective existence." People treat it as "background"—as a *scene*—that "underscores not only our identity and presence but also our history."[6]

By the early decades of the nineteenth century, many places in the new American nation were already famous for providing this sort of experience. Increasingly, Americans were schooled in the symbolism of their national landscape, and those who could afford to became occasional practitioners of the leisure discipline of "picturesque touring" that had become popular in England before that century's turn. Picturesque touring is what the American landscape painter, Thomas Cole, had been doing in the southern Adirondacks on July 8, 1837, when he recorded in his journal, "Have just returned from a tour in search of the Picturesque."[7] The purpose of Cole's excursion had been to seek places that display symbols worth recording, and his recording of them was the practice of rendering scenery rhetorical. Barbara Warnick shows how the belletristic rhetoric that dominated this era in both Britain and America treated "taste" as the primary perceptual faculty that enabled reception and judgment.[8] Normalized and improved by instruction and experience, an individual's taste would enable recognition of the collectively good and true when their symbolic representations are encountered. To encounter such symbols and then to publicize them was the purpose of picturesque touring.

The practice of picturesque touring was first theorized in England by William Gilpin. His 1792 essay, "On Picturesque Travel" (reprinted the following year in the *New-York Magazine*), makes its rhetorical work clear: "If [nature's] great scenes can inspire [the picturesque traveler] with a religious awe; or its tranquil scenes with that complacency of mind which is so nearly allied to benevolence, it is certainly for the better."[9] That is because people are most delighted and edified

> when some grand scene, though perhaps of incorrect composition, rising before the eye, strikes us beyond the power of thought. . . . In this pause of intellect; this *deliquium* of the soul, an enthusiastic sensation of pleasure overspreads it, previous to any examination by the rules of art. The general idea of the scene makes an impression, before any appeal is made to the judgment. We rather *feel,* than *survey* it.[10]

Thomas Cole had strong feelings about the role of this sort of rhetorical experience. His "Essay on American Scenery," first delivered as a lyceum lecture and published in 1836, described the influence of scenery in terms that direct it toward the work of transforming individuals who live in America into *Americans.* The experience of "delight" afforded by such scenes "is not merely sensual" or temporary, he said. Rather, "in gazing on the pure creations of the Almighty," the observer "feels a calm, religious tone steal through his mind, and when he has turned to mingle with his fellow-men, the chords which have been struck in that sweet communion cease not to vibrate." Cole's preference was for the untamed and "sublime" scenery that he saw as characteristically American, but he could also acknowledge the civic value of an individual encounter with "cultivated scenery":

> [I]t encompasses our homes, and though devoid of the stern sublimity of the wild, its quieter spirit steals tenderly into our bosoms, mingled with a thousand domestic affections and heart-touching associations human hands have wrought and human deeds hallowed all around. And it is here that taste, which is the perception of the beautiful and the knowledge of the principles on which nature works, can be applied and our dwelling places made fitting for refined and intellectual beings.[11]

That Cole was speaking for many of his fellow citizens is evident in the elaborately illustrated publications on American scenery that would soon begin to appear. In 1851, Benson Lossing published *A Pictorial Field-Book of the Revolution,* a copiously illustrated account of his picturesque tour of the scenes of the Revolutionary War. The following year *The Home Book of the Picturesque: or, American Scenery, Art, and Literature* collected essays by Irving, Bryant, Cooper, and others, as well as engravings from paintings by Cole and the other prominent landscape painters of the day—Kensett, Durand, Cropsey, and Church. Its avowed purpose was to celebrate "the diversified landscapes of our country [that] exert no slight influence in creating our characters as individuals, and in confirming our destiny as a nation."[12] A generation later came the massive *Picturesque America; or, The Land We Live In: A Delineation by Pen and Pencil of the Mountains, Rivers, Lakes, Forests, Waterfalls, Shores, Canons [sic], Valleys, Cities, and Other Picturesque Features of Our Country.*

Published first in 1870 as a periodical series of "views," *Picturesque America* was soon to be a two-volume compendium of well-known and meaning-laden American scenes. Its rhetorical function, according to historian Sue Rainey, was to enable "Americans, after the trauma of the Civil War, to construct a national self-image based on reconciliation between North and South and incorporation of the West." Rainey continues:

> Its more than nine hundred pictures also provided graphic testimony of the variety, uniqueness, and potential wealth of the American landscape and the advanced civilization of its cities. This composite image both promoted and reinforced a resurgence of nationalism rooted in the homeland.[13]

In Kenneth Burke's resonant phrase, such scenes invited the Americans who experienced them, actually or vicariously, "to make [themselves] over in the image of the imagery" presented there.[14]

Places that function in this way are fundamentally rhetorical in Burke's primary sense of that term: they prompt in individuals a transformation of identity. For Burke, the "simplest case of persuasion" is less a sort of argument than it is a kind of human relationship: "you persuade a man only insofar as you can talk his language by speech, gesture, tonality, order, image, attitude, idea, *identifying* your ways with his."[15] Rhetoric is at work whenever people interact using symbols and are influenced by that interaction to understand themselves and their relation to each other differently. That different understanding prompts a change of identity, and this change "may involve identification not just with mankind or the world in general, but with some kind of congregation that also implies some related norms of differentiation and segregation."[16]

To prompt individual Americans to identify themselves with a national "congregation" was what Congress seems to have had in mind when, in 1864, during some of the most difficult weeks of the Civil War, it passed a bill that assigned the federally owned Yosemite Valley and Mariposa Grove of sequoias to the state of California with the mandate that these places be made available for "public use, resort, and recreation."[17] A year later, members of the newly appointed California Yosemite Commission assembled in the valley within earshot of Yosemite Falls to determine how they might implement this mandate. The commission chairman was Frederick Law Olmsted—philosopher of American landscape and designer of the nation's great urban parks. During America's "darkest hours," Olmsted began, Congress enacted "the will of the Nation . . . that this scenery shall never be private property, but that like certain defensive points upon our coast it shall be held solely for public purposes."[18] Particularly in times of crisis, he continued, places like this must be preserved as a refuge where Americans can gather to experience beauty and serenity in their homeland. And doing that is directly in the public interest, it being "a scientific fact that the occasional contemplation of natural scenes of an impressive character" not only "increases the subsequent capacity for happiness" but also decreases the incidence of the sort of "mental and nervous excitability, moroseness, melancholy, or irascibility" in individuals that prevents their "proper exercise of the intellectual and moral forces."[19] The particular experience afforded by those places can prompt individual visitors to adopt for themselves the essentially civic virtues that are "intrinsically and mysteriously associated . . . with moral perception and intuition."[20] At Yosemite, anyone can witness its great "union of the deepest sublimity with the deepest beauty of nature, not in one feature or another . . . not in any landscape that can be framed by itself, but all around and wherever the visitor goes."[21] And that is why such places must be made accessible to all Americans—why "the establishment by government of great public grounds for the free enjoyment of the people . . . is thus justified and enforced as a political duty."[22]

That is also why Congress subsequently designated, in quick succession, the Yellowstone Basin and the Grand Canyon of the Colorado as the first national parks. "Like certain defensive points upon our coast," as Olmsted had put it, places like these should "be held solely for public purposes."[23] In the late nineteenth century, the United States was a farflung and unwieldy collective of people trying to recover from a catastrophic civil war. To transcend their considerable differences and enact together a national identity, its citizens needed a new sense of their commonality. These were places that no American could own. Here individual Americans could transcend their diverse local identities and share the common experience of inhabiting together a spectacular place designated as a public symbol of their nation. That is what national parks and monuments were, and are, for.

The man appointed in 1915 to organize the separately administered national parks into what became the National Park Service used the government printing office to publicize that purpose. One of Stephen Mather's first acts as a new assistant to the secretary of the interior was to oversee the compilation, publication, and wide distribution of an ambitious compendium of photographic images from each park that he titled the *National Parks Portfolio*. Mather himself introduced the volume with a "Presentation" page that proclaimed, "This Nation is richer in natural scenery of the first order than any other nation; but it does not know it." Consequently, he continued, "The main object of this portfolio . . . is to present to the people of this country a panorama of our principal national parks set side by side for their study and comparison" for the purpose of turning "the busy eyes of this Nation upon its national parks long enough to bring some realization of what these pleasure gardens ought to mean, of what so easily they may be made to mean, to this people."[24]

From the beginning, American national parks and monuments have been "made to mean" something more to the American public than mere pleasure. Stephen Mather's rhetorical project was to prompt citizens to invent for themselves the sort of identity from which *national* purposes would follow. Mather was the first of many who worked to make the national parks and monuments places where Americans would learn who they are as citizens of a nation, members of a "congregation" that, in the modern era, has shaped individual and collective identity in the same ways religion did in premodern times. Benedict Anderson observes that the "dawn of nationalism at the end of the eighteenth century coincide[d] with the dusk of religious modes of thought."[25] And yet, as Ernest Renan has put it:

> A nation is a soul, a spiritual principle. Two things, which in truth are but one, constitute this soul or spiritual principle. One lies in the past, one in the present. One is the possession in common of a rich legacy of memories; the other is present-day consent, the desire to live together, the will to perpetuate the value of the heritage that one has received in an undivided form.[26]

As Benedict Anderson has explained, a nation is necessarily an imagined community realized in shared symbols. What those symbols display is an ideal human identity that encompasses values and beliefs, desires and commitments of the people that community comprises. A nation's officially designated public places display that identity. Individuals may encounter those places separately, but the meaning they encounter is collective—it is the soul of the nation they share. And that brings us back to Thomas Cole's claim that the experience of "delight" afforded by such scenes "is not merely sensual" or temporary. Rather, "in gazing on the pure creations of the Almighty," the observer "feels a calm, religious tone steal through his mind, and when he has turned to mingle with his fellow-men, the chords which have been struck in that sweet communion cease not to vibrate."

At the national parks and monuments of the United States, these places are implicitly sacred. The "nature" parks—such as Yellowstone, Yosemite, and Grand Canyon—are rendered sacred as "pure creations of the Almighty" that are protected as relics of a sublime and pristine American nature and, at the same time, made accessible for public pilgrimage. The "history" parks—such as Gettysburg and Saratoga—are rendered sacred as relics of redemptive sacrifice made manifest through the interpretive work of the park service. This sacred character becomes explicit only rarely. The 1933 Yellowstone National Park master plan included a map designating the area immediately surrounding the Grand Canyon of the Yellowstone a "sacred area"[27] and mandating that it be restored to its natural state. The Grand Canyon National Park's 1994 *Architectural Character Guidelines* begin with a foreword that ends with the matter-of-fact statement that, as development proceeds in that national park, "we must always remember that we are building on holy ground."[28] But the sacred "vibration" of these places can be felt by those who visit regardless of whether it is made explicit in interpretive materials. Historian James McPherson, for example, tells of how he and his students experienced emotions so powerful as to call forth tears while they walked the "hallowed ground" of Gettysburg.[29]

Displaying a Sacred Place: The Neilson Farmhouse

But what exactly does it mean for a place to be "sacred"? According to Mircea Eliade, religious people live in a world where "the sacred" is something that can irrupt anywhere. A deity can manifest itself in a rock, a tree, a river, anything at all. Humans are then put in immediate contact with a realm that is "wholly other," and the everyday, profane world takes on meaning. A bush bursts into flame. A carpenter climbs a hill and is transfigured before his companions. Or, the sacred object might appear unchanged to the mortal senses and yet manifest itself to the spiritually alive person as wholly other. A grove of trees might reveal itself as the abode of a god, though it continues to look and sound and smell like nothing more than a grove of trees. Eliade's central point is that "the sacred" and "the profane" are fundamentally distinct realms. To experience the sacred is to confront something radically other to the world of everyday, profane experience. And yet some connection with the realm of the sacred is essential to the religious person, for whom the profane world is in itself meaningless. Eliade invents the term "hierophany" to name the irruption of the sacred.[30]

Jean-Paul Sartre theorizes an experience that moves in a parallel but opposite direction, an experience he calls "the absurd." Exemplified in a key episode in his novel *Nausea*, the absurd is a kind of atheistic double of Eliade's hierophany. The root of a chestnut tree suddenly manifests itself to Sartre's protagonist, Roquintin, as wholly other in its brute indifference to human purposes and defiance of human reason. It overflows his efforts to say what it is, and he is filled with revulsion. Like Eliade's sacred object, it is *de trop,* too much to be comprehended by rational categories such as color and shape. For Sartre—essentially a disillusioned child of the Enlightenment—it is these rational categories that give meaning to the everyday world, and so, in contrast to hierophany, the experience of the absurd renders that everyday world meaningless. Hence, as the hierophany fills the religious person with reverential awe, the absurd fills the existential person with disgust.[31]

Both hierophany and the absurd can be understood as versions of what eighteenth-century rhetoricians called "the sublime." Drawing on an ancient text attributed to Longinus, writers like Edmund Burke and Hugh Blair characterized the sublime in language that combines the reverence of which Eliade speaks and the horror associated by Sartre with the absurd. The common quality is contact with a dimension that is radically different from the world of everyday experience, a dimension that is "wholly other." Theorists of the sublime most frequently exemplified it in natural scenery, especially the torrential waterfalls, great mountains, and wild forests that were a common subject of Thomas Cole's paintings. It was primarily the sublimity of the American landscape that Cole had in mind when he wrote of the religious and civic inspiration that could be found in contemplating it, though he also recognized the civic importance of scenery that was aesthetically pleasing without the alien character of the sublime.

As described by Eliade, hierophany seems of itself to entail no rhetoric of display. The sacred simply "shows itself to us"[32] with no human intervention. Sartre's absurd is likewise the gratuitous manifestation of a wholly other reality. To live in what Eliade calls a "sacralized world" is to live amid the constant possibility of hierophany, to be continuously alive to the immanence of a sacred reality that may break through the veil of the ordinary at any time. Religious people may engage in rhetorics of display that enshrine some object or event that has revealed itself as sacred, but in itself the hierophany is a pure and gratuitous manifestation of the wholly other. The transfiguration of Jesus, for example, was a gratuitous manifestation, but afterward the apostle Peter wanted to erect three tents to mark the site. Those tents would have constituted a rhetoric of display that would show the sacred character of the place. And the liturgical rites that are central to many organized religions can be understood as rhetorics of display that attempt through rituals of language and gesture to show the sacred character of what might otherwise appear to be ordinary objects—a wafer of bread, a cup of wine, a book, a fragment of cloth or bone. In the Christian tradition, we are accustomed to distinguish sects by the elaborateness of their rhetorics of display—high-church sects engage in high-style rhetorics, low-church sects engage in plain-style rhetorics.

Whatever else it did or did not accomplish, the European Enlightenment "desacralized" the world, to use Eliade's term. But Eliade argues—and we agree—that the project of making a wholly profane world has not been and probably never can be complete. "To whatever degree he may have desacralized the world, the man [sic] who has made his choice in favor of a profane life never succeeds in completely doing away with religious behavior."[33] Our view is that the rhetorics of display at work in the national parks are secular remnants or echoes of what Eliade calls "religious behavior," specifically of the liturgical formulae that constitute rhetorics of sacred display. The rituals of observation enacted at the national parks are, we argue, liturgical rites of a civic religion.

Our example is the tour road at the Saratoga National Historical Park in upper New York State, with particular emphasis on the Neilson farmhouse, an eighteenth-century building that served as a makeshift headquarters for American officers and is now situated and displayed at one of the principal stops on the tour road. But if our analysis stands up, it should cast light on a wide range of sites at which objects are held up to public view by rhetorics that transform seemingly mundane things into the sacred objects of a "religion" whose purpose is to unite us as a "congregation" of citizens—in short, a civic religion. A shapeless lump of metal is placed behind glass and becomes a musket ball that wounded a patriot soldier. A sign names a patch of blackened sand as "cryptobiotic soil," an especially fragile form of life deserving of respect because its endurance exemplifies the endless wonder and bounty of the American land. A mangled fire truck is put on display as a relic of the collapse of the World Trade Center towers and becomes a sacred reminder of heroes who rode in it to their death. The object puts us in contact with a realm having something of the radical otherness associated by Eliade with the sacred. Like an experience of the religious sacred, the contact transforms and gives new meaning to ordinary reality. McPherson speaks of finding "inspiration" on the sacred ground of Gettysburg.[34] We think of this realm as "the civic sacred" in recognition of its place in civic religion, and we see landscapes —our national parks in particular—as major loci of the civic sacred.

The notion that one's native landscape has a sacred character goes back at least to the ancient Greeks, who took pride in being *autochthonous,* or born from the soil on which they lived. Americans are not unique in attributing cultural significance to the land we inhabit, though we may be more emphatic than many on this point. It is revealing that our first distinctly American movement in art, the Hudson River School (of which Thomas Cole is the generally recognized "founder"), took the landscape as its great subject. There is some irony here; the only "Americans" who might claim to be *autochthonous* are those whose identity as Americans is qualified by the adjective "native." Perhaps non-native Americans make so much of the American land because, for some, it was a refuge their ancestors chose and, for others, it was a prison to which their ancestors were taken in chains. Like Eliade's sacred, this land is to us something radically other to which we have a powerful attraction. We apostrophize its "spacious skies" and proclaim that it was "made for you and me" in song. We build highways and establish great parks to display the landscape as a sacred object that defines who we are as a people. For many Americans of the second and third quarters of the twentieth century, a Sunday afternoon drive through the countryside was a liturgy of civic religion as surely as the church service earlier that day was a liturgy of the Christian religion.

For some, the ritual drive through the American countryside might include the Saratoga battlefield. The scene of a 1777 military engagement that historians have characterized as the turning point of the Revolutionary War, the Saratoga battlefield became a New York State historical park in 1927, when the Model T Ford was introducing millions of Americans to the ritual of scenic tourism. A little more than a decade later it was transferred to the federal government to become a national park. The principal visitors' experience at the Saratoga National Historical Park today is a one-way tour road for automobiles and bicycles marked by ten stops at which signs and audiotapes chronicle particular events and characters in the battle. The tour road itself and most of the interpretive materials on it were developed during the 1960s and early 1970s.

Riding the tour road is analogous to the Catholic ritual known as the stations of the cross, in which devout persons travel symbolically the journey of Christ from the garden of Gethsemane to the tomb, stopping for prayer and meditation at fourteen "stations" marking specific episodes. The conventional design of a Catholic church includes pictorial representations of each episode placed around the walls of the nave for use in "saying the stations," and open-air sites marked by the stations are fairly common. The stops on the tour road similarly are marked by pictorial as well as textual aids to assist the visitor in visualizing the events of the battle. The first stop on the battlefield tour road is at Freeman's farm, scene of the first encounter between British and colonial troops; the last stop is at the burial site of Simon Fraser, a British officer whose death was instrumental in the American victory. As in the stations of the cross, one follows a narrative by moving through an actual or imagined landscape, pausing along the way to meditate on specific persons and events understood to be meaningful in establishing collective identity, in the one case Christian, in the other American. Through the experience, one enters ritually into what Eliade would call a sacred time, a time set apart from and radically other to the flow of "clock time" in which we live our everyday lives.

There is no evidence that our analogy between the stations of the cross and the battlefield tour road was on the minds of those who designed and marked the tour road at Saratoga or any of the other tour roads that are standard features of most national parks. The idea of the battlefield as a sacred place was nonetheless current among the many who made the pilgrimage there starting shortly after the battle itself and continuing throughout the nineteenth and twentieth centuries. The accounts of Timothy Dwight, Daniel Webster, Benjamin Silliman, and many others are marked by a reverential tone and occasional use of explicitly religious references to "martyrs," "relics," and the like.[35]

Like many religious pilgrimages, visits to the battlefield were (and are) simultaneously exercises in the tradition of scenic tourism that Americans imported from Great Britain in the early nineteenth century. The landscape of the battlefield has the hilly and wooded character canonized by the British and American artists and writers who developed that tradition, making it a suitable locale for picturesque touring in the tradition of Gilpin. Among the early visitors to the battlefield was Timothy Dwight, one of the first and most diligent American practitioners of scenic tourism.[36] French naturalist Jacques Milbert included the Saratoga battlefield in his 1823 picturesque tour of upper New York State.[37] Others who visited Saratoga to witness the scene of a momentous battle were simultaneously enjoying what Cole would recognize as the "delight" of an encounter with "cultivated scenery."

While better known as a work of popular history, Benson Lossing's two-volume *Field Guide to the American Revolution* (1851) deserves an important place in the tradition of scenic-tourism literature. Lossing set out in 1848 on a trip up the Hudson that followed in reverse direction the course of "Gentleman Johnny" Burgoyne's 1777 campaign to isolate the New England colonies, and he eventually traveled some eight thousand miles over numerous battle scenes of the Revolutionary War. His account weaves conventional picturesque description of the countryside together with historical narrative of the events that had taken place there some seventy years before. (In the margins of the book, passages are marked "1848" or "1777" to assist the reader in keeping the strands of the story clear.) The book is liberally illustrated with woodcuts of Lossing's own drawings of the places he visits.

Figure C10, for example, is Lossing's full-page montage of Bemis Heights, site of fortifications constructed by the American Continental army in its effort to stop Burgoyne's push southward toward Albany. At the top of the page is the Neilson farmhouse as it stood in 1848; Lossing tells us that only the small wing to our right existed in 1777. Moving clockwise down the page, the next image is another farmhouse that had been demolished a few years before, as reconstructed by Lossing from a sketch made by Charles Neilson; it served as the headquarters for Gen. Horatio Gates, the American commander in the battle of Saratoga. Below that is the interior of the original section of the Neilson farmhouse, which Lossing tells us "is carefully preserved [by the Neilson family] in its original condition," that is, in its condition when it served as field headquarters for colonial officers.[38] At the bottom of the page is a view looking eastward across the Champlain Canal and the Hudson River toward the hills of Washington County and Vermont; in the foreground is a barge similar to the one Lossing traveled in from Waterford to Bemis Heights. Above that is a map to which Lossing will refer in narrating incidents of the battle. To the left of the map is a halberd that, he says, was "plowed up in the neighborhood, and is in the possession of Mr. Neilson. When found it had a small British flag . . . which soon occupied the utilitarian and more peaceful position of patches in the bed-quilt of a prudent housewife."[39]

The rhetoric of display at work in this montage (and throughout Lossing's book) has characteristics that distinguish it from the rhetoric governing display on the tour road that now occupies this same site. Most noticeable are the emphasis on marks of human civilization and the easy juxtaposition of past and present. Lossing has no hesitation in showing on the same page a canal barge such as the one that brought him to Bemis Heights in 1848 and a map on which visitors (and readers) can trace events of the battle that took place there some seventy years earlier. The sacredness of the past is acknowledged: the portion of the Neilson farmhouse that existed in 1777 and served as headquarters for two American officers has been preserved by the Neilson family, and Lossing's drawing shows it to us "in its original condition." But the house itself has been greatly expanded, and it is in daily use as the dwelling of a prosperous family. Lossing calls it a "mansion,"[40] and his drawing displays the prosperity of the Neilson family in the form of livestock and a fence that seems to be enclosing a substantial estate.

The drawing of the canal boat offers evidence of the more general prosperity achieved through improvements that have opened an area that was in 1777 an isolated frontier to the commercial markets of Albany and New York City. The past that Lossing displays is not really all that distant in years: during the barge trip from Waterford to Bemis Heights, he speaks with the son of a man who fought at Saratoga, and while touring the battlefield he meets a woman who can recount personal memories from the time of the battles. In displaying the past, he simultaneously exhibits the progress that has propelled his audience beyond the material realities of that past and continues to move them ahead. He expresses concern that collective memory of the Revolution be preserved. This is in fact his stated purpose in publishing the book. But what makes the battle of Saratoga worth remembering is, paradoxically, what is working to efface that memory: the social and material progress set in motion by the transformation of British colonies into free and independent states. The past displayed in his account seems not so much "wholly other" as it is prelude to the present and future. Considered from the vantage point of Eliade's analysis, its "sacredness" is metaphorical at best, though Lossing and his contemporaries certainly recognized the battlefield as "sacred ground."

We turn now to the treatment of the Neilson farmhouse by the National Park Service. Before the park service took over the battlefield in 1939, the state of New York had transformed the farmhouse from a living residence into a museum piece. The nineteenth-century

8. The Nielson farmhouse at the Saratoga National Historical Park. Photograph by
S. Michael Halloran

additions that had made it a mansion in Benson Lossing's eyes were removed during the
1920s, but the farmhouse was by no means in its original condition. The siding and interior
plastering had been redone in 1927, and a number of other features were of nineteenth- and
twentieth-century vintage, though contrived to look much older. The house had been
moved from its original foundations to a new site, and a couple of other buildings had been
erected near it in order to create a cluster of "colonial era" structures, including a block-
house fort said to include beams from a barn that had been fortified during the battle of
Saratoga. The cluster of buildings, formed as an imaginative reconstruction of the year 1777,
constituted the center of the New York State historical park.

When the National Park Service took over the park, its policy was to remove all post-
Revolution structures and restore the site as fully as possible to its original state. The block-
house fort, whose design was more appropriate to the period of the French and Indian War
than the Revolution, was removed sometime in the 1970s to a field outside the park
boundaries, where it stood until 1999 when it was moved to the nearby town of Stillwater
to serve as a visitors' center. A number of stone monuments that had been erected starting
in the late nineteenth century were allowed to remain on the battlefield, though some of
them were moved and at least one whose inscription was found to be inaccurate has been
placed in long-term storage. Historical highway markers that had been placed by the New
York State Education Department as aids to motorists were removed from the battlefield
regardless of their accuracy. The public thoroughfares that had run through the battlefield
when it was farmland were torn up or converted to hiking or horse trails, and a closed-cir-
cuit tour road was constructed for the sole purpose of giving access to the battlefield sites.

The park service conducted extensive archeological, architectural, and historical studies from 1957 to 1960 to determine the original structure of the Neilson farmhouse and the use to which it was put during the battle of Saratoga. The reports documenting the conclusions drawn from these studies are meticulous. The 1960 "Furnishings Plan," for example, lists 102 specific items to be displayed in the sixteen-by-seventeen-foot common room that is the building's main interior space, and the report includes five pages of architectural drawings to show exactly where each item should be placed. Among those items is a small mirror, whose presence is justified in the report as an expression of the known personal vanity of Benedict Arnold, one of the officers who probably quartered at the Neilson farmhouse. The building itself was moved back to its original site and restored as accurately as possible to its physical state in 1777, using as much of its original fabric as possible. Where structural members had to be replaced, the new materials were marked in unobtrusive places so that later investigators could distinguish the replacements clearly from originals.

Today the house stands at stop two on the tour road, atop a hill that was fortified by the Continental army against a British assault from the north. The tour road likewise approaches the house from the north, along gently rising ground. At the high point of the road there is a parking lot from which a trail leads up to the house itself. From the parking lot, the road then circles around the house in a broad, counterclockwise, downhill arc along a steeper slope, so that after stopping to view the house up close, one has a continuously changing scenic view reminiscent of a cinematic pan. The house thus recedes and rises to the left as one proceeds along the road toward the next stop, eventually disappearing behind another hill.

While the door of the house is usually left open, visitors are not permitted to enter. The furniture and objects on display inside are mostly reproductions chosen to represent the house as a makeshift military field headquarters rather than the home of the Neilson family. The 1960 furnishing plan says that it should "look as if the staff had just dashed outside to view some near and unexpected commotion" and expected to return within a few minutes.[41] Objects such as a uniform coat draped over the back of a chair and a quill pen lying on the table help to convey the sense of a momentary interruption. Costumed interpreters are frequently in attendance at the farmhouse to answer questions, and during commemorative "encampments," Revolutionary war reenactors pitch their tents, cook meals, and conduct drills in the long, sloping field to the southeast of the house. Lines of posts mark fortifications that have been identified by archeologists.

A few yards in front of the house is a viewing stand with an interpretive sign and a button marked "History Now." Pushing the button activates an audiotape whose script goes as follows:

> I'm John Neilson. I built that frame house a year or so after I leased this parcel of land. What with my duties in Colonel McCrea's Regiment of Albany County Militia and there bein' only my wife, Lydia, and myself to do the labor, I had little time for farmin'. However, I cleared and fenced what I could and put in maize, potatoes, and flax.
>
> When the invaders drew nigh and 'peared a battle was imminent, I hurried Lydia into an ox cart and took her south beyond Stillwater. I had to return, since I was on command, carryin' military stores 'twixt Albany and Lake George.

I'd as lief not, for t'was a sorry sight. The soldiers dug trenches and piled great
walls of earth and logs all about my farm. They chopped my fences for firewood, cut
hay from my mowin' ground and dug up my potatoes. They even trampled Lydia's
little sauce garden—pumpkins, turnips, and all. Two officers of high rank quartered
in my house . . . another in one of my barns.

Yet, all the farms in this neck of the woods received the same treatment . . . some
worse than mine.

As my captain explained . . . the approach of the enemy was of the greatest
concern . . .

The tape station is so positioned that, as you listen, you stand before the actual farmhouse
of John Neilson. It is painted the barn red that research has revealed as its original color.
The details described by the voice on the tape, including the fortifications and the attendant damage done to Neilson's crops and fences, have likewise been carefully documented
by historical research. But the trenches, the walls of earth and logs, the hay stubble, and the
trampled garden described by the voice are not visible. The house stands on a field of mown
grass next to a grove of mature trees and shrubs. The farmhouse as we see it today is neither what it was in 1777 nor what it became as the Neilson farm grew and flourished in the
nineteenth century. Rather, it is an idealization displaying a version of what John Neilson
and the others were fighting for at Saratoga. As such, it has something of the "luminosity"
Rosenfield speaks of. It "gleams," as Burke would say, with the vitality of a time held sacred
in American collective memory.

We might think of the house as a kind of screen upon which the voice on the audiotape
invites us to project an imagined picture of the Neilson farmhouse as it was in September
and October of 1777. The resultant experience is an image that flickers back and forth
between the reconstructed farmhouse actually before us and a mental picture of the disorder into which it was thrown by the necessities of warfare. The image of an idealized pas-
toral America alternates with the image of John and Lydia Nielson's sacrifice in pursuit of
that ideal. It is like a cinematic montage that we can enjoy while pausing on a brisk bike
ride or a quiet drive through the scenic countryside, depicting the Jeffersonian ideal of a
United States made up of self-sufficient farmers living on land won by sacrifice, determination, and labor. And yet there is a trace of disillusion in the voice of John Neilson, an
undertone that, despite the encouraging words of "my captain," the sacrifice demanded of
John and Lydia feels too great. Where does this undertone come from and what does it
mean? How might it affect the experience of those who come to witness this symbol of our
national identity, and, in Rosenfield's felicitous phrase, to "give thought to what [they]
witness"?

In her 1995 review of the literature on collective memory, Barbie Zelizer asserts that
"collective memory is usable" in the sense that it is "always a means to something else" having to do with the present social order.[42] In this, the articulation of collective memory can
be seen as a kind of epideictic on Perelman and Olbrechts-Tyteca's understanding of that
term, according to which it asserts value commitments in the interest of strengthening
adherence to those values.[43] On this view epideictic is a celebration in the present moment,
oriented toward action in the future. In contrast, Rosenfield offers a reading of Aristotle,
according to which the purpose of epideictic is simply and solely to display the luminosity
of a timeless excellence:

How the listener may behave tomorrow . . . is of less import than his power to behold, to reach out through the speaker's representation to a potential for mortal perfection which envelops us but ordinarily chooses to hide from the common view of men [sic]. Insofar as auditors can join the speaker as spectators of the noble and excellent in this fashion, they will rejoice with him in their liberation and thereby make more permanent in the collective memory this confirmation of momentarily disclosed reality.[44]

Rosenfield's view makes of epideictic something very like Eliade's hierophany—an irruption of the timeless into the flow of everyday time. The epideictic moment is *kairotic,* but it is an opportunity for contemplation rather than action, for quiet rejoicing that humans are capable of this sort of excellence.

The contrast between these two views of epideictic and collective memory turns on a question of time. Epideictic is about something out of time (say, the sacrifice and dedication exemplified by John and Lydia Neilson), but it must happen in time (say, at the moment we stand before their reconstructed farmhouse and press the "History Now" button to hear John's voice). As hierophany is an irruption of the timeless at a specific moment in time, epideictic attempts to illuminate the timeless in some specific here and now. The collective memory that is nourished by epideictic aspires to the state of timelessness, but it subsists in time. It feeds on rituals, festivals, and observances that we attend at specified times, after which we return to everyday activities. On Perelman and Olbrechts-Tyteca's view, the timeless aspect of epideictic and collective memory is consumed in timeliness. It is *for use* on subsequent deliberative occasions. On Rosenfield's view, the true epideictic occasion is itself a moment out of time, a pure gift of rejoicing in the presence of excellence.

The John Neilson tape quoted above was created in preparation for the U.S. bicentennial. Like similar audiotapes at other stops along the tour road, it was scripted in the early 1970s, which is to say in the waning years and immediate aftermath of the war in Vietnam. The note of disillusionment in Neilson's voice is echoed in the voices that speak at other "History Now" stations; together those voices echo the disillusionment of a time marked by the resignation of an American president and the final bankruptcy of our adventure in Southeast Asia. The tapes are very much of their time, as epideictic rhetoric inevitably must be. The restoration of the Neilson farmhouse itself was done in conformity with standards of historic restoration that came into use only in the mid-twentieth century, standards that further developments in the field of historic-preservation architecture may one day make outdated. The design of the tour road and the landscaping of the stops along it reflect aesthetic standards developed in the eighteenth and nineteenth centuries and then adapted to forms of scenic tourism afforded by twentieth-century technology. The inscriptions on stone monuments that were placed on the Saratoga battlefield in the late nineteenth century and still stand there are in a style recognizably Victorian, and they speak to ideals of reconciliation and transcendence rooted in post-Reconstruction culture.

Timeliness is never absent from the epideictic. The question is whether, or perhaps to what extent, its timeliness dims the luminosity of "momentarily disclosed reality." This may be as much a question of the audience's openness to the gleam of that disclosure, of our own readiness to experience what Rosenfield calls "beholding wonder,"[45] as it is of the artfulness of a rhetoric whose purpose is to display symbols that invite this sort of response.

From the vantage point of the post-9/11 era, the time of Watergate and Vietnam seems like a moment of self-doubt for America, of apostasy from a civic religion that had defined an American "congregation" for two centuries. It is this self-doubt that is audible in the scripted and taped voice of a John Neilson imagined three decades ago. Like the deeds of the men and women who prevailed at Saratoga in 1777, our national moment of apostasy is a part of collective memory. It will not be forgotten, but what remains to be seen is whether it becomes another turning point in our national narrative, one that will eventually transform us from a Burkean "congregation" of wrangling believers into an assemblage of cynics.

Rosenfield believes that epideictic discourse in the mode he theorizes is rare because "its necessary constituents—openness of mind, felt reverence for reality, enthusiasm for life, the ability to congeal significant experiences in memorable language—are also rare."[46] The staff of the Saratoga National Historical Park is now engaged in developing a new master plan and interpretive strategy. Whether they and the National Park Service generally can find within themselves those constituents of epideictic discourse is a matter of some consequence. Of even greater consequence is our own readiness to discover those qualities within ourselves, to "reach out . . . to a potential for mortal perfection" when it is made present to us.

Notes

1. W. J. T. Mitchell, *Iconology: Image Text, Ideology* (Chicago: University of Chicago Press, 1986), 9.

2. Lawrence W. Rosenfield, "The Practical Celebration of Epideictic," in *Rhetoric in Transition: Studies in the Nature and Uses of Rhetoric,* ed. Eugene E. White, 133 (University Park: Pennsylvania State University Press, 1980).

3. Kenneth Burke, *Language as Symbolic Action: Essays on Life, Literature, and Method* (Berkeley: University of California Press, 1966), 378–79.

4. J. B. Jackson, *A Sense of Place, A Sense of Time* (New Haven: Yale University Press, 1994), 157–58.

5. J. B. Jackson, *Landscape in Sight: Looking at America,* ed. Helen Lefkowitz Horowitz (New Haven: Yale University Press, 1997), 301.

6. Ibid., 305.

7. Thomas Cole, *Thomas Cole: The Collected Essays and Prose Sketches,* ed. Marshall Tymn (St. Paul, Minn.: John Colet Press, 1980), 143.

8. Barbara Warnick, *The Sixth Canon: Belletristic Rhetorical Theory and Its French Antecedents* (Columbia: University of South Carolina Press, 1993), 17.

9. William Gilpin, *Three Essays: On Picturesque Beauty; On Picturesque Travel; and On Sketching Landscape: to Which Is Added a Poem, On Landscape Painting* (London, 1792), 47.

10. Ibid., 49–50.

11. Cole, *Thomas Cole: The Collected Essays,* 199–200.

12. *The Home Book of the Picturesque: or, American Scenery, Art, and Literature* (New York: G. P. Putnam, 1852), 3.

13. Sue Rainey, *Creating Picturesque America: Monument to the Natural and Cultural Landscape* (Nashville: Vanderbilt University Press, 1993), xiii.

14. Kenneth Burke, *The Philosophy of Literary Form* (Berkeley: University of California Press, 1973), 281.

15. Burke, *A Rhetoric of Motives* (Berkeley: University of California Press, 1960), 55.

16. Burke, "Rhetorical Situation," in *Communication: Ethical and Moral Issues,* ed. Lee Thayer, 268 (London: Gordon and Breach Science Publishers, 1973).

17. Frederick Law Olmsted, *Yosemite and the Mariposa Grove: A Preliminary Report, 1865* (Yosemite National Park, Calif.: Yosemite Association, 1993), vii.

18. Ibid., 9.

19. Ibid., 12.

20. Ibid., 19.

21. Ibid., 8–9.

22. Ibid., 18.

23. Ibid., 9.

24. Stephen T. Mather, "Presentation," *National Parks Portfolio* (Washington, D.C.: U.S. Department of the Interior, 1915).

25. Benedict Anderson, *Imagined Communities: Reflections on the Origin and Spread of Nationalism,* rev. ed. (London: Verso, 1991), 19.

26. Ernest Renan, "What Is a Nation?" *Nation and Narration,* ed. Homi Bhabha (London: Routledge, 1990), 19.

27. As mentioned by Yellowstone National Park historian Lee Whittlesley, in conversation on October 28, 2002.

28. U.S. Department of the Interior, *Grand Canyon National Park Architectural Character Guidelines* (Washington, D.C.: National Parks Service, 1994), 6.

29. James M. McPherson, "Gettysburg," in *American Places: Encounters with History,* ed. William E. Leuchtenburg, 265 (New York: Oxford, 2000).

30. Mircea Eliade, *The Sacred and the Profane: The Nature of Religion,* trans. Willard R. Trask (New York: Harcourt, Brace and World, 1959), 8–18.

31. Jean-Paul Sartre, *Nausea,* trans. Lloyd Alexander (New York: New Directions, 1964), 126–35.

32. Eliade, *The Sacred and The Profane,* 11.

33. Ibid., 23.

34. McPherson, "Gettysburg," 266.

35. See William L. Stone, ed., *Visits to the Saratoga Battle-Grounds 1780–1880* (1895; repr., Port Washington, N.Y.: Kennikat, 1970).

36. Ibid., 105–9.

37. J. Milbert, *Picturesque Itinerary of the Hudson River and the Peripheral Parts of North America,* trans. Constance D. Sherman (1826; repr., Ridgewood, N.J.: The Gregg Press, 1968), 47–49.

38. Benson J. Lossing, *The Pictorial Field-Book of the Revolution; or, Illustrations, by Pen and Pencil, of the History, Biography, Scenery, Relics, and Traditions of the War for Independence* (New York: Harper and Brothers, Publishers, 1851), 1:47.

39. Ibid.

40. Ibid., 1:45.

41. Agnes M. Downey and John Luzader, "The John Nielson House, Stillwater, New York, Furnishings Plan," typescript report in the archive of the Saratoga National Historical Park at the park visitors' center, 1960.

42. Barbie Zelizer, "Reading the Past against the Grain: The Shape of Memory Studies," *Critical Studies in Mass Communication* 12 (1995): 226.

43. C. Perelman and L. Olbrechts-Tyteca, *The New Rhetoric: A Treatise on Argumentation,* trans. John Wilkinson and Purcell Weaver (Notre Dame, Ind.: University of Notre Dame Press, 1969), 47–51.

44. Rosenfield, "The Practical Celebration of Epideictic," 140–41.

45. Ibid., 138.

46. Ibid., 150.

7

*E*nvisioning Postcommunism
Budapest's Stalin Monument

On October 23, 1956, Budapest students held a demonstration to publicize a set of sixteen demands for democratic reform and national sovereignty. Several of the demands were symbolic, including the removal of a massive statue of Stalin that stood on the edge of City Park. Over the course of the day, hundreds of thousands of sympathizers spontaneously took to the streets. By evening, a crowd estimated at one hundred thousand had converged at the Stalin monument, and as impatience gave way to performance, the bronze effigy was brought crashing to the ground. Meanwhile, another group went to the central radio head-quarters in an effort to force the station to broadcast the list of demands. As the crowd tried to enter the building, the guards fired, sparking a violent uprising that was crushed after the Soviet army launched an attack on November 4. Reform leader Imre Nagy took refuge in the Yugoslav embassy, and János Kádár was installed as the head of a new government. The consolidation of the new government's authority involved months of purges, mass arrests, show trials, and executions. Betrayed by the Yugoslavs, Nagy was abducted to Romania, then taken back to Hungary where he was executed on June 16, 1958.[1]

In the immediate aftermath of the uprising, the government tried to paint the events as an attempted coup by fascists, criminals, or U.S. agents. But this transparently false account was soon dropped, replaced by a blanket of silence intended to suppress all memories of the humiliating defeat. In exchange for their silence and political compliance, Kádár offered the Hungarian people a comfortable life through the implementation of economic and cultural reforms. The policy was evidently successful, as Hungary achieved the repu-tation of "the happiest barracks" in the Soviet camp.[2]

After the unraveling of communism in 1989, a new, democratic Hungarian republic was proclaimed on October 23. As the selection of that date suggests, memories of 1956 were never far below the surface of the nation's consciousness. As the political transforma-tion unfolded, 1956 took on the status of a foundational myth, with the bloody events of that fall widely regarded as the first volley in a long revolution that culminated in the cere-monial reburial of Nagy on June 16, 1989, free elections in the spring of 1990, and the with-drawal of the last Soviet soldiers on June 19, 1991.

Following the groundbreaking work of Hobsbawm and Ranger on the invention of tra-dition and Anderson on the creation of national consciousness, a vast body of literature on the politics of public memory in the formation of collective identity has appeared.[3] Two interrelated points have become axiomatic in this developing literature. First, scholars emphasize that there is a political dimension to historical writing and other modes of constructing the past. The politics of history is most pronounced during the frenzied aftermath of ruptures within political cultures when they are reconstituted through conscious breaks from the past involving active creation of new national myths, rituals, and symbols. Yampolsky calls this the "double semiotics of iconoclasm."[4] Symbols that embody the ideals of a vanquished *ancien regime* are destroyed, while new symbols that represent the ideals of the *nouveau regime* are displayed in their place. Monuments and memorials are replaced, streets and public squares are renamed, old holidays are repealed and new ones celebrated. All redirect public political processes of remembering and of forgetting in ways that legitimate the actions of those wielding newly acquired power.

Second, scholars also stress that a nation is not some preexisting entity that expresses its ideals through its culture, but that culture produces "the nation" by selecting and weaving together fragments—images, myths, heroes, martyrs—from the available supply of cultural materials.[5] As Noyes and Abrahams put it, "nations are neither primordial bodies nor constitutional arrangements, but ideological constructs."[6] Anderson locates the embryo of national consciousness in the standardization of vernacular languages and their appearance in print,[7] but other symbolizing systems were equally important in nation building. National literatures drew upon familiar legends about the heroes, saviors, and deliverers of the people; national dances, costumes, handiwork, and cuisine grew out of folk traditions; state holidays evolved out of pagan rituals and religious ceremonies. Today, much of the ideological work through which the nation is produced and maintained is mass mediated, but the basic process—the production of imagined communities through the use of symbols —remains the same.

The postcommunist Hungarian experience affirms these twin axioms. The 1956 revolution was a primary source of cultural materials for imagining the new Hungarian nation's ideals. Political acts redirected public memory through swift replacement of socialist symbols with the new 1956 iconography. Places named for Communist heroes were renamed for 1956 icons, with, for example, Zoltán Schönherz Road becoming October 23 Road and Elek Bolgár Square becoming Imre Nagy Square.[8] This "memory work" is visually striking, with hundreds of new monuments, reliefs, and plaques ceremoniously unveiled in city and village squares, parks, courtyards, schools, churches, cemeteries, and other public spaces throughout the country.[9]

This chapter is concerned also with a third, less-noticed axiom that is indelibly interwoven with the first two: that the politics of public memory and the corresponding formation of "the nation" are *rhetorical* processes, whatever else they may be. Thus, the rhetorical function of both discourse and visual communication is linked necessarily with *selections* from among potentially available cultural fragments and their integration within a more or less coherent vision of "the nation." The integrated vision of a new polity, then, is contingent upon rhetorical selections that, necessarily and at one stroke, encourage remembering and forgetting.[10] I want to trace an important episode in the shaping of public memory about the new Hungary as an exemplar for study of the rhetoric of display: the spontaneous destruction of the Stalin statue during the 1956 uprising and its subsequent rhetorical depictions.

The Budapest crowd's spontaneous destruction of the massive Stalin monument and subsequent retellings of that iconoclastic event through film and other media attest to the rhetorical power of that now-absent symbol. One commentator noted how a monument such as the statue of Stalin might otherwise have remained an unremarkable dot on the urban landscape rather than a super symbol central to the mythology of the 1956 uprising without the transforming impact of this sudden destructive act. Yampolsky writes, "The moment of explosion is, from the point of view of spectacle, undoubtedly the most significant in the whole biography of the monument."[11] The mythic power of the now-absent likeness of Stalin is indeed largely a function of the visceral, anarchic joy experienced as the city was purged of its presence, but the carnivalesque atmosphere surrounding the statue's destruction also attests to something more: the roles of master and subject were reversed, and retributive justice was symbolically served.[12]

The destruction of monuments is a powerful interruption of the flow of time because of their intended durability. Cast in bronze or carved of marble, the monument is designed to cheat history through the eternal commemoration of an individual, an event, or a concept. As a result, images of ruins or scenes with fragments of broken, abandoned statuary take on a special poignancy. It is the hubris of the "King of Kings" in Shelley's "Ozymandias" that makes the image of his "colossal wreck," half-buried in the desert sand and long forgotten, so powerful.[13] Similarly, Peter Blume's surrealistic take on Italian fascism, *The Eternal City*, draws its strength from the ideals of democracy that lie broken in the form of shattered sculpture as a jack-in-the-box head of Mussolini leers over their remnants.[14]

Beyond its original ideological intentions and the emotional force of their exorcism, the Stalin monument's "phantom existence"[15] is further infused with meaning as a result of the repression of memories of that glorious moment during the thirty-one years of the Kádár era. I will argue that the public reconstitution of these memories of the iconoclastic act in the postcommunist period is best understood as epideictic commemoration along the lines suggested by Lawrence Rosenfield. Epideictic, he writes, "suggests an exhibiting or making apparent (in the sense of showing or highlighting) what might otherwise remain unnoticed or invisible."[16] It is concerned with the luminosity or radiance that emanates from noble acts or thoughts, and it beckons us to join with our community in recognizing and celebrating what is—grace, goodness, courage. "Such thoughtful beholding in commemoration constitutes memorializing," he writes.[17]

I am intrigued with Rosenfield's reference to the act of beholding. Beholding, in one sense, applies readily to visual modes of propaganda. The power of monumental art as visual propaganda is bound up with its ability to captivate observers, a point well understood by Lenin.[18] The Stalin monument illustrates that sort of beholding. The visual presence of Stalin's likeness demanded that the Hungarian public acknowledge its relationship to the all-powerful state. But Rosenfield points to another sense of beholding that applies more to the monument's destruction and subsequent absence than to its once-imposing visual presence. This is the sense he characterized as involving commemorative qualities of thoughtful "epideictic" beholding. The differences in these two senses of beholding are important, but they cannot be set out fully without first examining the constraints under which the Stalin statue was created, displayed, received, destroyed, and, ultimately, resurrected as an absent but central symbol within the mythology of the 1956 revolution.

To establish how the destruction of the monument has carried so much rhetorical weight over the decades, we need to explore the act of beholding in its different dimensions. The statue was conceived during the aesthetic and political era of high Stalinism, when socialist-realist art served as the cornerstone of official doctrine[19] and when Hungary's leader, Mátyás Rákosi, reigned as "Stalin's best pupil." It was toppled shortly after Krushchev's denunciation of the cult of personality at the Twentieth Party Congress in 1956, which ushered in a period when "rigid adherence to the 'monolithic' Marxist theory of the arts was no longer obligatory."[20] And its memory was actively resurrected in the present period of multiparty democracy and liberal economics, where public art is generated through an uneasy alliance between state and private interests and where commemorative activities are often a flashpoint for competing political agendas. In other words, the codes that governed (or were intended to govern) the collective consciousness of Hungarians were radically revised several times over the course of the monument's life and afterlife. We begin with the inception of the plan for a monument honoring Stalin.

Revolutionary Art in Hungary

On August 20, 1949, a holiday honoring St. Stephen, the founder of the state, Hungary adopted a new constitution. Modeled after the Soviet Union's 1936 constitution, Hungary became a people's republic aimed at building a socialist, popular democracy with the support of the Soviet Union. Four months later, on December 21, 1949, Stalin's seventieth birthday was marked by a feverish display of loyalty to the Soviet ruler, led by the fawning Rákosi, whose adulation of Stalin was practically boundless. Stalin had long cultivated the image of the firm but compassionate father of the Soviet people. Now that he embraced the nations of Central and Eastern Europe, his birthday offered an opportunity for his adopted children to display loyalty.[21] No one was more enthusiastic in taking on the role of loyal son than Rákosi. In conveying his greetings at the birthday celebration in Moscow's Bolshoi Theater, Rákosi gushed that "the Hungarian workers and peasants recognize Comrade Stalin as our dear father." The tens of thousands of gifts offered by Hungarians to their dear father ranged from fine art (Zsigmond Kisfaludi Strobl's "Family Statue") to folk art (the homespun creations of peasant women) to kitsch (a Kremlin-shaped floor lamp with a clock that chimed Radio Moscow's break signal every half hour).[22] But the main offering was a pledge to create a monument to Stalin "worthy of the Generalissimo in its artistic quality and in its size."[23]

In research conducted during the twilight of communism, the historian János Pótó traces the maneuvering behind the scenes as plans were worked out for the design and setting of the monument.[24] The secretariat of the Hungarian Workers' Party made all of the important decisions, which often were fronted by ad hoc committees such as a selection committee formed to decide among entries or by existing bodies such as the Budapest City Council. The Ministry of Culture and the Budapest mayor's office jointly announced a competition for the commission, inviting twenty-five artists to take part. The sculptors were instructed to submit 1:10 scale plaster models of works that would ultimately stand between five and six meters and be rendered of either bronze or marble. The guidelines also spelled out the ideological aura that the work was to radiate: "The submission must express on behalf of us all the beloved, great Stalin as the leader of the world's socialists and peace-loving people, the commander of the glorious Soviet Army that liberated Hungary, and the protective father of the People's Democracies."[25]

The results were appalling. The designs were submitted to Kálmán Pongrácz, chairman of the Budapest City Council's executive committee. The press had reported that a second round of the competition would be held, but Pótó found a press release in which Pongrácz's report to the council is quoted as saying that the entries "are atrociously bad. . . . They are figures that are so deformed that investigations of their creators should be immediately launched."[26] Based on photographs of the submissions, art historian László Prohászka maintains that chairman Pongrácz was not overstating the case. "We can imagine that some of them weren't thrilled with the assignment," he writes, "but nobody would hardly have thought to caricature the figure of Stalin intentionally."[27] The majority of the artists, he believes, were simply afraid. One of the competitors, Károly Antal, recalled years later how the State Security Force launched a search for perpetrators of "sabotage" after the nose on a plaster cast of Stalin's face used in some ceremony was damaged. Prohászka underscores the point: "it's not possible to create great works of art with shaking hands"; the artists had reason to be nervous.[28]

József Révai, Hungary's minister of culture from 1949 to 1953, had the power to force conformity to an ill-defined, socialist-realist aesthetic. Aczél and Méray describe Révai as an erudite man and an outstanding writer whose essays on Hungarian literature and history are national treasures. As minister, however, he became a "haughty despot" driven single-mindedly to advance a cultural revolution that would destroy class barriers to the universities, operas, museums, and theaters.[29] In a lengthy speech delivered at the Second Congress of the Hungarian Workers' Party early in 1951, Révai bluntly identified the Soviet Union as the source of inspiration for Hungary's cultural revolution: "The model, the school master of our new socialist culture: Soviet culture."[30] He then deflected criticism from the charge that Hungary was mechanically reproducing Soviet culture: "They babble on about how we're 'Russianizing' Hungarian culture. It's not worth spending many words arguing against this stupid slander. They dare to say this, those people whose cultural life of chewing gum, Coca Cola, and American detective movies is eroding the national character."[31]

Despite such disclaimers, Soviet cultural forms and aesthetic principles were imposed monolithically in all of the new people's democracies. The Sovietization of Eastern Europe was resented because it was alien, because it was felt to be "not ours."[32] Hungary had its own avant-garde movements, dating from the fin de siècle and culminating in the politically charged art of the Hungarian Soviet Republic in 1919.[33] The central theme of this earlier generation of socialist artists and writers was the nation's semi-feudal status, and they looked to the West in their search for progressive politics and modes of expression.[34] Péter Hanák emphasizes the pull of Western Europe:

> Here, where Asia was the product of the soil and of dreams, the time had come when they were catching up with Europe. Europe was there in the subject matter, the way they perceived things, in their depth of thinking—in short, in the society's way of responding to the challenges and problems of becoming bourgeois. And much more than that, it was in their power of expression, their aesthetic treatment, their modern approach to the language of music, painting, and writing.[35]

A period of white terror followed the collapse of the 1919 Hungarian Soviet Republic, and many of the nation's most creative artists and intellectuals—Béla Bartók, László Moholy-Nagy, Béla Balázs, György Lukács—were forced into exile. Those who remained in Hungary were subject to the repressive cultural dictates of Miklós Horthy, whose conservative regime would last almost until the end of World War II, when he was forced to concede power to the extreme right. Ignác Romsics writes that the war took a heavy toll on Hungary's cultural, intellectual, scientific, and educational spheres. "Yet destructive as the devastation was," he writes, "it also resulted in the release of new forces, fresh energies; the brake was suddenly taken off the impetus for democratic reform, which had been given so little scope before and during the war."[36] While the left consolidated its political power, diverse literary and artistic styles found expression as novelists, poets, musicians, painters, and graphic designers built upon the residual cultural formations of early twentieth-century modernism in Hungary, enriched by trends introduced by returning exiles.[37] But with the establishment of the Communist Party's hegemony in the late 1940s, backed by the Kremlin, innovation and experimentation were suspended in favor of the clichéd iconography of socialist realism as formulated in the Soviet Union of the 1930s.

Following the failed first competition for a monument to Stalin, the city council invited the top four contenders to submit new designs. They selected that of Sándor Mikus, leading the press to dub him "the happiest Hungarian sculptor." Mikus was a well-established artist, talented by any measure. He had exhibited pieces in the Venice Biennale in 1930 and had won a gold prize in the Paris World Exhibit in 1937. The bronze female figure was his favored mode of expression, rendered in his early work in small-scale sculptures and then later in full scale. Reminiscent of Degas's ballerinas, Mikus's figures radiate a simplicity, sensitivity, and serenity that transcend politics to touch the observer's soul.

Early in 1951, Mikus went to work in a studio specially built to hold the gargantua. The source of the bronze that would be used in casting the monument is of particular interest. The Budapest City Memorial Authority had at its disposal some twenty-three tons of bronze in the form of statuary that had been damaged during the war or dismantled after the war for political reasons. The figures represented included János Hunyadi, who led the struggle against the Ottoman Turks in the fifteenth century; Artúr Görgey, a Hungarian army officer who chased the imperial forces out of Hungary during the 1848–49 War of Independence; Ignác Darányi, a cabinet minister in the Wekerle government of 1906 to 1910; and Counts Gyula Andrássy and István Tisza. Some of the damaged monuments were to be repaired and returned to their original sites. However, the Hunyadi statue was the only one that was ever restored. The rest, Pótó writes, "disappeared before our eyes forever; probably these counts and 'traitors' were 'amalgamated' into the bronze figure of Stalin."[38]

Pótó is correct when he states that the bronze disappeared before Hungarian eyes, but the story of the provenance of the bronze used for the Stalin monument is part of the lore that surrounds it: observers of the Stalin monument "saw" reflected in its patina the heavy hand of the state, with its clumsy attempt to recast history. Thus, in his recent account of the events of October 23, 1956, Romsics writes, "Quite apart from the fact that Stalin, along with Rákosi, was the prime symbol of everything bad, people held a grudge that the bronze for this eight-metre monstrosity, on its ten-metre-high podium, had been obtained by melting down the statues of a host of still widely respected Hungarian figures, such as István Tisza, Gyula Andrássy and Artúr Görgey."[39]

As work on the statue proceeded, party leaders decided to locate it at the axis of Gorkij (now Városligeti) Avenue and Dózsa Road, a major thoroughfare that fronts City Park. Here, they would construct Procession Square, with the base of the monument serving as a reviewing stand for party and state dignitaries on May Day and other obligatory mass spectacles. The monument—a statue of Stalin standing rigidly with his right arm bent at the elbow—was unveiled before a crowd of eighty thousand on the morning of December 16, 1951.

Révai gave the inaugural address, hailing Stalin as "the leader of the people of the Soviet Union, the teacher of the whole world's working class, the flag bearer of the entire progressive humanity, whom all people, big and small, hold dear to their hearts." He proceeded to extend the gratitude of the Hungarian people to Stalin for all that he had done for them: "We thank Stalin that the soil of our homeland was not ravaged by civil war after the Liberation. We thank Stalin that the tree of reactionary conspirators did not grow to the sky, that the alliance of the Hungarian working class and peasantry victoriously fought the struggle with the internal reactionaries to inaugurate the peaceful building of socialism."[40] Then, to the hushed tones of the Soviet national anthem, a gigantic sheet covering the statue fell to the ground.

Reflecting the proportional excesses of Stalinism—what Schöpflin refers to as the "romance of size"[41]—the most remarkable feature of the monument was its dimensions. The statue itself was eight meters tall, approximately five times the "Man of Steel's" actual height, and weighed six-and-a-half tons. It stood on a four-meter-high limestone pedestal, which was supported by the six-meter-high tribune. Altogether, the monument reached eighteen meters, or about six stories high. Even official paeans to the creation could not contain the awe observers experienced at the sheer size of the thing. In the lead article of *Irodalmi Újság,* the publication of the Hungarian Writers' Union, the writer stammers, "How huge it is: This is our first thought. Then immediately after that: How good it is."[42]

Documentary clips of the inaugural ceremony reveal the complex relationships among observers and observed that were established through the proportions and configuration of the monument. The dignitaries on the tribune, including Rákosi, the Soviet ambassador, and members of the Politburo, stand high above the crowds. Literally and figuratively backed up by the force of the towering Stalin, they survey the scene with satisfaction. The cheering masses crowded into the square lift their faces as they pay homage to the iconic Stalin and the living Rákosi from street level. The soldiers in the military parade are similarly dwarfed by the monument. They march past in lockstep with their gazes fixed straight ahead, displaying their unwavering obedience to authority. And the enormous bronze Stalin dominates the entire scene, eclipsing not only the crowds but his own functionaries with his imposing shadow.

Beholding the Stalin Monument as Visual Display

The Stalin monument could only be considered remarkable from the twisted aesthetics of socialist realism. The Swedish art historian Anders Aman calls it "a figure with no artistic authority." Similarly, Prohászka writes that it was "essentially vacant of meaning."[43] Still, Mikus was awarded the Kossuth Prize, Hungary's highest artistic honor. His contemporaries applauded him for capturing simultaneously the two faces of Stalin: the modest, avuncular mortal who patted small children on the head and the "mysterious, omniscient, all-powerful" being who "needed only one quality to become God—immortality."[44] Later picked up by other commentators, this reading was initially crafted by Révai, when he stated in his inaugural address that Mikus had depicted Stalin as "great in his simplicity and simple in his greatness."[45]

9. Stalin statue,
May Day, 1953.
Photograph by Jenő
Virág. Courtesy of the
Hungarian National
Museum

Christina Lodder provides a good starting point for analyzing the visual dimensions of the Stalin monument in her description of socialist-realist sculpture. She writes:

> The hallmark of Socialist Realism in sculpture is an essential descriptiveness which is reliant for its impact on a stark monumentality combined with a degree of simplification of the figure, and an idealisation of its facial and physical features in accordance with the "heroic" qualities of the socialist man.[46]

Stalin's humanity was conveyed by the simplicity of the composition. The statue is immediately recognizable as a visual descriptor of Stalin, an iconic sign in the Peircean sense. The figure is standing still; the only suggestion of motion is the right arm, which is extended from the elbow. Similarly, the facial expression appears insignificant, devoid of signs that might complicate its claim to referential candor. The modesty and familiarity of the figure's clothing—Stalin's simple, trademark military tunic, buttoned up to the chin— further enhance the wise father's humanity. Bonnell notes that by the war's end, "Stalin had exchanged the plain military tunic for a handsomely tailored military uniform, complete with epaulets and insignia of a generalissimo."[47] Here, however, the only symbol of military rank or decoration is a single medal on the left side of the figure's chest, the Hero's Gold Star of the Soviet Union. Stalin is a vision of serene modesty.

But when we look again, we see the other Stalin: "the infallible leader who stood above other men by virtue of his superhuman powers, iron willpower, and contagious magic."[48] Let us start with the hands and the head, "the most naturally expressive parts of the human body."[49]

The extension of the hand loses its innocence when we notice the similarity of the gesture to Christian iconography of the Savior. In countless biblical scenes such as Giotto's fresco *Christ Entering Jerusalem* or Rembrandt's etching *Christ Preaching*, Christ is shown with his arm or arms extended or lifted as he greets his disciples, instructs the faithful, or entreats the skeptics. In the Rembrandt etching, the Jews of Amsterdam huddle around Christ. Holz uses the term "dream theater" to refer to this device of integrating the viewer into a work of art, and he notes that it was frequently used in socialist-realist painting. In such scenes, a central character is surrounded by observers. Viewers of the painting identify with these "doubles" and experience the same emotions they display in the painting: pride, wonder, acclamation, or awe. "Aesthetically manipulated," Holz writes, "the viewer thus becomes physically and psychologically part of the 'ideological dream reality.'"[50]

A number of sculptors who competed for the Stalin commission created such dream theaters by surrounding the central figure with secondary characters—honor guards bearing flags, young people presenting wreaths or flowers, soldiers marching with rifles, and peasants with scythes. In some cases, the figures are free standing, and in others they are carved into friezes on the base or on separate walls. The most intrusive of these secondary characters appears in András Beck's composition. A boy is standing alongside the figure of Stalin. Both are facing forward, slightly turned toward one another, and Stalin's hand appears to be on the boy's shoulder. Stalin looks off into the distance while the boy gazes up at his face, reaching toward it in a gesture that suggests he is presenting Stalin to observers as an object of wonder. Beck was not invited to the second round of competitions; evidently he overshot the mark by placing the secondary figure on the same level and scale as Stalin. Mikus's composition included sixty-two larger-than-life figures carved in high relief in a red limestone base. Completed only after Stalin's death in 1953, the frieze circles the base of the monument and depicts the story of the Soviet army liberating Hungary and the building of socialism.

Just as the figures on the base draw the observer into the Mikus monument, the absence of inscribed meaning on the face compels the viewer to fill in the blanks. Prohászka describes the face as Sphinx-like. A quick glance reveals nothing, he writes, but if a person looks at it for a long time, he can read anything in the expression.[51] Barthes would argue that the interpretive process is never so free. The bronze face is a metonym for the man, a signifier *designed* to propagate the myth of a Stalinist utopia. According to Barthes, myth hides itself behind the literalness of the sign. Even as it interpellates the listener, mythic speech "suspends itself, turns away and assumes the look of a generality: it stiffens, it makes itself look neutral and innocent."[52] However, socialist realism refuses this coy stance, brashly proclaiming its ideological work. In Barthes's words, while the mythology of the right is "well-fed, sleek, expansive, garrulous," the mythology of the left is poverty stricken:

It does not know how to proliferate; being produced on order and for a temporally limited prospect, it is invented with difficulty. . . . Whatever it does, there remains about it something stiff and literal, a suggestion of something done to order. As it is expressively put, it remains barren. In fact, what can be more meagre than the Stalin myth? No inventiveness here, and only a clumsy appropriation: the signifier of the myth . . . is not varied in the least: it is reduced to a litany.[53]

But while the monument was blatant propaganda, it still had the power to convey Stalin's "contagious magic." Its rhetorical force was a product of the "privileging of the eye in the task of political education" that dated back to the Bolshevik revolution. As Bonnell explains, "Visual methods for persuasion and indoctrination appealed to Bolshevik leaders because of the low level of literacy in the country and the strong visual traditions of the Russian people."[54] This emphasis on the visual in Russian culture grew out of the Eastern Orthodox tradition, where the icon was not simply a representation of a sacred person or object, but rather the incarnation of holiness. In other words, both communist ideology and Eastern Orthodox thinking were articulated through symbolic systems where distinctions between the sign and the referent are absent or at least obscure.[55] Regardless of its cultural fit, the exaggerated attention to visual communication persisted as the Zhdanovian model of revolutionary art was applied in the various people's republics. The formula that was issued from the Kremlin was ill suited indeed to postwar Hungary, where the literacy rate was over 90 percent, where Roman Catholicism and Reform Protestantism were the dominant religions, and where poetry had long held pride of place in the cultural pantheon.

In any case, likenesses of Stalin were designed to do more than represent the authority commanded by the leader of the Communist Party of the Soviet Union. They were to function totemically, to be experienced not analytically but directly as the instantiation of obedience and submission. Sinkó writes, "Stalin statues were not 'statues' in the Western, secularized and artistic sense of the term; instead they were cultic objects which served to introduce the great man's mystical presence."[56] In 1952, before disillusion led the Communist writers to split with the party, Tamás Aczél offered a "proper" reading of the monument:

Until now, Stalin *was* with us. From now on, he *is* with us. With his eyes, he watches our work; with his smile, he lights our path. . . . Up until now we have consulted his writings for advice; now we will go to him and personally "discuss" what we must do; we'll tell him about our difficulties and our joys. And it is certain that the father and protector of our peace will never deny us his counsel.[57]

Cast in bronze, this relationship was projected into an infinite future. But Berger raises an interesting point when he argues that precisely because of their long-term nature, statues —as opposed to, say, posters or flyers—are inherently unsuited for propaganda purposes. He writes:

Works which are intended to have a long-term effect need to be far more complex and to embrace contractions. It is the existence of these contractions which may enable them to survive. . . . It is to the great advantage of the Russians that they think of art as prophetic. It is their tragedy that under the autocracy of Stalin, the belief in the prophetic quality of art was subtly but disastrously transformed into the belief that art was a means of definitively deciding the future now.[58]

The iconography of the Stalin monument thus offered Hungarians a visual display that invited them to behold in his gargantuan likeness a theater of dreams. Through symbol, myth, and prophesy, the Stalin monument offered Hungarians what amounted to a singular, omnipresent, restrained vision of political possibility. Yet, as I shall next show, the destruction of this display and its removal from public view would afford Hungarians opportunities for thoughtful beholding far richer in political possibilities.

Epideictic Beholding of the Stalin Monument's Destruction

With little subtlety to recommend it, the Stalin statue soon became the primary symbol of an alien ideology. Most of the hard-line Communists who rose to power after the war, including Rákosi and Révai, had been exiles in the Soviet Union. The returning Muscovites "were the outposts and representatives of a foreign power's interest in their own fatherland."[59] Using their famous salami tactics to methodically slice away the opposition, these Soviet-backed Communists had gained decisive control of the government and major institutions by 1948. By the time the Stalin monument was erected in 1951, their ruthlessness had become hard to ignore.

From the outset of Hungary's postwar coalition government, the Communists controlled the security forces, including the police and the interior ministry. The primary weapon used in the consolidation of the Communist Party's control was the State Security Department, known by its acronym, ÁVO (Államvédelmi Osztály). ÁVO grew out of an organization established in 1945 to hunt down war criminals. But from early on, its operatives were charged with gathering incriminating evidence or cooking up false charges to discredit opponents such as Cardinal József Mindszenty, arrested in 1948, or potential political rivals such as László Rajk, executed in 1949. More broadly, ÁVO functioned as an instrument of mass terror, as thousands of people were subjected to surveillance, arrests, torture, secret trials, imprisonment, and, in extreme cases, executions. This reign of terror lasted from 1945 until 1953, when the system was reformed under the leadership of Imre Nagy following the death of Stalin.[60]

In the absence of press or radio coverage, this dark realm of public life was shrouded in mystery, suspicion, and rumor. But with the closure of detention camps in 1953, the former prisoners came home, and information about the suspected brutalities was confirmed. Aczél and Méray tell of the horror with which young Communist writers listened to the stories of their colleagues who had been imprisoned: "The tortures, the hangings, the suffering faces of those in the cells unrolled before their inner eyes like a film."[61] As the rift between the party and its former supporters widened, artists, writers, and other intellectuals could no longer deny the price that Rákosi had paid for sitting next to Stalin on his birthday.

With the Stalin era now over, the monument lost any pretense to inspirational or seductive power. Following Krushchev's criticism in early 1956 of the cult of personality, Hungarian authorities had begun to discuss the removal of all symbolic references to Stalin, including the monument. But before this could happen, history took its own course as the events of October 1956 unfolded.

Some two hundred thousand Hungarians left the country after the uprising was suppressed. Over the years, exiled writers and historians produced scores of monographs about the events, peppered with descriptions of the dramatic scene surrounding the monument.[62] In Hungary itself, totalitarian practices of concealing political developments through complete silence or the use of absurd, Orwellian inversions softened after order was restored. However, certain topics—chief among them the 1956 uprising—could only be broached with great circumspection, following the party line. For example, a history of the Hungarian workers' movement that appeared in a series of historical picture books describes Nagy as a traitor and, in both photographs and text, emphasizes the shameful behavior of the "counter-revolutionaries": the burning of books, the seizure of the Budapest party headquarters, and the lynching of its guards.[63] Books such as this, designed for popular audiences, are silent on the matter of the Stalin statue, but references to it do appear in more specialized texts. Rezsõ Szíj's 1977 book on Mikus, for example, includes a page about the competition and Mikus's creation, although it is telling that Szíj has little to say about the aesthetics of the statue itself, concentrating instead on the reliefs. About the destruction of the monument, he writes only, "The Stalin statue was toppled in the fall of 1956. Some people say it was the only good statue of Stalin."[64]

Still, visible traces of the absent Stalin endured. The iron-reinforced concrete base was left intact and continued to serve as a reviewing stand. The ghostly presence of the demolished monument was a constant reminder of the euphoric act of iconoclasm, pure in its bloodlessness, majestic in its audacity. The base was finally dismantled in 1990. By that time, the "counterrevolution" had been officially upgraded: first to a popular uprising and then, according to the 1990 Law on the Memory of the Revolution, to a revolution and freedom struggle. The story of the Stalin statue is prominent in the discursive revisions that have ensued. Let us look at some examples.

In 1989 Miklós Ómolnár published a collection of documents related to the revolution and descriptions of events by those who witnessed or participated in them. Several of these personal stories include references to the toppling of the Stalin statue, including that of Aurel Molnár, a retired Magyar Radio reporter. He tells of learning about the destruction of the monument from his children when he returned home the night of the twenty-third:

> Jaj, if only I'd known, I would have gone over there! Because when Comrade Révai unveiled it, I gave the introductory speech! So beautifully, according to a lot of people, that tears came to their eyes. . . . Of course, I would gladly have watched how they toppled to dust the colossus that I helped inaugurate.[65]

The writer Tamás Aczél mentions the statue in his 1994 account of the reestablishment in exile of *Irodalmi Újság:*

> At the time of my escape, it turned out that I'd brought with me in my little suitcase not only some worn shirts, underwear, and socks, but the Stalin statue's *nose,* which I then sold to an American millionaire for thousands of dollars. I lived high off the hog in Vienna with that money.[66]

Népszabadság, Hungary's leading newspaper, ran a piece on the fortieth anniversary of the revolution that consisted of recollections of 1956 distilled from oral histories collected by the 1956 Institute. Several of them are eyewitness accounts of the scene at Procession Square and are worth quoting in their entirety. From Ferdinand Szabó, a civil servant in 1956:

> An incredible crowd was at the Stalin statue. I was standing on the steps of the builders' headquarters [across the street]. The crowd yelled, "Let's take it down,

let's topple it!" Twenty-five or thirty trucks showed up, and they attached the winch cables to Stalin's neck. A signal was given and they took off, but they didn't take into account that this was a massive statue, so that every one of the trucks' back ends were lifted up. Then there was a shout, "Let's go to it!" In minutes, forty or fifty people had climbed up on cars. It was impossible to pull them down from there. From somewhere or other, they brought a blowtorch. They cut around the two legs under the knees. It fell to the railing, from there it spun around once, and then plunged to the ground. Everybody who could get close to it spat on it and kicked it.

From Gábor Karátson, a law student:

The toppling of the Stalin statue took a long time; it was difficult to bring it down. The people were really funny. It had a great impact on me when they shouted, "Hold on, Little Joe!" This was absolutely not a Stalinist shout, but a kind of folksy sporting, that no matter how big he was, he was alone, and we numerous people had to make sure that he hold on. Meanwhile, the star from the Trade Union building was also pushed off. When the statue came crashing down, we sang, "The intriguer has died, the vile hostility is over."[67] The crowd sang this very quickly, it had an interesting operatic effect.

And from Tamás Mikes, a student:

This was the story of Gulliver and the Lilliputians. They tugged at that carcass up there with every possible kind of tool, and it still wouldn't move, until somebody realized it would have to be cut off at the boots with a blowtorch. This was beautiful. It had already gotten a little bit dark, and the sparks flew all the way to the edge of the boots. The large numbers of little people finally brought the big piece of garbage to the ground. This was the moment when—it's a terrible phrase and I never want to say it again, but really—I felt the majesty of the people.[68]

As these examples show, narratives about the statue are laced with irony: the radio announcer who laments missing the spectacular destruction of the idol he himself had eulogized; the gifted writer who once gave his soul to communism and then sold the nose of its personification for U.S. dollars. The scene is recounted through language that is highly metaphoric, with its references to Gulliver and the Lilliputians, and highly visual, with its images of fiery sparks flying against the clear, black October night. Such recollections are reinforced by black-and-white photographs that have been brought out of hiding and are now widely reproduced and circulated as dominant forms of postcommunist iconography.[69] Images that have achieved iconic status include antlike figures scaling the statue on ladders that looked as if they were made of matchsticks; the massive, severed head lying ignominiously in the street; the gigantic boots, all that remained of the statue, with twisted reinforcing steel jutting awkwardly out of their tops.

The images of the empty boots are particularly evocative. As Aradi explains, the boot was a motif frequently used in socialist iconography to represent the brutal repression of a people by force, either internal or external. While the boot was associated throughout Europe with militarism, particularly the goose step of fascism, in Hungary it also resonated with feudal images of the barefoot peasant who lived at the mercy of the boot-wearing landlord. The intensity of the symbol is demonstrated in one of the best examples of socialist

10. Dismembering of the Stalin statue. Photograph courtesy of the Hungarian National Museum

11. The empty boots of the Stalin statue. Photograph courtesy of the Hungarian National Museum

expressionism in Hungary, Gyula Derkovits's 1930 painting *Kenyérért* (*For Bread*). This graphic indictment of the white terror that followed the suppression of the Hungarian Soviet Republic depicts a slain worker lying in a snow-covered street next to the boots of an armed soldier.[70]

The rhetorical force of the Stalin statue's boots was further exaggerated by a piece of lore that still circulates. Regnum Marianum, a Roman Catholic church, was built in Budapest's City Park in 1931 as an expression of gratitude for the crushing of the Hungarian Soviet Republic. One of the most beautiful churches in the city, Regnum Marianum stood on the site selected for Procession Square and was unceremoniously leveled in August 1951. Popular belief claims that Stalin's bronze boots stood on the very spot where the altar had been. Pótó reports that the statue was actually erected some 150 to 200 meters from the church, but the story is still spun today. In 1992, the fathers of Regnum Marianum marked the site with a simple crucifix and sign on which it was written, "Here stood the Regnum Marianum Church. Mátyás Rákosi destroyed it in 1951."[71]

But what is most striking about the narratives is how the visual imagery illuminates the courage and will to freedom that motivated the destruction of the monument. The memory of that episode takes on an epideictic quality as the spectator-storytellers position themselves among the crowd and bear witness to the collective experience of jubilation and autonomous action. Rosenfield insists that epideictic is concerned with the *acknowledgment* of goodness, not its assessment or evaluation. Appealing to Pericles, he writes that "no one could award the Athenians an 'A' for courage; rather, their courage would make a claim on men's respect for all time."[72] The intoxicating moment when the monument was brought crashing to the ground would make such a claim during the dark days of terror and the monotonous years that followed. It would be resurrected openly and joyously when the old regime crumbled, enveloping the public in memories of resistance to tyranny.

Conclusion

Tamás Mikes's embarrassment about experiencing "the majesty of the people" on that October night betrays our resistance to beholding the world with the openness that epideictic demands. In Rosenfield's words, we "confuse the mental act of reaching out to welcome reality with those counterfeit emotions comprising sentiment. We thus find ourselves dismissing as 'maudlin' the very acknowledgment of radiance that is necessary to comprehend epideictic."[73] But as Rosenfield has developed the concept, epideictic has a subversive potential that is worth exploring in the pursuit of human autonomy, hardly a closed book in Hungary or anywhere else. Epideictic commemoration frees us from the narrow channels of cognition and trusted lines of reasoning, creating a mental sanctuary where we can collectively affirm our human capacities.[74]

The kind of experience involved in epideictic beholding is thus predicated on being open, unself-consciously, to restoration in public memory of an ideal once embodied in a fleeting but wonderful event. Visual and narrative acts of commemoration are not necessarily mere propaganda, recirculating the clichés and commonplaces of established thought. They can involve efforts to sort out for recollection ideals amidst the early rumblings of political changes. And herein is epideictic's subversive dimension, so largely overlooked in previous studies. We now can see that the act of toppling the gargantuan statue, so freighted with assumptions of totalitarian power, was not mindless iconoclasm, but a significant event conducive to emancipatory political thought; it embodies for collective consideration the sheer wonder at unrestrained possibility as a foundation for political community. In contrast with public responses to visual propaganda such as the Stalin statue, the experience of epideictic beholding is founded on openness, not subservience; it inspires an unsentimental sense of awe at ideals for a free and open community and not a quasi-religious sense of obedience that is always laced with fear; it invites gratitude and appreciation; it does not compel obedience.

The ultimate fate of the monument and its place in the history of Hungarian national mythology is caught in a story Prohászka tells. The actor Sándor Pécsi, an art collector, was able to secure the right hand of the fallen idol and take it home with the help of an entrepreneurial taxi driver. When the Soviets crushed the revolution, he buried the historic bronze document in his garden where it lay hidden for thirty-five years. In 1991, his widow sold it to the Modern History Museum for forty thousand forints (roughly five hundred dollars).[75] In the panoptics of power, the relationship between viewer and viewed was finally turned on its head, as fragments of the iconographic stand-in for an all-knowing, all-seeing dictator became objects of morbid curiosity for the citizens who were once his target. But then, the story of the Stalin monument has been one of multi-directional gazes.

Of the students' sixteen points that sparked the revolution, other symbolic demands would be quietly addressed during the years of Kádárian appeasement. The star on the coat of arms would be shrunk; the calendar of holidays would be revised. But the most potent symbol of the regime had been destroyed at the hands of the people, a moment that will endure in Hungary's history. If socialist realism loomed large in its physical scale and in its ability to inspire terror, the destruction of its epitome by a people armed only with the tools of their trade was great indeed. It was an event, I have said, conducive to wonder at political possibility. The humiliation and physical suffering inflicted on the people during the period of reprisals was (bitter)sweetened by this memory, and when the end of the long revolution finally came, the memories would come out of the mothballs as objects to behold, just like Pécsi's hand.

Notes

1. The best introduction to the uprising is György Litván, ed., *The Hungarian Revolution of 1956: Reform, Revolt and Repression, 1953–1963* (New York: Longman, 1996). First published in Hungarian just two years after the fall of communism, it was written by members of the 1956 Institute in Budapest to fill the critical need for a textbook that accurately describes the events and their antecedents and thoughtfully interprets their significance. Of the many histories and analyses published by Western scholars or exiled Hungarians in the years after the revolution, I particularly recommend Tibor Méray, *That Day in Budapest: October 23, 1956*, trans. Charles Llam Markmann (New York: Funk and Wagnalls, 1969). A devoted member of the Communist Party who joined the opposition circle that formed around Imre Nagy in 1954, Méray's graceful prose is written from an insider's position.

2. Litván, *The Hungarian Revolution*, 147–48.

3. Eric Hobsbawm and Terence Ranger, eds., *The Invention of Tradition* (Cambridge: Cambridge University Press, 1983); Benedict Anderson, *Imagined Communities: Reflections on the Origin and Spread of Nationalism*, rev. ed. (London: Verso, 1991). Other seminal works on memory, history, and identity include Paul Connerton, *How Societies Remember* (Cambridge: Cambridge

University Press, 1989); Maurice Halbwachs, *On Collective Memory,* trans. and ed. Lewis A. Coser (Chicago: University of Chicago Press, 1992); David Lowenthal, *The Past Is a Foreign Country* (Cambridge: Cambridge University Press, 1985); Pierre Nora, ed., *Realms of Memory: The Construction of the French Past,* vol. 2, *Traditions,* trans. Arthur Goldhammer, ed. Lawrence D. Kritzman (New York: Columbia University Press, 1997); Raphael Samuel, *Theatres of Memory,* vol. 1, *Past and Present in Contemporary Culture* (London: Verso, 1994).

4. Mikhail Yampolsky, "In the Shadow of Monuments: Notes on Iconoclasm and Time," trans. John Kachur, in *Soviet Hieroglyphics: Visual Culture in Late Twentieth Century Russia,* ed. Nancy Condee, 100 (Bloomington: Indiana University Press, 1995).

5. David Morley and Kevin Robins, *Spaces of Identity: Global Media, Electronic Landscapes and Cultural Boundaries* (New York: Routledge, 1995), 45.

6. Dorothy Noyes and Roger D. Abrahams, "From Calendar Custom to National Memory: European Commonplaces," in *Cultural Memory and the Construction of Identity,* ed. Dan Ben-Amos and Liliane Weissberg, 77 (Detroit: Wayne State University Press, 1999).

7. Anderson, *Imagined Communities,* 44.

8. Schönherz was arrested and executed during World War II as a result of his involvement with the illegal Communist Party. A political exile, Bolgár served as an officer in the Soviet army during World War II and participated in the liberation of Hungary. After the war, he represented Hungary as a diplomat to Czechoslovakia and then to Great Britain.

9. Boros's appendixes indicate that by 1996, 126 monuments, 38 reliefs, and 234 plaques to 1956 were placed at public sites. See Géza Boros, *Emlékművek '56-nak* (Budapest: 1956-os Intézet, 1997).

10. On these rhetorical dimensions of public memory, see Carole Blair, Martha S. Jeppeson, and Enrico Pucci Jr., "Public Memorializing in Postmodernity: The Vietnam Veterans Memorial as Prototype," *Quarterly Journal of Speech* 77 (1991): 263–88; Stephen H. Browne, "Reading, Rhetoric, and the Texture of Public Memory," *Quarterly Journal of Speech* 81 (1995): 237–65; Stephen H. Browne, "Remembering Crispus Attucks: Race, Rhetoric, and the Politics of Commemoration," *Quarterly Journal of Speech* 85 (1999): 169–87; Sonja K. Foss, "Ambiguity as Persuasion: The Vietnam Veterans Memorial," *Communication Quarterly* 34 (1986): 326–40; and Cheryl R. Jorgensen-Earp and Lori A. Lanzilotti, "Public Memory and Private Grief: The Construction of Shrines at the Sites of Public Tragedy," *Quarterly Journal of Speech* 84 (1998): 150–70.

11. Yampolsky, "In the Shadow of Monuments," 101.

12. Mikhail Bakhtin, *Rabelais and His World,* trans. Helene Iswolsky (Bloomington: Indiana University Press, 1984), 10–15; Richard Stites, "Iconoclastic Currents in the Russian Revolution: Destroying and Preserving the Past," in *Bolshevik Culture: Experiment and Order in the Russian Revolution,* ed. Abbott Gleason, Peter Kenez, and Richard Stites, 3 (Bloomington: Indiana University Press, 1985).

13. John Berger, *Art and Revolution: Ernst Neizvestny, Endurance, and the Role of Art* (New York: Vintage International, 1969), 75.

14. Nóra Aradi, *A szocialista képzőművészet jelképei* (Budapest: Kossuth Könyvkiadó / Corvina Kiadó, 1974), 226; Frank Anderson Trapp, *Peter Blume* (New York: Rizzoli, 1987), 57.

15. Yampolsky, "In the Shadow of Monuments," 101.

16. Lawrence W. Rosenfield, "The Practical Celebration of Epideictic," in *Rhetoric in Transition: Studies in the Nature and Uses of Rhetoric,* ed. Eugene H. White, 135 (University Park: Pennsylvania State University Press, 1980).

17. Ibid., 133.

18. See Vladimir Tolstoy, Irina Bibikova, and Catherine Cooke, eds., *Street Art of the Revolution: Festivals and Celebrations in Russia 1918–33,* trans. Frances Longman, Felicity O'Dell, and

Vladimir Vnukov (London: Thames and Hudson, 1990); Christina Lodder, "Lenin's Plan for Monumental Propaganda," in *Art of the Soviets: Painting, Sculpture and Architecture in a One-Party State, 1917–1992,* ed. Matthew Cullerne Bown and Brandon Taylor (Manchester: Manchester University Press, 1993).

19. Czeslaw Milosz, introduction to *On Socialist Realism,* by Abram Tertz [pseud.] (New York: Pantheon Books, 1960), 10.

20. Ernst Fischer, *The Necessity of Art: A Marxist Approach,* trans. Anna Bostock (New York: Penguin Books, 1963), 111.

21. Jeffrey Brooks, *Thank You, Comrade Stalin! Soviet Public Culture from Revolution to Cold War* (Princeton, N.J.: Princeton University Press, 2000), 69–70, 219–23.

22. Gábor Murányi, "*Sztálin-őrület '49,*" *HVG,* December 18, 1999, online archive at http://hvg .hu (last accessed July 15, 2005).

23. Quoted in János Pótó, *Emlékművek, Politika, Közgondolkodás* (Budapest: MTA Történettudományi Intézet, 1989), 75.

24. Ibid., 75–81.

25. Quoted in ibid., 76.

26. Ibid., 77.

27. László Prohászka, *Szoborsorsok* (Budapest: Kornétás Kiadó, 1994), 162, 164.

28. Ibid., 164.

29. Tamás Aczél and Tibor Méray, *The Revolt of the Mind: A Case History of Intellectual Resistance behind the Iron Curtain* (Westport, Conn.: Greenwood Press, 1959), 82–83.

30. József Révai, *Révai József Elvtárs Felszólalása a Magyar Dolgozók Pártja II. Kongresszusan, 1951 Február 26–án* (Budapest: A Magyar Dolgozók Pártja Központi Vezetősége Agitácios és Propaganda Osztály, 1951), 32.

31. Ibid., 33.

32. György Schöpflin, *Politics in Eastern Europe, 1945–1992* (Oxford: Blackwell, 1993), 84.

33. György Lukács oversaw the Hungarian Soviet Republic's cultural sphere. Like many of the initiatives undertaken during the 133 days of the republic, Lukács's programs aimed at making art accessible to the masses were brash and daring and thus subject to severe criticism. For instance, thousands of *objets d'art*—including paintings by El Greco, Rembrandt, Botticelli, Monet, and Renoir—Chippendale furniture, and Gobelin tapestries were confiscated from private collectors and organized into an exhibit shown free of charge to trade unionists. See Árpád Kádárkay, *Georg Lukács: Life, Thought, and Politics* (Cambridge, Mass.: Blackwell, 1991), 220–21. This radical democratization of art was a far cry from the highly restrictive policies pursued in the early 1950s. Still, Lukács advocated limits on intellectual and artistic autonomy. In an article on freedom of the press published in *Vörös Újság,* he wrote, "The proletarian state must deal with freedom as it does with banks and prostitutes. It will not tolerate any pretense that seeks to poison the human soul." The quote is in Kádárkay, *Georg Lukács,* 227; on Lukács's heavy-handed actions, also see Lee Congdon, *The Young Lukács* (Chapel Hill: University of North Carolina Press, 1983), 156.

34. See Judit Frigyesi, *Béla Bartók and Turn-of-the-Century Budapest* (Berkeley: University of California Press, 1998); Péter Hanák, *The Garden and the Workshop: Essays on the Cultural History of Vienna and Budapest* (Princeton, N.J.: Princeton University Press, 1998); John Lukacs, *Budapest 1900: A Historical Portrait of a City and Its Culture* (New York: Weidenfeld and Nicolson, 1988).

35. Hanák, *The Garden and the Workshop,* 81.

36. Ignác Romsics, *Hungary in the Twentieth Century,* trans. Tim Wilkinson (Budapest: Corvina, 1999), 254.

37. James Aulich and Marta Sylvestrová, *Political Posters in Central and Eastern Europe 1945– 95: Signs of the Times* (Manchester: University of Manchester Press, 1999), 21.

38. Pótó, *Emlékművek*, 76.

39. Romsics, *Hungary in the Twentieth Century*, 305.

40. I transcribed Révai's remarks from documentary footage included in Márta Mészáros's 1987 feature film *Napló Szerelmeimnek* (Budapest Filmstúdió, MOKÉP, Hungarofilm).

41. Schöpflin, *Politics in Eastern Europe*, 86.

42. Iván Boldizsár, "*Sztálin szobra Budapesten*," *Irodalmi Újság*, December 20, 1951. In the months leading up to the completion of the mammoth project, the press had kept the public well informed about its progress, pointing with pride to its projected size. For example, a newspaper article in October reported, "We can illustrate with an example how huge the statue will be. The coat pocket is 1.2 meters long, and the diameter of a button is more than 10 centimeters." In "*Így készül a Sztálin-szobor*," *Magyar Nemzet*, October 7, 1951, Open Society Archives, Budapest, fonds 300, subfonds 40, series 1, box 1243, file Műemlék 1951–1959.

43. Anders Aman, *Architecture and Ideology in Eastern Europe during the Stalin Era: An Aspect of Cold War History* (New York: The Architectural History Foundation, and Cambridge, Mass.: MIT Press, 1992), 194; Prohászka, *Szoborsorsok*, 164.

44. Tertz, *On Socialist Realism*, 92.

45. Quoted in Aman, *Architecture and Ideology*, 192.

46. Lodder, "Lenin's Plan for Monumental Propaganda," 17.

47. Victoria E. Bonnell, *Iconography of Power: Soviet Political Posters under Lenin and Stalin* (Berkeley: University of California Press, 1997), 252.

48. Ibid., 254.

49. Berger, *Art and Revolution*, 141.

50. Wolfgang Holz, "Allegory and Iconography in Socialist Realist Painting," in *Art of the Soviets*, 77.

51. Prohászka, *Szoborsorsok*, 164.

52. Roland Barthes, *Mythologies*, trans. Annette Lavers (New York: Hill and Wang, 1972), 125.

53. Ibid., 147–48.

54. Bonnell, *Iconography of Power*, 3.

55. Aulich and Sylvestrová, *Political Posters in Central and Eastern Europe*, 7–8. Many of the symbols and motifs of socialist realism grew directly out of Eastern Orthodox iconography: the heavy use of red and gold, an overabundance of heavenly light directing believers toward utopia, the Christlike depictions of Lenin and Stalin. See Holz, "Allegory and Iconography in Socialist Realist Painting," 76–77.

56. Katalin Sinkó, "Political Rituals: The Raising and Demolition of Monuments," in *Art and Society in the Age of Stalin*, ed. Péter György and Hedvig Turai, 81 (Budapest: Corvina, 1992).

57. Tamás Aczél, "*Sztálin szobra—A béke jelképe*," *Szovjet Kultúra*, January 1952, 6.

58. Berger, *Art and Revolution*, 55.

59. Aczél and Méray, *The Revolt of the Mind*, 9.

60. Romsics, *Hungary in the Twentieth Century*, 227, 272.

61. Aczél and Méray, *The Revolt of the Mind*, 254.

62. See, for example, Méray, *That Day in Budapest*, 238–40; Miklós Molnár, *Victoire d'une défaite: Budapest 1956* (Paris: Fayard, 1968), 128; Ferenc Váli, *Rift and Revolt in Hungary* (Cambridge: Harvard University Press, 1961), 268.

63. János Blaskovits, "*A szocializmus alapjainak lerakása Magyarországon* (1948–1962)," in *Míg megvalósul gyönyörű képességünk, a rend: A magyar Munkásmozgalom Története, 1918–1978*, ed. Sándor Borbély and Béla Esti, 123–25 (Budapest: Móra Ferenc Könyvkiadó-Kossuth Könyvkiadó, 1978).

64. Rezső Szíj, *Mikus Sándor* (Budapest: Corvina, 1977), 8.

65. In Miklós Ómolnár and others, *Tizenkét nap, amely—1956 október 23–november 4: Események, emlékek, dokumentumok* (Budapest: Szabad Tér Kiadó, 1989), 79.

66. Tamás Aczél, "*Kezdők az Oxford Streeten: Kísérletek egy korszak idézésére,*" in *Évkönyv 3,* ed. János Bak and others, 79 (Budapest: 1956-os Intézet, 1994).

67. The line "*Meghalt a cselszövő, elmúlt a rút viszály*" is from the first great Hungarian national opera, Ferenc Erkel's *Hunyadi László.* Composed in 1844, the opera was set in the fifteenth century to avoid problems with Austrian censors. *Hunyadi László* contrasts the heroic Transylvanian Hunyadi family with the weak Habsburg boy king, László V, a pawn of his manipulative relative, Ulric Cilli. The death of the traitorous Cilli at the hands of Hunyadi's supporters precipitates the joyous lyrics. On the Hunyadi family, see Joseph Held, *Hunyadi: Legend and Reality* (Boulder: East European Monographs, 1985), 172. On the cultural-historical significance of the opera, see John Tyrrell, "Russian, Czech, Polish, and Hungarian Opera," in *Oxford Illustrated History of Opera,* ed. Roger Parker, 246–49 (Oxford: Oxford University Press, 1994).

68. András B. Hegedûs and Zsuzsanna Kõrösi, "*Szikrák futottak a csizmák peremén: Hogyan emlékezünk 1956. október 23-ra?*" *Népszabadság,* October 22, 1996, online archive at http://www .nol.hu (Last accessed July 15, 2005).

69. See, for example, Gábor Jobbágyi, *Szigorúan titkos emlékkönyv / Top Secret Memoir, 1956* (Hungary: Szabad Tér Kiadó, 1998).

70. Aradi, *A szocialista képzõmûvészet jelképei,* 60–61.

71. I have omitted several layers of the fascinating story of the succession of symbols that were built and destroyed on this site. István Kiss's massive monument to the 1919 Hungarian Soviet Republic was erected in 1965 and transferred to Budapest's Statue Park Museum in 1992. Prohászka (*Szoborsorsok,* 170) claims that this monument did stand on the site of the former altar. In the fall of 2000, a group of high-school students from Jewish families sawed down the Regnum Marianum crucifix, painting on its base a red star and the name of a nonexistent group, the Budapest Liberation Guard. In the culture wars of postcommunist Hungary, the action touched off a storm of accusations, with the right claiming that the high school—an "anti-Christian, anti-Magyar nest of Bolshevism"—bears responsibility. See Szilvia Varró, "*Díszei hullanak,*" *Magyar Narancs,* December 21, 2000, 14.

72. Rosenfield, "The Practical Celebration of Epideictic," 135.

73. Ibid., 136.

74. Ibid., 149.

75. Prohászka, *Szoborsorsok,* 167.

Victoria J. Gallagher

8

isplaying Race

Cultural Projection and Commemoration

On the outskirts of Atlanta stands Stone Mountain, the site of an honorific memorial to three Confederate heroes. Stone Mountain Park's commemorative walk, devoted to the secession of the Confederate states from the Union, and its re-creation of plantation life contrast starkly with the Chapel of All Faiths, the eternal flame, and the tomb at the Martin Luther King Jr. Memorial and Center for Nonviolent Social Change, located just forty-five minutes away in the Sweet Auburn Historic District of downtown Atlanta. While both are designated as parks, the former contains elements of a theme park: water slides, a petting zoo, cable car and paddle-wheel boat rides, a nightly laser show during the summer months, and hosts of other amusements. The latter, by contrast, is a set of buildings, walkways, and architectural features devoted to the memory and mission of one man and the social movement of which he was a part. If, as Michael Kammen argues, memory is activated by contestation and amnesia by the desire for reconciliation, these two sites would seem to provide very different means for shaping visitors' sense of racial and cultural identity, past, present and future.[1] But do they? And, more important, how are our racial identities tied to the images we encounter, interact with, and present, both in day-to-day life and in public, commemorative activities?

Political scientist Richard Merelman argues that racial identity is informed by cultural projection, defined as "the conscious or unconscious effort by a social group and its allies to place new images of itself before other social groups, and before the general public."[2] The goal of this chapter is to further our understanding of how racial identities are tied to commemorative activities by (1) extending and critiquing Merelman's model of cultural projection and (2) using the resulting theoretical framework to analyze the rhetorical manifestation of racial identities in these two southern memorial sites. Comparing and contrasting their symbolic, material, and linguistic elements reveals how each site displays particular visions of racial identities and social relationships. Specifically, such analysis reveals how Stone Mountain has come to enact a commodified, "de-raced" reinvention of the South, a reinvention that is made possible, to a large extent, *because* of the King memorial's syncretic, albeit "raced," qualities.

This chapter unfolds in two sections. In the first section, I explore theoretical issues related to commemoration, cultural projection, and display and use the insights garnered to formulate a theoretical framework. This framework encourages a comparative analysis between various forms of cultural projection and/or displays of racial and cultural identity. In the second section, I use this framework to guide analysis of the two sites.

The Rhetorical Display of Race

In his book *Representing Black Culture: Racial Conflict and Cultural Politics in the United States,* Richard Merelman asserts that there is a growing debate about American national identity due to changes in American culture. Merelman argues that the last thirty years have witnessed a growth in black cultural projection, particularly in the areas of entertainment media, schools, universities, periodicals, research foundations, and, to a lesser extent, government. Thus, according to him: "The scene is set for a struggle between a changing American Culture—in which black cultural projection plays an increasing role—and white domination exerted through the normal processes of American politics."[3]

Merelman describes four forms that cultural projection may take and reads various events and artifacts, including the establishment of the Martin Luther King Jr. national holiday, through this framework.[4] *Syncretism* is a form of "mutual projection" that occurs when "dominants accept some of the subordinate cultural projection, and subordinates accept some of the dominant projection."[5] Because it incorporates subordinate (as well as dominant) cultural imagery, syncretism may work to "weaken the cultural foundations of political domination in a society." *Hegemony* is an exclusive form of cultural projection in which "dominant groups control the flow of cultural projection." Thus, the dominant group's cultural imagery becomes the "common sense" for all groups. As a result, "Hegemony . . . undercuts the ability of subordinates to resist domination." *Polarization* is described as a failed form of cultural projection that occurs when groups both "experience the pain of having their own projections rejected by others" and "struggle to fight off the projections of these same others." Finally, *counterhegemony* is a form of cultural projection that involves the conversion of "dominants to subordinate versions of the world." Dominants gradually become more accepting of subordinates and thus begin to adopt a worldview that "immediately and definitively questions their right to power and which demands they cede power to subordinates."

The cultural projection model is important because it focuses attention on the extent to which power struggles among dominant white and subordinate nonwhite racial groups, especially blacks, have taken on a "*cultural* dimension, as opposed to traditional forms of economic struggle (over, say, the distribution of income) or political struggle (over, say, the distribution of elected representatives)."[6] The cultural projections that Merelman maps with his model, including Spike Lee's films, the discourse of multicultural education, and television news, also function as rhetorics of display that advance some cultural images while concealing others, thereby imbuing particular individuals, communities, social groups, and practices with value and significance. Until recently, according to Merelman, black cultural projection has typically been restricted to entertainment media, sports, and music. However, the number and types of images of blacks that invite "respect, commendation, debate and engagement" rather than negative stereotyping is increasing throughout the society. Among the rhetorical sites of cultural engagement that have proliferated over the last fifteen years are civil rights museums and memorials. Significantly, the images presented both visually and verbally at/in these sites are of black people engaging in political action in the face of great opposition and danger—images that command attention and invite rhetorical inspection.

A rhetorical perspective on cultural displays, including displays of racial identity, can address some gaps in Merelman's project. A rhetorical analysis, for instance, would examine the cultural projections of different groups that compete for public attention and approval. Merelman, though indicating all cultural groups engage in cultural projection, devotes little attention to comparative examination of dominant and subordinate group projections. He defines dominant and subordinate groups as follows:

> A politically, economically and socially subordinated group engages in cultural projection when its allies put forth new, usually more positive pictures of itself beyond its own borders. By inviting respect, commendation, debate and engagement, these new images contest the negative stereotypes that dominant groups typically apply to subordinates. For its part, a dominant group engages in cultural projection when it and its allies develop a newly positive set of self-images, and put forth such images to subordinate groups. These new images not only contend that dominant groups deserve the right to rule, but also ask subordinate groups to approve rather than resist or distrust rule by dominants.[7]

A rhetorical perspective on cultural display also involves examining both the substance of the images themselves and the formal, structural features that audiences use to make meaning. Merelman's approach, in contrast, focuses on "apparent outcomes" or effects of cultural projection (for instance, polarization is characterized by cultural projection that fails) with the consequence that it is difficult to account for the multiple kinds of experiences and readings that result when people encounter artifacts and sites of memory. Finally, a rhetorical study of display attempts to understand the specific means through which cultural projections come to influence specific audiences, as well as the culture at large. Merelman's model does little to explain these inner workings of cultural projections; instead the model is deployed to determine whether a particular image or set of images—verbal, visual, or material—has succeeded or failed at converting dominant group members to subordinate perspectives. In my view, it would seem more profitable to determine what kind of resources these often-competing projections provide for diverse audiences who must act together to construct social meaning, including social meanings related to racial identities.

To address these issues, and thereby extend Merelman's model, I turn to recent scholarship on genre theory and public memory. As communication becomes increasingly multimodal (oral, written, visual, material), genre theory can provide a framework for describing and theorizing this complexity as well as the patterns of regularity that cut across artifacts.[8] This is particularly important for sites of memory, because they are not exclusively linguistic in nature. Rather they are composed of layers of oral, written, visual, and spatial "statements" that combine to form complex wholes, simultaneously symbolic and material in nature. Because an emphasis on genre requires looking comparatively across discourses and artifacts, considering similarities as well as differences between what Merelman would classify as dominant and subordinate forms of cultural projection is important. This is particularly the case when dealing with sites of memory such as Stone Mountain and the King memorial because, as historian W. Fitzhugh Brundage points out, "The recalled past of all societies is inherently relational; no group fashions its memory [and, we might argue, its racial identity] without reference to others."[9]

Genre is also helpful to understanding how cultural projections related to public memory lead to the development of social, racial identities, since, as individuals, we "reproduce patterned notions of others." Carolyn Miller proposes that genres "help do our rhetorical thinking for us" by providing the "mutual, cultural knowledge that enables individual actors to communicate as competent participants."[10] She argues for an understanding of genre as a "specific, and important *constituent* of society, a major aspect of its communicative structure, one of the structures that institutions wield."

> Genre we can understand specifically as that aspect of situated communication that is *capable of reproduction,* that can be manifested in more than one situation, more than one concrete space-time. The rules and resources of a genre provide reproducible speaker and addressee roles, social typifications of recurrent social needs or exigencies, topical structures (or "moves" and "steps"), and ways of indexing an event to material conditions, turning them into constraints or resources.[11]

This emphasis on patterns of regularity across artifacts and sites as essential to our participation in social life is echoed by Brundage in his attempts to explain how historical and personal memory interact to form an essential component of the social identity of groups and individuals. He writes:

> Expressions of historical memory require precise articulation. Culturally influential historical narratives typically acquire an accepted form that is free of the idiosyncrasies and nuances that shade personal memory. Memories that deviate too much from convention are unlikely to be meaningful to large audiences or to be spread successfully. Consequently, groups labor to create stable social memories that are resistant to eccentric or unsanctioned interpretations. . . . Yet in any collective memory there is an inherent dialectic between stability and innovation. . . . The identity of any group goes hand in hand with the continuous creation of its sense of the past. No enduring memory can be entirely static. . . . For a historical memory to retain its capacity to speak to and mobilize its intended audience, it must address contemporary concerns about the past. Consequently, although the crafters of historical memory often resolve to create a vision of the past that is impervious to change, their very success depends on its ongoing evolution.[12]

Brundage goes on to argue that "power and access to it are central to the creation and propagation of historical memory," an argument very similar to Merelman's regarding cultural projection. Both note that representations of African Americans have often been conspicuously ignored, while white social memory and representations have been treated as both public and universal in their claims.[13] Not until the 1960s, according to Brundage, "did blacks command the political power necessary to insist on a more inclusive historical memory for the South."[14] However, it has taken even longer for museums and memorials that feature any type of black and/or African American perspective to emerge. And, as Donna Graves notes, it is only in the last decade that there has been an increase in scholarly attention devoted to identifying and analyzing the "symbols and patterns that characterize attitudes toward race and difference in American culture."[15]

These three perspectives, on cultural projection, genre, and public/collective memory, indicate that there is an important shift occurring in the public arena, namely that epide-ictic discourses of display are being foregrounded even as the culture is experiencing sig-nificant changes in demographic makeup and in social and political structures. Certainly, discourses related to values tend to predominate when conflict and/or diverse perspectives emerge within social groups. And in times such as these, productions and uses of the past as means to assert values deserve thoughtful consideration. Building on the insights of the three perspectives summarized briefly above, the following questions provide a guiding framework for examining the Stone Mountain and King memorials:

What are the patterns of regularity between the two memorials/parks? What do they come to mean, and how?

How is the dialectic between stability and instability, similarity of structure and unique instantiation, played out at the sites? How does this dialectic relate to the issues of power and access?

What types of relationships between dominant and subordinate groups are displayed and/or constructed at the sites (syncretic, hegemonic, counterhegemonic, polarized)?

Are particular visions of social relationships and civic participation displayed at each site? If so, what are these visions?

Displaying Race in the New New South

In his comparative discussion of the memorial sculptures in Kelly Ingram Park and the Montgomery Civil Rights Memorial, Dell Upton argues that the commemorative activity surrounding the civil rights movement of the twentieth century promotes a rehabilitation agenda similar to the creation of the "New South" at the end of the Civil War period. He writes: "A century later, Southern leaders frame the civil rights movement as a second pain-ful rebirth—'the payments our history required,' in the words of one tourist publication —that transformed the New South into a New New South."[16] Most major southern cities now feature both the Confederate memorials that were erected in great numbers in the early part of the last century, as well as the more recent memorials and museums that honor and recount the experiences of African American leaders and the civil rights movement. This results in what Brundage terms "a symbiotic relationship between the remembered past of dominant groups and the counter memories of the marginalized" within these cities.[17] Certainly, both Stone Mountain and the King memorial participate in a common genre of commemoration, and both are tied geographically, historically, and culturally to the city of Atlanta and the state of Georgia in symbiotic ways.

Commemorative Contexts

From the beginning, it appears that the Stone Mountain memorial was conceived as an "answer" to the memorial building of the northern or Union states. As David Freeman notes in his history of the Stone Mountain memorial, William Terrell first suggested (in May 1914) building a memorial at Stone Mountain because he was "disturbed by the per-ception that the Southern perspective had been neglected in modern histories and that Northern states and the Grand Army of the Republic ha[d] spent millions of dollars on memorials to their heroes while the South had not."[18] Geographically, Stone Mountain was perfect because it was visible from downtown Atlanta and large enough to fit the grand scale with which its originators hoped to "answer" their Northern counterparts.

Stone Mountain had also become the annual gathering site for the newly revived (at the time) Ku Klux Klan organization headed by "Colonel" William Simmons. Freeman downplays the connection between the Klan and the Confederate memorial as circumstantial, yet he notes that Simmons "possibly selected Stone Mountain as the place for the nocturnal ceremony [of cross burning] precisely because of the planned Confederate Memorial" and that Sam Venable, the owner of the majority of the mountain, was also a Klansman.[19] In addition, he recounts that just three weeks after Simmons burned the first cross on the mountaintop, Helen Plane, the woman who was most influential in getting the Confederate memorial project off the ground, wrote to Gutzon Borglum, the initial sculptor, with the following news and suggestion: "The 'Birth of a Nation' will give us a percentage of the next Monday's matinee. Since seeing this wonderful and beautiful picture of Reconstruction in the South, I feel that it is due to the Ku Klux Klan which saved us from the Negro domination and carpet-bag rule, that it be immortalized on Stone Mountain. Why not represent a group of them in their nightly uniform approaching in the distance?"[20]

The project was besieged by difficulties almost immediately. In quick succession, World War I, the Great Depression, and World War II intervened to halt or delay its progress. But there were also financial difficulties, infighting, and possible corruption within the Stone Mountain Confederate Monument Association (an audit conducted in the wake of the Great Depression revealed that only 27 percent of the expenditures up to that point in time had gone for actual construction).[21] Borglum (who himself joined the Klan in the 1920s) completed the head of Lee and an outline of his horse by 1924 but refused to continue working unless he was paid. When he was offered, and then accepted, the Mount Rushmore commission, the Stone Mountain association fired him and brought in Augustus Lukeman, who basically started over. He, too, produced a head of Lee, but the Great Depression and a general lack of funds put an end to the carving. It was not until 1958 that the State Park Authority brought back to life the dream of a Confederate memorial carved into the face of Stone Mountain.

That year saw the creation of the Stone Mountain Memorial Association, which engaged in a lengthy study regarding whether and how to proceed with the carving.[22] The design and technical issues were not resolved until January 16, 1964, when Walker Hancock was chosen to complete the Lukeman carving and to design and oversee the building of a memorial plaza. While Hancock's design work was important (he corrected several flaws in Lukeman's original design), his other projects kept him from visiting the actual site more than two or three times a year. It was George Weiblen (who had served as superintendent of the carving thirty-five years earlier and who made the successful bid for the carving contract this third time around) and Roy Faulkner, one of Weiblen's crew, who brought the project to completion. It is not clear to what extent, if any, the Ku Klux Klan was involved in the project at this point, but the Klan was certainly active in Atlanta and other areas of Georgia during this time, particularly in "responding" to the activities of the civil rights movement of the 1950s and 1960s. In his address at the dedication of the memorial, May 9, 1970, then vice president Spiro Agnew made a connection between the memorial and the cause of civil rights in the South, albeit in a convoluted manner, warning, "just as the South cannot afford to discriminate against any of its own people, the rest of the nation cannot afford to discriminate against the South."[23]

In 1996, when Stone Mountain was designated as an Olympic venue, the Stone Mountain museum exhibit "removed all mention of the Ku Klux Klan, in a hasty cleaning up of its image before the world."[24] Stone Mountain had been transformed, in the words of Louis Harlan, from a country village into "a suburb of the Atlanta megalopolis, a playground for yuppies."[25]

By contrast, Coretta Scott King founded the Martin Luther King Jr. Center for Non-violent Social Change in order to carry on her husband's work and honor his memory. Concerned about the impact of urban renewal on the neighborhood in which her husband was raised, she purchased property on Auburn Avenue, just east of the Ebenezer Baptist Church in downtown Atlanta, and in 1971, King's remains were moved to the site. Coretta Scott King worked successfully with the National Park Service to have the area declared a historic district. In October 1980, federal legislation established the Martin Luther King Jr. National Historic Site and Preservation District to "protect and interpret for the benefit, inspiration, and education of present and future generations the places where Martin Luther King, Junior, was born, where he lived, worked, and worshiped, and where he is buried."[26] As described in the *National Historic Site Historic Resource Study,* the site is located "in an urban area that has suffered significant deterioration in recent decades and continues to be threatened."[27]

It was not always so. Between 1853 and 1906, the Auburn street district was primarily a white residential and business district that included a substantial black minority.[28] However, following the bloody September 1906 race riot, during which whites attacked many blacks and black-owned properties in downtown Atlanta, Auburn Avenue became a haven for black businessmen who were fleeing the increased hostilities and rising rents in the central downtown business district. Between 1910 and 1930, "Sweet Auburn" became the center of black culture in Atlanta: "Black Masonic leader John Wesley Dobbs tagged the area 'Sweet Auburn' because its churches, homes, and commercial buildings were highly visible emblems of black achievement. The avenue and its vicinity was the site of influential black businesses, churches, and a diverse black residential community."[29] While the area remains residential with a mix of primarily black-owned businesses, it has indeed deteriorated. In writing about the impact of the civil rights movement on black neighborhoods in the South, Dell Upton describes the kind of scenario that led to Sweet Auburn's current state:

> As downtown services and accommodations were opened up to African Americans, black merchants could not compete, the black banks and insurance companies that financed urban development declined and collapsed, and the former black business district was transformed into a "blighted" landscape ripe for redevelopment. The devastation of the landscape that was so painstakingly built through the efforts of the black middle class is shocking. The few churches and commercial structures that survive among the open fields and parking lots—and even more appropriate, the fields and parking lots themselves—constitute another kind of monument to the movement, for it is commemorated at the site of its significant events, but in a setting that bears virtually no resemblance to its historical self.[30]

The geographic locations of these two memorials—one in a beautiful park with stunning natural features, including the mountain itself (583 acres of exposed granite), trees, wildflowers, and a lake; the other in an urban neighborhood that reflects the tumultuous path of race relations in the South—are indeed symbiotic. There is no little irony in the suburban versus urban context, the natural beauty of a real park versus the ugliness of urban renewal and housing projects around a constructed "park." Indeed, it would be striking if the King memorial were located in a part of town where middle- and upper middle-class blacks and African Americans are clearly living out the opportunities gained as a result of the civil rights movement. Instead, the King memorial and its related structures exist in an ambivalent relationship to the neighborhood that surrounds them. The newness of some of the buildings and the ideals embodied in the site are made all the more poignant by the fact that they are located in an area where black people continue to strive to eke out a living.

The fact that, after years of financial problems, political bickering, and technical difficulties, the Stone Mountain memorial was finally brought to completion during the 1960s (with heavy state involvement) and dedicated in 1970 is also indicative of the symbiotic nature of these two memorials. The Confederate memorial did, after all, serve as an answer to something, but in the timing of its completion, it would appear to have become the Old South's answer to the modern civil rights movement.

Patterns of Regularity and Unique Instantiations

As indicated above, these two memorials share a common commemorative purpose: they seek to honor purportedly virtuous persons and/or events, thereby shaping historical memory and asserting values to inform current and future deliberations. It is perhaps not surprising, then, that the two memorials share certain formal features in common, although the instantiations of these structures are distinctive at each site. For instance, both parks feature a birth home of sorts. In the case of the King memorial, the birth home is the actual structure in which King was born and where he lived his young life. The home has been preserved and restored, as have many neighboring homes and buildings. Tours of the home, provided by the National Park Service staff, and a video that features the home (*Our Friend Martin*) present King as a hero who was also just a regular child, a regular person. King's mythical, larger-than-life status in contemporary culture is intentionally downplayed somewhat in order to create the impression in visitors' minds that they, too, like King, could and would do the heroic thing, if called upon.

At Stone Mountain Park, the birth home is a restored plantation, the generalized symbolic birth home of the Confederacy or, certainly, of the "lost" way of life that is so central to nostalgic, romanticized visions of the antebellum South. While the houses and other buildings were carefully selected after "years of research and planning" and purportedly provide a "realistic view of the lifestyle of antebellum Georgians," very little information is provided as to how these buildings would have actually fit together in a real plantation or about the people who lived there. Freeman provides some interesting and, again, from a comparative perspective, highly ironic, historical context: "The plantation, originally dubbed Stone Acres Plantation, opened to the public in April 1963. The star attraction was not the plantation itself, but Butterfly McQueen, the actress who played the role of Prissy in the film version of *Gone with the Wind*. McQueen worked there as one of the tour guides on weekends until July 1965, when she ran into conflict with the management."[31] While Freeman claims that once McQueen departed, all overt references to *Gone with the Wind* at the park disappeared, as recently as Labor Day 2001 the plantation featured an exhibit

12. Plantation home, Stone Mountain Park. Photograph by Victoria J. Gallagher

of Margaret Mitchell's clothes and artifacts in the main house. In addition, the museum at Memorial Hall, billed in promotional literature as a symbol of the park's commitment to history and education, featured an exhibit devoted to *Gone with the Wind*, and the author of a book on Margaret Mitchell's life was the featured guest.

The placement of the Margaret Mitchell display in the main plantation home implicitly leads visitors to experience the plantation through the images of a fictionalized story (*Gone with the Wind*) and/or through the lens of Margaret Mitchell's own life. Even without the special displays, it is difficult to construct an adequate historical sense of plantation life. Did more than one wealthy family live on any given plantation, as this layout seems to suggest? Would there really have been only two slave quarters for a plantation of this size? The descriptive narrative texts in the homes refer to servants and the work they would have done. The word "slave" appears only on the placards at the two slave cabins. Were there really two separate classes on plantations, slaves and servants? Or, as most historical accounts suggest, were there two types of slaves: field slaves and house slaves? In the main house there is a reference to the mammy who raised the children of the house and taught them table manners. Clearly, plantations were defined by race/class, yet there is no effort to describe these issues—and the silence is deafening. Instead, a mythical, fantasy version of antebellum life is strongly perpetuated.

Another feature found at both sites is a commemorative walkway. At the King memorial, the Freedom Walkway extends up the side of the reflecting pool where King's tomb is located. Visitors walk from the base of the pool, having passed through the Chapel of All Faiths, up the side past the fountains, and to Freedom Hallway, where they can view exhibits pertaining to the lives of Martin Luther King and Coretta Scott King, as well as Gandhi. The initial plans called for the walkway to feature commemorative art, but that phase has

13. Freedom Walkway left of reflecting pool, King Memorial. Photograph by Victoria J. Gallagher

not been completed. In the new visitors' center, completed by the National Park Service just prior to the 1996 Olympics, the main display room also features a freedom walkway, with life-size statues marching together on a road that begins at ground level and angles upward toward a wall of tempered glass windows. Given the extent to which freedom marches were used as modes of political action during the civil rights movement of the 1950s and 1960s, the inclusion of these freedom walkways makes rhetorical and symbolic "sense." They also evoke the ongoing journey metaphor that is often used to depict the struggle for civil and human rights.[32]

At the Stone Mountain memorial, the commemorative walkway extends down both sides of the lawn between Memorial Hall and the carving. There are thirteen viewing terraces along the walks, representing the states of the Confederacy. At the entrance to each terrace, there is a granite stone on which is carved an outline of the state and its date of secession, admission to the Confederacy, and readmission to the Union. Each terrace also features a low rock wall, trees, shrubs, and flowers. Facing Memorial Hall and proceeding up the left walkway, the states are positioned in the order of dates of secession, beginning with South Carolina and moving on: Florida, Louisiana, Virginia, Tennessee, and North Carolina. To preserve the order, one must go back down to the right side of the lawn and begin again, this time with Georgia, Mississippi, Alabama, Texas, Arkansas, Kentucky, and Missouri. A special placard stands beside both of the last two viewing spots. It reads: "Kentucky and Missouri were not 'readmitted' to the Union because they did not officially secede. Splinter groups in these Border States declared for the Confederacy and were recognized by the Confederacy but they did not represent the official state government. The Confederacy claimed thirteen states but the Union recognized eleven as being in secession." At the base of the walkways, on both sides of the lawn, are two memorial plazas, each

14. *Valor*, Stone Mountain Park.
Photograph by Victoria J. Gallagher

15. *Sacrifice*, Stone Mountain Park.
Photograph by Victoria J. Gallagher

containing a statue and blocks of stone inscribed with quotations from key heroes of the Confederacy and of the American states. Freeman describes the statues as follows:

> *Valor* measures seventeen feet tall and stands on a five-and-a-half foot high base of pink granite. Carved in the base are the words, "Men who saw the night coming down upon them somehow acted as if they stood at the edge of dawn." This is attributed to a Confederate soldier just before his death. The statue of *Sacrifice* stands fourteen feet high, or over nineteen feet on its granite pedestal. Inscribed in the base is the phrase, "The country comes before me," uttered by the wife of General P. G. T. Beauregard.[33]

The commemorative walkway at Stone Mountain Park thus appears to fit the larger-than-life scale of the figures memorialized on the face of the mountain. In promotional accounts of the memorial, much is made about the scale and permanence of the carving. One such publication, titled *Georgia's Stone Mountain Park,* features the following quote, taken from then Virginia governor E. Lee Trinkle's dedicatory address on June 18, 1923:

> We shall have erected a monument which will outlive the centuries and which will carry the history of our Southern War to a Future so distant that the mind of man is not gifted to grasp it . . . Centuries will be born to die—age will follow age down the unending pathway of the years; cities, government, people will change and perish— while yet, our heroes carved in stone, still stand on guard—custodians of imperishable glory, the sentinels of time.[34]

Louis Harlan, however, provides a very different reading of the monument in relation to the larger context of the mountain and of history: "[T]he chief problem of carving the Stone Mountain monument was not that it was too large a feat, but that the scale was too small to make a big impression. . . . Today, the three Confederate leaders on horseback, seen from the distance below, appear too small for grand effect, about the size of a postage stamp or the Stone Mountain commemorative half-dollar. The men do not match the mountain" (see figure C11).[35]

Certainly, the commemorative walkways and the related statuary and structures at both sites are imbued with a similar sense of reflective purpose, yet the actual experience of the walkways at these sites is quite different. At the King memorial, the walkways serve to aid visitors in contemplation and, as a result, they are part of the main attraction—this is what people come to see and do. At Stone Mountain, however, the walkway serves as a sort of framing structure: it prescribes the boundaries of the wide-open lawn stretching in front of Memorial Hall, the staging area for the nightly laser show. In my visits to the site, I have rarely seen visitors follow the commemorative walkway from start to finish or gather at the commemorative statues, yet all summer long, families and groups of friends set up chairs and blankets on the lawn hours before the start of the laser show, picnicking on food brought from the many concession areas in the park.[36] The commemorative walkway and even the carving, to a certain extent, serve as a backdrop for these other activities.

Thus, at Stone Mountain, the memorial's (and, as a result, the park's) theme and purpose are diffused in many respects. In fact, park management personnel have struggled over the question of the primary mission/message of the park—educational, historical, amusement?—as well as how to appeal to various audiences. Publications and promotional materials emphasize a mix of all three missions, but amusement tends to be featured most centrally, with history and education programming thrown in.[37] This diffuseness is also seen in the rather strange relationship between the park and the state: all publications, the Web site, and other official references describe the park as "Georgia's Stone Mountain Park." Indeed, the state played a significant role in getting the project off the ground the third time around, purchasing the land and forming the association that brought the carving to completion.[38] Yet, the park is privately run and dominated by private, for-profit concessions.

At both sites, the dynamic between what is amplified and what is muted is central to visitors' experience of the memorials. The invited reading or experience at Stone Mountain, as indicated above, is one of nostalgia and mythology wherein issues of race are muted while the virtues of valor, sacrifice, and genteel living are offered as foundations of the Old South. Yet there are gaps in the "text," and visitors get glimpses of the complexity of race relations in the South. For example, the ubiquitous Confederate flags—in display cases, on flagpoles, on souvenirs, on T-shirts, including one with sparkles and sequins that reads "GRITS (Girls Raised in the South) Rule"—promote a form of southern pride which may be seen, by at least some people, as exclusionary, if not divisive. At the same time, however, African American families hold weddings and reunions on and near the plantation site. Over Labor Day weekend 2001, an African American couple was married in the formal gardens of the plantation house, and two African American families held reunions in the picnic areas adjacent to the plantation grounds.

By contrast, the invited reading or experience at the Martin Luther King memorial is highly functional, even ritualistic. The formal elements that mimic a mausoleum—the casket housing the remains of a dead loved one by an eternal flame and chapel of all faiths—combine with the buildings and the visitors' center to evoke memories of and to educate about the past. The homes and displays provide evidentiary support for the overarching theme that social change can occur through the lives and work of individuals. However, the emphasis on King's life and times, particularly when combined with the national significance granted to the site, serves to mute the complex story of the civil rights movement and the many individuals and events that contributed to social change. The journey or pilgrimage at the King memorial, ending as it does at the Freedom Hall, points to education as the essential tool or goal for the future. The road in the visitors' center has a less clearly-defined end and thus may suggest that the journey itself is the important lesson or goal.

Reading these two sites comparatively demonstrates how instantiations of generic structures are always idiosyncratic and innovative even as they provide us the stability (via similar structures and forms) by which to interpret and agree on social experiences. In the case of Stone Mountain and the King memorial, the differences in instantiation suggest differences in the cultural projection as well as in the type of persons, events, and social practices that are imbued with value. While genre analysis provides the means for examining both the substance of images themselves and the formal, structural features that audiences use to make meaning, Merelman's model provides a way of understanding the impact of these meanings on racial identities and politics.

Cultural Projections and Social Visions

Using Merelman's model, we may characterize Stone Mountain as a form of hegemonic cultural projection since the dominant group—in this case, southern whites and/or the state

—controlled (and, for the most part, continue to control) the flow of cultural projection. However, as indicated earlier, simply looking at who "controls" a memorial site fails to account for the multiple kinds of experiences and readings that result when people encounter commemorative displays. What would be considered offensive racial projections in other contexts are no longer polarizing at Stone Mountain, because they have been sublimated underneath entertainment, nostalgia, and fun activities. The overt reliance on the theme park model, which serves to diffuse or mute the asserted commemorative focus, leads to a point of view geared toward entertainment and fun. A not-too-deep, de-raced, history "lite" becomes the "common sense" perpetuated by the park. Yet, the potential for reinvigoration, and therefore polarization, is still there. In addition, the extent to which Stone Mountain's racial projections have been sublimated also provides the grounds for making a contrary case, namely, that segregationists have become a subordinate group and integrationists the dominant.

The King memorial, on the other hand, with the involvement of the National Park Service and the new visitors' center, is characterized by a more syncretic relationship wherein dominants accept some of the subordinate cultural projection, and subordinates accept some of the dominant projection. The efforts of Coretta Scott King, the members of the Ebenezer Baptist Church, and the surrounding community led to the cultural projection *of* African Americans *by* African Americans. The partnership with the National Park District and historic preservation groups served to merge dominant group projections with subordinate group projections. Yet it is difficult today to interpret the King memorial site as a truly mutual projection for two reasons. First, the majority of people who visit the site are black and/or African American. In a sense, then, large numbers of whites reject, or at

16. Visitors' Center and new Ebenezer Sanctuary viewed from Eternal Flame, King Memorial. Photograph by Victoria J. Gallagher

least, ignore the images displayed at the site, one of the characteristics central to polarization in Merelman's typology. Secondly, the recent addition of new buildings across the street from the original site seems to separate the previously merged dominant and subordinate projections into two sides of the street. The King Memorial and Center for Nonviolent Social Change, the original Ebenezer Church Sanctuary, and King's birth home are all located on one side of Auburn Avenue. Prior to 1996, the view across the street from the King memorial was of an empty lot, designated in 1992 as the future site of a community center to be named after King. Instead, the National Park Service constructed a new visitors' center on this property. The contrast between the new, larger building, set back from the sidewalk and surrounded by extensive landscaping and statuary, on one side of the street, and the older, smaller structures, set directly off the sidewalk on the other side of the street, is quite noticeable. Additionally, in the King center, the birth home, and the original Ebenezer sanctuary, members of the community and church serve as hosts. At the visitors' center, uniformed park rangers greet visitors. The Ebenezer congregation has also built a huge new sanctuary across the street, adjoining the visitors' center, but the doors are locked to visitors except on Sunday mornings.

The original structures at the King memorial thus provide a vision of social relationships based upon individual motivation and purpose. As mentioned earlier, the structures are highly functional and direct in purpose: a casket, a building housing archives and displays, a church sanctuary, homes. While both sides of the street have bookstores where visitors can purchase postcards, posters, wall hangings, T-shirts, and books by and about African Americans and blacks in the United States, the activity and identity of being a consumer is clearly secondary. Instead, in the new visitors' center, individuals are offered the opportunity to participate as writers of history (there are stations within the display room equipped with pencils/pens and books of blank pages where visitors sit and write their reactions, experiences, feelings, memories). On the other side of the street, the Chapel of All Faiths, the eternal flame, and the tomb instruct visitors to reflect and remember the person and impact of Martin Luther King Jr. Ultimately, the memorial, in its coupling with the Center for Nonviolent Social Change, indicates both structurally and symbolically that an individual's commemoration can lead to social action and change.

A very different set of actions and relationships is encouraged by the structures and symbols of Stone Mountain. There, relationships are built on consumption, whether it is the consumption of "Southern" food (fried chicken, pork rinds, sweet tea, and lemonade are featured fare at the park) or the consumption of amusements (the cable car ride, the train ride, the laser light show, the paddle-wheel boat ride, and a host of others). This difference in activity between the two sites is indicated as soon as a person arrives at the park, since at Stone Mountain, you must pay to enter, pay to ride the rides, pay to eat. While at both sites the commemorative-related activities are free, Stone Mountain's commemorative features end up providing a kind of backdrop for a host of other activities. In this way, the commemorative features and what they commemorate (the "Lost Cause") become an omnipresent, albeit sublimated, background narrative for whatever other activities occur. Since no reflection is encouraged (at the park, you "do" rather than "think"), the strange ironies that pop out all over are left unexplored, and the assertion of a mythologized Old South system of social relationships and values is made to seem harmless, even desirable. After all, African Americans and whites, international tourists and locals, Olympians and weekend joggers all share in the use of the park. Yet assertions of southern pride are ever present, and, unlike the King memorial, where the focus is on the relationship between the individual, his or her conscience, and his or her participation in the community and in history, at Stone Mountain the emphasis is on families and groups coming together to engage in activities of consumption and entertainment.

Conclusion

As the analysis above indicates, Merelman's model of cultural projection provides an interesting point of analysis for artifacts that display images of social/cultural groups and their racial identities. It provides an explanation for why rhetorics of display increasingly dominate our cultural and political scene as well as a framework for understanding the impact of such displays on racial identities and politics. But a model based largely on who initiates the display and how or whether it is received provides little information regarding the types of symbolic and interpretive resources deployed or the experiences evoked by them—in other words, *why* they may be received and perceived in one way or another. A rhetorical, comparative analysis informed by the conception of genre as social action provides a more nuanced examination and thereby some explication regarding how sites of memory, such as Stone Mountain and the King memorial, may *come to mean*. Genre analysis does this by emphasizing comparative analysis across cases—cases that may share formal features and underlying exigencies in common, yet differ widely in terms of actual instantiations and substance. In this analysis, both sites have been shown to share features that enable them to be categorized collectively by all visitors as state-sponsored commemorative sites that seek to honor purportedly virtuous persons who served purportedly worthwhile causes. They also share, as described above, many formal characteristics or features in common—commemorative focus, designation as set-aside space (national park and historic site, state park), birth homes, commemorative walkways, visitor participation opportunities, bookstores / gift shops. However, the experience of these formal characteristics and the meanings that may be drawn are unique at each site: for example, the birth home as mythologized and romanticized (Stone Mountain) compared with the birth home as demythologized but ritualized (King memorial); the commemorative walkway as framing structure for diffuse activities (Stone Mountain) compared with the commemorative walkway as central to both commemoration and the actual activities of visitors (King memorial).

While genre analysis emphasizes formal and structural stability across rhetorical displays responding to similar exigencies, it also demarcates the constraints, the potential for generic violation or instability. As this analysis reveals, there are glimpses of instability in the display of values at each site. At Stone Mountain, the amplification of virtues of valor and sacrifice, southern hospitality, and a gloried past are undercut by the park's lack of a clear focus. The current amalgamation of many different activities and features has no one coherent storyline holding it all together, except the ubiquitous presence of symbols of southern pride. And, as a result, both GRITS and African American family reunion groups use the site, separately but equally. At the King memorial, the amplification of the role of the individual (King) and of communities in social action and change is undercut somewhat by the physical context, the overriding presence of the state in the form of the park rangers, and the experience of the two sides of the street evoked by the new visitors' center structure. And, while anyone could, theoretically, have access to either site, at Stone

Mountain the cost of things as well as the location out of town restricts particular people (city dwellers, the poor, those without transportation) in particular ways, while at the King memorial, the location in a "deteriorated area" is also seen as potentially restrictive by some people (suburban whites, the middle/upper classes).

Finally, genre-informed rhetorical analysis leads to a judgment regarding the success or failure of verbal, visual, and/or material images in accomplishing rhetorical ends. For Upton, the South's memorials dedicated to civil rights are

> tombstones of racial strife and heralds of a new order. Taking their cues from the spectacular economic success of Atlanta, which billed itself during the years of the civil rights movement as "The City Too Busy To Hate," Southern urban leaders herald the birth of a (non)racial order that fulfills the "nation's commitment to liberty and justice for all" and forms the social basis for a reinvigorated, globalized regional economy.[39]

This comparative analysis of Stone Mountain and the King memorial reinforces Upton's judgment. Stone Mountain is able to enact an economic, commodifed reinvention of the South by amplifying southern "virtues" and muting issues of race. Yet, without the heraldic, syncretic qualities of the King memorial, without the acknowledgment and documentation of progress, of social change, of history and memory that it provides, Stone Mountain (and the South itself) would be unable to sustain such "rehabilitation" in the eyes of the nation and world and instead would continue to be polarizing and polarized. As Brundage so aptly puts it:

> At first glance, both white and black southerners have felt the tension between "what was" and "what ought to have been" in their pasts. For different generations of whites the Civil War and then, more recently, the economic and social transformation that C. Vann Woodward has called the "Bulldozer Revolution," have broken the ribbon of time, severing the present from the preceding eras. Twice over the white past has been rendered obsolete. The traumas of the southern past, as Woodward has explained, ensured that white southerners could not easily depict their history as one of unbroken success and progress. Yet the appearance of abrupt and wrenching change, especially the modern civil rights movement, has enabled white southerners to see parts of their past as conveniently obsolete. Their eagerness to forgive the past for the sins of the past is encouraged by regional boosters, southern politicians eager to erase the stigma of provincialism, and a tourist industry that promotes nostalgia.[40]

As examples of cultural projection, then, memory sites that participate in a commemorative genre instruct us as to our racial identities through the visions of civic participation and social relationships they display. At the King memorial, visitors are provided the resources for social action (the structural forms, their physical relationships with one another, the activities they "recommend," the geographical context), based on a syncretic view of racial identity and dominant and subordinate group relationships. We are invited to see ourselves as individuals who are raced but who can meet together and experience one another's viewpoint and, ultimately, make change. At Stone Mountain we are directed to act as if we are not raced, consuming and being entertained with no sense of who we are and where we have come from, while at the same time we are offered a permanent view of a fantasized past in which everyone knew their place and the world was right. Comparatively analyzing dominant and subordinate projections such as these enables a clearer understanding of the process of amplification and muting that is central to rhetorics of display. And in both of these memorials, what is to be commemorated and valued is displayed, not solely via discourse or argument, but through enacted experiences of visual, material artifacts and environments.

Notes

1. Michael Kammen, *Mystic Chords of Memory: The Transformation of Tradition in American Culture* (New York: Vintage Books, 1993), 14, 704.

2. Richard M. Merelman, *Representing Black Culture: Racial Conflict and Cultural Politics in the United States* (New York: Routledge, 1995), 3.

3. Ibid., 25.

4. In his analysis of the King holiday, Merelman argues both that it represents the ritualization of black cultural projection and that elements of syncretism are present in the various celebrations and ceremonies. However, he concludes that these ceremonies do not lead to complete syncretism since "[n]o single, qualitatively revised version of 'being American' emerges from" them.

5. These descriptions are summarized from Merelman, *Representing Black Culture,* 5–6.

6. Ibid., 26.

7. Ibid., 3.

8. Gunther Kress provides supporting arguments for this claim in his keynote speech, "Multimedia, Multimodality, and the Idea of Genre," presented at the Genre 2001 conference titled "Genres and Discourses in Education, Work and Cultural Life: Encounters of Academic Disciplines on Theories and Practices," in Oslo, Norway, in May 2001. In that speech, Kress suggested that genres provide a set of particulars in multimodal events, just as they do in primarily linguistic events. Yet, he warned, we must be careful not to treat images as if they are quasilinguistic or a parallel mode to language. Rather, representation in different modes reconfigures social interactions in particular ways. For instance, if speech is organized in time, visual images are organized in space, leading to the simultaneity of all things occurring in a picture. A picture, then, is not a story. Rather it is a display, an event structure. Writing and speech may appear in relation to it, providing a story line, a structure in time.

9. W. Fitzhugh Brundage, "No Deed but Memory," in *Where These Memories Grow: History, Memory, and Southern Identity,* ed. W. Fitzhugh Brundage, 22 (Chapel Hill: University of North Carolina Press, 2000).

10. C. R. Miller, "Rhetorical Community: The Cultural Basis for Genre," in *Genre and the New Rhetoric,* ed. Aviva Freedman and Peter Medway, 72 (London: Taylor and Francis, 1994).

11. Ibid., 71.

12. Brundage, "No Deed but Memory," 9–10.

13. Ibid., 11, and Merelman, *Representing Black Culture,* 5–6.

14. Brundage, "No Deed but Memory," 11.

15. Donna Graves, "Representing the Race: Detroit's Monument to Joe Louis," in *Critical Issues in Public Art: Content, Context, and Controversy,* ed. Harriet F. Senie and Sally Webster, 215, 220 (New York: Harper Collins Books, 1992).

16. Dell Upton, "Commemorating the Civil Rights Movement," in *Design Book Review* 40 (1999): 32.

17. Brundage, "No Deed but Memory," 22.

18. David Freeman, *Carved in Stone: The History of Stone Mountain,* (Macon, Ga.: Mercer University Press, 1997), 56.

19. Ibid., 61.

20. Ibid., 61–62.

21. The historical information summarized here is based upon Freeman, *Carved in Stone,* and Louis R. Harlan, "Climbing Stone Mountain," in *American Places: Encounters with History,* ed. William E. Leuchtenburg, esp. 160, 161, 167 (New York: Oxford University Press, 2000).

22. The historical information summarized here is based upon Freeman, *Carved in Stone,* 157–77.

23. For a more complete account of the dedication ceremony, see Freeman, *Carved in Stone,* 176–77.

24. This is how Louis Harlan summarizes author Tony Horwitz's description of the preparation of Stone Mountain for the 1996 Olympics in the book *Confederates in the Attic.* Horwitz further noted that, as a result, "The Invisible Empire became, well, invisible." See Harlan, "Climbing Stone Mountain," 167.

25. Ibid., 167.

26. Pub. L. No. 96–428, October 10, 1980, summarized in Robert J. Blythe, Maureen A. Carroll, and Steven H. Moffson, *Martin Luther King, Jr. National Historic Site Historic Resource Study* (Atlanta, Ga.: Cultural Resources Planning Division, Southeast Regional Office, National Park Service, U.S. Department of the Interior, 1994).

27. Ibid., 8.

28. Alexa Henderson and Eugene Walker, *Sweet Auburn: The Thriving Hub of Black Atlanta, 1900–1960* (Atlanta, Ga.: National Park Service, 1983), 5–10.

29. Blythe, Carroll, and Moffson, *Martin Luther King, Jr. National Historic Site Historic Resources Study,* 19.

30. Upton, "Commemorating the Civil Rights Movement," 31.

31. Freeman, *Carved in Stone,* 149.

32. A visual depiction of the journey metaphor is found in the following civil rights–related museums: the Birmingham Civil Rights Institute, the National Civil Rights Museum (in Memphis), and the Martin Luther King Jr. Memorial Visitors Center (in Atlanta). The journey metaphor, sometimes also described as a pilgrimage or exodus, is used in Martin Luther King Jr.'s writings and speeches, as well as in tourist publications geared toward African and black Americans. See, for instance, Wayne C. Robinson, *The African-American Travel Guide* (New Jersey: Hunter Publishing, 1998).

33. Freeman, *Carved in Stone,* 181.

34. Because Robert E. Lee, a native Virginian, was to be the first figure carved by Borglum, the Virginia governor was invited to dedicate the chisels and make the dedicatory address. For a full account of the day, see Freeman, *Carved in Stone,* 70. The quote is found in Deborah Yost, *Georgia's Stone Mountain Park* (Kennesaw, Ga.: Ariel Photography Services, 2000).

35. Harlan, "Climbing Stone Mountain," 167.

36. The secondary nature or role of the commemorative walkway and plaza is substantiated by Freeman: "Compared to the dedication of the Confederate Memorial, the one for the plaza was largely ignored. Most people viewed the plaza ["plaza" refers here to the two plazas and statues—*Valor* and *Sacrifice*—as well as the commemorative walkways] as a nicely appointed but ultimately unnecessary expenditure" (*Carved in Stone,* 182).

37. Freeman gives some examples of park management's efforts to determine the best balance between amusement, history, and recreation. He argues that recreation and entertainment have remained the primary focus. See *Carved in Stone,* 155, 183–88.

38. For a summary of the state of Georgia's involvement in the memorial project and park, see Freeman, *Carved in Stone,* 141–56.

39. Upton, "Commemorating the Civil Rights Movement," 32.

40. Brundage, "No Deed but Memory," 15.

Lawrence W. Rosenfield

9

*A*fter Walter Benjamin
The Paradise at the End of the Rainbow

The larger terms of this project have been set by Walter Benjamin in his massive, unfinished (and only recently translated into English) *Arcade Project*.[1] Begun in 1927 and left as fragments in folders of notes and clippings at his death, this magnum opus charts, among other things, the nineteenth-century transformation of the urban landscape from multiple gathering places in which citizenship might appear into a showcase for the display of goods best suited for man-the-consumer. The ramifications of this mutation on the life of our times are vast, embracing as they do most features of what we today regard as culture and public life.

I have elsewhere examined other aspects of this aestheticization of the public realm with respect to the growth and evolution of museums and department stores as well as public parks and palatial gardens.[2] Many other venues remain to be investigated, including exhibition halls, shopping malls, amusement parks, historical districts, leisure centers, even educational and correctional institutions. All are united in being devoted to what Benjamin refers to as a commodity fetish,[3] a quasi-religious enthusiasm for the objects displayed in these settings, together with the correlative activity of collecting such objects for themselves and apart from any particular use they might have.

In such an age, rhetoric transforms into marketing, the artful display of objects in order to tantalize and arouse the consumer's appetites. Benjamin foreshadows my contribution when he notes in passing that, in such a romantic climate, "gambling converts time into a narcotic."[4]

This commentary considers only one example—the culminating paradise of the consumer culture; the convergence of museum, emporium, park, video arcade, movie palace, sideshow, Catskill resort, strip mall, and world's fair exhibit; that temple of blessed excess: the Las Vegas or Atlantic City casino. These protean dream façades, which currently include such adult theme-park confections of glitz, flicker, and sleaze as replicas of New York, Paris, Venice, imperial Rome, the Taj Mahal, Rio (replete with regular enactments of Carnival), Luxor, the Old West, assorted riverboats, and a Caribbean treasure island, among others, employ the most blatant rhetoric and marketing to loosen the consumer's wallet. Arthur Goldberg, late chief executive officer of the largest of these "gaming" corporations, Park Place Entertainment, sums up the core of his industry:

It's the only business . . . where one can actually influence demand through smart marketing and imaginative products rather than just try to steal market share from competitors. We've got so much working in our favor: increasing affluence and leisure time, good demographics, and an entertainment product that appeals to people's desire for instant gratification and an exciting social experience.[5]

Or, as one casino executive confided to me, "We stroke them [the visitors] and they excrete money."[6]

In a word, the contemporary casino employs rhetoric in a topsy-turvy manner to privilege fantasy, where traditional rhetoric suppressed imagination in favor of prudence and common sense. The casino venue envelops the patron in a virtual fantasy world designed to lower all inhibitions in him while simultaneously encouraging the arousal of all human appetites. The fundamental rhetorical claim is the pious folly that desires aroused set one free. On this fundamental enthymeme claim rest the rhetorical proofs that encourage the spasms of spending and indulgences of the orifices that make Las Vegas ("the meadows"), nestled in the "Valley of the Dollars," the consumer wonder that it is.

To amplify my theme, let me again cite a few excerpts from the annual financial reports of these corporate titans. Here is how one report describes the corporation's product:

Life is what you make of it. We make dreams. . . . When we dream, we escape to a world outside of our everyday lives. Dreaming allows us to transcend reality, to be calmed when we need to relax or to be thrilled when we need excitement. Often, our dreams involve a place where life is easier, carefree and more exciting than our lives at home.[7]

Ergo, gambling is self-medication. More to the point, gambling is now a commodity similar to petroleum, orange juice, pork bellies, airline seats, autos, cola, or rolled steel. Casinos can be differentiated, like cigarettes, only by price or image. And image is rhetoric's province.

On its face, the claim that desires aroused set one free would seem to defy lifetimes of hard experience and psychoanalytic theory[8] for all but a few devotees of Dionysius. Yet, illuminated by the central romantic mantra ("The world is my idea"), it awakens dormant longings (my dreams can come true in spite of my common sense) using topoi that have been staples of Western rhetorical thought for almost a millennium.

To clarify this, think for a moment of the hordes of pilgrims who today trek to Las Vegas by bus, car, or plane as though to Lourdes—for what are they seeking, cures? Las Vegas, located in the Mojave Desert, the most parched landscape in the Western Hemisphere (and second only to the Sahara as the most desolate on earth), might not seem the ideal natural location for a dream paradise. And, indeed, the political, legal, and real estate factors leading to its development are well known. No one really minded gambling and other sins in such an uninviting location, as close to hell-on-earth as a sinner might get.[9]

However, the very transformation of the site has rhetorical features that may well speak to those who feel left behind by life or captives of destiny. There is a hollow, even bewildered, forlorn look to so many who transit the arid, smoggy, inhospitable landscape, almost a metaphor for forsaken lives. In a real sense they have "gone to hell."

And how are they greeted on arrival in "the meadows" that are Las Vegas? By water —vital, flowing, abundant water—in all its protean variations: pools, rushing streams, tropical waterfalls, gushing fountains, wave pools, Asian monsoons, overhead mists, trickling basins, roaring cascades, and, most spectacular of all, industrial-size fish tanks and aquariums, all sparkling pure and vital and primal in the hot desert sun.

Where once—before the hotels themselves became part of the entertainment package—the hoteliers embraced their arid location (the Sands, the Dunes, the Sahara, Algiers, Mirage, Luxor), the newer hotels use water as well as labels (Bellagio, the Venetian, Treasure Island) to play off and defy the arid setting to suggest a luxuriant dream world of water and vegetation. Indeed, as Rothman claims, water is no problem—it is a surrogate commodity for money; so long as there is money around, the water will flow to Las Vegas, diverted from other uses for the state of Nevada.

Students of classical rhetoric will immediately recognize in this cornucopia of waterworks the venerable topos of abundant water as a sign of life and vitality.[10] Originating with the biblical Hanging Gardens and Alhambra's Generalife gardens (1391) and spreading throughout the Italian Renaissance, the rhetorical topos was turned back upon itself to signify the Edenic pleasure of a lush and fertile place.[11] Thus, whatever the historical, legal, or economic reasons for siting Las Vegas as a center for gaming and hedonism, the use of abundant water as a topical theme to celebrate voluptuous excess is an excellent illustration: gushing water as a "strike-it-rich," "get-rich-quick," "there's-no-tomorrow" invitation to excess.

The water topos is echoed by a second theme that defies the logic of Hades: in spite of wilting heat, our movements are effortless. Be it the slot machines (source of 75 percent of gaming revenues and based on no skill, relying only on the Fates) or pedestrian transit, the Las Vegas experience is effortless. With the plethora of escalators, trains, monorails, assorted shuttle buses, moving sidewalks, trolley buses, stretch limos, pedicabs, and more (and even extending to financial devices such as automated teller machines, credit allotments, and casino comp cards to calculate complimentary perks), participation is effortless. While there may not be a free lunch in life, the Las Vegas topoi system and the reasonably priced buffets and pedestrian movers are almost as good.

While the Disney theme-park ride connotation is obvious, it is the underlying topos—the celebration of effortless movement as an aspect of effortless joy, of the illusion of a free lunch—that marks the rhetorical illustration of the underlying enthymeme: to surrender to desires of all sorts and be free is ecstasy.

To these dual topoi made material—rushing water and effortless motion—that defy the intuitive understanding of this desolate location is now added the fantasy mirage of the megaresort-casino itself. The casino ("little house" in Venice, where gambling was tolerated) has been morphed into a Hollywood dream temple that worships innocent hedonism and Baroque, over-the-top adoration at the feet of Robert Venturi.

Three elements characterize the arousal of the themed casino hotels. First, each conforms to its popular stereotype through artful appropriation and pastiche (an equivalent of modern art's deference to montage and collage).[12]

The Rio hotel has its carnival.

The Paris hotel has a pint-sized Eiffel Tower.

New York New York has a deli and a Coney Island roller coaster, even though the original at Coney Island is long gone.

The Venetian has its Grand Canal—although it is indoors and on the second floor (above an indoor parking lot).

And Bellagio generates Lake Como's summer showers on the quarter hour.

Secondly, each is meant for those who have never had the experience of the original place and so have only their popular stereotype to compare with the casino. Thus, the Mirage, Tropicana, and Mandalay Bay, though lush with vegetation, are all generic knock-offs of exotic, tropical paradises from a Hope-Crosby "Road" movie. Once inside Treasure Island, the Caribbean pirate fantasy resorts feebly to lame titles (Buccaneer's Restaurant, Candy Reef Fudge Shop). And the Excalibur hotel stages nightly dinner-theater "medieval tournaments" that are less medieval than they are Errol Flynn.

Thus, Las Vegas Boulevard is a street of sweet dreams, and each Strip casino hotel is a stage set, a self-contained Hollywood fantasy in which visitors can lose themselves.[13] Nearly all of them include shopping arcades. The Bellagio Hotel has the Via Bellagio, a glass-domed retail knockoff of the belle époque Galleria Vittorio Emanuele in Milan. The Luxor features the Giza Galleria, including a replica of King Tut's tomb. The Desert Passage at Aladdin's Resort Casino (itself the fourth incarnation of this desert theme in forty years) is designed to evoke a Middle Eastern souk, with more than 140 stores—among them Tommy Bahama, Billy Martin's, and Aveda.[14] It is nothing more than an American shopping mall done up with Hollywood flourishes.[15]

Recognizing that most of its clientele come to its resorts for excitement (but only safe, familiar novelty, nothing too exotic—mango-flavored margaritas, but no sautéed rattails—this is family fare, after all), Las Vegas, "the land that taste forgot," has demolished the neon-bedecked garish reminders of an earlier Mafia-controlled era for safe, spotless, Disney-influenced replicas of the most common, popular destinations of carefree tourism. After all, why risk the excitement of a visit to New York—where you might get mugged or step in dog excrement—or Venice—where you surely will be soaked on the dollar exchange rate—when you can have the fake version, together with bountiful buffets, and still feel right at home?[16] It should come as no surprise that a menu special at the Paris resort's French Bistro offered prime rib and crab leg, perhaps a Gallic variation on the all-American surf and turf.

Or as one of the thousands of couples from all over the country who seek out Las Vegas for their costume-drama Elvis weddings puts it, their Vegas wedding was "new, clean, efficient, and organized—everything is first class."

This speaks for the entire virtual experience of entering into the make-believe stereotype.[17]

Like grand opera, these sensual casino emporia operate often as sheer display for its own sake, from the carefully planned "hook" (moment of arrival) through the family-certified "quirky" novelties of erupting volcanoes, dolphins (in a desert, no less), white tigers, dancing fountains, pirate ships sinking on cue, the artificial aromas of lush botanical gardens, and even a full-scale, high-end art museum—all elements intended to arouse and distract (and thus to shut down the consumer's critical faculties) and thereby "to appeal to our guests' every impulse and passion."[18] It should thus come as no surprise that retail shopping attractions featuring boutiques of the most exclusive fashion arbiters (Armani, Hermes, Prada, Gucci, Tiffany) grace these pleasure domes. After all, "How can one ever imagine a complete vacation experience without the promise of a shopping spree?"[19]

Perhaps "experience" is too delicate a word; what we have here is massive engorgement. Whereas in 1997, gambling was the top attraction for visitors to Las Vegas, now it has slipped to second place. It was replaced in 2002 by "entertainment," comprising shopping, dining, and floor shows. What Victorians quaintly referred to as "innocent diversions" or "follies" have become, in our day, legal addictions.[20]

Hence, the third rhetorical feature of the themed casino is a counterintuitive one: Where the rhetorical tradition aims to enhance *phronesis* and praxis for the betterment of the commonwealth, the casino becomes a destination to isolate the individual in a narcoleptic trance wherein he becomes separated from his civic self and daily life. This theatrical distraction transports one into Dionysian realms that are ordinarily experienced only through illicit drugs.[21] Nor is the Las Vegas magic any longer limited to casinos: recall Las Vegas's ill-fated flirtation with high culture's fast-food temple to "fine art," the whorish (and now shuttered) Las Vegas branch of the Guggenheim Museum (located at the Venetian), a theme park / franchise.

As art critic Deborah Soloman noted,[22] this museum has had a troubled relation with serious art in recent years, prompting some to compare its administration to corporate calamities such as Enron, Tyco, and WorldCom. One is not reassured by the fact that the Guggenheim Las Vegas had no curators or that the chairman of the Guggenheim Museum, Peter Lewis, crows, "I bought myself the job" by outbidding cosmetics heir Ronald Perelman, the previous chair. The bottom line is that—in Richard Serra's memorable phrase— "the art is a kind of sideshow,"[23] while the focus is on the franchise, the corporate logo, and the building's architecture.

This was surely the case with Guggenheim Las Vegas, but it reflects the casino in general. It was designed by Rem Koolhaas, a Dutch architect previously known for his design of the Prada store in New York's SoHo—and currently proposing to design the new flag of the European Union to resemble a supermarket bar code. His "museum's industrial trappings," with Frank Gehry interiors (he of Guggenheim Bilbao notoriety)—"overhead cranes and a hangar door in the main gallery . . . fulfills . . . the fantasies . . . that art is rooted in [SoHo] industrial lofts"—are alien to Las Vegas as serious art. But it fit well in the Las Vegas jumble of stereotypes. That it is housed in a completely different stereotype (the Venetian) is a small matter in this world of distractions.[24] It merely highlights the "gawking" mode of seeing encouraged in these houses for the disconnected, as if the opium den of previous centuries had been reincarnated, with Lysol spray replacing the narcotics of earlier days.[25]

Yet, the peculiarity of Las Vegas, a sort of necropolis for legendary tourist stop offs, is that it actually follows a grand European tradition of nostalgic fakes, epiphanies in epoxy. After all, the quaint medieval Belgian town of Bruges is a nineteenth-century re-creation, as are the French Carcassonne, the Venetian campanile, and Brussels's Grande Place, some more fanciful than others. And even the chockablock array of architectural follies (Venice hard on the heels of a generic tropical jungle, for instance) traces its origins to Copenhagen's Tivoli Gardens, where an Arabian pavilion cohabits with a Chinese pagoda. It is merely its rhetorical peculiarity that I highlight here.

Even New York City's SoHo, center of the art gallery world-cum-exclusive shopping, is a fairly new "zoned" historical district meant to preserve the cast-iron façades of nineteenth-century factories, which in turn imitate eighteenth-century European marble palaces, so that SoHo constitutes layers of artificial architectural references. Should we then fault Caesar's Palace for its pastiche of polyurethane replicas of Greek-Roman-Renaissance statuary? Placed out of reach of curious human hands, they suggest at least the illusion of Roman gravitas in the midst of a playhouse. At the very least, they improve on the dusty plaster reproductions of classic sculpture stranded in so many college art history basements. The Italian frescos replicated on the walls of the Venetian are a harmless conceit: wallpaper.

Americans drive fast and eat fast, and they prefer fast, glib, and superficial architecture. Why restore or renovate when we can gobble down tourist destinations on the fly?[26] We find in these casinos a realm that devalues any authenticity, preferring to celebrate the fake, not as a scam but as a rhetorical trope. To preserve, restore, or renovate resonates with Roman virtue—they bespeak fealty to some past virtues. The casino reveals an impulse to replicate a few iconic details; they are fakes with a wink, rather like Ramada motels that dress up a bit like antebellum southern plantations, or Martha Stewart merchandise, or re-packaged fashion knockoffs. Are they copies? Homages? Inspired by . . . ? They are brazen fakes, and that appears to suit vox populi just fine. We relish the Madame Tussaud imitation in preference to the real thing, and we strike a familiar pose to get the payoff: a photo joke of appearing to hug the celebrity. Just so, the casino: it detaches us from reality and grants admission to fantasia—on the quick.[27]

In sum, far from being add-ons to the quaint, time-gambling narcotic posited by Benjamin, the pleasure casinos at the dawn of the new millennium engulf their customers in a virtual fantasy world where the light of day and common sense are obliterated, as is inhibition, in a total surrender to indulging one's appetites. The casino's rhetoric presents the inn at the end of the rainbow, hell-on-earth devoid of unsettling surprises, civic sense, or indeed any sense whatsoever except display in the service of sheer, gnawing desire. Is any price too much to pay for such bliss? The lords of the gaming tables think not.

Notes

1. See W. Benjamin, *The Arcade Project,* trans. H. English and K. McLaughlin (London: Belknap Press, 1999).

2. L. W. Rosenfield and J. F. Leontiou, "*Museus e magazines: O nexo entre a museu e a loja de departamentos,*" ANAIS 96, vol. 1 (São Paulo: Associacão Nacional de Pasquisadores em Artes Plasticas, 1996), 83–90; L. W. Rosenfield, "Central Park and the Celebration of Civic Virtue," in *American Rhetoric: Context and Criticism,* ed. T. W. Benson, 221–66 (Carbondale: Southern Illinois University Press, 1989).

3. Benjamin, *The Arcade Project,* 3–26.

4. Ibid., 12.

5. Quoted in J. R. Laing, "King of Craps," *Barron's,* August 23, 1999, 23–26.

6. For her encouragement with this project, I remain indebted to Beth Braun of Reno's Monarch Casino.

7. Mirage Resorts, Annual Report, 1998, 1–2.

8. See W. Muensterberg, *Collecting* (Princeton, N.J.: Princeton University Press, 1994); and P. Monaghan, "Collected Wisdom," *Chronicle of Higher Education,* June 28, 2002, sec. A.

9. See Hal Rothman, *Neon Metropolis* (New York: Routledge, 2002).

10. L. W. Rosenfield, "Central Park and the Celebration of Civic Virtue," 250.

11. See T. Comito, *The Idea of the Garden in the Renaissance* (New Brunswick, N.J.: Rutgers University Press, 1978), 49–50.

12. See E. Gibson, "Renaissance Vegas Style," *Condé Nast Traveler,* August 2002, 87.

13. Yet lurking behind each stage set is a tall, hovering, almost menacing monolith that is the hotel itself, unadorned but for a stylistic frill at its summit—and to disguise its true nature in a landscape of desolation.

14. R. La Ferla, "Travel to Exotic Places and Buy, Buy, Buy," *New York Times,* August 12, 2001, sec. 9.

15. See T. Rozhon, "Las Vegas Makes Shopping a Sport," *New York Times,* October 9, 2002, sec. C.

16. Architecture critics have noted the American taste preference for the recycled fake over the authentic, epitomized by the casino. See Ada Louise Huxtable, "Living with the Fake, and Liking It," *New York Times,* March 30, 1997, sec. 2; Paul Goldberger, "Casinos Royale," *New Yorker,* September 14, 1998, 72–79; Peter Marks, "Playing Poker with the Medicis," *New York Times,* June 13, 1999, sec. 5.

17. See Gibson, "Renaissance Vegas Style," 120.

18. Mirage Resorts, Annual Report, 1999, 6–10. This trend of bringing the dream to the consumer will culminate in the next stage of casino design, in which various casinos will be interconnected so that the gambler may wander in a somnambulant state among different venues owned by the same corporation, changing settings as easily as if the dream were real. For example, the Park Place Grand Casino Tunica incorporates no less than four theme venues: Gold Rush San Francisco, Victorian Mississippi River Town, New Orleans Mardi Gras, and Great American West. See Park Place Entertainment, Annual Report, 1999, 17.

19. Mirage Resorts, Annual Report, 1999, 10.

20. This trend is confirmed by the recent announcement by Park Place Entertainment and The Gordon Group of plans to transform the venerable, tacky Atlantic City pier into a Monopoly-themed retail and entertainment complex. The new marketing category, "entertainment retail," involves mall shops that amuse. See R. S. Gubbe, "New Century Vegas," *Las Vegas* (Las Vegas: V.I.P. Publications, 2001), 16–25.

21. Oddly enough, there is reason to believe that such epideictic celebration, apart from practical civic business, returns us to the primordial roots of rhetoric. See J. Walker, *Rhetoric and Poetics in Antiquity* (New York: Oxford University Press, 2000); L. S. Pangle, *Aristotle and the Philosophy of Friendship* (New York: Cambridge University Press, 2003), 82–83.

22. Deborah Solomon, "Is the Go-Go Guggenheim Going, Going?" *New York Times Magazine,* June 30, 2002, 36–41. See also M. Kimmelman, "An Era Ends for the Guggenheim," *New York Times,* December 6, 2002, sec. E.

23. Solomon, "Is the Go-Go Guggenheim Going, Going?," 41.

24. See G. E. Thomas, letter to the editor, *New York Times,* April 28, 2002, sec. 2; A. Rawsthorne, "Museum or Amusement Park?" *Travel and Leisure* (October 2000), 147–52.

25. See G. and S. Collins, "Gawkers in Paradise," *New York Times,* December 28, 2003, sec. 5, Travel section.

26. See M. J. Lewis, "It All Depends on How You Define 'Real,'" *New York Times,* June 23, 2002, sec. 4, Weekend section.

27. The philistine whose sneering "What's the difference?" between authentic and phoney betrays a crude ignorance that typically confuses culture and kitsch. Caesar's Palace may knock one's socks off, but it is neither Roman nor Classical—it is trite and sterile. See M. J. Lewis, ibid.

Richard Morris

10

eath on Display

As fundamentally rhetorical and cultural in origin and orientation, overt responses to death reveal worldviews, cultural premises, manners of organizing, parsing, combining, interpreting, and responding to the world.[1] When displayed in public space, they also commonly rehearse explicit cultural lessons. This is not difficult to fathom. The "sacral power of death," as William May termed it, looms so ominously that humans marshal all their energies to cope with the chaos death introduces into their lives.[2] In attempting to puzzle through that chaos, as Ernest Becker well understood, they bring to bear all the resources at their command—their knowledge, beliefs, principles, experiences, attitudes: the culture that has nurtured and perplexed and shaped their lives.[3] In such moments, human confrontation with death bodies forth concentrations of the culture(s) we are.

Those concentrations in turn regularly issue forth through material responses (memorials) that, as Richard Meyer notes, "establish patterns of communication (and even dynamic interaction) with those who use or view them"; in so doing, they "allow us to achieve a better understanding of ourselves—what we are, what we have been, and, perhaps, what we are in the process of becoming."[4] Gravescapes—memorials and the landscape containing them—provide an ideal setting for unraveling such patterns of communication because each memorial is a sacred symbol given both to the deceased and to the living. Sacred symbols "function to synthesize a people's ethos—the tone, character, and quality of their life, its moral and aesthetic style and mood—and their world view—the picture they have of the way things in their sheer actuality are, their most comprehensive ideas of order."[5]

As a sacred symbol, each memorial partially epitomizes the ethos and worldview of the gift-giver. Each manifests concretely what/who is memorable, as well as how and why the memorable ought to be remembered. Each privileges, preserves, and advances the gift-giver's worldview and ethos over all others. Considered collectively, memorials coalesce into describable traditions that reflect richer, more complex, more complete images of the *ethoi* and worldviews they seek to maintain and perpetuate. When deliberately located in sanctified public space, memorials and the traditions to which they belong endeavor to speak to present and future generations not only of how and why that past ought to be remembered, but also of how and why the present and future ought to be shaped and lived. Passing from one person to the next, through contiguous generations, this culture, this "historically transmitted pattern of meanings embodied in symbols,"[6] helps ensure the culture's survival and the possibility of its continuing influence on public memory. The rehearsal of cultural lessons through death displays thus reflects a deeply informed yearning to extend one's mortality by attaching oneself to something larger and less ephemeral.

Drawing on field research conducted in forty states across the United States, this chapter examines three markedly different memorial traditions articulated in gravescapes dating from 1632 to the present as a means of understanding the interplay between death displays and culture.[7] The chapter begins with an exploration of death displays indicative of a memorial tradition that gave rise to the memento mori gravescape, turns second to an examination of death displays belonging to a tradition from which the garden gravescape emerged, turns third to a consideration of the memorial tradition that gave rise to the lawn gravescape, and concludes with a discussion of the implications toward which this study points.

Memento Mori

From the beginning of colonization until after the turn of the nineteenth century, mainstream graveyards routinely were located at the community's center, typically adjoined community church grounds, and uniformly presented visitors with a singular rhetorical and cultural imperative: remember death, for the time of judgment is at hand. Although others later largely would succeed in altering a great many of these memento mori gravescapes and establishing alternative settings that articulated quite different *ethoi* and worldviews, the location and ostensibly neglected condition of this gravescape, as well as the discursive and iconographic representations found therein, were and are culturally and rhetorically consistent and appropriate (see figure 17).

In the most obvious sense, the memento mori gravescape serves as a convenient place to dispose of the dead. But its more significant purpose—its cultural and rhetorical significance within this worldview—derives from a formal capacity to evoke or establish memory of death, which serves to remind the living of their own fragility and, hence, of their urgent need to prepare for death. Culturally and rhetorically, as Charles Grandison Finney knew, centrally displaying death helps to ensure that the living will witness the gravescape's message regularly as a reminder "to manifest that this world is not their home" and "that heaven is a reality."[8] From a different frame, as Herbert Marcuse observes, devaluation of the body's significance minimally means that "the life of the body is no longer the real life, and the negation of this life is the beginning rather than the end."[9]

The physical and ideological features that members of other cultural groups most disliked and later most rapidly sought to change about this gravescape—its seemingly neglected, decaying condition, its constant displays of death-related icons, and the demand that viewers keep death ever in their thoughts—constitute critical signifiers of a cultural message that discernibly separates the here and now from the forever after. That separation is a direct reflection of the belief that humans should not "trust too much in an arm of clay"; for the day of death "is fast approaching. It hastens on,—it comes surely and steadily, —nothing can arrest, nothing can retard it. And are we prepared?—prepared to meet our God?"[10]

To locate the dead away from the living, to enclose burial grounds with fences as if to separate the living from the dead, to embellish and gild the gravescape, or to order the

17. Memento mori gravescape, Granery Burial Ground, Boston, Mass. Photograph by Richard Morris

graveyard according to dictates of efficiency and structural linearity, which others would later accomplish in the construction of their own gravescapes, contravenes this worldview. The constant struggle to embrace and encourage others to embrace the view that life is nothing more than preparation for death, that one's preparation for death is a preparation for eternity, demands unvarying attention if one seeks to merit eternal bliss and avoid everlasting damnation. The formal unity of memorials displayed in this gravescape both ensures its identity and energizes and sustains its rhetorical and cultural purpose.

Even from a distance, the common size and shape of such memorials speak to visitors of their singular purpose. Despite the possibilities of variation, an overwhelming majority of the memorials belonging to this tradition are relatively modest structures (between one and five feet in height and width and between two and five inches thick), and most are variations of two shapes: single and triple arches (see figure 18). Together with location and general appearance, such minimal uniformity undoubtedly helps to ensure that culturally informed viewers will not mistake this gravescape for a community pasture or a vacant lot. But a more specific link between manifestation and purpose—between the gravescape and its rhetorical and cultural significance—derives from iconography, mottos, and inscriptions, which in one form or another incessantly and almost univocally remind viewers of death and time—hence, of the limited time humans have to prepare for their own death. As Dickran and Ann Tashjian note, these display elements reaffirm and reassert "the broad cultural goals and ideals" of the communities to whom they speak.[11] In this sense, as Lucien Agosta points out, a gravescape "may thus be seen as an emblem book with each separate stone a page in that book."[12]

As a significant part of that book, marker inscriptions characteristically provide only the deceased's name, age, date of death, and, less frequently, date of birth, cause of death, and family or community status, with by far the largest number providing nothing more than a very brief inscription. To do otherwise—to draw attention to the heroic deeds or accomplishments of the deceased or to implore visitors to remember the deceased through their emotional experience, for instance—would run contrary to the cultural imperative of this worldview, thereby imperiling the deceased and the community.

For those steeped in the traditions that gave rise to this gravescape, brief inscriptions and inscription-only memorials add to an explicit chorus: "Let their memories live but let their ashes be forgotten."[13] By focusing on the deceased's age and date of death and by conspicuously excluding all or most of what occurred between birth and death, memento mori displays draw attention away from the deceased and toward an explicit display of the finality of death. In turn, display serves to teach or remind the living that "this world is not our abiding place," which well complements the ethos viewers are expected to adopt:

> Our continuance here is but very short. Man's days on the earth, are as a shadow. It was never designed by God that this world should be our home. Neither did God give us these temporal accommodations for that end. If God has given us ample estates, and children, or other pleasant friends, it is with no such design that we should be furnished here, as for a settled abode, but with a design that we should use them for the present, and then leave them in a very little time. When we are called to any secular business, or charged with the care of a family, if we improve our lives to any other purpose, than as a journey toward heaven, all our labour will be lost. If we spend our lives in the pursuit of a temporal happiness; as riches, or sensual pleasure; credit and esteem from men; delight in our children and the prospect of seeing them well brought up, and well settled &c.—All these things will be of little significance to us. Death will blow up all our hopes, and put an end to these enjoyments.[14]

For those who embrace this cultural framework, as Tashjian and Tashjian observe, death is "an occasion for teaching the congregation a religious lesson as well as for commemorating the dead."[15] Brief inscriptions are but one part of that lesson.

Another part of the lesson comes through mottos such as "*memento mori*" ("remember death") and "*fugit hora*" ("time flies" or "hours flee"), which are inscribed on countless early memorials and leave little doubt as to what viewers are to remember (see figure C12). To restate and reinforce the lesson, displays relentlessly confront viewers with time- and death-related icons—skulls, crossed bones, coffins, shovels, picks, funeral shrouds, leaves, vines, flowers, fruits, vegetables, crashing waves, assorted winged creatures, hourglasses, allegorical scenes, the curtain of death, and the exceptionally popular winged death's head.

Culturally and rhetorically, iconographic representations such as these are far from horrific. Their purpose, like the purpose of brief inscriptions and the gravescape of which they are such an integral part, is not to instill a mind-numbing fear, but to provide viewers with continual reminders of the distinctions between physical life and spiritual life, between the ephemeral and the everlasting. Early practitioners turned time and again to the winged death's head (and other similar symbols) because it clearly states the point and implies a faint hopefulness that shuns hubris yet invites comfort. Simplicity, clarity, and cultural embeddedness collectively ensure that everyone schooled in the tradition's basic values, whether literate or not, will "understand the carvings and profit from their didactic import."[16]

18. Single- and triple-arch memorial forms, Old Colony Burying Ground, Norfolk, Conn. Photograph by Richard Morris

In the graveyard and beyond, those who create, sustain, and perpetuate the memento mori displays struggle against the chaos that death continuously represents by filtering experience through a worldview that finds its most salient memorial expression in the form of a dichotomy between body and soul. At the very least, that dichotomy serves as a synecdoche for primary cultural principles, values, and beliefs (for example, good/evil, eternal/ephemeral, order/chaos, reward/punishment, sacred/secular, clean/dirty, hope/fear, reality/illusion, health/disease, self/other, life/death) and as a vehicle for expressing and displaying primary cultural realities that undergird and constitute this worldview. Here, one of the primary realities from which this tradition's death displays emerge and in which they are ultimately meaningful is the view that life is a vertical journey through an ephemeral existence that constantly challenges and reinforces human frailty in order that deity may judge individual fidelity and worth. Each action, each event, each desire, each hope—everything—exists for this purpose and this purpose alone.

Purpose thus both derives from and rearticulates the cultural qualities of a necessary tension between ephemerality and the journey, which lends to time a dual character. On the one hand, "time is death" serves as a guiding metaphor that characterizes temporality as an enemy against which viewers must ever struggle. This elevation of time signifies body, which is ephemeral, all too human, and even pornographic because time/body is always the opposite of eternality, which refigures deity within the self. Therein emerges a second sense of time as goad and friend, for eternality—stretching infinitely forward but cosmically limited rearward—is timelessness: deity's time. This is the time of mortal immortality.

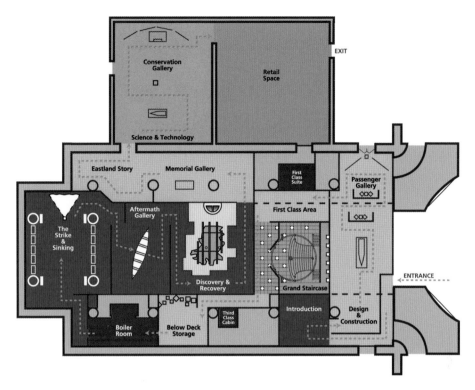

C1. *Titanic* exhibition floor plan, Chicago Museum of Science and Industry. Used with the permission of RMS *Titanic* Inc. and Clear Channel Exhibitions

C2. The *Titanic*'s bell. Photograph by Dirk Fletcher. Used with the permission of RMS *Titanic* Inc. and Clear Channel Exhibitions

C3. The *Titanic*'s grand staircase. Photograph by Dirk Fletcher. Used with the permission of RMS *Titanic* Inc. and Clear Channel Exhibitions

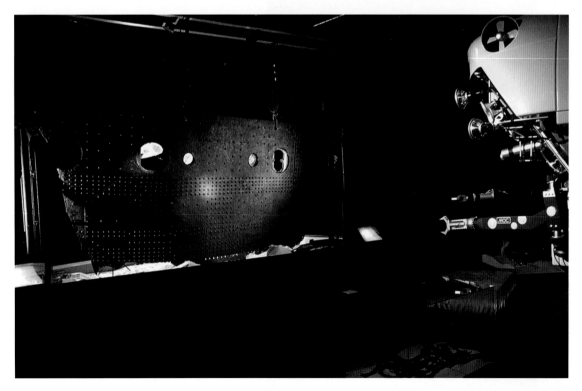

C4. The "Big Piece." Photograph by Dirk Fletcher. Used with the permission of RMS *Titanic* Inc. and Clear Channel Exhibitions

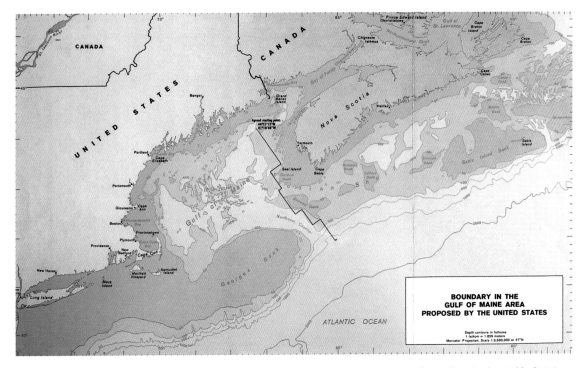

C5. United States base map with proposed boundary line. Originally figure 30, "Boundary in the Gulf of Maine Area Proposed by the United States," memorial submitted by the United States of America, September 27, 1982, International Court of Justice. Depths in fathoms. Mercator Projection. Scale 1:3,500,000 at 42°N

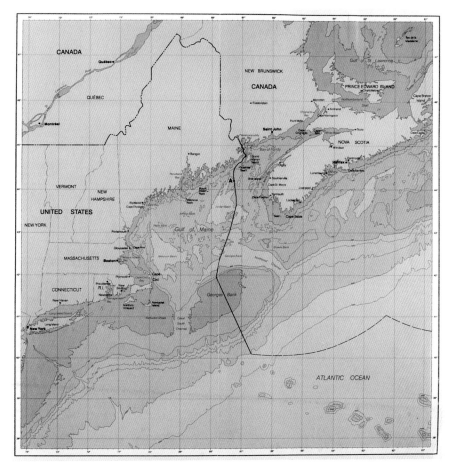

C6. Canada's base map with proposed boundary line. Originally figure 57, "The Canadian Line Respects the Geography of the Gulf of Maine Area," counter-memorial submitted by Canada, June 28, 1983, International Court of Justice. Depths in meters. Mercator Projection. Scale 1:4,700,000 at 41°N

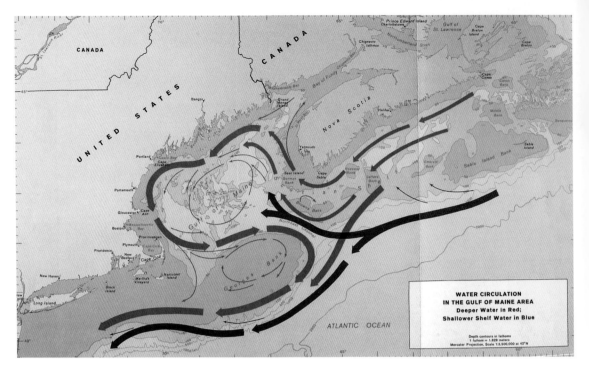

C7. "Water circulation in the Gulf of Maine area." Originally figure 5, memorial submitted by the United States of America, September 27, 1982, International Court of Justice. Depths in fathoms. Mercator Projection. Scale 1:3,500,000 at 42°N

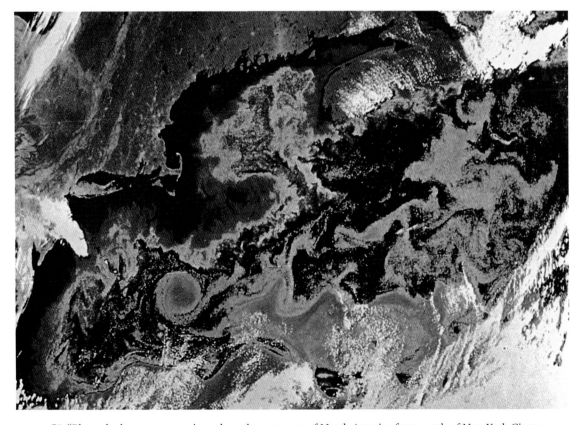

C8. "Phytoplankton concentrations along the east coast of North America from south of New York City to Nova Scotia." Originally figure 6, memorial submitted by the United States of America, September 27, 1982, International Court of Justice

Fishable Quantities of Individual Stocks Occur as Indicated by Bars

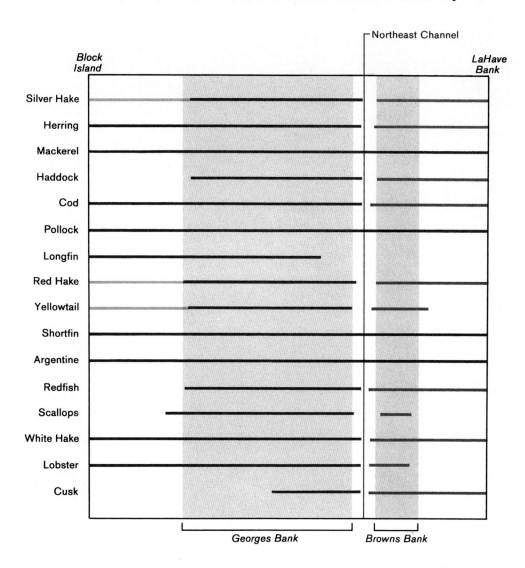

C9. "Ranges of stocks of sixteen commercially important species, in a zone extending from Block Island (Rhode Island), across Georges Bank, the Northeast Channel, and Browns Bank to LaHave Bank." Originally figure 7, memorial submitted by the United States of America, September 27, 1982, International Court of Justice

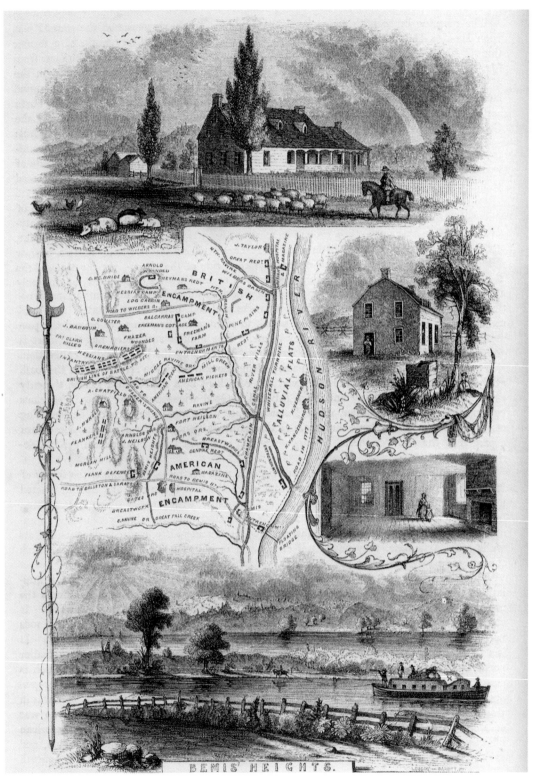

C10. Illustration from Benson Lossing's *The Pictorial Field-Book of the Revolution* (New York: Harper and Brothers, Publishers, 1851), vol. 1

C11. Stone Mountain carving viewed from Memorial Hall. Photograph by Victoria J. Gallagher

C12. Memento mori motto,
the Burying Point, Salem, Mass.
Photograph by Richard Morris

ABOVE, LEFT C13. A new aesthetic in an alien context: Edward Wright Memorial (thirty inches by fifty-two inches, slate), 1825, Author's Ridge Burying Ground, Concord, Mass. Photograph by Richard Morris

BELOW C14. Heart stereogram. Generated by John Shotter

ABOVE, RIGHT C15. A hate tattoo. Watercolor on paper by George Burchett, early 1900s

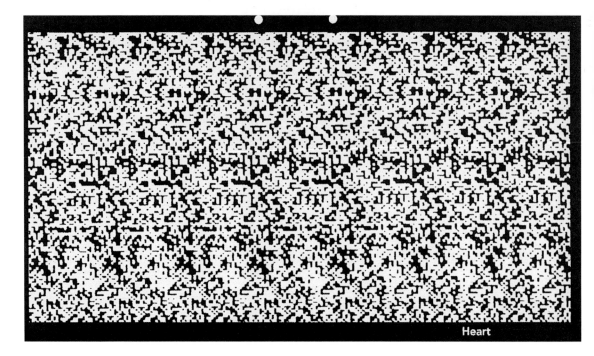

Heart

Space/place projects a similar duality.[17] One part of this duality reflects the relationship between human space/place and the space/place of deity. Significantly, although human space/place is severely restricted, deity relaxes that restriction by lending to sanctified space/place the possibility of infinitude through the qualities of mind, thought, and spirit as appositions of body. Then, again, the relationship between the location of humans in a presumably neutral world that is wedged between absolute good and absolute evil lends to space/place the qualities of animal instinct and body-as-husk. Even as husk, body both houses deity's qualities and is a bearer of ephemerality. Duality here reinstates the urgency and significance of maintaining sanctified spaces/places as sanctuaries (graveyards and churches) within strictly human spaces/places (towns and cities), as well as the need to place the dead inside boundaries of sanctified space. Sanctified space/place recapitulates the relationship between deity and human-as-deity (soul/spirit), provides specific locations where the living may feel closer to deity, and designates sanctuaries where the living may retreat from the temptations of ephemeral space/time and where the dead may begin the final stage of the journey toward judgment.

Death and death displays serve within this arrangement as constant reminders that viewers must avoid the temptations of secular life and attend assiduously, tenaciously to cultural dictates that promise to ensure deity's affirmative judgment, which underwrites immortal bliss. Concomitantly, death also serves socially as the bond of community, the common adversary and friend—a corporeal visitation of the eternal that ever reminds viewers of duty, responsibility, right conduct, right attitudes, and, most important, the possibility of mortal transcendence.

So constituted, death displays instruct witnesses to adopt a method or mode of conduct and attitude that "moves" them ever "upward" away from the absolute evil that threatens their immortal souls by pulling them "down." Since some individuals may be more "up" (hence, more deity-like) or "down" than others, ethos becomes an expression of worth and authority through hierarchical differentiation, which makes this largely (though not wholly) a qualitative matter insofar as judgment assays the quality of human existence. At the larger cultural and social levels, the vertical structure that stretches between good and evil positions the collectivity such that their possibilities for investigating alternatives are considerably abbreviated.

In one direction, this means that culturally informed viewers live in a world so carefully controlled and delimited by definition that interpretation is scarcely problematic. In another direction, those who embrace this tradition are continually impelled to restrict interpretations and alternatives of those outside the community both for their own sake and for the sake of their obligation to demonstrate their cultural membership rhetorically by bringing others into the community. Internally and externally, death's display continually surfaces through cultural survival as motive.

A Garden Romance

A very different manner of displaying death, which began to emerge in the middle of the eighteenth century and came into full bloom at the turn of the nineteenth century, schools viewers to appreciate and celebrate the emotionality, unity, and beauty of death as a moment immersed in and engaged with natural processes. Within this cultural space, death is inspirational; display focuses attention specifically on the individual as a source of loss and grief; loss and its attendant emotions bring the living into congregation with themselves, community, and nature; and art and nature combine in the presence of death to create a form of display that seeks to impel viewers toward sublime and homeopathic feelings, thoughts, and attitudes.

Initially, those who embraced and articulated this naturalistic, sublime, homeopathic perspective created displays that voiced these values as a means of celebrating the deceased's life and death as extensions of nature and art. Early efforts thus replaced the memento mori tradition's scant information with poetic pathos, substituted "In Memory of" for "memento mori," and replaced death icons with nature and/or art icons (see figure C13). And yet, because early memorials of this sort displayed themselves in memento mori gravescapes, surrounded by an entirely different voice and an environment that spoke of an altogether different set of values that too easily overwhelmed and negated the message of this emerging tradition, the enunciations of a clear, unimpeded voice would have to wait for the development of an unreservedly different kind of gravescape.

That moment of clarity resoundingly arrived with the consecration of Mount Auburn Cemetery in the autumn of 1831, when Joseph Story proudly proclaimed that places of the dead ought to be environments from which the living can derive pleasure, emotional satisfaction, and instruction on how best to live their lives—a place where visitors, sitting by the graves of loved ones, would be able "to hear the tone of their affection, whispering in our ears." In such a space the living will be able to shed their tears—not "the tears of burning agony," but the tears of relief that allow the living to "return to the world," where they feel themselves "purer, and better, and wiser, from this communion with the dead."[18]

In place of memento mori gravescapes, where visitors found "the head-stones broken, or swayed half over, the intervals choked up with briers, elders, and fat-weeds," with "the whole place" bearing "the impress of the most frigid indifference,"[19] visitors now would find a place of serenity, of repose, in rural areas outside the limits and disciplines of towns and cities where the dead might sleep restfully and the living might find their place among the dead, art, and nature. Instead of headstones bearing reminders of death, churchyards reminiscent of the viewer's need to prepare religiously for death and judgment, and other things associated with the memento mori tradition, visitors found in Mount Auburn an extraordinary garden luxuriously adorned with nature and appointed with the most remarkable works of art money could supply.

As America's preeminent landscape architect Andrew Jackson Downing pointed out, "no sooner was attention generally raised to the charms of the [garden cemetery], than the idea took the public mind by storm." Within a matter of months travelers from near and far began to make "pilgrimages to the Athens of New England, solely to see the realization of their long cherished dream of a resting place for the dead, at once sacred from profanation, dear to the memory, and captivating to the imagination."[20] Part of the reason for Mount Auburn's immediate popularity, perhaps, was due to this gravescape's novelty. Yet, Mount Auburn was still being satisfyingly displayed long after its novelty had worn off.[21] More, the garden romance of this gravescape was "rapidly imitated in all parts of the United States."[22] By 1849, Downing was able to observe with due pride that "there is scarcely a city of note in the whole country that has not its rural cemetery." Philadelphia alone, he continued, has "nearly twenty rural cemeteries at the present moment—several of them belonging to distinct societies, sects or associations, while others are open to all."[23]

Seemingly every garden cemetery fostered one or more guidebooks designed to provide visitors with a detailed description of the gravescape and "a walking tour" calculated to conduct visitors "within every occupied spot, and every object of interest."[24] As precursors to and even blueprints for city and town parks, garden cemeteries quickly became "pleasure grounds" where ordinary folks encountered "a programmed sequence of sensory experiences, primarily visual, intended to elicit specific emotions, especially the so-called pleasures of the melancholy that particularly appealed to contemporary romantic sensibilities."[25] Family life, social life, courtship, aesthetic education, and connection to nature blossomed in spaces speaking volumes about how life could and should be lived.

Ever sensitive to the needs of cultural growth, garden cemetery owners nurtured these sensibilities in an effort to capture the hearts and imaginations of visitors. A significant portion of that effort aimed at ensuring that visitors would greet nature's many splendors by taking great care to select sites that would reveal "Nature's own easy and graceful outline" and by purchasing and importing extensive varieties of exotic shrubs, bushes, flowers, and trees.[26] At Laurel Hill in Philadelphia, for instance, the owners immediately purchased and planted "almost every procurable species of hardy tree and shrub" to make it "a better arboretum than can easily be found elsewhere in the country."[27] Beneath the trees' canopies, visitors discovered a forested garden filled with opulent artwork thoroughly expressive of the worldview that invented this gravescape. Thus, "a visit to one of these spots has the united charm of nature and art,—the double wealth of rural and moral association. It awakens at the same moment, the feeling of human sympathy and the love of natural beauty, implanted in every heart."[28] To effect this union of nature and art, cemetery

19. A garden display, Mount Auburn Cemetery, Cambridge, Mass. Photograph by Richard Morris

owners went to great lengths—and often great costs—to commission and obtain aesthetically appealing objects to adorn the cemetery and to set a standard for those wishing to erect memorials to their deceased friends and relatives (see figure 19).

What is perhaps even more important—and what constitutes one of the most striking features of this gravescape—is the constancy with which its diverse cemeterial iconography articulates a uniform worldview and ethos. A less concentrated constancy had begun to emerge even in the early years, to be sure; but with the introduction of a cemeterial form that specifically encouraged lot owners to create memorials designed as works of art that praise nature and promote pathetic responses, those attracted to this perspective now had the requisite positioning to create a gallery of art embraced by nature bejeweled.

With so much freedom at their disposal, lot owners freely displayed death through an impressive variety of memorials. Without minimizing that variety, one might fairly say that death displays belonging to this tradition generally animate one of two related expressions. The first abides principally by the creed that memorials are or ought to be works of art insofar as they draw attention either to the memorial as a work of art or to the work of art as a memorial. In either case, what seems most immediately notable about these displays is that someone with sufficient wealth cared enough about the deceased (or their status in the community) to commission a work of art to their memory. Given the extent to which those who embraced the garden gravescape relied on the "rural" burial practices of ancient civilizations to justify the need for their new cemeterial form, the prominence of Egyptian, Greek, Gothic, and Roman influences in these displays is culturally and rhetorically inevitable (see figure 20).

20. Ancient influences in a new American context, Mount Auburn Cemetery, Cambridge, Mass. Photograph by Richard Morris

21. Garden pathos, Mount Auburn Cemetery, Cambridge Mass. Photograph by Richard Morris

The second expression, which we might term "pathetically evocative works of art," intensely focuses on pathetic sentiments. Displays of this sort typically feature representations such as the faithful animal, emotionally engaged and engaging angels, women and children (similarly engaging and engaged), emblems of nature, or artistically re-created artifacts associated with the deceased (see figure 21).

The union of art and nature in these kinds of death displays consistently and continually recapitulates a view of time as cyclical, which places a premium on living within the present moment because, as isochronal, the present incorporates both present and past. This fortifies the experiential emphasis on emotions as essential to well-being so central to worldview's homeopathic impulse. Placing images of the memorable at the forefront of memory ("In Memory of"), on the other hand, necessarily makes the present subordinate to the past because the present derives its character from the past. This is moderately a consequence of the temporal position of the memorable; but it is principally a consequence of a worldview that steadfastly encourages the living to define themselves in terms of the past —for example, by borrowing from ancient civilizations to create, justify, and express this tradition.

While the past thus sanctifies the present and creates the possibilities of the future, space/place contrastingly is always already sanctified, springing as it does from nature. What remains is for humans to recognize their place within a preexisting harmony so they may better protect nature from the "unnatural" acts and actions of those who fail to understand the "natural" sanctity of space/place. As the garden romance makes entirely clear, however, preservation as an impulse and motive carries with it a responsibility to create a harmonious relationship between humans and nature through the production of art. This confluence in turn transforms space/place into a medium through which individuals may actualize their potential to achieve a harmonious relationship with nature by protecting it from the "unnatural."

Ethos here becomes an expression of equality and similitude where difference dissolves into universality. Because some things within this worldview may be more "natural" than others, there is always at least the potential for implementation of a hierarchy that generates and sustains a vertical mode of conduct and attitude within a supposedly horizontal, egalitarian environment. Such a hierarchy may constitute grounds for disagreement over elements and degrees of authenticity (for instance, the kinds of "natural" activities in which one engages and the degree to which one engages such activities), which index the quality of one's cultural membership. Ethos expands hierarchy by separating the "natural" from the "unnatural," which serves as boundary between inclusion and exclusion.

Although nature in this scheme is itself goodness, the belief that human efforts can somehow improve nature (for instance, through art) insinuates that goodness is at least fairly a human product because human beings and their productions are "natural." Yet, the equally central belief that some actions and/or acts and some individuals are more "natural" (qualitatively) attenuates this belief by introducing the distinct possibility that human actions are not always or inevitably "natural." Nature thus serves not only as the metric by which all things are measured, but also as origin of and justification for hierarchy.

Hierarchy, perpetuated socially, partially dissolves through application of emotions, which serve as media through which the living sustain their attachment to nature, as the primary means through which individuals establish and perpetuate their relationships with others, and as the foremost vehicle for attending to one's physical and spiritual well-being. As media, emotions articulate nature and provide the living with a lens through which nature's mysteries emerge, which accentuates the privileged place of pathetic memorials. As relational conduit, emotions provide the basis on which individuals seek to conjoin with one another and, more, with the world at large. As vehicle, emotions serve to move individuals into harmony with themselves so that they might be in greater harmony with nature.

Taken together, the elements that constitute this tradition constitute and manifest a very particular worldview and ethos. Within that particularity, confrontation with death is far less a struggle against chaos than an opportunity to understand and become part of unity and universality within a seemingly specific disunity, which focuses attention and experience both on living in the moment and on the dichotomy between the "natural" and the "unnatural." As with the previous dichotomy between body and soul, this dichotomy serves as a synecdoche for primary cultural principles, values, and beliefs (where "natural" equates with "good" and where "unnatural" equates with "bad" or "wrong") and as the axial mode for identifying and expressing cultural realities.

One such reality is that culturally informed viewers must adopt a wholly "natural" ethos —one grown out of and belonging to the moment; perfectly suited to time and place;

immersed in and content with being immersed in the inevitable process of being happy in the sight of nature and art; imaginative; guileless; in touch with one's feelings; sublime; and, above all else, appreciative of the unity and universality of all things. Moreover, because living in the moment is a "natural" expression of the past, just as the future is a "natural" expression of the present, emotions (the most obvious and immediate manifestations of lived experience from this perspective) both identify the authenticity of the individual's lived experience and promote authentic experience, thereby freeing individuals by encouraging them to cast off the burdens of the past and the anxieties of the future.[29] Ethos thus presupposes and seeks to perpetuate a "natural" horizontality.

At the level of cultural community, that horizontality positions the collectivity such that the insistence on unity dissolves difference, which simultaneously makes interpretation an apparently open-ended but clearly constrained matter. Ostensibly, that is, any interpretation is permissible; yet, only "authentic" interpretations are acceptable, which makes worldview the boundary that restrains and disciplines the freedoms of ethos. No less than the memento mori tradition, then, this cultural perspective on display must restrict interpretations and alternatives of those outside the community, both for their own sake and for the sake of their obligations to community.

Epic Heroism and the Lawn Cemetery

As with the tradition that gave rise to the garden gravescape, the third display tradition that draws our attention here first emerged in alien gravescapes where both voice and freedom of articulation met with cultural inconstancies and even aggressive resistance. Initially borrowing display forms from other traditions (for example, the cippus and obelisk from the garden gravescape) and locating them in gravescapes that muted and often diluted their cultural message, those who sought to nurture and perpetuate this new tradition early on developed their own gravescape and, surprisingly, created sanctified public spaces for their displays beyond the usual bounds.

The creation of sanctified places for the dead in towns and cities, as already noted, was a widespread practice since the beginning of colonization, and the effort to move garden cemeteries away from towns and cities met with an immediate and expansive success that continues into the present. By the 1840s those who embraced this third tradition were finding ways to return their death displays to town and city centers while keeping them clearly detached from churches and graveyards. One of the earliest such efforts resulted in the Washington Monument—a prototypical, unadorned obelisk in Washington, D.C. (see figure 22). Measuring more than 555 feet from the ground to its crown, this white marble shaft, which was begun in 1848, does not invite viewers to contemplate nature or art or one's "finer sentiments." Quite the contrary. One need not indulge in fanciful psychologizing about its phallic appearance to recognize that this display is an accomplishment of labor rather than of artistic skill, that it equates size with significance, that it asserts its dominance over its environment, over nature—that it speaks of power over, of control. Rather than being an expression of a need to live in harmony with that against which all things are measured within the tradition of the garden gravescape, a structure of such monumental proportions announces both the dominance of the species over nature and the consequences of epic heroism.

That announcement, echoed again and again across the nation's cities and towns, provided those who embraced this burgeoning tradition with abundant, powerful opportunities

22. The Washington
Monument, Washington,
D.C. Photograph by
Richard Morris

to articulate their ethos and worldview to an ever-expanding populace. No longer bound by the confines of cemeterial habits or restricted to death displays circumscribed by the personal or social identity of a single individual, memorials strategically erected in bustling business centers, in town squares, and in governmentally sanctioned public spaces constructed an aura of official authenticity. Beyond their inherent ability to speak *to* the people, death displays now newly seemed to possess the power and authority to speak *for* the people. Increasingly, representative memorials encompassing groups of individuals emerged to express their worldview and ethos as America's worldview and ethos (see figure 23).

Efforts to articulate that ethos and worldview by erecting memorials beyond the gravescape were fecund, but they did not provide a broad populace of individuals with opportunities to participate in cultural articulation and ascendance. Nor did efforts outside the gravescape apostrophize what those who belonged to this third tradition regarded as the overly sentimental, expensive, and arrogant features of the romance gravescape. The same cultural logic that resulted in the erection of romantic memorials stripped of their romantic associations again surfaced when this new tradition created a new American gravescape signifying an entirely different worldview and ethos.

Unknowingly, those who embraced the garden romance greatly assisted in the production of this newest effort by being generally willing to acknowledge that they had given lot owners too much latitude in developing their lots. At the same time that Downing was heaping praise on the rural cemetery of its natural beauty, for instance, he also complained that any such beauty was considerably diminished "by the most violent bad taste; we mean the hideous ironmongery, which [rural cemeteries] all more or less display." "Fantastic conceits and gimcracks in iron might be pardonable as adornments of the balustrade of a circus or a temple of Comus," he averred, "but how reasonable beings can tolerate them as inclosures to the quiet grave of a family, and in such scenes of sylvan beauty, is mountain high above our comprehension" (see figure 24). Worse, "as if to show how far human infirmity can go," he continued, "we noticed lately several lots in one of those cemeteries, not only inclosed with a most barbarous place of irony, but the gate of which was positively ornamented with the coat of arms of the owner, accompanied by a brass door-plate, on which was engraved the owner's name, and city residence."[30]

Beyond the disruptive character of hideous ironmongery, many citizens also willingly acknowledged the "deforming effect of those little terraces and angular disturbances of the surface, which result from leaving this work to the taste and caprice of individuals."[31] Having admitted this much, even those who embraced the garden romance found it necessary to institute rules to govern not only what they would permit visitors to the cemetery to do, but also what they would allow lot owners to do by way of "improving" their lots. In turn, instituting rules to limit the actions of visitors and lot owners shifted much of the decision-making power from lot owners, who often were also part owners of the cemeteries, to a newly created professional position, the cemetery superintendent.[32]

One of the most important consequences of the admission that the form of the garden cemetery could be improved by restricting individualism is that it provided those who sought to advance this new tradition with an opportunity to create their own cemeterial

23. U.S. Marine Corps War Memorial, Washington, D.C. Photograph by Richard Morris

form. In 1855, only ten years after Spring Grove Cemetery in Cincinnati had announced its splendors as a rural cemetery, according to the design of "John Notman, who also planned Laurel Hill Cemetery, near Philadelphia,"[33] Adolph Strauch submitted and put into effect a plan to alter its form. Originally, the plan to redesign Spring Grove appears to have been directed primarily at removing the "hideous ironmongery" and "little terraces and angular disturbances" that people found unappealing. But Strauch took the plan several steps further.

After removing "the numerous and crowded enclosures," Strauch eliminated burial mounds, hedges, stone fences, numerous trees, and "the innumerable tombs and gravestones [that] break up the surface of the ground, cut it into unsymmetrical sections, destroy the effect of slopes and levels, and chop up what should be the broad and noble features of one great picture into a confused and crowded multitude of what seem like petty yards or pens."[34] The result was not simply a streamlined romance garden, but an altogether different kind of cemeterial form that placed authority and discipline directly in the hands of corporate owners and superintendents.

Where the memento mori gravescape quietly prayed for the possibilities of spiritual ascendance and the garden cemetery celebrated the glorious union of nature and art, the "landscape lawn method" or lawn cemetery, as it was later termed, promised a deathless place for the dead driven by several distinct advantages. Here, visitors encounter an open vista, unobstructed by fences, memorials, aesthetic renderings, and flora (see figure 25), where "the mind is not disturbed by the obtrusion of bounds and limits that seem to claim superiority and respect, or to assert rights of ownership and contrast of station, even among

24. Ironmongery, Augustus Flagg, Mount Auburn Cemetery, Cambridge, Mass. Photograph by Richard Morris

25. Lawn cemetery gravescape, Princeton Memorial Park, Princeton, New Jersey. Photograph by Richard Morris

the dead."[35] Second, this new gravescape allows cemetery superintendents to make the most efficient use of the land in the cemetery, thereby affirming the view that "individual rights must be subordinated to this general plan." "Civilization," according to one advocate, "consists in subordinating the will of the individual to the comfort and well-being of all."[36] Third, by eliminating fences, hedges, "unnecessary" trees, and other things associated with the garden cemetery, and by requiring markers to be small enough to be level or nearly level with the ground so "they do not appear in the landscape picture," proponents of the lawn cemetery sought to eliminate completely "the old graveyard scene."[37] Together, Sidney Hare remarked, these "improvements" allow citizens to eliminate, albeit gradually, "all things that suggest death, sorrow, or pain"[38]—clearly a direct and distinctive move away from the *ethoi* and worldviews other gravescapes articulate.

The advantage that proponents of this new gravescape seemed to advertise most robustly, however, was that it created an efficient and inexpensive place for ordinary citizens to bury their friends and family. When Mount Auburn was first opened for public burials, a single lot of three hundred square feet cost $60. By the time Adolph Strauch had finished redesigning Spring Grove in 1855, the price of a lot at Mount Auburn had increased to $150,[39] and by 1883 lot prices ranged from $225 for an "unexceptional lot" to $750 for "choice lots."[40] Add to this the cost of an elaborate memorial, of creating a burial mound, of landscaping the lot, of an iron or stone enclosure, as well as the cost of the funeral, and the total was well beyond the modest means of most citizens. By contrast, as late as 1875 the lot prices at Spring Grove ranged from $90 to $150 for a lot of three hundred square feet.[41] Having eliminated virtually all of the features that elevated rural cemeteries to the status of social attractions, those who turned to lawn cemeteries encountered few costs to add to the price of the funeral itself.

Lawn cemeteries did not take "the public by storm," as the rural cemetery had, but they did increase in number nearly as rapidly as rural cemeteries had; in the years following the Civil War they gradually became the most common type of gravescape—a clear measure of the influence this tradition was beginning to have at the national level. Instead of presenting viewers with markers to remind them of their need to prepare for death or with elaborate displays nestled in sylvan scenes, the modern lawn cemetery presents viewers with "a landscape more spacious and parklike"[42] and with memorials that suggest very little in the way of artistic skill, individuality, or death. As a particularly apropos summation, cemeterial regulations require memorials in the lawn cemetery to be "unobtrusive," which translates into small, unadorned plaques sealed into the ground—a strategy that puts death out of sight and significantly increases maintenance efficiency (see figure 26).

Taken collectively, the lawn cemetery and the placement of death displays in town, city, and national centers gave a strong, lucid voice to this newly emerged tradition's worldview and ethos. Central to that voice is an unambiguous and irrevocable dichotomy between emotion and reason. Like the dichotomy between body and soul in the memento mori tradition and the dichotomy between "natural" and "unnatural" in the garden romance, the dichotomy between reason and emotion serves as a synecdoche for primary cultural principles, values, and beliefs (where reason defines the "good" and emotion defines the "bad" or evil) and, in its various manifestations, as a vehicle for expressing primary cultural realities.

26. Lawn cemetery memorial, Anna M. Accardi memorial (twenty-three inches by fourteen inches, brass), 1979. Princeton Memorial Park, Princeton, New Jersey. Photograph by Richard Morris

Among the primary realities from which this tradition's memorial displays emerge and from which they obtain their significance is the view that life is a journey toward success, toward an immortality that individuals must strive to merit through their heroic actions. That view emphatically and immediately brings into focus the necessity of providing mechanisms for identifying the means by which individuals can achieve and measure success. Here, the dichotomy between reason and emotion (as synecdoche and as vehicle for expression through display) indexes key elements of the ethos individuals are expected to adopt. Reason, from this point of view, dictates that individuals must be prepared to triumph over adversity, maintain a quiet persistence and fearlessness, tirelessly advance through a toilsome journey of promotion, maintain an honesty and steadiness of purpose, believe that their grasp of reason is self-sufficient and universal, understand and act on their duty to dominate and control nature (and death), discharge their duties even amid times of change and peril, lead and fashion transcendent success, demonstrate their ability to grasp a great subject and strip it of all its mysteries, revere and promote efficiency, recognize and work within the laws of nature, and be above all else a person of action.

Within the vertically structured community this meritocracy demands, ethos presses forward both as boundary and as discipline. As boundary, ethos serves the purposes of worldview by restricting and identifying cultural members (for example, by reducing all topoi of mode to quantity as the primary principle for determining individual merit or by insisting on the principle of efficiency as a fundamental measure of success). As discipline, ethos assists in maintaining the integrity of community by promoting individuality yet insisting on uniformity so measurement and merit remain autonomous of difference. Thus constrained and disciplined, community achieves interpretation uniformly (that is, there can be one and only one correct interpretation) and autonomously (that is, because the laws of nature over which individuals must triumph make "reality" transparent).

Socially, death displays within this tradition specifically reinforce ethos and worldview through the cultivation of homogeneity and fragmentation. Homogeneity (as so visibly demonstrated in the lawn cemetery) publicly announces the tradition's power and dominance, and fragmentation serves both to sustain the place of the individual and to stifle voices outside the community. Then again, because efficiency and success (and other similar values implicit in this tradition) are outcomes that privilege the future over the past and present, judgment is inherently teleological, which focuses cultural memory and display on progress and thus brings death under cultural control via elimination. Elimination reciprocally offers comfort against the chaos that death proposes.

Conclusion

As one of the truly great mysteries—perhaps even the foundation for the *mysterium tremendum* itself—death insinuates ominous demands. With those demands comes an urgency that death thereby imprints on the living as one of its most salient consequences—the mandate to create spaces of comfort and discomfort, sources of safety and danger, and cognitive and emotional domains into which the living can retreat and into which they must not go. Death displays both materialize from and respond to that mandate.

The memento mori tradition materializes from and responds to that directive through a host of vehicles. Most obviously, it develops, perpetuates, and communicates discomfort and its solution, comfort, as a means of giving death its due, which concomitantly underscores the place of the tradition and the culture whence it comes as the only legitimate sources of comfort. Death here comes fully into view as a dreadful passage through which each and every individual's eternal fate is determined. The risks and consequences of failure are tremendous, as they must be within this arrangement. And yet, an infinitude of bliss, which awaits those who have prepared well for death's dark visitation, is equally inscribed inside this terror. The balance, or perhaps the possibility of imbalance, must weigh heavily on the minds of those who understand the world through this lens—never knowing precisely how much each infraction will count against, how each good deed will count toward, whether one's goodness in the here and now will be enough to warrant deity's affirmation, how much or which moment will tip the scales.

Hope in this arrangement becomes a fickle ally—always a possibility because reward for fidelity is faithfully promised, but even the most assiduously faithful understand that they can bank no real reassurance when the rules of currency are not only unexplained but also unexplainable. Memento mori displays and the worldview and ethos from which they emerge thereby demote hope to a strained version of what is simply possible. The point, of course, is to create an opportunity for eternal bliss as a solution to the mysteries and mystifications of death but to do so in such a way that demands fidelity to the selfsame worldview and ethos that create and nurture the dichotomy in the first place. Only thus can fidelity qua ethos reinforce and draw strength from the danger/safety dichotomy so central to ethos. Put differently, to don the apposite ethos is to respond appropriately to death's demands, which response has the potential for creating a zone of safety but also can never fully resolve the reality of danger. Re-creating worldview through ethos in turn reasserts the reality of death's significance as the penultimate danger that can be addressed only through a worldview that again reasserts ethos.

Such a tenuous hold on comfort and safety leaves certitude as the only reliable emotional and cognitive domain into which the living can retreat. Only those who know without question that they have been fully faithful to the demands of ethos and worldview can look on death displays from this tradition knowing that their fate is secured. Since certitude of this magnitude is improbable even among the chosen (as demonstrated, for example, by the paucity of memento mori displays that *assert* hope and comfort), emotional and cognitive reassurance, like comfort and safety, become destinations rather than stable locations.

Far from being a matter of cruelty or confusion, this configuration is an absolute necessity in the sense that alteration of any one of these elements would undermine the entire structure. To provide stable sources of hope regarding the outcome even in a particular case challenges death's status, which diminishes the role of ethos, which questions worldview's adequacy. To provide any more than a suggestion of comfort would reintroduce the possibility of hope, with the same cascading consequences. And to provide cognitive spaces into which the living might firmly retreat would too easily intimate that both hope and comfort are realities onto which one might reliably cling, which makes danger, discomfort, and even death inutile and placeless. Oppositions accordingly exist for one another, and death displays play integral roles at every cultural and rhetorical turn.

Death displays belonging to and indicative of the romance garden invite and communicate a strikingly different understanding of comfort, safety, and cognitive/emotional retreat. Beginning not with a vertical metaphor defined by its oppositions but with a cyclical metaphor defined by becoming, death displays here recognize vulnerability as an asset.

Comfort inevitably arrives through the process of becoming more of what one already is (natural) and can be enhanced infinitely through one's infinite becoming. This grand cycle domesticates death, makes it ordinary, thus eliminating (at least culturally) the need for a danger/safety dichotomy—all things belonging to the same order. What one *feels* displaces the danger/safety equation and calls forth an emotive response to salve one's feelings—like treating like, in a classic homeopathic remedy.

With discomfort defined as something wholly within the individual's capacity to address and resolve, danger's place is as a restorative for those who stray from nature. Failure to heed death's call to heal emotion with emotion, to become more natural, carries as its most significant penalty the failure to heal oneself; yet, because humans are unaffectedly natural, they must return to nature regardless of how they act or what they do or do not do. To heed death's call is to create for oneself a cognitive and emotional place of retreat that renaturalizes the self. Feeling and knowing blend seamlessly: what one knows, one also feels—not only about death, but about all things natural—because feeling is knowledge. Art on this scale explicitly becomes an expression of feelings and, because knowledge equates with feeling, an extension or alternative way of manifesting knowledge. This brings display to a level well beyond production and into the domain of communication, which serves the ends of both art and nature. Death displays thus enlarge this composition by bringing art, nature, emotion, and knowledge into a homeopathic nexus. The "unnatural" against this backdrop becomes anathema—the place into which one must not go.

Death displays belonging to and expressive of epic heroism transpire from and construct an altogether different constellation that reconfigures death, which is nothing more than a disease to be conquered and an opportunity to turn crisis into a fighting chance to live. As a disease, death is a subject to be investigated, understood, explained, manipulated, predicted, controlled, eliminated. As an opportunity, death is one among many potentially powerful antagonists but not so powerful that human effort cannot prove itself superior. Far from being mere hubris, the cultural logic here places destiny in the hands of the individual whose heroic deeds can transform discomfort into comfort, danger into safety, and death into a thing of the past.

Discomfort and comfort, which in this arrangement are equivalent to danger and safety, here return to an oppositional status, where the former appears in the figure of an inability to enact ethos directly. Since one cannot act heroically in the face of death proper, which creates discomfort (and danger), acting against death's intermediaries becomes discomfort's resolution (for example, locating memorials below ground so that viewers need not confront what they cannot act against). What this means pragmatically is that comfort and discomfort (as well as safety and danger) pivot on an axis of merit as a medium of exchange; for one who would exchange discomfort for comfort must enact ethos in order to produce actions that merit comfort, which comes in twin forms. The first is knowing that one can do nothing about death and, consequently, that one must take whatever action one can to deal with the consequences (or intermediaries) of death. The second is knowing that immortality issues forth through heroic actions such that one survives beyond death through cultural memory. In both instances one exchanges heroic actions for the desired result so that consequence is ever a product of ethos.

Exchanges of this sort derive primarily from a worldview that divides emotions (and, thus, cognitive and emotional retreats and spaces into which one must not go) into two sorts: those that perpetuate and those that impede cultural ends. Those that perpetuate cultural ends and celebrate ethos (bravery, courage, and the like) often play the role of motive and become natural resources that are valuable for their instrumentality. Those that impede cultural ends by distracting those who would be heroic from their journey toward success are much more likely to be subject to harsh discipline, as both inaction and inappropriate action call ethos into question.

Rather than indexing deity and absolute evil (despite a similar cast), ethos here indexes success and failure, which emerge as quantities rather than qualities. Linking backward to the size-equals-significance motif so obvious in city-based displays from this tradition, one might conceivably merit immortality on the basis of a single act or action, but the accumulation of acts and/or actions across time seems a far more common basis of celebration. At any rate, the privileging of quantification over and against other modes of being and understanding immediately and directly results in the need for identifying the "best" (fastest, largest, most, and so forth) as the primary means of determining worth. Without this mechanism of competition (along with quantitative means of measuring outcomes and the witnesses who verify such outcomes), those who embrace this tradition would have no method of achieving immortality through the accumulation of merit.

Epic heroism, the garden cemetery, and the memento mori gravescape variously construct universes of meaning in which displays of death rehearse cultural lessons that radiate in multiple directions. Each tradition creates specific modes of understanding and responding to the world at large and to death in particular. Each emanates from and speaks through a cultural logic that is internally impeccable and externally always suspect. Each seeks in its own ways and at the very least to provide reassurances against the ultimate unknown. If we are rotten with perfection, as Kenneth Burke proposed,[43] we are doubly rotten with a thirst for perfection's fulfillment through immortality. However much we may struggle against the chaos, seek to become the best of our nature, climb the heroic ladder of success, or elsewise display ourselves against death, without a framework larger than ourselves, larger even than death, we are left to consider the stubborn possibility that the only thing remaining to us in the end is the end.

Notes

I wish to express my gratitude to Professor Larry Prelli, whose foresight, patience, and acumen have made this volume and my contribution herein possible.

1. Although not part of the formal structure of this chapter, two points merit parenthetical notice from the outset. First, this essay makes no attempt to comprehend all memorial traditions, all American memorial traditions, or even a majority of American memorial traditions; death may favor no one, but death displays most certainly do. Second, some of the ideas contained in this chapter reconsider ideas articulated in previous publications and presentations; readers interested in a more in-depth exploration of these and related issues may wish to consult *Sinners, Lovers, and Heroes: An Essay on Memorializing in Three American Cultures* (New York: State University of New York Press, 1997).

2. William F. May, "The Sacral Power of Death in Contemporary Experience," in *Perspectives on Death*, ed. Liston O. Mills, 168–96 (New York: Abingdon, 1969).

3. See Ernest Becker, *The Denial of Death* (New York: Free Press, 1975).

4. Richard E. Meyer, introduction to *Cemeteries and Gravemarkers: Voices of American Culture*, ed. Richard E. Meyer, 1, 5 (Ann Arbor, Mich.: UMI Research Press, 1989).

5. Clifford Geertz, *The Interpretation of Cultures* (New York: Basic Books, 1973), 89.

6. Ibid.

7. Namely, Alabama, Arizona, Arkansas, California, Colorado, Connecticut, Delaware, Illinois, Indiana, Iowa, Kansas, Kentucky, Louisiana, Maryland, Massachusetts, Michigan, Minnesota, Mississippi, Missouri, Montana, Nebraska, Nevada, New Jersey, New Mexico, New York, North Carolina, Ohio, Oklahoma, Oregon, Pennsylvania, Rhode Island, South Dakota, Tennessee, Texas, Utah, Virginia, Washington, West Virginia, Wisconsin, and Wyoming.

8. Charles Grandison Finney, *Lectures on Revivals of Religion,* 6th ed. (New York: Leavitt, Lord, 1835), 132.

9. Herbert Marcuse, "The Ideology of Death," in *The Meaning of Death,* ed. Herman Feifel, 68 (New York: McGraw Hill, 1959).

10. Thomas Robbins, *Diary of Thomas Robbins, D.D., 1796–1854,* ed. Increase N. Tarbox (Boston: Beacon, 1886), 1:86.

11. Dickran Tashjian and Ann Tashjian, *Memorials for Children of Change: The Art of Early New England Stone Carving* (Middletown, Conn.: Wesleyan University Press, 1974), 10.

12. Lucien L. Agosta, "Speaking Stones: New England Grave Carvings and the Emblematic Tradition," *Markers* 3 (1985): 48.

13. Frederick T. Gray, *New Years' Sermons, Preached in the Bulfinch Street Church, on Sunday, January 3, 1847* (Boston: Hall, 1847), 24.

14. William Bentley, *The Diary of William Bentley, D.D., Pastor of the East Church, Salem, Massachusetts,* ed. Peter Smith (Gloucester, Mass.: Essex Institute, 1905), 2:127.

15. Tashjian and Tashjian, *Memorials for Children of Change,* 36.

16. Ibid., 52.

17. Space and place clearly are not synonymous and clearly would merit a separate and more complete treatment in a longer or differently focused essay.

18. Joseph Story, "An Address Delivered on the Dedication of the Cemetery at Mount Auburn, September 24th, 1831," in *A History of the Cemetery of Mount Auburn,* ed. Jacob Bigelow, 148–49 (Boston: Munroe, 1859).

19. Henry Ward Beecher, *Star Papers, or, Experiences of Art and Nature* (New York: Derby and Jackson, 1859), 124.

20. Andrew Jackson Downing, "Public Cemeteries and Public Gardens," in *Rural Essays by Andrew Jackson Downing,* ed. George W. Curtis, 154 (New York: Da Capo, 1974).

21. Stanley French, "The Cemetery as Cultural Institution: The Establishment of Mount Auburn and the 'Rural Cemetery' Movement," in *Death in America,* ed. David E. Stannard, 69 (Philadelphia: University of Pennsylvania Press, 1974).

22. Jacob Bigelow, *A History of the Cemetery of Mount Auburn* (Boston: Munroe and Brothers, 1859), vi.

23. Downing, "Public Cemeteries and Public Gardens," 154–55.

24. Nehemiah Cleveland, *Green Wood: A Directory for Visitors* (New York: Green Wood, 1850), 4.

25. Blanche Linden-Ward, "Strange but Genteel Pleasure Grounds: Tourist and Leisure Uses of Nineteenth Century Cemeteries," in *Cemeteries and Gravemarkers: Voices of American Culture,* ed. Richard E. Meyer, 295 (Ann Arbor, Mich: UMI Research Press, 1989).

26. Cleveland, *Green Wood,* 250.

27. Downing, "Public Cemeteries and Public Gardens," 155–56.

28. Ibid., 155.

29. See, for example, Martin Heidegger, *Being and Time,* trans. John Macquarrie and Edward Robinson (New York: Harper and Row, 1962); Peter Koestenbaum, "The Vitality of Death," *Journal of Existentialism* 5 (1964): 139–66; and Peter Koestenbaum, *The Vitality of Death: Essays in Existential Psychology and Philosophy* (Westport, Conn.: Greenwood, 1971).

30. Downing, "Public Cemeteries and Public Gardens," 156.

31. Cleveland, *Green Wood,* 250.

32. See, for example, James J. Farrell, *Inventing the American Way of Death* (Philadelphia: Temple University Press, 1980).

33. D. J. Kenny, *Illustrated Cincinnati: A Pictorial Hand Book of the Queen City* (Cincinnati: Clarke, 1875), 318.

34. F. B. Perkins, "Sepulture, Its Ideas and Practices," *Galaxy* 11 (June 1871): 841–42.

35. Ibid., 843.

36. As quoted in Farrell, *Inventing the American Way of Death,* 118.

37. Edward Evarts Weed, *Modern Park Cemeteries* (Chicago: R. J. Haight, 1912), 94.

38. As quoted in Farrell, *Inventing the American Way of Death,* 120.

39. Bigelow, *A History of the Cemetery of Mount Auburn,* 23.

40. Moses King, *Mount Auburn Cemetery, Including Also a Brief History and Description of Cambridge, Harvard University, and the Union Railway Company,* 19th ed. (Cambridge: Moses King, 1883), 27.

41. Kenny, *Illustrated Cincinnati,* 319.

42. John Brinkerhoff Jackson, *American Space: The Centennial Years, 1865–1876* (New York: Norton, 1972), 70.

43. Kenneth Burke, *Language as Symbolic Action: Essays on Life, Literature, and Method* (Berkeley: University of California Press, 1966), 16.

Part 3

Demonstrations as Rhetorical Display and Rhetorical Displays as Demonstrative

Gerard A. Hauser

11

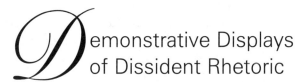

Demonstrative Displays of Dissident Rhetoric

The Case of Prisoner 885/63

In 1994, South Africa became an inclusive democracy. That there is a democracy in South Africa is a testimony to political vision and perseverance in the struggle that overthrew apartheid. With most opposition leaders imprisoned and its citizens of color subjected to the harsh social, economic, and political realities of the Afrikaner regime, the odds were stacked against organizing a successful resistance movement; they were even greater against a spirit of truth and reconciliation prevailing should one succeed. But the movement did succeed, and a principal reason for its success was the instruction in political identity and organization that occurred in the least likely place, the state prison on Robben Island.

Robben Island is located eight miles to sea off the Cape Town coast. Its history as an exile for the damned dates to 1525, when a Portuguese ship reportedly left some prisoners there. Since then it has been the place of banishment for South Africa's outcasts: the chronically ill, insane, lepers, and prisoners. By 1931 the chronically sick, insane, and lepers were no longer treated on the island and the sanitariums were burned to the ground, but the prison remained. The island itself is inhospitable: the waters surrounding it are frigid, the weather conditions tend toward the extremes, and its landscape is poorly suited for agriculture and offers only meaningless labor in its rock quarry.

Beginning in the early 1960s, Robben Island became the principal place of incarceration for political prisoners convicted of crimes growing out of their opposition to apartheid. Its population included most of the opposition leaders, Nelson Mandela among them. White prisoners were transferred to other facilities, leaving only black, common-law prisoners as inmates with the newly arriving politicals. The common-law prisoners had organized into rival gangs and, although segregated in lockup from the political prisoners, included them among their targets for intimidation, sexual assault, and physical brutality. The guards, who typically were uneducated and/or without prospects for professional advancement, were sadistic and racist. Their treachery included using the prison gangs to totalize its environment of terror. The island, in short, was a location in which South Africa's racist structure was mirrored by the racial composition of the inmates and conduct of their warders.

Confronted by conditions so extreme that survival had to be each man's foremost concern, the political prisoners soon determined that they could not count on the state or the prison system to initiate humane reform and took it upon themselves to change the prison's culture. Were we to follow the panoptic theory of power set forth in Foucault's *Discipline and Punish*,[1] we would predict their efforts were doomed to failure. Remarkably, however, they succeeded in transforming the prison from a culture of violence to one that recognized the prisoners' human dignity and from an environment in which physical survival was paramount to a "university of resistance."[2] Their success is all the more interesting in that it challenges the Foucauldian position, which focuses on how the operations of power constitute subjects and their knowledge, by suggesting that resistance has its own productive capacity, that it is capable of both halting an oppressive power and constituting power of its own. We are led to ask, what made such a transformation possible?

Clearly no single factor can account for it. My endeavor is to explore one facet that contributed to this success by initiating a changed consciousness within the prison of the political prisoners' identity: *demonstrative* aspects of political conscience in the political prisoners' *displays* of dissent. I will begin this exploration by considering a suggestive lead in Quintilian's *Institutio Oratoria* regarding the rhetorical character of display that links it to demonstration. I will argue that the prison is an ironically potent rhetorical site in which resistance is enacted through performances of vernacular rhetoric. The most potent of these vernacular resources is the political prisoner's body, which becomes the locus of a deadly political struggle with the state. Within prison, and to those observing from outside, displays of resistance function as a vernacular mode of epideictic in which "showing" may acquire the demonstrative power of irrefutable proof. Such public performances interrogate power in a way that denaturalizes its equations as imposed by prison warders and induces in those who observe them, as it does in those who read about them, a fantasia, an imagined visualization, of political conscience. Their bodily resistance, in short, serves as an inventional locus. It frames the terms of affiliation through graphic displays that transform the political prisoner's identity into a prisoner of conscience[3] and demonstrate political commitments that conscience beseeches its attending public not to abandon. I will use as my evidentiary basis for these considerations Indres Naidoo's memoir of his incarceration as a political prisoner in South Africa's facility on Robben Island, *Island in Chains*.[4]

Demonstrative Rhetoric and the Fantasia of Display

In *Institutio Oratoria*, book 6, Quintilian takes up the topic of emotional appeals. In candor, he observes, a great many pleaders are capable at discovering arguments adequate to prove their points. While he does not "despise" such adequate arguments, he allows that their true function is to instruct pleaders of genuine eloquence in the facts of the case. The real work of the orator, and the place where a person earns distinction, is arousing the judges' emotions. Making strong proofs, he admits, will incline judges to think our case superior to our opponent's, but when we arouse their emotions, they will want it to be better. "And what they wish, they will also believe" (6.2.5).[5] By this line, Quintilian is led to conclude that emotions more than reason lie at the heart of eloquence. "For it is in its power over the emotions that the life and soul of oratory is to be found" (6.2.7).

In Quintilian's opinion, the first requirement for stirring emotions in others is to feel them personally. We cannot counterfeit grief, anger, or indignation. These and other emotions arise from a certain disposition evoked when we suffer events of personal magnitude and consequence. How else, he wonders, can we explain the eloquence of mourners expressing their grief or the fluency of an unlettered person stirred to anger? These are sincere expressions of feelings, and they are powerfully moving. Consequently, if we wish to give our words the appearance of sincerity and move the judges to share them, we must first adapt ourselves to the emotional state of those whose emotions are genuinely felt.

We achieve this emotional simulacrum by a special experience, which the Greeks called *fantasiai* (fantasia). Fantasia occurs when we imagine the absent persons and events so vividly that we respond as if they were before our very eyes.

> Shall I not bring before my eyes all the circumstances which it is reasonable to imagine must have occurred in such a connexion? Shall I not see the assassin burst suddenly from his hiding-place, the victim tremble, cry for help, beg for mercy, or turn to run? Shall I not see the fatal blow delivered and the stricken body fall? Will not the blood, the deathly pallor, the groan of agony, the death-rattle, be indelibly impressed upon my mind? (6.2.31)

This remarkable passage, juxtaposed against the orthodoxy of reasoned argument as legitimating public judgment, resituates the force of rhetoric in emotions and our emotions in the undeniable evidence of what we see. And what do we see? Quintilian offers us a sensuous image of the embodied orator whose corporeal experience is authenticated by its individual immediacy. It is authenticated by the orator's verbal display of the physical scene and by a response of strong emotions.

Those who are most sensitive to these passing impressions of lush imaginative representation will achieve the state of *enargeia*. In this state we seem not to narrate, Quintilian says, but to exhibit. Our words acquire the immediacy of an eyewitness whose emotions are so actively stirred as to leave the audience with an indelible impression.

> For oratory fails of its full effect, and does not assert itself as it should, if its appeal is merely to the hearing, and if the judge merely feels that the facts on which he has to give his decision are being narrated to him, and not displayed in their living truth to the eyes of the mind. (8.2.62)

Enargeia is the source of sincere emotional expression, which, Quintilian insists, the orator is duty bound to perform on behalf of his client whose interests are at stake. The emotional state induced by witnessing the scene (*enargeia*) is complemented by the stylistic quality that captures the energy of the action occurring in the scene. In book 8, Quintilian adds his voice to those of other leading Greek and Roman rhetoricians by instructing the incipient orator to infuse his verbal portraits with *energeia,* which "finds its peculiar function in securing that nothing that we say is tame" (8.3.89). The audience experiences powerful feelings not just by being told what took place, but by seeing in its details actions in agreement with nature. For this reason, the orator must strive for stylistic qualities in his depiction of the scene that capture *energeia:* energy or vigor through action that an actual observer would witness. "Fix your eyes on nature and follow her," he advises. "All eloquence is concerned with the activities of life, while every man applies to himself what he hears from others, and the mind is always readiest to accept what it recognizes as true to nature" (8.3.71).

The Roman rhetorics, which inseparably link *verba* and *actio,* were exquisitely sensitive to the fact that action requires engagement of situated deeds and that audiences become engaged by such deeds when the issues they raise touch their lives. Life-engaging decisions, such as those enacted in the law courts and the forum, necessarily involved emotions. While an audience convulsed with emotion would be a public menace, sound judgment on practical conduct requires an ability to experience the pleasures and agonies occasioned by public and private relationships. The classical tradition's rendition of rhetoric as an architectonic productive art couples emotional and rational engagement as tandem necessities for sound public judgment. Quintilian's reference to the orator's duty suggests he thought emotional engagement was essential for a judge to ponder proportion between acts and consequences so that prudence might prevail and that such engagement requires rhetorical display.

The concern with display that Quintilian emphasized in his discussion of emotional engagement was not confined to matters of style. Roman rhetoricians also accorded it paramount importance in their discussions of epideictic oratory, in which they captured display aspects of this genre when they changed its name from "epideictic" to "demonstrative." This switch, seemingly reliant on a different sense of display than in the passages above, ultimately returns to its energizing/actional features in a way that is both informative of display's *dunamis,* or rhetorical power, as the Greeks expressed it, and bears on the evocative power of rhetorical displays by political prisoners we shall consider momentarily.

Harry Caplan expresses the traditional interpretation of this shift from "epideictic" to "demonstrative" in his translation of *Rhetorica ad Herennium.* In a note on epideictic, Caplan states:

> The Greek term "epideictic" did not primarily emphasize the speaker's virtuosity, nor was the Latin equivalent *demonstrativum* intended to imply logical demonstration. Whereas in both deliberative and judicial causes the speaker seeks to persuade his hearers to a course of action, in epideictic his primary purpose is by means of his art to impress his ideas upon them, without action as a goal.[6]

Even if the Romans did not mean to imply that demonstrative oratory was logical demonstration, Richard McKeon makes the important point that the transformation of Greek philosophical method into a rhetorical form was nonetheless a significant change of focus on what counted as proof.[7] Caplan's point about not confusing the shift from "epideictic" to "demonstrative" with scientific demonstration is well taken, but it also reminds us that the Romans considered "display oratory" as a special mode of proof.[8]

A transformative spirit is at work in two additional and related aspects of Roman rhetoric relevant to this discussion: the primacy of the audience's criteria over the foundational ones of metaphysics or epistemology as the standards for judgment, and the relationship of performance to rhetorical invention. These tandem innovations are illustrated by Cicero's permutation of Greek philosophical categories, particularly Aristotle's, in his consideration of loci as an extension of Aristotle's topical theory.

Aristotle developed his theory of dialectical discourse, set forth primarily in his *Topica* and *Categories,*[9] on an a priori system of first principles to which all possible meaningful statements had to conform. Cicero's appropriation of Aristotle's theory replaced its metaphysical foundations with the primacy of rhetorical experience. Cicero regarded rhetorical experience as culminating in the audience's determination of a claim's truth status based on whether it withstood the test of argumentation.[10] His *Topica* transformed Aristotle's dialectical system of topoi into a rhetoricized system of loci suited to analyze the needs of practical affairs or the conduct of public business that sought audience assent.[11]

By replacing metaphysical assumptions with the rhetorical act of gaining audience assent as the basis for knowledge and truth, Cicero captured the importance of loci for rhetorical invention in practical affairs and in philosophical systems. By this shift, Cicero also linked the inventional moment to enacted performance conducted in concert with the audience (*actio*), as well as to prior preparation.[12]

Cicero's emphasis on the primacy of the audience's judgment brings us back to Quintilian on emotions. The demonstrative speech was concerned with honor, a public virtue exhibited by deeds worthy of praise and emulation. Praise always pursues a double objective: to recognize the personal virtue of the extolled, which commands the honor that is their due, and to impart the civic lessons their lives exemplify to a public called upon to witness the honor being bestowed upon them.[13] The rhetor's challenge was to awaken the community's desire to live its public life in ways that endorsed the values for which the extolled person stood, if not emulate this person's exemplary qualities. The orator did not inspire admiration and emulation by *reasoning* about past deeds but by *exhibiting* them. The same means that Quintilian argued were necessary to make the judges *believe* were equally the rhetorical means deployed to *exhibit* public virtue and, thereby, to offer a rhetorical form of demonstration. But there is more.

Quintilian's account attributes the invention of the most powerful appeals to an internal state of fantasia. Fantasia is equally operative as an audience's inventional prompt in discourse that relies on a narrative of deeds to support claims of praise and offer instruction on how to live a virtuous public life. As Nicole Loraux's study of funeral orations shows, Athenians' understanding of their city was a rhetorical invention, a fantasy of the social imaginary constructed through the epideictic form.[14] Depictions of deeds extolled and condemned move us beyond abstractions. They teach us how to live our lives by bringing the scene before our mind's eye; they make us witnesses in our imaginations to acts that require our affirmation or condemnation for them to live in collective memory as concrete realities. The community teaches its citizens that courage is a virtue through the rhetorically constructed fantasy of seeing brave deeds performed. Such displays demonstrate, through their imagined showing, both what we mean by bravery and that the honored citizen was brave. Our collective understanding of both the praiseworthy deeds and their call for a common response is evoked by the fantasy of our collective seeing. By this simulacrum in the collective imaginary we also witness a demonstration of sorts that has the force of rhetorical certainty—a symbolically constituted reality.

The rhetorical inflection that moves demonstration from a claim of knowledge to one of understanding cuts across the grain of general scholarly usage. The academy's perspective is predisposed to understand "demonstration" as referring to mathematical, logical, or scientific arguments that purportedly prove conclusions to a level of certainty that defies reasoned refutation. The history of science and of logic is replete with exceptions to that view. To take a famous example, the Holy Office of the Inquisition's response to Galileo's *Dialogue*, printed in 1632, shows that the logical derivation of purportedly certain claims to knowledge can be challenged by changing the axioms on which demonstration of the claim's truth must rest. Even among scientists, one scholar's demonstration has been grist for another's refutation. René Descartes, for example, writing in the same century as Galileo, used a geometric model of deductive reasoning to establish his philosophical system as a basis of certain knowledge and scientific method, only to have it refuted by the empiricists, most notably Sir Isaac Newton, who turned his system on its head to establish a new observational basis for scientific proof.[15] In either case, the linkage of "demonstration" with display of logical or observational grounds for "proving" displaced all association of the concept with rhetorical displays that called upon audiences to imagine and thereby witness actions that exhibited incontestable qualities of virtuous conduct that, in turn, bound them together in civic community.

The instability of demonstration as a concept and a reasoning practice is underscored further by the street rhetoric that became a staple for dissident displays of political disaffection during the twentieth century. Mesmerizing performances of pageants and spectacles and displays of mass demonstration, so much a part of contemporary, mass-mediated culture, are not unique to our time. The ubiquity of mass media representations has simply made us more conscious of, if not more critically reflective about, iconic representations and the vernacular rhetoric of street-level displays occurring beyond the halls of power. Such displays of political sentiment transform the ancient rhetorical practice of exhibiting communal values through demonstrative oratory to political demonstrations that carry the aura of self-evidence. The bridge from the Roman transformation of a rhetorical genre into a special mode of proving to political demonstrations in the street telescopes the long history of rhetorical performance based on the fantasia of "seeing is believing." As Graham Nash exhorted Americans through song during the tumult of the celebrated Chicago Seven trial, they could "change the world, rearrange the world" if they would simply "come to Chicago."[16]

These performances, enacted as if they conveyed social truths, underscore important conclusions about demonstrative rhetoric and the fantasia of display that are relevant to the discourse and action of dissident rhetoric. First, the demonstrations of rhetorical performances parallel qualities inherent in the demonstrations of logical and scientific "proving." Both purportedly are grounded, as Quintilian noted, "in the nature of the object with which they are concerned." Both also induce commitment through "showing" or "exhibiting": the rhetorical demonstration exhibits in discourse or action virtuous or vicious qualities of conduct that invite communal recognition and judgment; in comparison, the logical demonstration exhibits all the proof's elements that, in turn, inescapably yield the conclusion, and the scientific demonstration exhibits the necessary procedural elements that, in turn, foster reliable observation. Finally, each also makes claims that follow from purportedly irrefutable premises: rhetorical demonstrations possess an air of moral certainty that parallels (1) the logical certainty inherent to proofs that work consistently from accepted premises to claims in accord with formal rules of reasoning, as well as (2) the scientific certainty inherent in the presumption that whatever one is trained to observe and see is empirically real.

Second, rhetorical displays also demonstrate in one or both of two ways. Rhetorical performance can be enacted before an immediate audience with all the added persuasive power implied by the presumption that "seeing is believing." Often, however, rhetorical performances must be reenactments of actions or events that the audience did not immediately witness. In that case, rhetorical displays must marshal verbal and formal resources that induce the audience to undergo the fantasia of imagined seeing. The fantasia of seeing, in which the audience is brought into the emotional ambit of eyewitnesses, then carries the demonstrative force of self-evident, valid proving.

These considerations are especially relevant to dissident rhetoric. As numerous demonstrations protesting wars, denial of civil rights, policies contributing to degradation of the planet's ecology, and the like illustrate, displays of dissent arguably are as influential as official rhetoric in shaping public opinion, informing social judgment, and consolidating social will.[17] For these rhetorical performances to exercise influence, they must organize social knowledge within a dialectic between official authority and moral conviction that makes displays of values and aspirations, as well as their disparity with lived realities, appear self-evident. At the same time, the reality of power differentials also requires that rhetorical displays of dissidence serve as a wedge to open the possibility of negotiation with the adversary.[18] Dissident rhetoric, we shall see, not only calls upon the persuasive powers of demonstration, whether before immediate or indirect audiences, but also requires a distinctive kind of rhetorical locus to generate rhetorical displays that can do so.

The Political Prisoner as Rhetorical Locus of Political Conscience

Political prisoners occupy a unique rhetorical position. They are unlike common felons in that their incarceration grows from the threat of their ideas. Often they have broken no law save the unspoken prohibition against disagreement with a totalitarian power. When their legal violations do involve acts of violence, they stem from embracing ideas at odds with the existing order. Their ability to display an alternative political vision to the existing order can be so compelling, as recent history has demonstrated, that repressive regimes remain willing to liquidate leading dissidents and even entire ethnic groups with genocidal fervor. The most recent report of Human Rights Watch cites such abuses on every continent, often with the eyes of world leaders averted when their national interests seem to warrant.[19]

Removing dissidents from society makes the calculated wager that once they are off the public stage they will be forgotten and, if their treatment is horrendous enough, quite possibly they will recant. Consequently, repressive regimes remain willing to take their chances at success in forcing the opposition to be silent. However, this wager is not without risk. The impulse toward a pogrom can be checked in cases where the opposition has made effective use of the publicity principle and its enemy status is defined less on group identity than ideological differences. There prudence dictates that mere incarceration may suffice. Against the risk that the political prisoner will quicken public imagination as a symbol of the state's alien ethos, the regime calculates that removal from public view will toll the dissident's political death knell and possibly deliver a mortal blow to the ideas for which he or she stands. For those still on the streets, the regime banks on intimidation forcing them to avoid the kinds of overt acts that will bring them to the same fate, as the former Soviet Union's practice of show trials grimly testifies. Without public displays of disaffection and alternative visions of the political order, the bet is that opposition politics will disintegrate or, at worst, go underground.

Underground resistance may breed disaffection, but without the remedy of leading dissident voices, disaffection often succumbs to the toxicity of cynicism, itself a form of display, albeit unlikely to captivate public understanding or overpower the existing order's claim to legitimacy. By the same token, the political prisoner remains alive as a viable political being only through channels outside those of the official political public sphere. For political prisoners to have political force they must find ways to be seen; they require a counterpublic sphere in which to lead and sustain dissident discourse.[20] Moreover, the prisoner must find ways to display political conscience and consciousness capable of inspiring resistance regardless of personal costs in the service of revolutionary change.[21]

Here we should note that not all political prisoners are prisoners of conscience. A political prisoner becomes a prisoner of conscience by choosing to remain a dissident in prison. For many, their resistance goes unnoticed by the outside world, being enacted in daily micropractices that refuse submission to an authority they regard as illegitimate. In the case of leading dissidents, this choice often is known publicly through their refusal to accept the authorities' Faustian bargain of their name for their freedom. Regardless of their status, by refusing to sign a loyalty oath, to recant their prior rhetoric, or to accept an offer of emigration, these political prisoners make an affirmation of conscience that accepts fidelity to the commitments of their advocacy over personal liberty. They are prisoners of their conscious commitments, which means their conscience defines their relationship with the state.

By refusing the state's deal, the prisoner of conscience accepts the terror of prison as the personal price for maintaining an authentic voice.[22] For the political prisoner who is not a leading voice, these same terms may or may not be offered. For most they are not, since their imprisonment stems from alleged violations of the criminal code. Nevertheless, as political prisoners, their relationship with their warders bears the indelible mark of oppositional identity. By insisting on retaining it, they situate themselves outside the narrative of the penal code and within a narrative of resistance. By choosing not to curry favor with their warders and thus to submit, they exhibit a fundamental opposition that reframes their incarceration from the official narrative of the sentence to an interrogation of the state's legitimacy.

In myriad ways political prisoners declare their oppositional identity through individual and collective displays of dissent, including overt confrontation between the individual and the overwhelming power of the state. Consequently, the prisoners become the very site—the place—of a political struggle, as they attempt to find their dissonant voices while the authorities use all available means to mute them. They are the particular place, as it were, where the contest occurs, and, as such, their sense of themselves as a concrete and relational manifestation of resistance precedes and creates the more abstract sense of space in which events occur.[23] As a place, their resisting bodies also double as loci (sometimes their most potent loci) for inventing displays of conscience that, otherwise, would remain silent and concealed from view.

These displays, as the prisoners' writings themselves, are heteroglossic. Their dialogue with their warders and readers arises out of social circumstances in which they typically and overtly interrogate and challenge—in Bakhtinean terms, dialogize—the legitimacy of the existing order.[24] Often they do so less through the rhetoric of political manifesto than by recounting the dialogue with authority that takes place between the prisoner of conscience and the authorities and warders within the prison. They indict the state through rhetorically constructed displays of its agents' ignorance, insensitivity, and disregard for basic human dignity and by their own displays of an alternative logic of political conscience. A central mode of this interrogation is the prisoner's use of the body as an inventional locus for enacting displays of conscience.

The particular case I wish to examine in light of the foregoing is the prison memoir of Indres Naidoo recounting his experiences in Robben Island Prison. Naidoo was one of the first volunteers for the armed wing of the African National Congress (ANC), *Umkhonto we Sizwe* (Spear of the Nation). He fell victim to a trap in which he was caught bombing a railroad signal box on the outskirts of Johannesburg. He was tried and convicted of sabotage in 1963 and sentenced to a ten-year prison term to be served at Robben Island.

After he completed his sentence, Naidoo was virtually banned from further involvement in South African politics; he was under house arrest weekends and evenings and forbidden to have contact with ANC members or to make public statements regarding his imprisonment. Still he used word of mouth to spread information about conditions on Robben Island and the continued resistance of the political prisoners there. These stories linked ongoing events, such as the uprisings in Soweto, to the larger political movement that Robben Island's political prisoners were struggling to keep alive. He finally determined, however, that he had to leave South Africa in order to give greater publicity to the ANC cause and keep the resistance movement alive on Robben Island. With the help of Albie Sachs, a lawyer who was also a noted dissident and prison writer banned from South Africa, Naidoo tells his story as prisoner 883/63 in his book *Island in Chains*.[25]

Naidoo's rhetorical burden was imposed by the leadership of the ANC prisoners, which charged released prisoners to publicize conditions in the prison so that others in South Africa and beyond would learn of the brutal conditions there and of their continued resistance. He keeps faith with those still in the prison by providing a first-person account of his treatment. On the surface, the memoir seems reportorial, even anecdotal, by contrast to the writing of noted resistance leaders who faced the rhetorical challenge of explaining their movement's political agenda or of overtly confronting the state it opposed. Consequently his memoir lacks Dietrich Bonhoeffer's analytical incision, Martin Luther King's argumentative dexterity, Adam Michnick's eye for political irony, Fleeta Drumgo's unrestrained political invective, Jacobo Timmerman's skill at constructing an etiology of torture, Irena Ratushinskaya's dialogical facility, Nelson Mandela's political vision, or Václav Havel's capacity to reflect on the deeper significance of his warders' ordinary acts of dehumanization.[26]

If *Island in Chains* is not marked by closely reasoned argument, neither is it mere *reportage.* Its serial displays of confrontation between sadistic practices that deny human worth and resistance that affirms human dignity construct an emotionally evocative presentation.[27] Naidoo brings his readers into the prison's world of moral and mortal political struggle during the decade from 1963 to 1973—a time of horrific treatment that the prisoners managed, eventually, to reverse—by making them eyewitnesses to its concrete, phenomenological manifestations. Even seemingly quotidian episodes in which prisoners exchange contraband, hide and circulate newspapers, or seek medical assistance for ailing comrades become displays of resistance and assertions of self-worth. At its heart, however, stands the prisoner's body as a contested rhetorical locus that the prison authorities attempt to control and mute and from which prisoners struggle to enact rhetorical displays of self-worth through defiant acts of civility and deception.

Prison and the Struggle for Rhetorical Place

The prison system arranges space and time in ways that suppress opportunities to enact rhetorical displays of political conscience. This is demonstrated in both the organizational structure and the substance of Naidoo's narrative. Both show how prisoners of conscience must struggle to overcome powerful obstacles in finding a locus from which to enact a political conscience.

Island in Chains is organized into three parts: the trip to the island; the island, which is itself demarcated into two phases of chains bound and chains loosened; and the trip from the island. The first and third parts are organized as coherent stories. The trip to the island tells of his crime and arrest, horrific treatment by the police, trial and conviction, and journey across South Africa to the penal facility on Robben Island. Each of its episodes bears narratival relationship to what preceded and what follows. The trip from the island details his final appearance before the parole board, the conditions of his release, the boat trip from the island, and his reunion with his family.

The island itself, which forms the center of the book and is the defining space for Naidoo's account of his time in prison, is organized differently. It consists of a series of disconnected episodes. Each is self-contained, and, in most instances, its order of appearance could be altered without discernable consequence to the narrative integrity of the whole. There is no apparent plot that organizes episodes or informs characters. There is no sense of temporal progression with a past or future or with a time frame that brackets episodes. Dates simply are not mentioned; calendar time is irrelevant. Its episodes are vignettes, illumining in themselves as stories of conflict with unreasonable authorities and ignorant warders, of repetitive and meaningless activity, and of small acts to sustain community among the damned. At the same time, these small acts that inform us about the political prisoners' daily realities acquire added meaning as they are fitted into an account of resistance. Each is a vernacular rhetorical act, an evocation that appeals in ways other than the discourse of official forums but that is grasped and internalized by a people sympathetic to the individuation of each prisoner's pain. On its own, each quotidian act might be regarded as a form of "gentle violence"[28] in its insistence on solidarity from the other prisoners to resist the reign of terror inside the prison. Within the frame of bodies under assault, however, their *dunamis* is anything but gentle. Each encounter with the warders becomes a condensed expression of the national struggle, a synecdoche that, by concentrating a people's struggle in the besieged prisoner's body, releases uncommon *energeia*.

From the moment they entered the penal system, South Africa's political prisoners experienced its world of regulation and control. As with the common prisoner, each one's sentence established an official chronotope[29] through its terms of space and time that tempered any and all of the prisoner's daily negotiations with power. For political prisoners this negotiation was complicated by an ever-present awareness, shared with the authorities, that the isolation of prison remained outward looking; although removed from society's normal places of civic and private concourse, the political prisoners never relinquished hope of engaging its consciousness. Consequently, the authorities did whatever they could to isolate the politicals from the outside world. They were denied newspapers, radios, or other means for learning of outside events. Their communication privileges of mail and visitors were limited and often abridged. The chronotope of each political's sentence was meant to sever any connection to an externally inhabited local place and historic time that might have reinforced the meaning of resistance by harboring an alternative understanding to the official chronotope of the prison.

They also experienced the common prisoner's reality of bodily insufficiency. They worked, slept, ate, and relaxed in a world of systematic control and ubiquitous observation.

Movement was confined to the cell, the latrine, the mess hall, the prison yard, the work-shop. When they passed beyond the prison walls, it was to march to the quarry, where labor was hard and dangerous. There was no personal space under their control, no privacy from the other's gaze. Unlike common prisoners, most politicals were housed in common cells holding at various times from forty to eighty men. These conditions prohibited even the illusion of privacy. Nor could they escape the prison's unremitting noise. Even visitation, we learn, occurred in a space constructed to maximize noise and frustrate the consolation of communicating with loved ones.[30] For South Africa's political prisoners, entering the penal system also meant entering a regime of systematic humiliation and terror. They now were vulnerable to the caprice of another who subjected them to physical and psychologi-cal abuse and used the prison's public spaces as arenas for displays of authority.

Put otherwise, beyond the physical and temporal arrangements of prisons, the spatial-ization of the penal system includes its historically conditioned spatiotemporal patterns of social action and routine reflecting a vision of a social world.[31] Robben Island Prison, as a specific place, refers not simply to a geographical location but to the dialectical relationship between its environment and the human narratives that occurred there. Its narratives were conditioned by a chronotope of degradation that denied prisoners access to a rhetorical place, an inventional location from which to argue back.

This helps to explain how, in facilities like Robben Island, those with power are able to subject other humans to monstrous forms of brutality so stunning that we can only won-der at their human possibility. Studies of Nazi death camps find that a regime based on inflicting pain requires a system of depersonalization that fits the prisoner's body into nar-ratives of the subhuman.[32] The prison must strip the individual prisoner of individuality, otherwise the guards have difficulty executing barbaric tasks that transgress the moral boundaries for respecting human dignity. Bodies are routinely stripped, which is not the way humans present themselves in public. We tend not to congregate with other naked bod-ies, reserving our nakedness for the restricted place and gaze of privacy. Bodies are assem-bled en masse. Naked, they appear as herds of animals, not individual persons. Bodies are starved to the point where they eat like animals, some driven to scavenging for extra morsels of food. Prisoners are stripped of their names, which communicate individual identities with personalities, histories, and agency, and given numbers, which reduce them to ledger entries. They are required to live in their own filth, so that their cells come to resemble pens of livestock unable to keep themselves clean. Guards do not engage them in face-to-face interaction, which would require recognizing them as individuals and persons able to be conversational partners. Such tacit recognition of the other's humanity would impose lim-its making it more difficult later when called upon to administer bodily abuse. Language barriers also serve as a mode of depersonalization, since they make it difficult for prisoners to communicate individual thoughts, feelings, needs, or responses to their warders and reduce them to following set commands, much as animals.

Bodily displays of this sort can function as a deceptive form of inducement to an atti-tude of exclusion—a misshapen but extremely effective *energeia* of sorts. Naidoo's account exhibits each of these depersonalizing modes on Robben Island and how the prisoners' resisting bodies reframe their warders' acts. Against the overwhelming physical power of the prison, their bodies became symbolic means for inverting power vectors within the prison. In circumstances that appeared to preclude debating political ideals, their physical treatment became an extension of the dialectic between the political prisoners and a racist regime. Their political identity framed their bodies so that each physical interaction was in some measure a statement of an alternative vision of the body politic. Their resisting bodies were, in this sense, a rhetorical locus from which to assert their personhood in the face of dehumanizing and depersonalizing treatment. Each mistreatment intended as a display of power could be read as a self-indicting response by the authorities and the state they represented to the dialogizing of the Afrikaner regime by the prisoners' bodies and their implied national alternative of South Africa as a multiracial place. We should linger a moment on the first part of Naidoo's story, then, because it alerts us to the commitments of the Afrikaner state that led to a regime of terror inside the prison. It also marks the start of Naidoo's journey from a political prisoner fearful for his life to a prisoner of conscience determined to resist his oppressors.

Naidoo's opening account of his arrest and interrogation is a ghastly and graphic display of physical and psychological torture that begins with his arrest (15–26). The police had been informed of the attempted midnight sabotage of a railroad signal box by Naidoo and two compatriots and captured them in the act of committing their crime. Naidoo was shot attempting to flee, but he tells us this did not stop the police from hitting him with their rifle butts. After receiving medical attention to remove the bullet, the police refused to let him be hospitalized, as the doctor had ordered, and instead took him to the interrogation center. He recounts hearing his comrades' screams of agony and cries for mercy as he waited to be questioned. When they emerged with faces disfigured beyond recognition, he is fixated by heightened dread, knowing he will be next.

He recalls being led into the interrogation room, where he counted twelve to fifteen police officers. Naidoo and his accomplices had concluded that Gammat Jardien, the person who had trained them, suggested the target, and supplied the dynamite, had laid their trap. When the interrogator asked who was in charge of the operation, he gave them Jardien. He describes how the police fell on him, punching and kicking until he cried with pain. When asked if he was going to make a statement, he kept repeating, "Ask Jardien, he knows everything."

People came and went. Naidoo lost track of who was in the room. The torture continued, and, to assure the reader that these were not rogue cops, he notes that the authorities in charge knew what was going on. Since they did not put a stop to it, apparently they approved.

Next a wet canvas bag was placed over his head, and his tormentors started squeezing its knot and choking him. "I gasped for air, and every time I breathed in, the canvas hit me in the face. I was choking, my nostrils and mouth were blocked by the wet canvas; the harder I tried to get air into my lungs, the tighter the bag clamped over me, cutting off the air, preventing my lungs from working." The police laughed and told him he was going to die that day. He recalls struggling and thrashing on the verge of unconsciousness from suffocation. There was more police laughter. "The bag was released and I swallowed air desperately, but then the canvas slapped into my mouth and once more I started to choke, my body in a total panic." After nearly suffocating him, they removed his shoes and beat the soles of his feet with a rubber baton. He lost sense of time in the shock waves screaming up his legs. Then they pinned him and attached wires to his body. He recalls seeing the wires leading from his body to a dry cell battery, the wires being attached, "and as they attached the lead to the battery I felt a dreadful shock pass into my body. My whole being seemed to be in shock—I learned afterwards that it was only for a few seconds, but at the time it seemed like five or ten minutes." All the while he screamed, "It's Gammat Jardien . . . Ask Gammat Jardien. Gammat Jardien knows everything." But the shock torture continued, convulsing every particle of his body. "I kept on screaming to them, begging, pleading with them to stop, but the more I cried the more they went on applying the shocks."

Finally, the torture ended. As an exercise of political power, torture has value only if it produces a confession that serves a larger political purpose. Killing Naidoo without securing his betrayal of the ANC movement would turn him into a martyr. It also would expose the cause of his death to public scrutiny in the wider courts of opinion and the judicial system. Having failed to crack his body, Naidoo tells us they went to work on his mind.

He says the police told him the others had given a full statement, his comrades had sold him out, he was a fool to resist. Then Lt. Steenkamp, head of the Natal Security Branch, interrogated him and offered Naidoo a deal for his cooperation:

> "Listen, man," he said confidently, "we can get you off if you cooperate; you know the maximum penalty for sabotage is death, and the prosecution will ask for the death sentence in this case—you were caught red-handed. I'm a personal friend of Balthazar, I play golf with him every Wednesday"—he was referring to Vorster [head of the prison system]—"We can send you anywhere in the country, give you money, buy you a car, buy you a house—you're a young man, twenty-six, you've still got a long way to go; we can send you out of the country, we have many friends overseas. What do you say?"

Without overtly depicting his effort as heroic or his body as politically inscribed, Naidoo's account of his arrest and interrogation brings his reader to a very dark place in human conduct. We become as witnesses to willing acts of dehumanization that are self-incriminations of the regime's moral economy while simultaneously underscoring his manifest threat to the Afrikaner order, to its way of life, to its power. Meanwhile, Naidoo does not present himself as posing a threat but as a victim of monstrous acts of cruelty who is struggling for survival. Since we are not told whether he knew more than the identity of his betrayer, we have only his palpable, consuming terror in the face of his torment to judge his responses. His ordeal reminds us not be judgmental of those who surrender. In Tzvetan Todorov's words, ". . . each victim stands alone and thus powerless before an infinitely superior force."[33] It also italicizes the prisoner's body as a contested site and source of political meaning with implications for the rhetoric of display.

Since his body is no longer under his own control, the torture inscribes his person as not just embodied but as a *public place:* a contested place, a political place, with multilocalities (the location of his body is many different places at the same time) and multivocalities (in each place we may hear many different voices) of empowerment and disempowerment —of the state, the police, the ANC, *Umkhonto we Sizwe,* South Africa, and Naidoo himself.[34] Its concreteness as a place opens his embodied person to interpretation as a rhetorical construction. More important for Naidoo's story, these ontological conditions of place provide an enriched sense of his embodied person as a rhetorical place, a locus of inventional possibility.

Naidoo's account of his physical and psychological torture thus prefigures Robben Island and the larger struggle in which he is engaged: the dialectic of the state's raw power pitted against the frailties of the individual prisoner. This dialectic is particularized in the spatialization of the prison as an institution and in the body of the political prisoner. His opening depiction as defenseless, isolated, outnumbered, and overwhelmed leaves us without a sense of him as a challenger of the Afrikaner regime. We wonder how he will be able to survive what lies ahead and remain true to his political convictions. Immediately after his sentencing our question is answered, as he joins the struggle for his body as the place of battle and a locus for political conscience.

Rhetorical Display and the Timely Enactment of Political Conscience

The hard realities of South Africa's prisons made them a regime of *kairotic* moments[35] to display white supremacy and conscious choice. Each concrete episode, complete unto itself, was a revelation of the warders' menace and the prisoners' resistance. The meaning of resistance did not come from publicists outside the prison—there was little opportunity to reach the outside[36]—but from bodily expressions of conscious commitments performed before other prisoners and the guards themselves.

Upon arrival at their first installation on the way to Robben Island, a prison outside Johannesburg called the Fort, Naidoo details how the prisoners were marched into the prison yard and ordered to strip. The guards mocked their naked bodies, prodded them with their batons, flicked their straps in the prisoners' faces, coming as close to their eyes as possible, and hurled racial insults at them. They were then given the command, *Tausa!* ("Dance!"). The guards were ordering the naked prisoner to leap in the air and spin while opening his legs and clapping his hands overhead. He was to land making a clicking sound with his mouth, legs apart and body bent forward to expose an open rectum to the warder's inspection (31).[37] Naidoo recounts this initiating moment as a line the political prisoners were unwilling to cross.

By performing the *tausa,* the prisoner became an obligatory participant in his own ritualized humiliation, enacted in public before affirming witnesses who also saw it as an assertion of their superiority. But the *tausa* also was a ripe inventional place for demonstrative performance of honor and dishonor, which the prisoners seized when they refused the command. The seriousness of resisting bodies as a locus for enacting a challenge of political conscience to the prison's authority became apparent when the guards then escalated their act of conscience into a carnival chase.

> The white warders moved away, leaving us to the mercy of the black warders, saying that we were the ones who had tried to blow up a train of black workers. *Kierekops* (sticks with heavy round knots at the top) flashed around us as the black warders chased us from one part of the yard to the other, threatening to beat the life out of us. We just ran and ran, exhausted and humiliated, knowing that our sentence had just begun (31).

The humiliation of the first day was repeated in countless ways as the prisoners were moved across the country on their journey to Robben Island. Naidoo recounts how the authorities gave them ripped clothes that did not fit, put them into frigid cells without sufficient blankets to retain body heat, shaved their heads, insulted them, poked them with their batons and tripped them as they ran during periods of forced exercise, served meager portions of inedible and unnourishing food or denied them food out of caprice, subjected them to physically exhausting labor and beat them when they showed signs of fatigue, and each afternoon upon returning to the prison yard from their work detail subjected them to a strip search:

> We were running naked, our clothes in our arms: a thousand of us streaming across a yard to place the clothes in a pigeon-hole, then racing, the cold air beating against our skins, to a door containing a metal detector, leaping through the doorway one after the other, and then grabbing the first set of clothes we saw in a pigeon-hole on the other side, irrespective of who had worn it the previous day, dressing as we ran, ducking blows and hearing insults as we sped towards the kitchen, grabbing a plate of food from prisoners handing out the evening meal—worried that if we missed we would go without food (45).

Naidoo's story continues episodically without any apparent organizing plot. In the penal system's life-world, it seems, there are only experiences. Each experience, however, contains competing displays of *energeia:* the warders using the spectacle of overt violence to control the prisoners' bodies as a demonstration of white supremacy; the prisoners responding with the gentle violence of mundane acts of resistance as a demonstration of their human dignity. The journey to Robben Island fades as Naidoo's organizing device, as the *energeia* of the prisoners' experiences is translated into the *enargeia* of verbal displays of the penal system itself. We are made witness to encounters that demonstrate how the ideology of white supremacy controls the penal system's steering mechanism and constrains the prisoners' apparent options. Its system logic, in which space is constricted to maximize control and temporal progression is replaced by episodic moments of humiliation, does not beckon heroic deeds; it dictates calculating each act for its survival value.

Finally Naidoo reaches Robben Island. He tells us that upon arrival the new prisoners were taken to the yard where they were forced to stand spread-eagle while the white warders subjected them to a humiliating hand frisk. The prisoners were further objectified when the guards insisted they be addressed only in Afrikaans. Insisting on Afrikaans was part of the mortification process to strip the prisoner of his sense of self. The language divide between warder and prisoner marked the initiate prisoner as lacking an essential human capacity to communicate. When Naidoo addressed a young guard in English, protesting that he did not speak Afrikaans, the guard ridiculed his use of English (which he could not speak). Mocking treatment of the initiate's English further marked him as a barbarian, not a person. When Naidoo continued to correct the guard for referring to the prisoners as "coolies" while persistently referring to the warder as "sir," the head warden was called to set Naidoo straight.

> "If you know what's fucking good for you [said the head warden], you will learn to speak Afrikaans bloody fast. Most of my warders don't speak English and what's more you must remember to address them as *Baas.* There's no "Sir" on the Island, only *Baas*" (66).

The warders' insistence on being called *baas* (boss) was particularly demeaning because it inscribed the prisoner as a slave, subject to the power of his masters. If the depersonalized prisoner was only a slave, then what was to prevent his masters from treating him as an animal?

Naidoo, on the other hand, was not responding as an animal. His refusal to code shift for his guards was an act of defiance.[38] His use of *sir* instead of *baas* refused to concede resignation, subservience, or unmitigated terror at the consequences for not acknowledging white supremacy.[39] Moreover, his defiance, expressed through respectful speech, evoked telling crudeness from the guard and celebration of his own ignorance. For readers outside the Afrikaner's life-world, Naidoo's display of civility and linguistic skill reverses the roles of power by interrogating the limited horizon of his guards and demonstrating a conscience that insisted on being treated as a human being.

There is power of another sort present in this exchange—the power of gentle violence to transform overt violence. Repeated acts of civility toward the guards were a strategy to transform the riot of Robben Island Prison into a facility that respected the human dignity of the prisoners. As a first step toward this transformation, the ANC prisoners insisted on maintaining civility in their forms of address and response to the guards and insisted, insofar as possible, that the guards do the same. Initially, polite speech may have been received as antagonistic, but over time its interrogation of the guards' limited horizons, it was hoped, would calm their threshold for inflicting pain.

After recounting this initiating exchange, the next day finds Naidoo commencing his sentence of forced labor at the lime quarry. He was to spend the next ten years of his life in the meaningless activity of crushing rocks. He recounts more beatings, more strip searches, the stench and mess of overflowing slop pots that make every confining moment in their cells a debasing misery, systematic degradation such as a prisoner buried up to his neck in the scorching sun for complaining about the extremity of that day's labor and later having his warder urinate on his face while taunting his thirst, medical neglect, refusal to acknowledge any communication not expressed in Afrikaans, and unrelenting insults to bodies in psychological and physical pain.

Naidoo's account is a relentless report of how the prison quotidian of language, oppressive work conditions, unreasonable orders, unnourishing food, physical and psychological abuse, and more defines torture and terror in small statements magnified by the conditions of repetition and idleness that, at the same time, fuel the counter chronotope of resistance. As time condenses to fit the confined and confining space of Robben Island, days, months, years flow together with no temporal referent beyond the episodes themselves. Each brings out the pointless cruelty of a world constructed to discipline and punish bodies that were neither difficult to handle nor overtly challenging the authority of the prison system.

Naidoo's account also displays a different organizational principle than the panoptic chronotope of discipline and punish. Public spaces dominated by a regime whose rule is enforced by armed guards are ill suited for deliberating prevailing conditions. As James Scott argues, under these conditions the subjugated counter the public transcript, recording who is in charge and the rules in play, with the hidden transcript of resistance constructed off stage.[40] In prison, where the idleness of prison time intensifies small things, clandestine conversations, private expressions of resentment, pilfering, sharing contraband, disseminating information, violating small rules, songs of identity and protest, speaking in one's native tongue, and so forth find their place—their inventional loci—in the larger context of political objectives. Every day on Robben Island provided its *kairotic* moments to exert the responding gentle violence of such mundane resistance. On a daily basis, conduct in public places may have been guided by the Ethiopian proverb "When the great lord passes the wise peasant bows deeply and silently farts." However, the cumulative indignities suffered in silence and recorded in the hidden transcript built pressure behind commitments of resistance seeking release.

Through a miscellany of such episodes, *Island in Chains* constructs Naidoo as a fundamentally decent man with engaging thoughts, feelings, values, and political convictions and whose organizing principle is not the prison but his own body. True, Robben Island is the site where his prison experiences occur. However the experiences themselves are developed through displays of physical and psychological resistance. In a world in which warders respond to arguments with logical absurdities, his body becomes his most effective means for making statements and counterstatements that cannot be ignored. Consequently, when his body resists the injustices of his warders, it is not merely bodily display that we witness. This is a person known to us; his identity is fused with his political values. This fusion gives his body uncommon inventional power as a fantasia of political conscience.

Fantasia and the Dialogue of Dignity

Naidoo's writing is doubly inscribed, reporting the episodes to which prisoners and prison personnel actually present were witness and presenting these scenes to us as readers. The treatment of prisoners is never fully visual in the sense of being open to documentation and sight. This is especially true of political prisoners, whose treatment often is fabricated in documents that deny their complaints or forge accounts of their treatment and that control the perceptions of external observers by steering them from the arenas of harsh treatment. Naidoo's account brings us into this world in a way that we might read as a report of what took place so that we might understand. It also brings the scene before our eyes in a way that invents Robben Island as a locale of incarceration and as a domain of conflict between political ideals. This fantasia is most pronounced at moments in which gentle violence will not work, including moments of political spectacle.

Perhaps the most poignant of these, and illustrative of this double inscription, is Naidoo's response to being publicly whipped (120–26). He tells us the prisoners had been ordered to enter barefoot a stagnant pool of water polluted with slime and dead seagulls and whose bottom consisted of jagged stone. Naidoo refused and defended his action with a reasoned defense based on the necessary conditions for an order to be valid. He was told his reason had no place in Robben Island's world. His only course was to follow orders blindly, and he was found guilty of insubordination. His punishment was to receive four lashes with a bamboo cane.

Whippings were ritualized events. They took place in the hospital courtyard every Tuesday and Thursday. Naidoo's account offers a moving fantasia of his ordeal and demonstration of political conscience. He tells us that as he was brought into the courtyard he noticed the warder who was to whip him holding a six-foot-long bamboo cane, the hospital physician, three or four prison officials, and twenty or thirty guards. "I heard the burly chief warder saying . . . that he was going to kill me that day, and that I would have scars for the rest of my life. He kept boasting about how efficient he was . . . and the other warders egged him on, almost hysterical with excitement." He was stripped naked and strapped to a wooden frame called the "whipping Mary."

I heard the whistle of the cane. Next moment it felt as though a sharp knife had cut across my backside. There was no pain immediately but suddenly, my whole body felt as though it had been given an electric shock. I grabbed hold of the Mary with both hands and clung tightly to it.

The chief warder commented sarcastically, "*Oj, die koolie wil nie huil nie*—the coolie doesn't want to cry," and all the warders joined in the chorus.

The next two strokes missed their mark, but the final one hit the same spot as the first. "The stroke was so painful that after it I could hardly see in front of me. I was dazed and strange shapes appeared in front of my eyes. I grabbed hold of the Mary and hung on to it as I tried to regain control of myself." Naidoo did not speak or groan. He was untied and told to return to his cell. His pain was so great he could not put on his pants and held his shirt up so its tail would not brush against his wound. He moved unsteadily across the yard to his cell, determined not to show signs of weakening. As he entered his cell, he noticed "for some reason or other, the prisoners had not been sent out to work that day. As I staggered inside there was absolute silence and the prisoners waited for me to say something. Then, in the midst of my comrades, with no warders around to see, I collapsed."

Naidoo's whipping was intended to inflict humiliation in the most mortifying way, by doing so before his peers. Eliciting cries like a wounded animal would be a sign that he had succumbed to pain and make a statement to the other prisoners that in breaking him their warders had once more asserted their superiority. It was intended as one more proof that he and they were objects in the life-world of apartheid. At the same time, displays of mortification before an assembly of prison guards, which can serve as a reinforcement of the social order, risk defeat should the intended victim somehow prevail. By not succumbing, Naidoo gained the momentary victory of silencing his warders and of seizing an opportunity for solidarity of conscience among the other political prisoners. The guards may have wanted the prisoners to see him break, but the prisoners most assuredly did not. In fulfilling the other prisoners' desires, is it not conceivable the *energeia* of his silence moved them to believe they also might prevail?

At the same time, the *enargeia* of Naidoo's account brings his readers into contact with a scene of political enactment that demonstrates the principle at stake. It is one thing to invent arguments against a political system one opposes and for a vision of civil society that might replace it and another to arouse an emotional response that brings an audience to both condemn one practice and endorse another. Similarly, it is one thing to arouse emotional responses to actions by portraying them in a scene brought before the audience and another to arouse emotional responses to principles by bringing them before a reader's eyes. The latter requires a fusion of language and idea in a way that is iconic, as occurs with Naidoo's body, now representative of resistance and a rhetorical place.

Naidoo's resistance provides material evidence that the political prisoners' quotidian had ceased to be merely a display of warder violence. It was a power struggle over the basis for how the guards and political prisoners would interact. Their resistance was more than bodies fighting back to protect themselves; it was an act of conscience performed out of fidelity to the underlying commitment that their human dignity should not be compromised. The demonstrative force of Naidoo's bodily display during the whipping is a material analog to reasoned argument. Moreover, it is an argument laced with Hegelian irony, as the silencing of the chorus of jeering guards by a broken body demonstrates its moral superiority. By rupturing the prison's surface of authority, Naidoo's challenge to the governing principle of "might makes right" renders his bodily display of self-possession an act of war, an aggression of spirit that reframes internal affairs between these prisoners and their warders as a power struggle in which the prisoners are not lacking resources.

Reading such deep consequences into Naidoo's refusal to break during the public caning is warranted by his narrative, which continues to develop a story of prisoner solidarity that leads to victories, however ephemeral, in the prisoners' struggle to realign the power vectors within the prison. It also suggests the need to revise my earlier characterization of *Island in Chains* as apparently lacking plot. Examining Naidoo's memoir in terms of its display rhetoric as a fantasia of political conscience discloses how its seemingly disjointed episodic structure and potpourri of dramatic moments and mundane acts are unified by the underlying manifestation of the power struggle that defined the prison experience at Robben Island as significant in advancing the ANC's cause to overthrow apartheid and establish South African democracy on the trajectory of truth and reconciliation. As the memoir continues, we read of prisoner solidarity in a hunger strike that achieved concessions from the prison authorities, of the warders' gradual lessening of racial slurs and increased address by name, of warders who spoke to prisoners in English and in some cases engaged in lengthy conversations. We learn that the prison department agreed to permit them to study and that the prisoners, many of whom were well educated, acted as tutors to guards who were struggling to pass their own high school and college courses. We learn of improved medical treatment, of access to outside observers from the Red Cross and the South African parliament to discuss conditions in the prison, of the formation of cultural clubs and activities that were either approved or permitted if not officially sanctioned. We learn of the formation of a soccer league and mini-Olympics that were organized and administered by the political prisoners. Finally, we learn of Naidoo's high esteem among the prisoners, as reflected in his numerous leadership positions. In short, the prisoners' spatialization of political conscience constructed an alternative political reality to the official chronotope of South Africa's penal system, projecting a multiracial civil society that was the antithesis of apartheid.

The visual possibilities of Naidoo's narrative, then, go beyond metaphoric reasoning, which portrays apparent differences as assimilated into a unity, and beyond irony, which portrays apparent unities as distanced from one another. It situates us in a story through the point of view of his voice, which, not incidentally, transports us to the scene through his bodily experiences. His bodily experiences have taken us from his paralysis with fear for his survival during the torture of his initial police interrogation, to acts of political resistance that seek realignment of power within the prison. The "as if" quality of what we see is not just Naidoo's body in pain, but a body fused with a political cause; what it does and what it suffers is iconic with the very principles for which it stands. If we hold as true what as readers we imagine "as if" present from Naidoo's point of view, we have experienced the state of belief Quintilian situated at the heart of eloquence. If we respond to his body in pain with the belief we would accord an eloquent demonstration, "as if" to a fusion of suffering and truth, it is the result of fantasia, a rhetorical invention wherein we experience the "hallucination of presence."[41] The *enargeia* of his memoir moves us beyond responding "as if" to a narrated story where we now respond "as if" present to its scene and participating in it.

Conclusions

This chapter has been concerned with the demonstrative possibilities inherent to display rhetoric: how the *enargeia* of display rhetoric can engage our emotions "as if" we were witnessing the scene, how the fantasia of witnessing can be so powerful as to induce a sense of certainty that compels assent, how bodily display may function as an inventional place or locus while simultaneously serving as a place of political contest, and how narratives of bodily display invent expressions possessing demonstrative force. These considerations have been particularized in demonstrations of political conscience performed through bodily displays by Robben Island Prison's political prisoners who contested the prison's disciplining of the body with their own bodily resistance.

My argument has recognized that the public arena of the prison yard is not an agora. In the agora, the public nature of community truths requires they be spoken. Politics requires that public realities be seen and heard; it cannot be practiced as a private monologue about one's convictions. Political prisoners, on the other hand, are denied voice. Without open political congress, prisoners of conscience must find alternative means to occupy a public arena in which to contest the way things are. Their resistance publicizes otherwise internal realities.

Prisoners of conscience, by definition, behave as public persons. Consequently, even public spaces constructed to serve as sites of humiliation and capitulation become opportunities to display commitments of conscience through the *energeia* of bodily acts within the prison and the correlative *enargeia* of verbal display in their narratives. Whereas the prisoner in prison time leaves the faint trace of a record—offense, sentence, time and place served, official actions—the prisoner of conscience leaves abundant traces through the *energeia* of dialogizing acts within the prison that can influence the minds and actions of others. Their defiance creates friction between assertions of personal identity and the depersonalizing system logic of the prison. This friction, in turn, becomes an inventional place for generating a fantasia of political conscience, a product of imagination.

Given the urgency of these prisoners' personal and political situations, I have argued that displays of bodily resistance are often the only but also the most effective means for inventing displays of conscience. They open a negotiation of sorts—with enemies, other prisoners, and possibly an external public—that counters the sentence's arbitrary boundaries of space and time and the muteness it enforces with the concrete place and time of their embodied political conscience. Within this negotiation, the evocative power of the prisoner's body can reach beyond immediate witnesses to distant readers by bringing the prisoner's dialogue with terror before their eyes. Presenting this confrontation with *enargeia*-inducing displays offers a form of argument that is difficult to refute.

Dorinda Outram, writing of the French Revolution, argues that bodies contesting the rights of the aristocracy "possessed the power, which the competing linguistic discourses obviously did not, to focus dignity and legitimacy in incontestable, because nonverbal, ways on the bodies of known individuals who acted as personifications of value systems."[42] Similarly, for sympathetic viewers and readers, bodily displays by political prisoners function demonstratively, as irrefutable proof of the existing order's moral culpability. Even allowing that many of these prisoners had committed illegal and possibly life-threatening acts, the reader still is confronted with a basic moral question about limits to disciplining the body of another human and to responses to defiance. The fantasia of manhandling compels the conclusion that these limits have been transgressed.

Depictions of the body in pain are, in the larger scope of an ongoing political struggle, inventional loci. The prison writer's rhetorical problem often is to dissociate his person from a perception of his deeds as criminal so that he can emphasize his identity as a prisoner with political status. Naidoo addressed this problem in an instructive way. Through episodic engagements that invented a political ethos, he dissociated his person from a perception of his deeds as criminal so that he could emphasize his political identity. This invented image, constructed through a fantasia of his engagements with oppression, engulfed the state's best efforts at framing and organizing the meaning of his incarcerations in criminal terms. At the center of his story was the place of his body, whose struggles served to strengthen an already formed dissident character while indicting the habitude of the regime that he opposed and that held him prisoner for acting on his beliefs. Bringing these displays of terror and resistance before our eyes offered a further fantasia of civil society born of the contrast between an Afrikaner regime that constructed political prisoners as animals to be dominated by cruelty and the prisoners' ongoing acts of refusal aimed at creating a space for negotiating conditions in the prison.

ANC leader and former Robben Island prisoner Neville Alexander has written, "What happens in a prison is a reflection of what happens in the surrounding society."[43] If we read the manhandling of political prisoners as indicative of a society with flagrant disregard for the human dignity of those who advance alternatives to the ruling social vision, surely Naidoo's embodied experience serves as an antidote inventing an alternative vision of civil(ized) society.

The contrasting images of society projected by the prison's disciplining of politicized bodies and the prisoners' bodily displays of resistance exhibit the recurring irony of the rhetorical domain occupied by prisoners of conscience. Symbolic resources in this domain are inherently entwined with the dissident body, transforming the apparent weakness of subjugated bodies into extremely potent rhetorical weapons against the powers that control them. Through juxtaposition of their treatment with their resistance, their displays of pain dialogize the rhetoric of the state by reversing the official and unofficial language of political appeal. Robben Island was, as Naidoo noted, intended to break the political spine of antiapartheid militants but instead became the center of resistance. The creative imagination driving its resistance belongs to a consciousness so committed to virtues of political conscience that its adherents refuse to cave. The mistreated body appears to us as driven to extremes, including the possibility of self-annihilation, over each principle it seeks to negotiate. Made visible, concrete, corporeal, personal, this fantasia of consciousness overtakes the prisoners' criminal status with a display of something far darker: the evil of treatment insensitive to their humanity.

Such bodily displays are demonstrative acts with strength analogous to logical force. By interrogating the state with performances embodying irrefutable and certain premises, they expose opposing premises as demonstrably bankrupt and weak. Wardens and warders who represent the state are presented through words and deeds that are crudely indecent in their intransigence and indifference before human pain. They seem unable to get beyond slang expressions of power lacking in historical consciousness or learned insight. Their performances reduce official speech to a parody of itself, uttering clichés as substitutes for

analysis. Through the place of the body, and the *kairotic* insertion of pain to steer its negotiation with power, prisoners of conscience confront their observing public with the monstrosity of a government that condones such acts out of refusal to recognize that this
disciplined body is also a human being. For a public situated in the fantasia of the resistor's
body, inflicting torture and abuse thus becomes a perverse self-interrogation by the regime
of its own lack of conscience. Self-interrogated, self-indicted, entrenched power explodes in
its dialectic with the dissident movement.

Being situated in the prisoner's body has theoretical significance in another way. The
persuasive power of particularity has been a staple of rhetorical thought since antiquity.
The culture of Western modernity, on the other hand, has contrary impulses to stress the
universal over the particular, to diminish the significance of the vernacular, and to favor the
disengaged and anonymous over the personal. This bent deflects us from those aspects of
rhetoric that have the greatest power to win the judges' hearts and thereby, as Quintilian
assessed matters, gain their assent. The edifice of objectivity and detachment encounters
heavy weather whenever our eyes are directed toward those very facets modernity tends to
discount.

Narratives of particular persons, as the Western tradition has recorded since Homer's
Iliad, are more than their individually embodied stories. Each person's story, by the very
fact that it is shared, means that this embodied being also inhabits a public place. It occupies a specific historical locale shared with other particular persons who have their own
stories, each of which interacts in some way with the others. For this reason, human engagements with place are always political and, therefore, concerned with power; the rhetoric of their narratives is always constitutive of an "as if" reality occupied by some people's
stories and not others. Against abstract and disembodied space, the specificity of place involves a dialectic between these narratives and their environment.[44] The demonstrative
consequence of this dialectic over power, in fantasia's thrall of this prisoner's bodily place,
compels assent to a particular history with an identifiable human pursuing a specific political pilgrimage toward an alternative destiny to what now exists. The dialectic situated in
the body as a place or locale of resistance also suggests how the contested body functions
as a rhetorical place or locus and, moreover, the dialectical character of rhetorical loci.
Extrapolating from the body as a place from which we invent, we may speculate that loci
generally are conditioned by and interactive with the context of inventing. As we move from
conceptualizing "place" as an abstract heuristic category to "place" as an inventional standpoint, loci become particular, concrete places that cannot avoid engaging their indigenous
multivocalities and multilocalities and whose meanings are interpretations of the dialectic
occurring there.

Finally, contrary to the early Foucauldian characterization of oppressed bodies as objects or symbols manifesting existing power relations, the demonstrative force of Robben
Island's resisting bodies suggests they may be active creators of new power relations that
sustain individuals in their confrontation with systems of power. Political conscience, enacted through bodily performances that resisted denial of their human worth, constructed
dignified individual bodies that became a source of authority among the other prisoners
and a public resource for their complaints. Within its counterfantasia to the state's totaliz-
ing myth of power, displays of pain can be more than an individual's anguish; each suffering body can become a synecdochic representation of an alternative body politic capable

of affirming an independent identity. The rhetorically constructed body in pain writes its appeal at the sensuous level of individual experience. Sensuous experience bypasses the a priori epistemology that buttresses official rhetoric with the immediacy of identification that grows out of each reader (as each prisoner) having a personal body. Over and against a discourse of power, which deciphers the criminal body with the abstractions of the existing social and political order that subjugates it, the body in pain produces its own knowledge through concrete sensory experience of the individual, which, transformed into abstractions, can transcend the body's temporal constraints to speak uncontested truths. Such bodily displays act as a demonstrative rhetoric exhibiting with irrefutable force where matters stand.

Notes

The author wishes to acknowledge Thomas Farrell, the late James McDaniel, Larry Prelli, and an anonymous reviewer for helpful criticisms of this essay in draft; Dilip Gaonkar for insightful suggestions regarding theoretical issues in this analysis; and the faculty and students in communication arts at the University of Wisconsin and communication studies at Northwestern University who responded to an earlier presentation.

1. Michel Foucault, *Discipline and Punish: The Birth of the Prison,* trans. Alan Sheridan (1977; repr., New York: Vintage, 1979).

2. For a convenient sample of prisoner accounts that testify to changes within Robben Island Prison over time, consult Jan K. Coetzee, ed., *Plain Tales from Robben Island* (Pretoria: Van Schaik, 2000).

3. The relationship of the common law prisoner and resistance of conscience are beyond the scope of this analysis. Nor do I assume criminal acts committed for a political cause are inherently praiseworthy, as the terrorist acts of September 11, 2001, made evident, at least from the perspective of the United States.

4. Prisoner 885/63 [Indres Naidoo], *Island in Chains: Ten Years on Robben Island,* as told to Albie Sachs (London: Penguin Books, 1982). Subsequent references to *Island in Chains* are provided in the text by page numbers.

5. Quintilian, *Institutio Oratoria,* trans. H. E. Butler (Cambridge: Harvard University Press, 1958). All references to *Institutio Oratoria* are provided in the text by book, chapter, and line numbers.

6. Cicero, *Rhetorica ad Herennium,* trans. Harry Caplan (Cambridge: Harvard University Press, 1964), 172–73nb.

7. Richard McKeon, "Discourse, Demonstration, Verification, and Justification" and "Proceedings," in *Démonstration, Vérification, Justification* (Louvain: Nauwelaerts, 1969), 37–92 passim.

8. The Greeks gave some foundation for this view when they characterized epideictic as a *deictic* form, or mode of proof, that is distinguishable from other modes of proof. Thus, rhetorical displays were *epideictic logoi,* demonstrations were *apodeictic logoi,* and historical indications were *endeictic logoi.* Moreover, in contrast with the Greek view, the Romans considered demonstration to be a mode of reasoning whose premises were grounded in the minds of judging audiences rather than in the nature of the subject undergoing demonstration. As Quintilian notes, speeches demonstrate through praise and blame the "nature of the object with which they [that is, the audience] are concerned" (3.4.14). The idea that standards for judgment of whatever is "demonstrated" are located within the audience rather than in some extrinsic metaphysical or epistemological foundation has as its corollary the need to discover resources for "proving" through rhetorical invention. An important example of this innovation is found in Cicero's consideration

of loci as an extension of Aristotle's metaphysically grounded topical theory. For a convenient review of the meaning associated with *deixis*, consult http://perseus.csad.ox.ac.uk/cgi-bin/resolve-form (last accessed February 25, 2002).

9. Eleanore Stump, *Boethius's De topicus differentius* (Ithaca, N.Y.: Cornell University Press, 1978), 159–78.

10. Michael J. Buckley, "Philosophic Method in Cicero," *Journal of the History of Philosophy* 8 (1970): 143–54.

11. In *Topica* 2.6, Cicero pays homage to Aristotle in a way that situates his work as an extension of Aristotle's own theory. He argued, contrary to the Stoics (and Aristotle's *Topica*, which he ostensibly was appropriating), that a method for inventing claims to be tested was required prior to testing their truth. His upbraiding of the Stoics for neglecting the other half of Aristotle's system, coupled with his assertion that Aristotle founded the subject and that he regards his work as following Aristotle's, suggests Cicero thought he was advancing Aristotle's system. However, his specific complaint, that the Stoics' almost exclusive focus on judgment paid insufficient attention to invention, ignores Aristotle's fixing the ends of dialectic as criticism and belief (albeit provisionally so), and that the emphasis of Aristotle's *Topica* is on testing the opponent's argument, or judgment (Cicero, *Topica*, trans. H. M. Hubbell [Cambridge: Harvard University Press, 1968]).

12. See Richard McKeon, "The Methods of Rhetoric and Philosophy: Invention and Judgment," in *The Classical Tradition: Literary and Historical Studies in Honor of Harry Caplan,* ed. Luitpold Wallach, 365–73 (Ithaca, N.Y.: Cornell University Press, 1966), for a discussion of this shift as illustrated by the four *stasis* questions, central to Roman rhetorical theory, as permutations of Aristotle's metaphysically based questions that guide scientific inquiry.

13. Gerard A. Hauser, "Aristotle on Epideictic: The Formation of Public Morality," *Rhetoric Society Quarterly* 29 (1999): 5–23.

14. Nicole Loraux, *The Invention of Athens: The Funeral Oration in the Classical City,* trans. Alan Sheridan (Cambridge: Harvard University Press, 1986).

15. Newton encouraged the moral philosophers of the Enlightenment to use the observational method for investigating the workings of the mind, which he explicitly recommended to them at the close of his *Optics.* See Isaac Newton, *The Mathematical Principles of Natural Philosophy,* trans. Andrew Motte (London: H. D. Symonds, 1803); and *Optiks,* 4th ed. corrected (1730; repr., London: G. Bell and Sons, 1931). The British empiricists' observation-based speculations on the workings of the mind, in turn, influenced the rhetorical and aesthetic theorists of the Scottish Enlightenment's psychological school. Speculative treatises by Archibald Alison, James Beattie, Hugh Blair, George Campbell, Alexander Gerard, Joseph Priestly, and Adam Smith, to mention the more noteworthy, maintained that qualities of vivid display rendered rhetorical and aesthetic creations mimetic of nature. I have discussed this relationship with regard to the centrality of visualization in "Empiricism, Description, and the New Rhetoric," *Philosophy and Rhetoric* 5 (1972): 24–44. For a provocative extension of this visual line of thought, see James P. McDaniel, "Fantasm: The Triumph of Form (An Essay on the Democratic Sublime)," *Quarterly Journal of Speech* 86 (2000): 48–66.

16. Graham Nash, http://www.garnettsites.com/GrahamNash (last accessed April 5, 2002). See also McKeon, "Discourse."

17. Gerard A. Hauser, *Vernacular Voices: The Rhetoric of Publics and Public Opinion* (Columbia: University of South Carolina Press, 1999), passim.

18. Erik Doxtader, "Characters in the Middle of Public Life: Consensus, Dissent, and Ethos," *Philosophy and Rhetoric* 33 (2000): 336–69.

19. Human Rights Watch, http://www.hrw.org (last accessed December 20, 2005).

20. For a discussion of the relationship of rhetoric to the counterpublic sphere, see Robert Asen and Daniel Brouwer, eds., *Counterpublics and the State* (Albany: State University of New York

Press, 2001). For a discussion of counterpublic spheres as hosting disparate modes of rhetorical possibility, see Hauser, *Vernacular Voices*, 111–60.

21. Gerard A. Hauser, "Prisoners of Conscience and the Counterpublic Sphere of Prison Writing: The Stones That Start the Avalanche," in *Counterpublics and the State*, 35–58.

22. See Nelson Mandela, *Long Walk to Freedom* (New York: Little, Brown and Company, 1994); Adam Michnik, *Letters from Prison*, trans. Maya Latynski (Berkeley: University of California Press, 1985); Wole Soyinka, *The Man Died* (New York: Farrar, Straus, and Giroux, 1972); and Jacobo Timmerman, *Prisoner without a Name, Cell without a Number*, trans. Toby Talbot (1981, repr. New York: Vintage, 1988) for a sampling of prisoners of conscience who make explicit professions of the personal costs they were prepared to pay to retain an authentic political voice.

23. For a discussion on the relationship of concrete "place" to abstract "space," see Philip Sheldrake, *Spaces for the Sacred: Place, Memory and Identity* (Baltimore: Johns Hopkins University Press, 2001), 7.

24. Heteroglossia refers to the situatedness of all speech as providing an unrepeatable set of conditions that make its meanings to particular listeners at a particular time unlike any before or since. Discourse is "dialogized" when the privileged positions of prevailing power structures and ideologies are challenged, making us aware of competing positions and interpretations. These radiant engagements instigate a dialogue among the respective cultural languages "that mutually and ideologically interanimate each other," giving new possibilities for understanding and expressing reality. See M. M. Bakhtin, *The Dialogic Imagination*, ed. Michael Holquist, trans. Caryl Emerson and Michael Holquist (Austin: University of Texas Press, 1981), "Discourse on the Novel," 284–85, "From the Prehistory of Novelistic Discourse," 47, and editor's glossary, 426–27.

25. *Island in Chains* was published by Penguin Books in Britain, and Random House in the United States and Canada. Its publication by commercial presses suggests that its contents were not dictated by the ANC, as might be alleged were it to have appeared from a press under its influence or control.

26. Dietrich Bonhoeffer, *Letters and Papers from Prison*, ed. Eberhard Bethge (New York: Macmillan, 1967); Fleeta Drumgo, "Letter from Fleeta," in *If They Come in the Morning: Voices of Resistance*, ed. Angela Y. Davis (New York: The Third Press, 1971); Václav Havel, *Letters to Olga*, trans. Paul Wilson (New York: Henry Holt, 1989); Martin Luther King Jr., "Letter from Birmingham Jail," http://almaz.com/nobel/peace/MLK-jail.html (last accessed October 18, 2001); Mandela, *Long Walk to Freedom*; Michnik, *Letters from Prison*; Irena Ratushinskaya, *Grey is the Color of Hope*, trans. Alonya Kojevnikov (New York: Vintage, 1989); Timmerman, *Prisoner without a Name, Cell without a Number*.

27. See chapter 6 of Richard Sennett, *The Fall of Public Man* (New York: Vintage, 1979), for a discussion richly suggestive of such presentation's rhetorical potential.

28. Pierre Bourdieu develops this thesis as an explanation for how a *habitus* of socially approved symbolic acts regulates social practices in ways that reflect the social and political economy of power. See *The Logic of Practice*, trans. Richard Nice (Stanford: Stanford University Press, 1990), 127.

29. My use of space and time is intended in the spirit of Bakhtin's observations on the chronotope in literature. See Bakhtin, "Forms of Time and of Chronotope in the Novel," in *The Dialogic Imagination*, 84–258. My extension of his lens is grounded, however, in the rhetorical sense of place as an inventional locus and the priority of place to space as a particularized manifestation of historicity within space.

30. The visiting area consisted of two facing arenas with wire mesh from floor to ceiling. Guards patrolled the section between them. Prisoners and visitors faced each other across the divide and had to shout to be heard above the din. The consequence was noise so loud as to make hearing what was being said impossible.

31. See Sheldrake, *Spaces for the Sacred,* 21.

32. Tzvetan Todorov, *Facing the Extreme: Moral Life in the Concentration Camps* (New York: Holt and Company, 1996), 158–78.

33. Ibid., 130.

34. See Sheldrake, *Spaces for the Sacred,* 21.

35. *Kairos* refers to the discursive moment that opens to the possibility of decisive change. It may be manifested in a well-timed remark or may be the moment in a debate when the time is ripe to introduce certain arguments to advantage. For an overview of this concept, see John Poulakos, *Sophistical Rhetoric in Classical Greece* (Columbia: University of South Carolina Press, 1995), 61–73 passim.

36. Naidoo reports that efforts to complain to external authorities were rebuked as trivial, seldom transmitted, never responded to as serious, frequently dismissed with fabricated notations that the prisoner chose to drop the complaint, and likely to carry consequences for being lodged. When outside observers came to monitor the prisoners' treatment, the authorities carefully orchestrated where the visitors went and whom they interviewed to craft a perception of humane conditions. It was not until the airing of *90 Days* on BBC in 1966 and subsequent public concern expressed by Helen Sussman in the South African parliament that national and world attention to Afrikaner treatment of political prisoners became a topic of public concern (Naidoo, *Island in Chains,* 162–63). Barbara Harlow also notes the visit of a Red Cross official who counteracted misleading government statements by filing a report highly critical of conditions in the prison (*After Lives* [London: Verso, 1996]).

37. Political prisoners commonly circumvent restrictions on communication by smuggling messages hidden in the body's orifices. Guards attempt to prevent this by subjecting prisoners to body searches. Prisoners regard this practice, even when performed without explicitly demeaning rituals such as the *tausa,* as a humiliating invasion of their bodies.

38. Naidoo's ignorance of Afrikaans may have been a ruse, since he recounts in Afrikaans what the guard was saying and uses Afrikaans throughout the book.

39. Neville Alexander, *Robben Island Prison Dossier: 1964–1974* (Cape Town: University of Cape Town, 1994), 15–27, discusses the political inflection of *baas.* According to Alexander, "Just as a non-political prisoner's life would be worth nothing if he did not do this [that is, call the warder *baas* or a similar term indicating submission], so in 1962–1964 the political prisoners who refused to kow-tow in this manner courted death in the most literal sense. Many assaults were caused by refusal to say Baas. Virtually all prisoners use this searingly, readily debasing terminology until a stand was taken by certain prisoners and followed by the rest" (ibid., 27).

40. James Scott, *Domination and the Arts of Resistance* (New Haven: Yale University Press, 1990).

41. Paul Ricoeur, *Time and Narrative,* trans. Kathleen Blamey and David Pellauer (1985; repr., Chicago: University of Chicago Press, 1990), 3:186.

42. Dorinda Outram, *The Body and the French Revolution: Sex, Class and Political Culture* (New Haven: Yale University Press, 1989), 4.

43. Alexander, *Robben Island Prison Dossier,* 50.

44. Sheldrake, *Spaces for the Sacred,* 1.

Jerry Blitefield

12

It's Showtime!
Staging Public Demonstrations, Alinsky-Style

Power is not only what you have, but what the enemy thinks you have.

Saul Alinsky (1909–72)

Generally understood, "display" reveals something, lays out something for others to see, shows off something. Despite the specific cause or occasion for each, public demonstrations inherently display power relationships. Whenever some government parades its armaments in patriotic array, the public demonstration exhibits prospects for unified allegiance behind the government's cause and the values that cause presumably serves. Whenever some activist group rallies its numbers to meet in a public square, the demonstration itself manifests collective grievance in behalf of some cause and the values it purportedly serves. In either case, collective power in service to a cause and its corollary values is manifested, "proven," or "demonstrated." The public showing or proof of collective power becomes more compelling the larger the gathering's size; yet, as I will show later, numbers alone do not tell the whole story.

Public demonstrations manifest both epideictic and political dimensions. A public demonstration can enact for participants a kind of epideictic celebration of the implied values of a cause and condemnation of those who are seen as opposing them. The cause and its corollary values are not usually open to criticism, at least among the participants and like-minded witnesses to the demonstration. At the same time, public demonstrations are a kind of political exhortation for desired "goods" and dissuasion from pursuit of harms purportedly sought by perceived adversaries. In that respect, public demonstrations are likely to place those who become audience to them in the role of political critics or judges, who decide whether those implied "goods" ought to be actualized in future political practice. Both epideictic and deliberative lines of thought are often manifested through and in responses to public demonstrations. Public demonstrations are often gauged according to a general pattern of thought that Aristotle associated with epideictic—the topic of "magnitude." From that vantage, public demonstrations are a visible amplification of the extent of a group's power and significance, which is seen as impressive (or not) depending upon the size or "magnitude" of the display. Suppose Martin Luther King spoke about his dream to a gathering of 250 rather than 250,000 people? At the same time, demonstrations are political exhortations about the future and, thus, invite speculation about probable outcomes and consequences—a general pattern of thought that Aristotle associated with the topic of "future fact."[1]

I contend that public demonstrations are, above all, political performances; they enact proofs of power with implications about the future that are contingent upon the quality of their execution. These performances function as a kind of enthymeme. A well-executed public demonstration establishes visible proof of power, but it also implies a decidedly deliberative premise that prophesies about the political future: "this display of power can be reenacted if necessary." When a protest group finds itself pressing a particular issue, an effective demonstration of concern for that issue becomes a down payment or promissory note on future popular displays and subsequent public pressure should the issue remain unresolved. For those organizing a display of power, the display in the present must serve as a persuasive political trope that constrains thought about the future (that is, that behind this current demonstration rests the skill and will to organize another). This political trope I call "premonitory proof": "proof" in a well-executed and visible performance of power; "premonition" in the implication that power displayed now can be reenacted in the future.

Public demonstrations, as performances, must manifest a clear perception of conflict between the demonstrating body and those who are demonstrated against. The effectiveness of demonstrations in mediating change depends upon convincing targeted audiences that they are challenges that can be reenacted. A public demonstration must not only be a coherent performance but a prototype, a harbinger of possibilities to come. In this chapter, I explore these and other rhetorical principles involved in enacting effective public demonstrations, with a focus on strategies articulated and practiced in Saul Alinsky's community organizing work. In the sections that follow, I first examine the origins and rhetorical dimensions of Alinsky's conflict-based approach to organizing power. I then explain rhetorical maneuvers involved in enacting the performance of organized power through public demonstration. Finally, I conduct a case study of an Alinsky-style "action" as a rhetorically enacted spectacle that reverses the roles of performing rhetor and spectating audience typically assumed by the more and the less powerful.

Organizing Power

Pro or con, at issue in public demonstrations is power's arrangement and potential rearrangement. Demonstrations, even when peaceful, are aggressive and supported by conflict. Through their public performance, demonstrations assert that power arrangements are not absolute and, thus, can be rearranged through demonstrative challenge. This assertion is ratified in a study of strategic nonviolent action by political scientist Gene Sharp, who confirms that (governmental) power is liquid, is not a "fixed quantum"[2] in either person or position, and, as such, is always up for redistribution. If power is held but not owned, then power is always for the taking.

Why, then, do disgruntled peoples not regularly snatch power rather than succumb to it? Sharp has several explanations for such obedience,[3] yet beneath them all, the one universal cause for obedience is simple consent of the ruled. Sharp contends that no ruler, not even the most criminal or brutal of them, maintains and exercises power without the subjects' cooperation.[4] This leads him to two conclusions: "Obedience is essentially voluntary,"[5] and "Consent can be withdrawn."[6] A ruler's distilled power is collective power relinquished. In all political systems, political subjects daily grant or withhold consent to the power hierarchy in which they find themselves through their own public displays. Action and inaction display opposition or support. Therefore, obedience to power is also a form of political demonstration. So, for instance, when a driver stops at a red light and waits for it to turn green, even though no other oncoming traffic is within sight, not only are the "rules" of the state obeyed, but the driver is publicly displaying consent to, and therefore affirmation of, the rules of the state. Begin to question the rules, however, hedge on the consent, and the stage is set for acts of political challenge. Public actions, then, call the rules into question publicly, and when they do, suddenly the power arrangement undergirding the rules gets called into question, too. Such public display on whatever scale exposes and asserts the instability of power's distribution and the potential for its redistribution.

Legendary community activist Saul Alinsky knew in practical terms what Sharp had expressed in academic terms: (1) that power is fluid, relational, always subject to changing hands and (2) that obedience to power is a matter of consent, or, at the very least, of cooperation. Those who acquiesce to another's power in essence cooperate with that superordinate power by accepting its terms and conditions and living accordingly. Yet, for Alinsky, simply resisting those terms and conditions would not in itself constitute an opposing power. For Alinsky, "power" is, generically, "organized energy."[7]

> When people agree on certain religious ideas and want the power to propagate their faith, they organize and call it a church. When people agree on certain political ideas and want the power to put them into practice, they organize and call it a political party. The same reason holds across the board. Power and organization are one and the same.[8]

"Power," then, is the ability to organize and exercise one's will, even when the "one" is many. In group terms, this means gathering together disconnected, disaffected individuals who share a common interest and connecting them within a larger body politic for the purpose of addressing their collective disaffection collectively. The whole becomes more than the sum of its parts, for not only does the newly organized body begin to exercise and display its will as one, but its members also begin to identify with the organization and its potential to mediate change in ways unavailable to atomized individuals. Organized collectively, power does not only generate outwardly toward some political object, it also generates inwardly, creating a wholly new political subject: *we*. Splayed, fingers are benign; curled and pulled tight, they create a fist—the same components, simply organized for power.

Throughout his career, Alinsky reorganized the energy of dissatisfied communities in ways that drew power to the community organization by drawing power away from those it organized against—established political elites. This called for a specific style of political engagement, one that sought to confront political elites publicly, incorrigibly, and, whenever possible, spectacularly, with the ultimate aim of prompting a direct public response. To foster that style of organizing, Alinsky established the Industrial Areas Foundation (IAF) in 1940 Chicago for the expressed purpose of preparing and dispatching professional organizers to underpowered (read: unorganized) communities seeking change (and willing to pay a fee). By the time of his death in 1972, Alinsky's iconoclastic and irreverent approach to community organizing had become legend, but his initial foray into community organizing is less remarkable.

Alinsky cut his teeth working with dispossessed communities while a University of Chicago undergraduate (and later graduate) student in the 1920s. He studied with sociologists Robert Park, Clifford Shaw, and, perhaps most significantly, E. W. Burgess, whose courses lifted Alinsky out of the academic stagnation of his first two years.[9] Park, Shaw, and Burgess—the "Chicago School" of urban sociology—"argued that social disorganization, not heredity, was the cause of disease, crime, and other characteristics of slum life . . . [and] showed that it was the slum itself, and not the particular group living there, with which behavior pathologies were associated."[10] In sharp contrast to the still resonant "eugenics movement" (that is, the "nineteenth century argument . . . that slums were populated by the genetically inferior"),[11] this theory inversion became the basis later on for Alinsky's more progressive and aggressive views on community activism.

From these early experiences, Alinsky likely formed one of the tenets of his thinking: no community is without power. Rather, disenfranchised communities suffer from an unawareness of their inherent power. Unacknowledged and untended, community power dissipates; Alinsky (and the IAF) worked to reverse the dissipation. Alinsky knew that only by tapping into and slowly building up homegrown power can any community begin to address its troubles.[12] To reverse dissipation and actualize the latent power in any community, then, organizers must literally sell the idea of that inchoate power and show that by working collectively—and only by working collectively—such power could be harnessed so that "things can change." Well before taking action, the IAF will canvas house to house and neighborhood to neighborhood, sometimes for a year or more, cultivating local leaders and selling the idea that each member of the community has a share and a stake in organizing the power of the community. At some point, however, their organizing efforts will have so ripened that rather than *go to* citizens homes and neighborhoods, the IAF and local leaders will need to *bring* those citizens to each other and have them witness the mass of, perhaps even massive, power at their ready. This is the point when the community organization must establish a public presence through public display and demonstration of its power. This is when the community's individuals have moved significantly forward enough toward collectivity so that a broad display will catapult group consciousness to a higher level of belief and commitment, to intone a new sense of political being: the fist they have become.

Students of rhetoric may see in this organizing strategy glimmerings of Kenneth Burke's "consubstantiality," an identification with others that does not claim to erase difference but rather attempts to build upon those shared segments of disparate lives about which people feel a commonality of concerns.[13] The IAF works to achieve consubstantiality through defining issues for collective community concern, but it also "corporealizes" this Burkean notion by finding occasions during which community members can experience each other en masse. As alluded to earlier, this creates a rhetoric of display that turns inward, not outward (or at least not exclusively outward). As a trope for change, mass organizing is predicated on the notion that political power inheres to some degree in numbers. The people will then need to see those numbers themselves in order to believe in the organization and, ultimately, to mobilize within it. Yet, like the letters of the alphabet scrambled and placed side by side, sheer numbers do not tell a story on their own; only by organizing the characters can a coherent story be told.

Conversely, nothing galvanizes an organization, a "we," as does a publicly defined and clearly demarcated "them." Surely "there is no point to tactics unless one has a target upon which to center the attacks."[14] Articulating and demonizing an opposition quickens community cohesion, especially if that opposition can be manifested in the open. Pugilistic in both language and demeanor, Alinsky-style organizing itches to fight; generally outmatched in strength, however, the strategy is one of wit whose gambit is often to have the enemy respond disproportionately. Alinsky wrote, "The enemy properly goaded and guided in his reaction will be your greatest strength."[15] This means that the "enemy" will at times provide an organizer with reactions—or better yet, overreactions—from which the community organization can then profit, sometimes hugely. In a *Harper's Magazine* interview Alinsky remarked, "A Bull Connor with his police dogs and fire hoses down in Birmingham did more to advance civil rights than the civil-rights fighters themselves."[16] That Connor's dogs and hoses were in response to "proper goading or guiding" on the part of the demonstrators is doubtful; that the cause of civil rights grew exponentially from his overreaction, however produced, is not. On the other hand, the absence of a strong reaction can be most deflating. Speaking again in *Harper's,* Alinsky hypothesized about the civil rights march from Selma to Montgomery: "Imagine what would have happened if instead of stopping the marchers that first day with clubs and tear gas, chief state trooper Lingo had courteously offered to provide protection and let them proceed. By night the TV cameras would have gone back to New York and there would have been no national crisis to bring religious leaders, liberals, and civil-rights fighters from the North to Selma."[17] What better way to solidify a community's self-identity and gain adherents than to have some *other* play its sinister part, or made to look sinister? Ergo, an "enemy" must be found, or, when necessary, created. And the more monstrous, the better.

Of course, what we are talking about is manifesting conflict. Publicly displaying conflict is the key to Alinsky's organizing, both theoretically and practically, and not just for tackling issues but for amassing and consolidating community power. Rather than avoided, conflict is to be embraced, even engineered, as a fulcrum of change. Central to Alinsky's philosophy, conflict as a political medium is traceable to his days as a sociology student.

The University of Chicago sociology department that Alinsky entered in the 1920s was founded in 1892 by Albion Small, who, twelve years later, translated and published in the *American Journal of Sociology* an essay by the German theorist Georg Simmel, "The Sociology of Conflict." In this essay Simmel claims that antagonism forms "sociations" between a group and some other. In a 1923 version of this essay, Simmel writes,

> it may sound paradoxical in the common view if one asks whether irrespective of any phenomena that result from conflict or that accompany it, it itself is a form of sociation. At first glance, this sounds like a rhetorical question. If every interaction among men is a sociation, conflict—after all one of the most vivid interactions, which, furthermore, cannot possibly be carried on by one individual alone—must certainly be considered as sociation. And, in fact, *dis*sociating factors—hate, envy, need, desire— are the *causes* of conflict; it breaks out because of them. Conflict is thus designed to resolve divergent dualisms; it is a way of achieving some kind of unity, even if it be through the annihilation of one of the competing parties.[18]

One of Simmel's basic themes, then, is that conflict constructs social relations and is not in and of itself negative. As a medium for social correction, conflict may be necessary for the formation of an in-group capable of forcing change. Simmel even speaks of external "hostility" as a sometimes necessary expedient for in-group formation.[19] "The more purely negative or destructive a given enmity is, the more easily will it bring about a unification of those who ordinarily have no motive for any community."[20]

Early on in the twentieth century, Small's translation of Simmel took hold. By the mid-1920s, Simmel's notions of conflict held great significance for the brand of urban sociology rooted in the Chicago School. A sociology student in the very department where Simmel was first translated, and under the radical tutelage of Burgess, Park, and Shaw, young Alinsky likely would have intuited conflict as a means of forming community "sociations" for reorganizing slum life. Profiling the role of the organizer as a community catalyst, Alinsky echoes Simmel:

> The organizer dedicated to changing the life of a particular community must first rub raw the resentments of the people of the community; fan the latent hostilities of many of the people to the point of overt expression. He must search out controversy and issues, rather than avoid them, for unless there is controversy, people are not concerned enough to act.[21]

Unsurprisingly, Alinsky's thirteenth rule of tactics in *Rules for Radicals* is "Pick the target, freeze it, personalize it, and polarize it."[22]

As part of a lecture series[23] delivered the same year Alinsky published *Rules for Radicals* (1971), Kenneth Burke coincidentally confirmed the value of Alinsky's thirteenth rule by amplifying conflict as an important resource for enacting identification—identification serving as "a kind of persuasion in which (you might say) we spontaneously, intuitively, and often unconsciously, act upon ourselves."[24] He speaks of three types of identification, two of which are outwardly nonconflictual. One is "quite dull . . . [and] flowers in such usage as that of a politician who, though rich, tells humble constituents of his humble origins."[25] Another "derives from situations in which it goes unnoticed. My prime example is the word 'we,' as when the statement that 'we' are at war includes under the same head soldiers who are getting killed and speculators who hope to make a killing in war stocks." But a third kind resonates well with Alinsky's conflict tactics: identification through antithesis.[26]

Burke typifies identification through antithesis with the case of "allies who would otherwise dispute among themselves [joining] forces against a common enemy."[27] Attention directed to the enemy becomes self-reflexive, and opposition to that enemy becomes the sinew of group bonds, group identification. Affirming the "more monstrous the better" value of the enemy, war history is replete with instances where identification through antithesis has benefitted from a caricaturist demonization of the enemy. U.S. World War II posters, for instance, commonly depict Germans with feral eyes and rat-like teeth and Japanese as apelike.[28] If demonizing the enemy, even inaccurately, will produce greater conviction at home, produce a stronger "we" with which to fight "them," then so be it. Directly or indirectly, Alinsky learned this lesson well: that in times of war there can be no equivocation about the enemy's evil, that the greater the evil perceived, the greater would be the rally against it. Identification through antithesis intensifies with exaggeration and political hyperbole, and Alinsky so understood the "we" building value of antithesis that where it did not occur naturally he sought to instigate it rhetorically by "rubbing resentments raw." Successfully leveraged conflict must, however, go beyond simply "fanning the latent hostilities to the point of overt expression." Conflict must be "performed," enacted; it must be displayed publicly. Conflict thus challenges the distribution of power outwardly and quickens the power of identification inwardly. Two examples follow: a hypothetical illustration Alinsky conjured but never employed and an actual post-Alinsky IAF "action."

Performing Power

While Simmel speaks about conflict in abstract and generic terms, Alinsky and his IAF prodigy make conflict tangible in public contests, in "actions," as performances by those pursuing greater power from those holding the power pursued.[29] These actions are literally performances that follow "scripts" that were fully conceptualized and rehearsed prior to actual public displays. In other words, at least in Alinsky terms, actions do not just "happen." As performances, they take planning, staging, practice—discipline. A mob does not an action make.

To a degree, any Alinsky-style performance can create a win/win situation for those pursuing power: on the one hand, the powerful could capitulate to demands, and the aggrieved could come away with a "victory" (a sort of "unification through annihilation," in Simmelian terms); on the other hand, the powerful might resist and thereby present the aggrieved with more fodder for antithetical identification and, thus, lend greater impetus to organizing efforts. Regardless of particular results, well-orchestrated performances enact three rhetorical maneuvers: (1) reversal of power relationships such that the underpowered gain power while the powerful lose power, even if only temporarily; (2) establishment of premonitory proof; and (3) heightening in-group solidarity. I shall discuss these three maneuvers in turn.

As a conflict tactician, Alinsky knew that in a showdown of physical force those enjoying the status quo always had the upper hand. Never wanting to play to anyone's advantage but his own, Alinsky would employ nonconfrontational, almost oblique forms of resistance and opposition. In such instances, leading with mind rather than muscle, Alinsky delighted in exploiting the sensed-but-unarticulated, extralegal realm of decorum. Decorum encodes informally agreed upon standards of socially acceptable behavior, usually predetermined by elites, that act largely as buffers against open conflict. But the "rules" of decorum are not legally binding and enforceable and, as such, are exploitable. An Alinsky and IAF strategy is to stage performances that openly violate decorum, thereby withdrawing from the power relationship implicit in that code of decorum. Immune from legal prosecution, those acting indecorously render elites frustrated, furious, and baffled but, best of all, powerless to effect a controlling response. Appearing to act lawfully while violating decorum is to perform in a place where elites are powerless to rule.

For instance, in November 1964, a Rochester, New York, community delegation had flown to meet with Alinsky in his Chicago IAF office. They sought his help in mounting a community campaign against the Eastman Kodak Company, charged with practicing racially discriminatory hiring. Alinsky had received other offers from other cities and so made no commitment at that time to the Rochester delegation (though he did later accept their bid). But, as Alinsky biographer Sanford Horwitt recounts:

> Before they left, Alinsky, who had never been to Rochester but who listened intently to accounts of the city's stuffiness and smugness, said, "There's a tactic I've always

wanted to try, and Rochester would be the perfect place." As earnest as Saul Alinsky could be when he was about to spin a story like this one, he continued: "You buy blacks three or four hundred tickets to the Rochester symphony. But before the performance, they'll all get together for dinner, except this won't be an ordinary dinner, it'll be a big baked-bean dinner. They'll go to the symphony and fart it out of existence. How would that go over in Rochester? Wouldn't people love that?"[30]

While this might be read as flippant mouthiness—in which Alinsky often took great delight—beyond the effrontery (or rather, due to the effrontery) there is a strategy at work, one that he follows up with more detail in *Rules for Radicals*. He includes the Rochester "sniffony" scenario in the chapter "Tactics," explaining the reasons why it might have proven effective.[31] His tactic presents an "I dare you" attitude, making the community organization's power present in an untrumpable way.

> First, the disturbance would be utterly *outside the experience* of the establishment, which was *expecting the usual stuff* of mass meetings, street demonstrations, confrontations and parades [that is, the usual displays of conflict]. . . . Second, all the action would ridicule and make a farce of the law *for there is no law,* and there probably never will be, *banning natural physical function.* Here you would have a combination not only of noise but also of odor, what you might call natural stink bombs. Regular stink bombs are illegal and cause for immediate arrest, but *there would be absolutely nothing here that the Police Department or the ushers or any other servants of the establishment could do about it. The law would be completely paralyzed* [emphasis added].[32]

Clearly the tactic was to move from appropriate behavior (buying tickets, sitting quietly, listening to the music—that is, accepting the house "rules" and the institutional power behind them) to inappropriate behavior (creating both an aural and olfactory subversion). Withdrawing consent from decorum, from the house rules, in the end would have had the effect of appropriating the concert hall experience and exposing the ultimate impotence of the institutional powers. One can imagine the giddiness of the "flatulents" farting away to the hog-tied horror of the genteel. Elias Canetti would term these Rochester subversives a "reversal crowd":

> Reversal presupposes a stratified society. A clear separation of classes, one enjoying more rights than the other, must have lasted for some time, and made itself felt in men's daily life before the need for reversal arises . . .
> Every command leaves behind a painful *sting* in the person who is forced to carry it out. . . . People who are habitually ordered about are full of them, and feel a strong urge to get rid of them . . . [so] if many [such] men find themselves together in a crowd, they may jointly succeed in what was denied them singly: together they can turn on those who, till now, have given them orders. A revolutionary situation can be defined as this state of reversal, and a crowd whose discharge consists mainly in its collective deliverance from the stings of command should be called a *reversal crowd.*[33]

Alinsky was not working on a Rochester revolution per se, but he intended to reverse the roles of power at one of the ruling elite's most high-profile symbols of cultural stratification and button-downed order. While not all actions will lend themselves to the kind of sophomoric high jinks Alinsky plotted for the Rochester symphony elites, an underlying message is that the activists are also an audience for their planned actions, and concern should be given to how the tactics will affect them, and not just the "enemy." "If your people are not having a ball doing it," Alinsky wrote, "there is something wrong with the tactic."[34]

A less ribald instance of play within display comes out of a 1990 publication celebrating the fiftieth anniversary of the Industrial Areas Foundation, *IAF 50 Years: Organizing for Change.*

"Banking on Victory"

Discriminatory practices in the banking industry had prevented many Baltimoreans from purchasing homes. BUILD [Baltimoreans United in Leadership Development] vowed to put an end to this and to see that Baltimore residents received fair treatment.

For months, BUILD leaders had been attempting to set up a meeting with the president of one of the largest banks in the city. Leaders had frequently written and phoned him. BUILD members became incensed at his consistent refusal to meet with or recognize the organization. BUILD had taken enough.

After several strategy and training sessions, 60 leaders gathered at the bank on an appointed date. Lining up single file outside of the bank, they shuddered as carloads of police with K-9 dogs on leashes came to "maintain order." Armed with the fact that they all had accounts at this bank, they filed in to "conduct business." The bank tellers and managers were totally unnerved as they attempted to serve their customers. Some brought in five-hundred pennies that they needed converted into dollars. Some wanted balances checked. Some wanted to talk about new or old accounts. Some were clumsy and dropped their change; others were forgetful and forgot their account numbers. All, however, after conducting one transaction returned to the back of the line to wait their turn to conduct more business.

At the same time, a delegation of leaders went upstairs to the office of the president. They said they wanted an appointment, and that the BUILD members who were in line downstairs could certainly conduct "business" as customers all day. They had brought lunch.

Responding to the phone calls from the frenzied employees downstairs, the president offered to meet immediately. BUILD leaders replied that they had come to schedule an appointment for a meeting. He quickly gave them a date. The delegation returned to the BUILD members who were still in line downstairs and reported their victory. Much to the relief of the besieged bank employees, they all exited to the front of the building. Outside, they joyfully greeted members of the media to report the great success.

As a result of that action, early in the history of BUILD, over 250 families received mortgage loans in the city at affordable rates. The BUILD organization sent signals to Baltimore power brokers that the BUILD organization was the new "kid" on the block and was there to stay![35]

Here, again, we see the Alinsky/IAF strategy taunting decorum. Yes, the customers' bodies "conducted business," but their motive was to disrupt business until they received the concession sought from the bank's president. The frustration of tellers and other account holders was a consequence of following "proper" bank operating procedures. Cashing in literally on this right to conduct business finally yielded the bank president's concession to meet. In finding and violating tacit rules of appropriate behavior, BUILD was able to slip through a loophole and, in so doing, appropriated—within the legal guidelines of the institution—the bank floor and its tellers, the entire place.

In these examples we see how the performances enact the trope of premonitory proof. Not only could BUILD have continued conducting "business" all day, but legally and logistically, the group could return to conduct business all day tomorrow, and the next day after that, and the next day after that, ad infinitum. And as long as *anyone* could purchase a concert ticket, the Rochester symphony hall was at risk. The beauty of handcuffing elites with their own rules of proper behavior is that, once discerned, the rules become topics for invention of additional actions, and each sly action becomes both proof of power and premonition for further action.

BUILD's disciplined, collaborative, and well-executed performance strengthened in-group solidarity and power, and, at the same time, it induced out-group recognition of that power. All BUILD participants performed parts in a political drama, parts that together reinforced the "us" versus "them" dynamic. And the performance before an audience of bewildered officers, tellers, and "real" customers achieved identification through form as much as substance. According to Burke, form is the arousing and satisfaction of audience expectations.[36] Every element of the performance contributes to the dynamic mix of formal violation and satisfaction. "We" are repeatedly set apart from "them" through myriad acts that violate conventional form.[37] Participants play their disciplined but unconventional parts of the performance, generating a "collaborative expectancy" unifying them as in-group members: "*we* do *this*, on the other hand, *they* do *that; we* stay *here*, but *they* go *there; we* look *up*, but *they* look *down*. . . ."[38] Repeated violations of conventional form become strongly anticipatory, with each unconventional element generating expectation of yet another, to be fulfilled by yet another, and so on. Indeed, a well-orchestrated performance overall takes on the formal qualities of a well-wrought argument, what Burke called "syllogistic progression."[39] We return to the idea that the performance is also a premonitory proof. "Our" enactment today can be reenacted against "them" tomorrow.

The Spectacle of Power: A Case Study

Public demonstrations are rhetorically produced to be witnessed, to be seen. As such, they are manifestations of spectacle. I saw firsthand how the IAF produced and performed a spectacle when I participated in an IAF Ten-Day Training session in July 1998. As part of my training, I participated along with ninety-nine other trainees in what the IAF called an action.[40] Working with United Power for Action and Justice (UPAJ), a congress of fledgling community groups looking to confederate themselves under a newly fashioned umbrella organization, the IAF sought to establish its own and United Power's credentials through a carefully planned inaugural event. Under IAF guidance, a caucus of member group leaders planned United Power's first public staging of that event to generate enthusiasm, exhibit organizing skills, and create confidence in United Power's leadership. Aristotle's dictum about ethos was that trustworthy character was created artfully through proof in the speech ("And this should result from the speech, not from a previous opinion that the speaker is a certain kind of person.").[41] The ethos of community leaders and the IAF did not depend so much upon what they said as upon what they *did* through performance of a well-staged event. In other words, this first meeting was a collaborative action that could largely influence how the public and establishment power brokers, as well as the membership itself, would view United Power's "trustworthiness" as a new organization.

The action took place in the First Church of God Christian Life Center in Evanston, Illinois, a bright, modern, somewhat panopticonnish sanctuary designed to accommodate five hundred worshipers. On the night of July 6, however, eight hundred people jammed its pews shoulder to shoulder and lined its walls elbow to elbow. Unable to find room within, a throng huddled in the front foyer to watch through a glass partition.

Once under way, in the presence of all, representatives of the various groups approached the pulpit and formally pledged membership to United Power. The assembled were then presented with something of an agenda for future United Power campaigns. Two campaigns mentioned were sweeping and amorphous: increased health care and improved child care across Cook County. These would require long-range planning and commitment. Two other more immediate concerns counterbalanced the long view of health care and child care: Evanston was moving toward privatized recycling, putting on the block the jobs of six city recycling workers; and a local religious group, the Vineyard Christian Fellowship, had been denied the right to hold services in a building they legally occupied by the capricious application of a zoning ordinance, allegedly so that, forced from their property, that property could then be redeveloped as a shopping area. Unlike the countywide concerns, the matters of the recycling workers and religious group presented the audience with occasions for direct action in the town of Evanston.[42]

The Evanston action exhibited the features of what David Procter described as a "dynamic spectacle." A dynamic spectacle, for Procter, is a symbolic event which becomes "a touchstone for community building"[43] by "crystallizing" the welter of arguments surrounding community concerns, if only temporarily.[44] Interest-group rhetors exert rhetorical influence through the event, which makes issues salient before the body politic from their own preferred perspective.[45] In this case, the IAF/UPAJ action induced members of the North Cook County community to see affordable health and child care as important problems that were not abstract but involved people; they were of public rather than private concern and, thus, required collaborative participation in a fight for change.

Procter's discussion of spectacle implies that interest-group rhetors possess a clear motive that guides production of an event conveying a coherent message to a desired, collective audience. Most spectacles do exhibit disciplined planning and design as means for conveying a coherent message that joins rhetors and audience. However, not all spectacles are clear in motive and coherent in message. For example, consider Michael Halloran's study of the 1927 sesquicentennial pageant celebrating the Battle of Saratoga (New York).[46] Crowds far in excess of those anticipated arrived, overran pageant events, and distended the tightly planned program. As the planned agenda unraveled, so too did "the image of social order [originally] encoded in the pageant script."[47] Once the crowd overwhelmed the event, the event itself became little more than a chaotic, purposeless human happenstance. Halloran, however, saw the chaotic result of the pageant's collapsed structure as itself a spectacle of sorts, comparable to Woodstock. Both lacked a clear motive and a coherent message.

The Evanston action resembles the kind of spectacle implied in Procter's work in that the entire event was fully orchestrated for *action* toward some clearly defined outcome. The IAF/United Power motive was to give witness to an organization whose whole had become greater than the sum of its parts. The coherence of the Evanston gathering, in contrast with the crowd at Saratoga, resulted from the fact that—appearances to the contrary—the entire event was planned down to the actual number of attendees.

The July 6 action was conceived as a gathering of identified community groups, so the IAF had asked those groups well in advance of July 6 for attendance commitments. Not an estimate, not a goal, but a commitment: *If you say you will bring ten people, we will expect ten people; if you say five, we will expect five. We will expect whatever number you choose, so choose realistically. No excuses.* When eight hundred people showed up at a five-hundred-seat venue, the IAF was not surprised. Quite to the contrary, they tabulated this number in advance, assured by the commitments they received.[48] Of course, most of the eight hundred attendees who crammed into the church did not expect that massive turnout. As a result, group identification was partly "manufactured" by compressing space—physical and psychological—between attendees.[49]

Halloran's analysis yields the additional insight that spectacles are not transacted according to the somewhat static rhetor-audience model that Procter presumes in his otherwise comprehensive study. Halloran defines "spectacle" as a "public gathering of people who have come to witness some event and are self-consciously present to each other as well as to that event."[50] Accordingly, for Halloran, spectacle is a "lived experience," during which "[m]embers of the audience become rhetors through their visible and audible reactions, transforming the event as it transpires in an enactment of the social order. To think of a rhetorical transaction as a spectacle is thus to blur the roles of rhetor and audience."[51] In contrast with Procter's more static, stable, and unilateral view, Halloran sees rhetor-audience relationships as dynamic, fluid, and multilateral. For Halloran, spectacles blur and shift the lines between rhetor and audience. That insight helps us understand an important aspect of the IAF/UPAJ action's rhetorical functioning.

At the Evanston event, the audience became rhetorical unto itself by its very presence; seeing so many others there, they became awed by and validated in their collective participation. The closing of ranks, so to speak, contributed to the burgeoning group identity; and the room packed with people provided the IAF/UPAJ inaugural the intended symbol of organizing power, which a room partially or poorly filled would not. Given that the audience present was not the sole audience (that is, that the IAF/UPAJ organizers knew the event would be covered by the invited media and read about by other "audiences"—friend, foe, and uncommitted), the packed room also symbolized unlimited community power. The room filled to excess raised important questions: How many others may have been turned away? Who can say how large an arena the IAF and UPAJ might have filled? Who can then assess the potential scope and reach of this group?

Surely, these are the kinds of questions the IAF intended to evoke by guaranteeing more people than the place could comfortably accommodate. Four hundred people in that five-hundred-seat sanctuary would constitute a far more ambiguous symbol of community power and organizing skill than the eight hundred who actually turned out; so, too, would the same eight hundred if they occupied a venue capable of seating twice that number. Spaces and gaps equate to questions and doubts, for both the assembled and outsiders. By ensuring that all spaces and gaps were closed, the IAF visually erased all questions and removed all doubts. Still, although closely gathered, the assembled had not yet been transformed consciously or actively from audience to rhetor, but they would be.

Toward the end of the evening, Tom Lenz, a local pastor and leader of United Power, stood at the pulpit and addressed the immediate audience. He began by assailing the injustice of laying off municipal workers to "shave a few bucks from the budget" and noting how the issue is not confined to the six workers, but rather is about "a huge trend toward less stable jobs, and toward jobs that don't pay a living wage." Lenz then went on to speak of the Vineyard Christian Fellowship, that "there was a time when religious congregations were valued members of a community," but that "now we know what our city council cares about . . . turning over a huge chunk of downtown to a developer to build a dozen cinemas and restaurants . . . so that our kids can have the latest Hollywood crud twelve hours a day, so we can have two-dollar lattes."

Prompted by "handlers"—unidentified audience plants whose job is to jumpstart crowd reactions—wild applause made the rest of the Lenz litany inaudible, but after the clapping subsided, he asked searchingly:

> The question is—tonight—do we do anything about it? [pause] Well we can. It's called "standing for the whole." It's what this whole meeting has been about. It's about transcending our narrow issues, moving outside our tribes and our individual traditions. It's written. It's a leap of faith. It's what unions call solidarity . . . to take an injury to one as an injury to all. [pause] With that, I'd like the recycling members and their families to please stand.

Lifted by another wave of applause, the six workers and their families arose above the sea of shoulders and bobbing heads. Standing awkwardly in the middle of the center pews, no doubt feeling self-conscious under 360–degree scrutiny, as the applause dropped off they quickly moved to sit down, but Lenz said commandingly, "No, no, no, we're not done with you yet. Stay standing. Back up." Lenz then offered a brief tribute to the recycling workers and the job they do and to their families.

With the recycling workers still on their feet, Lenz said, "Now I'd like the parishioners of Vineyard Christian Fellowship to please stand," which they also did to applause. Following words of praise, they, too, were asked to remain standing. So, at this point toward the end of the evening, in this room of eight hundred people, a total of approximately thirty recycling workers, their families, and Vineyard Christian parishioners stood uneasily, self-consciously clustered among themselves as the seated crowd watched and applauded.

When the sanctuary again grew quiet, and with the thirty still on their feet, Lenz lowered his voice and asked, "The question of all of us is, will we let them stand alone, or will we rise up and show them that we stand with them in solidarity? [Emphatically] Will you stand for the whole with me?"

Sparked by the enthusiastic reply of the handlers, the entire assembly rose to its feet as if one, erupting in applause, the standing "whole" tightly surrounding the recycling workers and parishioners, absorbing "them" into "us." Lenz continued to speak, but the raucous standing ovation made him pause, smiling. The moment had not only "coalesced" the issues, it also carried the audience forward to understanding itself not as "me" and "thee" but rather "we." What had been an audience of eight hundred was now a single rhetor speaking as one. What had been eight hundred fingers had now closed into a fist. It was a brilliant rhetorical performance.

And it was *the* defining moment of the evening. Yet there was another, somewhat-more-ambiguous defining moment earlier, which harkens back to both Sharp and Canetti, mentioned previously in this piece. A handful of local politicians had been unceremoniously ushered in to take seats toward the front of this gathering of hundreds of attendees at the First Church of God Christian Life Center. Invited to attend, they had not been asked to address the group as elected officials. At one point, however, the politicians were asked to stand and be recognized as allies, which they did, acknowledging the polite applause before resuming their seats.

As the public face of politics is always a display of dense symbols, this gesture toward the politicians is rich in implications. Recognizing the politicians for their support of UPAJ goals raised questions about other local politicians *not* present: *Who* wasn't there? *Why* weren't they there? But this formal recognition differed from that afforded the recycling workers and the Vineyard Christian Fellowship worshipers. The politicians were "recognized," but they remained separate from those assembled, suspended between "us" and "them." They received polite acknowledgment for their support, but depending on their future actions, they could as readily become the targets of blame as of praise.

Further, while seated, the politicians may have gotten a sense of the crowd's dimensions by scanning the room, but much of their depth perspective would have been obscured by the heads and bodies of those sitting around them. By asking the politicians to rise, the IAF/UPAJ organizers presented them with an unobstructed view from which to take in the massive crowd, a constituency that could be reanimated for or against them. Here they witness the display of a premonitory proof of power. The assembled here, after all, could be reassembled elsewhere. The politicians were acknowledged, but in return they also had to acknowledge the young organization's impressive power.

Here again, we see the shifting roles of rhetor and audience within a spectacle, inverting the traditional roles of *politician as speechifying rhetor* and *citizenry as speechless audience*. The assembled citizenry here became the speechifying rhetor, delivering a very clear message of strength to politicians assembled as a speechless audience. The spectacle, by design, flipped the assumed rhetor-audience roles and thus, as Halloran might put it, "the image of social order [traditionally] encoded" in public demonstrations.

We see here, too, the rhetorical manifestation of Cannetti's "reversal crowd." The politicians stood silently before public scrutiny, stripped of traditional resources for exercising their power (speechmaking) and made to witness a powerful organization comprised of less-powerful individuals. The IAF/UPAJ arrangement said, in essence: "Tonight, we hold the podium, we do the talking. We have brought you here to listen, not to speak. You will not speak." Those hundreds in attendance may have felt a certain surge of power with this rearrangement of rhetorical roles. But that surge could only have come about by first "recognizing" the politicians, singling them out from the larger gathering, and then recognizing their obedient silence. No doubt, the politicians sensed the brownout of their own formal power.

The IAF/UPAJ leaders orchestrated an unequivocal display of their newly organized power before the politicians, the public, and, most important, their members. The spectacle proved their power. Equally as important, the spectacle cast the mold for future displays.

This spectacle produced the organizational genes for reproducing itself again and again, and that prospect is the Evanston spectacle's greatest significance as rhetorical performance.

Conclusions

Successful organizing requires rhetorical skill as much as political will. Organizing power among the disenfranchised is a gradual process involving conversion of the traditional "audience" into a unified "rhetor" ("the people speaking") and of the traditional rhetor ("members of the elite") into a responsive audience. Alinsky showed that power is expressed in relationships and that power relationships can be subverted or reversed through rhetorical performance. From his perspective, then, proof of power is acquired through well-executed performance of collaborative actions rather than eloquent use of words. Thus, power must be "demonstrated" through performance, not simply asserted. The point is reversible: inability to "demonstrate" power through effective performances is tantamount to proof of power's absence. From Alinsky's vantage, then, both organization and reorganization of power relationships require rhetorical performances that display those relationships.

The Alinsky/IAF study shows that contesting power relationships is not simply a matter of a group's size. Wrested power results from artful performance. Sixty people do not constitute a mass demonstration; yet, when strategically deployed, sixty people can totally incapacitate a bank's power to do business. The important lesson this teaches us is that even without overwhelming numbers, power relationships can be reversed—if only temporarily —through the well-orchestrated performance of a number of small acts.

There is no guarantee that even a planned and well-executed performance will result in a complete turnabout. Those holding power often have time on their side, and time often erodes resolve. Thus, the first response when "answering" demonstrators often is to play a waiting game: maintain recalcitrance, and eventually the malcontents will go home. But those seeking power rather than just attention know that power requires demonstration of the kind that I have called "premonitory proof." If power is enacted effectively today, it creates the anticipation that it can be reenacted effectively again tomorrow. The malcontents may go home, but they will return. For friends and foes alike, a successful performance creates an "if, then" situation: if we/they succeed today, then we/they can succeed tomorrow.

Any performance that challenges power relationships requires the reversal of conventional rhetor and audience roles. The Alinsky/IAF examples illustrate that this reversal sometimes can occur when the less powerful brazenly violate decorum at the sacred sites of power and thereby disrupt, if not rearrange, power relationships. Less audaciously, reversal of rhetor and audience roles can be achieved by inviting the powerful to the less powerful's own turf so that they can witness newly found power harnessed through organization. In either case, role reversal of usual rhetorical relationships occurs, and through that reversal, opportunity is afforded for the display of organized power before those far more accustomed to wield power than to witness its presence in others.

Reversal of rhetor and audience roles so that the less powerful can enact an orchestrated performance of organized power extends to demonstrations other than those examined in this chapter. When civil rights activists dared go into "whites only" domains (bus terminal waiting areas, lunch counters), they were reversing rhetorical relationships through performance of a shift in power relationships. When graffiti artists from Greenpeace use a corporation's own properties to denounce that corporation (for example, hanging a banner from a Dow Chemical water tower in New Jersey; thrashing a message into a Monsanto cornfield in the Midwest), they, too, are reversing usual rhetorical and power relationships through performance. In each case, we see rhetorical roles reverse through performance of power's rearrangement.

Well-executed public demonstrations are visible proof of the ultimate vulnerability of status quo power; they challenge established relationships. At the same time, rhetorical performances "demonstrate" unforeseen possibilities for rearrangement of those relationships: *Your dominant power is assailable. Our acts demonstrate to you, to ourselves, and to a world looking on that we have placed a limit on your power and, in forcing you to respond, have shown power of our own.* And it is precisely this revelation of previously concealed power relationships that makes the performance of public demonstrations an important rhetoric of display.

Notes

Special thanks to Lawrence J. Prelli and S. Michael Halloran for their critiques of and suggestions for earlier versions of this essay. It has been much improved with their help.

1. Aristotle, *On Rhetoric: A Theory of Civic Discourse,* trans. George A. Kennedy (New York: Oxford, 1991). See Aristotle's discussion of epideictic and deliberative at 1358b8–28. His connection of these two kinds of rhetoric with these otherwise widely applicable, general topics is found at 1392a1–7.

2. Gene Sharp, *The Politics of Nonviolent Action, Part One: Power and Struggle* (Boston: Porter Sargent Publishers, 1973), 9.

3. These include (1) *habit* (humans have for a long time obeyed ruling elites), (2) *fear of sanctions* (potential negative responses from the ruling elite, often manifested physically), (3) *moral obligation* (belief that obedience serves the interest of the common good; belief that the ruler is imbued with suprahuman authority—that is, a religious leader), (4) *legitimacy of command* (for example, the issuance of a command from the president of the United States of America), (5) *conformity of commands to accepted norms* (that is, subjects conform with the command because it calls for behavior that they believe to be right unconditionally), (6) *self-interest* (obedience that leads to corporate or personal gain), (7) *psychological identification with the ruler* (obedience or cooperation based upon strong emotional identification with a leader or regime or system), (8) *zones of indifference* (when rules do not stir enough reaction to resist them), and (9) *absence of self-confidence among subjects* (that is, subjects feel as though they lack the intelligence, fortitude, and so forth, to resist) (Sharp, *The Politics of Nonviolent Action,* 19–23).

4. We should not confuse *power* with *force.* A despot resorting to physical force—violence, or threat of violence—against his or her subjects has in the very exercise of physical force admitted to a loss of power, which the physical force then seeks to restore. The breakdown of social order, chaos, and open revolt manifest that the ruler's power has been taken back by the ruled and set free in disorder. Brutality is the means by which the ruled are convinced to give it back.

5. Sharp, *The Politics of Nonviolent Action,* 26.

6. Ibid., 30.

7. Saul D. Alinsky, *Rules for Radicals: A Practical Primer for Realistic Radicals* (1971; repr., New York: Vintage, 1972), 51.

8. Ibid., 113.

9. Sanford Horwitt, *Let Them Call Me Rebel: Saul Alinsky, His Life and His Legacy* (New York: Vintage, 1992), 11.

10. Ibid., 13.

11. Ibid.

12. Contemptuous of academics in general, Alinsky derided "school trained" social workers— that is, those without training in "the Alinsky way"—who go into communities making a beeline for the issues without first building community power. "Basically the difference between their goals and ours is that they look to get rid of four-legged rats and stop there; we organize to get rid of four-legged rats so we can get on to removing two-legged rats" (Alinsky, *Rules for Radicals,* 68). In other words, regardless of good intentions, do-good social work may remedy a particular community ill, but it will leave intact the very power arrangement that allowed the condition to develop in the first place.

13. Kenneth Burke, *A Rhetoric of Motives* (Berkeley: University of California Press, 1950), 20.

14. Alinsky, *Rules for Radicals,* 131.

15. Ibid., 136.

16. Marion K. Sanders, *The Professional Radical: Conversations with Saul Alinsky* (New York: Harper and Row, 1970), 42.

17. Ibid., 42.

18. Georg Simmel, *Conflict and the Web of Group Affiliations,* trans. Kurt H. Wolff and Reinhard Bendix (New York: Free Press, 1955), 13.

19. Ibid., 28–34.

20. Ibid., 103.

21. Alinsky, *Rules for Radicals,* 116.

22. Ibid., 130.

23. Kenneth Burke, *Dramatism and Development* (Barre, Mass.: Clark University Press, 1972).

24. Ibid., 28.

25. Ibid.

26. Ibid.

27. Ibid.

28. For samples of visual as well as verbal antithesis in war rhetoric, see Sam Keen, *Faces of the Enemy: Reflections of the Hostile Imagination* (New York: Harper and Row, 1986).

29. Surely there are secondary audiences for such public displays, but those audiences are only of consequence insofar as they either join the demonstrating group or bring influence to bear on the struggle—that is, as public opinion. I do not mean to underestimate the value and potential of these secondary audiences, but for the sake of this discussion I think it prudent to think in a simple challenger/challenged binary.

30. Horwitt, *Let Them Call Me Rebel,* 457.

31. Alinsky did eventually take up the Rochester cause; curiously, although he alludes to the "sniffony" scenario both in interviews and in his own writing, he never actually employed it as a tactic. In neither interviews nor his own writing does he explain why.

32. Alinsky, *Rules for Radicals,* 139.

33. Elias Canetti, *Crowds and Power,* trans. Carol Stewart (New York: Farrar, Straus, Giroux, 1962), 58.

34. Alinsky, *Rules for Radicals,* 128.

35. Industrial Areas Foundation (IAF), *IAF 50 Years: Organizing for Change* (Chicago: Industrial Areas Foundation, 1990), 19.

36. Kenneth Burke, *Counter-Statement* (1931; repr., Berkeley: University of California Press, 1968), 31, 124.

37. Thus, the elements of disciplined, enacted performance not only violate what Burke called conventional form but do so in multiple ways through what Burke defined as repetitive form. See *Counter-Statement,* 125–26.

38. Burke, *Rhetoric of Motives,* 58.

39. Burke, *Counter-Statement,* 124.

40. Starting with only a handful of organizers in 1940, the IAF has since sent hundreds into the field and continues to train new organizers each year. Working in communities around the country (and some even outside the country), the IAF has grown immensely, and in order to maintain continuity, establish clear philosophical and strategic foundations, and identify organizers with promise, the IAF has held biannual ten-day training sessions for many years. By the graciousness of Ed Chambers, Alinsky's successor as director of the IAF, I was allowed to attend the July 1998 training session despite the fact that I was then a graduate student doing research and did not intend to enter the field of community organizing.

41. Aristotle, *On Rhetoric,* trans. Kennedy, 38 (1356a4).

42. The IAF distinguishes between "problems" and "issues." "Problems" constitute concerns that are sweeping in nature: health care, economic justice, environmental policy, and so forth. "Issues" constitute limited and highly specific concerns that can be addressed directly and immediately and that can be "won." As a matter of policy, the IAF seeks to work on both problems and issues so that long-range change can occur, supported by the confidence that short-term victories bring. In Evanston, then, health care and child care served as problems; the recycling jobs and right to worship served as issues.

43. David E. Procter, "The Dynamic Spectacle: Transforming Experience into Social Forms of Community," *Quarterly Journal of Speech* 76 (1990): 119.

44. Ibid., 118.

45. Ibid., 119.

46. S. Michael Halloran, "Text and Experience in a Historical Pageant: Toward a Rhetoric of Spectacle," *Rhetoric Society Quarterly* 31 (Winter 2001): 5–17.

47. Ibid., 6.

48. As further evidence of how much public demonstration can become theater, the one hundred trainees who took places within the assembly, and who were indistinguishable from the larger group but with no connection to it, were still part of the visual "proof" of this event.

49. This is a creative application of the topos of magnitude insofar as the perception of the gathering's size and the association of that gathering with an impressive display of power were quite intentionally manufactured for rhetorical impact.

50. Halloran, "Text and Experience in a Historical Pageant," 5.

51. Ibid., 6.

John Shotter

13

reating Real Presences

Displays in Liminal Worlds

Certainly, we still wish to capture in our arts the invisible currents that rule our lives.

P. Brook[1]

The "otherness" which enters into us makes us other.

G. Steiner[2]

There is something very special hinted at in the notion of display—to do with "the uncon-cealment of things in their 'thisness'"[3]—that has not been properly acknowledged in the current, self-centered, self-contained, self-consciously intellectual forms of thought we have pursued in Western, modernist philosophy and still pursue in our academic inquiries today. As Rosenfield further points out, "the term 'epideictic' comes from *epideixis* ('to shine or show forth'). Hence our translation of the word as 'display' (in the sense of show *off*) is only literally correct. More precisely the word suggests an exhibiting or making apparent (in the sense of showing or highlighting) what might otherwise remain unnoticed or invisible."[4] Our modernist categories, however, can easily lead us back into treating a "display" as merely a representation of one kind or another, as a form that requires our individual and subjec-tive interpretation if its content or meaning is to be understood. Thus, rather than allow-ing ourselves the possibility of encountering something uniquely new, something radically other than anything already known to us—something with, so to speak, a life of its own— the very requirements of our academic disciplines can (mis)lead us into ignoring what dis-plays can "say" to us. Confronted with an alien display—a sculpture, a painting, the outline of a sacred ceremony or ritual, a monument, a museum, and so forth—it is all too easy for us to approach it as we might any other "problem" of an objective nature: to first analyze it into a set of already well-known elements and then to explain it in terms of a speculative theory, working in terms of a hidden set of rules or principles said to be responsible for its supposed influences on us.

But to analyze it in this way is to fail to grasp the uncanny or extraordinary nature of what occurs, or can occur, in certain of our displays. Indeed, it is to fail to grasp the crucial element of *aletheia* at work on all those occasions when we simply express ourselves to those around us in some way (including those occasions when we offer each other supposed theoretical explanations of a phenomenon)—namely, the working of the godlike agency Lethe, the god of oblivion, who can lead us to be forgetful of the merely mundane and allow us a momentary contact with *Being* "as it is." For even the theoretical rules or principles we propose are not merely empty, mechanical shapes or forms (themselves requiring interpretation by us, individually) but are themselves god-ideas, invisible but real "presences" issuing their own commands to us, to which we all must be answerable (if we have satisfied the requirements of our professional colleagues) in the same way. Our modernist modes of inquiry, especially as developed by Descartes, in functioning (they claim) only in relation to an external, mechanistic world, miss just those influences at work "within" our lived or living worlds. Aimed at mastery rather than at understanding, they function to keep us at a distance from the things around us. Thus, rather than "entering into" a display's world and becoming a witness to the nature of its being, its original otherness, we aim simply at using it for our own ends; rather than celebrating it, we think of manipulation; rather than embracing it, we evaluate it for its worth or gain to us; and so on.

In what follows below, I want to explore what has been lost (or seemingly lost, because of it having become rationally invisible to us, so to speak) in our debilitated, modernist notion of cultural representations. I want also to explore not only how we might regain a sense of the uncanny power that can be exerted on us by at least some of the displays we encounter, but also of how that power is still at work, in fact, unnoticed, in many of our modes of intellectual inquiry. Indeed, to go further, I want to suggest that that uncanny effect, along with the (often unwarranted and misleading) persuasive power of many scientific claims, is due to something very special in the nature of living expression that is not properly acknowledged in our current forms of inquiry: its capacity within the dynamic, spontaneously responsive relations unfolding between itself and those encountering it to give rise to "real presences"[5]—that is, it can give rise to an invisible but nonetheless real agency that, so to speak, has a "life of its own" and as such can exert its own "demands" and "judgments" on our reactions to it. Rather than our having to interpret it to understand what its meaning might be for us, we find "it," so to speak, "telling" us its meaning, as if we are answerable to it, not it to us.

Seeing an Invisible Presence

As I intimated above, the phenomenon of a real presence is something very special that occurs *only* when we enter into mutually responsive, dialogically structured, living, embodied relations with an other or otherness in our surroundings—when we cease to set ourselves, unresponsively, at a distance from them and allow ourselves to enter into an interinvolvement with them. Then, in the intricate "orchestrated movement" occurring in the unfolding, contingent, or paired[6] interplay between our own outgoing, responsive expressions toward them and their equally responsive, complementary expressions incoming toward us, a very special kind of *felt* understanding becomes available to us. We can begin to get a palpable sense of their "inner nature" or the "character of their lives." In other words, the indivisible whole sensed here is not an independent spatial form with all its parts present at once, but a dynamic form, a temporally unfolding, "shaped" movement occurring within the interplay and dependent upon it for its existence.

Two paradigm instances of such real presences are very familiar to us: we hear or see a meaning in a person's speech or in the array of print spread out before us on the page of a book. Having learned our mother tongue, or to read, long ago, we find ourselves "called" to pay a certain form of outward attention by the word-forms occurring before us. As we encounter each word-form, with each word contributing to the inner articulation of the very same unitary whole that gives it its meaning, we begin to develop a kind of understanding quite different from the passive, representational-referential kind that is currently much more familiar to us in our intellectual lives. Following Bakhtin, I will call it an active, relational-responsive form of understanding. In it, we gain more than merely a configurational "picture," so to speak, of a state of affairs. For, in adopting "an active, responsive attitude toward" a piece of speech or text, a reader or listener "either agrees or disagrees with it (completely or partially), augments it, applies it, prepares for its execution, and so on. And the listener adopts this responsive attitude for the entire duration of the process of listening and understanding, from the very beginning—sometimes literally from the speaker's first word."[7]

In other words, in our encounters with a text or with any other expressive display by an other or otherness in our surroundings, "the 'otherness' met with is not," as Steiner puts it, "'a thing out there,' is not, first and foremost, an 'object.'"[8] Such othernesses are "'presences,' 'presentments' whose existential 'thereness' (Heidegger's word) relates less to the organic . . . as to the 'transubstantional'";[9] that is, such invisible othernesses can be sensed as being "there" in the text and as such have a "life of their own" with its own unique character.

Another well-known paradigm is a rainbow.[10] A rainbow, of course, has no objective existence or location in space in itself; it only makes a unique appearance to a unique individual in the dynamics of interaction occurring between them and the sunlight from behind them. As Barfield comments, "Look at a rainbow . . . *Is it really there*? . . . [I]f you walked to the place where the rainbow ends, or seems to end, it certainly would not be 'there.' In a word, reflection will assure you that the rainbow is the outcome of the sun, the raindrops and your own vision."[11]

Here, however, because of their unusual nature and because their well-worked-out technical nature makes the "orchestrated" character of our interinvolvement with them describable in detail, I want to begin the exploration of such invisible but real presences with another quite different exemplar: a "presence" that, paradoxically, can become visible to us in a visual display. I am speaking here of the 3-D stereograms that many of us have tried (often quite unsuccessfully) to see in certain specially created, two-dimensional, random-dot displays—displays that, frustratingly, only become visible to us if we can let them instruct us in how to see them. Like learning a new dance step or how to cut our own hair in the mirror, this is not always easy. Nonetheless, in scanning over the two-dimensional, random-dot-stereogram on figure C14, there is a way to begin to visually *sense* a 3-D "heart" within it; not an outlined heart, but a heart shape marked out in depth before us.

This is because, although we may move our two eyes over the page before us as we please, the dots are arranged on the page in such a way that they can be said to have a set of unique requirements of their own. Like the autofocus mechanism on many modern cameras, as we point our two eyes in different directions in scanning over the display, our two eyes achieve for us, bodily and spontaneously, a fused and focused point of fixation at a certain sensed distance from us—a sense intimately related to where we feel we can reach out with our fingers to achieve a touch (for a point near to us) or where we must bodily travel (for more distant points). The principle behind the arrangement of the (seemingly random) dots in the display lies in what is called the "wallpaper" effect, discovered by Sir David Brewster (1781–1868), the inventor of the stereoscope. He noticed that Victorian wallpaper printed with a repeating pattern would jump to a new plane of depth if he looked at it with crossed eyes; for then, instead of both eyes focusing *and* converging on the *same* piece of pattern, while one eye focused on one piece of pattern, the other focused on the next (or even the next but one) in the repeating cycle. Thus, as already mentioned, as we look in one direction toward the display, we can find a convergent focus at *this* distance, in another direction at *that* distance, in another at *another* distance, and so on. So as we continue to look over the display on the page before us, we gain in the course of our surveying or scanning it a felt sense of a heart-shaped form before us—a felt sense that is identical for everyone, an embodied awareness that is shaped by the way the display, so to speak, "calls" us to "look over" it, if we are to sustain the sense of a unitary object before us.

Indeed, it is as if we must almost "feel over" what is before us with our eyes, point by point, place by place, just as we must in feeling something with our fingers. Merleau-Ponty describes the process of "looking" involved thus: "The look . . . envelops, palpates, espouses the visible things. As though it were in a relation of pre-established harmony with them, as though it knew them before knowing them, it moves in its own way with its abrupt and imperious style, and yet the views taken are not desultory—I do not look at a chaos, but at things—so that finally one cannot say if it is the look or if it is the things that command."[12] Rather than simply looking *at* a "thing," it would perhaps be more accurate to say that I see *according* to it, or *with* it, for "it" is a guiding agent in my looking. In other words, no "things" as such reveal themselves to us instantaneously, as mere passive observers of them; seeing requires an active looking from us.

Thus, once we "see" the "object" in the display, we "see" it not by finally being able to "work it out" as one might solve a problem, not by imposing this or that particular interpretation on it, but in terms of a quite-specific range of spontaneously occurring, bodily reactions and anticipatory responses—seeing parts of the "object" as near to us and others as far from us, not just as large and small, as in a two-dimensional display. And this is a crucial point, for when we do "see" it (the heart), we locate it neither "on" the page nor "in" our heads, but in fact "out" in the space between us and the page, that is, "out in the world." For that is where, dynamically, the different two-dimensional views from my two eyes cohere into a 3-D unity, just as a real object that I caress with my hand is "out there," too. But, to repeat, the "heart" is not a real object but an invisible presence, present only in the unfolding temporal course of our visual involvement with the special patterning of the dots on the two-dimensional page. It emerges and is only there in our orchestrated interaction with the whole distribution of the dots on the page. But once in possession of the appropriate "way of looking," we can "look from" one part of the display—having allowed it to "call out" a certain response from us—while "looking toward" another with a certain adjustive anticipation, and so on, and so on.[13] Indeed, it is just as if each element we encounter and respond to tells us how to prepare ourselves to go out to meet the next, so that, as it were, we can turn toward it with our hand already raised to shake its hand. Thus it is that our bodies create in us a qualitatively new set of relational dimensions, joining retrospective experience to prospective anticipations.

The Creation of Real Presences in "Orchestrated Interplays"

Above I suggested that it is in the realm of dialogically structured activity, and only in this realm, that such agentic presences as I have outlined above can be created. So what is so special about this realm? Well, one thing that is special about it is that it is a corporeal and not a cognitive phenomenon; it comes into existence only in our living responses to what we treat as living expression. As Wittgenstein notes: "Our attitude to what is alive and to what is dead, is not the same. All our reactions are different."[14] While we can come to an understanding of a dead form in terms of objective, explanatory theories representing the sequence of events supposed to have caused it, a quite different form of engaged, responsive understanding becomes available to us in our engagement with what we treat as the expressions of living things. They can "call out" spontaneous reactions from us in a way that is quite impossible for forms that do not seem to us to be the products or outcomes of living expression.

A classic example of such an event in this realm is Giambattista Vico's account of the emergence of a first possible "sensory topic."[15] While modern theories of knowledge begin with something already present to the mind—for example, Descartes begins with clear and distinct ideas—Vico begins by asking how it is that the mind comes to have anything stable present to it at all. For the minds of the first men were "little better than the minds of beasts, [in] which each new sensation cancels the last one."[16] How do human beings manage to create and establish, within the flow of experience between them, a shared "stopping place" (topos), an "is," within the flow of sensation that can be "found again"? How can a shared anchor point be established? For Vico, it is not a matter of "seeing" in common, but of "feeling" in common, with the giving of a shared significance to shared feelings in shared circumstances.

In paragraphs 374 through 399 of the *New Science,* Vico discusses what he calls the "civil history" of the saying that it was "from Jove that the muse began." Taking it seriously, he suggests that it was from a fear of thunder that the first sensory topic—and the first great "imaginative universal," that is, the god Jove—was established. For, in everyone within a social group being startled in the same way, the opportunity arose for them all to act responsively in common, to run in a state of fear into the caves to shelter from the thunder. Although the source of the great sounds in the sky might be invisible, the fact that all respond to it in the same way—as if, metaphorically, they were the angry words of a giant being—provides, we could say, a moment of common reference to a "presence" shared between them. For, as Vico points out, this kind of fear, the fear of thunder, is not like one's fear of an immediately obvious dangerous event. There is no such immediately obvious practical response to thunder; its meaning is unclear. It is "not a fear awakened in men by other men, but fear awakened in men by themselves," says Vico.[17] To this extent, it is a kind of fear that seems to point beyond the thunder. When people hear it, they become confused and disoriented; they move hesitatingly and with concern for each other—the thunder's presence is the mute explanation of their actions. And often, "when men are ignorant of the natural causes producing things, and cannot explain them by analogy," says Vico, "they attribute their own nature to them."[18]

Thus, at this point, "The first theological poets created the first divine fable, the greatest they ever created: that of Jove, king and father of men and gods, in the act of hurling the lightening bolt; an image so popular, disturbing and instructive that its creators themselves believed in it, and feared, revered and worshiped it in frightful religions."[19] The fable of Jove, the first great "imaginary universal," lends form to and is rooted in the "sensory topic" established in that first startling moment in people's shared responses to thunder. In all spontaneously responding to thunder as if to big words, they are acting imaginatively—but, "in their robust ignorance, [they] did it by virtue of a wholly corporeal imagination," says Vico.[20]

In other words, the initial beginnings of a people's "common sense" (*sensus communis*), their attributing of a shared meaning to shared events, began to emerge spontaneously, in specific contexts in relation to specific concrete events. The sensuous topos established here is a totality linking thunder with shared fears at the limits of one's being and with recognizing the existence of similar such feelings in others through shared bodily responsive activities. In their fear, they took up the otherness of the world around them into themselves, and in their wonder they set themselves off from it. The first great imaginary universal of Jove was created, not out of a heterogeneous amalgam of elements held together externally, within a systematic framework of thought, but by developing a totality of specific relations, existing just for a moment among a group of people, from within, by internal articulation. Thus, just as other complex, living wholes, like oak trees, grow or develop from origins in simple, living wholes, like acorns, so the complex image of Jove is developed from a sensory topic in which it is possible to "re-feel" everything present at those times when "Jove" is active. And while such feelings are gradually articulated into more specific forms of symbolic expression—into rituals, ceremonies, and so forth—the originally inarticulate feelings remain on hand as standards, so to speak, against which the more explicit forms of response may be judged, that is, sensed, as to their adequacy or not.

Such moments of being struck by or entered into by a novel otherness, thus to be informed by something capable of changing the nature of one's very being in the world, is central also to Fisher's important work.[21] He begins his study of how Descartes sets out his step-by-step method for the achievement of certainty in the *Regulae*, or *Rules for the Direction of the Intellect*, similarly—with Socrates' claim (in the *Theaetetus*) that "philosophy begins in wonder" and with the importance of phenomena that "strike" us. He then turns to some remarks of Wittgenstein's in the "Brown Book," to do with our being struck by what is unfamiliar to us. For both Descartes and Wittgenstein suggest that we do not have an experience, as such, of the ordinary: "Unfamiliarity is much more of an experience than familiarity," says Wittgenstein.[22] "By a feeling or experience here," says Fisher, "we mean that we have a definable moment of a special kind that might be noticed, remembered, formulated in description, something discrete within the flow of time, something clear, self-contained, separable from what came before and after . . . a patch of experience, a *this* with its own duration and quality."[23] Next, Fisher suggests, it is within such memorable and "feelingful" moments that an experience of "seeing connections" can occur: "Being struck by something is exactly the opposite of being struck dumb. The tie between wonder and learning is clear in the moment when after long confusion and study you suddenly say, 'Now I get it!' . . . the moment of 'getting it' is extremely clear in mathematics. In an instant, unexpectedly, the answer is seen for the first time, and all that was a puzzle of unrelated facts up to that instant turns into clarity and order."[24]

Given such moments of "getting it," Descartes' achievement, Fisher suggests, was to "design a way to make sure that every necessary fact is visually present to the mind at the moment when [a] next step [in one's reasoning] is being weighed and that, as in chess, pieces that have been made inactive have been removed from sight."[25] Each methodical step sets the stage for such an instantaneous act of "seeing," we complete it with confidence and move on to arrange the next. And in his *Regulae,* Descartes set out a set of simple exercises for coming to a recognition of what such a certainty feels like; they give one a feel for "what one step looks like, what adequate symbolism is at any given moment, what the distinction between relevant and irrelevant details feels like, but above all, what the feeling of 'getting it,' of crossing the small gap of the unknown is like."[26]

Now, as I have already intimated above, it is *only* in the two-way, orchestrated interplay occurring in those embodied, living, spontaneously responsive relations, occurring between our own outgoing expressions toward an other or otherness and their incoming expressions toward us, that this special kind of practical understanding becomes available to us. In it, to repeat, we grasp the nature of these others and othernesses, not as passive and neutral objects, but as real, agentic presences to which we must be responsive and toward which we must adopt an "evaluative attitude."[27] But such understandings—which, to repeat, we can call relationally responsive understandings—do not occur in all our interactions. They occur only in those circumstances in which expressions and their perception[28] are at issue. From now on, I will call this "the realm of the dialogical."

The Realm of the Dialogical: Its Strange and Special Features

We can outline some of its relevant features as follows: as embodied living beings, we cannot escape from being spontaneously responsive, both to those around us (others) and to other aspects (othernesses) of our surroundings. Thus, in meetings or encounters with others of our kind, instead of one person first acting deliberately and individually, independently of the other, and the other then replying individually and independently of the first, both act in the responsive presence of the other. And they do this straightaway, bodily, in a "living" way, without having first to work out how to respond to each other. This means that when someone acts, their activity cannot be accounted as wholly their own activity, for one person's acts are partly shaped by the acts of the others around them. Indeed, they all act within the mutually responsive atmosphere of each other's activities. This is where all the strangeness of the dialogical, of dialogically structured activities, begins.[29]

Within this realm of jointly constituted activity, none of our actions are truly yours or mine alone; they are ours. Those acting within this realm act participatively within it as a "collective we"; as such, their joint actions are distributed amongst them. No actions are self-contained. Indeed, all the theoretical concepts usually pertaining to inner lives of individuals—such as utterances, thoughts, ideas, meanings, understandings, even intentions, and especially ethical issues—need to be reconsidered in this light. As Bakhtin remarks with respect to the notion of an idea, the idea, dialogically, "is not a subjective individual-psychological formation . . . in a person's head; no, the idea is inter-individual and inter-subjective—the realm of its existence is not individual consciousness but dialogical communion *between* consciousnesses. The idea is a *live event* played out at the point of dialogic meeting between two or several consciousnesses."[30] Ethically too, in the context of our participation within a collective we, we find ourselves with certain obligations to our joint affairs: only if you respond to me in a way sensitive to the relations between your actions and mine can we act together to sustain ourselves as a collective we. And further, if

I sense you as not being sensitive in that way, then I feel immediately offended in an ethical way—I feel that you lack respect for our affairs.

What is produced, then, in such spontaneous conversational or dialogical exchanges is something very intricate. In fact, it is a very complex mixture of not wholly reconcilable influences—as Bakhtin remarks, both centripetal tendencies inward toward order and unity at the center, as well as centrifugal ones outward toward diversity and difference on their margins or borders. Indeed, within such exchanges we can find, occurring spontaneously, preintellectual precursors to our later deliberations. Thus we will mislead ourselves if we mischaracterize this precursor world in our usually taken-for-granted philosophical categories. Aware of this danger, after having noted that modern philosophy "prejudges what it will find," Merleau-Ponty suggests that, to overcome this tendency, philosophy "once again . . . must recommence everything, reject the instruments reflection and intuition had provided themselves, and install itself in a locus where they have not yet been distinguished, in experiences that have not yet been 'worked over,' that offer us all at once, pell-mell, both 'subject' and 'object,' both existence and essence, and hence give philosophy resources to redefine them."[31] In other words, we must install ourselves in what he, Bakhtin, and Wittgenstein all call "the primordial." We must develop a sense of what it is like to live in the precursor world, to what previously we took to be the "external world" as set out by Descartes. How might it be characterized?

Well, first let us note what was mentioned above, that because the overall outcome of any exchange cannot be traced back to the intentions of any of the individuals involved, such activity cannot be accounted simply as action (for it is not done by any individuals alone, thus it cannot be explained by their reasons). Nor can the outcome of the exchange be accounted simply as behavior (as a causal regularity), for as a human activity, it still has intentionality, that is, it is such that it seems to point to, to contain, to mean, to be a means to, or, in short, to be related to something other than or beyond itself—even if that something might not exist. As a consequence of these two properties, the dialogical reality or dialogical space participants construct between them is experienced not only as an external reality, but also as a third agency (an "it") with its own (ethical) demands and requirements. "The word," as Bakhtin remarks, "is a drama in which three characters participate (it is not a duet, but a trio)."[32]

If we take our conversational exchanges as a paradigm for all such exchanges, it is easy to see that, although they may be, as first-time formative events, quite specific in one sense —in being responsively shaped in accord with a specific set of occasioning circumstances —they are also still always open to further inner articulation. In other words, in being unfinished, all such activities within this realm lack a finalized specificity. They are ever only partially specified. Indeed, they remain a complex mixture of many different kinds of influence. This makes it very difficult for us to characterize their nature; for they have neither a fully orderly nor a fully disorderly structure, neither a completely stable nor an easily changed organization, neither a fully subjective nor fully objective character. Spatially, too, they are not easy to identify, for they are nonlocatable in the sense that they are spread out or distributed amongst all those participating in them; neither are they wholly inside people, nor are they wholly outside them. They have their being in that space between them, where what is outside is also partially inside, and vice versa. Temporally also we run up against similar problems, for as Bergson points out with respect to the nature of a flow of activity, "real time has no instants."[33] There are no separate befores and afters in a flow of activity; each moment has within it a carryover from the past and a quite specific anticipation of the future—just as the recipient of a question feels a compelling need to reply with an answer to it.

In short, the flow of activity within this third realm of dialogically structured activity is an indivisible whole, meaningful in different ways at different moments for all those who are participants within it, but that cannot be divided into separable parts—observable as such by a nonparticipant outsider—and still retain its identity as the whole that it is. Indeed, it is precisely its lack of any predetermined order, and thus its openness to being specified or determined just by those involved within it—while usually remaining quite unaware of having done so—that is, in practice, its central defining feature. And it is precisely this that makes this sphere of activity so rhetorically interesting. For it opens up for study how, from beginnings in new, first-time reactions, we might refine, elaborate, and develop the spheres of activity already existing between us into novel ways as yet unknown to us. "The origin and primitive form of the language game is a reaction," notes Wittgenstein; "only from this can more complicated forms develop. Language—I want to say—is a refinement, 'in the beginning was the deed' [Goethe]."[34]

Like Merleau-Ponty, Wittgenstein also takes it that Western philosophers have (mostly) come onto the human scene far too late in the day, and they have then looked in the wrong direction for the wrong thing. In treating human beings as self-conscious intellectuals, they have looked backward and inward, seeking supposedly already existing, single, sovereign centers of influence at work hidden within them as individuals—centers that can be expressed in terms of rules, systems, or principles. In an effort to come on the scene much earlier, Wittgenstein remarks that "when you are philosophizing you have to descend into primeval chaos and feel at home there."[35] While with regard to language he suggests that "I want to regard man . . . as an animal . . . As a creature in a primitive state . . . Language did not emerge from some kind of ratiocination."[36] "But what is the word 'primitive' meant to say here?" he asks. "Presumably that this sort of behavior is *pre-linguistic:* that a language-game is based on it, that it is the prototype of a way of thinking and not the result of thought."[37] And, one might add, this sort of behavior—people's initial, spontaneous bodily responses to the events around them—constitutes prototypes for ways of seeing, hearing, touching, and so forth, ways of valuing, and most importantly, styles of expression.

Wittgenstein, like Merleau-Ponty, wants to consider people's activities in a world prior to individual people acting willfully and intellectually, a precursor world, a sphere in which people act unthinkingly, in spontaneous response to the events occurring around them. And furthermore, rather than looking inward and backward to seek their supposed hidden intentions or thoughts, he wants to look outward and forward, toward how people create and establish between them, in their spontaneous and nondeliberate acts now, ways of "going on," the beginnings of new "forms of life" within which they can later come to act willfully and intellectually. It is in the realm of these precursor activities that the notion of real presences has its point and purchase. As transitional entities, with only a partial, fleeting existence, they can only exist as possible candidates for later conceptualization. To attempt to conceptualize such presences clearly and completely would be to distort their "living" nature.[38]

Applications

In this section, because the sphere of science is, perhaps, the last place one might expect the notion of real presences to play a role, still less a central role, I want to explore the important part such presences in fact do play in this sphere. We can begin with Hanson's Wittgensteinian critique of the misrepresentation by philosophers of microphysics. Why is it so misrepresented, he asks? Because, he replies, "they have regarded as paradigms of inquiry not unsettled, dynamic, research sciences like microphysics, but finished planetary systems, planetary mechanics, optics, electromagnetism and classical thermodynamics."[39] If one is to capture what is at stake in understanding the conduct of inquiry in such as-yet-unfinished spheres of research—and in fact, as we shall see, in understanding our conduct of inquiry in all such unfinished spheres of social life at large—we shall find that, as Hanson puts it, "the issue is not theory-using, but theory finding. . . . Let us examine not how observation, facts and data are built up into general systems of physical explanation, but how these systems are built into our observations, and our appreciation of facts and data."[40]

As is well known, the first time novices look down a microscope at a cell structure, they find it difficult to know what to see. Hanson discusses looking at an X-ray tube (he supplies an illustration of just such a tube viewed as if from the cathode end). "Would Sir Lawrence Bragg and an Eskimo baby," he asks, "see the same thing when looking at an X-ray tube? Yes, and no. Yes—they are visually aware of the same object. No—the *ways* in which they are visually aware are profoundly different. Seeing is not only the having of a visual experience; it is also the way in which the visual experience is had."[41] The appropriate aspects of an entity are brought out and made determinate—that is, specified—in the context of expressions (talk and other gestures) within which it appears. As Wittgenstein puts it: "My relation to the appearances here is part of my concept."[42] But the context as such need not be set out explicitly; indeed, it cannot be. It must be displayed in how I orchestrate my performance within it, my interweaving of my pointing with my words, the precise vocabulary from which I choose my terms, the questions I phrase, the answers I accept, the timing of my actions to complement those of others, and so on, and so on.

Hanson begins his discussion by remarking that what is involved here is not, as is so often assumed, a matter of interpretation.[43] Following Wittgenstein, he points out that a mere interpretation made after the fact of observing a "something" will not do the work required of it: it will not provide us with the *way of seeing* required to orient us toward the different aspects of our surroundings as we might meet them in practice. Further, as he points out: "To interpret is to think, to do something; seeing is an experiential state. The different ways [in which various ambiguous figures] are seen are not due to different thoughts lying behind visual reactions. What could 'spontaneous' mean if these reactions are not spontaneous? When the [ambiguous figure of a] staircase 'goes into reverse' it does so spontaneously. One does not think anything special."[44] So if it is not a matter of interpretation, how might we capture this aspect of our seeing?

Hanson tries to capture this aspect of the display in question by suggesting that "seeing is a 'theory-laden' undertaking."[45] But he immediately remarks on the inadequacy of these terms, for it seems to suggest that the kind of seeing in question is merely a seeing in the visual sphere, that is, a matter of "seeing as," of seeing something as an exemplar of something already well known to us. Rather, the task is to capture the kind of constitutive seeing we manifest—as mentioned above—in our actual, practical performances within the settings of a research science, the seeing of unfinished entities not yet well known to us. To capture this kind of seeing, Hanson proposes the term "seeing-that," by which he means that to see *that* something is the case is to see that if certain things were done, or were to happen, to the object before one's eyes, certain other things would result. As Wittgenstein puts it, a kind of understanding is involved "which consists in 'seeing connections.'"[46] It is a kind of seeing with "*an aetiology and a prognosis*"[47]—that is, the seeing of an object (in terms of visible forms), mingled in with a felt sense of it as an agent (with invisible powers) in its own right. In other words, what Hanson is alluding to here is, it seems to me, precisely what we have tried to capture above with the notion of a "real presence."

Ochs and her colleagues show how the orchestrated responsive performances of neophyte and experienced research physicists can still nonetheless display the felt presence of a "something" not yet (scientifically) stabilized and finished as a reputable finding.[48] They describe in detail how—in their gestured relations toward their measurement curves written on blackboards, toward their overhead-projected diagrams, and in the timing of their talk about them, and so on—they create, in concert with their colleagues, "liminal worlds" that enable all concerned "to understand physical worlds which are not directly accessible to their perceptual abilities."[49] Such worlds are *liminal* worlds in that "sharp boundaries are not drawn linguistically between subject (i.e., researcher) and object (i.e., the physical phenomena under study) . . . the physicists' grammatical choices deconstruct place and identity, and a referential indeterminacy results."[50] Thus, in being still indeterminate, they are not simply open to yet further specification, but they invite or call for their own further responsive shaping. But how might that further responsive shaping be done and be done especially in a nonmisleading way in which all can share?

Interestingly, it seems to be done by the physicists in question talking within such liminal worlds, once created, in terms of certain personified agencies. Seemingly spontaneously, such agencies come into existence in their own right, with their own demands and their own requirements that the physicists who create them must respect, in the dialogical spaces the physicists create between them. These agencies are given voice in such utterances as: "I'm in the paramagnetic state"; "why am I breaking into domains?"; "you're inside a barrier and all you're doing is fluctuating inside that barrier on that time scale"; "When I come down I'm in the domain state"; and so on.[51] In other words, like Levy-Bruhl's primitive peoples, the physicists here treat any special such entity of which they speak as if a "definite influence emanates from it, or is exercised upon it,"[52] and they talk with a "belief in forces and influences which, although imperceptible to the sense, are nevertheless real."[53] Thus, strangely, although seeming to be vague and imprecise, given the "situated" or "indigenous" nature of an audience's responses to it, such a form of communication—because of the power of the real presences displayed in it to move all involved, spontaneously, in the same way—can be made as precise as necessary both to progress and to criticize the research in hand. So, although the physicists concerned do not yet know what they are talking "about" —for they have not yet completed their investigations—they are nonetheless able, in their talk-entwined performances in relation to their projected diagrams and suchlike, to create a shared sense of the real presences at work between them.

The point can be generalized: in all the claims made by scientists (in whatever fields they might operate), intermingled in with the objective and mechanical realms of phenomena they describe in their claims is another unnoticed realm of invisible agencies. And it is these invisible agencies that are, in fact, responsible for bringing off the results of the mechanisms they suppose. In another terminology: accounts of natural processes couched solely in terms of natural laws, principles, or rules fail to account for how purely mechanical impacts, in the context of an inert void, could ever give rise—in the face of the second law of thermodynamics—to (self-sustaining) organic, living unities or wholes; agencies are needed.

Among other spheres of inquiry, in which precisely this issue has been raised, are biology and evolutionary theory. Here I will mention just the work of Keller, although clearly, the work of many others is relevant here too.[54] As Evelyn Fox Keller remarks: "What Darwin brought to biology, at least as we interpret it in the twentieth century, is a way of thinking about the living world as a gas phenomenon, as a composite of autonomous individuals characterized by an internal notion of fitting, engaged in interactions very much like those in the competitive world of Adam Smith."[55] What such a view fails to allow is any process of "internal development," that is, development by internal articulation from an already-organized but simple organic whole to a more richly differentiated whole. "Darwin himself contributed, perhaps more than any other thinker," Keller remarks, "to the erasure of the relational dimensions of the world,"[56] to the erasure of that kind of understanding that consists in seeing connections. In the rhetoric of neo-Darwinian evolution, the necessities of blind chance and the elimination of those unfit seem sufficient to account for the development of those fit to their surroundings. But if this is the case, if blind chance is all that is at work, why should entities able to hold themselves together as an organized whole develop? How could entities able to sustain their own distinct identities, in the face of perturbations from the selfsame surroundings selecting them for their fitness, develop? Why should not random chaos continue into eternity? Again, the formative or organizing power of an agency of some kind is in fact missing from the theory; it is supplied rhetorically in the metaphor of the "survival of the fittest."

In the sphere of DNA research too, Keller also raises similar problems. As she sees it, the introduction by Watson and Crick of the metaphor of "information" into the repertoire of biological discourse, "was a stroke of genius."[57] For, in the move of "the collapsing of *information* with *program* and *instruction* [they] vastly fortified the concept of gene action."[58] But to attribute to genes the capacity to issue and to follow instructions, to talk of DNA as providing the program for synthesizing protein molecules is, again, to talk of genes, not simply as mechanical objects, but as agencies. As Keller notes, the tendency for this slippage or carryover to occur in biology was noted some time ago by Schrödinger, the distinguished physicist. About the very notion of a code-script, he comments, "[T]he term code-script is, of course, too narrow. The chromosome structures are at the same time instrumental in bringing about the development they foreshadow. They are law-code and executive power—or, to use another simile, they are architect's plan and builder's craft—in one."[59]

Bewitched or charmed by the methods of science, "we are under the illusion that what is sublime, what is essential, about our investigation consists in grasping *one* comprehensive essence."[60] As a consequence, as professionals trained into a discipline, we have sought, and often still do seek, regularities, patterns, or orderliness, which we then proceed to try to express in terms of general rules, laws, or principles. But in so doing, we fail to notice that even in the propositional claims displayed on the page before us, real presences are at work, calling us to respond to them as if a "definite influence emanates from [them]" (Levy-Bruhl) —we are thus "bewitched" into seeing such propositions as having somehow captured the essence of the phenomena in question, when in fact they have not.[61]

Conclusions

There is something very special in our works of art, in performances of human expression: we expect them to touch us, to move us, to deliver up to us new meanings or new meaning potentials, new possible understandings of a circumstance that we cannot attain in any other way. What, then, after all the explorations undertaken here, can we say about what is special in the nature of living, human "displays?"

Let us begin by noting the liminal nature of the realities within which they have their role. Although to be sure, in these so-called postmodern times, when little is stable and can be taken for granted as of shared value, less and less of our interactions with each other now take place in a stable, well-established, and well-known world. More and more they occur in pluralistic, only fragmentarily known, and only partially shared social worlds. Indeed, we might argue that, in such circumstances, what can be displayed or made manifest as of value will be treated as such—hence the emerging importance of the topic in these times. But I cannot embark on that argument here. Instead, I will simply note that if we are to move beyond our present times, we need more than problem-solving forms of inquiry, more than arguments as to "best outcomes." We need access to those forms of expression, displays, that move us spontaneously to respond in ways shaped by "the invisible currents that rule our lives"[62]—all those forms of expression, such as monuments, plays, paintings, staged protests, and many other such displays that make in some way the invisible visible to us. Although by their very nature vague and incomplete, such events can provide us with new beginnings.

Central to their capacity to do this, to induce new forms of understanding in us, is— to repeat what has been almost a mantra throughout this chapter—their ability to provoke new embodied responses from us, new reactions from which "more complicated forms can develop." But more than just being momentarily moved by a displayed event is often required. Besides being merely poetic, our displays must also be dramatic. More than merely touching on a "something" and then moving on, as we do in our daily routines, we must somehow make the connections between the invisible currents shaping our lives also visible to ourselves in some way. We must, as in an artistic presentation or performance, embed them in an unfolding drama in some way.[63] For what is done in an unfolding drama is to foreground and make sensibly graspable the *whole* shape or *whole* character of what, nonetheless, still remains invisible—its presence as a unitary whole is portrayed or displayed in the performance or display (just as Marcel Marceau shows us all the outlines of an invisible wall in his hand movements as he struggles to find an opening in it).

While in the past it has been thought that critical argument and debate over theoretical matters has been central to the growth of knowledge, consideration of the power of display shows that knowledge and understanding can grow in other quite different ways also —not just through our works of art, but through all those aspects of our expressions in which we mingle our representational talk of our shared circumstances, as they are objectively, in with our talk of them in terms of the real presences we feel to be at work as agencies within them. Indeed, Rorty's claim that in philosophy, "[i]t is pictures rather than propositions, metaphors rather than statements, which determine most of our philosophical convictions"[64] would seem to be justified. For it is the invisible presences at work in the more visible aspects of our texts that work to shape and direct our urges and compulsions, our needs and wants and desires, as well as our judgments of worth, and the place we accord each particular judgment in the general scheme of values we apply in deciding what it is best to do within those aspects of our lives we share with others.

Thus, as Hanson notes, in finishing off his comments as to what seems to be important in scientific research: "The paradigm observer is not the man [or woman] who sees and reports what all normal observers see and report, but the [one] who sees in familiar objects what no one else has seen before."[65] So, although two scientists might not differ at all in doing calculations, in making predictions, and in providing explanations when working with scientific formulae, differences could still occur between them in the connections and relations they sense as existing within the phenomena of their inquiries. But these would show up "only in 'frontier' thinking—where the direction of new inquiry has regularly to be redetermined."[66] And that can be our task, too, in this book: to see in displays what no one has seen before, thus to show (display) why now, at this moment in history, this topic is a topic of such crucial importance.

Notes

1. P. Brook, *The Empty Space* (New York: Simon and Schuster, 1968), 45.

2. G. Steiner, *Real Presences* (Chicago: University of Chicago Press, 1989), 188.

3. L. W. Rosenfield, "The Practical Celebration of Epideictic," in *Rhetoric in Transition: Studies in the Nature and Uses of Rhetoric,* ed. Eugene E. White, 131–55 (University Park: Pennsylvania State University Press, 1980).

4. Ibid., 135.

5. Steiner, *Real Presences*.

6. Conversation analysts have advanced the notion of "adjacency pairs," that is, the fact that many utterances addressed by a speaker to a listener spontaneously occasion in the listener a felt obligation, a "conditional relevance," to respond to the utterance in a certain normatively "preferred" manner—a greeting with a return greeting, a question with an answer, a request with a compliance, and so on. But the preference here is not a matter of a participant's desires or wishes. The felt obligation is a *presence* with its own requirements, such that if one fails to respond in the preferred manner, one must offer an *account* (a justification or excuse) as to why one is acting in such an unexpected manner. See H. Sachs, E. Schegloff, and G. Jefferson, "A Simplest Systematics for the Organization of Turn-taking for Conversation," *Language* 50 (1974): 696–735. I am indebted to Professor Sally Jacoby for this connection.

7. M. M. Bakhtin, *Speech Genres and Other Late Essays,* trans. Vern W. McGee (Austin: University of Texas Press, 1986), 68.

8. G. Steiner, "'Critic'/'Reader,'" in *George Steiner: A Reader* (Harmondsworth: Penguin Books, 1984), 84.

9. Ibid., 85.

10. Used by Philip Fisher on the cover of his very important book *Wonder, the Rainbow, and the Aesthetics of Rare Experiences* (Cambridge, Mass.: Harvard University Press, 1988).

11. O. Barfield, *Saving the Appearances: A Study in Idolatry* (London: Faber and Faber, 1965), 15.

12. M. Merleau-Ponty, *The Visible and the Invisible* (Evanston, Ill.: Northwestern University Press, 1968), 133.

13. See also in this connection J. Shotter, "'Now I Can Go On': Wittgenstein and Our Embeddedness in the 'Hurly-Burly' of Life," *Human Studies* 19 (1996): 1–23.

14. Wittgenstein, *Philosophical Investigations* (Oxford: Blackwell, 1953), no. 284.

15. Giambattista Vico, *The New Science of Giambattista Vico,* ed. and trans. T. G. Bergin and M. H. Fisch (Ithaca, N.Y.: Cornell University Press, 1968).

16. Ibid., par. 703.

17. Ibid., par. 382.

18. Ibid., par. 180.

19. Ibid., par. 379.

20. Ibid., par. 376.

21. Fisher, *Wonder.*

22. L. W. Wittgenstein, *The Blue and the Brown Books* (New York: Harper Torch Books, 1965), 127.

23. Fisher, *Wonder,* 20.

24. Ibid., 21. Being struck by a similarity, suddenly "seeing connections," is a crucial but very complex experience. As Wittgenstein comments in *Philosophical Investigations* (211): "Is being struck looking plus thinking? No. Many of our concepts *cross* here." Fisher does rather take the simplicity of the moment of being struck for granted.

25. Fisher, *Wonder,* 61.

26. Ibid., 66.

27. Bakhtin, *Speech Genres,* 84.

28. E. Cassirer, *The Philosophy of Symbolic Forms,* vol. 3, *The Phenomenology of Knowledge* (New Haven, Conn.: Yale University Press, 1957); M. Merleau-Ponty, *Phenomenology of Perception,* trans. C. Smith (London: Routledge and Kegan Paul, 1962); and Merleau-Ponty, *The Visible and the Invisible.*

29. See the accounts of "joint action" in J. Shotter, "Action, Joint Action, and Intentionality," in *The Structure of Action,* ed. M. Brenner, 28–65 (Oxford: Blackwell, 1980); J. Shotter, *Social Accountability and Selfhood* (Oxford: Blackwell, 1984); J. Shotter, *Cultural Politics of Everyday Life: Social Constructionism, Rhetoric, and Knowing of the Third Kind* (Milton Keynes: Open University Press, 1993); J. Shotter, *Conversational Realities: Constructing Life through Language* (London: Sage, 1993).

30. M. M. Bakhtin, *Problems of Dostoevsky's Poetics,* ed. and trans. C. Emerson, (Minneapolis: University of Minnesota Press, 1984), 88.

31. Merleau-Ponty, *The Visible and the Invisible,* 130.

32. Bakhtin, *Speech Genres,* 122.

33. H. Bergson, *Duration and Simultaneity* (New York: Bobbs-Merrill, 1965), 52.

34. L. Wittgenstein, *Culture and Value,* trans. P. Winch (Oxford: Blackwell, 1980), 31.

35. Wittgenstein, *Culture,* 65.

36. L. Wittgenstein, *On Certainty* (Oxford: Blackwell, 1969), no. 475.

37. L. Wittgenstein, *Zettel,* ed. G. E. M. Anscombe and G. H. V. Wright, 2nd ed. (Oxford: Blackwell, 1981), no. 541.

38. The claim that such presences are at work in those displays that powerfully touch or move us is not at all new. It was Chaim Perelman and L. Olbrechts-Tyteca, *The New Rhetoric: A Treatise on Argumentation,* trans. J. Wilkinson and P. Weaver (Notre Dame, Ind.: University of Notre Dame Press, 1969), and Chaim Perelman in "Choice, Presence, and Presentation," in Chaim Perelman, *The Realm of Rhetoric* (Notre Dame, Ind.: University of Notre Dame Press, 1982), who reintroduced American rhetorical scholars to the notion of presence, that is, to the agentic power of unnoticed or imperceptible images, after its eradication from modern thought by Descartes' rationalism. Recently, Tucker extended Perelman's observations in a phenomenological account

of "standing-out-ness" in "Figure, Ground and Presence: A Phenomenological Account of Mean-ing in Rhetoric," *Quarterly Journal of Speech* 87, no. 4 (2001): 396–414. However, I wish to be criti-cal of both accounts as individualistic and psychological. They fail to take the very special nature of the realm of dialogically structured social activities into account. Others who made important contributions to the notion of presence, in ways that are compatible with it as a dialogical phe-nomenon, are L. Levy-Bruhl, *How Natives Think* [*Les functions mentales dans les sociétés inférieurs*], trans. L. A. Clare (London: George Allen and Unwin, 1926); Cassirer, *Philosophy of Symbolic Forms;* Rosenfield, "Practical Celebration of Epideictic; and Steiner, *Real Presences.* All these writers feel that, prior to our seeing of the world around us in terms of stable and static forms, we under-stand it from within our inescapable embedding within a ceaseless, two-way flow of spontaneously responsive, living activity—we have a *participative* understanding of it. Thus, as Steiner puts it in "'Critic'/'Reader,'" in our reading of a text, we proceed "*as if* the text was the housing of forces and meanings, of meanings of meaning, whose lodging within the executive verbal form was one of 'incarnation.' [We read] *as if* . . . the singular presence of the life of meaning in the text and work of art was 'a real presence' irreducible to analytic summation and resistant to judgment in the sense in which the critic can and must judge" (85). I have also myself attempted a comprehensive exploration of these issues with respect to our attempts to understand linguistic meaning in J. Shot-ter, "'Real Presences': Meaning as Living Movement in a Participatory World," *Theory and Psychol-ogy* 13, no. 3 (2003): 577–609.

39. N. R. Hanson, *Patterns of Discovery* (Cambridge: Cambridge University Press, 1958), 1.

40. Ibid., 3.

41. Ibid., 15.

42. Wittgenstein, *Zettel,* no. 543.

43. Here we might note Tucker's (2001) claim that the oscillations between one or another understanding of an ambiguous figure is a matter of "a conscious choice between two interpre-tations" ("Figure, Ground and Presence," 401).

44. Hanson, *Patterns of Discovery,* 11 (my additions).

45. Ibid., 19.

46. Wittgenstein, *Investigations,* no. 122.

47. Hanson, *Patterns of Discovery,* 21.

48. E. Ochs, S. Jacoby, and P. Gonzales, "Interpretive Journeys: How Physicists Talk and Travel through Graphic Space," *Connections* 1 (1994): 151–71; E. Ochs and S. Jacoby, "Down to the Wire: The Cultural Clock of Physicists and the Discourse of Consensus," *Language in Society* 26 (1997): 1–27; and E. Ochs, P. Gonzales, and S. Jacoby, "'When I Come Down I'm in the Domain State': Grammar and Graphic Representation in the Interpretive Activity of Physicists," in *Interaction and Grammar,* ed. E. Ochs, E. Schegloff, and S. Thompson, 328–69 (Cambridge: Cambridge Uni-versity Press, 1996).

49. Ochs, Jacoby, and Gonzales, "Interpretive Journeys," 163; also see Ochs and Jacoby, "Down to the Wire."

50. Ochs, Jacoby, and Gonzales, "Interpretive Journeys," 164.

51. Ochs, Gonzales, and Jacoby, "When I Come Down I'm in the Domain State," 328–69; and Ochs, Jacoby, and Gonzales, "Interpretive Journeys," 151–71.

52. Levy-Bruhl, *How Natives Think,* 38.

53. Ibid.

54. See especially R. Doyle, *On Beyond Living: Rhetorical Transformations of the Life Sciences* (Stanford, Calif.: Stanford University Press, 1997).

55. E. Fox Keller, "Dialogue," in *New Paradigms, Culture, and Subjectivity,* ed. D. F. Schnitman and J. Schnitman, 38 (Cresskill, N.J.: Hampton Press, 2002).

56. Keller, "Dialogue," 38.

57. E. Fox Keller, *Refiguring Life: Metaphors of Twentieth-Century Biology* (New York: Columbia University Press, 1995), 18.

58. Ibid., 19.

59. E. Schrödinger, *What Is Life? The Physical Aspect of the Living Cell & Mind and Matter* (Cambridge: Cambridge University Press, 1967), 23.

60. Wittgenstein, *Zettel*, no. 444.

61. Wittgenstein, too, makes a very similar comment in remarking: "The proposition seems set over against us as a judge and we feel answerable to it. It seems to demand that reality be compared with it." L. Wittgenstein, *Philosophical Grammar,* ed. Rush Rhees and trans. A. Kenny (Oxford: Blackwell, 1974), 132, no. 85. Also, in Wittgenstein, *Philosophical Investigations,* he speaks of the "battle against the bewitchment of our intelligence by means of language" (no. 109), and in *On Certainty,* of "[t]he propositions that one comes back to as if bewitched—these I should like to expunge from philosophical language" (no. 31).

62. Brook, *The Empty Space,* 45.

63. As Ochs, Jacoby, and Gonzales note, "Visual representations are treated [in their] collaborative interpretative activity as stages on which scientists dramatize understandings of their own and others' work" ("Interpretive Journeys," 152).

64. R. Rorty, *Philosophy and the Mirror of Nature* (Princeton, N.J.: Princeton University Press, 1979), 12.

65. Hanson, *Patterns of Discovery,* 30.

66. Ibid., 118.

Part 4

*E*pideictic Identifications and Divisions

John C. Adams

14

$\mathcal{E}$pideictic and Its Cultured Reception
In Memory of the Firefighters

The enduring cultural practice of epideictic rhetoric has undergone extensive scholarly commentary. Once considered "mere" entertainment or superficial self-display,[1] ancient epideictic is now accorded, by some commentators, greater cultural significance relative to education, building and maintaining community, and the oratory of politics and law.[2] The enduring importance of this ancient practice is nowhere better illustrated than during a political community's experience of a palpable need for words to cope with calamitous events, a need that Lincoln fulfilled exceptionally at the Gettysburg battlefield.[3] Yet, it seems evident from the aftermath of the September 11 terrorist destruction of New York City's twin towers that leaders may fail to deliver epideictic rhetoric suited to their immediate occasion even as citizens and commentators feel the need for speeches to revisit and appropriately memorialize their painful loss.[4]

This chapter argues for an account of epideictic that emphasizes the ways in which its appropriate reception requires deeply cultured ways of being that are shared by speakers and listeners. Central to this position is what I call a "linguistic predisposition," an "open" inclination toward the potential of speech to console, commemorate, inspire, or otherwise lend meaning to events of importance in the life of a political community. I consider as an example former president Clinton's speech delivered in memory of firefighters who lost their lives in the Worcester warehouse fire of December 3, 1999.

If one is unable to observe virtue in the firefighters' commemorated deeds, it may be because one lacks the culturally prompted predisposition toward speech and language needed to do so competently. For epideictic to serve an educative civic function, as some have claimed,[5] both orator and audience must share the same linguistic predisposition toward the potential of speech to reveal as incontestably good the actions exhibited as morally exemplary. I take the position, then, that the experience of epideictic as educative requires both the display of moral virtue through exemplary actions *and* a culturally prompted recognition of the display as a commemorative speech act *requiring* its reception as a celebration of civic virtue. Together, the linguistic display and its competent reception enable the commemoration of what is best in human community. Once commemorated, the actions are established as paradigms of virtue and may be summoned as precedents to future cases of moral reasoning.

Epideictic's Educational Function: Observing Virtue

"Epideictic" is derived from the transliterated Greek *epideixis*—making known or manifest, an exhibition, a display. Aristotle, in his *Rhetoric*, theorized that epideictic exhibited or manifested qualities of a person's actions as exemplary of virtue (or of vice) and, thus, as worthy of praise (or blame) or, as Rosenfield put it, of acknowledgement (or disparagement).[6] Eulogies, for example, are epideictic speeches delivered at memorial services to praise or acknowledge the virtues of the dead. Wills reminds us that eulogies are traceable to Pericles' famous *epitaphios logos,* or state funeral oration, and that Lincoln's speech at Gettysburg used some of the stock antithetical topoi found in Pericles' speech.[7]

Perelman and Olbrechts-Tyteca articulated a contemporary perspective on epideictic founded on its purported educational or didactic function. As they put it:

> The speaker engaged in epideictic discourse is very close to being an educator. Since what he is going to say does not arouse controversy, since no immediate practical interest is ever involved, and there is no question of attacking or defending, but simply of promoting values that are shared in the community. . . . For it is not his own cause or viewpoint that he is defending, but that of his entire audience.[8]

Perelman and Olbrechts-Tyteca took Isocrates as their classical starting point for developing their view of epideictic as didactic. Gerard Hauser claimed that Perelman and Olbrechts-Tyteca used an Isocrates quote to amplify their claim that "the values emphasized by this genre [epideictic] must be ones already deemed worthy of providing guidance,"[9] but more important, the citation showed that the two scholars presumed that "the educative function they emphasize for epideictic spans from the present to the period when its theory originated."[10]

Christine Oravec, another contemporary commentator on epideictic, further illuminates the educative function. According to Oravec, any didactic or educative qualities of epideictic must be rooted in the performance of a social function. The most important aspect of that social function involves the reciprocal relationship between speaker and audience—the speaker and listeners together supply the materials for the speech, and the listeners seek illuminating and important statements made by the speaker from the materials they both supply. For example, if the speaker and listeners share a common sense of the meaning and value of the virtue of courage, the listeners judge the speech with respect to the speaker's ability to take their shared beliefs about courage and apply them so they are able to recognize and celebrate courage as it is exemplified by the person who is the subject of the speech—to participate together in appreciating and sharing a concept of the good. Or, as Oravec has written:

> The epideictic speaker formulates principles derived from the common store of his audience, then applies these principles to well-known or typical objects or persons. From this act of application the audience "learns" or "understands" the connection between the principle and the manifestation of the principle, an act of comprehension which illuminates their own experience and increases their trust in the speaker's judgment.[11]

In this view, the epideictic speaker gives voice to the otherwise unexpressed virtues admired by the audience as they are exemplified in a particular case or manifestation (for example, a firefighter who sacrificed his life to rescue a person from a burning building). Only when the epideictic speaker succeeds in making apparent a mutual sense of the praiseworthy (or blameworthy) can the audience participate as *theoroi* rather than as judges and reflect on the meaning of the virtues the exemplary actions display. As Walker put it, "[T]he role of an epideictic's audience is not a *krites* but a *theoros,* that is, one who is to make 'observations' (*theoriai*) about what is praiseworthy, preferable, desirable or worthy of belief in the speaker's *logos.*"[12]

Speakers exhibit that they are persons of practical wisdom, or *phronesis,* through their demonstrated grasp of the praiseworthy in their speeches. They can recognize in particular cases ideas held by their audiences that bear on virtue. As Hauser said with respect to Aristotle's formulation, the speaker in this sense also models *phronesis* for the listeners, gathering and projecting his or her ethos as *phronimos*—as a bearer of practical wisdom. Aristotle's implied idea of the model rhetor is the bearer of practical wisdom who displays its qualities through the act of speaking and the substance of the speech, providing a source of rhetorical and ethical *mimesis* for the listeners.[13] Thus, when such a person speaks of "courage" (for example), the person is trusted only insofar as he or she displays through the speech an understanding of what courage is. That understanding must resonate with the audience through fitting exhibition of courage enacted in particular deeds performed by those whose actions the speech commemorates.

The speakers who praise or blame demonstrate at one stroke their own characters and the characters of their audiences through the virtues displayed in their speeches. A speaker becomes for all assembled the voice of the virtuous and good in the immediate occasion. That sets a demanding challenge for all who take up the obligation to make epideictic speech. As Oravec put it:

> The epideictic orator, then, faces a most difficult test, because the value of his discourse depends not upon the audience's faculty of choice concerning things which are already past or are to come but upon the common and present experience of the praiseworthy object's distinctive quality.[14]

As such, epideictic speech may become the "measure" against which future and past deeds are put. As Aristotle notes, forensic and deliberative rhetoric often partake of epideictic's "attributions" insofar as audiences often judge past deeds or proposed future deeds in light of the very ideas of virtue that epideictic extols. For example, one spur to future action is the belief that the action, once performed, will prove virtuous and, therefore, worthy of praise during some future epideictic celebration when one is remembered for good works. Aristotle raised this point to the level of a strategic, persuasive principle in his *Rhetoric* when he stated, "[I]f you desire to praise, look what you would suggest; if you desire to suggest, look what you would praise."[15]

In summary, epideictic, in this formulation, serves an educational function in the sense that its practice occasions the enacted display and observation of virtue. Since virtuous qualities are presented as incontestable, the rhetorical means for displaying them are not arguments per se, but paradigmatic examples designed to *amplify* in narrative form the qualities being exhibited for public commemoration and celebration. I shall turn next to that feature of an educational epideictic.

Epideictic's Practical Function: The Paradigm Case

The educative function of epideictic is redeemed when speaker and audience are capable of joining together in contemplating, as Oravec puts it, "the common and present experience of the praiseworthy object's distinctive quality."[16] This experience requires display of distinctive moral qualities through concrete actions as well as the speaker's and audience's cultured predisposition to recognize those actions as exemplary of virtue and, thus, meaningfully participate in commemorative observance. I shall address these two dimensions respectively in this and the next section.

Epideictic displays paradigm cases that embody presently operative, but contingent, concepts of virtue. As concrete and vividly depicted exemplars of the good drawn from the actual deeds of community members, they forcefully display virtue's reality. Rosenfield puts this point well:

> Closely related to *epideixis* is *paradeigma* ("concrete example"), used as a force for inducing belief. . . . The example used to amplify does not support a contention so much as it inspires the listener by "setting an example" before his eyes for admiration. Its authority issues from its capacity to invite the auditor to *listen,* to take heed of its meaning. . . . The epideictic orator seizes on and embellishes particular incidents in his subject's career (*episodioi*) in order to set free on the audience the radiance incorporated in the events (compassion in the case of Lincoln, humility in Saint Francis).[17]

To extend this point generally, the excellence exhibited in the *humanity* of those praised not only is revealed for acknowledgement, but it becomes a common point of identification, which, at a minimum, enables recognition that one of "us" exemplifies virtue. The recognition may induce pride in one's community and inspire auditors with a sense of *their* potential to also act virtuously.

As the rhetorical devices of amplification are woven around the deed's commemoration and spun into the observers' communal awareness (*sensus communis*), the actor's attachments to the community become palpable and may evoke a mixed emotional response —sorrow, joy, gratitude, awe. The emotional experience completes the observers' intellectual grasp (understanding) of the relationship between the concept of virtue and its concrete manifestation in an exemplar. For example, the audience must appropriately *feel* the influence of a community member's courage to fully interpret the exemplar's significance. It is the unquestionable quality of communal feeling as much as the conceptual grasp of the narrated paradigm case's exemplification of virtue that fixes the exemplar's place in public memory. Once memorialized through epideictic display, the exemplar of virtue becomes a settled case employed as a point of reference in deliberations regarding the "good" and its place as a motive—attributed or avowed—in judging the virtue of other actions the case typifies.[18]

As much as they may be experienced as indubitable at a given time and place, the virtues that epideictic speakers exemplify through paradigm cases are contingent and, thus, are subject to change. That is, while the virtues' names persist (for example, "gentleness"), the deeds that exemplify them necessarily shift and change across contexts. This sort of change is inevitable in many cases and possible in all cases, but epideictic rhetoric as practiced does not serve an interest in change. Rather, it takes up relatively enduring, commonplace concepts of the good and perpetuates them through fresh exemplars that manifest virtue's continuing presence across the contingencies of time and circumstance that life's flow manifests. So, remarkably (or maybe unremarkably), Aristotle's commonplace concept of courage is still affirmed by exemplars that are continuously rediscovered in concrete cases and commemorated by epideictic across centuries of human travail.[19] In a way, and as I shall argue later, epideictic exemplification opposes the kind of critical consciousness that operates to contest or "unmask" virtues or the actions that purportedly exemplify them. That is, even epideictic's employment to blame critically reaffirms the virtues that give instances of vice their meaning to a given community.

Any concept can in principle be contested, but epideictic rhetoric runs counter to such critical awareness and functions instead to enable recognition of and regard for notable deeds. Without discourse that is valued in its own right for acknowledging, celebrating, and deepening one's adherence to operative concepts of the good, social community would be rent by endless semiosis or *aporia*. Again, there has to be a settled starting point in order to get somewhere—with no beginning there is no end, both in the temporal and axiological senses. For example, I will not be able to love if I am able only to endlessly ask "What is love?" in the recognition that there are infinite possible answers to the question and in the belief that further questioning is the aim of questioning. Epideictic rhetoric, on the other hand, gives answers in the form of concrete exemplars that may manifest the appearance of love in human experience.

We can better understand the operations of exemplary actions in epideictic in relation to paradigm cases deployed in moral reasoning. In moral reasoning, paradigm cases are used as points of reference to determine whether a proposed course of action or an action already performed is morally efficacious. The paradigm case is taken as the indubitable starting point for moral reasoning. It is the premise or precedent that is used as a criterion for gauging deeds. Where proposed lines of action or past deeds fall at the edges of the paradigm case, deliberations take place to determine whether, or if, they may be acceptable as marginal cases. Where cases clearly fall outside the range of the paradigm case, they are judged to be morally inefficacious, and from there determinations are made whether to sanction a deed already performed or to abstain from a proposed course of action that would fall beyond the paradigm case's range of coverage. In addition, in rare instances an anomalous case can itself become accepted as a "type case" in the face of unprecedented moral exigencies brought about by new technologies or other innovations (for example, cloning, "harvesting" fetal tissue).

Jonsen and Toulmin present the characteristics of paradigm cases involved in moral reasoning or casuistry that have persisted at least since the Renaissance.[20] There is remarkable stability in the "paradigms of virtue" that work their way through the practice of moral reasoning and form the basis of case ethics. This stability indicates, among other things, that there is social value ascribed to understanding moral reasoning in their light. Epideictic, similarly, draws upon the presumptive power of exemplary actions that "carry conclusive weight, absent 'exceptional' circumstances."[21] In so doing, it displays what is worthy of praise and narrates the example as a contemporary point of reference. Drawing on the rhetorical power of *ekphrasis* to enable a verbal vision of virtue, the commemorated deed's depiction scripts out possibilities for *mimesis*. That is, the ascription of virtue to deeds enables their categorization as charges to action. The paradigm case assists moral deliberation by bridging the uniqueness of every event with a settled and embodied point of comparison. In essence, in their deliberations casuists seek analogies or disanalogies between present cases and paradigm cases.

Epideictic rhetoric continuously rehearses and updates the paradigms of virtue to perpetuate passionate and reasonable ways of thinking about virtue and vice. But again, the employment of paradigms of virtue in moral reasoning is a practice that has had its critics. For example, Blaise Pascal's *Provincial Letters* probably served to contribute to casuistry's disrepute and widespread mistrust of its efficacy as a means of resolving moral quandaries.[22] His criticisms are readily extended to the practice of epideictic as far as it may uncritically contribute rhetorically compelling examples to the casuistry mill. Pascal's hostility toward casuistry was related to the emergent philosophic "faith" in scientific modes of reasoning and the belief that abstract, context-free principles would in their own right become the measures of moral worth. Paradigm cases of virtue were rejected as starting points, along with rhetoric, in part because of the cases' status as examples and rhetoric's role as the technique of their persuasive portrayal as particular, concrete, sensuous, pathos-charged instances. The cases' particularity ran contrary to philosophy's interest in employing disembodied "axiomatic" principles as motives to right conduct. Philosophically derived ethical principles, or axioms, were viewed by contemporaries as correctives to rhetoric's fixation on the "particular case" and its practitioners' perceived quest for effectiveness instead of truth.

The perceived inappropriateness and ineffectiveness of casuistry among a group of people, just as the failure of epideictic to prompt virtue's acknowledgment, may be occasioned by a group's disposition toward language, life, and learning that forecloses the possibility of its reception. When the very idea of epideictic as a valued cultural performance with worthwhile communal purposes becomes threatened, or consequently goes unperformed, its educational function loses legitimacy to the point that the "way of being" its practice perpetuates may cease to exist. Hauser points to this prospect:

> [T]he didactic function of epideictic suggests that as a public sphere ceases to celebrate public morality and, instead, substitutes a scientistic or a bureaucratic model of public relations for political relations, the public that inhabits this sphere is denied the very instruction on which its survival as a politically relevant body depends. . . . A public illiterate in models of proper conduct and inarticulate in expressing the moral bases for its beliefs soon becomes moribund and relinquishes the discursive basis for its political actions to authority or force.[23]

To this I will now add that a public bereft of the right predisposition for enabling the production and *appropriate reception* of epideictic will not be able to recognize virtue, let alone celebrate or learn about it. Such a public is not inclined to be open to the potential of speech to reveal excellence in human experience and, thus, cannot learn from it. Unless inclined positively toward speech's potential to reveal virtue, people called upon to observe epideictic speech will lack the capacity to take its exemplars of excellence to heart, to find in them sources of social inspiration, and to share them with others as manifesting qualities essential to a good civic life.

Epideictic's Cultural Function: The Predisposition to Observe Virtue

Whenever epideictic speakers display actions, there is the presumption that speakers and audiences are joined in a cultured predisposition to observe those actions as exemplary of community virtues. On this point, commentators concerned with the ethics of rhetoric in general, and with epideictic in particular, seem to be in accord. For example, Richard Weaver argued that all of culture crystallizes around fundamental sentiments or dispositions toward the world and other people. This is what he calls the "metaphysical dream," which is "an intuitive feeling about the immanent nature of reality."[24] The metaphysical dream is pre-rational and, it goes almost without saying, precritical. As he put it, "If the disposition is wrong, reason increases maleficence; if it is right, reason orders and furthers the good."[25] Rosenfield, similarly, discusses the experience of epideictic in terms of a disposition that is open to experience reality's disclosure in itself or to its re-presentation through epideictic speech.[26] Those ill disposed toward openly participating in epideictic celebration close off the potential to experience that which is no less than wonderful in human life, seeking "closure" with the unsettling experience by returning to familiar partisan preferences and divisive inclinations. But it is through grateful contemplation and acknowledgement of that which is wonderful that people become joined in fundamental attitudes necessary for meaningful civic life.[27]

Based on these commentaries, I suggest that we may (or may not) possess an inclination toward speech's potential to reveal virtue, which I call a "linguistic predisposition." Linguistic predispositions, like any other kind of fundamental attitudinal orientation, vary. One may hold a closed linguistic predisposition, attitude, or inclination toward speech's potential to exhibit virtue and be unreceptive to efforts at actualizing that potential in particular, situated speech acts. On the other hand, one may embrace an open linguistic predisposition toward the potential of speech to reveal virtue and be receptive to situated efforts at its actualization. Nor is it unusual to experience tensions between the two contrary dispositions in particular cases. In any case, however, one's capacity to witness or observe displays of virtue, to take them to heart and reflect upon them, is decided at least partly—if not largely—from one's prior inclinations about speech's potential to display, and thereby teach, virtue.

Linguistic predispositions are revealed in speech-community members' talk about talk —in widely accepted maxims and metaphors that indicate people's shared assumptions about (1) speech's place in their lives, (2) what speech can or cannot do, and (3) why and how it can or cannot do it. What some have called "linguistic values" are also expressions that manifest inclinations ranging, on the one hand, from the tendency to denigrate or trivialize speech and related efforts to re-present virtue in words to, on the other, the inclination to remain open, if only provisionally, to speech's potential to reveal virtue.[28] For example, the statements "talk is cheap" and "faith comes through hearing" express quite different expectations about the quality of experience enabled through speech. They may be among the different beliefs about language that express underlying inclinations toward speech's potential to reveal virtue.

Clearly, under the assumption that all the stories of speech's place and accounts of its capabilities are cultural constructions, it is not necessary to adhere to any particular belief about speech and, in this case, any given concept of epideictic rhetoric. The idea of epideictic rhetoric expounded in this chapter and its relation to teaching and learning and setting paradigm cases is not derived from a scientific description of natural order where failure to believe it and embrace it would be a sign of error, as, for example, if one persisted in believing that the earth is flat in the face of evidence to the contrary. One's refusal to believe or embrace a given idea of speech is a matter of choice—a choice that has consequences, ultimately, for the kind of community constituted through acts of communication and one's membership in it. Some linguistic predispositions will enable one to see and experience virtue when it is publicly displayed in exemplary cases. Others may foreclose that possibility. The choice reveals one's preferred orientation toward words for whatever reason. In the final analysis, that choice is founded on fundamental inclinations toward language's potential. The shared beliefs and values that express those inclinations do no less than exhibit a social order wherein the range of aims constituted by the play of speech acts —their culturally prompted recognition, competent performance, and appropriate reception—induces characteristic qualities of experience at occasions of being together that are constitutive of ways of life.

The notion of a linguistic predisposition is at least compatible with Weaver's metaphysics of culture and Rosenfield's phenomenology of the epideictic experience, but I suggest that linguistic predispositions can be redirected and reformed through cultural promptings and are not solely a function of personality nor of social inspiration alone. Ours is a culture that demonstrates on an almost daily basis its distrust of public words, whether effectively and movingly used or artfully or dully expressed. But the values and beliefs expressing that underlying predisposition to distrust language, like any other cultural phenomena, are not written in stone. People can be made to see how different values and beliefs about speech could, in some cases, afford them qualities of experience they will find desirable. They can be induced to adopt, if only provisionally, alternative beliefs and values that work to redispose them toward speech.

Addressing the issue of how to redirect fundamental tendencies so that the unreceptive become receptive to speech's potential to exhibit virtue requires a full reconsideration of the types of rhetoric that takes us beyond the bounds of what is possible in this one chapter. For example, the eloquence of an epideictic speech can exhibit *itself* as a virtue as it powerfully marshals words to display qualities of excellence in the persons it praises. Exhortation, as a rhetoric of comparative goods and their consequences, can work to prompt shifts in beliefs about speech and language and thereby redispose those who bear them toward greater openness to commemorative speech. Commentators stress that epideictic exhibits qualities of excellence that often are reshaped into the leading premises of deliberative and legal rhetoric. It is plausible that deliberation about the value of speech can incline people to become more open to speech's potential to publicly celebrate virtue, if only provisionally, to reveal the qualities of excellence that constitute a civic community.

In Memory of the Firefighters

The experience of epideictic requires display of distinctive moral qualities through portrayals of concrete actions as well as the cultured linguistic predisposition to observe in speech actions that are exemplary of virtue. Meaningful commemorative observance cannot proceed otherwise. Accordingly, I contended (1) that epideictic speech may serve a civic educational function (2) by the rhetorically competent exhibition of exemplary cases of virtue (3) for a community of rightly predisposed observers (4) who, as a consequence, observe the exemplars as self-evident or indubitable and (5) take them up as paradigms to be employed in subsequent cases of moral reasoning. In this section I propose to show how epideictic assumes linguistic predispositions that enable listeners to participate in observance of virtuous action during a eulogy of six firefighters killed in Worcester, Massachusetts.[29]

On Friday, December 3, 1999, in Worcester, Massachusetts, there was a terrible fire that took the lives of six firefighters who went into a flaming warehouse in the belief that there were two homeless people trapped inside. Initially, two firefighters went in to save them. When the two firefighters became trapped, four additional firefighters went in to rescue their comrades and the homeless people. All six firefighters died in the fire. Subsequently, it was discovered that the two homeless people had actually started the fire by knocking over a candle as they quarreled. However, they were not in the warehouse when the firefighters entered.

An outpouring of grief and the commemoration of the firefighters' courageous deeds spontaneously arose throughout the community. The spontaneous outpouring indicates that the community of Worcester was appropriately disposed to value acts of commemoration. In keeping with this disposition, a memorial ceremony was held specifically to publicly honor the firefighters, commemorate their deeds, and assuage the community's grief.

Among others, President Clinton gave a speech at the memorial held in Worcester (December 9, 1999). He began his speech by remarking on how words are not sufficient to "alleviate the pain you feel now."[30] He went on to acknowledge the losses of the family members and the friends and colleagues of the firefighters and thereby enlarged the circle of identification by acknowledging that the presence of thousands of people at the event indicated, better than words, that "your tragedy is ours; your men are ours; our whole country honors them and you." As president, Clinton was able, and probably expected, to bring to awareness the national (rather than merely local) character of the firefighters' virtue as exemplars of the spirit of public service that animates those who work on behalf of the community and, in its most general manifestation, the nation.

Clinton went on to quote Benjamin Franklin's "Brave Men at Fires," in which Franklin said that the motive for fighting fires is "not for the sake of reward or fame; but they have a reward in themselves, and they love one another." This further established that one of the virtues of firefighters, as a corollary of their courage, is their selfless willingness to risk their lives *together* in service to their community. The six men who died were referred to as "brave men who found a reward in firefighting, who loved one another. Six men who, in turn, richly rewarded this community." The play on the word "reward" emphasizes the impact on the community of their selfless desire to serve together.

As the speech developed further, Clinton ascribed part of the motive for the firefighters' deeds to divine forces—to God's "still, small voice." This is important, for it imbues their actions with an order of grace and, in the context of the eulogy, assures that they acted in accord with God's will and will, therefore, rest in peace. Clinton characterized their inspiration as their "dream to serve, to save lives, and to stick together" and attributed this inspiration to their listening to God's voice.

He drew the firefighters' deeds further into a circle of national and international import, emphasizing that their deeds were driven by virtues that transcend regional interests, as evidenced in the crowd gathered to commemorate their deeds: "Like their fellow firefighters everywhere, they embodied the best of our nation." To be sure, this statement raises the significance of their deeds to national and international levels, emphasizing the deeds' transcendence and imbuing them with a spiritual quality. Clinton ended his speech by bearing witness to the community's "love" of the firefighters, showing the community's ethos as appropriately with, and responsive to, the firefighters' virtuous deeds—their communal debt of gratitude is paid as their love parallels God's love, bringing heaven and earth together by their mutual regard for the deceased firefighters and the courageous sacrifice they selflessly performed for the good of the community.

In keeping with classical epideictic's engagement of encomia, Clinton's speech is replete with references to the firefighters' conscious striving after high ideals that took them in harm's way and took their lives. Their deeds are screened through scriptural passages and condolences to family members, comrades, and friends, indicating that there is a spiritual sensibility assumed by Clinton to be operative in the audience.

The conclusions the speech reaches regarding the virtues exemplified by the firefighter's deeds are indubitable. This is evident because the speech simply tells the story without guile and clearly without an intended audience in view that is resistant to its assertions—it does not "make a case." Similarly, the references to family, comrades, and friends poignantly provide them with words of comfort recognizing the significance of these kinds of social ties and grief's depth at the loss of loved ones.

The speech displays the firefighters' actions as paradigms of virtue. Again, as Clinton stated:

> Like their fellow firefighters everywhere, they embodied the best of our nation— of commitment and community, of teamwork and trust—values at the core of our character, values reflected in the daily service not only of those we lost, but in this awesome parade of men and women who have come from all over our country and from some countries beyond our border to honor their comrades and console their families.

The passage above exhibits the firefighters' virtues as though they are noncontroversial "facts of the matter" that must be acknowledged, provided that the audience has acquired the cultured predisposition to do so. Clearly, the Worcester community *was* predisposed to do so. The spontaneity of the community's outpouring of grief and the speech's content and positive reception (as reflected in many accounts) clearly illustrate epideictic's educative function. As the firefighter's deeds are taken up into public memory, they become paradigm cases of public virtue that can serve as points of departure in future talks about duty's laudable motives, the necessity of a community's grateful acknowledgement, and the prospect of individuals' inspired emulation.

As Worcester's case clearly illustrates, there *are* communities of listeners able to recognize together the unquestioned virtue of selfless acts of courage—of risking one's life to rescue others—not simply because one may be a bystander presented with an opportunity for doing so, but because one has consciously devoted one's own life to public service. The virtues extolled through the firefighters' exemplary actions are as much about Worcester's citizens as they are about the firefighters who died. The firefighters exemplified selflessness in public service, courage, religiosity, and love of family and comrades. These are the qualities that Clinton's epideictic speech amplifies not only about the dead firemen, but about the community. That is what it means to be a citizen of Worcester or, more broadly, an American citizen (however idealized).

Together, as they publicly commemorate the firefighters' selfless acts built on foresworn commitments, the audience and Clinton perform a way of being together that privileges the social over the individual and reaffirms their mutual commitment to perpetuate its existence through the depths of grief and gratitude the speech evokes. In a way, the memorial and its speeches constitute a public thanksgiving as much as mourning the loss of community members, parents, spouses, and comrades.

If one is only able to frame Clinton's speech, and the memorial ceremony itself, with a spirit of distrust rooted in an ethic of cynicism, the speech and its occasion may become sources of derision rather than inspiration—nothing is learned, nothing is gained. In this interpretation, it could very well be the case that one is not "culturally competent" in the reception of epideictic. Put slightly otherwise, one is unable to open oneself to the influence of the speech in one's life because one is not rightly disposed toward the speech's potential to reveal excellence in human experience. In short, there must be a predisposition to be affected by the speech per se prior to its utterance. One must find the "good reasons" for being so affected in one's community and in oneself as representative of the community.[31] One must be linguistically predisposed to recognize epideictic's aim and value its social function in order to practice its reception by the enabling virtue of *charitable* observation.[32] For example, if one is predisposed to position oneself as if "all the world's a courtroom," one may be unaffected by epideictic. That is, insofar as it does not present arguments appropriate to one's projected sense of its litigious scene, and one's seemingly fitting role as a juror therein, epideictic fails because it fails to make a case.

As a speech act, epideictic may be understood as an avowal. As such, *it must be taken seriously* if one is to take it to heart—if one is to appropriately "observe" it. However, this is not to say that a predisposition toward openness to epideictic speech will preclude the rejection of its substantive claims. For example, if a speaker cites an act of reckless abandon (for example, a stunt in the movie *Jackass*) as an example of courage, there may be no good reason even for a charitably disposed listener to accept it as exemplary of courage. Thus, the predisposition toward openness can be altered by good reasons during the course of the discourse. The speaker's cited example must align with accepted "like" examples in order to associate it with the listener's operative concept of virtue. For it is the impression of the cited example's identification with similar and settled examples that enables its induction into the pantheon of the community's type cases. As such, the cited example becomes the most current operative representative case. Oftentimes the example's identification will be made evident as a strategy of amplification by comparing the present case with past cases, as Clinton did with his citation of Franklin's "Brave Men at Fires" and passages from the Bible.

As in interpersonal encounters, there is great risk involved in being so open to the influence of others as to take their every word at their word—to trust in their sincerity. However, without a predisposition to be open and trusting (alluded to by Rosenfield), the opportunity to "theoretically" encounter, and be moved by, virtue's exemplars is utterly lost.[33] As with any genre of discourse, one may be predisposed critically (or uncharitably) to tune it out as unworthy of notice or out of fear of being influenced by it. For example, in the case of television "commercials" (a genre of discourse), there is technology specifically designed to engage a negative predisposition toward them by skipping over them in the course of recording or playing back the desired programming. Similarly, one may choose to forego attendance at a memorial service because of a negative predisposition toward memorial services per se and the kinds of speeches their cultured scene requires.[34]

Participation in epideictic observance cannot transpire without exemplary actions that are incontestable and without the right disposition for competent, cultured reception of speech commemorating those actions *as* embodiments of virtue. One cannot have an "observance" with the "right" disposition alone; one needs incontestable actions that are exemplary of virtue. Nor can one have incontestable actions if the audience is not predisposed to acknowledge them gratefully as manifestations of excellence in human life. In sum, epideictic's moral exemplars "teach" virtue by virtue of their influence on appropriately open, trusting, and willing observers—listeners willing and able to construct themselves as observers.

Conclusion

By making the cultural scene of this chapter's focus on epideictic a paramount concern, I have intended to make as transparent as possible that the quality of experience one may have at the reading or hearing of speeches is significantly impacted by one's deeply cultured linguistic predispositions. The sensibilities they instantiate may be understood as competencies insofar as they motivate practices serving valued social functions. In addition, as explained in this chapter, linguistic predispositions set interpretive frames that, in the case of epideictic, may enable or disable its educational, social, and practical functions.

The competency I describe entails aptly putting together what culturally belongs together—an inclination toward charitable observation and celebratory epideictic speech. This predisposition toward alignment gives precedence to taking encomium seriously—it instantiates a bias similar in many respects to the truth bias we bear in everyday life, where we take for granted that people are telling us the truth unless we have good reason to believe otherwise. The "good reason to believe otherwise" is usually the result of discovering that we have been lied to. One's global mistrust of public encomium, one's predisposition to deride its sincerity and not take it seriously as it is publicly performed may be valorized as a given listener's enabling critical apparatus. However, in fact, it may actually *disable* one from enacting one's solidarity—from *being* in solidarity—with any given community. That is, global distrust of public praise may be a source of alienation or anomie, as one is unable to affect a disposition that is to the point. A disposition on point delivers one from the position of outsider and, perhaps, might even fulfill a longing to belong. In a similar sense, failure to acknowledge—to take to heart—the virtues displayed in Clinton's speech actually positions one outside, or in opposition to, the assembled Worcester community, as well as the national and international communities Clinton's speech evokes.

The citizens of Worcester possessed a linguistic predisposition that enabled them to join in meaningful recognition of their solidarity as members of a shared community. Their membership is betokened by their common desire to assuage their grief and deepen their commitment to the civic virtues they celebrated together. At the same time, they remained unique individuals capable of becoming, at other times and places, members of partisan groups locked in conflict over dissimilar political interests. The common inspiration of the transcendent idea of community afforded by the epideictic occasion and their being together at the commemoration the occasion instantiated enabled them to acknowledge and reflect on their *community*'s sense of civic virtue amidst all diversity. At that occasion, they are all citizens of Worcester, gratefully commemorating the virtue of the firefighters who sacrificed their lives for the community's good.

The assembly gathered at the memorial observance becomes itself a paradigm case of a virtuous pluralistic community teaching a lesson that may be referred to by its members as future exigencies arise that must be dealt with in solidarity as a unified community. In sum, the firefighters' celebrated civic virtue respects the *people* who make up the community they serve—not the white people, or the elderly people, or even the men and the women, but *people* who populate a city conceived to serve public as well as individual interests.

Finally, Clinton's speech publicly celebrates the virtues of courage, self-sacrifice, comradeship, religiosity, and service exemplified by the concrete reality of the firefighters' deeds. After September 11, 2001, similar themes and epideictic purposes were enacted across the United States, indicating that there are occasions in contemporary culture when people are willing and able to downplay their differences and join together as citizens. They found an identity on such occasions, a way of being together, that was based on unity, mutual understanding, and shared gratitude for civic virtues exhibited by those among them who put the good of community before their self-interest.

The nearly universal recognition of the excellence of public servants engaging in risk taking on behalf of the people celebrates the principle of unity in diversity that keynotes a healthy republic's ethos. That is, the epideictic celebration of civic virtue publicly manages the dynamic play of unity's and diversity's dialectical opposition. Community servants are praised for their identification with the humanity of those they serve—as people—without reference to competing identifications that in other contexts, rightfully or not, would set them apart. Audience members predisposed by the sentiment of charity to observe epideictic as the guileless and sincere commemoration of virtuous deeds will learn by the deeds exemplified that there are ways of being and being together that hold an otherwise diverse community together after all.

There are, then, signs of epideictic's endurance today. The question that remains for epideictic—this most ancient "rhetoric of display"—is whether people can maintain the requisite shared linguistic predisposition to observe virtue through speech within a culture inclined increasingly toward skepticism, if not cynicism. This chapter optimistically contends that such a predisposition can be not only maintained but instilled in those who lack it—it can be learned. Whether we are as motivated to search out the qualities of concord as much as those conducive to discord is no mere academic matter; it goes to the heart of our prospects for common identity as members of a civic community in a pluralistic world.

Notes

1. J. Richard Chase, "The Classical Conception of Epideictic," *Quarterly Journal of Speech* 47 (1961): 293–300.

2. See, for example, Jeffrey Walker, *Rhetoric and Poetics in Antiquity* (New York: Oxford University Press, 2000); Edward Schiappa, *The Beginnings of Rhetorical Theory in Classical Greece* (New Haven: Yale University Press, 1999); Gerard A. Hauser, "Aristotle on Epideictic: The Formation of Public Morality," *Rhetoric Society Quarterly* 29 (Winter 1999): 5–23; Thomas Cole, *The Origins of Rhetoric in Ancient Greece* (Baltimore: Johns Hopkins University Press, 1991); John C. Adams, "Ramist Concepts of Testimony, Judicial Analogies, and the Puritan Conversion Narrative," *Rhetorica* 3 (1991): 251–68; Lawrence W. Rosenfield, "The Practical Celebration of Epideictic," in *Rhetoric in Transition,* ed. Eugene White, 131–55 (University Park: Pennsylvania State University Press, 1980); Christine Oravec, "'Observation' in Aristotle's Theory of Epideictic Rhetoric," *Philosophy and Rhetoric* 9 (1976): 162–74; Chaim Perelman and Lucie Olbrechts-Tyteca, *The New Rhetoric* (1969; repr., Notre Dame, Ind.: University of Notre Dame Press, 2000).

3. Garry Wills, *Lincoln at Gettysburg: The Words That Remade America* (New York: Simon and Schuster, 1992). It should be noted, however, that Lincoln's speech was not unitarily acclaimed in its own time—there was controversy concerning its appropriateness.

4. For example, some commentators (including Wills) indicted leaders at New York City's memorial anniversary for failing to even *look for* the right words. See Janny Scott, "The Silence of the Historic Present: Sept. 11 Leaves Speakers at a Loss for Their Own Words," *New York Times,* August 11, 2002, late edition, sec. 1, 29.

5. For examples, see Hauser, "Aristotle on Epideictic," Oravec, "'Observation' in Aristotle's Theory of Epideictic Rhetoric," and Perelman and Olbrechts-Tyteca, *The New Rhetoric.* These authors consider how epideictic (among other things) couples abstract concepts of virtue (for example, "courage") to specific deeds, thereby "showing" auditors the connection between the abstract idea and its concrete manifestation. Hauser, most notably, shows how this connection-making serves an interest in "exhibiting public morality." Thus, he argues "we learn it [public morality] through the *mimesis* of deeds unfathomable were they not publicly exhibited and validated" ("Aristotle on Epideictic," 19).

6. Rosenfield, "The Practical Celebration of Epideictic," 134.

7. Wills, *Lincoln at Gettysburg,* 41–62.

8. Perelman and Olbrechts-Tyteca, *The New Rhetoric,* 52.

9. Hauser, "Aristotle on Epideictic," 10.

10. Ibid., 10. Most commentators agree that epideictic performs an educative function, though there is some controversy over the interpretation and use of Aristotle's formulation of epideictic in staking out that position. For example, although Rosenfield did not oppose Perelman and Olbrechts-Tyteca's updating of epideictic for contemporary application, he worried that the unwary reader might wrongly interpret Aristotle's epideictic as serving an educational function. Doing that would project modernist thinking about inculcating "values" onto Aristotle's original formulation. Recently, Hauser contended that Aristotle's epideictic did serve an educative function because it was predicated on Aristotle's "model rhetor"—a "*phronimos*" or bearer of *phronesis* (practical wisdom) who is, therefore, capable of "helping others . . . in matters of practical conduct"—and an audience competent to understand virtues exhibited before them (ibid., 11). Teaching is involved in the implication that hearers would be disposed to emulate virtues exhibited in the actions displayed in their own public conduct. I shall not enter this debate, since I plan to offer a distinct position on epideictic's educative function that is suitable for application to contemporary manifestations of epideictic. See Rosenfield, "The Practical Celebration of Epideictic," 132–35.

11. Oravec, "'Observation' in Aristotle's Theory of Epideictic Rhetoric," 166. The parts of this section that draw on Oravec are based on my introduction to *Voices of a Proud Tradition: A Collection of Aggie Muster Speeches* (Bryan, Tex.: Brazos Valley Printing, 1986).

12. Walker, *Rhetoric and Poetics in Antiquity,* 9.

13. Hauser, "Aristotle on Epideictic," 11–17.

14. Oravec, "'Observation' in Aristotle's Theory of Epideictic Rhetoric," 173.

15. See Aristotle's *Rhetoric,* trans. John Henry Freese (1926; repr., Cambridge: Harvard University Press, 1975), 1.9.36–37.

16. Oravec, "'Observation' in Aristotle's Theory of Epideictic Rhetoric," 173.

17. Rosenfield, "The Practical Celebration of Epideictic," 135–36.

18. See Albert R. Jonsen and Stephen Toulmin, *The Abuse of Casuistry: A History of Moral Reasoning* (Berkeley: University of California Press, 1988), 322–25.

19. Aristotle's definition of courage from the *Rhetoric:* "Courage makes men perform noble acts in the midst of dangers according to the dictates of the law and submission to it" (1.9.8). It

should be noted though, that there *has* been a shift in English-speaking cultures (especially in North America) that rightfully adds "and women" or substitutes "people" for "men."

20. Jonsen and Toulmin, *The Abuse of Casuistry*, 306–7.

21. Ibid., 322.

22. Ibid., 231–39.

23. Hauser, "Aristotle on Epideictic," 19–20.

24. Richard M. Weaver, *Ideas Have Consequences* (1948; repr., Chicago: University of Chicago Press, 1984), 18.

25. Ibid., 19.

26. See Rosenfield, "The Practical Celebration of Epideictic," 134–39.

27. See Rosenfield's concluding remarks, "The Practical Celebration of Epideictic," 150.

28. See Ann Kibbey, *The Interpretation of Material Shapes in Puritanism: A Study of Rhetoric, Prejudice, and Violence* (Cambridge: Cambridge University Press, 1986), where she explains how the shared beliefs that contemporaries have concerning speech's place in their lives and how their beliefs about what speech can and cannot do may induce qualities of experience different from people who have different beliefs. Kibbey calls these shared beliefs linguistic values. I employ the concept of linguistic predispositions (instead of values) to emphasize their place as motives in the recognition and judgment of the different kinds of speech acts—for example, the predisposition to judge public avowals as insincere or public constatives as untrue. This predisposition may constitute what some would call a "crisis of confidence" where the public generally mistrusts the speech of politicians. Most likely, though, conflicting predispositions toward speech may be borne by individuals when, for example, they try to decide which talk is "cheap" and which talk is not. Herein I emphasize the choices listeners make about how to listen and how these choices may open and foreclose different qualities of experience, including "learning" about virtue from the public speech of others.

29. President Bill Clinton, "President's Remarks," December 9, 1999, http://www.telegram .com/fire/president.html (last accessed July 27, 2002). The speech is appended to the notes for this chapter. Ruth Smith and John Trimbur wrote an excellent essay on the speeches delivered eulogizing the firefighters. While they accept my contention that epideictic serves an educational function, they find fault with my "assumption of a single 'transcendent point of identification.'" In contrast to my imputation of unitary identification among participants at the occasion, they argue that "the presidential voice of Clinton . . . [is] partial amidst the multiple locations of speakers at the Worcester service. The lessons each speaker wishes to teach present not only a pedagogical message but more tellingly a deliberative intervention into the terms of the social contract among firefighters, the public, and the state in its various geographical configurations and affiliations" (see their note 3). While this may be the case, the succession of speakers framed their addresses from their respective positions (union leaders, mayor, senator, president) as a display of solidarity, teaching that the same qualities of virtue are observable from different positions. The acknowledged differences are sources of credibility for each speaker's part in the ceremony. Together, they constitute an ensemble of voices that, despite differences, exhibit a quality of unity expressed through the speakers' common ground. Nevertheless, perhaps "concord" (rather than unity) is a better way to express the occasion's quality of being together. In either case, after the event, the ensemble will reengage its members' separate, and possibly conflicted, interests. Smith and Trimbur draw attention to the fact that multiple voices speaking on the same occasion from different social, geographic, or role-related positions deeply complicates epideictic's reception and may inevitably prompt listeners to take on the role of "judges" rather than observers. But at Worcester a common idea of civic virtue was voiced from different positions *and* observed by the audience. See Ruth Smith and John Trimbur, "Rhetorics of Unity and Disunity: The Worcester Firefighters Memorial Service," *Rhetoric Society Quarterly* 33 (Fall 2003): 7–24.

30. Here is a case where the "words/deeds" hierarchy is transcended, as Clinton's talk about talk characterizes the assembly's presence as a kind of nonverbal communication that "speaks louder than words in saying that your tragedy is ours; your men are ours; our whole country honors them and you." Its presence, then, may help to alleviate the pain. As Clinton uses words to attribute a motive to his and the assembly's presence and imbue it with meaning, he performs the epideictic function of aptly putting words to deeds that Oravec describes ("'Observation' in Aristotle's Theory of Epideictic Rhetoric," 166). Moreover, he shows sensitivity to the fact that being together with others can help one to manage one's grief—sometimes we just *need* to be together to lighten the burden of human suffering.

31. I use "good reason" here in line with Karl Wallace's usage. See Wallace's "The Substance of Rhetoric: Good Reasons," *Quarterly Journal of Speech* 49 (1963): 239–49. See also Walter Fisher, "Toward a Logic of Good Reasons," *Quarterly Journal of Speech* 64 (1978): 376–84, and "Rationality and Good Reasons," *Philosophy and Rhetoric* 13 (1980): 121–30. Here, I apply "good reason" to the value one may attribute to a genre of speech. Below, I employ it as a criterion for making substantive judgments of a given speech's claims—not its value as a genre of speech.

32. See Adams, "Ramist Concepts," where I explain how Puritans adopted the Pauline "rule of rational charity" in their judgments of conversion narratives, which enabled them to frame their reception as a "celebration" of spiritual values rather than as the "judgment" of courtroom testimonies. I believe this rule applies to the "appropriate" reception of secular epideictic discourse as well, where part of the observer's cultural competence relates to employing an interpretive frame that "fits" the culturally determined occasion and intention of the speech. With the Puritans, reframing from a "litigious" to a "loving" reception was a consequence of respected contemporaries' arguments that charitable reception is more "fitting" to the spiritual values and collective ethos of the members of the congregation, as well as to the narrative's intention. Another way of looking at it would be to consider an observer's "misframing" as a failure to "observe" the speech's generic intention, due perhaps, to cultural difference or incompetence, alienation, cynicism, misanthropy, poor attention span, or any number of interpretive impediments disabling one's desire or ability to be influenced by the speech in the interests of *its* cultured aim.

33. Seemingly, as a site of "theoretical encounter," epideictic speech has a constative dimension. As such, its validity claim may be that of truth rather than sincerity. As Jürgen Habermas characterizes it, then, the theoretical encounter alluded to would be a judgment of the validity of its truth claims. However, in the spirit of the epideictic occasion, truth claims are not called into question without good reason—as when the motive imputed to a deed is categorically wrong (as in the *Jackass* example, where courage may be imputed to senseless risk-taking). As an avowal, it is the perceived *sincerity* of the imputation of motive to the commemorated deed that renders it, as a trusted sign, exemplary of virtue. Even so, if at any point during the speech the speaker's imputation of motive is observed as inept (no matter how sincere), the celebration is over. In another respect, epideictic speech may be characterized as a regulative speech act so far as its overall intention is to guide one's behavior by the inculcation of virtue. The *mimesis* it intends to foster can be read as "model obedience" to its paradigmatic command. It is beyond the scope of this chapter to engage the permutations of speech act theory's locution-illocution-perlocution complex. Suffice it to say that my references to "misframing" play into the complex of misadventures with speech engaged by all the possible misalignments between a speech act's intention and its "mis-reception." I am grateful to Elizabeth Collar for drawing my attention to this complex mix of crisscrossed possibilities. For an excellent summary of Habermas' uses of speech act theory, see Sonja K. Foss, Karen A. Foss, and Robert Trapp, *Contemporary Perspectives on Rhetoric*, 2nd ed. (Prospect Heights, Ill.: Waveland Press, 1991), 241–72.

34. This sort of global, negative predisposition is reflected every year around college grad-
uation time in the *Doonesbury* comic strip's humorous portrayal of the vacuity of "typical"
commencement addresses. The comic strip's portrayal ironically advances paradigm cases of commencement speech, reaffirming its place as a debased form of public address. The idea of an
"ironic epideictic" suggested by a rhetorical discourse that disparages rhetoric underscores that
"observation" or theoretical encounter *can* be viewed as critical insofar as it is prompted by an
interest in affecting an interpretative frame that is to the point—that is consistent with the speech
act's intent. In this sense, one's theoretical encounter may *subsequently* prompt appreciation or
denigration, praise or blame. Moreover, as in the maxim "one person's hope is another person's
fear," the occasion of observing epideictic, as far as it may prompt identification or alienation,
reveals one's position in the community the speech addresses. Although one may be physically
present at the occasion and be a part of the demographer's headcount, one's standpoint and the
sensibilities it enables or disables may form the basis of one's acceptance or rejection of the paradigmatic display of virtue the speech projects. As in the maxim "one person's heroes are another
person's fools," one may see that the same deed can be characterized in diametrically opposed
ways. The epideictic speaker does not make a case for the side she or he speaks from. For rightly
disposed members of the community addressed, the aptness of a speaker's imputation of courage
to a given deed is self-evident—those who may call the same deed "foolish" may themselves be
vituperated as enemies of the community. The question of where to draw the line in judgments
of virtue and vice have vexed humanity since it was first realized that different people may see the
same thing differently, and under the Aristotelian primary axiom, the differences may be signs of
error rather than different perspectives stemming from different social positions or cultural sensibilities. Conflicted positions and sensibilities may be deemed legitimate in their own right as
signs of affiliation—of membership in different communities of interest making up a city or
some other politically bordered and geographically depicted collective of bodies. Nevertheless,
without a site of concord culturally capable of prompting people to transcend their partisan preferences in celebration of what appear as self-evident signs of virtue, the power of "we the people"
is dissipated in the flow of partisan conflict that may be seen as democratic social order's highest
aim, when in fact it is simply one side of the dialectic of concord and discord constituting a
healthy republic's communal ethos. Within the horizon of some higher sensibility as a body
politic, we share a commitment to perpetuate the dialectic of concord and discord in acceptance
of our imperfection, as a sign of our freedom, and toward the fulfillment of our desire to be
autonomous agents *and* bearers of civic virtue enmeshed in social arrangements underwritten by
rhetoric's interest in justice, virtue, and expediency.

Appendix

Presidential Speech

President Clinton's Remarks

Thank you. First, to the wonderful families of our six fallen heroes, who the Vice President
and I had a chance to visit with before the beginning of this service. To their colleagues in
the fire department, their friends in this wonderful community. To the thousands of men
and women in uniform who have come here to join the Mayor, the Governor, the Senators,
the members of Congress, the Bishop and members of the clergy. President Whitehead, and
members of the firefighters. Especially to Chief Budd and Frank Raffa, and all the grieving
members of this fire department, too.

I hope you can all sense how clearly we know, in spite of our talks, that words have a
poor power to alleviate the pain you feel now. But as you look around this vast hall, and

know that there are thousands and thousands more standing outside and other places, we hope that by our collective presence we will speak louder than words in saying that your tragedy is ours; your men are ours; our whole country honors them and you. We grieve with you, and we will stay with you.

More than two and a half centuries ago, Benjamin Franklin wrote an essay entitled, "Brave Men at Fires." He might have written it last week. This is what he said: "Neither cold, nor darkness will deter good people from hastening to the dreadful place to quench the flame. They do it not for the sake of reward or fame; but they have a reward in themselves, and they love one another."

Today we honor six brave men who found a reward in firefighting, who loved one another. Six men who, in turn, richly rewarded this community. So they hastened to the dreadful place to save others. For them, there was no other way.

In the book of Isaiah, God asks, "Whom shall I send, and who will go for us?" And Isaiah says, "Here am I. Send me."

When the question again rang from the smoking skies last week, Paul Brotherton, Timothy Jackson, Jeremiah Lucey, Jay Lyons, Joseph McGuirk and Thomas Spencer also answered with a single voice: Here am I. Send me.

They were firefighters to the core, heroes already, as we have heard, to their friends and loved ones, not to mention the people they saved through the years. For all six, being a firefighter was more than a job, it was in their blood. So when they went into that building that night, they were following their dream to serve, to save lives, and to stick together.

Like their fellow firefighters everywhere, they embodied the best of our nation—of commitment and community, of teamwork and trust—values at the core of our character; values reflected in the daily service not only of those we lost, but in this awesome parade of men and women who have come from all over our country and from some countries beyond our borders to honor their comrades and console their families.

Too often, we take them for granted, our firefighters. In the days ahead, I hope every American will find an occasion to thank those in their communities who stand ready every day to put their lives on the line when the alarm bell rings.

In the Book of Kings, we find the wonderful story of the prophet Elijah, who climbs a mountain to seek the voice of God. A wind shatters rocks in pieces, but the Bible says, the Lord is not in the wind. Then, there's an earthquake and then a fire, but God is not in the earthquake or in the fire. But then, the Scripture says, "after the fire, a still, small voice."

It is that still, small voice that spoke to those six good men, that moved their souls to service and sacrifice. The still, small voice that endures through the ages, that inspires the songs and words we have all shared today, that must now carry this group of grieving families through their grief to going on.

Today, we thank God for the lives our fallen firefighters lived. We hope their families can remember the good and happy times, and bring some smiles through their tears. We commend their souls to God's eternal loving care, and we pray that His still, small voice will bring strength and healing to these families and to this wonderful community who loved them so much.

John Nguyet Erni

15

*F*launting Identity
Spatial Figurations and the Display of Sexuality

Margins and centers shift with subjectivities constantly in motion . . . The boundaries of physical geographies are rebuilt in mental images.

Sally Munt[1]

Introduction

On Twelfth Street and Ocean Drive in the spectacular South Beach in Miami, Florida, stories and legends are being inscribed on this beach city through the everyday movements of queer life, especially after more than a decade of a visible influx of "gay capital" into the city. Visible if clichéd, these queer movements are thematized by sultry imageries of a resort town populated by a colorful and exuberant multitude: imageries of sweaty human flesh, rollerblades, tight spandex shorts, bicycles, hair flowing in the air, nudity on the beach, and the ever-moving bric-a-bracs of everyday gossip. An additional type of queer energy found in "SoBe"—the affectionate nickname given by the hip elites—is amply supplied by queer and queer-friendly celebrities who have inhabited the beach city as transient local entrepreneurs (for example, Madonna, Ricky Martin, Gloria Estefan, and the late Gianni Versace). If some or all of these queer imageries and energies are characteristic signs of sex and sexuality, then there are at least two important consequences: sexuality is here rendered a moving landscape, and it is itself a moving figure within that landscape.

This chapter is a theoretical exercise that attempts to utilize postmodern theories developed in cultural studies, critical geography, and urban studies to rethink matters of identity, community, and belonging for a particular mode of queer culture found in a particular locale. I would like to insist, at the outset, on the particularisms of this adventure: the uniqueness in pursuing a spatial theory of identity (and of related questions of culture and history); the specificity of a visible sexual culture on high parade as part of a cultural "method" of community making; and the singularity of a mixed space known as Miami Beach or South Beach as a rhetorical exemplar of "displaying" a cosmopolitan sexuality that is neither dominant nor marginal. These particularities will be assembled—and staged rhetorically—in order to construct a queer scene where pressing questions about the space-based politics of identity and difference can be posed and examined anew.

Two main reasons motivated the writing of this essay. First, in recent years, there has been a proliferation of work in cultural studies that privileges theories of space in an attempt to reformulate our understanding of the politics of cultural identity.[2] In these works, however, the question of sexuality—particularly queer sexual identity—is often left by the roadside. In working through the problem of "display," I would like to intervene into this body of work by considering how queer sexuality and queer community can be rendered more visible in the field of critical postmodern geography.

Second, also in recent years, both the gay and straight media have consistently been fascinated by the phenomenon of so-called gay capital—that is, a discourse about a resourceful and affluent gay middle-class lifestyle—and how it intersects with "gay despair" brought on by the AIDS crisis since the mid-1980s. Socioeconomics meets psychology, displaying a certain paradoxical condition of gay life in the 1990s and beyond.[3] Gay life has never been so visible in our culture. But what is the cost of this visibility that increasingly depends on the construction of a gay middle-class population purportedly ravaged by an epidemic?

The case of South Beach arose as a pertinent example of the *constructed* intersection between gay affluence and gay despair when *Out,* a popular, glossy gay lifestyle magazine in the United States, dubbed the city "God's waiting room," deliberately recasting this popular retirement spot for senior citizens into a kind of hospice space for gay middle-class "retirement" due to a disease. Glenn Albin, who authored the *Out* article, "To Live and Die in South Beach," writes:

> This is not the first time in its history Miami Beach has been referred to as God's Waiting Room. In the past it was the warmest place in America to die. Today it has become the *hottest* place in America to die. Gay men living with HIV are relocating to sunny Florida by the score. For some, South Beach is a nurturing, warm city that has laws to protect its gay citizens as equals. For others, it is a palm-lined cliff that mighty buffalo throw themselves over.[4]

This recasting of the mythologized gay predicament in SoBe requires a serious examination, not only because it has implications for HIV prevention efforts, but, more important, for broader critical concerns about community formation and sustainability in a growing number of cities where gay capital and HIV/AIDS are often copresent and relatively visible. In other words, implicit in the name "God's waiting room" is a class designation linked to a complex but transient sense of queer community development borne out of a changing epidemic. At stake here is an emerging rhetorical definition of queer sexuality that is being linked to a sense of place constructed through notions of gay "middle-classness," gay migration, and an epidemic that is still inflected with meanings of a fast-lane gay lifestyle. As Albin asks rhetorically, "Are gay people the driving force behind this image [of gay decadence and risk taking], or have they become sucked into the undertow of a town whose purpose has always been escape and fantasy?"[5] Because of this sense of place (for example, the "waiting room"; the beach city), the emerging definition of queer sexuality is necessarily a performative description. That is to say, it is a definition predicated on picturing a scene that can approximate and animate the various meanings of class, mobility, and disease clustering around the figure of the queer.

In this chapter, I want to trace the rhetorical performance of queer sexuality that is being displayed through media rhetorics on the "gay boom" phenomenon in the city and through other historical narratives about the city's development. My proposed method here is to read the city space through an alternating juxtaposition of media rhetorics, historical narratives, and postmodern theories in critical geography. I subject these elements to a kind of turn-taking re-presentation—redisplay, really—of the figure of the "queer" in order to open a new way of thinking about what Ruth Fincher and Jane Jacobs have called a "located politics of difference" as a sustained feature of city spaces.[6] Queerness thus becomes a spatially performative category endowed with everyday scene-making and, by extension, scene-transforming capacity. It is thus important to note here that this method is not aimed at generating a composite picture of South Beach in any realist fashion.[7] In short, I would like to attempt to offer a reading of South Beach with respect to the spatial modalities of movement, mobility, and transient identity.

South Beach as a locale and an emerging conjuncture of cultural narratives about queers indeed raises many questions about the relationship between city development and queer economics, about politics of migration (and exile) in the Sun Belt, and about queer history marked by an epidemic. But my essay here approaches those questions in a theoretical framework formed by everyday "surface" activities—lounging in the sun, rollerblading through crowds, turning heads on gorgeous people, tourism, driving, passing through, stopping for a beer, stopping again for another beer, another turning of heads on gorgeous people. I want to connect these spatial movements and use them to engender effects of queerness, belongingness, and identity. This exercise thus strongly echoes Doreen Massey's description of space as a product of "the intricacies and the complexities, the interlockings and the non-interlockings, of relations from the unimaginably cosmic to the intimately tiny."[8] I will therefore invite the reader to imagine various scales and levels of intensity located on the surface of queer everyday life in South Beach, where we shall note a series of images that serve as passing road signs, if you will, indicating a new sense of queer belonging through the complex interdisplay of sexuality, class, style, consumption, and mobility. We do not need to agree with these images—they are not something we agree to or not—but we might want to frame them, and perhaps displace them, without necessarily defacing them. So here we go.

Cultural Billboards on South Beach

Let us take a drive through South Beach. The legend has it that queers migrated to South Beach during the high commercial tides of queer gentrification.[9] The origin of their coming—mostly gay men from the Northeast United States, Latin America, and Europe—is insignificant, because in the sociological and popular imagination about gay migration, they came from nowhere and everywhere—wherever. The fact that they ended up on South Beach throughout the last decade and a half or so, however, suggests a loaded psychosexual narrative that works to resituate their relationship with the AIDS epidemic and reframe the very sexual landscape of South Beach. Lounging, sipping their beer, or simply striking a pose as urban cowboys on Twelfth Street and Ocean Drive, their story is a mundane metaphor for the representative *fin-de-siècle* gay male: he is a middle-class urban migrant, a "homo-spectating" traveler, whose life is likely to be marked by AIDS one way or another and whose personal and political needs can potentially be met in a Florida resort beach city, which allegedly doubles as a hospice city. His is also a story of the queer *flaneur,* to borrow a term from Walter Benjamin, who used it to theorize the voyeuristic figure of the mobile city dweller at the onset of modern consciousness.[10] The journey of the queer flaneur is famous only for its "invisible visibility," in a small and moderately paced resort city, but big in its queer significations and fast in its transient desires.

On South Beach, gays, lesbians, transvestites, tourists, Cuban exiles, Latin drug traffickers, and retirees alike move through the city with restless relaxation. Social and cultural interactions are typically at a high volume. Yet the mode of interaction seldom inflates into an immersed and sustained deliberation over differences or conflicts; here, there are no grand metaphysical claims, no big community news in any easily unifying way. Nonetheless, I want to put up two road signs—"cultural billboards"—indicating a certain direction we want to go. First, a road sign that suggests that the colorful story of South Beach produced by (1) practices of tourism, (2) social and architectural gentrification, and (3) exile politics, is articulating a "queering" of the spatial operations that those processes depend on. Put in another way, there is a special sensibility about the historical and sociopolitical making of South Beach that is best understood in queer spatial terms. Second, another road sign can be erected to suggest that this queer spatiality is engendering a way of being queer that need not invest itself in a deep metaphysical search of meaning and identity in places. The suggestion is that there is a spatial theory of identity that does not necessarily amount to a representable "map" or even a coherent "geography" of identity or community formation. It is a theory, in other words, that is not necessarily built on rocks.

Cultural Billboard One: Space and Sensibility

In the recent boom of studies about cities and urban spaces, postmodern theories have had a definitive influence over social scientific and humanist research, such as that in geography, urban planning, sociology, architecture, anthropology, and political economy, as well as in literary-based interpretation of urban experiences.[11] Enthralled, on the one hand, by the visible diversity of lived experiences and community formations in urban settings and, on the other hand, by the rapid commercialization of everyday life through a highly saturated media environment typically found in the city, researchers have recognized that old sociological models for understanding city life are inadequate. They have recognized that these models are largely insensitive to multiple differences, imprecise in differentiating materiality from more symbolic processes, and are thus politically naïve in assessing boundaries of identities and their struggles. As a result, Jane Jacobs and Ruth Fincher have argued:

> "The city" as an object of analysis has been irredeemably unsettled, and many of the more resilient ways urban processes are understood have been rendered problematic. What happens, for example, to the quest for a broadly applicable "theory of urbanization" when we are confronted with the postmodern critique of meta-narratives? What happens to our capacity to produce normative models of cities in this context of a new sensitivity to the politics of difference? What happens to studies of housing, suburbia, the inner city, ghettos, gentrification, social polarization, and urban social movements when framed not by a theory of "the city" but by theories of difference?[12]

The theories and politics of difference in the studies of cities suggest that things do not, and need not, line up neatly together. Put in another way, identities, spaces, behavior, lifestyles, and politics are seldom latticed into rigid correspondences. Power relations need not work in accordance with the dominant/subordinate, center/periphery, or top/bottom axes. Instead, city spaces are notoriously slippery—sandy in the case of South Beach—producing porous neighborhoods of identities and open districts of experience.

27. Rainbow-tipped poles displaying gay pride, hoisted not upon rocks, but on sand. Photograph by John Nguyet Erni

To echo Bakhtin, the city is "carnivalesque" in nature, where the logic of identity display and performance often involves associations and switching between locations, bodies, social differences, symbolic practices, psychological experiences, and so on. Such displacements of display are not imposed upon the urban subject from the outside; instead, they are the core operating terms of a flexible network, an economy of social, topographical, historical, linguistic, and bodily flow—in short, of spatiality.

In what ways, then, can we see South Beach as a carnivalesque city in spatial terms? The renaissance being enjoyed by South Beach since the 1990s—the revival of the built and social environments, the infusion of investments in hip cultural forms and the consequent proliferation of spectacles, the orgiastic commercialization of everyday life—is but one in a series of revivalist narratives written about the city. These narratives run in a form of boomeranged surfing on the wrong side of the economic tidal waves. By that I mean that the history of South Beach is filled with recurrent narratives of social and capital rejuvenation that took place during widespread economic down times, first in the late 1920s, and then in the late 1970s, and again in the early 1990s.[13]

One of the things that makes South Beach famous is, of course, art deco, which is an art movement and a pseudopolitical consciousness borne out of a cynicism toward capitalism, a movement generally recognized by art historians as a stylized effect of and response to the Depression era. Most of the eight hundred buildings that characterize the Art Deco Historic District on South Beach were built between 1923 and 1943. Between 1929 and 1939, the number of deco-style beachfront hotels, houses, and apartments jumped three- to fourfold.[14] The rapid development of the city in size and in style underscores an important underlying nature of the town that can be characterized as "boom in the gloom." In many ways, the attempt by the art deco movement to redefine history and the environment in grand geometric terms (such as simplicity, slim vertical and horizontal emphases, spatial austerity) steeped in minute aesthetic details, helps to secure a particular sensibility of South Beach as a space of contradiction between style and economics. The so-called excesses of this space may indeed have something to do with this contradiction, this continual tension between cultural voluptuousness and economic deprivation, rather than with the tired assertion of runaway flamboyance.

In the mid-1970s, the legend of the great preservationist of South Beach, a debutante by the name of Barbara Baer Capitman, emerged during yet another economic hard time. Her tenacious battle with city officials who wanted to demolish the art deco buildings in order to make room for high-rises essentially kept alive the contradiction between style and economics. The legend goes that Capitman's perseverance eventually prevailed, leading to her founding of the Miami Design Preservation League in 1976 and the nomination of the art deco district to the National Register of Historic Places in 1979.[15] Once again, the narrative of the boom in the gloom was rehabilitated.

So, it seems that the city development of South Beach was based on a revivalism that privileges a sensibility and a rhetorical style over realism and authenticity. One might add that the current boom on South Beach since the early 1990s (that began in part with the migration of gay capital) also repeats this pattern: the swelling of postmodern sensibility in the midst of the trend of economic and social downsizing. Against the kind of scholarly contemplation upon postmodern spatiality and hyper-reality made famous by writers such as Mike Davis, Edward Soja, Jean Baudrillard, and others, South Beach is usefully self-reflexive.[16]

Cultural Billboard Two: Queering the Politics of "Community"

What is "queer," and how is it linked to concepts of place, space, and display? In what manner has this category been inscribed upon the city as an available form of experience as well as a form of political contestation against "heteronormativity"?[17] Does sex have territories? And does queer sex always reside "in the outside," at the periphery, as it were?

Broadly speaking, the burgeoning work in queer social theory in recent years formulates "queer" as something that refers to nonnormative, curious, and imaginatively ambiguous objects and relations. A queer mode of sociality is theorized as a fluid space of "production" in Foucault's sense, involving a dissident array of sexual (and sexualized) identities, identifications, bodily senses and sensations, textual relations, and institutions. Eve Sedgwick explains, "The word 'queer' itself means across—it comes from the Indo-European root—*twerkw*, which also yields the German *quer*, Latin *torquere* (to twist), English *athwart*."[18] She goes on to note that passionate queer things are "loose ends where representation, identity, gender, sexuality, and the body can't be made to line up neatly together."[19]

Queer theory is not exactly identical to gay and lesbian studies in terms of the conceptual definition of sexual difference, methods, or even objects of analysis. As Amy Kaminsky reminds us:

> The shift from gay and lesbian studies to queer studies has been marked by a move away from studying an already available body of work by homosexual writers toward producing theory in an open field; away from questions of identity (coming out, claiming a voice) to questions of subjectivity (what is the queer subject, and how

is such a subject constituted?); away from community, in, for example, a perhaps idealized notion of a lesbian-centered women culture and a lesbian-separatist politics, to the relation of the queer subject to the body politic and to the nation; from representation of preexisting and retrievable gay themes to the performance of transgressive behavior as constitutive of categories like sexuality and gender.[20]

Briefly then, "queer sexuality" can be defined as a practice of discursive excess that twists normal notions of gender, sexuality, and even space. "Queer identity" represents unfixed political and social positionings against heteronormativity. And the "queer body" is an adventure in surplus representations. In short, queer studies is concerned with the identity politics that construct and impact those who move on the outside of foundationalist gender and sexual norms. Yet queer studies is less concerned with queerness as an object than as a *process*. By refusing to operate in the paradigm of essential categorization or in the center/margin model, queer studies focuses on the lines of movement across ideas, expressions, relationships, spaces, and desires that innovate different ways of being in the world. The epistemology of such a nonnormative construction of identity has been widely termed "queer performativity."[21]

Perhaps one of the most significant claims made by queer theory is that the accepted dominant "norms" of society, of identity, and so on, are possibly already riven with contradictions. In other words, it suggests that the status of the dominant is not as secure and stable as previously assumed; rather, dissonances, lapses, relapses, multiple articulations, contradictions, incohesiveness, excesses—in short, queerness—may have been ever present in the prevailing social order. As an analytical category, queer thus designates an "antifoundational" mode of philosophical thinking. To be anti-foundational signifies more than taking a philosophical stance. It also carries significance in terms of space: an antifoundation signifies a resistance to essentialized concepts of space.

There has been a somewhat parallel development in critical geography and postmodern urban studies, in the sense that key concepts of space, place, identity, and community development have been rethought as having no necessarily fixed or essential foundation.[22] In particular, those critical geographers and researchers in urban studies who have researched on the "geography of sexuality" have recently pushed their own disciplines to move away from positivist traditions and suggested alternative frameworks for analyzing the presence, growth, and political struggles of situated queer life. They have looked at the complex spatial relations of queers with the state, with processes of urbanization and gentrification, urban consumerism, problems of migration and tourism, controversy of public sex, problems of racism, and so on.[23]

Central to the current critical debates in these fields are two concerns: how to make claims of a "queer community," given the perplexing array of factors contributing to the formation of queer visibility in any given place, and how to forge a sense of "queer citizenship" and "belonging" as a discourse whose legitimacy (in the civil and political sense) need not necessarily rest upon the state or the hegemonic legal apparatus.[24] Geography has a unique role to play here; its focus on the social formation of space and place allows for analytical considerations made at multiple levels of abstraction. In other words, the performative "emplacement" of queerness in place and as space should allow us to invent new and innovative forms of community belonging and cultural citizenship for queers.

28. SoBe gay boys in a circuit party. Photograph by John Nguyet Erni

One such form—that which is being proposed in the present exercise—may take queer consumption of varied spatial stimulations as a major clue for tracing out the contour of queer community belonging. Such spatial stimuli include elements that move on the surface of queer everyday life, such as media images, billboards, moving figures in a crowd, staged public events, and popular culture. While it is important to see that these elements carry with them social, cultural, historical, and even political significance, it is their status as visceral showpieces, as nitty-gritty, mini performances of queer sensibilities and desires —in short, as display—that is our focus here. The shift toward this approach may indeed be a deliberate distortion, that is to say, the forging of a different kind of treatment for, and body politics around, the common core of concerns in queer community development and identity politics. Take, for example, a major focus in analyses of queer geography and political economy: that of class difference.

To be sure, the critical analyses of queer experience tend to be strongly underpinned by class concerns. Since John D'Emilio's groundbreaking essay on the relationship between capitalism and gay identity, researchers have focused on class difference as a central problematic in their consideration of queer life, especially that in advanced consumerist societies.[25] Amy Gluckman and Betsy Reed's important book a few years ago, *Homoeconomics: Capitalism, Community, and Lesbian and Gay Life,*[26] places an implicit emphasis on the same, to an extent that differences between gay male and lesbian consumption and among diverse racial groups are examined as differences subsumed under class politics. For lesbians and gay men in the United States, the onset of the "gay marketing moment" signals an increasing recognition of the interaction—and elision—among identity, commerce, and politics. Yet more than anything else, this recognition of gay commercial visibility has brought home an important fact: visibility does not apply evenly to all gay people. In the

United States, the impressive demographics, profligate spending habits, and high levels of discretionary income boasted of the gay community by marketing organizations, and appropriated by conservative political voices, have produced a new mythology of gay affluence, which of course turns out to be a class-based mythology.[27] Accordingly, critical analyses of this new cultural mythology rightfully emphasize the politics of class in order to illuminate underlying conflicts in the phenomenon of gay consumption lifestyle.

However, to understand the formation of cultural community and identity as they are shaped—and imagined—by acts and displays of consumption, it is perhaps important to note the distinction between a politico-economic logic and a consumption logic. Broadly speaking, the former stresses various forms of economic practices, including labor relations and modes of production and consumption, as the basis of ideological experience. Social life is abstracted into economic life. The same conceptual abstraction also exists in a cultural logic of consumption, for it stresses that both the producers and consumers of culture acquire their (commodified) experience and identities through various modes of representation, figuration, fetishization, reification, and so on.[28] With consumption logic, then, social life is abstracted into discourse. It is not my purpose here to delineate the validity of each approach. Instead, in the present discussion of finding a new and innovative way to reconceptualize queer community formation and queer cultural citizenship, I want to highlight the role of consumption logic in the formation of an emerging identity politics. Specifically, I suggest that a performative logic of consumption through the continual act of display and redisplay, of figurative flaunting, in fact constitutes the basis for a visible but flexible sense of community and citizenship of desire.

Seen in these ways, queer performative consumption becomes something that moves across space, place, and the body and, in doing so, *bypasses* class and economic concerns in order to enable a reworking of a queer sense of belonging. This logic of consumption generates a community of desire that is weakly, if at all, tied to class politics per se. With this, we can then refute the simplistic but politically charged claim that gay capital (and the "middle-classness" of gay people) alone forms the basis for gay visibility and community organizing. This claim needs to be challenged because the privileging of the discourse of gay capital has enabled a conservative backlash against progressive queer politics in many urban centers. Class politics has been a hijacked political discourse working to deny the struggle of queers for political justice. It has in fact become a contaminated discourse against queer people in the United States.[29] It is with new and innovative definitions of a queer sense of belonging that queers can reclaim an organic form of community and citizenship, through a struggle whose basis need not be class or capital oriented. Given this purpose, how can South Beach be read so as to insinuate a more flexible symbolic economy implicating, and implicated by, a nondogmatic queerness?

Not Yet a Home: On Pseudo-places, Spaces, and Belongings

There are some possible encumbrances in any attempt to *read* spaces. Since the 1950s, there has been a fairly consistent fascination in urban sociology to study cultural groups marked by race, gender, foreignness, and sexual deviance. Those studies tend to minoritize these cultural groups' social status by way of a determination of their social deprivation based on spatial deprivation. The study of ghetto spaces for racial, ethnic, and sexual communities in the United States is exemplary of so much writing of this kind in urban sociology. Aside

from the obvious problem of sociological pathologization, this approach is largely motivated by a desire to *fix* the object of reading, as it were. These works are quite attentive to
the significance of practical narratives that people have in places, such as that of social networking, common rituals of everyday life, and subcultural codification of difference and
identity. But the attention to such narratives is strictly in relation to the realist notion of
places as fixed surfaces upon which narratives of deprivation are inscribed. In this way, the
working-class ghetto, the gay bar, the housing project, the casino, the black and Hispanic
neighborhood, and the city in general all appear as denotatively blank text waiting for connotation. "Identity" correspondingly is secured in a logic of textual fixity that informs the
research project.

   But, the trouble with spaces like South Beach as a site of analysis is that they frame "textual connotation," "identity," and "subjectivity" through constant markers of movements
and transience. Identity is subjected to a different sort of logic that is more performative
than connotative and less contemplative. So the project of reading South Beach—and other
notoriously slippery spaces—requires us to retreat from the "text" and perhaps begin with
the motion of the moving figures, or the figure of movement, and its performative operations in space and time. This is what Michel de Certeau calls the "popular practice" of place
and placing.[30] And as Nigel Thrift argues, identity must be theorized as "space-time distribution of hybrid subject-contexts constantly being copied, constantly being revised, sentenced, and enunciated."[31]

   Thus, another way to spend time on South Beach by way of the idea of sensibility over
sense is to see it as a transit space. Seasonally, geographically, and even symbolically speaking, South Beach is a stopover en route to or from somewhere else. However, the temptation of the city must be taken seriously. What I have in mind is something similar to what
Meaghan Morris calls the "calculated readability" of "pseudo-places."[32] As a tourist herself
passing through a resort motel in Australia, she writes, "True places are opaque to the passing observer and 'require' active response . . . Pseudo-places achieve an artificial trans-
parency, inducing the passivity typical of 'tourism.'"[33] I take it from Morris that a radical
constructedness that induces readiness, availability, or contextual openness in those pseudo-
places can engender a mode of reading practice that is engaging and unrigid at the same
time. I reckon that South Beach qualifies as a pseudo-place; it is always poised with a *poten-
tiality* for narrative. It promises a seduction *at large* by way of the adventure of the eye, a
poignant catch of a stranger's delicious gaze, a good lay, a clandestine rendezvous, a wanted
intimidation, a brush with stardom, or even an alienating longing for love. Passing through
South Beach's self-referential artificiality and constructedness, we are perhaps cynical, but
always open to seduction.

   Whether you come here to be romantic, to score, or just to strike gold, you encounter
a self-reflexive transit space that is not demanding on its claim to authenticity or metaphysics, but a space that nonetheless always offers scripts of possibilities for you to linger
and evaluate. Whether we call this cinematic effect or not because of the resemblance between the cinematic space and the transit space, there is a well-developed, colorful pseudo-
place like South Beach that can enumerate an array of transient subject positions and
identifications. To borrow from film theorist Laura Mulvey, this pseudo-place is embedded
with a "to-be-looked-at-ness" without demanding on any one or any kind of subjectivity
too forcefully or explicitly. In this way, the relationship among the touristic-spectatorial, the

neighborly, the entrepreneurial, the poser, and the transient is not about categorical opposition, but rather about a continuum marked and divided by degrees of "being-thereness."
One may say that identity on South Beach is what Larry Grossberg calls the "mattering
map" that expresses not a metaphysical quest for selfhood but a radical and intense sense
of belonging actuated through the performative give-and-take, display-and-consumption,
of space, place, and the body.[34] As a SoBe-ite once told me, on South Beach there is no
imposition over where, when, or how you stop being a tourist and start acting like a local,
as long as you stay busy as a beachgoer, a barhopper between roving and kinky parties like
those at the Warshaw or the Kremlin or Twist, a shopper on Collins Avenue, a body wor-
shiper at the News Café, a restaurateur at Café Manana or the Sushi Rock Café, or even just
an indifferent passerby on the Lincoln Road Mall. And in all or any of the above, looking
pretty and walking light of course helps, as a local tourist or a touring local.

This is perhaps why South Beach as a cultural sign projects itself on billboards posted
around the city with essentially one and only one theme: the theme of flow, as evident in
all those advertisements for walking tours, bicycle tours, circuit parties, mobile tea dances,
and pedestrian malls. Not to mention the thousand vectors of desiring gazes that network
the city into a giant flux. The conventions of beachdom and pastel-and-neon tourism render an aesthetic of what Richard Sieburgh calls "accelerated impressionism."[35] With characteristic intensity, the sun worshippers on any good sunny day on South Beach, and the
gyrating barflies and cowboys on ecstasy in any sultry evening, can provide plenty of Sieburgh's imagery.

The identity of South Beach as *place* is indeed founded on movement and temporality.
The city's history and genesis are in fact best learned through the references to movement
and migration. After all, the legends about the historical figures who discovered and subsequently developed Miami Beach and Florida in general, such as Henry Flagler, John
Collins, and of course Carl Fisher, reveal their common tie to and passion for the transportation industry. It was those turn-of-the-century entrepreneurs' characteristically modernist spatial vision of territoriality that has brought about an expansive mobility of elites,
laborers, travelers, adventurers, and merchants through the automobile, the train, and the
boat and that gave birth to a geographical space marked by the chronic consciousness of
movements, place, and speed.[36] Throughout the successive slumping and rehabilitation
periods on South Beach over the years, such an originary moment continues to deliver the
city, especially the preservationist rhetorics attached to the city, as a projection of identity
and community in (and into) space and time.

Back on Twelfth Street and Ocean Drive, in the midst of a comfortable mix of longings
and transient excitations, one defines his or her queer sense of belonging along multiple
sidelines. Elspeth Probyn coined the term "queer belongingness."[37] A particularly striking
image in her book *Outside Belongings* is when she cruises up and down the streets of Montreal in the winter, and she gathers a splendid sensibility about how identity is lived out: in
"the inbetweenness of belongingness, of belonging not in some deep authentic way but
belonging in constant movement, modes of belonging as surface shifts."[38] Once out in the
brisk winter cityscape that comprises an "ensemble of immanent signs of difference,"[39] you
could assess the multiple lines of intersection offered by city life in a cold climate that does
not permit you to linger for too long. Moving on, but not moving out or moving away:
this seems to be a useful metaphor for how identity is formulated on the surface of our

everyday life. So in spatializing the events, one can claim one's social identity in momentary singularities.

Drawing on a Deleuzian framework, Probyn distinguishes two modes of belonging into "specificity" and "singularity":

> I understand "specificity" to refer to zones of possible forms of belonging: being lesbian, being Welsh, being woman, being red, etc. To use yet other terms, the movement from specificity to singularity can be understood as processes that render the virtual actual—the ways in which the general becomes realized by individuals as singular. . . . Zones of specificity and difference, at different times and under certain circumstances, then may be yielded and lived out as singular. . . . Singularity is thus *rendered* not posited, it is to be produced in the processes of reducing possibility (as with a sauce or stock).[40]

Each route might define a different kind of longing and belonging. And each might be perfectly realistic, but they do not necessarily add up to a generalizable geography of identity. Still, in any case, you can transport yourself—hurriedly, of course, in the howling wind—along lines and directions of everyday life only to encounter their radical rearrangeability, that is to say by extension, their radical queerness. Traveling in this way ceases to be a metaphor for mapping a geography of identity when singularizing forms of belonging come to characterize everyday life in a way that exceeds the teleology of identity or subjecthood. According to Probyn, this excess, however, is an operation of "adding to" without "adding up."[41] Key to Probyn's conceptualization of belonging is the idea of surfaces—of living according to "what emerges from what is said now, here, and nowhere else."[42] If the surfaces of the city or the self are layered with the modality of space, the operation of walking in the howling wind, and the enunciation of here and now, they can in turn expose the rigidity in formulations of identity through generalization or essentialism.

Further, this mode of operationalizing identity and belonging, which I have associated with queerness, stands in contrast to other political modes of belonging staked out by other minority groups. On South Beach, queers are multiracial and multinational in origin. Yet the configuration of pseudo-spatiality discussed above renders it necessary for the queers to generate multiple discursive flows of display in their quest for belonging. Reified categories such as race, ethnicity, and nationality may be subjected to the logic of pseudo-spatiality, producing new forms of political engagement that are not necessarily routed through those identity tags. This is in contrast with many other minority groups living in borders (real and discursive). For instance, in delineating the discursive strategies used by Chicana feminists residing in border terrains in the United States (for example, the Southwest region) to reclaim their authentic sense of identity and community, Lisa Flores argues that such a political vision to employ rhetorics of difference is important for Chicana feminists to create a sense of "home."[43] In this way, the politics of rhetorical work and the politics of home are symbiotic. What is being sketched in the case of South Beach is rather different, neither because there are no racially oriented political struggles in the city nor because a sense of home is unimportant for SoBe-ites. What is being proposed here, instead, is that the current of rhetorical displays found in the city may be shaping a rather different longing for togetherness in terms of sense, style, fluidity, and scale. When applied to this case, the political tradition associated to the discursive quest for home may smack of what

Charles Morris III calls "determined interpretation" incapable of discerning the "hidden transcripts."[44]

Not in Kansas Anymore: Conclusion

The potential seduction of the theory of queer belonging discussed in this chapter might be summed up by Probyn, in a short passage somewhat reminiscent of the scene on Twelfth Street and Ocean Drive on South Beach:

> As an ex-bartender and waitress, I have learned a lot in bars. And as I sit [in a lesbian bar] musing on dyke difference, I am reminded of the two important bar tips: one, do not ground your identity in bars; two, do not search for depth in bar talk—take it in its very *quelconque*-ness, its so-what-ness. Thus instructed, I move to engage in the sowhatness, to trace the scratched surface of belonging here.[45]

Back on South Beach (en route to Montreal in order to get direction, so to speak), we assess the display of queer sexualities through the theory of singularity and through the enunciation of "so what." Historically, for many queers, it has been over the deepening of a queer collectivity that serves as the primary definition of belongingness: "the gay and lesbian community," "the gay and lesbian movement," "gay and lesbian identity politics," "queer nation," and so on. And homophobia may be precisely a mode of mobility, a spatial territorialization, that limits the movements of queers and ghettoizes queer spaces. But, as a closing remark that, I insist, could only be made at a particular locale (like South Beach), for now and nowhere else, I suggest that the kind of claim of queer belonging that I am trying to make in this chapter does not seek its grounding in queer historical truth, or even in queer politics in its general and generalizing sense. I have to admit that this makes for a more difficult sort of queer theory and queer cultural politics. Yet perhaps what it attempts to do is to gesture toward some kind of direction, like a road sign, that permits a certain queer trajectory in which it becomes possible for some to linger in the landscape, to open roads, form communities, and build homes, and for others to simply keep on moving, riding their singularizing desires on the road.

So the road sign that we encounter in the opening of this chapter about gay migration as a result of an epidemic is just that: a road sign and no more. Queers may indeed be migrating to South Beach. But whether they mark the space as "God's waiting room" or not, we must not totalize the sign. To do that is simply to turn a blind eye on the fluid multiplicity that characterizes ordinary life in SoBe. That would be too unqueer!

Notes

1. Sally Munt, "The Lesbian Flaneur," in *Mapping Desire: Geographies of Sexualities,* ed. D. Bell and G. Valentine, 118 (New York: Routledge, 1995).

2. See, among others, N. Alsayyad, ed., *Hybrid Urbanism: On the Identity Discourse and the Built Environment* (Westport, Conn.: Praeger, 2001); G. Bridge and S. Watson, ed., *A Companion to the City* (Oxford: Blackwell Publishers, 2000); K. Hetherington, *Expressions of Identity: Space, Performance, Politics* (Thousand Oaks, Calif.: Sage Publications, 1998); D. Massey and P. Jess, ed., *A Place in the World? Places, Cultures and Globalization,* (Oxford: Oxford University Press and Open University, 1995); S. Pile and N. Thrift, ed., *Mapping the Subject: Geographies of Cultural Transformation* (New York: Routledge, 1995); S. Pile and M. Keith, ed., *Geographies of Resistance* (New York: Routledge, 1997); E. W. Soja, *Thirdspace: Journeys to Los Angeles and Other Real-and-Imagined*

Places (Cambridge, Mass.: Blackwell, 1996); E. Soja, *Postmetropolis: Critical Studies of Cities and Regions* (Malden, Mass.: Blackwell Publishers, 2000); P. Yaeger, ed., *The Geography of Identity* (Ann Arbor: University of Michigan Press, 1996).

3. See among others, K. De Witt, "Gay Presence Leads Revival of Declining Neighborhoods," *New York Times,* September 6, 1994, A14; T. Drummond, "Not in Kansas Anymore," *Time,* September 25, 1995, 54–55; V. Hersch, "Pink Dots Target Gay Customers: How Come? Check Out How Affluent Gays Are," *Restaurant Business,* September 20, 1992, 46; F. Prose, "Splashy, Flashy Miami," *New York Times,* March 1, 1992, 15; G. Trebay, "Babes in Boyland," *Village Voice,* August 4, 1999, 49–50.

4. G. Albin, "To Live and Die in South Beach," *Out,* May 1995, 74.

5. Ibid.

6. R. Fincher and J. M. Jacobs, ed., *Cities of Difference* (New York: The Guilford Press, 1998).

7. The scenes and sights that will be briefly visited throughout this chapter will represent a series of selective, but noteworthy, stopovers or vignettes. The focus will be on rhetorico-discursive and not teleological representations of the beach-city space. To take a visible point of interest found on South Beach as an example, the art deco buildings that make SoBe famous are, at an important level, material sites not so much to be tallied and mapped out for geographical consumption. In a far more interesting way, they are a display of a certain excess, in terms of style, sensibility, and even migrant history. In this chapter, my interest rests more on tracing, and not mapping, the city and what stories the traces can tell us about the queer class.

8. D. Massey, "Spaces of Politics," in *Human Geography Today,* ed. D. Massey, J. Allen, and P. Sarre, 283 (Cambridge, U.K.: Polity Press, 1999).

9. See for instance, Albin, "To Live and Die in South Beach," 74; Drummond, "Not in Kansas Anymore," 54–55; L. Gross, "From South Beach and SoBe," in *Voices in the Street: Explorations in Gender, Media, and Public Space,* ed. S. Drucker and G. Gumpert, 201–10 (Cresskill, N.J.: Hampton Press, 1997); J. Nordheimer, "Miami Beach Sees Signs of a Revival," *New York Times,* November 3, 1985, 26; Prose, "Splashy, Flashy Miami," 15.

10. Briefly put, the "flaneur" is a desiring traveler whose restlessness embodies the modern consciousness that privileges movement, transience, and cosmopolitan openness. In "The Lesbian Flaneur," Sally Munt appropriates Benjamin's modernist (anti)hero to read fictional accounts of sexual adventures of lesbian characters in New York.

11. See, among others, R. Ainley, ed., *New Frontiers of Space, Bodies and Gender* (New York: Routledge, 1998); K. Anderson and F. Gale, ed., *Inventing Places: Studies in Cultural Geography* (Melbourne, Australia: Longman Cheshire, 1992); E. Carter, J. Donald, and J. Squires, ed., *Space and Place: Theories of Identity and Location* (London: Lawrence and Wishart, 1993); D. Morley and K. Robins, *Spaces of Identity: Global Media, Electronic Landscapes and Cultural Boundaries* (New York: Routledge, 1995); Pile and Thrift, *Mapping the Subject;* E. Wilson, *The Contradictions of Culture: Cities, Culture, Women* (London: Sage, 2001).

12. Fincher and Jacobs, introduction to *Cities of Difference,* 1–2.

13. See J. Beverley and D. Houston, "Notes on Miami," *boundary 2,* 23, no. 2 (1996): 19–46; "City of Miami Beach," http://ci.miami-beach.fl.us/ (last accessed June 2, 2002).

14. M. Bethany, "Soho in the Sun," *New York,* January 13, 1992, 18–27.

15. Nordheimer, "Miami Beach Sees Signs of a Revival."

16. An interesting case of a self-reflexive cultural moment associated with South Beach and Miami more generally can be found in the popular television program in the mid-1980s *Miami Vice.* Lawrence Grossberg's discussion of the show is relevant here: "*Miami Vice* is, as its critics have said, all on the surface. And the surface is nothing but a collection of quotations from our collective historical debris, a mobile game of trivia. It is, in some ways, the perfect televisual image,

minimalist (the sparse scenes, the constant long shots, etc.) yet concrete (consider how often we are reminded of the apparent reality of its scene). The narrative is less important than the images.... Such ironic gestures are common across a wide variety of programs." See L. Grossberg, "The Indifference of Television, or, Mapping TV's Popular (Affective) Economy," in *Dancing in Spite of Myself: Essays on Popular Culture* (Durham, N.C.: Duke University Press, 1997), 125–44, esp. 126–27.

17. "Heteronormativity" can be defined as the historical and discursive privilege of the ideas and practices associated with heterosexuality as the stable center of subjectivity and sociality. But while such stability is achieved through a binaristic structure that produces nonheterosexuality as other, it is not permanently stable. For a useful discussion of the discursive interdependence between "hetero" and "homo," see J. N. Erni, "Eternal Excesses: Toward a Queer Mode of Articulation in Social Theory," in *American Literary History* 8, no. 3 (1996): 566–81; D. Fuss, "Inside/Out," in *Inside/Out: Lesbian Theories, Gay Theories,* ed. D. Fuss, 1–10 (New York: Routledge, 1991).

18. E. K. Sedgwick, *Tendencies* (Durham, N.C.: Duke University Press, 1993), xii.

19. Ibid., 13.

20. A. Kaminsky, "The Queering of Latin American Literary Studies," *Latin American Research Review* 36, no. 2 (2001): 210.

21. See, for example, J. Butler, *Gender Trouble: Feminism and the Subversion of Identity* (London: Routledge, 1990); J. Butler, *Bodies That Matter: On the Discursive Limits of "Sex"* (New York: Routledge, 1993); E. Probyn, *Outside Belongings* (New York: Routledge, 1996); E. K. Sedgwick, *Epistemology of the Close* (Berkeley, Calif.: University of California Press, 1990); Sedgwick, *Tendencies;* M. Warner, *Fear of a Queer Planet: Queer Politics and Social Theory* (Minneapolis: University of Minnesota Press, 1993).

22. See, for instance, M. Davis, *Ecology of Fear: Los Angeles and the Imagination of Disaster* (New York: Metropolitan Books, 1998); M. Davis, *Magical Urbanism: Latinos Reinvent the U.S. City* (New York: Verso, 2000); A. Forsyth, "Sexuality and Space: Nonconformist Populations and Planning Practice," in *Journal of Planning Literature* 15, no. 3 (2001): 339–58.

23. See, among others, J. Binnie and G. Valentine, "Geographies of Sexuality–A Review of Progress," in *Lesbian and Gay Studies: An Introductory, Interdisciplinary Approach,* ed. T. Sandfort, J. Schuyf, J. W. Duyvendak, and J. Weeks, 132–45 (London: Sage, 2000); Bell and Valentine, ed., *Mapping Desire: Geographies of Sexualities;* M. Brown, *Replacing Citizenship: AIDS Activism and Radical Democracy* (New York: Guilford Press, 1997); P. Califia, *Public Sex: The Culture of Radical Sex* (Pittsburgh, Penn.: Cleis Press, 1994); N. Duncan, ed., *Bodyspace: Destabilising Geographies of Gender and Sexuality* (London: Routledge, 1996); L. Knopp, "Sexuality and Urban Space: A Framework for Analysis," in *Mapping Desire: Geographies of Sexualities,* 149–61.

24. Binnie and Valentine, "Geographies of Sexuality," 132–45.

25. J. D'Emilio, "Capitalism and Gay Identity," in *Powers of Desire: The Politics of Sexuality,* ed. A. Snitow and others, 100–117 (New York: Monthly Review Press, 1983).

26. A. Gluckman and B. Reed, ed., *Homoeconomics: Capitalism, Community, and Lesbian and Gay Life* (New York: Routledge, 1997).

27. M. V. L. Badgett, "Beyond Biased Samples: Challenging the Myths on the Economic Status of Lesbians and Gay Men," in *Homoeconomics,* 65–72.

28. R. Goldman, *Reading Ads Socially* (New York and London: Routledge, 1992).

29. The backlash, which is based on the presumption of gay affluence and gay political power, has in recent years resulted in cuts in public funding for HIV prevention programs. In addition, it has caused escalated conflicts internal to the gay and lesbian community due to class, gender, and racial differences with the community.

30. M. de Certeau, *The Practice of Everyday Life* (Berkeley: University of California Press, 1984), 1.

31. N. Thrift, *Spatial Formations* (London: Sage, 1996), 126.

32. M. Morris, "At Henry Parkes Motel," in *Too Soon Too Late: History in Popular Culture* (Bloomington: Indiana University Press, 1998), 35.

33. Ibid.

34. Grossberg, "The Indifference of Television," 142.

35. R. Sieburgh, "Sentimental Traveling: On the Road (and off the Wall) with Laurence Sterne," in *Scriptsi* 4, no. 3 (1987): 203.

36. See, for example, P. Hamill, "Flagler's Fantasy," in *Travel Holiday,* February 1992, 56–63, 97; "City of Miami Beach," http://ci.miami-beach.fl.us/; *Mr. Miami Beach,* dir. Mark (and) J. Davis, WGBH Educational Foundation, 1998.

37. Probyn, *Outside Belongings,* 63.

38. Ibid., 19.

39. Ibid., 26.

40. Ibid., 22–24.

41. Ibid., 24.

42. Ibid.

43. L. A. Flores, "Creating Discursive Space through a Rhetoric of Difference: Chicana Feminists Craft a Homeland," *Quarterly Journal of Speech* 82 (1996): 142–56.

44. C. E. Morris III, "Contextual Twilight / Critical Liminality: J. M. Barrie's *Courage* at St. Andrews, 1922," *Quarterly Journal of Speech* 82 (1996): 208.

45. Probyn, *Outside Belongings,* 33–34.

Phebe Shih Chao

16

attoo and Piercing

Reflections on Mortification

In such cultures, it might be argued, the skin, the border zone between the bounded self and the social world thought to encompass that self, a membrane that protects but may also conceal, must be a zone of fascination and danger of a particularly charged kind.

Susan Benson[1]

On most days, but especially in the summer, when people wear less concealing clothing, tattoos pass us on the street, wait on us at tables, gaze back at us from magazines and television screens, flaunt themselves on the beach. We see Maori armbands, Chinese characters, bellicose dragons, delicate rosebuds. In a duplicating reflexive mode, as tattoos appear on more bodies, the media report on them, the fad spreads further—in a seemingly unending cycle. Many models (Linda Evangelista, Christy Turlington, or Tyson Beckford, a striking Ralph Lauren male model, to name a few) are photographed with their tattoos prominently displayed. Celebrities, like Eminem, but including basketball, movie, and rock stars, sport tattoos, spawning growing circles of imitators and copycats. A-list Madonna allows her tattoo to be seen; down the list Drew Barrymore has a page on a tattoo Web site. The tattoo has become an emblem of transformation that visually announces the bearer's new identity. There are specials on tattoos run on National Public Radio and some of the cable channels. Every week it seems that the newspapers carry some sort of tattoo item. Some are short fillers, like the one about the ex-marine who sued a tattoo parlor for spelling "villain" incorrectly on his arm. Others are featured stories, such as one describing the painful process of tattoo removal.

Somewhat surprising in the context of the growing phenomenon of tattoos, mature bourgeois women are getting tattooed, though as yet nothing approaching the numbers of teenagers, college students, and yuppies. Middle-class women sport both open and concealed tattoos—on upper back edge of shoulder (to be displayed when a wide-neck shirt slips) or on the stomach (near the navel, for low trousers) or on the ankle (to catch the downward roving eye). In other words, the gender and class of those getting tattooed has changed: from mostly men to almost equal numbers of women; from people at the periphery (convicts, gang members, punks, sailors, prostitutes, circus freaks) to members of the establishment. Mark C. Taylor, an art history professor at Williams College, notes that except for a brief popularity "among European royalty and aristocrats at the turn of the [twentieth] century," tattoos have "generally been associated with marginal individuals and social groups."[2] Taylor refers to an early benchmark of modernism, the1908 essay on "Ornament and Crime" by Adolph Loos, in which the latter went so far as to say that he who was tattooed was "either a criminal or degenerate aristocrat. If someone who is tattooed dies in freedom, then he does so a few years before he would have committed murder."[3] Whatever the brief spurt of interest among a tiny elite group and the prison population, it was not until the late twentieth century that we have seen the growth of the phenomenon among the masses.

These introductory remarks place the author on the outside, as one gazing at the phenomena of tattooing and piercing, a scopophiliac who loves to see visual variety. The chapter is not based on first-person experience nor does it attempt to take the point of view from inside the tattooed or pierced body. To the outsider, the differences between tattoo and piercing are located in areas of emphasis and focus.

Tattoo and piercing often blend into one entity, one category, in public perception. Both require the skin to be pierced, though in varying degrees. Both are ways of decorating/transforming the body. The fact that "tattoo parlor" is the generic term for a place where tattooing and piercing take place also helps us think of the two as parts of the same phenomenon. What remains unseen is that both practices are symbolic acts of transformation through what Kenneth Burke called "mortification."

A Burkean reading shows that both tattooing and piercing are symbolic acts that expiate hierarchical guilt through purifying acts of mortification. Both the tattooed and the pierced have enacted dramas of transformation and redemption. The convict's racist epithets and the schoolgirl's rose, the barbell in the tongue and the ring in the nose, are enactments of a symbolic mortification ritual that purifies those who wear them and leaves a lasting display of their identification with and place within some desired tribe.

The first three sections of this chapter offer a focused examination of Burke's ideas in relation to tattooing and piercing: (1) Burke's redemptive model of communication and how it accounts for tattooing and piercing as purifying symbolic actions; (2) Burke's analysis of redemptive identification as a prime motive of symbolic action in general and, thus, of tattooing and piercing specifically; and (3) based on Burke's explanation of "division," my consideration of concealment as part of display, with attention to visibility and placement as important variables. The next three sections presuppose Burke's theory while considering special issues associated with tattooing or piercing: (4) the popularity of tattoos as corporeal emblems of transformation; (5) the significance of the concepts "civilized" and "primitive" as they bear upon tattoos and piercings; and (6) the phenomenon of piercing considered as more extreme (literally, deeper) than tattooing.

Burke's Model of Redemption

On the topic of the growing and widespread phenomenon of the tattoo in the Western world, a culture critic could begin by speculating on postmodern eclecticism—in other words, the acquirer of tattoos is choosing his expression, perhaps from the "primitives." A Freudian might continue with a discussion of tattoos in terms of fetishism. Or, going a different route, the film scholar could approach the subject on the basis of visual pleasure.

Scopophilia, Freud's term for just what the root words mean, love of looking, is closely connected to the idea of the primacy of the eye/vision/visual that art historians write about. Tattoo as art. The social scientist might hypothesize the postglobalization need for community—in other words, McLuhan's global community with Vietnam in your living room is only virtual reality; one still needs the community of material others of flesh and blood. Indeed, McLuhan might claim that the practices of tattooing and body piercing are emblems of a new tribalism that, he predicted, would permeate the new postliterate, media age. But Kenneth Burke would draw attention to these practices as enactment of symbolic dramas laced through and through with human motivations. It is instructive to read Burke again.[4]

Burke would contend that human communication is predominantly a symbolic drama enacted to alleviate guilt and to achieve redemption.[5] Humans as symbolizing beings are "goaded by a spirit of hierarchy" and "moved by a sense of order."[6] Hierarchy involves authority, levels of authority, and individuals up and down those levels.[7] Individuals caught in the pull of hierarchic impulses to move up, down, and across symbolic "orders" are simultaneously moralized by the negative, by the incompatible and often competing rules, norms, and strictures that define their relationships to the hierarchies that permeate their daily lives.[8] Since, as Burke points out, it is impossible to obey all hierarchical "thou shalt nots," individuals find themselves caught between competing commitments, desires, and values. Inevitably they violate "commandments" and undergo a secular version of the Fall. The experience of one's own imperfections, flaws, and limitations in the face of exacting and often competing hierarchical strictures culminates in the awareness of one's own transgressions, or "pollution," to use Burke's vocabulary. One suffers guilt, as Burke would have it, and the guilty turn to symbolic acts of identification in pursuit of redemption.[9]

There are two kinds of redemptive identification through which the "guilty" undergo a purifying symbolic rebirth: "victimage" and "mortification." Victimage achieves symbolic rebirth by transferring guilt for one's own "pollution" onto some external "vessel" or "scapegoat" that, through symbolic sacrifice, purges that guilt. Burke defined the projection device in his classic study of Hitler's *Mein Kampf*:

> . . . the "curative" process that comes with the ability to hand over one's ills to a scapegoat, thereby getting purification by dissociation. This is especially medicinal, since the sense of frustration leads to a self-questioning. Hence, if one can hand over his infirmities to a vessel or "cause," outside the self, one can battle an external enemy instead of battling the enemy within.[10]

The second kind of redemptive identification involves confronting one's pollution through an act of mortification, an act of self-sacrifice that "cleanses" one's self of guilt. As Burke explains it, mortification "must come from within. The mortified must, with one aspect of himself, be saying no to another aspect of himself."[11]

Though the redemptive dramas enacted through tattooing and body piercing involve both kinds of identification, this chapter will stress how those practices are purifying acts of self-sacrifice, or mortification, that yield visible emblems of transformation, or rebirth. One reason for this emphasis is that tattooing and body piercing are, in varying degrees, overt and quite literal acts of mortification in the sense of self-willed mutilation, or direct violation of the body. These practices thus resonate with the theologically tinged meaning of mortification that, as Burke puts it, involves "subjection of the passions and appetites, by penance, abstinence or painful severities inflicted on the body."[12] In varying degrees, the practices of tattooing and body piercing involve voluntary, self-chosen infliction of bodily pain that requires, according to Burke, "a kind of governance, an extreme form of 'self-control,' the deliberate disciplinary 'slaying' of any motive that, for 'doctrinal reasons,' one thinks of as unruly."[13] Though there are many useful studies of Burke's guilt-purification-redemption cycle,[14] few examine the purifying symbolism of overt, literal acts against the bodies of others (through acts of scapegoating) or of ourselves (through acts of mortification).[15]

For example, the prisoner has gone against authority, rejected the morality of his society, is made to feel guilty for his crime and also for his difference (or his lawless indifference); in prison, his act of crying out a loud, metaphorical "*no*" takes the form of a nonverbal gesture of defiance—a tattoo. That it is an act against the establishment (because he is not allowed the tools for tattooing, he must find or make some kind of sharp instrument to prick himself and acquire the ashes to rub into the wound) does not lessen the fact that in a Freudian way he is also punishing himself, inflicting pain on himself in the process, or, as Burke defines mortification, "carrying-out . . . judgments pronounced . . . against the self."[16] In terms of the position of the subject—the man in prison—his act of tattooing himself is an act of mortification, his wish to purify himself. And, part of his action is motivated by his wish to be accepted into the normative order of prison inmates, an inversion of the conventional, law-abiding order.[17]

At the same time, to the subject (the prisoner), the tattoo is a symbol of his victimage by society/authority. Here I should point out that although Burke speaks of "property," as making for "embarrassments,"[18] an individual's body is his property, even if he owns nothing else, and property that cannot be physically taken away from him short of death. From society's point of view, the control of the prisoner's body at some level is scapegoating, which purifies society. The authority (the legal system) does make claims on his body by putting it behind bars, limiting his movements, and does so definitively when it takes his life. In other words, the act of tattooing himself is an act that announces his proprietary interest in his own body. But the act also becomes redemptive, from the objective point of view, in the sense of catharsis it bestows on the law-abiding viewer. His incarceration is a "ritual resolving of civic tensions,"[19] and the tattoo is a symbolic acknowledgment of his antisocietal stance. Or one could say, as Burke does, that it is "'redemption' through *victimage*."[20] The public can achieve a kind of "social cohesion" by focusing on one who has drawn attention to himself by means of the symbolic tattoo, figuratively renaming himself as a transgressor. (Though fewer and fewer law-abiding citizens have a continuing problem with tattoos, nevertheless, historically those who wore them seemed like thugs or pariahs outside the acceptable bounds of society.) To state a generalized paradigm: the tattooer mortifies his flesh, whereby he becomes a societal scapegoat. But we must qualify that generalization to include the fact that the fashion model or the trendy teenager might not have the same motive as the convict. More than likely, they identify solely with their own subset among the tattooed while rejecting any or some "other" subset. Even in diverse subsets, however, the individual's conflict involves turning one part of the self against the purportedly polluted other part. The mortification mechanism remains the same.

Redemptive Identification as a Motive of Rhetoric

Central to redemption is the concept of identification that is based on the dual need for transformation and for community. Burke uses *Samson Agonistes* to introduce the subject of identification, specifically Milton's own "identification with a blind giant who slew himself in slaying enemies of the Lord" (an identification between Puritans [Milton] and Israelites [Samson], Royalists and Philistines). He highlights "a more complicated kind of identification: here the poet presents a motive in an essentially magnified or perfected form, in some way tragically purified or transcended; the imagery of death reduces the motive to *ultimate* terms [Burke's italics]." In other words, the imagery of slaying enacts a symbolic process of purification through transformation. Burke takes the "imagery of slaying (slaying of either the self or another)" as a "special case of transformation, and transformation involves the ideas and imagery of *identification*."[21] Thus, Samson's slaying of himself is a way to transform himself, but it also is a way for Milton to put himself into the action within the Samson story, thus achieving purifying transformation of his self through identification with the righteousness of Samson's cause and with his towering strength, more moral, even, than physical.

Following Burke's model, a person who acquires tattoos identifies with those who wear tattoos; one who pierces, with those who are pierced. The putative tattooer wants to transform himself, not just to acknowledge some inner change, but to make a noticeable statement, to display what I later call a "corporeal emblem of transformation." We cannot underestimate the need to be noticed. "Hey, look at me. I've changed." She/he wants to be thought of as someone who has not conformed to the norm, mere ordinariness to her/his way of thinking. Considered in these terms, the tattooed person gets to enjoy her/his in-your-face statement of difference. She/he becomes one with all those who are tattooed, who are protesting or, at the very least, resisting some aspect of the dominant society. Tattooing is a way of marching in the Gay Pride Day parade even if one is heterosexual. Transformations could be gender pronouncements: unempowered women motivated to look more like macho men. Or they could be self-criticizing proclamation: the unnoticed woman or man opting to declare her or his sexual appeal. Or class longings: liberated bourgeois determined to look more like underclass workers. Or age impersonations: young punks needing to look like more intimidating older punks, at the same time that middle-aged men and women yearn to join the youth culture.

Burke's identification is associated with what he calls "consubstantiality"; when one person identifies with another, the ambiguity remains that he is "'substantially one' with a person other than himself," while at the same time "he remains unique, an individual locus of motives . . . both joined and separate, at once a distinct substance and consubstantial with another."[22] This ambiguity would be one way of explaining the diversity among the people who get tattooed. They are consubstantial in their need to show how they are one with a group, part of a community, but they still remain distinct as individuals, having had their own unique histories for transforming themselves. Burke reminds us that "[w]e need never deny the presence of strife, enmity, faction as a characteristic motive of rhetorical expression."[23] Indeed, he delves into "the possibilities of identification in its *partisan* aspects . . . ways in which individuals are at odds with one another, or become identified with groups more or less at odds with one another . . . [at odds because] 'identification' is . . . to confront the implications of *division*."[24] Burke's insight is to see in the concept of identification "its ironic counterpart: division."[25] He states the paradox: "Put identification and division ambiguously together, so that you cannot know for certain just where one ends and the other begins, and you have the characteristic invitation to rhetoric."[26] Born into one order, the person acquiring the tattoo is joining another. Among paradoxes, consider that the tattoo is its own form of conformity—that is, conformity to another norm—at the same time that it is usually perceived by both the tattooed and the viewer as rebellion against the status quo, whatever it is, since the status quo is at any given moment made up of differences.

Division, Display, Concealment

I have shown that Burke points to the operation of division within one person. For example, the convict is mortifying himself in ways that divide him from his old conventional, law-abiding life at the same time that he is purifying himself within the prison hierarchy. Each individual is divided between the wish to transform himself *and* the Fall ("pollution") that accompanies the transformation, hence, the need to purify himself. I shall consider next how Burke's account of division extends to concealment as part of the manifestation of visual display.

Featured in an article in *Time* magazine on John William King, the white supremacist who dragged African American James Byrd Jr. to his death in east Texas, are photographs of King, one fully dressed without a sign of tattooing on his face and neck and one that shows a partial torso, mainly his underarm and upper arm, densely covered, "cataloguing some of King's racist tattoos, which cover 65% of his skin."[27] King is the kind of marginal person who acquired his tattoos while serving time in prison. And he is an example of one kind of concealment. You cannot see his tattoos when he is clothed to appear in court. But when he was arrested, the tattoos became public. The prosecution used their content—hate messages and signs—in their opening presentation against him. But his tattoos cannot be seen unless he is stripped of clothing; they are not supposed to be seen unless he means them to be seen. When they are seen, they are self-display as confrontation. When they are seen, he presents himself as a monster. Though a felon generally loses his rights to privacy, still, one wonders if he is not entitled to privacy when he has deliberately concealed markings on his body. In another close-up of a hate tattoo, an arm is thrust out from behind bars, with a swastika prominently featured inside the crook of the elbow (an attempt at concealment?). The essay that follows this lead photo states that prison guards are often racist, so except for the fact that the arm is extended out from behind the bars, it could be the arm of a guard. The ambiguity is worth noting. On the next page, the caption for a photograph of tattooed prisoners states that "inmates of most American prisons tend to segregate themselves into race-based gangs."[28]

Of course, such tattoos often are revealed for the impact they will have on viewers. Figure C15 exhibits a hate tattoo, confrontationally racist, intense—a flash, or a tattoo design on paper that customers can choose from. What social circumstances led to this flash? It is clearly anti-Asian: the eyes, specifically Chinese; the queue. Was it created in the context of the glut of railroad workers taking jobs away from Americans, white men who had arrived in the West a short while earlier? What is clear is that it goes against the values of the social norm in its violence, assuming the values of the hegemonic, white Christian—that is, it is not only a head severed at the neck, but cleaved in two as an added gratuitous measure.

One assumes that hate tattoos today express the wearer's racism. Defiance is often a motivation, as are related reactions of protest, resistance, and rebellion against the authorities, the establishment. That tattoos are permanent, or at least troublesome to remove, makes them even more defiant. The permanence of tattoos is critical. It is not as if one could say, "Could you remove your offensive tattoo please?" (as one might ask the thoughtless theatergoer to take off her hat). Clearly the need to make a statement applies generally to the marginalized groups I have named. But the individual sense of alienation that most people share to some degree is what led to their marginalization in the first place. And the marginalized tend to end up in groups to achieve some sense of belonging, of community. The reinforcement of individual alienation to group marginalization to group alienation seems to be a dynamic progression that continues.

Generally speaking, certain kinds of images are hidden. Usually, their statement is too extreme in some way; most people would consider them offensive. King's are too racist. Others are too erotic, pornographic, brutal, violent. One man in a tattoo parlor pulled up his pant leg to show me an erect penis the length of his shin, a small, out-of-scale cowgirl rider impaled on it.

On the other hand, the need to *display* the hidden is always there. I recently heard of a woman who has a large pair of beautiful sinuous carp covering her entire back, perhaps following some old Japanese design. Yet she wanted to display her tattoo, which was on a normally private part of her. The massage therapist thought the client came for a massage because she needed someone to see them.

The question of whether to display or conceal and the urge to have it both ways have led to an uneasy tension illustrated in a matchbook cover found in a bar (see figure 29).

Burke's discussion of division can be extended to consider the divisions among the different bodies that are tattooed. Keep in mind that the rhetoric of tattoos is not rooted in words so much as in the display of images on the body, a wide variety of different images in different styles. There is no agreement that the same image means the same thing to different wearers. Generally, display sites depend on personal preference (unless they are club

29. To reveal or conceal? An uneasy tension

or gang related). Further, the idea of display is complicated by the strategies of concealment even though they are ultimately about display. Possibly somewhere along the way, a wearer discovered that concealing the tattoo could still deliver the satisfaction of being a rebel, albeit a secret one. One has only to view the range of what is being displayed, the motivation behind individual choices, the sites of various displays, including what most of us consider very private parts, to realize that the notion of concealment is merely a way to limit the more public aspects of display, to save secrets for the favored few. Showing or concealing can be seen as part of the larger dialectic, or we can understand them in terms of Burke's "ironic counterpart," the division (one of many divisions) possible within the tattooed.

A very large division is the one between underclass tattoos and bourgeois/fashion tattoos. The media treat these two groups differently, tending to exploit the tattoos of criminals and punks by making the tattoo the entire point of the photo. Candids of movie stars and models that picture them with their tattoos showing, on the other hand, do not focus on the tattoos per se; they are merely present, at most secondary to beautiful hair blowing in the wind or the person with whom the star is chatting.

Another way of categorizing the divide is to point to those who acquired tattoos: historically involving few in number, currently endemic in its popularity. Surely there is a difference between these groups, some would challenge. I would argue only in degree in terms of a need for *transformation*. The non-tattooed wonder: why insist on a permanent rose when one could choose to change to a lily, to a daisy, to a plumeria, or to a dragon for that matter, in washable colors? But the fashion statement of tattoos for a Linda Evangelista or a Christy Turlington might mean: I'm giving up the rapid transience of fashion, a different outfit for each walk on the runway, a different look for each designer, occasion, or season, for the very permanence that the non-tattooed have a hard time understanding.

Corporeal Emblems of Transformation

I asked the psychotherapist Janna Malamud Smith, who wrote a book on privacy, *Private Matters*, a basic question.[29] Why did she think tattoos had become such a fetish? She speculated that perhaps "most people feel too anonymous and want to have something that announces them." She added, "I suppose it somehow says your body is yours. Someone else *looks*, but you've been there first."[30] It seems reasonable to see this need to assert an identity, assert one's claim to one's own body, and to suggest that tattooing can be seen as a landmark along the lifelong path of establishing identity.

In a more formal mode, Susan Benson, in a fine, even-handed essay on contemporary tattoo and piercing in Europe and America, comes to a similar conclusion, building on Alfred Gell's insightful analysis and theory in his study of Polynesian tattoos: "the puncturing, cutting and piercing of the skin; the flow of blood and the infliction of pain; the healing and closure of the wound; and the indelible trace of the process, a visible and permanent mark on yet underneath the skin . . . [create] 'an inside which comes from the outside . . . the exteriorization of the interior which is simultaneously the interiorization of the exterior.'"[31] Benson emphasizes the idea of interiority by examining cultures such as the European and American, where she finds that "self-realization and self-mastery . . . central to conceptions of personhood" lie within the person, or "inside." "In such cultures," she continues, "it might be argued, the skin, the border zone between the bounded self and the social world thought to encompass that self, a membrane that protects but may also conceal, must be a zone of fascination and danger of a particularly charged kind."[32] This is a compelling view of the appeal of tattoos. She arrives at the point, where Burke considers motives, in her own way: "[In the United States there is] a kind of *corporeal absolutism* [my italics]: that it is through the body and in the body that personal identity is to be forged and selfhood sustained."[33]

Corporeal absolutism leads to the idea that one can transform identity if one changes the body. Tattoos and body piercings are corporeal emblems of transformation that at once symbolize purgation of some undesired feature from oneself and purification through identification with some alternate, normative order. Consider, for example, how less-confrontational tattoos display a less-confrontational but nonetheless self-transformative project. Many of the people getting tattooed are conscious of tattoos merely as a fashion statement. At their most visible, tattoos decorate the body as clothes do. We wear clothes because it is the custom among "civilized" countries to do so. That said, we make the wearing of clothes into statements or displays of our personal attractiveness, our sexuality, our economic status, our aesthetic taste, ourselves. Even when the clothes are hidden most of the time, as in underwear, we might buy at Victoria's Secret. Many women who have tattoos consider them sexy, not unlike lace underwear. Sexuality is simultaneously endorsed and condemned by the self-contradictory bourgeoisie that most people claim to have come from. So the spirit of rebellion against the stodgy, puritanical tendency of the entrepreneurial class is recombined with the wish for freedom from constraints and freedom of self-expression, in the manner of Helen Gurley Brown's sermon of transformation that is the strategy for selling *Cosmopolitan*. The popularity of both the image of the *Cosmo* girl and the magazine tells the story.

Burke speaks of "autonomous" activities: "The fact that an activity is capable of reduction to intrinsic, autonomous principles does not argue that it is free from identification with other orders of motivation extrinsic to it . . . [it is] in the region of rhetoric when considering the identifications whereby a specialized activity makes one a participant in some social or economic class. 'Belonging' in this sense is rhetorical."[34] The office worker now turned *Cosmo* girl belongs to a new and, she perceives, trendier group.

One used to take for granted that wishing to "belong" meant upwardly striving. But today, "belonging" can be downwardly mobile, as among certain liberal, economically comfortable women whose yearning to belong to some utopian idea of sisterhood allies them with welfare mothers, minimum-wage earners. At the same time, for years haute couture has been borrowing from street kids. In the complex world of fashion, the white middle class, in part copying high-society/jet-set/fashion-designer fashion, appropriates as well a certain look from black ghetto kids or punks or the noticeably marginalized, who in turn have been influenced (and are openly appealed to) by high cost design (as in two-hundred-dollar sneakers). The tattoo has become that kind of fashion look. Although fashion per se dilutes the tattoo intention of ex-cons or Hell's Angels, still those who choose to be tattooed for fashion's sake know what the connotations of tattoos are and evidently are willing, if not fully consciously, to be lumped with the stereotypes that had already been established: rebel/outlaw/counterestablishmentarian.

It *is* difficult to find order in the seeming incoherence of tattoo images among contemporary youth and middle-class women. Women seem to be striving for something not connected to the typically male tattoos, caught as they are between the old, underclass images and the new uses of "other"/ritual symbols. There is a trend among young men to display Chinese characters that mean some abstract quality such as "strength." However, it is notable that they cannot read the images with which they adorn themselves. Permanent they may be, but unreadable to wearer or viewer, who must rely on the tattoo "artist" to be the dependable authority for getting the "authentic" meaning. The hazard of misinterpretation is at least as present as physical infection. There is also a trend among young men to copy the fierce look of primitive warriors. Perhaps these signs are part of the new-age spirituality, feeling the "magic," the spirit of the symbol. Many of those who are tattooed stress the celebratory nature of their acquisition of tattoos. I assume it is a celebration of their freedom to express themselves in the way they choose. That this celebration requires initial pain returns us to the Burkean notions of purification and the quest for redemption.

Burke would take as a given, that in order to assert our individuality (always a high priority in being American) or feel as if one is an innovator, we insist on some announcement, some *display*, of "this is me." In the specific case of women's bodies as a locality to be illustrated, I would suggest that claiming the body as the site of the display might have been furthered by the feminist movement's emphasis on the concept of *Our Bodies / Ourselves* (1970), the title of a central document/book for the movement. The right to abortion is one aspect of reclaiming our bodies; the right to fulfilling female sexual desires is another. The theater event *The Vagina Monologues* is yet another (the repeated calls for audiences to shout "cunt"—eighteen thousand voices in the 1999 performance at Madison Square Garden—toned down to "vagina" in some university productions, is a strategy to raise consciousness, to reaffirm one's body without shame). And tattoos could be said to belong in this category, too. Hence we see the rise of tattoos on intellectual, mature women. An extreme image of individual female rights also illustrates the division between (open) display and (sometime) concealment. There are women with radical mastectomies who celebrate with tattoos where their breasts used to be. These tattoos are normally hidden under their clothing, as their breasts were when they had breasts. But in order to make the big statement, they proudly exhibit them at parades, for photographs.[35]

A Dialectic: Civilized versus Primitive

We are used to thinking that wearing clothes is "civilized." Civilized, as opposed to primitive, is a loaded word. It is analogous to the range of meaning of "Culture" with an uppercase *C,* representing high culture a la Matthew Arnold (or "Kultur," as Ezra Pound called it) versus "culture" with a decidedly lowercase *c,* as anthropologists use the term, meaning "the concepts, habits, skills, arts, instruments, institutions, etc. of a given people in a given period."

It is now politically correct to give all cultures (lowercase *c*) an equal status, not privileging one culture as "civilized" over another as "primitive." The fact is that the recent renewed interest in body decoration among all groups is a real phenomenon of the late twentieth century, with no end in sight in the twenty-first. And I might reiterate here that Burke would see all tattooing and piercing, including in non-Western cultures, as a mortification ritual. We tend to see more clearly when our culture is estranged from original practices. Body decoration is a site where one can observe what happens when (old dichotomies of) civilized and primitive coincide, when (old dichotomies of) bourgeois and fringe classes seem in collusion, when high art and popular—even low—art come together. In an unexpected way, body decoration has become a visual rhetoric of liberty, equality, and fraternity, at the same time that it is an expression of globalization.

Indigenously, Americans have always been inordinately fond of visible signs—in Puritan times, the big white mansion on the hill was a visible sign of grace. It was a public display of God's blessings on (and this was the point) a man of virtue. By the late twentieth century, among a large group of the innerly disaffected, tattoos and piercings had become visible signs of dissatisfaction with hegemonic culture. The surface is cool, so cool we do not have to be heated in our discussion of what's wrong with the world and the older generation; we wear our disaffection and disdain on our body. Man, y'know? Worn on the outside, the surface is what you get; it is a way to exhibit deeper meaning. Or, is the unarticulated emblem all there is to it? The tattoo began as a visible sign of the rebel, a badge of difference. One could observe that a plethora of wearers of the same badges becomes its own conformity.

Taylor explains that at the end of the nineteenth century, one of the contributing factors to tattooing was the "emergence of the field of anthropology" and "the creation of ethnographic museums."[36] Europe had never seen anything like the artifacts brought back from Africa, Asia, and the South Pacific and, in archetypal Eurocentric hubris, named the art and the culture brought back from the field "primitive." As Taylor says, "European modernism invented itself by inventing primitivism."[37] It is invention in this sense: once having seen the exotically different, we label it primitive, thus transforming the objectivity of what we have seen into our subjective notion of what primitive is. Like Said's Orientalism, we declare *this* is what the "other" is. Taylor goes on to state plainly what the words imply: "Primitivism represents the infantile state of humanity and modernism epitomizes maturity."[38] In this argument, whereas the primitive, the child, knows only to do his thing, Picasso (like those who elect to be tattooed) *chooses* to include the "primitive."

To continue from Taylor's lead, clearly *National Geographic* magazine contributed to the availability of images that were "primitive." Many of us saw our first fully naked men and women in the *National Geographic,* and they were always in the context of the modern West looking at the exotic, primitive "other" in godforsaken corners of the world. The exchange of goods globally includes the commodification of body art. Might not viewing photographs of scarification, still practiced among peoples in Africa, initiate a new fashion practice among those affected by its aesthetic? In several firsthand accounts that I have read, the person getting a tattoo mentioned the *National Geographic* as a first awakening to the culture of body transformations.

New primitivism is a dissatisfaction with civilized life. But often that progresses to a need for community, a yearning for return to "better" earlier times. Except now, you no longer have to be born into the tribe; you can choose to join the tribe. It becomes a new tribalism—tribalism borrowed, colonialized, and the result of globalization. Globalization has taught us, and we have learned, to identify with "others," with wanting to show our ability to reconnect with the essential biorhythms by looking like them as, for instance, Rasta dreadlocks adopted by blond kids.

Some Thoughts about Piercing

The avant-garde exhibitions of the seventies had an impact on the piercings that were to follow in their wake. As Taylor phrases it, conceptual art extended "abstraction to dematerialization. . . . As a counter to the veneration of abstraction and immateriality, the body artist offers his or her own flesh and blood as the artistic medium."[39] There is the hearsay of a video performance that showed a German artist slicing his penis, piece by piece; others claim that this demonstration, in fact, never occurred. The media disseminate actual and rumored images and happenings with the speed of sound. Here, too, imitation plays a part.

In both tattoo and piercing, we have an emblem of difference from the majority, the mainstream, the social norm; an emblem of identification as a member of the fuck-you group, an emblem of what the owner considers beautification and decoration. So display is certainly part of it. Like the tree crashing in the forest, there is no sound if no one is there to hear it. Tattoos and piercings must be acquired, and they are meant to be seen, if not by all, at least by someone. A piercing of the clitoris would certainly be known to her lover; but in a photograph, it is also displayed to a photographer, and in books that feature extreme piercing, to untold numbers of readers.

But tongue piercings, nipple and penis piercings, and tattoos (on the rump, for example) that are covered by clothes are clearly not meant to be seen by the world—only by certain people, for erotic purposes; they are meant to turn your partner on. Here, we enter a world that is normally relegated to pornography. Is part of the titillation that here we are really on the edge of a precipice? Like the climber of Everest or the dope addict, how far can we go and still return from the journey? As a researcher in this subject, when will I have to close my eyes? We have taken the whole journey from scopophilia to scopophobia.

Piercing can be seen as a more extreme form of tattooing, which itself requires piercing but at a shallower level (one millimeter deep). And, as I mentioned earlier, the fact that "tattoo parlor" is the generic term for a place where both tattooing and piercing take place helps us think of the two as similar. We tend to think of tattooing versus piercing as yet another example of division within identification: some people identify with tattooers, while others identify with piercers. The rhetoric of the pierced true believer emphasizes pride in difference, ability to take pain, but the repulsion of the critical spectator, the unconvinced, is expressed in pejorative analysis. The effects of piercing on the outsider are consistently more intense than reactions to tattoo.

Piercing penetrates deeper into the body, beyond the skin, into the flesh. Gell's "interiorization of the exterior" is taken to an extreme degree. Piercing has almost all the requisites for "pure" mortification: punishing one's body through pain; a relative lack of other considerations such as the aesthetic (the tattooed one's belief that his designs are beautiful or that they enhance his look in terms of desirability or fashion). The motives for piercing include some need to make private pain public. Rueckert uses two examples of self-victimage: one is of a nun who "flagellates herself in the privacy of her cell to mortify the flesh (to negate . . . what her creed tells her is a negative)" and the other is of a "holy man in India . . . [who] does public penitential acts, who somersaulted fifty miles."[40] While Rueckert does not develop the notion of difference between the two acts of self-victimage —the one private and the other public—the examples open our eyes to what is happening today. The private is moving into the arena of the public.

Early Christian saints and martyrs mortified their flesh, or were mortified, for religious reasons and died for their beliefs. The icon of an ecstatic St. Sebastian pierced all over by arrows still sticking in his body is a particular kind of Christian archetype—painful suffering in the flesh for ultimate union with God. Because an alarming number of early Christians rushed to martyrdom in their zeal to be redeemed, St. Augustine felt it necessary to condemn suicide. In general, historically, exception has been made for mortifiers among religious penitents, but the more extreme phenomena among those who claim neither belief nor cult have been regarded as irrational. Until recent times, slashing oneself, piercing oneself, or mortifying one's own flesh were cause enough to assure one's place in an asylum for the insane. And yet literal mortification continues to exist in "decorative" piercing.

In the name of beautification, many cultures have had customs that have offended other cultures: plugs in ears or lips, elongating the neck, scarification, foot binding. Some mutilations are in the name of health and religious morality, such as circumcision or clitorectomy. These all alter the body unnaturally.

Is piercing decoration or mutilation? Let us consider first its least extreme form. Tattooing is a kind of piercing with color added. As we consider, keep in mind what else society "allows" or "tolerates": painting the lips, shaving (facial, body, pubic), waxing, electrolysis hair removal, plastic surgery (face-lifting, nose jobs, eye jobs, liposuction, breast implants —whether silicone or salt water in plastic bags—the latest Botox injections). In the documentary *The Eyes of Tammy Faye* (2000), directed by Fenton Bailey and Randy Barbato, we learn in the course of the film portrait that Tammy Faye, the ex-television evangelist, cannot be given a makeover look because her eyebrows and lip outline are tattooed on, are permanent. Only a degree of difference raises questions and tests viewer boundaries. Tattoos make boundaries unstable. What, then, about acts of piercing through tissue other than skin—piercing, pricking, entering? Freud has engaged this aspect. Earrings for pierced ears are acceptable. Then why are nose rings or diamond studs—common in India, for example —problematic? What about belly button rings, studs in the eyebrow, barbells in the tongue, rings through the nipples, rings and rods through the penis, through the clitoris? What is within the range of "normal"? When is it perverse? Of course, we all have subjective responses. Objective reasoning is a little more difficult. Tattoo and piercing destabilize our ways of seeing, thinking, and analyzing. In Burke's scheme of things, both are part of a code of resistance. Burke's rhetoric of motives sheds light on the phenomena of tattoos and piercing. And even as his theory explains why the faddist, the follower of fashion, does as she or he does, it is the ever-expanding world of tattoo and piercing that tells us how much more urgent those motives are than anyone had suspected.

Summarizing Observations

Burke's analysis of identification and division within the symbolic purification process lies at the base of this discussion on tattoo and piercing. Burke begins with the identification we share— namely, that we are all "fallen"—and goes on to the complexities of division, those within the self, where one part says no to another part, and those among various people who, though agreed on certain aspects (tattoos, say), disagree on others (racist and violent lifestyle versus new-age spirituality, for example). The purification process itself takes two forms: making others victims (scapegoating) and making ourselves victims (mortification). Both are at work in tattooing and body piercing as symbolic actions.

Redemptive identification in either form manifests tension between consubstantiality and individualism and, thus, contains the seeds of division. To explore the many divisions among those tattooed, I chose to focus on display and concealment, what is hidden and why. Closely related to that discussion is the idea that tattoos are corporeal emblems that symbolize transformations in identity; the wearer displays them for others to behold as tangible manifestations of having acquired a "purified" identity, with corresponding implications for division and identification. Display of identity is thus linked indelibly to the dynamic between revealing and concealing tattoos. The contrast between having oneself engraved with polite images (rosebuds and butterflies) or with erotically confrontational or politically inflammatory images (swastikas and hard-ons) serves as an obvious illustration of the implications of revealing and concealing in disclosing identity through display.

I also discussed how the terms "civilized" and "primitive," a difference that the "civilized" invented, become tangled. The civilized world not only takes credit for discovering "primitive" iconography, but also rushes to emblazon these deliciously "other" images on their own pampered flesh. With globalization, body decoration becomes yet another kind of commodity that can be purchased to display the right aesthetic and the desired identity. Even so, the "civilized" largely remain blind to the mortification rituals that they themselves enact when acquiring these images, though they would be quick to see "ritual" in similar images when emblazoned on "primitive" bodies. As Burke would contend, both are symbolic acts of mortification, whatever else they might be said to be.

Finally, I considered body piercing in comparison with tattooing. The pierced, too, enact a redemptive drama through display and concealment of a corporeal emblem of transformation before potential beholders. But piercing exemplifies, to a greater extent than tattooing, literal as well as symbolic mortification.

There are at least two implications that follow from the analyses in this chapter. One follows from the presumption that our identities—while certainly not formed and re-formed arbitrarily—are not permanently fixed or otherwise static; rather, they are dynamic and continue to develop within the ongoing drama of human life. The guilt-purification-redemption cycle is continuous and is not terminated by any single symbolic action. But tattoos, unlike most body piercings, are corporeal emblems of transformation that designate a new identity in a permanently fixed, tangible form. The possibility always remains open that identifications and divisions will shift and that those emblems of redemptive transformation could eventually become enduring, tangible symbols of a polluted identity in need of purification. Removal of the tattoo then becomes the painful act of symbolic—and literal—mortification through which the wearer again seeks purifying redemption.

The second implication is that a Burkean perspective on the symbolic acts of tattooing and piercing inescapably implicates both those who exhibit them and those who behold them within symbolic drama. Those of us who might react negatively to the exhibition are ourselves performing purifying symbolic acts, perhaps in the form of victimage or scapegoating. I am right thinking, clear thinking; she is not. And, of course, others might see the display as exemplary of a path to transformation of the self and, perhaps, pursue redemption through similar purifying acts of mortification manifested in the corporeal form of a tattoo or a piercing.

Throughout this inquiry I invited readers to join me in an us/them relationship with the tattooed and pierced. Any such division turns into a subject/object model. In this case, "we" do not participate in tattooing or piercing, but "they" do. The emphasis of this inquiry is to view "them" from "our" nonparticipatory perspective. Even as I acknowledge that we all are caught within the implications of perspective, I also insist that all of us—the tattooed and the pierced and the untattooed and the unpierced—are participants in symbolic dramas. Displays of tattoos or of piercings and responses to those displays are symbolic actions laced with attitudes. If Burke is at all right—and I think that he is—those symbolic actions, however variable, implicate us all in the dramatic cycle of expiating guilt in pursuit of redemption through symbolic acts of mortification, victimage, or both.

Notes

This paper is dedicated to Larry Prelli, generous editor, scholar, and friend.

1. Susan Benson, "Inscriptions on the Self: Reflection on Tattooing and Piercing in Contemporary Euro-America," in *Written on the Body: The Tattoo in European and American History,* ed. Jane Caplan, 235 (London: Reaktion Books, 2000).

2. Mark C. Taylor, "Skinscapes," *Pierced Hearts and True Love: A Century of Drawings for Tattoos* (New York: The Drawing Center, 1998), 30.

3. Ibid., 32. Taylor explains Loos's "emphasis on tattooing" immediately following the citation: ". . . because he [Loos] sees in the practice the origin of all forms of ornamentation associated with the primitivism that humanity is destined to overcome. The movement from the primitive to the modern is characterized by the gradual disappearance of decoration."

4. For a clear and incisive analysis of and commentary on Burke's theory of dramatism, see William H. Rueckert, *Kenneth Burke and the Drama of Human Relations,* 2nd ed. (Berkeley: University of California Press, 1982). For critical discussions of Burke's works, see Barbara A. Biesecker, *Addressing Postmodernity: Kenneth Burke, Rhetoric, and a Theory of Social Change* (Tuscaloosa: University of Alabama Press, 1997), and Robert Wess, *Kenneth Burke: Rhetoric, Subjectivity, Postmodernism* (New York: Cambridge University Press, 1996).

5. And Burke's perspective for studying symbolic drama, his "dramatism," designates "those [terms] that begin in theories of *action* rather than in theories of *knowledge.*" Kenneth Burke, "On Human Behavior Considered 'Dramatically,'" appendix to *Permanence and Change: An Anatomy of Purpose,* 3rd ed. (Berkeley: University of California Press, 1984), 274. Burke's model of redemption is detailed within the context of his dramatistic vocabulary in this appendix, 274–94. Useful summary discussions of this model are found in Sonja K. Foss, Karen A. Foss, and Robert Trapp, *Contemporary Perspectives on Rhetoric* (Prospect Heights, Ill.: Waveland, 1985), 178–82; Bernard Brock, "Rhetorical Criticism: A Burkean Approach," in *Methods of Rhetorical Criticism: A Twentieth Century Perspective,* ed. Bernard L. Brock, Robert L. Scott, and James W. Chesebro, 3rd ed., 184–86 (Detroit, Mich.: Wayne State University Press, 1989); and especially Rueckert, *Kenneth Burke and the Drama of Human Relations,* 128–52.

6. Burke, "Definition of Man," in *Language as Symbolic Action: Essays on Life, Literature, and Method* (Berkeley: University of California Press, 1966), 15.

7. Burke, "On Human Behavior," 282. Burke's discussion of Coleridge's use of the staircase as a theoretical plan illustrates this idea, 279–81.

8. Burke, "Definition of Man," 9–13.

9. Kenneth Burke, *The Rhetoric of Religion: Studies in Logology* (Berkeley: University of California Press, 1970), 4–5.

10. Kenneth Burke, "The Rhetoric of Hitler's 'Battle,'" in *Philosophy of Literary Form: Studies in Symbolic Action,* 3rd ed. (Berkeley: University of California Press, 1973), 202–3; also see his discussions in "On Human Behavior," 283–89, 292–94; and *Grammar of Motives* (Berkeley: University of California Press, 1969), 406–8. Burke also reflects on the scapegoat mechanism in poetics in *Philosophy of Literary Form,* 39–51. For a useful commentary, see C. Allen Carter, *Kenneth Burke and the Scapegoat Process* (Norman: University of Oklahoma Press, 1996).

11. Burke, *The Rhetoric of Religion,* 190. Burke makes a similar point in his discussion about how in poetics—as in life itself—"symbolizing of an old self is complemented by the emergence of a new self." See *Philosophy of Literary Form,* 39. Burke also discusses mortification in "On

Human Behavior," 289–90. An analysis and application of the mortification mechanism that has informed my position is Floyd D. Anderson and Kevin R. McClure, "Teddy Agonistes: Redemptive Identification in Edward M. Kennedy's 1980 Presidential Primary Campaign" (paper presented at Eastern Communication Association, May 1998).

12. Burke, *The Rhetoric of Religion,* 190.

13. Ibid., 190.

14. See, for examples, Mari Boor Tonn, Valerie A. Endress, and John Diamond, "Hunting and Heritage on Trial: A Dramatistic Debate over Tragedy, Tradition, and Territory," *Quarterly Journal of Speech* 79 (1993): 165–81; Brian L. Ott and Eric Aoki, "The Politics of Public Tragedy: Media Framing of the Matthew Shepard Murder," *Rhetoric and Public Affairs* 5 (2002): 483–505; Barry Brummett, "Symbolic Form, Burkean Scapegoating, and Rhetorical Exigency in Alioto's Response to the 'Zebra' Murders," *Western Journal of Speech Communication* 44 (1980): 64–73; and Barry Brummett, "Burkean Scapegoating, Mortification and Transcendence in Presidential Campaign Rhetoric," *Central States Speech Journal* 32 (1981): 254–64.

15. For exceptions, see Jeanne Y. Fisher, "A Burkean Analysis of the Rhetorical Dimensions of a Multiple Murder and Suicide," *Quarterly Journal of Speech* 60 (1974): 175–89; and Beth A. Messner and Jacquelyn J. Buckrop, "Restoring Order: Interpreting Suicide through a Burkean Lens," *Communication Quarterly* 48 (2000): 1–18. Also see Kara Shultz, "Every Implanted Child a Star (and Some Other Failures): Guilt and Shame in the Cochlear Implant Debates," *Quarterly Journal of Speech* 86 (2000): 251–75.

16. Burke, "On Human Behavior," 289–90.

17. For a reading on the subject of inversion of the conventional law-abiding order, based on Foucault's antiscience project, see Michael Huspek and Lynn Comerford, "How Science Is Subverted: Penology and Prison Inmates' Resistance," *Communication Theory* 6 (1996): 335–60.

18. Burke, "On Human Behavior," 278–79.

19. Ibid., 285.

20. Ibid., 284.

21. Kenneth Burke, *A Rhetoric of Motives* (Berkeley: University of California Press, 1969), 19–20; also see 3–6, 16–17.

22. Ibid., 21.

23. Ibid., 20.

24. Ibid., 22.

25. Ibid., 23.

26. Ibid., 25.

27. *Time,* March 8, 1999, 28–30.

28. Southern Poverty Law Center, *Intelligence Report* (Fall 2000), 24ff.

29. Janna Malamud Smith, *Private Matters* (Boston: Wesley Addison Publishers, 1997).

30. Smith, from a telephone interview, August 18, 2002.

31. Susan Benson, "Inscriptions of the Self: Reflection on Tattooing and Piercing in Contemporary Euro-America," 237. Gell is quoted in Benson's essay. His book is a landmark study on tattoos: Alfred Gell, *Wrapping in Images: Tattooing in Polynesia* (Oxford: Oxford University Press, 1993).

32. Benson, "Inscriptions," 235.

33. Ibid., 236.

34. Burke, *A Rhetoric of Motives,* 27–28.

35. Matuschka, the artist whose self-portrait "Beauty out of Damage" (exposing her mastectomy) appeared on the cover of the *New York Times Magazine,* August 15, 1993, has since had a design of flowers and insects tattooed over her concave mastectomy scar. In her as-yet-unpublished

autobiography, "Last Letter to Florence," she details her motivation on her particular choice of a way to deal with her surgery and her breast loss. She does not minimize the almost unbearable pain of tattooing over scar tissue. *Portsmouth Herald Sunday,* September 26, 2004, sec. E, cover and 8–9.

36. Taylor, "Skinscapes," 30.
37. Ibid., 30.
38. Ibid., 31.
39. Ibid., 34.
40. Rueckert, *Kenneth Burke and the Drama of Human Relations,* 147.

17

*C*olin Powell's Life Story and the Display of a "Good" Black Persona

In the late summer of 1995, retired four-star general Colin Powell divulged to reporters that his approaching twenty-six-city publicity tour for his forthcoming six-million-dollar autobiography, *My American Journey,* would serve as a "coming-out party" for a possible presidential bid.[1] Launched via excerpts in *Time* and *Reader's Digest,* televised interviews with Barbara Walters, Larry King, Tom Brokaw, David Frost, Jay Leno, and Katie Couric, and print interviews with *People, Parade,* and the *New Yorker,* the memoir leaped to the best-seller list and further fueled media frenzy about Powell's speculative candidacy.[2] By early fall, several polls placed the still-unannounced "candidate" as leading the field of several declared contenders.[3]

Few clues, however, emerged in the 613–page tome about the likely policy direction or even political party orientation of a Powell administration. In fact, in the memoir's final pages, the potential candidate rationalized omitting engaging with "abortion, gun control, welfare, [and] affirmative action" by contending that such "headline issues" held far less significance for the voting American public than did their "yearning" and "searching for a guiding star" to remedy a disintegrating social order.[4] Powell's policy-opaque approach to testing the presidential waters extended to his lucrative "stump" speeches,[5] the heart of which chronicled his climb from Harlem and the South Bronx as a child of Jamaican im-migrants to become the first black appointed both as national security advisor and chair-man of the Joint Chiefs of Staff.[6] Such striking emphasis on Powell the person led both *Newsweek* and *Time* to conclude that this prospective presidential hopeful believed his "life" was sufficient platform.[7]

Yet the potent symbolic allure of Powell's life story had long generated considerable ink. In 1989, *Parade* magazine had seized upon the symbolic patriotic themes implicit within the black national security advisor's "great American [life] story" for its July 4 cover story.[8] In the months surrounding the first Persian Gulf War, features in *National Review, News-week, U.S. News and World Report,* and elsewhere pulled heavily from Powell's humble beginnings in floating him as a potential "black Eisenhower,"[9] with *Newsweek* drawing the analogy even before a shot had been fired in the conflict. By 1993, two biographies of Pow-ell had devoted entire chapters speculating on whether the inspiring life odyssey of this politically enigmatic black Horatio Alger would reach full fruition in the Oval Office.[10] As speculation mounted over Powell's possible announcement, observers such as *Newsweek*'s Joe Klein championed Powell with the headline "Character, Not Ideology," and *U.S. News and World Report*'s Morton Zuckerman concluded his editorial endorsement, "If he declares, Powell, the candidate of biography and not ideology, has a chance to be a breakthrough president of the United States."[11]

As a Vietnam veteran who presided over what was then perceived to be the nation's swift Persian Gulf "victory,"[12] Powell undoubtedly functioned for many Americans as the perfect symbolic tonic for the nation's polarizing military failure in Southeast Asia. But his disciplined, soldierly ethos merely compounded his more salient appeal as symbolic medicine man for racial discord and disorder. Biographer Howard Means, for example, contended the black Powell's widespread popularity had performed a kind of racial "exorcism" for a country where, since its inception, "race has been [its] abiding schism, its inner continental divide."[13] Likewise, broadsheets of at least one Draft Powell for President committee heralded its hand-picked nominee as singularly able to "heal" racial divisions by fostering "racial harmony."[14] Most noticeably, Powell as "racial healer" became a leitmotif in literally dozens of media features on Powell. For example, months prior to his exploratory "campaign," *Time* framed the potential of a Powell presidency in metaphors of racial disease and cure: "A black President could become a major healer of the racial divisions that plague this country."[15] Following Powell's abrupt, late-November 1995 withdrawal from presidential consideration, the weekly pointed to the dashed hopes of Americans who had looked to this "black man on a white horse" as a chance to "reinvent race relations" or "to heal . . . 200 years of racial divide."[16]

The overt exploitation of Powell's personal biography by the prospective candidate and the mainstream media[17] invite critical evaluation of the ways in which such widely distributed renderings of Powell's life story contributed to his appeal as a symbol of racial "redemption" among certain audiences, especially given his far higher favorable ratings among whites than minorities—a reversal of conventional racial trends.[18] Others have emphasized that biographies and autobiographies are textured rhetorically.[19] Likewise, I contend that Powell's memoir, biographies, and various other interpretations of his life in widely circulated media venues produced prior to and coincident with his dalliance with a presidential run *argue* by enabling Americans outside of the nation's lowest racial caste—descendants of America's slaves—to view racial matters through what social critic Shelby Steele termed "seeing for innocence."[20] These accounts selectively absolve and indict on matters of race by enacting what I describe as a "good" black narrative, which both reflects and perpetuates what ethnographers claim is a prevalent mythos used to distinguish "superior" blacks holding *immigrant* credentials, such as Powell, from "inferior" blacks whose forebears were American slaves.[21] Because "immigration" status is the most salient defining feature of the "good" black narrative, this mythos vividly illustrates Kenneth Burke's contention that "terministic screens" or discursive filters accommodate a particular selection and deflection—a preferred reading—of a social order even as these same screens may reflect certain social "realities" they have aided in constructing.[22]

The versions of Powell's life examined in this chapter contain two overarching features ethnographers claim are means by which immigrant blacks work to accrue "good" black status. First, their emphasis on Powell as the son of industrious Jamaican immigrants comports with the common practice ethnographers locate among second-generation black immigrants of consciously telegraphing their ethnic heritage as a means of "filtering" themselves for the dominant culture so that they can ward off downward social mobility still linked to a black racial identity in the United States.[23] The inclusion of ancestry in life stories by political hopefuls is not in itself remarkable, but the Powell stories so conspicuously emphasize his distinctive black heritage that they suggest a peculiarly potent symbiotic relationship between its utility both for Powell the "candidate" and for the dominant culture. Second, Powell's "superior" black narrative endorsed and enacted the strategy of racial "exiting" rather than of "voice" to effect social entry[24] or, to use Steele's terms, the strategies of "bargaining" for white racial innocence rather than "challenging" it.[25] Many American blacks have long gravitated toward collective political "voice" to redress racial inequities, but some immigrant blacks—particularly those with strong ethnic identities—have favored individual strategies for mobility designed to elude the stigma of stereotypical "inferior" blackness. Steele contends that because whites yearn for a clear racial conscience, the most accepted and, therefore, successful blacks are not racial "challengers" but racial "bargainers," those blacks willing to grant "white society its innocence in exchange for entry into the mainstream" by saying, in effect, "I already believe you are innocent (good, fair-minded) and have faith that you will prove it"; black challengers, by contrast, annoy by confronting white society with the goad, "If you are innocent, then prove it," thereby holding white innocence captive until some ransom is paid.[26] Thus, racial bargaining accommodates "exit" symbiotically: individual blacks escape the taints of blackness while members of the dominant culture escape the taints of racism.

This chapter illuminates how this racial bargain was sealed through Powell's self-portrayals and others' portrayals of him. I first discuss the social constructions of "good" immigrant blacks versus "bad" native blacks and then explore how these constructs engage with the complex issue of blacks' personal agency in a dominant society enamored with racial bargaining. I next analyze how various tactics for displaying "good" black immigrant ethnicity function to bargain for white racial innocence, using Powell as exemplar. Powell's unprecedented appeal as a black "candidate" to the public at large is illuminated by the "good" black narrative that, I argue, invites a less heartening reading of racial healing, racial progress, and racial harmony than a cursory glance at his remarkable white following initially permits.

"Good" versus "Bad" Blacks

Since the turn of the twentieth century, black migration, predominantly from the West Indies, has dramatically altered the racial terrain in certain major American urban areas, such as New York City, where black immigrants currently comprise roughly a quarter of the black population.[27] Entering primarily in two waves, the preponderance of these black islanders has arrived on the heels of revised 1965 immigration laws.[28]

Combined with their industriousness, these immigrant blacks' devotion to education, family, church, the American-dream mythos, and "racelessness" rapidly earned them cultural capital among whites as "good" blacks purportedly "superior" to American-born or indigenous blacks, roughly a third of whom still remained mired in poverty at the time of Powell's speculative candidacy.[29] By the late 1960s, blacks of West Indian extraction reportedly earned 52 percent more than native blacks and by the 1980s controlled approximately

half of all black-owned businesses in New York City, although then numbering but 10 percent of the black population. In fact, second-generation black Jamaicans who came of age
during the dismantling of legal segregation in the United States, such as Powell, earn a
median income even higher than their white counterparts.[30] Given such impressive records
of achievement, some black West Indians—particularly first-generation and ethnically
identified descendants—tend to believe that "while racism still exists in the United States,
it can be effectively overcome through hard work, perseverance, and the right values and
attitudes."[31] Folklore has it, for example, that black Caribbean women first integrated the
garment trades in New York City in the 1920s by simply ignoring the "no blacks need apply" signs and walking in and demanding employment.[32]

The sharp disparity in upward mobility between these two black groups not only has
strengthened stereotypes of "bad" or "inferior" native blacks as indolent, criminal, illiterate,
government-dependent, unduly obsessed with racism, and morally remiss toward family
but also has lubricated the transfer of racial guilt over the nation's record of institutionalized racism from its white architects to native blacks themselves. To observers such as Ira
Reid, Thomas Sowell, Mona Charen, and others, the successes of black immigrants strongly
imply that white racism no longer seriously compromises the nation's fabled meritocracy,
an argument often advanced[33] and critiqued about accomplished individual blacks more
generally.[34] Dana L. Cloud, for example, maintains that the construction of Oprah Winfrey's successful black persona in popular biographies services dominant readings of race
by "implying the accessibility of [the American] dream to black Americans despite the
structural economic and political obstacles to achievement and survival posed in a racist
society."[35] But the extraordinary *group* success of black immigrants even more powerfully
enables attributing the onus for disproportional black poverty, prisoner rates, and other
grave inner-city conditions chiefly to the conduct of a native-black underclass itself.

Yet other evidence paints a more complex portrait, insisting upon a more reflective
reading. If and when black West Indians begin to assimilate, becoming less distinguishable
from American blacks in language, accent, dress, and other customs, they jeopardize and
sometimes lose the economic and social edges black islanders themselves openly concede
they enjoy.[36] Most particularly, the marked preferences expressed by white employers in
recent studies for hiring West Indians over native blacks[37] mirrors what Jack Miles terms as
"the comfort factor" whites feel towards immigrants of color. As illustration, he points to
the "unofficial but widespread preferential hiring of Latinos [over blacks]—the largest
affirmative-action program in the nation, and one paid for, in effect, by [native] blacks."[38]
So, too, the significantly lower social and economic status of black West Indians in countries without the buffer of large indigenous black populations confounds theories that the
remarkable mobility of black islanders in the United States results solely from behavioral
attributes accrued in West Indian culture rather than from structural features of a dominant white culture. In Toronto, as illustration, black Jamaicans inhabit the popular imagination as "welfare queens and gun-toting gangsters and dissolute youth"—roles typically
reserved for native blacks in the United States—and are nearly thirty times more likely to
face incarceration for crimes than are similarly charged whites.[39] Similarly, in her comparative analysis of black immigrant experiences in the United States and Britain, ethnographer
Nancy Foner writes that West Indians reign as "good" in "the context of black America"—
law abiding and entrepreneurial, for example—but they are stigmatized in predominantly

white London as "inferior" and "dangerous," bear the blame for an array of social ills, and are skittish about investing personal savings in small businesses largely dependent upon patronage by hostile English whites.[40]

Contributing to this sorting of "good" blacks from "bad" in the United States are the rival national narratives each group respectively embodies: on the one hand, the proud tale of bold immigrants *voluntarily* fleeing tyranny or poverty to pursue the promises of the American dream; and, on the other, the shameful countertale of *forced* black immigration —slavery—the greatest rebuke to the egalitarian mythos of the American dream. While native blacks irritate the dominant culture as constant physical and psychological reminders of a guilty racial past, immigrant blacks soothe as living testaments to America's political and economic allure, its essential "goodness," even for persons of color. As ethnographer Mary C. Waters reports, the narrative of black "immigration tends to erase the slave narra-tive"[41] for both whites and blacks of island extraction. Cornel West argues that the mere presence of black bodies makes even whites of good will uncomfortable,[42] but black "West Indians," Waters writes, "provide a black face for whites to look into without seeing the sor-ry history of American race relations mirrored back," thereby putting whites "at ease."[43] Thus, the "good" and "bad" racial histories associated with members of these different black groups enhances the allure of "bargaining" for white racial innocence. Indeed, a unique con-sequence of Powell as a black immigrant Horatio Alger is that some segments of the pub-lic invoked the force of this hallowed rags-to-riches mythos to court the candidate rather than the customary reverse, as evident both in numerous draft-Powell campaigns and in explicit or thinly veiled media endorsements. These themes of mythologized immigration and institutionalized racism converge in one white employer's comments that, in describing hiring preferences, transfer the nation's centuries-long racial obsession—intimated simply as "this"—to bigotry's traditional victims: native blacks purportedly fixated unduly on race:

> Island blacks who come over, they're immigrant. They may not have such a good life here they are so they gonna try to strive to better themselves and I think there's a lot of American blacks out there who feel we owe them. And enough is enough already. You know, this is something that happened to their ancestors, not now. I mean, we've done so much for the black people in America now that it's time that they got off their butts.[44]

Such sharp criticisms are not peculiar to whites. Rather, such critiques are echoed by those ethnically identified black immigrants who claim native blacks carry racial "chips on their shoulders," "sulk and cry about [race] without doing much to help themselves," and use racism as an "excuse" for their own various shortcomings or "lack of success."[45] These black immigrants and their children do not completely discount or ignore racism, but in-stead tend to protest racial injustices selectively and individually and with an eye toward the incident's bearing upon their individual fortunes.[46] Ironically, some black immigrants cast the white engineers of the racial caste system more charitably than they do native blacks consigned to its lowest rung who resent, directly challenge, or internalize their "inferior" grade. Even black West Indians openly sympathetic to the peculiar native-black predica-ment, according to both Foner and Waters, nonetheless generally describe themselves as "different" blacks in terms translatable as "superior": more ambitious, hardworking, confident, comfortable, and dignified in dealing with whites than indigenous blacks who purportedly are more cynical about effort reaping rewards and, thus, adopt a self-defeating "adversarial stance" towards the dominant culture.[47] Powell likewise draws numerous explicit and implicit comparisons between immigrant and other blacks throughout his memoir. For example, in writing of his admiration for southern black military officers struggling with their first exposure to integration, he inserts his "difference" from them this way: "I had never felt uncomfortable around whites; I had never considered myself less valuable."[48] And often these "differences" are easily readable through the filters of "good" black versus "bad" black mythology. "My parents came to this country looking not for government support," he writes in the memoir's final pages, "but for job opportunities."[49]

Such black ethnic stereotyping is often mutual. For their part, some American blacks frame West Indian blacks as arrogant, selfish, unfriendly to native blacks, oblivious to racial politics, and willing to endure workplace exploitation,[50] early on derisively dubbing these industrious newcomers as "Jewmaicans."[51] Such sweeping characterizations, of course, ignore an unmistakable history of militancy by blacks with islander heritage,[52] not least of which is Malcolm X, an icon for many young, native, inner-city blacks.[53] Nonetheless, black immigrants still reign among the favored targets for common epithets hurled by native blacks at other blacks whose personal enterprise, commitment to education, achievements, social networks, or even modes of dress or talk incur charges of acting "white"—"Uncle Tom," "Oreo," "Afro-Saxon," or "incognegro."[54] Powell himself writes that his courtship and marriage to a native black engendered initial concern and suspicion by both families, particularly his future father-in-law, who had tried to avoid "'damn West Indians'" all his life.[55] Given such experiences, many immigrant blacks perceive racial tensions in black-black rather than black-white terms.[56]

In no small contradiction, even as some blacks of island ancestry adamantly discount the significance racism bears on individual fortunes, they candidly concede that their own "better treatment" by whites—advantages in hiring, promotion, and other social venues— depends upon whites' awareness of their island ethnicity.[57] In fact, ethnographers report "reactive ethnicity" emerging among some new black arrivals who live in close proximity to native blacks facing severe racial discrimination.[58] Reaping the rewards bestowed upon "good" blacks, then, requires that such blacks differentiate themselves from those indigenous blacks whom they otherwise physically resemble. Consequently, despite publicly disdaining "racialism"—which they define as exaggerated racial pride, identity, and sensitivity to racism—these blacks of immigrant descent consciously broadcast their *ethnic* heritage through language patterns, accents, dress and hairstyles, or, most commonly, by creating strategies to work immigrant ancestry routinely into conversations. Illustrative is the report by one adolescent black islander of carrying a key chain emblazoned with an island map so as to provoke interrogation by curious whites.[59] So widely recognized are the social and economic advantages conferred on black immigrants relative to native blacks that some lower-class indigenous blacks have begun to poach ethnic markers such as speaking patois or sporting Caribbean fashion, in part, to accrue cultural benefits concomitant with foreign status,[60] a type of "passing" some native blacks employed during segregation to access the relative freedoms available to black immigrants and black foreigners.[61] Beyond advertising their distinctive immigrant credentials, many black newcomers and their progeny emphasize the kinds of "exiting" approaches to survival and advancement long associated with "exceptional" blacks in general: hard work and higher education, personal diplomacy and networking, and a scrupulous aversion to racial politics. Some black immigrants further disassociate from "blackness" by denying the applicability of the designator to themselves,[62] by confining their social networks to other black immigrants or to influential whites holding tickets to social mobility, and by parroting the dominant culture's negative stereotypes of native blacks.[63]

Racial "Bargaining" and Agent Status

The strategy of racial bargaining predicated on the distinction between "superior" and "inferior" blacks requires consideration of the complex issue of personal agency. In a society rife with hierarchy, agency necessarily is an ambiguous, fluid, and complicated concept, particularly for members of groups continually forced to negotiate that hierarchy. Much of the liberal-versus-conservative debate surrounding contemporary native-black conditions is couched in the stark polarities of *environmental* and *behavioral* theses, what Burke would term "scene" and "agent," respectively. But West and Henry Louis Gates Jr. contend that both scenic factors and individual choices and actions must be considered in assessing black conditions, because, in West's words, "structures and behavior are inseparable. . . . How people act and live are shaped—but in no way dictated or determined—by the larger circumstances in which they find themselves."[64] Only in "confronting the twin realities of white racism, on the one hand," they write, "and [black] failures to seize initiative on the other" can perplexing problems such as disproportionate black poverty be honestly and effectively addressed.[65]

Steele's emphasis on racial bargaining as the correct means to achieve black mobility reveals a variation of the behavioral or agent-centered thesis that is more akin to a Burkean sense of "agency": a pragmatic means by which to negotiate a dominant racial scene for purposes of advancement or survival.[66] In Steele's arguments, individual agency oscillates between black agents and the dominant racial scene, even as free will and choice are used to account for the circumstances (favorable or unfavorable) in which blacks find themselves. For example, Steele argues that decades after the razing of legal apartheid, blacks still continue to display themselves primarily as injured victims of white oppression both as leverage for collective entitlement and as an alibi for neglecting individual initiative, a victimization mentality that renders blacks perpetually infantile. Yet despite his withering critique of black preoccupation with white racism and power, he tacitly concedes white culture's enduring dominance as an arbiter of black mobility, a gate-keeping authority that positions blacks as not-fully-constituted agents per se, but what Burke might term "agent-minus[es]."[67] Because whites covet racial innocence, Steele writes, pragmatic "bargaining is now—today—a way for the black individual to *join* the larger society, to make a place for himself or herself."[68] In fact, he maintains that because black bargainers wield the power to grant whites their holy grail of racial absolution, the most gifted racial bargainers often doubly profit; beyond gaining access and acceptance, masterful bargainers may benefit from "the gratitude factor," finding themselves "cherished beyond the measure of [their] achievements."[69]

Steele situates racial bargaining in a post–civil rights era where racial challenging purportedly has been rendered obsolete, but his recipe for black mobility bears striking resemblance to the conciliatory demeanor long expected of severely oppressed blacks in exchange for white largesse. Toni Morrison, for example, argues that slave narratives generally featured supplicant black protagonists who strategically "veiled" the anguish of their racial injuries and their attendant anger for purposes of appealing to white change agents capable of altering black circumstance. Aiming for a sympathetic rather than alienated reading, slave writers "were silent about many things, and they 'forgot' many other things," revealing little or none of the pain and outrage of an "interior life" that might offend. Rather than challenging the evils of white supremacy, such stories, she writes, strategically complimented the "nobility of heart" and "finer high-mindedness" of whites, so as to encourage them to exercise it.[70] This discursive veiling reflects the "performance tradition in African-American culture" described by D. Soyini Madison where "the 'mask,' or presentation of self, constructed for white people" is displayed as "a matter of survival,"[71] a motif that still emerges in numerous analyses of black/white relations, Steele's among them. His pointing to Louis Armstrong's "exaggerated smile" as emblematic of the racial bargaining he advocates, for example, echoes Thomas Kochman's contention that blacks "still *front* in the presence of whites . . . even suppressing anger where expressing it would involve social risk."[72]

Even as Steele incessantly couches personal agency for blacks in the traditional "agent" terms of unfettered free will, his actual privileging of *pragmatic* black agency is perhaps nowhere more salient than in his prescient profile of the type of black presidential candidate he predicted could elicit widespread popular support. Years before Powell's name appeared on the public's presidential radar screen cloaked in metaphors of innocence, guilt, and redemption, Steele wrote of this hypothetical black leader:

> Whether it is right or wrong, fair or unfair . . . no black candidate will have a serious chance at his party's nomination, much less the presidency, unless he can convince white Americans that he can be trusted to preserve their sense of racial innocence . . . Such a candidate will have to use his power of absolution; he will have to flatly forgive and forget . . . [and] offer a vision that is passionately raceless, a vision that strongly condemns any form of racial politics.[73]

The remainder of this chapter treats Powell's biographies, autobiography, and other versions of his life as primers for and endorsements of this type of racial bargaining. In Powell's case, such tactics, I argue, grounded the frequent framing of him as racially redemptive presidential material by locating persistent social problems implicated by race primarily in the alleged shortcomings of native blacks. Although history provides various examples of black politicians who have proven themselves adept at negotiating and even alleviating white racial guilt,[74] Powell, I argue, benefitted from and exploited the "terministic screen" of black immigrant ancestry, a filter by which American culture, whites and some blacks alike, traditionally has sorted "good" blacks from "bad." In the Powell tales, the pronounced display of his immigrant credentials, coupled with themes typifying the talk both of ethnically identified black immigrants and many whites reported in ethnographic studies, coalesce to form what I term a "good" or "superior" black narrative.

Bargaining for White Racial Innocence: Displaying a "Good" Black Persona

Efforts by immigrant blacks to "exit" the category of pejorative blackness entail a variety of strategies, but my focus here is on *rhetorical* tactics embedded within narratives both by and about "good" blacks. Various renderings of Powell's life story present him, dominant society, and other blacks in terms of "bargaining for white racial innocence." Involved within the bargain are tactics of portrayal used by both Powell and the media that construct a "superior" black ethnic identity that is set against qualities attributed to an "inferior" native black identity. In this section, I inventory some of those tactics as they are exemplified in renderings of Powell's life story.

The Jamaican Horatio Alger

On its face, Powell's conspicuous appropriation of American-dream ideology to launch his presidential book-tour "campaign" was not exceptional. Among the most enduring and appealing American myths, the Horatio Alger tale has become a rhetorical staple for political aspirants of humble origins who use their rise from rags to riches both to certify their personal mettle and to confirm the nation's allegiance to unbridled opportunity.[75] This myth so attracts the public imagination that political hopefuls or their champions might embellish the actual distance of a candidate's climb. Powell's sister, for example, dryly noted that each published account of the Powell family progressively rendered the middle-class clan "poorer and poorer,"[76] a discursive embroidery Cloud notes in the "Oprah" tales.[77]

When the hero is both black and of recent immigrant stock, this hallowed American myth acquires exponential allure to a dominant culture seeking racial absolution. Impressive achievements of blacks in general can be touted as triumphs not only for the individual but for society as concrete exemplars of its belated repudiation of an undeniable racist past. But highly successful blacks with immigrant lineage are particularly enticing, because they enable more complete voiding or e-racing of that racist history. As Burke observes, "[A] thorough job of symbolic rebirth . . . require[s] the revision of one's ancestral past itself. . . . [I]n becoming wholly transformed one not only can alter the course of the future but can even remake the past."[78] The force black immigration can play in historical racial revisionism is intimated in Jim Cullen's extensive treatment of the American-dream mythos. The United States, he writes, "is a nation that has been *re-created* as a deliberate act of conscious *choice* every time a person has landed on these shores. Explicit allegiance, *not involuntary inheritance,* is the theoretical basis of American identity [emphasis added]."[79] Powell's symbolic power to license racial amnesia in recasting that American identity is vividly illustrated in broadsheets of one Draft Powell for President committee, which asserted in boldfaced copy: "The American Dream—as it was in *the beginning*— and as it remains today—is about freedom and opportunity. . . . Powell personifies that Dream [italics added]."[80]

The intense appeal to the dominant culture of appropriating the immigrant dimension of Powell so as to refashion America's racial identity as egalitarian is manifest in the longstanding and continuing play given his immigrant ancestry in various venues. As early as 1987, an installment of *Biography* trumpeted the then black national security advisor as "the embodiment of the American Dream" by featuring a tribe of Powell's Jamaican relatives witnessing to his "can-do" attitude and immigrant "work ethic";[81] tellingly, former secretary of defense Robert McNamara's review of the segment on amazon.com begins not with Powell's extensive military or professional record, but by immediately filtering this black man as "the son of Jamaican immigrants."[82] Likewise, several media cover stories and features coincident with the first Gulf War grounded the four-star general's promise as a "black Eisenhower" as much in his Jamaican family history and culture as in his military prowess, with *U.S. News and World Report,* as illustration, committing roughly a third of its feature story to his immigrant pedigree and upbringing.[83] With the 1996 election on the horizon, the displaying of Powell as the "son of Jamaican immigrants" had literally become a media mantra, nearly appearing to be an extension of the general's name. So routinized has the parading of Powell's black lineage become that CNN's Bill Schneider inserted the then secretary of state's immigrant heritage into commentary on Powell's February 2003 speech to the U.N. Security Council detailing Saddam Hussein's alleged weapons capabilities.[84]

Powell's two biographies by white authors, on which he closely cooperated, also prominently advertised his distinctive black genealogy in dangling him both as a presidential prospect and a symbol of racial reconciliation. The dust jackets on the Means and David Roth biographies respectively read, "General Powell emerges as the embodiment of the American Dream: the son of Jamaican immigrants, he rose from the hard life of the South Bronx to become the most talked about military leader since World War II" and "The son of Jamaican immigrants, Colin Powell grew up in the tenements of New York. . . . Colin Powell is . . . the embodiment of all that is good about America." On its back cover, testimonials to the Roth biography include the following praise: "*Sacred Honor* is a classic American drama . . . General Colin Powell's greatness is understood in the light of his very special family background." For his part, Means devoted an entire chapter to explicating the history and social lessons of the black Powell's Jamaican roots.

Powell's autobiography followed these leads with striking congruity, conspicuously telegraphing his "good" black ethnicity when testing the presidential waters. As Waters notes, whereas ethnicity declines among white immigrants as they strive for advancement by absorbing themselves into the larger culture, "the more socially mobile [immigrant blacks] cling to *ethnic* identity as a hedge against a *racial* identity [emphasis added]," which they recognize spells downward social mobility.[85] Thus, not surprisingly, the terministic screen of immigration emerges immediately, both in the first sentences of the inside dust jacket of *My American Journey*—"Colin Powell is the embodiment of the American Dream. He was born in Harlem to *immigrant parents from Jamaica* [emphasis added]"—and the book's frontispiece via a "My Roots" gallery of captioned photographs of Powell's Jamaican relatives and the island cottage in which his father, Luther, was born. In the preface to the book, Powell reiterates, "Mine is the story of a *black kid* of no early promise from an *immigrant family* of limited means [emphasis added]."[86] The first paragraph of the book's official first chapter follows suit, trailing Powell during his adult pilgrimage to his parents' Jamaican homeland. In the book's opening pages and throughout, Powell fused his "American Dream" odyssey, marketed explicitly on the dust jacket's exterior, with his parents' separate, elective passages to the states, "act[s] of courage and hope," he wrote, that "would help shape the destiny of their son."[87] So, too, embedded within his early, quite-extensive talk of Jamaican homeland, customs, and a legion of islander kin, is Powell's claim he had no "sense of [racial] identity" during his formative years. "Most of the black families I knew had their roots in Jamaica, Trinidad, or Barbados, or other islands of the West Indies," he writes, a point he shares in multiple articulations.[88] Yet the attention Powell lavishes on his island heritage throughout the memoir is strikingly at odds with his own admission in the opening pages that he could only speculate upon his parents' motivations for emigrating, given he had never discussed with his father, even as an adult, either the details of his father's early life in Jamaica or his parent's motivations for emigrating to a strange land.[89] Despite this seemingly longstanding disinterest in his ancestral homeland and his parents' psyche, Powell nonetheless chose to launch his book-tour presidential "campaign" via a Barbara Walters special containing recently filmed footage of him duplicating his parents' passage to America from Jamaica.[90]

Scapegoating Blackness

The redemptive tactic of the "Jamaican Horatio Alger" appealed to the dominant culture's desire for racial innocence, but symbolic purification rituals attending quests for escaping social taint rarely are benign. Rather, they traffic in division, hierarchy, power, mortification, and victimage, a cathartic process wherein guilt or social pollution is transferred to vessels "outside."[91] Since terministic screens simultaneously unite and divide, they unavoidably "set up the conditions for [a] particular kind of scapegoat."[92] Steele concurs, arguing that the search for "innocence imposes—*demands*—division and conflict."[93] Not surprisingly, native blacks in the Powell narrative bore the cost incurred for Powell's restoration of white racial innocence in myriad ways.

Many of the accounts, for example, engaged implicitly or explicitly in a black immigrant variation of what Thomas K. Nakayama and Robert L. Krizek and others have described as discourse that collapses whiteness and nationality, thereby intimating that being "black" and "American" are mutually exclusive. "To conflate nationality and 'race,'" they write, "is an expression of power since it relegates those of other racial groups to an [*sic*] marginal role in national life."[94] West concurs, arguing that discussions of race frequently contain the "implication . . . that only certain Americans can define what it means to be an American, and the rest must simply 'fit in.'"[95] Powell's immigration status, however, greatly eased the move to consigning native blacks to "alien" or "un-American," as suggested in Cullen's thesis that the "theoretical basis for American identity" is not "involuntary inheritance" but "conscious choice." Beyond the constant drumbeat of Powell as the incarnation of American-dream mythology, a 1994 *Newsweek* cover story, for example, asking "Can Colin Powell Save America?" baldly resorted to italics to cast this "son of Jamaican immigrants" as "an African-American who . . . seems a distinctly *American* character [emphasis in original]."[96] The following year, coverage in *U.S. News and World Report,* notably christened "An American Tale," claimed that "Colin Powell's vast extended family has lived a classic immigrant story, a classic American story"; the feature was almost entirely devoted to expounding upon the exceptional qualities of black Jamaican transplants whom it liberally quotes. "This sprawling clan," it argued, "has prospered for the same reasons many other immigrants have: strong families, discipline, hard work, high standards."[97]

To be sure, the Powell narrative approached the nation's inescapable record of institutionalized racism in various purifying ways: completely ignoring it, deploying therapeutic euphemisms such as racial "healing" that summoned slavery or Jim Crow, or, most commonly, neutralizing structural racism's enduring significance through the purifying comparative lenses of "superior" versus "inferior" blacks. As Cloud contends, minority biographies that service hegemony generally "pry into and recognize oppression while at the same time disclaiming its salience with regard to an individual's success or failure."[98] But the Powell "good" black narrative is especially noteworthy in that it frequently moved well beyond merely discounting racial obstacles to upward mobility to enact a kind of scapegoating ritual that Burke argues is a common approach to removing guilt or perceived taint. "[S]ymbolic transformation," he writes, "involves a sloughing off [of impurities]. . . . So, we get to the 'scapegoat,' the 'representative' or 'vessel' of certain unwanted evils, the sacrificial animal upon whose back the burden of these evils is ritualistically loaded."[99] For whites, such "impurities" entailed collective guilt over past racial sins, but for black immigrants and their descendants the "impurity" most needing "sloughing off" was the inferior mark of blackness. These dual purifying purposes were evident in the numerous media features on Powell that deployed the testimony of "good" blacks to locate native black circumstance primarily and sometimes exclusively in the attitudes of native blacks rather than the dominant culture. *U.S. News and World Report* wrote in 1991, "'An immigrant's son like Powell,' argues [Judge] Watson, [Powell's Jamaican-American] cousin, 'is not as burdened as other African-Americans by the legacy of slavery and racism,'" an assertion with some merit given the differing reception within dominant society of these respective black groups. But the next sentence clarified that the attitudinal "problem" of racism lay *only* with American blacks and not the receiving social order: "[Powell] has no sense of himself as a victim or a belief 'that somebody owes him something.'"[100] Four years later, the periodical rehashed the same three-part, racially redemptive formula of comparative U.S. and British slavery systems, relative black group psychology, and the invaluable corroborating testimony from Powell's Jamaican kin: "There were no limitations put in people's minds [in the West Indies] about what they could do," reported one Powell cousin in describing differing psychological profiles of Jamaican-Americans and native blacks. "As a result, we don't say, 'I can't.' We say, 'I'll try.'"[101] For its part, *Newsweek* described Powell's firsthand knowledge of the extreme violence greeting black demands for legal equality in the South during the 1960s, but then nonetheless unmistakably and unreflectively implied that racism as an obstacle—*even then*—was always and ever an individual *choice* made by blacks. "Powell seems never to have *allowed* his race to be a disadvantage [emphasis added]." Rather, "[h]e has approached the question [of race] in a distinctive West Indian way," an attitudinal "way" articulated by a Powell cousin: "'We tended to see it [race] differently from Southern blacks [at the time] . . . They saw the glass as mostly half empty. We saw it half full, and we were coming to fill up the rest.'"[102]

Powell's two biographies and memoir proceed in similar fashion, effectively canceling out their obligatory treatment of the nation's sordid racial record with generous discussions of black Jamaican-American accomplishments relative to other blacks. Means's entire Jamaican chapter, for example, expounded upon various behavioral and cultural theses to underscore marked disparities in achievements between transplanted black West Indians, including Powell's extended family, whom he liberally quotes, and their American black counterparts. There, however, the variable of a guilty slave history in influencing black mobility is not expunged but rather is emphasized as a potent *a fortiori* argument. Black West Indian immigrants, Means writes in a paraphrase of Sowell, have prospered impressively in the United States despite "the fact that the treatment of island slaves was generally even harsher than the treatment of slaves kept on plantations of the [American] South," who experienced a "paternalism" absent in a West Indian slave system demanding more self-sufficiency. (Powell likewise advances this "paternalistic" reading of U.S. versus West Indian slave systems in the opening pages of his autobiography, wherein he distinguishes himself from native blacks in numerous respects.) As a result, Means writes, the Powell family "story is not just another story of immigrants finding success in the New World. It is a far rarer tale: one of immigrants whose ancestors had once been chattel making that success," a tale he claims has a "moral."[103] The book's final paragraph revisited the immigrant theme displayed on its cover, opening pages, and throughout, asserting, "The Colin Powell story is . . . the classic tale of the immigrants' child, pushed by his parents to exceed the[ir] accomplishments. . . . It is a West Indian story and a Bronx story, an Army one and an American one. Most of all perhaps, it is a story of . . . human exceptionalism . . . [of] ris[ing] above the norms."[104]

In this coda to the Powell parable, Means married in one stroke the themes of black immigration and exceptionalism that second generation black islanders commonly report about their experiences with whites who perceive them as not "really black" according to the "norms," to borrow Means's term. But whereas white society has always been captivated by individual black "exceptionalism" as corroboration of the dominant culture's fair-mindedness, the alleged *group* "exceptionalism" of blacks possessing immigrant ancestry is wrought with irony. "Whites tend to let those of the second generation [of black immigrants] know that they think of them as exceptions to the rule, the rule being that most blacks are not good people," ethnographer Waters reports. "However, these [of the second generation] also know that unless they *tell* people of their ethnicity, most whites have no idea that they are not black Americans [emphasis added]."[105] Such ironic experiences go to the heart of Burke's thesis that terministic screens are but interpretive "fictions," his central point that he himself underscores with typographical emphasis: "[M]any of the 'observations' are but implications of the particular terminology in . . . which the observations are made . . . Pick some particular nomenclature, some one terministic screen . . . [t]hat you may proceed to track down the kinds of observation implicit in the terminology you have chosen."[106]

This perception that blacks of immigrant extraction are not *really* "black" evidences West's claim that "race"—generally meaning "blackness"—in the United States is, at bottom, a social, political, and ethical construct comprised of white guilt rather than a biological category arbitrarily comprised of factors such as the proportions of ancestral blood.[107] Thus, Powell's distinctive "good" black immigrant status helps to explain the frequent billing of him in the popular media as a black man who "transcends race." Not surprisingly, many of these racially transcendent claims invoked invisible, normative standards of "whiteness" described by Nakayama and Krizek, among others.[108] Means, for example, applauded the public perception of Powell as "a man without race," both noting that he "has no trace of race . . . in his voice" and quoting a bevy of political and military figures who praised the black general as a man who has "totally transcended the issue of race . . . He's such a tremendous role model from the standpoint that his race is not his identity."[109]

Many observers pointed to Powell's unprecedented popularity among whites as tolling the waning power of oppressive racial stereotypes, but the talk often surrounding his alleged "racelessness" strongly suggested the reverse: freer license by the dominant culture to cast "race" or, more accurately, "blackness" in uniformly pejorative terms. As Malcolm Gladwell writes, rather than sounding the demise of racism, the valorization of the "good" immigrant black "makes the old blanket prejudice against American blacks all the easier to express . . . without fear of sounding . . . racist."[110] Hailing Powell as a black man who "transcends race," a 1994 *Newsweek* cover story under the subhead "Carib Advantages" intimated that the weekly equated "race" solely with whiny, idle native blacks: "Powell has refused to countenance the bitterness and pessimism—the overwhelming sense of aggrievement—that has paralyzed much of the African-American community," it claimed, also noting his counsel to young blacks to not use racism as an "excuse."[111] And frequently, commentary couching Powell as a racially transcendent "healer" illustrated West's argument that the dominant culture places the burden on native blacks "to do *all* of the 'cultural' and 'moral' work necessary for healthy race relations [emphasis added]."[112] Emblematic of this trend is an editorial in *U.S. News and World Report,* which asserted that Powell "has proved by his life and work ethic that the American Dream is alive . . . and rendered the color of his skin irrelevant." In expanding further on Powell's alleged racelessness, however, the editorial located his promise as a racial medicine man primarily in this *black's* potential to discipline a dysfunctional, even degenerative, *black* culture, one framed as prone to playing the race card as an all-service alibi for various deficiencies:

> Powell . . . is not defined by his race . . . [T]here is no sense in him of the bitterness and cult of victimization that has skewed so much of the African-American dialogue. He boldly exhorts young men not to let racism be an excuse for shortcomings. . . . He can address race issues in a way no white person can . . . And he might well help to bind the racial wounds that still pain America.[113]

Silencing Black Voices and the Racial Excuse Trope

This latter story also typifies another element of the Powell narrative: native blacks function in the tale as *objects* of critique—"the 'problems' they pose for white people," as West puts it[114]—but nonetheless remain largely invisible in the narrative in at least two significant respects. A critical rhetoric, Raymie McKerrow argues, necessarily must interrogate *absence* as well as *presence* to illuminate discursive and nondiscursive mechanisms of power.[115] First, the "good" black Powell narrative is built almost exclusively from white voices (his biographers and autobiographical collaborator, "mainstream" journalists, and testimony from his military and political superiors) and from the voices of blacks of immigrant extraction (especially Powell himself and his Jamaican kin). To a remarkable extent, native black voices are confined to luminaries such as Jesse Jackson who are authorized to speak only on Powell's enchanting "racelessness" for the public at large rather than on common native-black experiences and culture. Second was the overwhelming absence amid the pervasive "hard work" theme in the Powell narrative of any of the millions of American blacks whose industriousness rivals or even eclipses Powell's immigrant parents' widely celebrated disciplined work ethic. This type of racial card-stacking epitomizes arguments by conservative behaviorists who, West claims, "rarely, if ever, examine the innumerable cases in which black people do act on the Protestant ethic and still remain at the bottom of the social ladder. Instead, they highlight the few instances in which blacks ascend to the top, as if such success were available to all blacks, regardless of circumstances."[116] Illustrative, but by no means uncommon, is commentary in *Life* magazine in 1993, which melds the common Powell narrative themes of immigration, industriousness, and the insignificance of racism on individual black success: "If the son of Jamaican immigrants has a message for black kids, it is that there is opportunity in America, that racism is the other guy's problem. There is no secret to his success, he says, 'I work hard.'"[117]

Ironically, the acknowledgment of racism in the Powell tales never constitutes a reason for individual circumstance but is rather couched as an excuse for personal failure. Consistent with its use by whites and many ethnically identified black immigrants, this racial excuse or "race card" trope in the Powell stories places responsibility for navigating racism on the shoulders of its recipients rather than pressing its perpetrators to reform. In 1991, *U.S.*

358 Mari Boor Tonn

News and World Report heralded Powell's "singular ability to bridge racial divisions," schisms it implied are more the fruits of native-black indolence than white prejudice: Powell's message to young blacks, it contends, "dwell[s] more on discipline than discrimination."[118] In 1994, *Newsweek* compared attitudinal differences of American and island blacks, noting that Powell "counsels young blacks" that "'You can't change [racism]. Don't have a chip on your shoulder . . . Don't use [racism] as an excuse for your own shortcomings.'"[119] Similarly, in one oft-quoted passage in Powell's memoir, he writes of speaking to black Fisk University students while Los Angeles still smoked in the wake of the Rodney King verdict. "The problem [of racism] goes beyond Rodney King," he acknowledged, still exhorting them to "[n]ever hide behind it or use it as an excuse for not doing your best."[120] Mere pages before, Powell—in the type of talk Cloud argues is representative of hegemonic minority biographies—recognizes structural oppression while simultaneously denying its influence on individual mobility. "Others may use my *race against* me," Powell writes, while on the same page expressing confidence in a "nation of *unlimited* opportunity [emphasis added]."[121] Such contradictory claims parallel a motif of narratives by immigrant blacks celebrated by the dominant culture as "good": although racism undoubtedly exists, it has little, if any, bearing on individual achievement.[122]

The extreme to which Powell takes the view that racism is an excuse rather than an obstacle influencing black circumstance is powerfully captured in a passage early in *My American Journey,* wherein Powell recounts his response to Jim Crow:

> I had to find a way to cope psychologically . . . I wanted, above all, to succeed at my Army career. I did not intend to give way to self-destructive rage, no matter how provoked. If people in the South insisted on living by crazy rules, then I would play the hand dealt me for now. If I was to be confined to one end of the playing field, then I was going to be a star on that part of the field . . . I was not going to let myself be emotionally crippled because I could not play on the whole field . . . And until the country solved [the problem of institutionalized racism], I was not going to let bigotry make me a victim instead of a full human being.[123]

Beyond Powell's couching black anger occasioned by segregation as "self-destructive" rather than justifiable is his stunning intimation here that those blacks legally denied employment, voting, schooling, and so forth had the luxury of electing either to be bigotry's "victim," a Burkean "agent-minus,"[124] or a self-actualized agent, a "full human being." Noticeably unexplored in this passage is how "the country" mysteriously might have elected to dismantle entrenched racial apartheid absent a *collective* political resistance, a movement without which the prospect of a Powell presidential candidacy would have been unimaginable. Moreover, his proffering of the individual and attitudinal solution of cooperating with racial "rules" rather than challenging their legitimacy typifies the individualistic therapeutic and religious approach to continuing racism and discrimination against gays and lesbians that Janice Peck and Bonnie J. Dow respectively argue is a motif on popular programs such as *The Oprah Winfrey Show* and *Ellen.* There, tenable critiques of systematic discrimination, warranted anger, and collective efforts for remediation are discredited by black guests or lesbian characters testifying to the benefits of individual psychological coping mechanisms.[125]

The appeal of the above passage to some segments of the dominant culture is evident in its selection out of Powell's 613–page memoir for whole or partial duplication by both *Time* and the *National Review* in laudatory coverage of Powell.[126] In fact, the passage's potential as fodder for reactionary racial arguments becomes abundantly clear in the *Review*'s editorial, notably titled "The Great Black Hope." Treating the issue of the "symbolism" of "Powell's race, and what he makes of it," this racial jeremiad repeats verbatim his pledge to triumph within his assigned racial place, arguing that "[t]hat credo, formulated at the time of the Montgomery bus boycott, suggests an alternative to the civil-rights movement— *clearly a superior alternative* to the black-power pork barrel the movement quickly became [emphasis added]."[127]

Scenic Pardoning

These accounts illustrate the relationship among scene, act, and agent that Mari Boor Tonn, Valerie A. Endress, and John N. Diamond argue occurs in social conflicts wherein the use of scene to absolve or indict depends upon an agent's position in a social pecking order. In these renderings, racism, racial categorization, and white norms ultimately become the duty of blacks to maneuver or romantically "transcend" as fully realized "agents" accountable for their individual choices or actions "in interacting with the competing community around them, a scene in which they are alien" by racial consignment.[128] In contrast, more powerful whites in such accounts are noticeably not prodded into accountable agenthood to alter further any racial norms that they have instituted as part of the racial landscape or "scene." In fact, in some of the Powell narratives, a hostile racist scene emerges as a catalyst rather than impediment to individual black success, a framing reminiscent of Sowell's attributions of immigrant blacks' industriousness to the more draconian slave system Caribbeans purportedly endured. In his memoir, for example, Powell writes of his responses to structural racism, "I occasionally felt hurt; I felt anger; but most of all, I felt challenged. I'll show you!"[129]

Despite purportedly having transcended race, Powell, self-described in his early televised *Biography* feature as a black man who "knew the [race] rules" and did not intend "to make waves,"[130] exhibited sentiments that nourish impressions reported in ethnographic studies of many black West Indians as "less willing to challenge the rules of the game, easier to get along with [than native blacks]."[131] Among various race rules for "exit" in the Powell tales were a scrupulous aversion to native black "racialism," meaning racial pride, identity, or sensitivity to racism even as he valorized his immigrant ethnicity and a good-natured tolerance for white racism.

Indeed, in the Powell stories, black ethnicity, along with "whiteness," often served as the terministic screens used for evaluating similar behaviors, judgments commonly rendered at the expense of American blacks. Terministic screens, Burke explains, produce "*different* photographs of the same objects, the difference being that they are made with different color filters."[132] In the Powell biographies and memoir, for example, the "clannishness among West Indians" and their intense ethnic "pride" are raised repeatedly. "My family," he writes, "socialized and found friends almost entirely within the Jamaican community."[133] Biographer Means likewise points out that the "special sense [of their own selves] tended to keep West Indians in the United States apart from native American blacks even when they lived in the same neighborhoods," and biographer Roth notes the "distinctive identity" and "strong . . . social cohesion" of West Indians who elected not to be "simply absorbed into the fabric of black American life."[134] As Waters notes, "the second generation [of immigrant blacks] reserves their ethnic status for use as an identity device to stress their distance from poor blacks and to stress their cultural values which are consistent with American middle-class values."[135] Hence, tellingly absent in the Powell celebrations of close-knit island ethnicity and pride are the repeated critiques by Powell of the self-sequestering of native blacks whom he worries reinscribe an "unhealthy" counterproductive resegregation and "isolation" by taking "black pride" to an "extreme." Moreover, black-black tensions exacerbated by West Indians' refusal to assimilate socially or professionally with native blacks is interpreted in the Powell biographies and autobiographies as native-black resentment, envy, or misunderstanding of immigrant blacks' hard-earned status as black elite. "American blacks," Powell himself writes, "sometimes regard Americans of West Indian origins as uppity and arrogant. The feeling, I imagine, grows out of an impressive record of accomplishments by West Indians."[136] Nor does Powell's concern with problematic black resegregation engage with the more salient phenomenon of white flight from schools and neighborhoods populated by blacks beyond a certain tipping point; currently, for example, 86 percent of white suburban Americans live in residential areas less than 1 percent black.[137] Again, the responsibility for racial integration and assimilation, as with other aspects of race relations, falls primarily upon native blacks.

As important, Powell brooks white racism but not black "racialism," as illustrated in his pardoning of racist incidents but not the black anger racism engenders. In his memoir, in fact, he explicitly acknowledges having "swallowed hard over racial provocations, determined to succeed,"[138] a philosophy echoing what W. E. B. DuBois described decades ago as the requirement for blacks to "endure petty insults with a smile" and "never fail to flatter" if they hoped to survive or advance.[139] A common theme emerging in media accounts of Powell is his lack of anger and his irreverent wit and good humor, including his willingness to "joke about ethnic differences in America in the face of tiresome political correctness," a quality a 1995 *Time* cover story illustrated in a lengthy account of one speech after which audience members solicited his candidacy.[140] And in *My American Journey,* references to routine injuries all blacks endured during segregation are rare, largely undeveloped, and noticeably clinical descriptions of an exterior rather than interior world, a quality resembling traits in slave narratives described by Morrison that strove "not to offend." More to the point, certain of the Powell tales reveal a black protagonist who responds to white racism with a conciliatory nod towards the high-ranking white offender. A 1990 *Newsweek* story, for example, points out "he forgave Reagan's sometimes insensitive remarks about race as a holdover from an earlier time."[141] In his autobiography, Powell himself writes that the infamous Willie Horton advertisement by the George H. W. Bush campaign was a "racist . . . political cheap shot," but in the very next stroke of his pen, he points to his own appointment in the Reagan and Bush administrations as tangible proof of their color-blind good faith. "I nevertheless tried to keep matters in perspective," he writes. "I took consolation . . . in the thought that their confidence in me represented a commitment to the American ideal of advancement by merit."[142] Similarly, Powell recounts a story in his autobiography of a white colonel advising him, as a young army officer, to play, in effect, what Powell rightly terms the "good Negro": resigning himself to a racist world. Powell reports, "I do not remember being upset by what he said. He meant well. Like all of us, [Colonel]

Brookhart was a product of his times and his environment . . . [H]e was a caring human being. I thanked him and left."[143]

But whereas Powell issues pardons for certain white racial infractions due to socialization, several of the Powell tales underscore his unwillingness to extend environmental reprieves to blacks angered by systematic racism, including soldiers under his command during the racially turbulent early Vietnam years. As Waters notes, ethnically identified black immigrants often view white purveyors of racism more charitably than they do those native blacks resentful over being forced to maneuver it. In his memoir, for example, Powell explicitly acknowledges the effects of rampant discrimination on the worldviews of some black recruits. "Less opportunity, less education, less money, fewer jobs for blacks," he writes, "equaled antisocial behavior in the United States, and those attitudes traveled." But in the same talk, he immediately professes harboring no "qualms" about disciplining black soldiers for such "antisocial behavior," which, the reader directly learns, includes organizing collectively over perceived civil rights grievances.[144] Here again, a dominant racial scene informs the respective excusing and affixing of individual liability for perceived transgressions. As Tonn, Endress, and Diamond argue, "Hierarchical status of an agent within a specific social scene may be central to determining when a scenic perspective can be employed to assign 'sin' as well as to remove it . . . In short, the agent's *relationship* to the scene may determine whether scene may be used successfully as alibi." In these cases, the white colonel, to use Tonn, Endress, and Diamond's words, "is defined by his intimate connection to the community in which he operates. He is at once controlled by scene and submerged in it." By contrast, disgruntled black soldiers experienced in facing racism are "set *against* scene" and therefore are "not allowed, as alien[s], to be controlled and therefore absolved by it."[145]

Simultaneous Distancing from / Capitalizing on "Blackness"

Finally, several accounts also illustrate Powell's pragmatic distancing from strategies of black collective "voice" unless and until such "voices" become authorized by the dominant culture. Numerous passages in Powell's memoir reassure readers that he took no part in nor then countenanced civil rights activities. He writes, for example, that he "heard the radical black voices—Stokely Carmichael, Eldridge Cleaver, and H. Rap Brown with his 'Burn, baby burn!'—with uneasiness" and was "not eager to see the country burned down," given he was "doing well in it."[146] But other passages suggest that Powell's distaste for civil rights agitation included even nonviolent resistance. For example, he proffers this immediate apologia over a spontaneous outburst triggered by an ordinary, personal, black experience with Jim Crow: "My emotional reaction, or at least revealing my emotions this way, was not my style. Ordinarily, I was not looking for trouble. I was not marching, demonstrating, or taking part in sit-ins." On the same page, he makes explicit his pragmatic preference for strategies of individually "exiting" the oppression borne of blackness over strategies of collective "voice" challenging that oppression: "My eye was on an Army career for myself and a good life for my family," a rationale he poses later as, "Had I been more militant, would I have been branded a troublemaker rather than a promotable black?"[147] Such overt privileging of self-interest over collective concern not only fits Cloud's framing of certain minority life narratives as "tokenist," where "group identity, politics, and resistance are traded for economic and cultural capital within . . . cultural spaces,"[148] but also West's critique of the current crisis in black leadership: "most present-day black political leaders appear too hungry for status to be angry, too eager for acceptance to be bold, too self-invested in personal advancement to be defiant."[149]

Powell's repeated and explicit privileging of the welfare of self and literal kin, however, contravenes the more expansive familial metaphor for race relations he repeatedly invokes in his memoir and media interviews, a perspective widely heralded to promote him as a symbol of racial "healing." "We have to start thinking of America as a family," he professes in his autobiography. "We have to stop . . . hurting each other, and instead start caring for [and], sacrificing for . . . each other."[150] *Time* magazine, in apprizing his lucrative, standing-room-only "campaign" speeches, notes, "His most powerful theme has been the importance of family, of America as a big national family and of reconciliation among warring forces" and extensively quotes Powell's familial philosophy: "We've got to start remembering that no member of our family should be satisfied if any member of our American family is suffering or in need and we can do something about it."[151] On its face, Powell's metaphor of color-blind kinship resembles West's argument that black nihilism is best tamed by a universal ethic of love.[152] Yet whereas West views the racial ethic of care through the wide lens of both spiritual and material nurturing, Powell's biographies and memoir make clear that concern for afflicted members of the "American family" would never entail shared "sacrifice" of the economic stripe: "I am put off by patronizing liberals who claim to know what is best for society but devote little thought to who will eventually pay the bills," he writes in *My American Journey*. "I question the priorities of those liberals who lavish so much attention on . . . entitlements that little concern is left for the good of the community at large."[153] Elsewhere, he tells young black audiences that the worst kind of poverty is not economic, but the "poverty of love." In such contradictory talk, "family," "community," and "love" emerge as mere therapeutic and psychological bromides rather than tangible material reforms and obligations, mirroring what both Peck and Dow variously describe as the discourse of relational love work and personal "liking" that entices the dominant culture because it espouses a commitment to harmony and equality without imposing political or institutional demands.[154]

In light of impressive civil rights victories across the globe, Powell concedes belated admiration for civil rights agitators who "[woke] up defenders of the status quo,"[155] most particularly the now iconic Nelson Mandela and Martin Luther King Jr., whose image bearing the words "Freedom has always been an expensive thing" ironically hangs in the White House conference room of the self-confessed career-cautious Powell.[156] In his memoir, Powell navigates between estranging himself from the "challenging" tactics of civil rights politics and simultaneously sharing in the credit for their hard-won victories by pointing to his tactic of "exit." "The crusade for equal rights requires diverse roles," he writes, not merely political activists but people such as himself who "serve by making an *example* of their lives," explaining, "I hoped then and now that my rise might cause prejudiced whites to question their prejudices, and help to purge the poison of racism from their systems [emphasis added]." But as elsewhere in the memoir, Powell concurrently blunts this critique of systematic racism with an encomium to the nation's proven commitment to unbridled egalitarianism. "My career," he writes, "should serve as a model to fellow blacks . . . in demonstrating the possibilities of American life."[157] In such talk, Powell succinctly captures the distinction West draws between movement icons and many contemporary black leaders: "Malcolm and Martin called for the realization that black people are somebodies with which America has to reckon, whereas black politicians tend to turn our attention to *their* somebodiness owing to *their* 'making it' in America."[158]

Conclusion

The sharp disparity in interpreting *similar* behaviors, attitudes, and experiences in markedly *differing* ways is a hallmark of the Powell tales, one Burke argues is endemic in terministic screens. Whereas native blacks whose self-respecting willingness to challenge unjust existing structural racial barriers are framed as blacks "looking for trouble" rather than justice, the "can-do" attitude of proud black immigrants refusing to bow to some "inferior" marker is continually celebrated. After all, nonviolent sit-ins at southern lunch counters in the 1960s that defied "whites only" signs differed little in kind from the legendary refusal of West Indian women during the 1920s to honor identical racial restrictions in the needle trades. So, too, Powell's affirming translation of the "clannishness" of ethnically proud West Indians contrasts sharply with his generally negative assessment of self-defeating "isolation" purportedly resulting from native blacks' extreme racial pride. As both feminists and blacks have long noted, qualities such as assertiveness, for example, are frequently assessed by the dominant culture negatively or positively depending upon whether such traits are exhibited by males or females, whites or blacks; while assertiveness in white males, as illustration, is commonly translated by the larger culture as "self-confidence," assertive females and blacks, in contrast, are often perceived by social power brokers respectively as "bitchy" and "uppity."[159] In Powell's case, the terministic screen accommodating such differing interpretations was not gender or even race, broadly speaking; rather, the "screening process" involved racial *immigrant ethnicity* as the cultural filter used by both whites and some blacks to sort and rank "good" or "superior" from "bad" or "inferior" blacks.

The elevation of the "good" black does not signal the death rattle of racism, but rather, as Burke argues often occurs in symbolic action, is merely the throwing out of something by one name—in this case, racism—and bringing it back by another.[160] At the same time that the Powell narratives valorized a man purportedly averse to racialism, the tales themselves engaged in their own brand of racial politics in various ways. Most obvious, of course, was the championing of Powell's successes through the lens of his immigrant ancestry as "proof" of the nation's color-blind meritocracy, even as his racial immigrant ethnicity was hoisted routinely to differentiate this *group* of "good" blacks from the *group* of "bad." Beyond telegraphing Powell's distinctive black ancestry were various other tactics that differentiated this particular black from native blacks: the scapegoating of native blacks in various ways, the use of the "race card" or racial "excuse" trope as the single explanation for dire black circumstance, a scenic pardoning of whites that placed the onus on blacks for negotiating racism, and his simultaneously distancing himself from blackness and black political resistance and "voice" while simultaneously associating himself with civil rights heroes and triumphs. All functioned to allow Powell to "exit" the pejorative category of blackness and, in the words of many observers, to "transcend" his race. Thus, Powell's appeal as the widely heralded "embodiment of the American Dream" lies not just in his impressive personal successes but also in a national racial history inescapably implicated in that myth, a history that was often constructed in ways that not only reified but furthered the view of American blacks as ultimate outsiders. As Gladwell writes, the embrace and elevation of the "good" or "superior" black becomes a protective front by which "discrimination against American blacks is given one last vicious twist: I am not so shallow to despise you for the color of your skin, because I have found people of your color I like. Now I can despise you for what you are."[161] Essayist Clarence Page argues the same point, specific to Powell, contending that the former general's engaging life story and his seemingly raceless comportment finally and more easily enabled "white Americans to say confidently, *No I am not opposed to all black candidates; I am only opposed to those black candidates who are not like Colin Powell.*"[162] For native blacks, then, immigration status simply adds another unattainable qualification beyond whiteness for eligibility into unrestricted social mobility. *U.S. News and World Report,* for example, applauds Powell as "not a Jesse Jackson" who "challeng[es]" white "values" and "power." "[Powell's] . . . humble origins validate their belief in their country." Instead of "mak[ing] whites feel guilty, he makes them feel good."[163] But noticeably unacknowledged in this passage is that Jackson is a black Horatio Alger of even more lowly beginnings than the second-generation immigrant Powell. Thus, the distinction lies not so much in the extent of a black rags-to-riches climb, but rather *the point of origin* of the respective "American journey." After all, one need only consider the probable public outcry occasioned by Jackson's choice to film a duplication of his ancestor's coerced passage to this country in the belly of a slave ship and display it for presidential campaign purposes.

Additionally, the incessant privileging of Powell's biography, including his unique black genealogy, over his policy positions or proven record of expertise replicates persistent habits by the dominant culture of evaluating or promoting blacks more on body or personal history than on mind.[164] This pattern of advertising Powell as more the black "exception" rather than political "expert" continued years beyond his aborted presidential "campaign." In a speech at Tufts University as late as November 2, 2000, reference to Powell's "birth to immigrant Jamaican parents in Harlem" preceded mention of his role as national and foreign policy advisor to three presidents both in promotional literature and introductions by local luminaries, a privileging of the personal that seems unimaginable for previous presenters such as former senator George Mitchell and former secretary of state Madeline Albright. To his own disservice, the capable, retired, four-star general himself resorted to the formula that had long entranced white audiences yearning for racial innocence, committing all but five minutes of a thirty-five-minute lecture advertised as "Management of Crisis and Change: The Middle East" to jokes, humorous yarns and impersonations, and personal anecdotes and biography, including lengthy accounts of his father's journey from Jamaica on a banana boat and his childhood in the South Bronx. Moreover, in those final moments of the speech specific to the Middle East conflict, he couched the tensions in the vague familial metaphors of caring he had commonly employed in approaches to race. But in a serious context of renewed and escalating strife in the Middle East and expectations for thoughtful political analysis, Powell's feel-good biography, comic demeanor, and familial abstractions lost their cachet. Widely panned as, for example, "little work" and "ad lib remarks on his upbringing" that strayed from the appointed topic, the speech and his controversial sizable honorarium clouded his nomination as secretary of state,[165] critiques that signal the possible costs as well as benefits of strategies of bargaining for racial innocence.

Moreover, this cultural ranking of "good" and "bad" blacks portends to further the long-standing estrangement, animosity, and scapegoating among members of these respective black groups, a consequence Burke argues, as I have said, is endemic in terministic screens. Whereas the celebration of Powell's "good" black life narrative may assuage white racial guilt, the interracial caste system from which it draws inspiration mitigates against racial harmony and progress, replicating, in fact, a kind of black status system that whites historically have nourished in various ways to diffuse the threatening power of black solidarity. Albeit in differing measures, the ranking of "good" and "bad" blacks mirrors not only the hierarchy of "color" gradations and other presumed European qualities long used to assign social standing in the Caribbean, but also what Gates describes as the longstanding "story of class tensions within the [American] black community."[166] In the islands where the light-skinned Powell would not be considered "black" but the more valued "colored,"[167] non-whites believe that black or colored complexion and non-Caucasian features sometimes can be offset by securing characteristics associated with white European culture—professional occupation, advanced education, manners, and relative wealth—enabling nonwhites to be perceived by some, Foner writes, "'as if' they were white."[168] So, too, Gates argues that plantation pecking orders among American slaves prefigured black class jockeying that troubled even the abolitionist movement. And by the Harlem Renaissance, he writes, explicit or implicit distancing from poorly educated, lower-class blacks by an aspiring black elite had become somewhat the norm.[169] And included in the complex tapestry of tensions and guilt that "superior" versus "inferior" black sorting produces are intergenerational clashes between some immigrant blacks and their children who reject their elders' negative stereotypes of native blacks and yearn to identify and assimilate as "American," as white immigrants have always had the promise of doing. Thus, ironically, the pragmatic perils of black immigrant assimilation as Americans turn the fabled American-dream mythos inside out.

To be sure, immigrant credentials may enable certain blacks to "exit" more easily a maligned black category in various ways, including the not-insignificant, self-fulfilling prophecy nourished by the "superior" versus "inferior" black designator. As one young black immigrant poignantly put it, "The West Indians tend to go that extra step because they, whites, don't usually consider them really black. . . . They see them as a *person* [emphasis added]."[170] Such comments implicitly acknowledge what Gates and West refer to as the unmistakable interplay between *behavioral* and *structural* features that inform conditions such as disproportional black poverty.[171] As Burke writes in his discussion of the concept of "entelechy," the import of social environment cannot be divorced from properties inhering in an individual in the process of growth and development. Entelechy, he writes, refers to a process of perfection, meaning that

> the seed "implicitly contains" a future conforming to its nature, if the external conditions necessary to such unfolding and fulfillment occur in the right order . . . [But] to think of the circumstances and the seed as composing a single process, then the locus of the entelechy could be thought of as residing not just in the nature of the seed, but *in the ground of the process as a whole.*[172]

Although a dominant white culture may find the coveted temporary solace in the racial forgetting that "inferior" versus "superior" black mythology affords, genuine and enduring racial reconciliation requires collective memory as well as collective moving forward. In his careful analysis of recent efforts for racial reconciliation in South Africa, Erik Doxtader

writes that the respective parties astutely recognized "[r]econciliation could not mean amnesia. Without devolving to victimization or persecution, it needed to be the hope of voices
long silenced, the assurance that perpetrators of violence would confront the human costs
of their actions, and a means of reconstruction." Thus the challenge of reconciliation entails a paradox. "The past," he explains, "is a referent for action even as that past must be
abandoned. History must be preserved and buried . . . The path from past to future must
be forged through acts of reconciliation that remember and transcend the past simultaneously."[173]

Notes

1. John F. Stacks and Michael Kramer, "I've Got to Make Some Choices," *Time,* September 18, 1995, 72. Different media accounts give differing numbers of the cities Powell visited during his book tour.

2. James Kelly, "Powell on Powell," *Time,* September 18, 1995, 57; Howard Fineman and Evan Thomas, "Powell on the March," *Newsweek,* September 11, 1995, 26–31.

3. Janis L. Edwards, "The Very Role Model of a Modern Major (Media) Candidate: Colin Powell and the Rhetoric of Public Opinion," *Communication Quarterly* 46 (1998): 167; Clarence Page, *Showing My Color: Impolite Essays on Race and Identity* (New York: Harper Perennial, 1996), 249.

4. Colin Powell with Joseph E. Persico, *My American Journey* (New York: Random House, 1995), 610–11.

5. Powell reportedly often received sixty thousand dollars for each speech, although some accounts reported that he received as much as two hundred thousand dollars for certain speaking engagements.

6. John Walcott et al., "The Man to Watch," *U.S. News and World Report,* August 21, 1995, 22.

7. Fineman and Thomas, "Powell on the March," 28; Michael Kramer, "Just Like Ike," *Time,* September 18, 1995, 74.

8. Powell with Persico, *My American Journey,* 406, 409. Powell explains that the periodical delayed the story originally planned for its July 4 issue to coincide with his appointment as chair-man of the Joint Chiefs of Staff.

9. See, for example, Steven V. Roberts with Bruce B. Auster and Gary Cohen, "What's Next, General Powell?" *U.S. News and World Report,* March 18, 1991, 50–53; John Ranelagh, "America's Black Eisenhower," *National Review,* April 1, 1991, 26–28; Eleanor Clift and Thomas DeFrank, "Bush's General: Maximum Force," *Newsweek,* September 3, 1990, 36–37.

10. Howard Means, *Colin Powell* (New York: Donald I. Fine, 1992); David Roth, *Sacred Honor: Colin Powell; The Inside Account of His Life and Triumphs* (Grand Rapids, Mich.: Zondervan, 1993).

11. Joe Klein, "Character, Not Ideology," *Newsweek,* November 13, 1995, 36; Morton Zucker-man, "Behind the Powell Phenomenon," *U.S. News and World Report,* August 21, 1995, 64.

12. In light of the second Gulf War against Iraq, the framing of the first Gulf War as a quick and decisive "victory" has been challenged by numerous observers.

13. Means, *Colin Powell,* 324, 328.

14. Webster B. Brooks III, "Colin Powell Calculus: The General's Road to the White House," promotional materials (18 Lebanon Street, Hartford, Conn., July 15, 1995), n.p.

15. John F. Stacks, "The Powell Factor," *Time,* July 10, 1995, 29.

16. Nancy Gibbs, "General Letdown," *Time,* November 20, 1995, 50, 56.

17. Since the issuance of his autobiography in the early fall of 1995, Powell publicly has staked out positions on contentious social issues such as affirmative action and abortion. The "good" black narrative posited and examined here, however, was promulgated most extensively when

Powell was widely and appropriately described as a "political enigma," an ideological "Rorschach inkblot test," a "classic blank canvass," an "empty ideological vessel," and "a riddle wrapped in a mystery" (Edwards, "The Very Role Model," 166; Page, *Showing My Color,* 254; Stacks, "The Powell Factor," 25; and Joe Klein, "Can Colin Powell Save America?" *Newsweek,* October 10, 1994, 20).

18. Walcott and others, "The Man to Watch," 44.

19. Various scholars have discussed the rhetorical nature of biographies and autobiographies, including Dana L. Cloud, "Hegemony or Concordance? The Rhetoric of Tokenism in 'Oprah' Winfrey's Rags-to-Riches Biography," *Critical Studies in Mass Communication* 13 (1996): 115–37; Thomas W. Benson, "Rhetoric and Autobiography: The Case of Malcolm X," *Quarterly Journal of Speech* 60 (1974): 1–13; Herbert Leibowitz, *Fabricating Lives* (New York: Alfred A. Knopf, 1989); Wayne J. McMullen and Martha Solomon, "The Politics of Adaptation: Steven Spielberg's Appropriation of *The Color Purple,*" *Text and Performance Quarterly* 14 (1994): 158–74; Toni Morrison, "The Site of Memory," in *Inventing the Truth: The Art and Craft of Memoir,* ed. William Zinsser, 101–24 (Boston: Houghton Mifflin, 1987); Martha Solomon, "Autobiographies as Rhetorical Narratives: Elizabeth Cady Stanton and Anna Howard Shaw as 'New Women,'" *Communication Studies* 42 (1991): 354–70.

20. Shelby Steele, *The Content of Our Character: A New Vision of Race in America* (New York: St. Martin's Press, 1990), 8.

21. Nancy Foner, "Race and Color: Jamaican Migrants in London and New York City," *International Migration Review* 29 (1985): 708–27; David Mittelberg and Mary C. Waters, "The Process of Ethnogenesis among Haitian and Israeli Immigrants in the United States," *Ethnic and Racial Studies* 15 (1992): 412–35; Mary C. Waters, "Ethnic and Racial Identities of Second-Generation Black Immigrants in New York City," *International Migration Review* 28 (1994): 795–820; and Mary C. Waters, "Explaining the Comfort Factor: West Indian Immigrants Confront American Race Relations," in *The Cultural Territories of Race: Black and White Boundaries,* ed. Michele Lamont, 63–69 (Chicago: University of Chicago Press, 1999). For a popular and more personal account, see Malcolm Gladwell, "Black Like Them," *New Yorker,* April 29 and May 6, 1996, 74–81. Gladwell is a second-generation Jamaican-American. For purposes of clarification in this essay, I follow the practices employed by various ethnographers and others in referring to blacks descended from slaves in the United States as "American," "native," or "indigenous" blacks to differentiate them from first- and second-generation blacks with roots in the Caribbean who also hold slave ancestry.

22. For a discussion of "terministic screens," see Kenneth Burke, *Language as Symbolic Action: Essays on Life, Literature, and Method,* 3rd ed. (Berkeley: University of California Press, 1966), 44–62. Walter Lippman also articulates such cultural designators this way: "For the most part we do not first see, and define, we define first and then see . . . [W]e pick out what our culture has already defined for us, and we tend to perceive that which we have picked out in the form stereotyped for us by our culture" (*Public Opinion* [New York Free Press, 1922], 54–55).

23. Waters, "Ethnic and Racial Identities," 817.

24. Steele, *Content of Our Character,* 75–76.

25. Ibid., 10–20.

26. Ibid., 10–11.

27. Gladwell, "Black Like Them," 75; Waters, "Ethnic and Racial Identities," 797.

28. Waters, "Ethnic and Racial Identities," 696–97. Whereas Jamaicans migrating to the United States always have been more skilled than the average Jamaican, the most recent influx has been marked by a higher percentage of professional, technical, and other nonmanual laborers. See Foner, "Race and Color," 710–11.

29. Jervis Anderson, "Black and Blue," *New Yorker,* April 29 and May 6, 1996, 62.

30. Roth, *Sacred Honor,* 35; Page, *Showing My Color,* 181.

31. Waters, "Ethnic and Racial Identities," 813.

32. Gladwell, "Black Like Them," 78.

33. See, as examples of such arguments, Ira De Augustine Reid, *The Negro Immigrant* (1939; repr., New York: Arno Press and New York Times, 1969); Thomas Sowell, *Essays and Data on American Ethnic Groups* (Washington, D.C.: Urban Institute, 1978); Nathan Glazer and Daniel Patrick Moynihan, *Beyond the Melting Pot* (Cambridge, Mass.: MIT Press, 1963); Mona Charen, "Will Anyone Listen?" Columnists, January 12, 2001, TownHall.com, http://www.townhall.com/columnists/monacharen/mc200010112.shtml (last accessed November 25, 2002).

34. Means quotes Roger Wilkins, *Colin Powell,* 97; Page, *Showing My Color,* 248–55; Cornel West, *Race Matters* (Boston: Beacon Press, 1993), 13.

35. Cloud, "Hegemony or Concordance?," 116.

36. Gladwell, "Black Like Them," 79; Waters, "Ethnic and Racial Identities," 800–801.

37. Waters, "Explaining the Comfort Factor," 67.

38. Jack Miles, "Blacks vs. Browns," *Atlantic Monthly,* October 1992, 54, 60.

39. Gladwell, "Black Like Them," 80–81.

40. Foner, "Race and Color," 715, 722. Foner concludes, "Structural features of British and American societies play a large role" in influencing black immigrants' self-perceptions, their own behaviors, and their social mobility within their respective dominant cultures (ibid., 724). Indeed, even as both Powell's biographer, Means, and the *National Review* point up the personal qualities and island culture of black Jamaicans as primary indexes of their successes, in their zeal to witness to America's unbridled opportunity, both share a letter to the editor of a British newspaper ironically testifying to structural influences on these black immigrant's mobility. Responding to a profile on Powell, the British reader wrote, "So General Colin Powell was born in Harlem, to . . . Jamaican, working-class immigrant parents. His good fortune is that they took the New York rather than Southhampton boat. If they had, he might have made sergeant" (Means, *Colin Powell,* 89).

41. Waters, "Explaining the Comfort Factor," 71.

42. Henry Louis Gates Jr. and Cornel West, *The Future of the Race* (New York: Alfred A. Knopf, 1996), 85.

43. Waters, "Explaining the Comfort Factor," 71, 85.

44. Quoted in Waters, "Explaining the Comfort Factor," 87.

45. Foner, "Race and Color," 717; Waters, "Ethnic and Racial Identities," 805, 813.

46. Waters, "Explaining the Comfort Factor," 76.

47. Foner, "Race and Color," 717; Waters, "Ethnic and Racial Identities," 805.

48. Powell with Persico, *My American Journey,* 114.

49. Ibid., 606–7.

50. Waters, "Ethnic and Racial Identities," 797.

51. Gladwell, "Black Like Them," 77; Roth, *Sacred Honor,* 34.

52. Among politically militant blacks with immigrant ancestry are Marcus Garvey, James Farmer, Stokely Carmichael, and Louis Farrakhan.

53. Numerous ethnographic studies reveal contradictory impressions of West Indians in the United States as both sophisticated racial "challengers" who unabashedly exert political "voice" and, conversely, conciliatory racial "bargainers" who elect to "exit" stigmatized blackness. Waters, for example, notes that black immigrants are couched, on the one hand, as "militant race leaders, with more advanced and confrontational racial ideologies and programs than American blacks. Yet they have also been seen as more conservative, less willing to challenge the rules of the game, easier to get along with [than native blacks]." See Waters, "Explaining the Comfort Factor," 89.

54. David K. Shipler, *A Country of Strangers: Blacks and Whites in America* (New York: Vintage Books, 1998), 46, 309; Waters, "Explaining the Comfort Factor," 67.

55. Powell with Persico, *My American Journey,* 70.

56. A comfort level with whites that surpasses comfort with blacks is a motif throughout ethnographic studies. See Waters, "Ethnic and Racial Identities" and "Explaining the Comfort Factor," and Foner, "Race and Color," as examples.

57. Waters, "Explaining the Comfort Factor," 67.

58. Waters, "Ethnic and Racial Identities," 801.

59. See Waters, "Ethnic and Racial Identities," 806; Foner, "Race and Color," 717; Mittelberg and Waters, "The Process of Ethnogenesis."

60. Waters, "Ethnic and Racial Identities," 808.

61. In his memoir, Powell writes of being interrogated by a waitress during segregation as to whether he was a foreign black before deciding if she could serve him (*My American Journey,* 108).

62. Gladwell, "Black Like Them," 74; Shipler, *A Country of Strangers,* 308.

63. Waters, "Ethnic and Racial Identities," 800.

64. West, *Race Matters,* 12.

65. Gates and West, *Future of the Race,* xv.

66. For a brief overview of the key terms of Burke's pentad, see Bernard L. Brock, "Rhetorical Criticism: A Burkeian Approach Revisited," in *Methods of Rhetorical Criticism: A Twentieth Century Perspective,* ed. Bernard L. Brock, Robert L. Scott, and James W. Chesebro, 3rd ed. rev. , 187–90 (Detroit: Wayne State University Press, 1989).

67. Kenneth Burke, *A Grammar of Motives* (Berkeley, Calif: University of California Press, 1969), 157.

68. Steele, *Content of Our Character,* 16.

69. Ibid., 12. Essayist Clarence Page makes a similar point in his analysis of black political hopefuls, Powell among them, arguing white Americans occasionally "award bonus points to a likable black candidate whose race can help them feel good about how open-minded they have always imagined themselves" (*Showing My Color,* 254).

70. Morrison, "The Site of Memory," 106, 110.

71. D. Soyini Madison, "'That Was My Occupation': Oral Narrative, Performance, and Black Feminist Thought," *Text and Performance Quarterly* 13 (1993): 223.

72. Thomas Kochman, *Black and White Styles in Conflict* (Chicago: University of Chicago Press, 1983), 61.

73. Steele, *Content of Our Character,* 13–14.

74. Shipler, *A Country of Strangers,* 429–32.

75. Mary E. Stuckey and Frederick J. Antczak argue, for example, that Bill Clinton's widely publicized struggle in surmounting adversity "represented a claim to competence potentially far more powerful than, say, experience in foreign policy, or personal friendships with foreign leaders." As important perhaps, "[a]s one who had lived the American Dream, Clinton was able to present his life as a parable for the nation, and to implicitly argue that by electing him, Americans would be able to restore the American Dream that they were in danger of losing [for themselves]" (Mary E. Stuckey and Frederick J. Antczak, "The Battle of Issues and Images: Establishing Interpretive Dominance," *Communication Quarterly* 42 [1994]: 125–26).

76. Roberts with Auster and Cohen, "What's Next, General Powell?," 52.

77. Cloud, "Hegemony or Concordance?," 122.

78. Burke, *Philosophy of Literary Form,* 41.

79. Jim Cullen, *The American Dream: A Short History of an Idea That Shaped a Nation* (New York: Oxford University Press, 2003), 6.

80. Charles J. Kelly Jr., "Citizens for Colin Powell for President," promotional materials (3018 N Street NW, Washington, D.C., 1996), 10.

81. "Colin Powell: A Soldier's Campaign," on *Biography* (Arts and Entertainment Channel, 1987).

82. Robert J. McNamara, "Editorial Reviews," *Biography,* "Colin Powell: A Soldier's Campaign." http://www.amazon.com/exec/obidos/search-handle-form/104–1350858–8454313?v=glance&s= video (last accessed November 21, 2002).

83. Roberts with Auster and Cohen, "What's Next, General Powell?"

84. Bill Schneider, "Play of the Week," CNN, February 7, 2003.

85. Waters, "Ethnic and Racial Identities," 817.

86. Powell with Persico, *My American Journey,* viii.

87. Ibid., 7.

88. Ibid., 23.

89. Ibid., 7–8.

90. Stacks, "The Powell Factor," 29. Powell's strategic marketing of his past is suggested further by the discrepancies between his early raceless sense of self and relatively tolerant childhood environment portrayed in his memoir's framing and his description in the earlier Means biography of the South Bronx as "not that much of a melting pot" where "you never lost your cultural identity" (Means, *Colin Powell,* 46).

91. Symbolic purification, particularly scapegoating, figures prominently in Burke's various works. For some discussions, see Kenneth Burke, *The Rhetoric of Religion* (Berkeley: University of California Press, 1961), 190–91, and Kenneth Burke, *The Philosophy of Literary Form,* 3rd ed. (Berkeley: University of California Press, 1973), 38–41, 202–3.

92. Burke, *Language as Symbolic Action,* 51.

93. Steele, *Content of Our Character,* 10.

94. Thomas K. Nakayama and Robert L. Krizek, "Whiteness: A Strategic Rhetoric," *Quarterly Journal of Speech* 81 (1995): 301.

95. West, *Race Matters,* 3.

96. Klein, "Can Colin Powell Save America?," 20.

97. Steven V. Roberts, "An American Tale," *U.S. News and World Report,* August 21, 1995, 27.

98. Cloud, "Hegemony or Concordance?," 122.

99. Burke, *Philosophy of Literary Form,* 39–40.

100. Roberts with Auster and Cohen, "What's Next, General Powell?," 52.

101. Quoted in Roberts, "An American Tale," 28.

102. Klein, "Can Colin Powell Save America?," 26.

103. Means, *Colin Powell,* 64, 66–67.

104. Ibid., 332.

105. Waters, "Ethnic and Racial Identities," 806.

106. Burke, *Language as Symbolic Action,* 46–47.

107. West, *Race Matters,* 26.

108. Nakayama and Krizek, "Whiteness: A Strategic Rhetoric," 293.

109. Means, *Colin Powell,* 19.

110. Gladwell, "Black Like Them," 79.

111. Klein, "Can Colin Powell Save America?," 26.

112. West, *Race Matters,* 3.

113. Zuckerman, "Behind the Powell Phenomenon," 64.

114. West, *Race Matters,* 2.

115. Raymie E. McKerrow, "Critical Rhetoric: Theory and Praxis," *Communication Monographs* 56 (1989): 107.

116. West, *Race Matters,* 13.

117. David Hume Kennerly and Sue Allison Massimiano, "The Demobilization of Colin Powell," *Life,* July 1993, 36.

118. Roberts, with Auster and Cohen, "What's Next General Powell?," 51.

119. Klein, "Can Colin Powell Save America?," 26.

120. Powell with Persico, *My American Journey,* 553.

121. Ibid., 534.

122. Such claims mirror premises that both Cloud and Bonnie J. Dow argue characterize popular culture artifacts treating individuals forced to confront various types of discrimination. The message, Dow writes, is that such persons "are, in fact, political subjects only when [they] allow [themselves] to be such" (Bonnie J. Dow, "*Ellen,* Television, and the Politics of Gay and Lesbian Visibility," *Critical Studies in Media Communication* 18 [2001]: 135).

123. Powell with Persico, *My American Journey,* 43.

124. Burke, *A Grammar of Motives,* 157.

125. Janice Peck, "Talk about Racism: Framing a Popular Discourse of Race on *Oprah Winfrey,*" *Cultural Critique* (Spring 1994): 91; Dow, "*Ellen,* Television, and the Politics of Gay and Lesbian Visibility," passim.

126. Excerpts from *My American Journey* in *Time,* September 18, 1995, 62; "The Great Black Hope," *National Review,* September 9, 1995, 10.

127. "The Great Black Hope," 10.

128. Mari Boor Tonn, Valerie A. Endress, and John N. Diamond, "Hunting and Heritage on Trial in Maine: A Dramatistic Debate over Tragedy, Tradition, and Territory," *Quarterly Journal of Speech* 79 (1993): 166–67.

129. Powell with Persico, *My American Journey,* 45.

130. "Colin Powell: A Soldier's Campaign."

131. Waters, "Explaining the Comfort Factor," 89.

132. Burke, *Language as Symbolic Action,* 45.

133. Powell with Persico, *My American Journey,* 23.

134. Means, *Colin Powell,* 68; Roth, *Sacred Honor,* 21.

135. Waters, "Ethnic and Racial Identities," 816.

136. Powell with Persico, *My American Journey,* 22.

137. West, *Race Matters,* 4.

138. Powell with Persico, *My American Journey,* 401.

139. Quoted by West in Gates and West, *Future of the Race,* 86–87.

140. Although dutifully noting the prospective presidential candidate's paucity of detailed policy positions, the weekly nonetheless applauded his performance in public as "superb," pointing to his skill in amusing audiences and soliciting pleas for his candidacy. The account reads in part: "[H]e parodied a pompous white military officer speaking in empty and orotund phrases. Then he mimicked a black sergeant talking about the coming war in the Persian Gulf: 'We gonna kick butt and go home.' Describing an encounter with Israeli Prime Minister Yitzhak Rabin at the White House treaty signing with Yasser Arafat, Powell put on a New York Jewish accent. And he even worked around the edges of gay sensibilities. 'Arafat . . . is so taken by the moment that he starts to pull me toward him and hug me and give me a two-cheek kiss. But I can only take so much new world order. . . . ' The audience laughed with him" (Stacks, "The Powell Factor," 25).

141. Clift and DeFrank, "Bush's General: Maximum Force," 37.

142. Powell with Persico, *My American Journey,* 400.

143. Ibid., 38.

144. Ibid., 190–92.

145. Tonn, Endress, and Diamond, "Hunting and Heritage," 178–79.

146. Powell with Persico, *My American Journey,* 124.

147. Ibid., 108, 401.

148. Cloud, "Hegemony or Concordance?," 122.

149. West, *Race Matters,* 38.

150. Powell with Persico, *My American Journey,* 611; see also 553.

151. Stacks, "The Powell Factor," 25–26.

152. West, *Race Matters,* 19.

153. Powell with Persico, *My American Journey,* 608.

154. Peck, "Talk about Racism," especially 117–18; Dow, "*Ellen,* Television, and the Politics of Gay and Lesbian Visibility," 131–37.

155. Powell with Persico, *My American Journey,* 124.

156. Roth, *Sacred Honor,* 159.

157. Powell with Persico, *My American Journey,* 400–401.

158. West, *Race Matters,* 38.

159. Shipler, *A Country of Strangers,* 296, 417.

160. Burke, *Philosophy of Literary Form,* 174.

161. Gladwell, "Black Like Them," 79.

162. Page, *Showing My Color,* 251–54.

163. Roberts, with Auster and Cohen, "What's Next General Powell?," 50.

164. See Shipler, *A Country of Strangers,* 276–316.

165. The author attended Powell's lecture at Tufts University on November 2, 2000, and took extensive notes, including timing his speech. Beyond the anecdotes described in the text, Powell also discussed the GI Joe action figure marketed in his likeness and his sponsorship of programs designed to encourage young people to excel, and he humorously rendered encounters with various dignitaries during his entire career. Only when pressed by frustrated audience members during the question-and-answer period following did this former high-ranking military commander during the Persian Gulf War discuss any specifics of Middle East relations, despite the title and purported purpose of his talk ("Management of Crisis and Change: The Middle East," the 2000 Issam Fares Lecture, Tufts University, November 2, 2000). Although most accounts in the news media and on the Internet reported that Powell had been paid two hundred thousand dollars for the speech, other reports ranged from sixty thousand to eighty thousand dollars. Powell defended the controversial speech by claiming it was "the kind I give all the time." Associated Press, "Colin Powell Defends Speaking Fee," January 9, 2001. (http://quest.com/stories/0109017670.shtml [last accessed August 13, 2005]). And much of the speech had strong affinities with a San Diego speech described in a *Time* cover story and earlier endnote.

166. Henry Louis Gates Jr., "Not Gone with the Wind: Voices of Slavery," *New York Times,* February 9, 2003, sec. 2.

167. Gladwell, "Black Like Them," 80.

168. Foner, "Race and Color," 713. Powell himself remarks in the Means biography, "[T]here's a great deal of status consciousness within West Indian families and Jamaican families especially between those who have a little bit of education and those who don't, between those who are light-skinned and those who are dark-skinned, between those who had British and Scottish relatives and those who didn't" (Means, *Colin Powell,* 72). As a result, the "serious handicaps" he describes his native black fiancée initially encountered both with his immediate and extended Jamaican family may have been neutralized by her fair skin, green eyes, and background from a "privileged," highly educated, professional Alabama family. See Powell with Persico, *My American Journey,* 64–70.

169. Gates, "Not Gone with the Wind."

170. Waters, "Ethnic and Racial Identities," 806.

171. Gates and West, *Future of the Race,* xiii–xv.

172. Burke, *Rhetoric of Religion,* 246–47.

173. Erik Doxtader, "Making Rhetorical History in a Time of Transition: The Occasion, Constitution, and Representation of South African Reconciliation," *Rhetoric and Public Affairs* 4 (2001): 247.

Joshua Meyrowitz

18

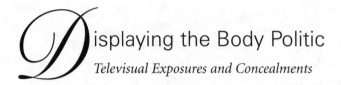

${\mathcal{D}}$isplaying the Body Politic
Televisual Exposures and Concealments

Introduction: From Disembodied to Embodied Leaders

If asked to conjure up an image of presidential greatness, many Americans would probably mention the Mount Rushmore National Memorial in the Black Hills of South Dakota. On the face of the mountain that rises fifty-seven hundred feet above sea level, sculptor Gutzon Borglum displayed the visages of presidents George Washington, Thomas Jefferson, Theodore Roosevelt, and Abraham Lincoln. The faces are scaled for men who would be 465 feet tall! Yet, no parts of their bodies below their heads are visible. The sculpture was meant to represent larger-than-life ideas and ideals, not the personal idiosyncrasies of the pictured men. Washington represents the fight for independence; Jefferson stands for the notion of self-government; Lincoln stands for the ideals of equality and the enduring union of the states; Roosevelt represents the emergence of the United States as a world power in the twentieth century.[1]

Gutzon Borglum worked on the Mount Rushmore monument from 1927 until his death fourteen years later. Even at the end of that period, the notion of disembodied, larger-than-life leaders continued to be supported by the public's lack of direct knowledge about the bodies of its presidents. By the time Mount Rushmore's creator died in 1941, Franklin Roosevelt had been president for eight of the twelve years he would be in office. Yet few Americans realized that FDR's legs were crippled, that he used a wheelchair, that he often had to be carried by staff, and that he essentially faked the ability to stand and walk on his own for selected public events.[2] The nature of FDR's relationships with his wife and his mistress, even with his White House staff, was out of public view.

For most of the history of the republic, the boundary between a president's private and public spheres remained thick. Until recently, few Americans had ever been in real or virtual close physical proximity with a president. The distance and mystery that surrounded presidents allowed those featured on Mount Rushmore to become symbols of ideals that transcended their physical beings. George Washington's ill-fitting false teeth and pock-marked face were invisible to most of his contemporaries. Thomas Jefferson's speech impediment, which led him to avoid speaking in public as much as possible, was unknown to most citizens. And although Abraham Lincoln's and Teddy Roosevelt's appearances were familiar through photography (and, for Teddy Roosevelt, through silent movies), most Americans did not know what their voices sounded like. To this day, few Americans know that Lincoln spoke in a rough, "backwoods" style or that he had a high, squeaky voice that went up an octave higher when he was nervous.[3]

Indeed, as late as the first term of President Eisenhower in the 1950s, even press conferences remained semiprivate affairs, where the press was not allowed to quote a president without his explicit permission.[4] The news media had to paraphrase the president's comments and answers, unless authorized to use word-for-word citations (which were often cleaned up for public distribution). That changed when President Eisenhower allowed the filming of his press conferences during his second term. For the first time, average Americans heard their leader stammer and stumble through impromptu or only half-prepared answers.

The new, more intimate view of presidents and presidential candidates worked to John Kennedy's advantage in televised debates with Richard Nixon during the 1960 campaign, where Kennedy presented a more pleasing personal style. As president, Kennedy was able to exploit a sense of intimacy between himself (and his family) and the public. Yet, Kennedy also managed to keep many of his health problems and his extensive extramarital sexual exploits out of public view.

Only thirty years later, however, the public realm was saturated with private information and intimate speculation about the president. In the scandal that erupted surrounding President Bill Clinton's relationship with White House intern Monica Lewinsky, the public reports and discussions dwelled on the sorts of detailed descriptions that had traditionally been kept behind closed American doors: fellatio, a cigar used as a dildo, phone sex, thong underwear, and semen stains on a blue dress. The intimate revelations and the political and legal maneuverings were beamed into U.S. homes, cars, and offices hour after hour, day after day, week after week, month after month.

Even the staid public affairs network C-SPAN (which normally carries dry, unedited coverage of Congress, congressional hearings, press conferences, speeches, interviews, and discussion panels) played hours of taped telephone conversations between the White House intern and her loose-lipped confidante, Linda Tripp. (This airing obviously involved a new definition for C-SPAN of their obligation to cover a "public affair," an obligation that overrode any concerns they might have had about cablecasting tapes of private conversations that had been captured illegally by Tripp in the state of Maryland, which has a two-party consent law for recordings.)

No adult, and few children, could escape the onslaught. Many anecdotal reports, consistent with my own experience, indicated that there was a sudden rise in sexual humor at corporations, universities, and other institutions that had previously moved to ban all such risqué topics in order to avoid complaints (and lawsuits) regarding "hostile work environments" or "sexual harassment." In keeping with the assumption that people of all ages already knew about the affair from other sources, even children's editions of news magazines used in schools—which normally "protect" young people from such adult scandals— apparently felt they could not maintain credibility with their young readers if they ignored the topic. They therefore included references in their articles to "the president's girlfriend."

The boundary between public and private had moved far into what was once considered the private realm. This situation prompted President Clinton to make an unprecedented direct plea to the public in August 1998 to work with him to restore a realm of privacy for the personal lives of presidents in order to simultaneously restore a public realm for attending to serious political issues.

This chapter will begin with an analysis of that 1998 Clinton speech. I will then assess the appeals in the speech in light of the way that the Clintons, as well as other politicians of both parties, had displayed themselves to the public just two years earlier in the 1996 presidential campaign. Then, I will outline what I call the "collaborative construction of intimacy" in American politics in general, along with its possible sources and implications. In part, I will argue that the evolution of communication media has been encouraging politicians, the public, and journalists to focus more on the intimate display of politicians as flesh-and-bones people while decreasing attention to issues that are not as easily linked to personal bodily experience. Thus, politicians lower themselves stylistically by explicitly employing in public the courtship displays typically used in intimate interpersonal interaction. At the same time, they often show implicit contempt for the public by largely bypassing discussion of topics of vital concern to a democracy. Finally, I will address some other reasons for the focus on the embodied experiences of political leaders and point to a potential source of a reversal of this trend.

Calling for a Public-Private Distinction

At around 10:00 P.M. on August 18, 1998, President Clinton delivered a four-minute television address to the nation in which he admitted that he had had a "relationship" with Monica Lewinsky that was "not appropriate" and that he had misled many people, including his wife. The main thrust of the very brief speech, however, was his own accusation that a line had been inappropriately crossed into the private life of a public figure and that he was going to reclaim his family life for his family. (For the full text of the speech, see the appendix to this chapter.)

Below are key excerpts from the speech, to which I have added emphases and a few explicating parentheticals. They highlight President Clinton's efforts to draw a clear distinction between private and public contexts:

> I answered . . . questions about my *private* life, questions no American citizen would ever want to answer.
>
> It constituted a . . . *personal* failure on my part. . . . I know my *public* comments . . . gave a false impression [but about a *private* matter].
>
> I was . . . very concerned about protecting my [*private*] family.
>
> I had . . . concerns about [a *public*] independent counsel investigation that began with *private* business dealings twenty years ago . . .
>
> The . . . [*public*] investigation moved on to my staff and friends, then into my *private* life.
>
> Now this [*private*] matter is between me, the two people I love most, my wife and our daughter, and our God. I must put it right. . . . Nothing is more important to me *personally*. But it is *private*. And I intend to reclaim my family life for my family. It's nobody's business but ours. Even presidents have *private* lives. It is time to stop the [*public*] pursuit of *personal* destruction and the prying into *private* lives and get on with our [*public*] national life.

I ask you to turn away from the [*public*] spectacle [over a *private* matter] of the past seven months, to repair the fabric of our [*public*] national discourse, and return our attention to all the [*public*] challenges and all the promise of the next American century.

President Clinton clearly implies here that the independent counsel's office, the press, and the public have inappropriately crossed a line into the Clintons' private lives. In the absence of a larger context, it is easy to agree with this argument. One need only recall the sanctimonious, gossipy, prying commentary and "reporting" that characterized the seemingly endless media discussions about the scandal. Additionally, the ways in which journalists and talk-show hosts assumed the language of intimacy when speaking about the Clintons was disturbing. They commented on what "Bill" should say to "Hillary," and on what "Hillary" should have said to "Bill," and on what "Monica" was thinking when she did this or that, and how "Chelsea" must be reacting to the whole matter—as if the reporters and pundits were family friends of the Clintons or professional therapists familiar with all the relevant intimate details. With this media coverage in mind, it is easy to sympathize with President Clinton or with anyone who might be targeted in a similar manner.

However, when one steps back from the framework presented by President Clinton in the speech, more complex questions arise. Did the Clintons themselves play a role in this blurring of their public and private lives *before* the Clinton-Lewinsky scandal? Was it simply the independent counsel and journalists and the public who crossed the line into President Clinton's private life? Or had President Clinton previously invited and encouraged the media and the public to cross that line in appealing for votes? I think the latter is clearly the case.

The Clintons Invite the Public into Their Private Sphere

Just two years prior to the 1998 Clinton apologia speech, the August 1996 Democratic convention offered President Clinton an opportunity to focus on the criteria by which he wanted his candidacy for reelection to be judged. Looking at representative excerpts from the films and speeches at that convention, one can ask whether President Clinton presents the national discourse on issues that he would later appeal for in his August 1998 speech, or whether he presented a discourse of personal appeal that was based on the strength of his relationships with his wife, Hillary, daughter, Chelsea, his brother, his mother, and even his mother-in-law.

In the film about President Clinton prepared for the Democratic Party's convention, there are many scenes of intimacy: a picture of Bill looking lovingly at Hillary on the day of their wedding; Bill and Hillary with baby Chelsea (Hillary is kissing the baby's head); a clip from a home video (dated February 1989) of Bill dancing with Chelsea; Bill taking the oath of office as governor with a smiling Hillary behind him; pictures of Bill and Hillary dancing; a scene of Bill Clinton and Al Gore hugging. The public is taken into what is presented as the president's "private" spheres and asked to judge his suitability for public office on the basis of the quality of his roles as husband and father and friend.

Hillary Clinton's speech at the convention continues the theme of a close marriage and shared parenting as virtues worthy of discussion in the public arena:

In October, Bill and I will celebrate our twenty-first wedding anniversary. [Pause for applause.] Bill was with me when Chelsea was born in the delivery room, in my hospital room, and when we brought our baby daughter home. [Viewers are shown live shots of a smiling Chelsea at the convention watching her mother speak.]

In another Democratic National Committee movie, Hillary's mother is called upon to "tell the truth" about President Clinton:

Everybody knows that there's only one person in the world that can really tell the truth about a man, and that's his mother-in-law. . . . I admire him . . . but I *love* him for the way he defended and loved my daughter. . . . I would love to have had the kind of intellectual partner that I could bounce off these great ideas . . . the good-natured ribbing and fun that they have with each other. These are both very complicated people. But their relationship is not. They just simply love each other. It's really a joy to see your daughter, your son-in-law, and your grandchild in that kind of environment. [The last few sentences are heard as the film dissolves between seven intimate photos of Bill and Hillary, with a final image of Bill and Hillary kissing Chelsea.]

In the next segment of the film, Bill Clinton is seated on a couch, dressed casually and speaking softly in an intimate, informal tone (with "ums" and "ahs"). He briefly displays and touches his wedding ring. He explains how "Chelsea normally doesn't want, uh, doesn't want to be involved in public affairs very much because she likes her privacy." But the film then violates Chelsea's privacy by showing image after image of her at public events and during political travels. (Thus, it is almost as if each viewer is being told that he or she is not a member of the mass public, but a friend, visiting in the Clintons' home, whom the Clintons trust to maintain Chelsea's sense of privacy from the scrutiny of the public at large.) The president continues, "We maintained a level of family intimacy with Chelsea that I'm very proud of and very pleased by and very grateful for. I'm going to miss her when she's gone."

Then, with more intimate talk and images, President Clinton describes two new nephews, one of whom, he tells us, reminds him so much of his deceased mother and in whose face he claims to see what his job in the presidency is all about. (We see video images of the young child playing in the Oval Office with the president and running into President Clinton's arms.)

In his convention speech, President Clinton makes other personal revelations. He describes how "Hillary and I still talk about the books we read to Chelsea when we were so tired we could hardly stay awake." He reveals that "[d]rugs nearly killed my brother when he was a young man. And I hate them." Clinton also talks about his mother's support during his first campaign and about how much he misses her now that she has died.

Even these brief excerpts suggest an incredible revelation of details and scenes of intimacy—marriage, romantic dancing, drug use in the family, births and deaths, toddlers in the Oval Office, grieving for a lost parent. After considering Bill Clinton's blurring of private and public, one could argue he has little grounds for complaining about the attention given to his "inappropriate" relationship with a White House intern. Once President Clinton uses his personal, loving relationship with his wife (as testified to by him, his wife, his mother-in-law, and numerous images of family intimacy) as part of his credentials for reelection to a public office, a reasonable person might argue that he has put his fidelity to that relationship on the political agenda. The video exposure of his playing with his nephew in the Oval Office also reverberates via later revelations. It is jarring to combine in one's mind the image of the toddler, who reminds Clinton of his mother and of what his work is all about, with the image of Clinton's sexual romps with Monica Lewinsky in the same office location.

Democrats Say "Come Home with Me"

Is intimate revelation in pursuit of political goals a peculiarity of the Clintons? Hardly. An examination of other speeches given at the same 1996 Democratic Party convention suggests that many of the other speakers make similar invitations to the public to enter their intimate spheres.

Representative Jesse Jackson Jr. of Illinois, for example, speaks about his father, saying:

> I want to take you home. Come home . . . with me to the breakfast table . . . where
> I learned about Jesse Jackson [Sr.]—the father, the husband, and my best friend.
> . . . [T]he greatest thing that Jesse Jackson ever did for me was that he married my
> mother.

Gov. Evan Bayh of Indiana makes a direct statement to his father in the presence of the convention and television audiences. (His father, a former senator, is sitting behind him, next to Evan Bayh's wife and twins and in view of the camera.) "I want to tell you, Dad, how proud I am and grateful for the love and guidance you've given me." Governor Bayh then describes how his mother was raised in the Dust Bowl during the Great Depression and "knew the meaning of work and the full measure of love." As with other convention speakers, he invites the public into private, intimate scenes normally off-limits to public display:

> I miss her. Mom died of breast cancer when she was forty-six. I'll never forget the
> last time we spoke. I sat at her bedside and held her hand in mine. We talked of the
> future, not of the past. . . . We talked of the girl I would marry, she would never meet,
> of the grandchildren she longed for but would never hold. Well, nine months ago,
> my wife, Susan, gave birth to those grandchildren, twin baby boys, Beau and Nick.
> And when we tiptoe into our children's room at night and look down at them sleep-
> ing there, we know that all of our hopes and fears for tomorrow lay quietly before us.
> [Viewers are shown live close-ups of his wife and twin baby boys, sitting next to his
> beaming father.]

Vice President Al Gore also engages in the discourse of intimacy at the convention. As Gore approaches the podium, ABC news anchor Peter Jennings comments on how President Clinton has a reputation for being "Mr. Smooth," while Al Gore has a reputation for being "Mr. Stiff." Al Gore does not need to hear Jennings's comment to address the crowd with a clear recognition of this widely held image. He starts by joking about the jokes about him. With extra stiffness for effect, he notes that President Clinton asked him to speak a day earlier than vice presidents usually speak at conventions because of "my reputation for excitement." He pauses for the laugh. He comments on having seen the convention attendees doing the Macarena dance and offers to do the "Al Gore version of the Macarena." He stands still like a statue. After a few seconds, he asks, "Do you want to see it again?" to audience laughter and, awkwardly, to his own.

As Gore becomes more serious, he spends the bulk of his time describing in excruciating and painful-to-listen-to detail the death of his only sibling from lung cancer.

> My sister, Nancy, was older than me. There were only the two of us, and I loved her more than life itself. She started smoking when she was thirteen years old. The connection between smoking and lung cancer had not yet been established, but years later the cigarettes had taken their toll. It hurt very badly to watch her savaged by that terrible disease. . . . When she was forty-five, she had a lung removed. A year later, the disease had come back, and she returned to the hospital. We all took turns staying with her. One day I was called to come quickly, because things had taken a turn for the worse. By then, her pain was nearly unbearable, and as a result, they used very powerful painkillers. And eventually it got so bad they had to use such heavy doses that she could barely retain consciousness. We sometimes didn't know if she could hear what we were saying or recognize us. But when I responded to that call and walked into the hospital room that day, as soon as I turned the corner, someone said, "Al's here." She looked up, and from out of that haze, her eyes focused intensely right at me. She couldn't speak, but I felt clearly, I knew she was forming a question: "Do you bring me hope?" All of us had tried to find whatever new treatment or new approach might help, but all I could do was to say back to her with all the gentleness in my heart, "I love you." And then I knelt by her bed and held her hand. And in a very short time, her breathing became labored, and then she breathed her last breath.
>
> Tomorrow morning another thirteen-year-old girl will start smoking. I love her, too. Three thousand young people in America will start smoking tomorrow. One thousand of them will die a death not unlike my sister's, and that is why, until I draw my last breath, I will pour my heart and soul into the cause of protecting our children from the dangers of smoking.

On ABC (and most likely on the other networks as well), the broadcast of this segment of Gore's speech was interspersed with shots of his parents struggling to keep their composure and with close-ups of the faces of teary-eyed convention attendees.

These excerpts from the Democratic Party's convention suggest the possibility that the Democrats may be trying a special strategy to show themselves as more human and compassionate than the Republicans. Yet, if one examines how the Republicans presented themselves at their own convention only two weeks earlier, we see further evidence of a trend toward collaborative intimate exposure.

Republicans Open Private Windows

Invitations to the public to come into politicians' intimate spheres appear early in the 1996 Republican convention with remarks from former president George Bush Sr., who addresses the large hall and millions of TV viewers as if he were speaking to friends in his living room.

> My friends, I must now confess that I've been going through a bit of an identity crisis. It is not easy being married to arguably the most popular woman in the United States of America.

After his speech, he and his wife hug their son, George W. Bush (later U.S. president), and then George Sr. and Barbara walk off stage holding hands.

Former first lady Nancy Reagan also addresses the convention in very personal terms. She speaks tearfully and with a voice breaking with emotion about her husband "Ronnie" (former president Ronald Reagan) and his struggle with Alzheimer's disease. Close-ups of crying audience members add to the emotional impact.

> I can't tell you what your cards and letters have meant to both of us. The love and affection from thousands of Americans has been and continues to be a strengthening force for Ronnie and me each and every day. We have learned, as too many other families have learned, of the terrible pain and loneliness that must be endured as each day brings another reminder of this very long good-bye.

Mrs. Reagan's speech is followed by a display of video images showing the loving relationship between Ronnie and Nancy. There are pictures of them hugging, gazing into each other's eyes, of Nancy looking lovingly and admiringly at Ronnie as he faces others. The last image is of the Reagans walking away from the camera, hand in hand. Then, in a final gesture of playful intimacy, Nancy bends her leg back and gives Ronnie a kick in the behind. There is not a word or image in the speech or film of any public policy issue. Voters are, in effect, encouraged to support the Republican agenda because Nancy loves Ronnie.

Within this spectacle of intimate exposure, the biggest challenge for the Republicans is the presentation of their candidate for the presidency, Bob Dole. Apparently trying to humanize the relatively stiff and seemingly aloof Senator Dole, convention planners have both Dole's daughter and wife display their emotional attachments to him.

Robin Dole says she is violating her father's wishes in order to tell convention attendees who her father is.

> My dad is a public man in a world where everyone feels qualified to offer opinions on the character of public men. But I am Bob Dole's only child. I have a private window I can open for you, and if I do, perhaps you, too, will see the man I'll always love best.
>
> When I close my eyes and call up the memories of my childhood, I feel the rock of my dad's love, his steadiness, and the absolute certainty that he would always be there. When I got lost at the amusement park, he found me. When I was scared on the roller coaster, he was behind me yelling, "Yippee!" When I thought he was lost after we got off, I found him around the corner buying tickets for a family of strangers. He'd found the children crying because they couldn't afford to ride. By example, more than words, I learned how to give of myself freely, and to be grateful to those who give to me. . . .
>
> Thank you, Dad, for giving me life and teaching me how to live it with a good and open heart. You have taught me how to find happiness and my own fulfillment. I am so proud to be your daughter.

By opening this private window and calling up memories from her childhood, Robin Dole offers to let us behind the public façade to show us the private man: the loving, supportive father who found her when she was lost and rode the roller coaster with her. (In other parts of her speech, she describes him teaching her to ride a bike, driving her on dates, lending—

and losing—a tie to one of her boyfriends, and teaching her to drive a car.) She conveys the experience of Bob Dole's bodily presence.

An even bolder attempt to humanize Bob Dole is made by his wife, Elizabeth Dole. In an unprecedented move, Mrs. Dole comes down from what she calls the "imposing podium" for two reasons: "One, I'm going to be speaking to friends, and, secondly, I'm going to be speaking about the man I love, and it's just a lot more comfortable for me to do that down here with you."

Addressing her husband, she notes that "if you're watching, let me just warn you, I may be saying some things that you, in your modesty, would never be willing to talk about." To Mrs. Dole's apparent surprise, Bob Dole then appears on a big screen behind her, waving and smiling. Mrs. Dole continues:

> He was born in a small town in Kansas. His parents were poor. In fact, at one point, when Bob was a boy, they had to move their family—parents and four children—into the basement and rent out their small home upstairs just to make ends meet. But while they were perhaps poor in material things, they were rich in values. Values like honesty, decency, respect, personal responsibility, hard work, love of God, love of family, patriotism—these are the values that led Bob to risk his life on the battlefields of Italy.

Following the style of some television talk-show hosts, Mrs. Dole speaks to and hugs individuals in the crowd. In an even more remarkable departure from typical convention speeches, Mrs. Dole pulls members out of the audience as the "evidence" for her claims. She introduces Pat Lynch, Bob's veterans' hospital nurse, who, we are told, used to wheel him around in his wheelchair to tell jokes to cheer up the other wounded soldiers. Mrs. Dole recounts (badly) one of Bob's more recent jokes. She hugs a senator. She tells of how U.S. Senate employees voted Bob "the nicest, friendliest of all one hundred senators." Mrs. Dole then displays Trudy Parker, the female Capitol police officer who, Mrs. Dole recounts, tearfully hugged Dole on his last day in the Senate. Oddly, neither Pat Lynch nor Trudy Parker is allowed to speak to tell her own story. They are used as mute visual displays of past embodied connections with Bob Dole.

In the campaign film presented at the convention, Bob and Elizabeth are shown sitting shoulder to shoulder, engaged in marital bantering. And in his convention speech, Senator Dole describes how he can never forget his mom and dad, whom he calls by their first names.

Politics as Personal: What's Missing?

In short, speaker after speaker at both 1996 conventions invited the public into the private realms of their lives—the loving connection between spouses, parent-child relationships, the breakfast table, the family living room, the birthing room, the deathbed, even the family trip to the amusement park. By conflating the personal and the political, Democrats and Republicans both did their part in making the private lives of politicians legitimate subject matter for public discussion and news coverage. This personalization of politics offers a challenge to President Clinton's plea for privacy. Once Clinton used his role as husband and father to promote his candidacy for public office, he lost some of his right to complain, "I intend to reclaim my family life for my family. It's nobody's business but ours. Even presidents have private lives."

The focus on the flesh-and-bones dimensions of politicians' individual lives certainly leads to a loss of privacy for politicians and their families. Yet what is lost to the public may be even greater. The display of politicians' bodies and intimate experiences deceptively diminishes attention to issues that should be central to democratic debate. Whatever traces of education, health care, tax policy, military expenditures, and so forth emerge from such intimate discourse tend to be tied in some way to the embodied experiences of the speaker. Especially remote are issues of foreign policy. Dwelling on Nancy's love for Ronnie, for example, makes it difficult to criticize President Reagan's endorsement of the training and arming of the Contras, who terrorized and killed thousands of Nicaraguan civilians, and the training and arming of soldiers who massacred thousands of Salvadoran men, women, and children, including more than seven hundred at the village of El Mozote.[5] Discussions of President Bush Sr.'s marriage to popular Barbara distract us from analyzing his role, as vice president, in building up Saddam Hussein's arsenal, an arsenal that the same George Bush later said needed to be destroyed in the 1991 Gulf War.[6] Admiring the cute toddler in Clinton's Oval Office obscures the need for public debate over Clinton's continuation of bombings and sanctions in Iraq, which, according to U.N. figures, killed thousands of Iraqi civilians every month.[7] When politicians open themselves up to us with such emotion and invite us into their private realms, it feels almost rude to raise these kinds of issues.

Even more direct contradictions seem off limits. For example, should one mention in response to Al Gore's passionate story about his sister's cancer and his vow to save other girls' lives that Gore continued to identify himself proudly as a tobacco grower and to accept tobacco campaign funds for years after Nancy's death?[8]

Some of the conditions of this new mix of exposure and concealment are suggested in Alexandra Pelosi's 2002 video documentary of the George W. Bush campaign bus, *Journeys with George.*[9] As portrayed in the documentary, Bush is remarkably playful, impish, and "accessible." He jokes freely with reporters about their behavior and his own. He gives Pelosi dating advice. He chews on a sandwich open-mouthed in a video close-up. He uses the bus's public address system to make fun of his own mispronunciations of words at public events. Yet, when Pelosi takes advantage of a campaign stop to confront George Bush, then governor of Texas, with a question in public about executions in his state, he later sits beside her, shoulders touching, and chastises her for going "below the belt." The clear implication is that her relationship with George Bush, and hence her career as a journalist, could be hurt by such "inappropriate" questions.

The focus on personality and style does not obliterate mention of ideas. Yet, many of the ideas that are highlighted are outside the realm of political debate and discussion. Elizabeth Dole, for example, notes that Bob Dole's family was poor in material things but rich in values: "honesty, decency, respect, personal responsibility, hard work, love of God, love of family, patriotism." Most of these are universal values that do not engage the public in civic debate. (Exceptions perhaps are "love of God," which might be challenged by atheists and agnostics, and "patriotism," which might be challenged, at least in its extreme forms, by internationalists.) Such abstractions give the *illusion of substance* to political discourse.

Clinical psychologist Renana Brooks has described the use of "empty language" in politics to induce the surrender of an audience to a speaker's will. Empty language, she says, "refers to broad statements that are so abstract and mean so little that they are virtually impossible to oppose." According to Brooks, such language is used to "conceal faulty generalizations; to ridicule viable alternatives; to attribute negative motivations to others, thus making them appear contemptible; and to rename and 'reframe' opposing viewpoints."[10]

Brooks claims that President George W. Bush is a master of empty language:

> Bush's 2003 State of the Union speech contained thirty-nine examples of empty language. He used it to reduce complex problems to images that left the listener relieved that George W. Bush was in charge. Rather than explaining the relationship between malpractice insurance and skyrocketing healthcare costs, Bush summed up: "No one has ever been healed by a frivolous lawsuit." The multiple fiscal and monetary policy tools that can be used to stimulate an economy were downsized to: "The best and fairest way to make sure Americans have that money is not to tax it away in the first place." The controversial plan to wage another war on Iraq was simplified to: "We will answer every danger and every enemy that threatens the American people."[11]

Brooks notes that while President Bush is often ridiculed for his mangling of words and phrases, he is, in fact, a master of "emotional language" and "personification." The word "you" is rarely used by President Bush in speeches, observes Brooks. "Instead, there are numerous statements referring to himself or his personal characteristics—folksiness, confidence, righteous anger or determination—as the answer to the problems of the country."[12]

Brooks focuses on George Bush's manipulative use of language, but her arguments could be extended to a description of trends in political discourse in general. She notes that politicians opposing Bush's policies cannot succeed merely by "proving the superiority of their ideas."[13] Her framework, like the analysis presented in this chapter, suggests that politicians must now compete in the realm of personal, embodied, and emotional appeals.

Reasons for the Change

I think it would be a mistake to try to single out one set of social actors—such as media executives, journalists, politicians, or the public—as creating the atmosphere of personal exposure in the United States. Instead, I argue that we are experiencing a *collaborative construction of intimacy,* where politicians, the media, and the public are all focusing more on the personal dimensions of politics. If this is so, it may be fruitful to ask whether there has been any social *environmental change* that has affected all these categories of people and that may have fostered this collective move toward displaying of the personal in public. Has there been any change in the last fifty years in the ways in which we see others and display ourselves in the United States (and many other countries) that might stimulate this increased blurring of the line between public and private, any change that might stimulate the focus on gesture, emotion, and family rather than on public roles and critical social and political issues?

One can make a strong case, I believe, that the rise and ever-increasing role of electronic media, particularly television and the World Wide Web, have encouraged these changes, altering the ways in which all members of society experience one another. The new behaviors of journalists, politicians, and members of the public can be seen, in this sense, as ways of adapting to, and trying to make the best of, more porous boundaries between different social settings.

When a man and a woman decide to move in together, they often find that they can no longer maintain many of the formal rituals of courtship. They come to know too many intimate details about each other to sustain the old formalities. Changes in media of communication can have an effect analogous to such changes in physical living arrangements. A shift in media of communication in a society can create more or less distance between members of society, altering the degree of formality of social interaction. This approach— contrasting the "environmental characteristics" of different media—is a key aspect of what I have called "medium theory." I use the singular "medium" to emphasize the focus on the unique features of each medium (or of each *type* of media), as distinct from the more common approaches to studying the influences of media messages and production variables.[14] The next section contrasts some of the characteristics of electronic media, particularly television, with the characteristics of print media in relation to the thickness of the dividing line between public and private.[15]

Characteristics of Media That Affect Privacy
Media Access Codes

Media vary in the amount of skill required to encode and decode their messages. *The more complex the codes used in a medium, the more the medium will serve to isolate social settings and separate the experiences of public and private, as well as isolate various technically public situations from each other. The simpler the codes used in a medium, the more the medium will tend to blur differences between different settings and between public and private behaviors.*

Learning to read and write is much more difficult than learning to watch television or to access visuals and sounds on the Internet. In contrast to the semantically meaningless shapes of letters, the images and sounds on television and in graphics- and audio-based Web sites are understandable to most people with minimal training and experience.

Mastering literacy requires years of practice and entails many stages of proficiency based on increasing linguistic, grammatical, and stylistic complexity. Because of this, young children and illiterates are excluded from all printed communication. Moreover, in a print-dominated culture, readers of all ages are divided into many distinct sets of information on the basis of different levels of reading ability and interest. For several centuries, written material served, in effect, as semiprivate communications among distinct categories of people.

The most discernible effect of varying media access codes is on children. With complex access codes, such as those of printed texts, children can be kept in the dark about many aspects of adult life. In contrast, simple access codes encourage exposure of many dimensions of private adult life that were once kept secret from children. Thus, while young children have no functional access to the sex acts described in the classic book *Fanny Hill,* even if the book is in their homes, they can experience the basics of a steamy scene from a TV soap opera on the family television or the images on a sexually oriented Web site if it is found on the family computer. They can also grasp some of the basics of a television discussion of a presidential sex scandal long before they could or would read the same material in a newspaper.

A similar trend occurs for adults. With simpler access codes, adults stray into areas of knowledge and experience that would have once seemed remote. A televised or webcast court trial or surgical operation, for example, makes for riveting viewing by the layperson, even though written descriptions or transcripts of such events would likely be read only by specialists. The simpler access codes of television and the images and sounds on Web sites encourage a blurring of different spheres. What would once have been functionally private becomes public.

As access to different types of situations and information becomes more homogenized and "democratic" as a result of simpler codes, social actors—including politicians and journalists—make less of an effort to maintain very distinct styles of behavior and discourse in different settings. As a result, the personal (and pseudopersonal) dimensions of life are allowed to permeate more settings.

Message-Object Link

The relationship between messages and media varies from medium to medium. *The more closely that particular messages are tied to specific objects, the more private and isolated the communications will be. The more that one object provides a multitudinous array of messages, the greater blurring there will be between public and private and among all types of communications.*

In print media, particular messages are inseparable from specific objects. Books, magazines, and newspapers, for example, must be acquired individually. Each particular message or set of messages must be actively sought out, actively carried into a house, actively placed somewhere—whether on the living-room coffee table or under a mattress. Children can easily be given access to one set of reading material (in certain sections of bookstores and libraries) without giving them access to other types of reading. Adults also tend to acquire only certain types of books, magazines, and newspapers matched to their areas of knowledge and interest.

With electronic media, however, a seemingly endless supply of different messages can be received through one acquired object (a radio, television, or computer). These media encourage much broader patterns of access to information, including what was once considered private (or was functionally private, in that its publicness was restricted to those physically present). In 2001, for example, controversy arose over the Internet posting of New York City voter registration records. These records have always been technically public but functionally inaccessible because of the time and travel needed to retrieve them. When the same information was put online, however, anyone in the world could type in the name and date of birth of any registered city voter and gain access to the voter's address and party affiliation. Privacy advocates were alarmed.[16]

The lack of a message-object link on television and the Internet encourages people to gain access to behaviors and information originally aimed at "others." Adolescent boys watch TV exercise programs aimed at young women or cruise Web sites aimed at adolescent girls. Women use search engines to research traditionally "male" topics (including using Web information to work around the still somewhat sexist and paternalistic male medical establishment). Average citizens use the Internet to research many foreign policy issues that were once restricted primarily to professional politicians and diplomats.

In short, books and other print objects are like guests in the home or office. They must be invited in and housed somewhere. But TV and the Internet are like new doorways to the home that bring in many invited and uninvited visitors—and blur old lines between public and private and between different social spheres.

Since electronic media tend to gather together demographically diverse audiences to the same "places," the messages that have the widest impact may be those that focus on "common-denominator topics." In this sense, it is not at all surprising that politicians increasingly focus on embodied experiences that we all share. A description of love be-tween a parent and child, or a story about the death of a sibling, is likely to resonate across more demographic categories than a particular analysis of tax policy.

The Association Factor

Media vary in relation to how much one's attending to them defines one's identity. *The more that a person's interaction with a medium involves a public choice and an explicit claim of identification, the more restricted will be the flow of information and experience. The more that monitoring a medium's content can be defined as simply "observing others," the more blurring there will be among types of experiences.*

Books and magazines are more than media of communication; they are also distinct objects and possessions. They serve not only as channels of information, but also as sym-bols of self and identity. In contrast, the television arena and cyberspace typically function more like street corners or marketplaces. That is, they serve as environments for us to mon-itor but not necessarily identify with.

Reading a newspaper requires an investment of reading effort and money and at least some minimal identification with its style and editorial policy. We have to reach out for the newspaper and embrace it—both literally and metaphorically. The same is true of other reading materials. Yet, with television, and with at least a subset of Web surfing, we simply sit back and let the information wash over us. While we usually select reading material that clearly reflects our own self-image, with TV and the Internet we often feel we are passively observing what *other* people like and are like.

Most Americans would feel uncomfortable stopping at a local store to pick up the cur-rent issue of a publication titled "Transvestite Times," "Male Strippers Review," "The Presi-dent's Sexual Preferences," or a magazine on incest, child abuse, or adultery. But millions of viewers feel quite comfortable sharing their homes, in effect, with transvestites, male strippers, and victims and perpetrators of incest, or almost anyone else who appears on a popular TV show, such as *Oprah* or the *Jerry Springer Show,* or is found on a computer Web site. Similarly, many Americans who would not buy books on such topics routinely pay at-tention to the personal styles of politicians on TV, just as millions of citizens watched hours and hours of discussions of President Clinton's sex scandal.

The relative lack of personal identification with content on TV and the Internet allows for an odd paradox: high ratings for programs and Web sites that many viewers claim to find disgusting. They watch while saying, "I can't believe people look at this stuff." Even many professional critics who condemn programs such as the *Jerry Springer Show* or *Howard Stern* comment on how difficult it is to *not* watch them once one comes across them. The same was true of endless hours of chat-show treatment of the Lewinsky presi-dential scandal. Ironically, our personal dissociation from TV and Internet content allows for widespread sharing of types of experiences across traditional categories of age, gender, education level, and location. Moreover, as content that would have only marginal popu-larity in print gains huge ratings on TV and Web sites, media corporations (which make profits by selling audiences to advertisers) produce more of that content.

Information Forms

One of the key differences between "word media" and "image media" is their primary reliance on different types of symbols: language "communications" versus images and "expressions." *The more that a medium relies on linguistic symbols, the greater its potential for abstract and nonpersonal discourse. The more that a medium conveys human expressions, the greater its tendency to expose concrete and personal dimensions of life.*[17]

Expressions include body and facial movements, gestures, and vocalizations. Expressions are both more direct and more ambiguous, more natural yet less precise, than linguistic statements. While one can start and stop communicating verbally, expressions are constantly given off. Expressions suggest how a person "really feels" and what they are "really like." Expressions are a rich and essential part of human interaction. Experiments by Albert Mehrabian and others have indicated that nonverbal cues have about twelve times the power of verbal cues in interactions.[18] Yet, like pictures without captions, their meanings are often unclear. As Paul Watzlawick and his colleagues have noted, a smile may indicate love or contempt, one can cry from happiness or sadness, subdued expression may be interpreted as tact or as indifference, and a clenched fist may suggest upcoming aggression or a decision of restraint.[19] Even when images and expressions are "captioned" with words, they can never be reduced to them.

Print media draw primarily on verbal communications, while television's power (and the power of the increasingly visual and aural dimensions of the Web) derives primarily from images and expressions. Of course, words are spoken and responded to on television. Indeed, we would probably turn off the set if TV newscasters or politicians refused to speak to us. Yet the role of language is dramatically altered, and often overshadowed, by the nonverbal. We usually *watch* television more than we listen to it. We listen to tone of voice and aural expressions at least as much as we pay attention to words spoken. We often *feel* good or bad about what we see and hear—more than we *think* about it.

The *words* "president," "governor," "senator," and "elected leader" still call forth awe and respect. These words refer to abstract, nonpersonal qualities. But the close-up *pictures* of the persons filling those roles are concrete and personal, and they are rarely as impressive. Whether or not politicians choose to highlight their embodied existence, we cannot help but notice the sweat on the brow, the bags under the eyes, the nervous twitch, the arrogant smirk.

Before TV, very few citizens ever met their leaders in the flesh, and virtually all those who did see leaders saw them at a distance too great to experience their facial expressions and subtle gestures. The speaker's platform once raised politicians up and away from the public. TV now lowers them to our level and brings them close for public inspection. Television gives voters the impression that they "really know" the politician as a person. This has diminished the mediating roles of political parties and journalists. TV also makes us more aware of aspects of politicians' relationships with those around them (both family and political advisors).

On television, even political "debates" often have relatively little to do with verbal communications. Most viewers do not respond to a television debate with ongoing comments such as: "That was an excellent argument"; "That's not historically accurate"; "He just contradicted what he said a few minutes ago"; or "Let me look that up in the encyclopedia to see if it's true." Much more commonly, people react by saying things such as: "He looks nervous"; "She's doing very well"; "He's tough!"; "I like her!"; "Look at those bags under his eyes"; or "I don't trust him."

Much more than print media, image media thrust dimensions of the personal, private realm into the public arena. One can choose, of course, to write about very personal matters, but unlike expression-based media, one's embodied existence is almost completely absent. Even when printed words describe intimate behaviors, the *form* in which the message is conveyed is impersonal and abstract. It often takes many chapters of a biography to convey what it would be like to interact with the book's subject. Yet, just a few minutes, or even seconds, of video can reveal something about the flesh-and-bones person that is almost impossible to capture in text.

With images and sounds, one can speak about very impersonal matters and yet find it nearly impossible to avoid sending a broad array of personal cues along with the non-personal "topic." Mediated images and sounds thrust the personal, private dimensions of life into the public arena. Television close-ups, for example, provide the type of information we are accustomed to responding to when we are with family members, lovers, and friends. Private emotion and public communication are blurred. The sudden loss of breath, the welling of tears in the eyes, the voice that cracks with emotion or moves steadily through a difficult passage—all these convey very personal information.

Private interactions have always been dominated by concrete appearance, gestures, and vocalization. We ask, "What is the person like?" and "Do I like him or her?" The public sphere, in contrast, was once tied closely to the more disembodied dimensions of language: "What has the person said, written, and accomplished?" We do not normally reject a potential lover or friend based on a weak résumé, and before television, voters had little opportunity to react negatively to national candidates because they were unpleasant to watch from a few feet away. Television, however, has increasingly fostered the use of "dating criteria" over "résumé criteria" in the public sphere.

In short, politicians can either try to fight the power of expressions in electronic media, or they can try to exploit them. It is not surprising, then, that both Democrats and Republicans strive to be the best "date." In a sense, presidential elections have become auditions for a four-year (or more) intimate television relationship with the public.

This is why Al Gore was seen to have such a disadvantage at the start of the 2000 presidential campaign. Gore was saddled with a reputation for knowing his facts but being a "cold fish." In a print-oriented résumé world, Gore would probably have been the strong front-runner against George W. Bush, who was never accused of being overly intelligent or well educated. But in a television era of image and style, Gore had a problem. The *New York Times* reported in May 2000, for example, how women voters were "unmoved" by Gore or had a "negative gut feeling" about him.[20]

With the help of advisers in and out of his family, Al Gore changed his style of dress to make him look more comfortable and approachable, and he practiced sounding less like an encyclopedia. He spoke about the mutual sexual passion he and wife still shared. His new "laid-back" style helped. At the August 2000 Democratic convention, his daughter ended her introduction of him by saying, "He's a really cool person, and I know you'd like him." And his best campaign gesture is generally seen to have been giving his wife, Tipper, a long, lustful kiss on the lips at the convention. Such public displays of affection were, until recently, viewed as very inappropriate in the United States (and were even banned from fictional movies by the Hollywood Production Code that was enforced from the 1930s to 1950s). Gore's poll ratings shot up, and he maintained enough strength to win the popular vote (and, many argue, was the real winner of the electoral-college vote as well).[21] Yet his lingering unease before the camera continues to limit his long-term political potential.

In the 2004 race for the White House, John Kerry also struggled with a personal style that turned off many TV viewers. He appeared arrogant and aloof. He, like Gore, was advised to "lighten up." Kerry struggled to display more emotion and a softer personality. At the Democratic National Convention, his daughters assisted in this effort by recounting personal family stories, including the one about their dad saving their pet hamster from drowning. In the campaign film shown at the convention, Kerry admitted to "crying like a baby" when his daughters Alexandra and Vanessa were born, adding—in case there was any ambiguity—"both of them." Ironically, not that long ago, candidates were seen as unfit for the presidency if they were known to cry.

Size and Sensitivity

Electronic media have evolved over time in terms of their size and their sensitivity to light and sound. *Larger and less sensitive media tend to support distinctions between public and private; the smaller and more sensitive to light and sound that a medium is, the more it will capture for the "public record" what was once private, "offstage" behavior.*

The exposure of what were once the private and relatively private spheres of life has been enhanced by the shrinking size and increased sensitivity of cameras and microphones. Even as late as the 1960s, politicians could control much of the flow of information about them because professional media equipment was bulky and needed special lighting and careful placement of a cooperative subject.

Now, sensitive microphones and small cameras that require no special lighting can capture the behaviors of unwilling and unknowing subjects. The reality program *Taxicab Confessions* is made possible by six lipstick-size cameras that fit in a single taxicab. Many citizens voluntarily expose (and preserve for viewing in unknown future contexts) scenes of their own private lives with the use of small, sensitive camcorders that can easily record family births, celebrations, even lovemaking. In the political realm, news organizations try to maintain a constant "body watch" on the president (ever since having to rely on an amateur's home movie of the assassination of President John Kennedy). As visual and aural media have become lighter, smaller, and more sensitive to light and sound, the zone of privacy for public figures has shrunk.

Speed and Bidirectionality

Media vary in their speed of transmission and in whether they are unidirectional or bidirectional (or multidirectional). *In general, slower and unidirectional media help to maintain distinctions between public and private, while faster and bidirectional (or multidirectional) media tend to break down traditional distinctions between public and private.*

A person writing a letter to be mailed to a relative is likely to summarize the nature of several months of family events. But if the same relative calls on the telephone or sends an e-mail requesting an immediate response, the same letter writer may respond with specifics of how he/she is feeling at that moment. In general, the more rapid and bidirectional the transmission, the more that intimate details of everyday life emerge in the public arena.

The increase in moment-to-moment behavioral display (in homemade videos, reality TV, journalistic reports, and so forth) is fostered by the rapidity of current electronic communication technologies. In contrast, President Eisenhower's press secretary, Jim Hagerty, was able to request the right to preview news media *films* of the president's press conferences because of the time delay in processing, editing, and broadcasting movies.

The instant or rapid bidirectionality of many current electronic media also enhances the exposure of intimate detail, as feedback encourages more exposure and discourages delays for thinking (and censoring). Similarly, the norm of rapid response to e-mail often leads to less-than-wise care in managing the technology. Often, a message is sent by accident before it is completed, and, even more embarrassingly, an intimate message aimed at a single person is sometimes sent by mistake to a whole list of e-mail addresses.

Presidential auras were once very well protected. A president's public statements were carefully edited and controlled. Now, at live television press conferences, presidents must start a sentence before they know how the sentence will end. On camera, even a five-second pause for thought may be viewed as a sign of stupidity or senility. (Yet surely our country would benefit from presidents who *do* take some time to think!) To adjust to this level of exposure, the wise politician develops an ongoing intimate persona that can tolerate minor errors, personal idiosyncrasies, and variations in mood. The resulting style is neither that of traditional, formal "onstage" performances nor that of private and informal "backstage" relaxation and rehearsal, but a blend of both, which I have called a "middle-region" style.[22]

There is a paradox inherent in these close, more intimate views of politicians. The public comes close to hunt for evidence of greatness; yet an image of greatness relies on distance and mystery. Thus, the close scrutiny in search of greatness destroys the possibility of seeing it. For their part, most politicians in the television era feel driven to act intimately with us; yet they often wake up to find we do not respect them in the morning. It is hard to imagine majority support for carving in a mountaintop the giant head of President Clinton, or of either president Bush, or of any other current politician to represent an ideal of our nation.

Conclusion

I have outlined some of the characteristics of our current communication environment that foster a collaborative display of "public intimacy" in the political realm. The present focus on the embodied characteristics of politicians certainly does not mark the first time that leaders have tried to shape the public's perception of them or to distract the public from various issues. Yet, it does represent, in many ways, a reversal of an earlier trend in image manipulation. As print media and literacy spread through western Europe in the sixteenth and seventeenth centuries, so did the ideas for influencing others from afar. This may be because printed texts literally hid the bodies of their authors and subjects, encouraging a more abstract and mystified image of leadership and authority. In the sixteenth century, Machiavelli noted that princes could take advantage of distance from their subjects to make it *appear* that they possessed certain princely qualities, since only a few people could come close enough to check out the reality. A century later, Balthasar Gracian, rector of the Jesuit College, advised priests to "[m]ix a little mystery with everything," because mystery "arouses veneration." Those who helped to shape the image of King Louis XIV worked to hide the "awkward discrepancies between the official image of the king and the everyday reality" of his body, including the facts that the king's "actual height" (five feet, three inches) was much smaller than his "social height" as portrayed by artists and that he had lost most of his hair due an illness in 1659.[23]

This chapter has suggested that, in an era of electronic media, such distinctions between the disembodied and the embodied images of leaders have become much more difficult to maintain. There are, however, other factors, not directly related to the characteristics of electronic media, that also encourage a mass-mediated intimate politics in the United States.

One of these factors is the basic structure of our political system. Unlike many other democracies, the United States has only two major parties, and our elections are based on a winner-take-all formula that diminishes the influence of nonmainstream viewpoints and candidates. Democrats and Republicans both receive funding from similar (often the same) sources. Were the two major parties to focus their public discourse primarily on issues, many voters would become more aware of how alike the two parties are with respect to many significant policies, such as so-called free-trade agreements, welfare reform, media deregulation, military spending, and foreign policy in general. A focus on issues might encourage more voters to explore positions and candidates that fall outside of this "bipartisan consensus." By focusing instead on personal style and embodied experiences, mainstream politicians project themselves as unique human beings, distinct from their political rivals. In 1996, Bob Dole seemed like a very different candidate than Bill Clinton, with a very different embodied "presence" on TV. Yet, the two candidates' positions on many major issues were relatively close.

Moreover, since so-called minor candidates are rarely given media forums in which to give extended displays of their personalities, life experiences, families, and so forth, the "major" candidates and officeholders create further distance between themselves and non-mainstream politicians by trying to create a "personal" relationship with the voters. In this sense, the seemingly fierce competition between the "major" Democratic and Republican candidates may actually mask a collaborative emphasis on themselves and on mainstream politics.[24]

News organizations could put pressure on politicians to deal more with substantive issues and less with their embodied experiences. Such pressure would fulfill the "watchdog" function of the press in its role as an unofficial "fourth branch" of the government. Yet corporate media have various disincentives to apply such pressure. "Talking heads" discussing issues at length are considered deadly for ratings. And those audiences that do tune in to a serious discussion may find that its substance distracts them from the ads, resulting in sabotage to the economic system that supports the media. In contrast, when politicians focus on their emotional and physical experiences, they often produce captivating TV, and, perhaps even more important, they project a philosophy of life that is compatible with the messages of most advertising. As the ads try to convince us, life's problems are mostly personal, and buying the right products brings one greater individual happiness and better relationships (often by improving one's body).

The emphasis on the personalities of mainstream politicians and the minimal attention given to extended political debate of issues (let alone to alternative views and non-mainstream candidates) is further enhanced by an even deeper symbiotic relationship between media corporations and the "major" politicians. Television news organizations have been reducing their preelection coverage of candidates and issues. This situation increases the role of expensive campaign commercials in elections, which creates an uneven playing field that favors "major" candidates and that benefits media corporations. The candidates who receive the most campaign donations—especially from media corporations—tend to be those who have supported the interests of the media. As Paul Taylor, a former

Washington Post political reporter who is an advocate for free airtime for candidates, has put it:

> Politicians give commercial broadcasters the public airwaves for free. During the campaign season, broadcasters turn around and sell air-time back to the politicians, while imposing a virtual news blackout on candidate discussion of issues. . . . By creating a pay-to-play model for political speech on the nation's premier medium for political communication, the television industry protects incumbents, starves challengers, and enriches itself.[25]

In all the ways discussed throughout this chapter, the current focus on the personal dimensions of politics, as represented in the embodied existence of politicians, is over-determined. Yet the pressures on the political arena are not unidirectional. Many advocacy groups, ranging from grassroots citizen groups to corporate-backed organizations, attempt to increase attention to issues.

The continuing significant role of *text* on many Internet sites, along with other key characteristics of this new medium, has been supporting a renewed focus on substantive issues in politics, even as other aspects of the Web (such as image and sound) have been enhancing the prior and continuing influence of TV. The ability to cheaply post, download, upload, cut and paste, create custom distribution lists, and forward messages has been changing the dynamics of political information flow. The Internet has been giving new access to nonmainstream politicians, issues, information, and perspectives, while also enhancing the range of debate about mainstream candidates and policies.

The Internet has fostered the rise of grassroots citizen movements that are not geographically defined. Such groups played a major role in spreading alternative perspectives and information about the United States' plan to invade Iraq in 2003. The Internet was the key tool used by average citizens to coordinate massive protests against the planned war throughout the United States and around the globe. The war was not averted, but some new, Internet-driven political dynamic seems to be at play (especially since the alternative media on the Internet were much more accurate than the mainstream media in predicting what would be found and not found in Iraq, including the strong resistance to "liberation" and the lack of stockpiles of weapons of mass destruction). The power of the Internet was seen again in the sudden outpouring of public opposition to an issue barely covered by the mainstream news media—the media's own further deregulation by the Federal Communications Commission (FCC) in June 2003. Though the issue remains in flux, the pressure from the public has led to both judicial and congressional roadblocks to the implementation of the FCC's decision. Similarly, by mid-2003, the Internet had helped to fuel a surge in the presidential candidacy of Governor Howard Dean, catapulting him from a media-designated "fringe" candidate into a major contender who could not be ignored by the mainstream media. (Consistent with the trends discussed throughout this chapter, however, once Dean gained mainstream TV attention, significant attention was paid to his "temperament," peaking in the torrent of media coverage of the "Dean scream"—his shouting to be heard over a crowd of twelve hundred of his volunteers following the Iowa caucuses in January 2004.)[26]

It is unlikely that the Internet and the resurgence of issue-based politics will completely displace the current focus on personal style of our leaders. As long as citizens turn to television to watch their leaders close-up, the criteria of intimate interactions will play an important role. Yet the Internet may foster a more balanced political realm, where citizens, while still searching for leaders they can "warm up to" via television, may demand (and take) more action on issues that extend beyond the bodies of particular leaders and shape the texture of life for the entire body politic.

Notes

I would like to thank Dr. Jeff Weintraub for inviting me to present an early version of this work as a colloquium at the Summer Humanities Institute on "The Question of Privacy" at Dartmouth College in July 1999. Dr. Jo Groebel's invitation for me to work on the international project "Privacy in the Public Sphere," organized by the European Institute for the Media, allowed me to develop this analysis further, and an earlier draft appeared as part of a more extensive report, Joshua Meyrowitz, "Post-Privacy America," in *Privatheit im öffentlichen Raum: Medienhandeln zwischen Individualisierung und Entgrenzung,* ed. Ralph Wieß and Jo Groebel, 153–204 (Opladen: Leske und Budrich, 2002). I also thank Renée H. Carpenter and Robin E. Sheriff for their comments and suggestions. Kimber Charles Pearce has my gratitude for his generosity in sharing videotapes of the 1996 political conventions.

1. This information is drawn from the Mount Rushmore Web site, http://www.MtRushmore.net (last accessed August 1, 2005).

2. See, for example, the memoir of White House correspondent Merriman Smith, who describes the difference between FDR's "literally lifeless" legs and what most of the public perceived in Timothy G. Smith, ed., *Merriman Smith's Book of Presidents: A White House Memoir* (New York: Norton, 1972), 30.

3. See Thomas Bailey, *Presidential Greatness: The Image of the Man from George Washington to the Present* (New York: Appleton-Century, 1966), for descriptions of the physical characteristics and ailments of many U.S. presidents. For a description of Abraham Lincoln's unusual voice, see William E. Barton, *Lincoln at Gettysburg* (Indianapolis, Ind.: Bobbs-Merrill, 1930), 30.

4. Elmer E. Cornwell Jr., *Presidential Leadership of Public Opinion* (Bloomington: Indiana University Press, 1965), 147, 187.

5. For an account of the U.S. role in creating and funding the Contras, see Christopher Dickey, *With the Contras: A Reporter in the Wilds of Nicaragua* (New York: Simon and Schuster, 1985). The extent of the initially covert U.S. role in Nicaragua was exposed as part of the Iran-Contra scandal. As for El Salvador, the Reagan administration denied that a massacre of hundreds of villagers had taken place in El Mozote in 1981, attempted to cover up other human rights abuses by U.S.-trained forces in the country, and attacked the credibility of the journalists who tried to report on them. Only years later were the atrocities confirmed by the mainstream U.S. news media. See, for example, Clifford Krauss, "How U.S. Actions Helped Hide Salvador Human Rights Abuses," *New York Times,* March 21, 1993, sec. A; and Mike Hoyt, "The Mozote Massacre," *Columbia Journalism Review,* January/February 1993, 31–34.

6. When a popular revolution in Iran in 1979 overthrew the U.S.-backed Shah of Iran, the United States (among other countries) sent massive aid to Saddam Hussein's Iraq and encouraged and supported Hussein's 1980 invasion of Iran. The CIA provided Iraq with intelligence from satellites and AWACS surveillance aircraft, which facilitated Iraq's use of chemical weapons against Iranians. See Murray Waas, "What Washington Gave Saddam for Christmas," in *The Iraq War Reader: History, Documents, Opinions,* ed. Micah L. Sifry and Christopher Cerf, 30–40 (New York: Touchstone, 2003); Russ Baker, "Iraqgate: The Big One That (Almost) Got Away," *Columbia Journalism Review,* March/April 1993, 48–54; and Rashid Khalidi, *Resurrecting Empire: Western Footprints and America's Perilous Path in the Middle* East (Boston: Beacon, 2004), 41–42 and 187–188n14.

7. The grim findings of the U.N. Food and Agriculture Organization (FAO) and the U.N. World Health Organization (WHO) regarding the impact of sanctions are summarized in Geoff Simons, *Iraq: From Sumer to Post-Saddam*, 3rd ed. (Houndmills, U.K.: Palgrave, 2004), 382. For UNICEF's estimate of the number of deaths of children under five that would *not* have occurred if Iraq's plummeting child-mortality trends during the 1980s had continued through the 1990s, see G. Jones, "Iraq—Under-Five Mortality," July 23, 1999, Child and Maternal Mortality Survey 1999 (Baghdad: United Nations Children's Fund [UNICEF]), http://www.casi.org.uk/info/unicef/irqu5est.pdf (last accessed August 1, 2005). For a description of declassified documents on the Pentagon's Web site that indicate that the U.S. government was aware of the resulting diseases and likely civilian death toll from its 1991 to 2003 policy of preventing Iraq from purifying its civilian water supply, see Thomas J. Nagy, "The Secret Behind the Sanctions," *The Progressive*, September 2001, 22–25, http://www.progressive.org/mag_nagysanctions (last accessed August 1, 2005). For a summary of some of the controversy over the sanctions, including the ways in which Saddam Hussein's government tried to manipulate public perceptions of their effects, see David Rieff, "Were Sanctions Right,?" *New York Times Magazine*, June 27, 2003, 41–46. Yet, the often-heard argument in the United States that it was Saddam Hussein's long-term disregard for his own people that led to the deaths during the sanctions period rings false in light of the Baath government's dramatic improvements in access to food, medical care, clean water, electricity, and education until the first Gulf War, contrasted with the devastating impact of the war and sanctions on those systems. See, for example, Ramsey Clark, *The Fire This Time: U.S. War Crimes in the Gulf* (New York: Thunder's Mouth Press, 1992), 59–84, and Simons, *Iraq: From Sumer to Post-Saddam*, 7–15 and 382–85. For a sample critique of the poor coverage of the sanctions in the mainstream U.S. news media, see Seth Ackerman, "*New York Times* on Iraq Sanctions," *Extra!* March/April 2000, 18–20, http://www.fair.org/extra/0003/crossette-iraq.html (last accessed August 1, 2005). For a more detailed critique of the poor coverage in the mainstream news media of U.S. wars with Iraq, see Joshua Meyrowitz, "American Homogenization and Fragmentation: The Influence of New Information-Systems and Disinformation-Systems," in *Media Cultures*, ed. William Uricchio and Susanne Kinnebrock (Heidelberg: Universitätsverlag, forthcoming).

8. While campaigning in North Carolina in 1988, four years after his sister's death, Gore told tobacco farmers of his experience with the crop: "I want you to know that with my own hands, all my life, I've put it in the plant beds and transferred it. I've hoed it, I've suckered it, I've sprayed it, I've topped it, I've cut it and spiked it and put it in the barn and stripped it and sold it. I know what tobacco is about." See Michael Kirk and Peter J. Boyer, "The Choice 2000," *Frontline*, PBS, October 2000 (transcript available at http://www.pbs.org/wgbh/pages/frontline/shows/choice2000/etc/transcript.html) (last accessed August 1, 2005).

9. Alexandra Pelosi, *Journeys with George*, Purple Monkey Productions, 2002.

10. Renana Brooks, "A Nation of Victims," *The Nation*, June 30, 2003, 20.

11. Ibid., 21.

12. Ibid.

13. Ibid., 22.

14. Joshua Meyrowitz, *No Sense of Place: The Impact of Electronic Media on Social Behavior* (New York: Oxford University Press, 1985), 16; Joshua Meyrowitz, "Medium Theory," in *Communication Theory Today*, ed. David Crowley and David Mitchell, 50–77 (Cambridge, England: Polity Press, 1994); Joshua Meyrowitz, "Multiple Media Literacies," *Journal of Communication* 48, no. 1 (Winter 1998), 96–108.

15. For a more detailed discussion of the environmental characteristics of media and their influence on "who knows what about whom" and "who knows what compared to whom," see Joshua Meyrowitz, *No Sense of Place*, chapters 5, 6, and 7.

16. Amy Harmon, "As Public Records Go Online, Some Say They're Too Public," *New York Times,* August 24, 2001, sec. A. The concerns apparently led to the site being disabled.

17. The distinction between communication and expression that I use here is drawn from Erving Goffman, *Strategic Interaction* (Philadelphia: University of Pennsylvania Press, 1969). My application of the communication/expression distinction to differences among media is developed more fully in *No Sense of Place,* 93–114.

18. Albert Mehrabian, *Silent Messages: Implicit Communication of Emotions and Attitudes,* 2nd ed. (Belmont, Calif.: Wadsworth, 1981), 76–77.

19. Paul Watzlawick, Janet Helmick Beavin, and Don D. Jackson, *Pragmatics of Human Communication: A Study of Interactional Patterns, Pathologies, and Paradoxes* (New York: Norton, 1967), 65.

20. Pam Belluck, "Women Appear Unmoved by Gore," *New York Times,* May 15, 2000, sec. A.

21. The consortium of news outlets that spent almost a year and close to one million dollars reviewing the Florida vote count discovered that, had a full reexamination of rejected ballots in Florida been conducted, using any of six different standards for what counted as a valid vote, Gore would have carried the state and won the presidency. The recount halted by the Supreme Court did not involve all rejected ballots. News reports on the consortium's findings, however, focused primarily on what the consortium determined would have happened had the limited recount halted by the Supreme Court been allowed to proceed, in which case Bush would have maintained a narrow lead. See Miranda Spencer, "Who Won the Election? Who Cares?" *Extra!* January/February 2002, 21–24, http://www.fair.org/extra/0201/fla-recount.html (last accessed August 1, 2005).

22. See Erving Goffman, *The Presentation of Self in Everyday Life* (New York: Anchor, 1959), for a discussion of "front region" versus "back region" behaviors in face-to-face interaction. See Joshua Meyrowitz, "The Rise of 'Middle Region' Politics," *Et cetera* 34, no. 2 (June 1977): 133–44, and Joshua Meyrowitz, *No Sense of Place,* for an adaptation of Goffman's framework to the study of social change and for a description of the development of new behavior patterns in politics and other spheres when the boundaries between traditional onstage and backstage settings become more permeable as a result of electronic media or other variables.

23. Niccolò Machiavelli, *The Prince,* trans. Harvey C. Mansfield (Chicago: University of Chicago Press, 1998), 70–71. Gracian is quoted in Hugh Dalziel Duncan, *Communication and Social Order* (New York: Bedminster, 1962), 218. For a fascinating and detailed analysis of the "management of the royal image" of Louis XIV, see Peter Burke, *The Fabrication of Louis XIV* (London: Yale University Press, 1992). The quote in the text is from Burke, 125. To my knowledge, none of these cited authors explicitly discusses the influence of printing. I make the case for the link between media and the evolution in image-manipulation strategies in *No Sense of Place.*

24. For a case study of how "national journalistic logic" may work in tandem with the major political parties' interests in obscuring the existence of "fringe" candidates, see Joshua Meyrowitz, "Visible and Invisible Candidates: A Case Study in 'Competing Logics' of Campaign Coverage," *Political Communication* 11 (April–June 1994): 145–64.

25. Paul Taylor, "Too Little Time," *Washington Monthly,* September 2000, 8.

26. For an excellent overview of the mainstream media's emphasis on Howard Dean's temperament, see Peter Hart, "Target Dean," *Extra!* March/April 2004, 13–18, http://www.fair.org/extra/0404/target-dean.html (last accessed August 1, 2005).

Appendix

The full text of President Bill Clinton's August 18, 1998, television address to the nation:

> Good evening. This afternoon in this room, from this chair, I testified before the office of independent counsel and the grand jury. I answered their questions

truthfully, including questions about my private life, questions no American citizen would ever want to answer.

Still, I must take complete responsibility for all my actions, both public and private. And that is why I am speaking to you tonight. As you know, in a deposition in January, I was asked questions about my relationship with Monica Lewinsky. While my answers were legally accurate, I did not volunteer information.

Indeed, I did have a relationship with Miss Lewinsky that was not appropriate. In fact, it was wrong. It constituted a critical lapse in judgment and a personal failure on my part for which I am solely and completely responsible. But I told the grand jury today, and I say to you now, that at no time did I ask anyone to lie, to hide or destroy evidence, or to take any other unlawful action.

I know that my public comments and my silence about this matter gave a false impression. I misled people, including even my wife. I deeply regret that. I can only tell you I was motivated by many factors: first, by a desire to protect myself from the embarrassment of my own conduct. I was also very concerned about protecting my family. The fact that these questions were being asked in a politically inspired lawsuit, which has since been dismissed, was a consideration too. In addition, I had real and serious concerns about an independent counsel investigation that began with private business dealings twenty years ago, dealings, I might add, about which an independent federal agency found no evidence of any wrongdoing by me or my wife over two years ago. The independent counsel investigation moved on to my staff and friends, then into my private life. And now the investigation itself is under investigation. This has gone on too long, cost too much, and hurt too many innocent people.

Now this matter is between me, the two people I love most, my wife and our daughter, and our God. I must put it right. And I am prepared to do whatever it takes to do so. Nothing is more important to me personally. But it is private. And I intend to reclaim my family life for my family. It's nobody's business but ours. Even presidents have private lives. It is time to stop the pursuit of personal destruction and the prying into private lives and get on with our national life.

Our country has been distracted by this matter for too long. And I take my responsibility for my part in all of this. That is all I can do. Now it is time, in fact it is past time, to move on. We have important work to do, real opportunities to seize, real problems to solve, real security matters to face.

And so tonight, I ask you to turn away from the spectacle of the past seven months, to repair the fabric of our national discourse, and to return our attention to all the challenges and all the promise of the next American century.

Thank you for watching and good night.

Selected Bibliography

Books

The books and essays listed below were selected by the editor or one of this book's authors because they thought these writings usefully address ideas relevant to the study of rhetoric and display. Given the vast literature relevant both to rhetoric and to display, the bibliography necessarily is incomplete. The aim is to provide a considered survey of scholarship that has historical, theoretical, or critical relevance, as well as potential value, for those who want to study rhetorics of display.

Alinsky, Saul D. *Rules for Radicals: A Practical Primer for Realistic Radicals.* 1971. Reprint, New York: Vintage, 1972.

Anderson, Benedict R. *Imagined Communities: Reflections on the Origin and Spread of Nationalism.* Revised Edition. London: Verso, 1991.

Bakhtin, M. M. *The Dialogic Imagination: Four Essays.* Edited by Michael Holquist. Translated by Caryl Emerson and Michael Holquist. Austin: University of Texas Press, 1981.

———. *Rabelais and His World.* Translated by Helene Iswolsky. Bloomington: Indiana University Press, 1984.

———. *Speech Genres and Other Late Essays.* Translated by Vern W. McGee. Austin: University of Texas Press, 1986.

Barfield, Owen. *Saving the Appearances: A Study in Idolatry.* New York: Harcourt, Brace and World, 1965.

Barnes, Trevor J., and James S. Duncan, eds. *Writing Worlds: Discourse, Text and Metaphor in the Representation of Landscape.* London: Routledge, 1992.

Bauman, Richard. *Verbal Art as Performance.* Prospect Heights, Ill.: Waveland, 1984.

Baxandall, Michael. *Giotto and the Orators: Humanist Observers of Painting in Italy and the Discovery of Pictorial Composition, 1350–1450.* Oxford: Oxford University Press, 1971.

———. *Painting and Experience in Fifteenth-Century Italy: A Primer in the Social History of Pictorial Style.* 2nd ed. Oxford: Oxford University Press, 1988.

Becker, Ernest. *The Denial of Death.* New York: Free Press, 1975.

Bell, David, and Gill Valentine, eds. *Mapping Desire: Geographies of Sexualities.* New York: Routledge, 1995.

Benson, Thomas W., and Carolyn Anderson. *Reality Fictions: The Films of Frederick Wiseman.* Carbondale: Southern Illinois University Press, 1989.

Berger, John. *About Looking.* New York: Pantheon Books, 1980.

————. *Art and Revolution: Ernst Neizvestny, Endurance, and the Role of Art.* New York: Vintage International, 1969.

————. *Ways of Seeing.* London: British Broadcasting Company and Penguin Books, 1972.

Black, Max. *Models and Metaphors: Studies in Language and Philosophy.* Ithaca, New York: Cornell University Press, 1962.

Blakesley, David., ed. *The Terministic Screen: Rhetorical Perspectives on Film.* Carbondale: University of Illinois Press, 2003.

Bodnar, John. *Remaking America: Public Memory, Commemoration, and Patriotism in the Twentieth Century.* Princeton, N.J.: Princeton University Press, 1992.

Boime, Albert. *The Unveiling of National Icons: A Plea for Patriotic Iconoclasm in a Nationalist Era.* New York: Cambridge University Press, 1998.

Bonnell, Victoria E. *Iconography of Power: Soviet Political Posters under Lenin and Stalin.* Berkeley: University of California Press, 1997.

Boorstin, Daniel. *The Image: A Guide to Pseudo-Events in America.* 1961. Reprint, New York: Harper and Row, 1964.

Bowers, John Waite, Donovan J. Ochs, and Richard Jensen. *The Rhetoric of Agitation and Control.* 2nd ed. Prospect Heights, Ill.: Waveland Press, 1993.

Bruner, M. Lane. *Strategies of Remembrance: The Rhetorical Dimensions of National Identity Construction.* Columbia: University of South Carolina Press, 2002.

Burgess, Theodore C. *Epideictic Literature.* Chicago: University of Chicago Press, 1902.

Burke, Kenneth. *Counter-Statement.* 1931. Reprint, Berkeley: University of California Press, 1968.

————. *A Grammar of Motives.* 1945. Reprint, Berkeley: University of California Press, 1969.

————. *Language as Symbolic Action: Essays on Life, Literature, and Method.* 3rd ed. Berkeley: University of California Press, 1966.

————. *Permanence and Change: An Anatomy of Purpose.* 3rd ed. Berkeley: University of California Press, 1984.

————. *The Philosophy of Literary Form: Studies in Symbolic Action.* 3rd ed. Berkeley: University of California Press, 1973.

————. *A Rhetoric of Motives.* 1950. Reprint, Berkeley: University of California Press, 1969.

————. *The Rhetoric of Religion: Studies in Logology.* 1961. Reprint, Berkeley: University of California Press, 1970.

Burke, Peter. *Eyewitnessing: The Uses of Images as Historical Evidence.* Ithaca, New York: Cornell University Press, 2001.

Clark, Gregory. *Rhetorical Landscapes in America: Variations on a Theme from Kenneth Burke.* Columbia: University of South Carolina Press, 2004.

Clark, Toby. *Art and Propaganda in the Twentieth Century: The Political Image in the Age of Mass Culture.* New York: Harry N. Abrams, 1997.

Cooke, Lynne, and Peter Wollen, eds. *Visual Display: Culture beyond Appearances.* New York: New Press, 1998.

Davis, Susan G. *Parades and Power: Street Theatre in Nineteenth-Century Philadelphia.* Philadelphia: Temple University Press, 1986.

Debord, Guy. *The Society of the Spectacle.* 1967. Reprint, Detroit: Black and Red, 1983.

DeLuca, Kevin Michael. *Image Politics: The New Rhetoric of Environmental Activism.* New York: Guilford Press, 1999.

Duncan, Carol. *Civilizing Rituals: Inside Public Art Museums.* London: Routledge, 1995.

Eco, Umberto. *Travels in Hyper Reality: Essays.* San Diego: Harcourt, Brace, Jovanivich, 1986.

Edelman, Murray. *Constructing the Political Spectacle.* Chicago: University of Chicago Press, 1988.

Edwards, Janis L. *Political Cartoons in the 1988 Presidential Campaign: Image, Metaphor, and Narrative.* New York: Garland, 1997.

Eliade, Mircea. *The Sacred and the Profane: The Nature of Religion.* Translated by Willard R. Trask. New York: Harcourt, Brace, 1959.

Fahnestock, Jeanne. *Rhetorical Figures in Science.* New York: Oxford University Press, 1999.

Fincher, Ruth, and Jane M. Jacobs, eds. *Cities of Difference.* New York: Guilford, 1998.

Finnegan, Cara A. *Picturing Poverty: Print Culture and FSA Photographs.* Washington, D.C.: Smithsonian Institution Press, 2003.

Fisher, Philip. *Wonder, the Rainbow, and the Aesthetics of Rare Experiences.* Cambridge, Mass.: Harvard University Press, 1998.

Foucault, Michel. *Discipline and Punish: The Birth of the Prison.* Translated by Alan Sheridan. New York: Pantheon, 1979.

Gabler, Neal. *Life the Movie: How Entertainment Conquered Reality.* New York: Knopf, 1998.

Galison, Peter, and Emily Thompson, eds. *The Architecture of Science.* Cambridge, Mass.: MIT Press, 1999.

Gates, Henry Louis, Jr. and Cornel West. *The Future of the Race.* New York: Knopf, 1996.

Geertz, Clifford. *The Interpretation of Cultures.* New York: Basic Books, 1973.

Gillis, John R., ed. *Commemorations: The Politics of National Identity.* Princeton, N.J.: Princeton University Press, 1994.

Gluckman, Amy, and Betsy Reed., eds. *Homoeconomics: Capitalism, Community, and Lesbian and Gay Life.* New York: Routledge, 1997.

Goffman, Erving. *The Presentation of Self in Everyday Life.* Garden City, N.Y.: Doubleday-Anchor, 1959.

Golinski, Jan. *Making Natural Knowledge: Constructivism and the History of Science.* Cambridge: Cambridge University Press, 1998.

Gombrich, E. H. *Art and Illusion: A Study in the Psychology of Pictorial Representation.* Millennium ed. Princeton, N.J.: Princeton University Press, 2000.

Grassi, Ernesto. *Rhetoric as Philosophy: The Humanist Tradition.* University Park: Pennsylvania State University Press, 1980.

Hardison, O. B., Jr. *The Enduring Monument: A Study of the Idea of Praise in Renaissance Literary Theory and Practice.* 1962. Reprint, Westport, Conn.: Greenwood Press, 1973.

Harris, Daniel. *Cute, Quaint, Hungry and Romantic: The Aesthetics of Consumerism.* N.p.: Da Capo Press, 2001.

Hass, Kristin Ann. *Carried to the Wall: American Memory and the Vietnam Veterans Memorial.* Berkeley: University of California Press, 1998.

Hauser, Gerard A. *Vernacular Voices: The Rhetoric of Publics and Public Spheres.* Columbia: University of South Carolina Press, 1999.

Hausman, Carl R. *Metaphor and Art: Interactionism and Reference in the Verbal and Nonverbal Arts.* New York: Cambridge University Press, 1989.

Hill, Charles A., and Marguerite Helmers, eds. *Defining Visual Rhetorics.* Mahwah, N.J.: Erlbaum, 2004.

Holly, Michael Ann. *Past Looking: Historical Imagination and the Rhetoric of the Image.* Ithaca, New York: Cornell University Press, 1996.

Huxtable, Ada Louise. *The Unreal America: Architecture and Illusion.* New York: New Press, 1997.

Jackson, J. B. *Landscape in Sight: Looking at America.* Edited with an Introduction by Helen Lefkowitz Horowitz. New Haven: Yale University Press, 1997.

———. *A Sense of Place, A Sense of Time.* New Haven, Conn.: Yale University Press, 1994.

Jacobson, David. *Place and Belonging in America.* Baltimore: Johns Hopkins University Press, 2002.

James, Beverly A. *Imagining Postcommunism: Visual Narratives of Hungary's 1956 Revolution.* College Station: Texas A&M University Press, 2005.

Jamieson, Kathleen Hall. *Eloquence in an Electronic Age: The Transformation of Political Speechmaking.* New York: Oxford University Press, 1988.

Jay, Martin. *Downcast Eyes: The Denigration of Vision in Twentieth-Century French Thought.* Berkeley: University of California Press, 1993.

Jencks, Charles. *The Language of Post-Modern Architecture.* 5th ed. New York: Rizzoli, 1987.

———. *Late-Modern Architecture and Other Essays.* New York: Rizzoli, 1980.

Jonsen, Albert R., and Stephen Toulmin. *The Abuse of Casuistry: A History of Moral Reasoning.* Berkeley: University of California Press, 1988.

Jordanova, Ludmilla. *Sexual Visions: Images of Gender in Science and Medicine between the Eighteenth and Twentieth Centuries.* Madison: University of Wisconsin Press, 1989.

Kammen, Michael. *Mystic Chords of Memory: The Transformation of Tradition in American Culture.* New York: Knopf, 1991.

Karp, Ivan, and Steven D. Lavine, eds. *Exhibiting Cultures: The Poetics and Politics of Museum Display.* Washington, D.C.: Smithsonian Institution Press, 1991.

Katriel, Tamar. *Performing the Past: A Study of Israeli Settlement Museums.* Mahwah, N.J.: Erlbaum, 1997.

Keller, Evelyn Fox. *Refiguring Life: Metaphors of Twentieth-Century Biology.* New York: Columbia University Press, 1995.

Kertzer, David I. *Ritual, Politics and Power.* New Haven: Yale University Press, 1988.

Kirshenblatt-Gimblett, Barbara. *Destination Culture: Tourism, Museums, and Heritage.* Berkeley: University of California Press, 1998.

Kochman, Thomas. *Black and White Styles in Conflict.* Chicago: University of Chicago Press, 1983.

Kress, Gunther, and Theo van Leeuwen. *Reading Images: The Grammar of Visual Design.* 1996. Reprint, London: Routledge, 2001.

Kunstler, James Howard. *The Geography of Nowhere: The Rise and Decline of America's Man-Made Landscape.* New York: Simon and Schuster, 1993.

Lacan, Jacques. *The Four Fundamental Concepts of Psycho-Analysis.* Translated by Alan Sheridan. Edited by Jacques-Alain Miller. New York: Norton, 1978.

Lakoff, George, and Mark Johnson. *Metaphors We Live By.* Chicago: University of Chicago Press, 1980.

Langer, Susanne K. *Philosophy in a New Key: A Study in the Symbolism of Reason, Rite, and Art.* 2nd ed. New York: New American Library, Mentor, 1951.

Leuchtenburg, William E., ed. *American Places: Encounters with History; A Celebration of Sheldon Meyer.* New York: Oxford University Press, 2000.

Levinson, Sanford. *Written in Stone: Public Monuments in Changing Societies.* Durham, N.C.: Duke University Press, 1998.

Linenthal, Edward T. *Preserving Memory: The Struggle to Create America's Holocaust Museum.* New York: Viking Penguin, 1995.

———. *Sacred Ground: Americans and Their Battlefields.* Urbana: University of Illinois Press, 1991.

———. *The Unfinished Bombing: Oklahoma City in American Memory.* New York: Oxford University Press, 2001.

Linenthal, Edward T., and Tom Engelhardt, eds. *History Wars: The Enola Gay and Other Battles for the American Past.* New York: Henry Holt–Metropolitan, 1996.

Lipovetsky, Gilles. *The Empire of Fashion: Dressing Modern Democracy.* Translated by Catherine Porter. Princeton, N.J.: Princeton University Press, 1994.

Loraux, Nicole. *The Invention of Athens: The Funeral Oration in the Classical City.* Translated by Alan Sheridan. Cambridge, Mass.: Harvard University Press, 1986.

Macdonald, Sharon, ed. *The Politics of Display: Museums, Science, Culture.* New York: Routledge, 1998.

Medhurst, Martin J., and Thomas W. Benson, eds. *Rhetorical Dimensions in Media.* 2nd ed. Dubuque, Iowa: Kendall/Hunt, 1991.

Merelman, Richard M. *Representing Black Culture: Racial Conflict and Cultural Politics in the United States.* New York: Routledge, 1995.

Merleau-Ponty, Maurice. *The Visible and the Invisible.* Edited by Claude Lefort. Translated by Alphonso Lingis. Evanston, Ill.: Northwestern University Press, 1968.

Meyrowitz, Joshua. *No Sense of Place: The Impact of Electronic Media on Social Behavior.* New York: Oxford University Press, 1985.

Miller, David C., ed. *American Iconology: New Approaches to Nineteenth-Century Art and Literature.* New Haven, Conn.: Yale University Press, 1993.

Mitchell, W. J. T. *Iconology: Image, Text, Ideology.* Chicago: University of Chicago Press, 1986.

———. *Picture Theory: Essays on Verbal and Visual Representation.* Chicago: University of Chicago Press, 1994.

Monmonier, Mark. *How to Lie with Maps.* 2nd ed. Chicago: University of Chicago Press, 1996.

Morley, David, and Kevin Robins. *Spaces of Identity: Global Media, Electronic Landscapes and Cultural Boundaries.* New York: Routledge, 1995.

Morris, Richard. *Sinners, Lovers, and Heroes: An Essay on Memorializing in Three American Cultures.* Albany: State University of New York Press, 1997.

Moss, Jean Dietz. *Novelties in the Heavens: Rhetoric and Science in the Copernican Controversy.* Chicago: University of Chicago Press, 1993.

Mountford, Roxanne. *The Gendered Pulpit: Preaching in American Protestant Spaces.* Carbondale: Southern Illinois University Press, 2003.

Nelkin, Dorothy, and M. Susan Lindee. *The DNA Mystique: The Gene as a Cultural Icon.* New York: Freeman, 1995.

Newman, Karen. *Fetal Positions: Individualism, Science, Visuality.* Stanford, Calif.: Stanford University Press, 1996.

Newman, Simon P. *Parades and the Politics of the Street: Festive Culture in the Early American Republic.* Philadelphia: University of Pennsylvania Press, 1997.

Ochs, Donovan J. *Consolatory Rhetoric: Grief, Symbol, and Ritual in the Greco-Roman Era.* Columbia: University of South Carolina Press, 1993.

Olson, Lester C. *Benjamin Franklin's Vision of American Community: A Study in Rhetorical Iconology.* Columbia: University of South Carolina Press, 2004.

———. *Emblems of American Community in the Revolutionary Era: A Study in Rhetorical Iconology.* Washington, D.C.: Smithsonian Institution Press, 1991.

O'Malley, John W. *Praise and Blame in Renaissance Rome: Rhetoric, Doctrine, and Reform in the Sacred Orators of the Papal Court, c. 1450–1521.* Durham, N.C.: Duke University Press, 1979.

Panofsky, Erwin. *Meaning in the Visual Arts.* Garden City, N.Y.: Doubleday-Anchor, 1955.

Perelman, C., and L. Olbrechts-Tyteca. *The New Rhetoric: A Treatise on Argumentation.* Translated by John Wilkinson and Purcell Weaver. Notre Dame, Ind.: University of Notre Dame Press, 1969.

Perlmutter, David D. *Photojournalism and Foreign Policy: Icons of Outrage in International Crises.* Westport, Conn.: Praeger, 1998.

Phillips, Kendall R., ed. *Framing Public Memory.* Tuscaloosa: University of Alabama Press, 2004.

Postman, Neil. *Amusing Ourselves to Death: Public Discourse in the Age of Show Business.* New York: Viking, 1985.

Poulakos, John, and Takis Poulakos. *Classical Rhetorical Theory.* New York: Houghton Mifflin, 1999.

Probyn, Elspeth. *Outside Belongings.* New York: Routledge, 1996.

Reynolds, Larry J., and Gordon Hutner, eds. *National Imaginaries, American Identities: The Cultural Work of American Iconography.* Princeton, N.J.: Princeton University Press, 2000.

Richards, I. A. *Philosophy of Rhetoric.* 1936. Reprint, London: Oxford University Press, 1976.

Rorty, Richard. *Philosophy and the Mirror of Nature.* Princeton, N.J.: Princeton University Press, 1979.

Rosteck, Thomas, ed. *At the Intersection: Cultural Studies and Rhetorical Studies.* New York: Guilford, 1999.

Rushkoff, Douglas. *Coercion: Why We Listen to What "They" Say.* New York: Riverhead Books, 1999.

Ryan, Mary P. *Women in Public: Between Banners and Ballots, 1825–1880.* Baltimore, Md.: Johns Hopkins University Press, 1990.

Savage, Kirk. *Standing Soldiers, Kneeling Slaves: Race, War, and Monument in Nineteenth-Century America.* Princeton, N.J.: Princeton University Press, 1997.

Scott, James C. *Domination and the Arts of Resistance: Hidden Transcripts.* New Haven, Conn.: Yale University Press, 1990.

———. *Seeing Like a State: How Certain Schemes to Improve the Human Condition Have Failed.* New Haven, Conn.: Yale University Press, 1998.

Sedgwick, E. K. *Tendencies.* Durham, N.C.: Duke University Press, 1993.

Seelye, John D. *Memory's Nation: The Place of Plymouth Rock.* Chapel Hill: University of North Carolina Press, 1998.

Selzer, Jack, and Sharon Crowley, eds. *Rhetorical Bodies.* Madison: University of Wisconsin Press, 1999.

Sennett, Richard. *The Fall of Public Man.* New York: Vintage, 1978.

———. *Flesh and Stone: The Body and the City in Western Civilization.* New York: Norton, 1994.

Sha, Richard C. *The Visual and Verbal Sketch in British Romanticism.* Philadelphia: University of Pennsylvania Press, 1998.

Sharp, Gene. *The Politics of Nonviolent Action, Part One: Power and Struggle.* Boston, Mass.: Porter Sargent Publisher, 1973.

Sheldrake, Philip. *Spaces for the Sacred: Place, Memory, and Identity.* Baltimore, Md.: Johns Hopkins University Press, 2001.

Shipler, David K. *A Country of Strangers: Blacks and Whites in America.* New York: Vintage, 1998.

Simmel, Georg. *Conflict and the Web of Group Affiliations.* Translated by Kurt H. Wolff and Reinhard Bendix. New York: Free Press, 1955.

Sontag, Susan. *On Photography.* New York: Farrar, Straus, and Giroux, 1977.

Stafford, Barbara M. *Visual Analogy: Consciousness as the Art of Connecting.* Cambridge, Mass.: MIT Press, 1999.

Steele, Shelby. *The Content of Our Character: A New Vision of Race in America.* New York: St. Martin's Press, 1990.

Steiner, George. *Real Presences.* Chicago: University of Chicago Press, 1989.

Steiner, Wendy. *The Colors of Rhetoric: Problems in the Relation between Modern Literature and Painting.* Chicago: University of Chicago Press, 1982.

Tashjian, Dickran, and Ann Tashjian. *Memorials for Children of Change: The Art of Early New England Stone Carving.* Middletown, Conn.: Wesleyan University Press, 1974.

Tufte, Edward R. *Visual Explanations: Images and Quantities, Evidence and Narrative.* Cheshire, Conn.: Graphics Press, 1997.

Vickers, Brian. *In Defense of Rhetoric.* Oxford: Clarendon Press, 1988.

Walker, Jeffrey. *Rhetoric and Poetics in Antiquity.* New York: Oxford University Press, 2000.

Wasserstrom, Jeffrey N. *Student Protests in Twentieth-Century China: The View From Shanghai.* Stanford, Calif.: Stanford University Press, 1991.

Weaver, Richard M. *Ideas Have Consequences.* 1948. Reprint, Chicago: University of Chicago Press, 1984.

West, Cornel. *Race Matters.* Boston: Beacon Press, 1993.

White, Hayden. *Figural Realism: Studies in the Mimesis Effect.* Baltimore, Md.: Johns Hopkins University Press, 1999.

———. *Tropics of Discourse: Essays in Cultural Criticism.* Baltimore, Md.: Johns Hopkins University Press, 1978.

Wills, Garry. *Lincoln at Gettysburg: The Words That Remade America.* New York: Simon and Schuster, 1992.

Wood, Denis. *The Power of Maps.* New York: Guilford Press, 1992.

Woodward, Gary C. *The Idea of Identification.* Albany: University of New York Press, 2003.

Young, James E. *The Texture of Memory: Holocaust Memorials and Meaning.* New Haven: Yale University Press, 1993.

Zaeske, Susan. *Signatures of Citizenship: Petitioning, Antislavery, and Women's Political Identity.* Chapel Hill: University of North Carolina Press, 2003.

Zanker, Paul. *The Power of Images in the Age of Augustus.* Translated by Alan Shapiro. Ann Arbor: University of Michigan Press, 1988.

Zelizer, Barbie. *Remembering to Forget: Holocaust Memory through the Camera's Eye.* Chicago: University of Chicago Press, 1998.

Essays

Adams, John C. "Ramist Concepts of Testimony, Judicial Narratives, and the Puritan Conversion Narrative." *Rhetorica* 3 (1991): 251–68.

Allison-Bunnell, Steven W. "Making Nature 'Real' Again: Natural History Exhibits and Public Rhetorics of Science at the Smithsonian Institute in the Early 1960s." In Macdonald, *The Politics of Display,* 77–97.

Alpers, Svetlana. "The Museum as a Way of Seeing." In Karp and Lavine, *Exhibiting Cultures,* 25–32.

Altman, Charles F. "The Medieval Marquee: Church Portal Sculpture as Publicity." *Journal of Popular Culture* 14 (Summer 1980): 37–46.

Andrews, James R. "Confrontation at Columbia: A Case Study in Coercive Rhetoric." *Quarterly Journal of Speech* 55 (1969): 9–16.

Armada, Bernard J. "Memorial Agon: An Interpretive Tour of the National Civil Rights Museum." *Southern Communication Journal* 63 (1998): 235–43.

Arthos, John, Jr. "The Shaman-Trickster's Art of Misdirection: The Rhetoric of Farrakhan and the Million Men." *Quarterly Journal of Speech* 87 (2001): 41–60.

Atkinson, David, and Denis Cosgrove. "Urban Rhetoric and Embodied Identities: City, Nation, and Empire at the Vittorio Emanuele II Monument in Rome, 1870–1945." *Annals of the Association of American Geographers* 88 (1998): 28–49.

Ausmus, William A. "Pragmatic Uses of Metaphor: Models and Metaphor in the Nuclear Winter Scenario." *Communication Monographs* 65 (1998): 67–82.

Ball, Edward. "Constructing Ethnicity." In Cooke and Wollen, *Visual Display,* 142–53.

Bann, Stephen. "Shrines, Curiosities, and the Rhetoric of Display." In Cooke and Wollen, *Visual Display,* 14–29.

Barbatsis, Gretchen S. "'Look and I Will Show You Something You Will Want to See': Pictorial Engagement in Negative Political Campaign Commercials." *Argumentation and Advocacy* 33 (1996): 69–80.

Bar-Itzhak, Haya. "'The Unknown Variable Hidden Underground' and the Zionist Idea: Rhetoric of Place in an Israeli Kibbutz and Cultural Interpretation." *Journal of American Folklore* 112 (1999): 497–513.

Barthes, Roland. "Rhetoric of the Image." In *Image-Music-Text*, 32–51. New York: Hill and Wang, 1977.

Barton, Ben F., and Marthalee S. Barton. "Ideology and the Map: Toward a Postmodern Visual Design Practice." In *Professional Communication: The Social Perspective*, edited by Nancy Roundy Blyler and Charlotte Thralls, 49–78. Newbury Park, Calif.: Sage, 1993.

Bauman, Richard. "Performance." In *International Encyclopedia of Communication*, 3:262–66. New York: Oxford University Press, 1989.

Bauman, Richard, and Patricia Sawin. "The Politics of Participation in Folklife Festivals." In Karp and Lavine, *Exhibiting Cultures*, 288–314.

Baxandall, Michael. "Exhibiting Intention: Some Preconditions of the Visual Display of Culturally Purposeful Objects." In Karp and Lavine, *Exhibiting Cultures*, 33–41.

Beale, Walter H. "Rhetorical Performative Discourse: A New Theory of Epideictic." *Philosophy and Rhetoric* 11 (1978): 221–46.

Benjamin, Walter. "The Work of Art in an Age of Mechanical Reproduction." In *Illuminations*, 1968; repr., ed. and introduction by Hannah Arendt, New York: Schocken, 1986, 217–51.

Bennett, Larry J., and William Blake Tyrell. "Sophocles' *Antigone* and Funeral Oratory." *American Journal of Philology* 111 (1990): 441–56.

Benson, Susan. "Inscriptions on the Self: Reflection on Tattooing and Piercing in Contemporary Euro-America." In *Written on the Body: The Tattoo in European and American History*, edited by Jane Caplan, 234–54. London: Reaktion Books, 2000.

Benson, Thomas W. "Joe: An Essay in the Rhetorical Criticism of Film." *Journal of Popular Culture* 8 (1974): 610/24–618/32.

———. "Killer Media: Technology, Communication, and the First Amendment." In Medhurst and Benson, *Rhetorical Dimensions in Media*, 378–97.

———. "Rhetoric and Autobiography: The Case of Malcolm X." *Quarterly Journal of Speech* 60 (1974): 1–13.

———. "The Rhetorical Structure of Frederick Wiseman's *High School*." *Communication Monographs* 47 (1980): 233–61.

———. "The Rhetorical Structure of Frederick Wiseman's *Primate*." *Quarterly Journal of Speech* 71 (1985): 204–17.

Benson, Thomas W., and Bonnie Johnson. "The Rhetoric of Resistance: Confrontation with the Warmakers, Washington, D.C., October, 1967." *Today's Speech* 16 (September 1968): 35–42.

Berman, Scott. "Public Buildings as Public Relations: Ideas about the Theory and Practice of Strategic Architectural Communication." *Public Relations Quarterly* 44 (Spring 1999): 18–22.

Biesecker, Barbara A. "Remembering World War II: The Rhetoric and Politics of National Commemoration at the Turn of the 21st Century." *Quarterly Journal of Speech* 88 (2002): 393–409.

———. "Renovating the National Imaginary: A Prolegomenon on Contemporary Paregoric Rhetoric." In Phillips, *Framing Public Memory*, 212–47.

Binnie, J., and G. Valentine. "Geographies of Sexuality—A Review in Progress." In *Lesbian and Gay Studies: An Introductory, Interdisciplinary Approach*, edited by Theo Sandfort, Judith Schuyf, Jan Willem Duyvendak, and Jeffrey Weeks, 132–45. London: Sage, 2000.

Birdsell, David S., and Leo Groarke. "Toward a Theory of Visual Argument." *Argumentation and Advocacy* 33 (1996): 1–10.

Black, Edwin. "Gettysburg and Silence." *Quarterly Journal of Speech* 80 (1994): 21–36.

———. "The Sentimental Style as Escapism, or the Devil with Dan'l Webster." In *Form and Genre: Shaping Rhetorical Action*, edited by Karlyn K. Campbell and Kathleen H. Jamieson, 75–86. Falls Church, Va.: Speech Communication Association, 1978.

Blair, Carole. "Contemporary U.S. Memorial Sites as Exemplars of Rhetoric's Materiality." In Selzer and Crowley, *Rhetorical Bodies*, 16–57.

Blair, Carole, Marsha S. Jeppeson, and Enrico Pucci Jr. "Public Memorializing in Post Modernity: The Vietnam Veterans Memorial as Prototype." *Quarterly Journal of Speech* 77 (1991): 263–88.

Blair, Carole, and Neil Michel. "Commemorating in the Theme Park Zone: Reading the Astronauts Memorial." In Rosteck, *At the Intersection*, 29–83.

———. "Reproducing Civil Rights Tactics: The Rhetorical Performances of the Civil Rights Memorial." *Rhetoric Society Quarterly* 30 (Spring 2000): 31–55.

———. "The Rushmore Effect: Ethos and National Collective Identity." In *The Ethos of Rhetoric*, edited by Michael J. Hyde, 156–96. Columbia: University of South Carolina Press, 2004.

Blair, J. Anthony. "The Possibility and Actuality of Visual Arguments." *Argumentation and Advocacy* 33 (1996): 23–39.

———. "The Rhetoric of Visual Arguments." In Hill and Helmers, *Defining Visual Rhetorics*, 41–61.

Blakesley, David. "Defining Film Rhetoric: The Case of Hitchcock's *Vertigo*." In Hill and Helmers, *Defining Visual Rhetorics*, 111–33.

Borda, Jennifer L. "The Woman Suffrage Parades of 1910–1913: Possibilities and Limitations of an Early Feminist Rhetorical Strategy." *Western Journal of Communication* 66 (2002): 25–52.

Bostdorff, Denise M. "George W. Bush's Post–September 11 Rhetoric of Covenant Renewal: Upholding the Faith of the Greatest Generation." *Quarterly Journal of Speech* 89 (2003): 293–319.

———. "Making Light of James Watt: A Burkean Approach to the Form and Attitude of Political Cartoons." *Quarterly Journal of Speech* 73 (1987): 43–59.

Bowie, E. L. "Early Greek Elegy, Symposium and Public Festival." *Journal of Hellenic Studies* 106 (1986): 13–35.

Boyle, Marjorie O. "A Likely Story: The Autobiographical as Epideictic." *Journal of the American Academy of Religion* 57 (1989): 23–51.

Brandt, Allan, and David Sloan. "Of Beds and Benches: Building the Modern American Hospital." In Galison and Thompson, *The Architecture of Science*, 281–302.

Browne, Stephen H. "Arendt, Eichmann, and the Politics of Remembrance." In Phillips, *Framing Public Memory*, 45–64.

———. "Encountering Angelina Grimke: Violence, Identity, and the Creation of Radical Community." *Quarterly Journal of Speech* 82 (1996): 55–73.

———. "'Like Gory Spectres': Representing Evil in Theodore Weld's *American Slavery as It Is*." *Quarterly Journal of Speech* 80 (1994): 277–92.

———. "Reading, Rhetoric, and the Texture of Public Memory." *Quarterly Journal of Speech* 81 (1995): 237–65.

———. "Remembering Crispus Attucks: Race, Rhetoric, and the Politics of Commemoration." *Quarterly Journal of Speech* 85 (1999): 169–87.

Brummett, Barry. "Burkean Scapegoating, Mortification, and Transcendence in Presidential Rhetoric." *Central States Speech Journal* 32 (1981): 254–64.

———. "Symbolic Form, Burkean Scapegoating, and Rhetorical Exigency in Alioto's Response to the 'Zebra' Murders." *Western Journal of Speech Communication* 44 (1980): 64–73.

Bruner, M. Lane. "Strategies of Remembrance in Pre-Unification West Germany." *Quarterly Journal of Speech* 86 (2000): 86–107.

Bruner, Michael S. "Symbolic Uses of the Berlin Wall, 1961–1989." *Communication Quarterly* 37 (1989): 319–28.

Bukatman, Scott. "The Artificial Infinite: On Special Effects and the Sublime." In Cooke and Wollen, *Visual Display*, 254–89.

Burke, Kenneth. "Dramatism." In *International Encyclopedia of the Social Sciences*, edited by David L. Sills, 7:445–52. New York: Macmillan, 1968.

Byer, Robert H. "Words, Monuments, Beholders: The Visual Arts in Hawthorne's *The Marble Faun.*" In Miller, *American Iconology,* 163–85.

Cameron, Duncan F. "The Museum: A Temple or the Forum." *Journal of World History* 14 (1972): 189–202.

Carlson, A. Cheree, and John E. Hocking. "Strategies of Redemption at the Vietnam Veterans' Memorial." *Western Journal of Communication* 52 (1988): 203–15.

Carter, Michael. "The Ritual Functions of Epideictic Rhetoric: The Case of Socrates' Funeral Oration." *Rhetorica* 9 (1991): 209–32.

———. "Scholarship as Rhetoric of Display; or, Why is Everybody Saying All Those Terrible Things About Us? *College English* 54 (1992): 303–13.

Cartwright, Lisa. "Gender Artifacts: Technologies of Bodily Display in Medical Culture." In Cooke and Wollen, *Visual Display,* 218–35.

Casey, Edward S. "Public Memory in Place and Time." In Phillips, *Framing Public Memory,* 17–44.

Chase, Richard J. "The Classical Conception of Epideictic." *Quarterly Journal of Speech* 47 (1961): 293–300.

Cherney, James L. "Deaf Culture and the Cochlear Implant Debate: Cyborg Politics and the Identity of People with Disabilities." *Argumentation and Advocacy* 36 (1999): 22–34.

Christiansen, Adrienne E., and Jeremy J. Hanson. "Comedy as Cure for Tragedy: ACT UP and the Rhetoric of AIDS." *Quarterly Journal of Speech* 82 (1996): 157–70.

Clark, Elizabeth B. "'The Sacred Rights of the Weak': Pain, Sympathy, and the Culture of Individual Rights in Antebellum America." *Journal of American History* 82 (1995): 463–93.

Clark, Gregory, S. Michael Halloran, and Allison Woodford. "Thomas Cole's Vision of 'Nature' and the Conquest Theme in American Culture." In *Green Culture: Environmental Rhetoric in Contemporary America,* edited by Carl G. Herndl and Stuart C. Brown, 261–80. Madison: University of Wisconsin Press, 1996.

Cloud, Dana L. "Hegemony or Concordance? The Rhetoric of Tokenism in 'Oprah' Winfrey's Rags-to-Riches Biography." *Critical Studies in Mass Communication* 13 (1996): 115–37.

———. "'To Veil the Threat of Terror': Afghan Women and the 'Clash of Civilizations' in the Imagery of the U.S. War on Terrorism." *Quarterly Journal of Speech* 90 (2004): 285–306.

Condit, Celeste Michelle. "The Functions of Epideictic: The Boston Massacre Orations as Exemplar." *Communication Quarterly* 33 (1985): 284–98.

Connor, W. R. "Tribes, Festivals and Processions: Civic Ceremonial and Political Manipulation in Archaic Greece." *Journal of Hellenic Studies* 107 (1987): 40–50.

Consigny, Scott. "Gorgias's Use of the Epideictic." *Philosophy and Rhetoric* 25 (1992): 281–97.

Cooper, Brenda, and David Descutner. "'It Had No Voice to It': Sydney Pollack's Film Translation of Isak Dinesen's *Out of Africa.*" *Quarterly Journal of Speech* 82 (1996): 228–50.

Crable, Richard E., and Steven L. Vibbert. "Mobil's Epideictic Advocacy: 'Observations' of Prometheus-Bound." *Communication Monographs* 50 (1983): 380–94.

Crowley, Sharon. "Afterword: The Material of Rhetoric." In Selzer and Crowley, *Rhetorical Bodies,* 357–64.

Daley, Patrick J. "Mapping the Environment: Contested Physical and Cultural Terrain in the 'Far North.'" *Journalism and Communication Monographs* 1 (2000): 263–300.

Darwin, Thomas J. "Intelligent Cells and the Body as Conversation: The Democratic Rhetoric of Mindbody Medicine." *Argumentation and Advocacy* 36 (1999): 35–49.

Dauber, Cori E. "The Shot Seen 'Round the World: The Impact of the Images of Mogadishu on American Military Operations." *Rhetoric and Public Affairs* 4 (2001): 653–87.

Daughton, Suzanne M. "The Fine Texture of Enactment: Iconicity as Empowerment in Angelina Grimke's Pennsylvania Hall Address." *Women's Studies in Communication* 18 (1995): 19–43.

DeLuca, Kevin Michael. "Unruly Arguments: The Body Rhetoric of Earth First!, Act Up, and Queer Nation." *Argumentation and Advocacy* 36 (1999): 9–21.

DeLuca, Kevin Michael, and Anne Teresa Demo. "Imaging Nature: Watkins, Yosemite, and the Birth of Environmentalism." *Critical Studies in Media Communication* 17 (2000): 241–60.

DeLuca, Kevin Michael, and Jennifer Peeples. "From Public Sphere to Public Screen: Democracy, Activism, and the 'Violence' of Seattle." *Critical Studies in Media Communication* 19 (2002): 125–51.

DeSousa, Michael A. "Symbolic Action and Pretended Insight: The Ayatollah Khomeini in U.S. Editorial Cartoons." In Medhurst and Benson, *Rhetorical Dimensions in Media,* 216–42.

DeSousa, Michael A., and Martin J. Medhurst. "Political Cartoons and American Culture: Significant Symbols of Campaign 1980." *Studies in Visual Communication* 8 (Winter 1982): 84–97.

De Vinne, Christine. "Conspicuous Consumption: Cannibal Bodies and the Rhetoric of the American West." In Selzer and Crowley, *Rhetorical Bodies,* 75–97.

Dickinson, Greg. "Joe's Rhetoric: Finding Authenticity at Starbucks." *Rhetoric Society Quarterly* 32 (Fall 2002): 5–27.

———. "Memories for Sale: Nostalgia and the Construction of Identity in Old Pasadena." *Quarterly Journal of Speech* 83 (1997): 1–27.

Dickinson, Greg, and Casey Malone Maugh. "Placing Visual Rhetoric: Finding Material Comfort in Wild Oats Market." In Hill and Helmers, *Defining Visual Rhetorics,* 259–76.

Dickson, Barbara. "Reading Maternity Materially: The Case of Demi Moore." In Selzer and Crowley, *Rhetorical Bodies,* 297–313.

Dieter, Otto A. "*Arbor Picta:* The Medieval Tree of Preaching." *Quarterly Journal of Speech* 51 (1965): 123–44.

Dow, Bonnie J. "*Ellen,* Television, and the Politics of Gay and Lesbian Visibility." *Critical Studies in Media Communication* 18 (2001): 123–40.

———. "The Function of Epideictic and Deliberative Strategies in Presidential Crisis Rhetoric." *Western Journal of Speech Communication* 53 (1989): 294-310.

Doxtader, Erik. "Making Rhetorical History in a Time of Transition: The Occasion, Constitution, and Representation of South African Reconciliation." *Rhetoric and Public Affairs* 4 (2001): 223–60.

Duffy, Bernard K. "The Platonic Functions of Epideictic Rhetoric." *Philosophy and Rhetoric* 16 (1983): 79–93.

Duncan, Carol. "Art Museums and the Ritual of Citizenship." In Karp and Lavine, *Exhibiting Cultures,* 88–103.

Duncan, Carol, and Alan Wallach. "The Universal Survey Museum." *Art History* 3 (1980): 448–69.

Eberly, Rosa A. "'Everywhere You Go, It's There': Forgetting and Remembering the University of Texas Tower Shootings." In Phillips, *Framing Public Memory,* 65–88.

Eco, Umberto. "Critique of the Image." In *Thinking Photography,* edited by Victor Burgin, 32–36. London: MacMillan, 1982.

Edwards, Janis L. "Echoes of Camelot: How Images Construct Cultural Memory through Rhetorical Framing." In Hill and Helmers, *Defining Visual Rhetorics,* 179–94.

———. "Running in the Shadows in Campaign 2000: Candidate Metaphors in Editorial Cartoons." *American Behavioral Scientist* 44 (2001): 2140–51.

———. "The Very Role of a Modern Major (Media) Candidate: Colin Powell and the Rhetoric of Public Opinion." *Communication Quarterly* 46 (1998):163–76.

———. "Wee George and the Seven Dwarfs: Caricature and Metaphor in Campaign '88 Cartoons." *INKS: Cartoon and Comic Art Studies* (May 1995): 26–34.

Edwards, Janis L., and Carol K. Winkler. "Representative Form and the Visual Ideograph: The Iwo Jima Image in Editorial Cartoons." *Quarterly Journal of Speech* 83 (1997): 289–310.

Ehrenhaus, Peter. "Silence and Symbolic Expression." *Communication Monographs* 55 (1988): 41–57.

———. "The Vietnam Veterans Memorial: An Invitation to Argument." *Journal of the American Forensics Association* 25 (1988): 54–64.

Erickson, Keith V. "Presidential Rhetoric's Visual Turn: Performance Fragments and the Politics of Illusionism." *Communication Monographs* 67 (2000): 138–57.

———. "Presidential Spectacles: Political Illusionism and the Rhetoric of Travel." *Communication Monographs* 65 (1998): 141–53.

Esherick, Joseph W., and Jeffrey N. Wasserstrom. "Acting Out Democracy: Political Theater in Modern China." In *Popular Protest and Political Culture in Modern China,* 2nd ed. Edited by Jeffrey N. Wasserstrom and Elizabeth J. Perry, 28–66. Boulder, Colo.: Westview, 1992.

Faigley, Lester. "Material Literacy and Visual Design." In Selzer and Crowley, *Rhetorical Bodies,* 171–201.

Finnegan, Cara A. "Documentary as Art in *U.S. Camera.*" *Rhetoric Society Quarterly* 31 (Spring 2001): 37–68.

———. "Doing Rhetorical History of the Visual: The Photograph and the Archive." In Hill and Helmers, *Defining Visual Rhetorics,* 195–214.

———. "The Naturalistic Enthymeme and Visual Argument: Photographic Representation in the 'Skull Controversy.'" *Argumentation and Advocacy* 37 (2001): 133–49.

———. "Social Engineering, Visual Politics and the New Deal: FSA Photography in *Survey Graphic.*" *Rhetoric and Public Affairs* 3 (2000): 333–62.

Finnegan, Cara A., and Jiyeon Kang. "'Sighting' the Public: Iconoclasm and Public Sphere Theory." *Quarterly Journal of Speech* 90 (2004): 377–402.

Fisher, Jeanne Y. "A Burkean Analysis of the Rhetorical Dimensions of a Multiple Murder and Suicide." *Quarterly Journal of Speech* 60 (1974): 175–89.

Fleming, David. "Can Pictures Be Arguments?" *Argumentation and Advocacy* 33 (1996): 11–22.

———. "Discourse, Democracy, and Design in the Classical Polis." *Rhetoric Society Quarterly* 32 (Summer 2002): 5–32.

Foner, Nancy. "Race and Color: Jamaican Migrants in London and New York City." *International Migration Review* 29 (1985): 708–27.

Foss, Karen A., and Kathy L. Domenici. "Haunting Argentina: Synecdoche in the Protests of the Mothers of the Plaza de Mayo." *Quarterly Journal of Speech* 87 (2001): 237–58.

Foss, Sonja K. "Ambiguity as Persuasion: The Vietnam Veterans Memorial." *Communication Quarterly* 34 (1986): 326–40.

———. "Framing the Study of Visual Rhetoric: Toward a Transformation of Rhetorical Theory." In Hill and Helmers, *Defining Visual Rhetorics,* 303–13.

———. "Judy Chicago's *The Dinner Party:* Empowering of Women's Voice in Visual Art." In *Women Communicating: Studies of Women's Talk,* edited by Barbara Bate and Anita Taylor, 9–26. Norwood, N.J.: Ablex, 1988.

———. "Rhetoric and the Visual Image: A Resource Unit." *Communication Education* 31 (1982): 55–66.

———. "A Rhetorical Schema for the Evaluation of Visual Imagery." *Communication Studies* 45 (1994): 213–24.

Foss, Sonja K., and Anthony J. Radich. "The Aesthetic Response to Nonrepresentational Art: A Suggested Model." *Review of Research in Visual Arts Education* 12 (Fall 1980): 40–49.

Furley, William D. "Praise and Persuasion in Greek Hymns." *Journal of Hellenic Studies* 115 (1995): 29–46.

Gallagher, Victoria J. "Memory and Reconciliation in the Birmingham Civil Rights Institute." *Rhetoric and Public Affairs* 2 (1999): 303–20.

———. "Remembering Together: Rhetorical Integration and the Case of the Martin Luther King, Jr. Memorial." *Southern Communication Journal* 60 (1995): 109–19.

Gieryn, Thomas F. "Balancing Acts: Science, *Enola Gay* and the History Wars at the Smithsonian." In Macdonald, *The Politics of Display,* 197–228.

———. "Two Faces on Science: Building Identities for Molecular Biology and Biotechnology." In Galison and Thompson, *The Architecture of Science,* 423–55.

Goggin, Maureen Daly. "Visual Rhetoric in Pens of Steel and Inks of Silk: Challenging the Great Visual/Verbal Divide." In Hill and Helmers, *Defining Visual Rhetorics,* 87–110.

Goodnight, G. Thomas. "The Firm, the Park and the University: Fear and Trembling on the Postmodern Trail." *Quarterly Journal of Speech* 81 (1995): 267–90.

Graham, John. "*Ut Pictura Poesis.*" In *Dictionary of the History of Ideas,* edited by Philip P. Weiner, 4:465–76. New York: Scribner's, 1973.

Greenblatt, Stephen. "Resonance and Wonder." In Karp and Lavine, *Exhibiting Cultures,* 42–56.

Gregg, Richard B. "The Ego-Function of the Rhetoric of Protest." *Philosophy and Rhetoric* 4 (1971): 71–91.

Grindstaff, Davin Allen and Kevin Michael DeLuca. "The Corpus of Daniel Pearl." *Critical Studies in Media Communication* 21 (2004): 305–24.

Gronbeck, Bruce E. "Rhetoric, Ethics, and Telespectacles in the Post-everything Age." In *Postmodern Representations: Truth, Power, and Mimesis in the Human Sciences and Public Culture,* edited by Richard Harvey Brown, 216–38. Urbana: University of Illinois Press, 1995.

Gross, Larry. "From South Beach and SoBe." In *Voices in the Street: Explorations in Gender, Media, and Public Space,* edited by Susan J. Drucker and Gary Gumpert, 201–10. Cresskill, N.J.: Hampton Press, 1997.

Grossberg, Lawrence. "The Indifference of Television, or Mapping TV's Popular (Affective) Economy." In *Dancing in Spite of Myself: Essays on Popular Culture.* Durham, N.C.: Duke University Press, 1997, 125–44.

Haas, Christina. "Materializing Public and Private: The Spatialization of Conceptual Categories in Discourses of Abortion." In Selzer and Crowley, *Rhetorical Bodies,* 218–38.

Hahn, Cynthia. "Seeing and Believing: The Construction of Sanctity in Early-Medieval Saints' Shrines." *Speculum* 72 (1997): 1079–106.

Haiman, Franklyn S. "Nonverbal Communication and the First Amendment: The Rhetoric of the Streets Revisited." *Quarterly Journal of Speech* 68 (1982): 371–83.

———. "The Rhetoric of the Streets: Some Legal and Ethical Considerations." *Quarterly Journal of Speech* 53 (1967): 99–114.

Haines, Harry W. "'What Kind of War?': An Analysis of the Vietnam Veterans Memorial." *Critical Studies in Mass Communication* 3 (1986): 1–20.

Halloran, S. Michael. "The Rhetoric of Picturesque Scenery: A Nineteenth-Century Epideictic." In *Oratorical Culture in Nineteenth-Century America: Transformations in the Theory and Practice of Rhetoric,* edited by Gregory Clark and S. Michael Halloran, 226–46. Carbondale: Southern Illinois University Press, 1993.

———. "Text and Experience in a Historical Pageant: Toward a Rhetoric of Spectacle." *Rhetoric Society Quarterly* 31 (Fall 2001): 5–17.

Happel, Stephen. "Picturing God: The Rhetoric of Religious Images and Caravaggio's *Conversion of Saint Paul.*" In *Rhetorical Invention and Religious Inquiry: New Perspectives,* edited by Walter Jost and Wendy Olmsted, 323–55. New Haven, Conn.: Yale University Press, 2000.

Haraway, Donna. "Teddy Bear Patriarchy: Taxidermy in the Garden of Eden, 1908–1936." *Social Text* 11 (Winter 1984–85): 20–64.

Hardie, Melissa Jane. "Beard." In Selzer and Crowley, *Rhetorical Bodies*, 275–96.

Hariman, Robert, and John Louis Lucaites. "Dissent and Emotional Management in a Liberal-Democratic Society: The Kent State Iconic Photograph." *Rhetoric Society Quarterly* 31 (Summer 2001): 5–31.

———. "Performing Civic Identity: The Iconic Photograph of the Flag Raising on Iwo Jima." *Quarterly Journal of Speech* 88 (2002): 363–92.

———. "Public Identity and Collective Memory in U.S. Iconic Photography: The Image of 'Accidental Napalm.'" *Critical Studies in Media Communication* 20 (2003): 35–66.

Harley, J. B. "Deconstructing the Map." In Barnes and Duncan, *Writing Worlds*, 231–47.

Harold, Christine L. "Tracking Heroin Chic: The Abject Body Reconfigures the Rational Argument." *Argumentation and Advocacy* 36 (1999): 65–76.

Harpine, William D. "'We Want Yer, McKinley': Epideictic Rhetoric in Songs From the 1896 Presidential Campaign." *Rhetoric Society Quarterly* 34 (Winter 2004): 73–88.

Hartnett, Stephen. "Fanny Fern's 1855 *Ruth Hall*, The Cheerful Brutality of Capitalism, and The Irony of Sentimental Rhetoric." *Quarterly Journal of Speech* 88 (2002): 1–18.

Hasian, Marouf A., Jr. "Anne Frank, Bergen-Belsen, and the Polysemic Nature of Holocaust Memories." *Rhetoric and Public Affairs* 4 (2001): 349–74.

———. "Jurisprudence as Performance: John Brown's Enactment of Natural Law at Harper's Ferry." *Quarterly Journal of Speech* 86 (2000): 190–214.

———. "Remembering and Forgetting the 'Final Solution': A Rhetorical Pilgrimage through the U.S. Holocaust Memorial Museum." *Critical Studies in Media Communication* 21 (2004): 64–92.

Hasian, Marouf A., Jr., and A. Cheree Carlson. "Revisionism and Collective Memory: The Struggle for Meaning in the *Amistad* Affair." *Communication Monographs* 67 (2000): 42–62.

Haskins, Ekaterina V. "'Put Your Stamp on History': The USPS Commemorative Program *Celebrate the Century* and Postmodern Collective Memory." *Quarterly Journal of Speech* 89 (2003): 1–18.

———. "Rhetoric between Orality and Literacy: Cultural Memory and Performance in Isocrates and Aristotle." *Quarterly Journal of Speech* 87 (2001): 158–78.

———. "Time, Space, and Political Identity: Envisioning Community in *Triumph of the Will*." In Blakesley, *The Terministic Screen*, 92–106.

Hauser, Gerard A. "Aristotle on Epideictic: The Formation of Public Morality." *Rhetoric Society Quarterly* 29 (Winter 1999): 5–23.

———. "Empiricism, Description, and the New Rhetoric." *Philosophy and Rhetoric* 5 (1972): 24–44.

———. "Incongruous Bodies; Arguments for Personal Sufficiency and Public Insufficiency." *Argumentation and Advocacy* 36 (1999): 1–8.

Hayden, Sara. "Family Metaphors and the Nation: Promoting a Politics of Care through the Million Mom March." *Quarterly Journal of Speech* 89 (2003): 196–215.

Helmers, Marguerite. "Framing the Fine Arts through Rhetoric." In Hill and Helmers, *Defining Visual Rhetorics*, 63–86.

———. "Painting as Rhetorical Performance: Joseph Wright's *An Experiment on a Bird in the Air Pump*." *Journal of Advanced Composition* 21 (Winter 2001): 71–95.

Helmers, Marguerite, and Charles A. Hill. Introduction to Hill and Helmers, *Defining Visual Rhetorics*, 1–23.

Hill, Charles A. "The Psychology of Rhetorical Images." In Hill and Helmers, *Defining Visual Rhetorics*, 25–40.

Hollis, Karyn. "Material of Desire: Bodily Rhetoric in Working Women's Poetry at the Bryn Mawr Summer School, 1921–1938." In Selzer and Crowley, *Rhetorical Bodies*, 98–119.

Hope, Diane S. "Gendered Environments: Gender and the Natural World in the Rhetoric of Advertising." In Hill and Helmers, *Defining Visual Rhetorics,* 155–77.

Hubbard, Bryan, and Marouf A. Hasian Jr. "Atomic Memories of the *Enola Gay:* Strategies of Remembrance at the National Air and Space Museum." *Rhetoric and Public Affairs* 1 (1998): 363–85.

Ivie, Robert L. "Literalizing the Metaphor of Soviet Savagery: President Truman's Plain Style." *Southern Speech Communication Journal* 51 (1986): 91–105.

———. "Metaphor and the Rhetorical Invention of Cold War Idealists." *Communication Monographs* 54 (1987): 165–82.

———. "The Metaphor of Force in Prowar Discourse: The Case of 1812." *Quarterly Journal of Speech* 68 (1982): 240–53.

James, Beverly. "Fencing in the Past: Budapest's Statue Park Museum." *Media, Culture and Society* 21 (1999): 291–311.

Jasinski, James. "Rearticulating History in Epideictic Discourse: Frederick Douglass's 'The Meaning of the Fourth of July to the Negro.'" In *Rhetoric and Political Culture in Nineteenth-Century America,* edited by Thomas W. Benson, 71–89. East Lansing: Michigan State University Press, 1997.

Jencks, Charles. "Rhetoric and Architecture." *Architectural Association Quarterly* 4 (1972): 4–17.

Jordanova, Ludmilla. "Medicine and Genres of Display." In Cooke and Wollen, *Visual Display,* 203–17.

Jorgensen-Earp, Cheryl R., and Lori A. Lanzilotti. "Public Memory and Private Grief: The Construction of Shrines at the Sites of Public Tragedy." *Quarterly Journal of Speech* 84 (1998): 150–70.

Katriel, Tamar. "'Our Future is Where Our Past Is:' Studying Heritage Museums as Ideological and Performative Arenas." *Communication Monographs* 60 (1993): 69–75.

———. "Rhetoric in Flames: Fire Inscriptions in Israeli Youth Movement Ceremonials." *Quarterly Journal of Speech* 73 (1987): 444–59.

———. "Sites of Memory: Discourses of the Past in Israeli Pioneering Settlement Museums." *Quarterly Journal of Speech* 80 (1994): 1–20.

Katriel, Tamar, and Aliza Shenhar. "Tower and Stockade: Dialogic Narration in Israeli Settlement Ethos." *Quarterly Journal of Speech* 76 (1990): 359–80.

Kennedy, George. "Antony's Speech at Caesar's Funeral." *Quarterly Journal of Speech* 54 (1968): 99–106.

Kiewe, Amos. "The Body as Proof: Franklin D. Roosevelt's Preparations for the 1932 Presidential Campaign." *Argumentation and Advocacy* 36 (1999): 88–100.

———. "Framing Memory through Public Eulogy: Ronald Reagan's Long Good-Bye." In Phillips, *Framing Public Memory,* 248–66.

Kirshenblatt-Gimblett, Barbara. "Objects of Ethnography." In Karp and Lavine, *Exhibiting Cultures,* 386–443.

Knopp, L. "Sexuality and Urban Space: A Framework for Analysis." In Bell and Valentine, *Mapping Desire,* 149–61.

Kostelnick, Charles. "Melting-Pot Ideology, Modernist Aesthetics, and the Emergence of Graphical Conventions: The Statistical Atlases of the United States, 1874–1925." In Hill and Helmers, *Defining Visual Rhetorics,* 215–42.

Krips, Henry. "Rhetoric, Ideology, and the Gaze: *The Ambassadors*' Body." In Rosteck, *At the Intersection,* 186–205.

Kuusisto, Riikka. "Heroic Tale, Game, and Business Deal? Western Metaphors in Action in Kosovo." *Quarterly Journal of Speech* 88 (2002): 50–68.

Lake, Randall A., and Barbara A. Pickering. "Argumentation, the Visual, and the Possibility of Refutation: An Exploration." *Argumentation* 12 (1998): 79–93.

Lancioni, Judith. "The Rhetoric of the Frame: Revisioning Archival Photographs in *The Civil War*." *Western Journal of Communication* 60 (Fall 1996): 397–414.

Lasch, Christopher. "Conversation and the Civic Arts." In *Revolt of the Elites and the Betrayal of Democracy,* 117–28. New York: Norton, 1995.

Lauer, Ilon. "Ritual and Power in Imperial Roman Rhetoric." *Quarterly Journal of Speech* 90 (2004): 422–45.

Lavine, Stephen D., and Ivan Karp. "Introduction: Museums and Multiculturalism." In Karp and Lavine, *Exhibiting Cultures,* 1–9.

Leff, Michael, and Andrew Sachs. "Words the Most Like Things: Iconicity and the Rhetorical Text." *Western Journal of Communication* 54 (1990): 252–73.

Lucaites, John Louis. "Visualizing 'The People': Individualism vs. Collectivism in *Let Us Now Praise Famous Men*." *Quarterly Journal of Speech* 83 (1997): 269–88.

Lucaites, John Louis, and Robert Hariman. "Visual Rhetoric, Photojournalism, and Democratic Public Culture." *Rhetoric Review* 20 (Spring 2001): 37–42.

Macdonald, Sharon. "Afterword: From War to Debate?" In Macdonald, *The Politics of Display,* 229–35.

———. "Exhibitions of Power and Powers of Exhibition: An Introduction to the Politics of Display." In Macdonald, *The Politics of Display,* 1–24.

Mackin, James A., Jr. "Schismogenesis and Community: Pericles' Funeral Oration." *Quarterly Journal of Speech* 77 (1991): 251–62.

Madison, D. Soyini. "'That Was My Occupation': Oral Narrative, Performance, and Black Feminist Thought." *Text and Performance Quarterly* 13 (1993): 213–32.

Matthews, Gray. "Epideictic Rhetoric and Baseball: Nurturing Community through Controversy." *Southern Communication Journal* 60 (1995): 275–91.

McDaniel, James P. "Fantasm: The Triumph of Form (An Essay on the Democratic Sublime)." *Quarterly Journal of Speech* 86 (2000): 48–66.

———. "Figures for New Frontiers, From Davy Crockett to Cyberspace Gurus." *Quarterly Journal of Speech* 88 (2002): 91–111.

McKenzie, Robert. "Audience Involvement in the Epideictic Discourse of Television Talk Shows." *Communication Quarterly* 48 (2000): 190–203.

McKeon, Richard. "Discourse, Demonstration, Verification, and Justification." In *Démonstration, Vérification, Justification,* edited by Philippe Devaux, 37–55. Paris: Nauwelaerts, 1968.

———. "The Uses of Rhetoric in a Technological Age: Architectonic Productive Arts." In *The Prospect of Rhetoric,* edited by Lloyd F. Bitzer and Edwin Black, 44–63. Englewood Cliffs, N.J.: Prentice-Hall, 1971.

McKerrow, Raymie, E. "Critical Rhetoric: Theory and Praxis." *Communication Monographs* 56 (1989): 91–111.

———. "Visions of Society in Discourse and Art: The Failed Rhetoric of Social Realism." *Communication Quarterly* 41 (1993): 355–66.

McMullen, Wayne J., and Martha Solomon. "The Politics of Adaptation: Steven Spielberg's Appropriation of *The Color Purple*." *Text and Performance Quarterly* 14 (1994): 158–74.

McNair, John R. "Computer Icons and the Art of Memory." *Technical Communication Quarterly* 5 (1996): 77–86.

Mechling, Elizabeth Walker, and Jay Mechling. "The Atom According to Disney." *Quarterly Journal of Speech* 81 (1995): 436–53.

———. "The Sale of Two Cities: A Semiotic Comparison of Disneyland and Marriott's Great America." *Journal of Popular Culture* 15 (Summer 1981): 166–79.

Medhurst, Martin J. "*Hiroshima, Mon Amour:* From Iconography to Rhetoric." *Quarterly Journal of Speech* 68 (1982): 345–70.

———. "Image and Ambiguity: A Rhetorical Approach to *The Exorcist.*" *Southern Speech Communication Journal* 44 (1978): 73–92.

Medhurst, Martin J., and Thomas W. Benson. "*The City:* The Rhetoric of Rhythm." *Communication Monographs* 48 (1981): 446–67.

Medhurst, Martin J., and Michael A. DeSousa. "Political Cartoons as Rhetorical Form: A Taxonomy of Graphic Discourse." *Communication Monographs* 48 (1981): 197–236.

Meister, Mark. "Meteorology and the Rhetoric of Nature's Cultural Display." *Quarterly Journal of Speech* 87 (2001): 415–28.

Messner, Beth A., and Jacquelyn J. Buckrop. "Restoring Order: Interpreting Suicide through a Burkean Lens." *Communication Quarterly* 48 (2000): 1–18.

Meyrowitz, Joshua. "Visible and Invisible Candidates: A Case Study in 'Competing Logics' of Campaign Coverage." *Political Communication* 11 (April–June 1994): 145–64.

Mitchell, Gordon R. "Placebo Defense: Operation Desert Mirage? The Rhetoric of Patriot Missile Accuracy in the 1991 Persian Gulf War." *Quarterly Journal of Speech* 86 (2000): 121–45.

Moore, Mark P. "The Cigarette as Representational Ideograph in the Debate over Environmental Tobacco Smoke." *Communication Monographs* 64 (1997): 47–64.

———. "Constructing Irreconcilable Conflict: The Function of the Synecdoche in the Spotted Owl Controversy." *Communication Monographs* 60 (1993): 258–74.

———. "From a Government of the People, to a People of the Government: Irony as Rhetorical Strategy in Presidential Campaigns." *Quarterly Journal of Speech* 82 (1996): 22–37.

Morris, Charles E., III. "Contextual Twilight / Critical Liminality: J. M. Barrie's *Courage* at St. Andrews, 1922." *Quarterly Journal of Speech* 82 (1996): 207–27.

———. "My Old Kentucky Homo: Lincoln and the Politics of Queer Public Memory." In Phillips, *Framing Public Memory,* 89–114.

Morris, M. "At Henry Parkes Motel." In *Too Soon Too Late: History in Popular Culture.* Bloomington: Indiana University Press, 1998, 31–63.

Morris, Richard. "The Vietnam Veterans Memorial and the Myth of Superiority," *Cultural Legacies of Vietnam: Uses of the Past in the Present,* edited by Richard Morris and Peter Erhenhaus, 199–222. Norwood, N.J.: Ablex, 1990.

Mortenssen, Peter. "Figuring Illiteracy: Rustic Bodies and Unlettered Minds in Rural America." In Selzer and Crowley, *Rhetorical Bodies,* 143–70.

Moss, Kenneth. "St. Patrick's Day Celebrations and the Formation of Irish-American Identity, 1845–1875." *Journal of Social History* 29 (1995): 125–48.

Mountford, Roxanne. "On Gender and Rhetorical Space." *Rhetoric Society Quarterly* 31 (Winter 2001): 41–71.

Murphy, John M. "Epideictic and Deliberative Strategies in Opposition to War: The Paradox of Honor and Expediency." *Communication Studies* 43 (1992): 65–78.

———. "'Our Mission and Our Moment': George W. Bush and September 11th." *Rhetoric and Public Affairs* 6 (2003): 607–32.

Nagel, Thomas. "Concealment and Exposure." *Philosophy and Public Affairs* 27 (1998): 3–30.

Nakayama, Thomas K., and Robert L. Krizek. "Whiteness: A Strategic Rhetoric." *Quarterly Journal of Speech* 81 (1995): 291–309.

Ochs, E., and S. Jacoby. "Down to the Wire: The Cultural Clock of Physicists and the Discourse of Consensus." *Language in Society* 26 (1997): 1–27.

Ochs, E., S. Jacoby, and P. Gonzales. "Interpretive Journeys: How Physicists Talk and Travel through Graphic Space." *Connections* 1 (1994): 151–71.

Olson, Kathryn M. "The Controversy over President Reagan's Visit to Bitburg: Strategies of Definition and Redefinition." *Quarterly Journal of Speech* 75 (1989): 129–51.

Olson, Kathryn M., and G. Thomas Goodnight. "Entanglements of Consumption, Cruelty, Privacy and Fashion: The Social Controversy Over Fur." *Quarterly Journal of Speech* 80 (1994): 249–76.

Olson, Kathryn M., and Clark D. Olson. "Beyond Strategy: A Reader-Centered Analysis of Irony's Dual Persuasive Uses." *Quarterly Journal of Speech* 90 (2004): 24–52.

Olson, Lester C. "Benjamin Franklin's Commemorative Medal, *Libertas Americana:* A Study in Rhetorical Iconology." *Quarterly Journal of Speech* 76 (1990): 23–45.

———. "Benjamin Franklin's Pictorial Representations of the British Colonies in America: A Study in Rhetorical Iconology." *Quarterly Journal of Speech* 73 (1987): 18–42.

———. "Portraits in Praise of a People: A Rhetorical Analysis of Norman Rockwell's Icons in Franklin D. Roosevelt's 'Four Freedoms' Campaign." *Quarterly Journal of Speech* 69 (1983): 15–24.

Ono, Kent A., and Derke T. Buescher. "Deciphering *Pocahontas:* Unpackaging the Commodification of a Native American Woman." *Critical Studies in Media Communication* 18 (2001): 23–43.

Oravec, Christine. "John Muir, Yosemite, and the Sublime Response: A Study in the Rhetoric of Preservationism." *Quarterly Journal of Speech* 67 (1981): 245–58.

———. "'Observation' in Aristotle's Theory of Epideictic." *Philosophy and Rhetoric* 9 (1976): 162–74.

Osborn, Michael. "Rhetorical Depiction." In *Form, Genre, and the Study of Political Discourse,* edited by Herbert W. Simons and Aram A. Aghazarian, 79–107. Columbia: University of South Carolina Press, 1986.

Ott, Brian L., and Eric Aoki. "The Politics of Negotiating Public Tragedy: Media Framing of the Matthew Shepard Murder." *Rhetoric and Public Affairs* 5 (2002): 483–505.

Parry-Giles, Shawn J., and Trevor Parry-Giles. "Collective Memory, Political Nostalgia, and the Rhetorical Presidency: Bill Clinton's Commemoration of the March on Washington, August 28, 1998." *Quarterly Journal of Speech* 86 (2000): 417–37.

Pauwels, Yves. "*Propagande Architecturale et Rhétorique du Sublime: Serlio et les 'Joyeuses Entrées' de 1549.*" *Gazette des Beaux-Arts* 137 (2001): 221–36.

Peck, Janice. "Talk about Racism: Framing a Popular Discourse of Race on *Oprah Winfrey.*" *Cultural Critique* 27 (Spring 1994): 89–126.

Perelman, Chaim. "Choice, Presence, and Presentation." In *The Realm of Rhetoric,* translated by William Kluback, 33–40. Notre Dame, Ind.: University of Notre Dame Press, 1982.

Peterson, Tarla Rai. "The Meek Shall Inherit the Mountains: Dramatistic Criticism of Grand Teton National Park's Interpretive Program." *Central States Speech Journal* 39 (1988): 121–33.

Poggenpohl, Sharon Helmer. "Doubly Damned: Rhetoric and the Visual." *Visible Language* 32 (1998): 200–233.

Poulakos, Takis. "The Historical Intervention of Gorgias's *Epitaphios:* The Genre of Funeral Oration and the Athenian Institution of Public Burials." *Pre/Text* 10 (1989): 90–99.

———. "Historiographies of the Tradition of Rhetoric: A Brief History of Classical Funeral Orations." *Western Journal of Speech Communication* 54 (1990): 172–88.

———. "Isocrates' Use of Narrative in the *Evagoras:* Epideictic Rhetoric and Moral Action." *Quarterly Journal of Speech* 73 (1987): 317–28.

———. "Toward a Cultural Understanding of Classical Epideictic Oratory." *Pre/Text* 9 (1988): 147–66.

Procter, David E. "The Dynamic Spectacle: Transforming Experience into Social Forms of Community." *Quarterly Journal of Speech* 76 (1990): 117–33.

Radley, Alan. "Artefacts, Memory and a Sense of the Past." In *Collective Remembering,* edited by David Middleton and Derek Edward, 46–59. London: Sage, 1990.

Richards, Jennifer. "Assumed Simplicity and the Critique of Nobility: Or, How Castiglione Read Cicero." *Renaissance Quarterly* 54 (2001): 460–86.

Ricoeur, Paul. "Between Rhetoric and Poetics." In *Essays on Aristotle's Rhetoric,* edited by Amelie Oksenberg Rorty, 324–84. Berkeley: University of California Press, 1996.

Rollins, Brooke. "The Ethics of Epideictic Rhetoric: Addressing the Problem of Presence Through Derrida's Funeral Orations." *Rhetoric Society Quarterly* 35 (Winter 2005): 5–23.

Rosenfield, Lawrence W. "Central Park and the Celebration of Civic Virtue." In *American Rhetoric: Context and Criticism,* edited by Thomas W. Benson, 221–66. Carbondale: Southern Illinois University Press, 1989.

———. "The Practical Celebration of Epideictic." In *Rhetoric in Transition: Studies in the Nature and Uses of Rhetoric,* edited by Eugene E. White, 131–55. University Park: Pennsylvania State University Press, 1980.

Ryan, Mary. "The American Parade: Representations of the Nineteenth-Century Social Order." In *The New Cultural History: Essays,* edited by Lynn Hunt, 131–53. Berkeley: University of California Press, 1989.

Ryder, Sean. "Reading Lessons: Famine and the Nation, 1845–1849." In *Fearful Realities: New Perspectives on the Famine,* edited by Chris Morash and Richard Hayes, 151–63. Dublin: Irish Academic Press, 1996.

Schilb, John. "Autobiography after Prozac." In Selzer and Crowley, *Rhetorical Bodies,* 202–17.

Schwartz, Barry. "The Social Context of Commemoration: A Study in Collective Memory." *Social Forces* 61 (1982): 374–402.

Schwartz, Barry, and Todd Bayma. "Commemoration and the Politics of Recognition: The Korean War Veterans Memorial." *American Behavioral Scientist* 42 (1999): 946–67.

Schwartz, Barry, and Horst-Alfred Heinrich. "Shadings of Regret: America and Germany." In Phillips, *Framing Public Memory,* 115–44.

Scott, Charles E. "The Appearance of Public Memory." In Phillips, *Framing Public Memory,* 147–56.

Scott, J. Blake. "Rhetoric and Technoscience: The Case of Confide." In Selzer and Crowley, *Rhetorical Bodies,* 239–74.

Scott, Linda M. "Images in Advertising: The Need for a Theory of Visual Rhetoric." *Journal of Consumer Research* 21 (1994): 252–73.

Scott, Robert L. "Diego Rivera at Rockefeller Center: Fresco Painting and Rhetoric." *Western Journal of Speech Communication* 41 (1977): 70–82.

Scott, Robert L., and Donald K. Smith. "The Rhetoric of Confrontation." *Quarterly Journal of Speech* 55 (1969): 1–8.

Selzer, Jack. "Habeas Corpus: An Introduction." In Selzer and Crowley, *Rhetorical Bodies,* 3–15.

Shaffer, Diana. "The Shadow of Helen: The Status of the Vision Image in Gorgias's *Encomium to Helen.*" *Rhetorica* 16 (1998): 243–57.

Shaw, Gordon, Robert Brown, and Philip Bromiley. "Strategic Stories: How 3M Is Rewriting Business Planning." *Harvard Business Review* 76 (1998): 41–50.

Sheard, Cynthia Miecznikowski. "The Public Value of Epideictic Rhetoric." *College English* 58 (1996): 765–94.

Shelley, Cameron. "Rhetorical and Demonstrative Modes of Visual Argument: Looking at Images of Human Evolution." *Argumentation and Advocacy* 33 (1996): 53–68.

Shotter, John. "'Real Presences': Meaning as Living Movement in a Participatory World." *Theory and Psychology* 13 (2003): 577–609.

Sipiora, Michael P. "Heidegger and Epideictic Discourse: The Rhetorical Performance of Meditative Thinking." *Philosophy Today* 35 (1991): 239–53.

Skow, Lisa M., and George N. Dionisopoulos. "A Struggle to Contextualize Photographic Images: American Print Media and the 'Burning Monk.'" *Communication Quarterly* 45 (1997): 393–409.

Smith, Ruth, and John Trimbur. "Rhetorics of Unity and Disunity: The Worcester Firefighters Memorial Service." *Rhetoric Society Quarterly* 33 (Fall 2003): 7–24.

Solomon, Martha. "Autobiographies as Rhetorical Narratives: Elizabeth Cady Stanton and Anna Howard Shaw as 'New Women.'" *Communication Studies* 42 (1991): 354–70.

Spencer, John R. Introduction to *On Painting*, by Leon Battista Alberti, translated by John R. Spencer. 2nd ed. New Haven, Conn.: Yale University Press, 1966, 11–32.

———. "*Ut Rhetorica Pictura:* A Study in Quattrocento Theory of Painting." *Journal of the Warburg and Courtauld Institutes* 20 (1957): 26–44.

Steiner, George. "Critic/Reader." In *George Steiner: A Reader*, 67–98. Oxford: Oxford University Press, 1984.

Stocking, George W., Jr. "The Spaces of Cultural Representation, circa 1887 and 1969: Reflections on Museum Arrangement and Anthropological Theory in the Boasian and Evolutionary Traditions." In Galison and Thompson, *The Architecture of Science*, 165–80.

Stormer, Nathan. "Embodied Humanism: Performative Argument for Natural Rights in the 'The Solitude of the Self.'" *Argumentation and Advocacy* 36 (1999): 51–64.

———. "Embodying Normal Miracles." *Quarterly Journal of Speech* 83 (1997): 172–91.

Strachan, J. Cherie, and Kathleen E. Kendall. "Political Candidates' Convention Films: Finding the Perfect Image—An Overview of Political Image Making." In Hill and Helmers, *Defining Visual Rhetorics*, 135–54.

Stroupe, Craig. "The Rhetoric of Irritation: Inappropriateness as Visual/Literate Practice." In Hill and Helmers, *Defining Visual Rhetorics*, 243–58.

Stuart, Charlotte L. "Architecture in Nazi Germany: A Rhetorical Perspective." *Western Journal of Speech Communication* 37 (1973): 253–63.

Stuckey, Mary E., and Frederick J. Antczak. "The Battle of Issues and Images: Establishing Interpretive Dominance." *Communication Quarterly* 42 (1994): 120–32.

Sullivan, Dale L. "A Closer Look at Education as Epideictic Rhetoric." *Rhetoric Society Quarterly* 23 (Summer/Fall, 1994): 70–89.

———. "The Epideictic Character of Rhetorical Criticism." *Rhetoric Review* 11 (Spring 1993): 339–49.

———. "The Epideictic Rhetoric of Science." *Journal of Business and Technical Communication* 5 (1991): 229–45.

———. "The Ethos of Epideictic Encounter." *Philosophy and Rhetoric* 26 (1993): 113–33.

———. "*Kairos* and the Rhetoric of Belief." *Quarterly Journal of Speech* 78 (1992): 317–32.

Tange, Andrea Kaston. "Envisioning Domesticity, Locating Identity: Constructing the Victorian Middle Class through Images of Home." In Hill and Helmers, *Defining Visual Rhetorics*, 277–301.

Taylor, Bryan C. "The Bodies of August: Photographic Realism and Controversy at the National Air and Space Museum." *Rhetoric and Public Affairs* 1 (1998): 331–61.

———. "'Our Bruised Arms Hung up as Monuments': Nuclear Iconography in Post–Cold War Culture." *Critical Studies in Media Communication* 20 (2003): 1–34.

Taylor, Mark C. "Skinscapes." In *Pierced Hearts and True Love: A Century of Drawings for Tattoos*, 29–45. Honolulu, Hawaii: Hardy Marks Publications, 1995.

Terrill, Robert E. "Irony, Silence, and Time: Frederick Douglass on the Fifth of July." *Quarterly Journal of Speech* 89 (2003): 216–34.

Teslow, Tracy Lang. "Reifying Race: Science and Art in *Races of Mankind* at the Field Museum of Natural History." In Macdonald, *The Politics of Display,* 53–76.

Tonn, Mari Boor, Valerie A. Endress, and John N. Diamond. "Hunting and Heritage on Trial: A Dramatistic Debate over Tragedy, Tradition, and Territory." *Quarterly Journal of Speech* 79 (1993): 165–81.

Torrens, Kathleen M. "Fashion as Argument: Nineteenth-Century Dress Reform." *Argumentation and Advocacy* 36 (1999): 77–87.

Trujillo, Nick. "Interpreting November 22: A Critical Ethnography of an Assassination Site." *Quarterly Journal of Speech* 79 (1993): 447–66.

Tucker, Robert E. "Figure, Ground and Presence: A Phenomenology of Meaning in Rhetoric." *Quarterly Journal of Speech* 87 (2001): 396–414.

Turner, Kathleen J. "Comic Strips: A Rhetorical Perspective." *Central States Speech Journal* 28 (1977): 24–35.

Twigg, Reginald. "Aestheticizing the Home: Textual Strategies of Taste, Self-Identity, and Bourgeois Hegemony in America's 'Gilded Age.'" *Text and Performance Quarterly* 12 (1992): 1–20.

Tyner, Judith A. "Persuasive Cartography." *Journal of Geography* 81 (July–August 1982): 140–44.

Vande Berg, Leah R. "Living Room Pilgrimages: Television's Cyclical Commemoration of the Assassination Anniversary of John F. Kennedy." *Communication Monographs* 62 (1995): 47–64.

Van Eck, Caroline. "The Structure of *De re aedificatoria* Reconsidered." *Journal of the Society of Architectural Historians* 57 (1998): 280–97.

Vickers, Brian. "Epideictic and Epic in the Renaissance." *New Literary History* 14 (1983): 497–537.

———. "Epideictic Rhetoric in Galileo's *Dialogo.*" *Annali dell'Istituto e Museo di Storia della Scienza di Firenze* 8 (1983): 69–102.

———. "Renaissance Reintegration." Chap. 5 in *In Defense of Rhetoric.*

———. "Rhetoric and the Sister Arts." Chap. 7 in *In Defense of Rhetoric.*

Waters, Mary C. "Ethnic and Racial Identities of Second-Generation Black Immigrants in New York City." *International Migration Review* 28 (1994): 795–820.

———. "Explaining the Comfort Factor: West Indian Immigrants Confront American Race Relations." In *The Cultural Territories of Race: Black and White Boundaries,* edited by Michèle Lamont, 63–96. Chicago: University of Chicago Press, 1999.

Watts, Eric King. "African American Ethos and Hermeneutical Rhetoric: An Exploration of Alain Locke's *The New Negro.*" *Quarterly Journal of Speech* 88 (2002): 19–32.

———. "Cultivating a Black Public Voice: W. E. B. DuBois and the 'Criteria of Negro Art.'" *Rhetoric and Public Affairs* 4 (2001): 181–201.

Weaver, Richard M. "Language Is Sermonic." In *Language Is Sermonic: Richard M. Weaver on the Nature of Rhetoric,* edited by Richard L. Johannesen, Rennard Strickland, and Ralph T. Eubanks, 201–25. Baton Rouge, La.: Louisiana State University Press, 1970.

Wells, Susan. "Legible Bodies: Nineteenth-Century Women Physicians and the Rhetoric of Dissection." In Selzer and Crowley, *Rhetorical Bodies,* 58–74.

Wilson, Mabel O. "Between Rooms 307: Spaces of Memory at the National Civil Rights Museum." *Harvard Design Magazine* (Fall 1999): 28–31.

Wollen, Peter. Introduction to Cooke and Wollen, *Visual Display,* 9–13.

Wright, Elizabethada. "Reading the Cemetery: *Lieu De Mémoire Par Excellance.*" *Rhetoric Society Quarterly* 33 (Spring 2003): 27–44.

Yampolsky, Mikhail. "In the Shadow of Monuments: Notes on Iconoclasm and Time." Translated by John Kachur. In *Soviet Hieroglyphics: Visual Culture in Late Twentieth-Century Russia,* edited by Nancy Condee, 93–112. Bloomington: Indiana University Press, 1995.

Yoos, George E. "How Pictures Lie." *Rhetoric Society Quarterly* 24 (Winter/Spring 1994): 107–19.

Zaeske, Susan. "Signatures of Citizenship: The Rhetoric of Women's Antislavery Petitions." *Quarterly Journal of Speech* 88 (2002): 147–68.

Zelizer, Barbie. "Reading the Past against the Grain: The Shape of Public Memory Studies." *Critical Studies in Mass Communication* 12 (1995): 214–39.

———. "The Voice of the Visual in Memory." In Phillips, *Framing Public Memory,* 157–86.

Special Issues

Birdsell, David S., and Leo Groarke, eds. "Visual Communication—Part 1." *Argumentation and Advocacy* 33 (Summer 1996): 1–39, 46–52.

———. "Visual Communication—Part 2." *Argumentation and Advocacy* 33 (Fall 1996): 53–80.

Hauser, Gerard A., ed. "Body Argument—Part 1." *Argumentation and Advocacy* 36 (Summer 1999): 1–49.

———. "Body Argument—Part 2." *Argumentation and Advocacy* 36 (Fall 1999): 51–100.

Levinson, Nancy, and William S. Saunders, eds. "Constructions of Memory: On Monuments Old and New." *Harvard Design Magazine* (Fall 1999): 2–93.

Vande Berg, Leah R., ed. "Space." *Western Journal of Communication* 63 (Summer 1999): 249–412.

Contributors

John C. Adams is visiting professor of rhetoric and communication at Hamilton College in central New York State and former dean/director of the Central New York Center of Empire State College in the State University of New York. He has published numerous essays with a particular focus on the history and philosophy of rhetoric and public address. His book *Delightful Conviction: Jonathan Edwards and the Rhetoric of Conversion* (coauthored with Stephen Yarbrough) won the 1994 Eastern Communication Association's Everett Lee Hunt Award for distinguished scholarship in rhetoric and public address.

Jerry Blitefield is associate professor of English at the University of Massachusetts–Dartmouth. His research interests include the physics of rhetoric and the interplay of the temporal and the material in the production of public discourse. His investigations examine how underpowered groups use the dynamics of "place" as a means of rhetorical agency.

Phebe Shih Chao is an independent scholar who has taught at Harvard University, Bennington College, Beijing University, and the University of New Hampshire. Her research interests include film criticism and the criticism of popular symbolic forms. She has several published essays in film criticism journals.

Gregory Clark is professor of English at Brigham Young University. He studies the varieties of rhetorical experiences inherent in American culture. Professor Clark's most recent book is *Rhetorical Landscapes in America: Variations on a Theme from Kenneth Burke* (University of South Carolina Press, 2004). He is editor of *Rhetoric Society Quarterly*.

John Nguyet Erni is associate professor of media and cultural studies and coordinator of graduate studies in the Department of English and Communication, City University of Hong Kong. He is author of *Unstable Frontiers: Technomedicine and the Cultural Politics of "Curing" AIDS*, editor of a special issue for *Cultural Studies* titled "Becoming (Postcolonial) Hong Kong" (2001), and coeditor of two books, *Internationalizing Cultural Studies* and *Asian Media Studies: Politics of Subjectivities* (both forthcoming). His work on gender, sexual politics, and media studies has also appeared in numerous journals.

James Michael Farrell is associate professor of communication at the University of New Hampshire, where he teaches courses in rhetoric and public address. He has authored numerous critical and historical studies of American public discourse, including several investigating the influence of Cicero on the career and writing of John Adams, and others on the oratory of Daniel Webster. Professor Farrell is a member of the American Conference on Irish Studies and currently is working on understanding the American response to the Irish famine. He was recipient of the National Communication Association's Karl R. Wallace Memorial Award and the University of New Hampshire's Liberal Arts Excellence in Teaching Award.

Victoria J. Gallagher is an associate professor in the Department of Communication at North Carolina State University. Professor Gallagher's work on the rhetoric of civil rights leaders and civil rights–related commemorative sites has appeared in *Quarterly Journal of Speech, Rhetoric and Public Affairs, Western Journal of Communication, Southern Communication Journal, Journal of Engineering Education,* and *Journal of College Admissions,* as well as in edited book collections. Her coauthored article on the rhetoric of Martin Luther King Jr. won the B. Aubrey Fisher Outstanding Journal Article Award, runner-up, from the Western States Communication Association. Professor Gallagher's current research projects include critical analysis of civil rights–related photographs and paintings and a book-length comparative analysis of civil rights and African American–related museums and memorials.

S. Michael Halloran retired recently from the Department of Language, Literature, and Communication at Rensselaer Polytechnic Institute, where he received his Ph.D. in 1973. He has published essays on a variety of topics in rhetorical theory and criticism and is coeditor (with Gregory Clark) of *Oratorical Culture in Nineteenth-Century America: Essays on the Transformation of Rhetoric* (1993). He is currently working on a book-length study tracing commemorations of the Battles of Saratoga through the nineteenth and twentieth centuries.

Robert Hariman is professor in the Department of Communication Studies at Northwestern University. He is author of *Political Style: The Artistry of Power* (1995), coeditor of *Post Realism: The Rhetorical Turn in International Relations* (1996), and editor of *Prudence: Classical Virtue, Postmodern Practice* (2003) and *Popular Trials: Rhetoric, Mass Media, and the Law* (1990). He has received the Distinguished Scholar Award from the National Communication Association.

Gerard A. Hauser is professor of communication at the University of Colorado at Boulder. He is a specialist in rhetoric and has published numerous articles and books on the subject of rhetorical theory and criticism, including *Introduction to Rhetorical Theory,* Second Edition (2002) and *Vernacular Voices: The Rhetoric of Publics and Public Spheres* (1999). Professor Hauser is a Fellow of the Rhetoric Society of America and Distinguished Scholar of the National Communication Association. He has received the National Communication Association's Hochmuth-Nichols Award for public address scholarship and the Rhetoric Society of America's Kneupper Article Award and George E. Yoos Award for Service. His research focuses on classical rhetorical theory, dissident rhetoric, and rhetorical features of public spheres. He currently is investigating the rhetoric of prisoners of conscience as a source of self-identity and as a call for civil society.

Beverly James is professor of communication at the University of New Hampshire. Her current work centers on postcommunist transformations in Hungarian culture, identity, and ideology and has appeared in *Critical Studies in Mass Communication, Javnost / The Public, Media, Culture, and Society,* and *Journalism of Popular Culture.* She is also author of *Imagining Postcommunism: Visual Narratives of Hungary's 1956 Revolution* (2005) and coauthor (with Patrick J. Daley) of *Cultural Politics and the Mass Media: Alaska Native Voices* (2004).

Cheryl R. Jorgensen-Earp is an associate professor of communication studies at Lynchburg College in Virginia. She has published articles in national and regional journals and is author of *The Transfiguring Sword: The Just War of the Women's Social and Political Union* (1997), a study of suffragette justifications for violent militancy. She also compiled and edited *Speeches and Trials of the Militant Suffragettes* (1999).

John Louis Lucaites is associate professor in the Department of Communication and Culture and adjunct associate professor in American studies at Indiana University. He also is a Fellow at the

Poynter Center for the Study of Ethics and American Institutions at Indiana University. He is the coauthor (with Celeste Michele Condit) of *Crafting Equality: America's Anglo-African Word* (1993). He has twice received the National Communication Association's Monograph Award. His current research focuses on visual rhetoric and the role it plays in the development and critique of twentieth-century liberal-democratic culture.

Joshua Meyrowitz is professor of communication at the University of New Hampshire. He is author of *No Sense of Place: The Impact of Electronic Media on Social Behavior,* which won the Book of the Year Award from the National Association of Broadcasters and the Broadcast Education Association, among other awards. Professor Meyrowitz has published dozens of articles about the media and culture in scholarly journals and anthologies, as well as general interest magazines and newspapers.

Richard Morris is professor of communication studies at Arizona State University. He is the author of *Sinners, Lovers, and Heroes: An Essay on Memorializing in Three American Cultures,* which won the Outstanding Book Award from the National Communication Association's International and Intercultural Division, "Educating Savages," which won the Outstanding Essay Award from the National Communication Association's International and Intercultural Communication Division, and more than thirty other books and essays dealing with ethnographic issues.

Lawrence J. Prelli is associate professor of communication and chair in the Department of Communication and affiliate associate professor in the Department of Natural Resources at the University of New Hampshire. His research examines rhetoric in relation to science, to environmental discourses, and to display. In addition to journal articles and book chapters in these areas, Professor Prelli has edited two special issues of international journals on rhetoric and science and is author of *A Rhetoric of Science: Inventing Scientific Discourse* (University of South Carolina Press, 1989), which won the 1990 Eastern Communication Association's Everett Lee Hunt Award for distinguished scholarship in rhetoric and public address. He received the 2004 Eastern Communication Association's Donald H. Ecroyd and Carolyn Drummond Ecroyd Teaching Excellence Award.

Lawrence W. Rosenfield is now retired from teaching and living in Lincoln, Nebraska. He is author of two books and several dozen chapters, monographs, and academic articles. He has received the Speech Association of America's Golden Anniversary Award for scholarship and the National Communication Association's Lifetime Teaching Excellence Award.

John Shotter is emeritus professor of communication in the Department of Communication at the University of New Hampshire. He is the author of *Social Accountability and Selfhood* (1984), *Cultural Politics of Everyday Life: Social Constructionism, Rhetoric, and Knowing of the Third Kind* (1993), and *Conversational Realities: The Construction of Life through Language* (1993). In 1997 Professor Shotter was an Overseas Fellow at Churchill College, Cambridge, and a visiting professor at the Swedish Institute of Work Life Research, Stockholm, Sweden.

Mari Boor Tonn is associate professor of communication at the University of Maryland at College Park. Her research on political rhetoric has appeared in major journals of communication and rhetoric and in book chapters. Professor Tonn's scholarship has earned her the National Communication Association's Karl R. Wallace Memorial Award for rhetorical scholarship, the Eastern Communication Association's Past Presidents Award, and the Organization for the Study of Communication, Language, and Gender's Best Essay of the Year Award. She also has received the Eastern Communication Association's Donald H. Ecroyd and Carolyn Drummond Ecroyd Teaching Excellence Award, the Eastern Communication Association's Distinguished Teaching Fellow Award, and the University of New Hampshire's Liberal Arts Excellence in Teaching Award.

Index

Page numbers in italics refer to illustrations.